New Directions in Elementary School Mathematics

New Directions in Elementary School Mathematics

Interactive Teaching and Learning

Emma E. Holmes

California State University, Fullerton

Merrill,
an imprint of Prentice Hall

Englewood Cliffs, New Jersey   Columbus, Ohio

Library of Congress Cataloging-in-Publication Data

Holmes, Emma E.
New directions in elementary school mathematics / Emma E. Holmes.
p. cm.
Includes index.
ISBN 0-02-356451-2
1. Mathematics—Study and teaching (Elementary) I. Title.
QA135.5.H587 1995 94-41854
372.7′044—dc20 CIP

Cover art: © Marjory Dressler

Editor: Linda James Scharp
Production Editor: Mary Harlan
Production Buyer: Laura Messerly
Editorial/production supervision and interior design: Spectrum Publisher Services

This book was set in Palatino by American-Stratford Graphic Services, Inc., and was printed and bound by The Banta Company. The cover was printed by Phoenix Color Corp.

Printed in the United States of America

10 9 8 7 6 5 4 3 2 1

ISBN: 0-02-356451-2

Prentice-Hall International (UK) Limited, *London*
Prentice-Hall of Australia Pty. Limited, *Sydney*
Prentice-Hall of Canada, Inc., *Toronto*
Prentice-Hall Hispanoamericana, S. A., *Mexico*
Prentice-Hall of India Private Limited, *New Delhi*
Prentice-Hall of Japan, Inc., *Tokyo*
Simon & Schuster Asia Pte. Ltd., *Singapore*
Editora Prentice-Hall do Brasil, Ltda., *Rio de Janeiro*

PREFACE

This book was written so that those who teach or are preparing to teach children mathematics understand new directions in teaching mathematics and use interactive teaching. Interactive teaching is based on the idea that to learn mathematics children must think mathematics and must construct knowledge that is meaningful to them. Interactive methods stress learner problem solving, reasoning, communicating, and making connections. It enables children to notice and use patterns and relations in numbers and space to better understand mathematics and their world. The National Council of Teachers of Mathematics advocates teaching and learning that encompasses these goals, and their publication, *Curriculum and Evaluation Standards for School Mathematics,* gives guidance to teachers in developing new directions in their teaching. Research supporting interactive teaching is cited throughout the book. You may wish to examine some of the references at the end of each chapter to explore further the notion of constructivist theories that form the foundation of interactive teaching.

All chapters discuss teaching a topic of elementary school mathematics using interactive teaching, and they give numerous examples in the form of teacher–pupil discussions, assignments for children, problem-solving activities, and games to enable the reader to understand interactive approaches to teaching and learning. By reading, reflecting, and discussing with others the ideas presented in the chapters, readers will be able to compare interactive methods for elementary school mathematics with those used by their teachers in the elementary school or the methods they are currently using in their classes. The numerous examples and the chapter discussions related to teaching elementary school mathematics will enable readers to understand interactive teaching and learning and so to be able to use this approach with confidence in their classes.

The book also includes many other features:

1. An introductory problem begins each chapter. The introductory problem requires a reader to think about the chapter contents in the context of its usefulness to children in understanding their world. The problems are open-ended, so that each reader can deal with the problems in his or her own way. Thinking about the problem solution and discussing ideas with others will lead to many insights about new directions in teaching and learning elementary school mathematics.
2. Reader activities are in each chapter. These help readers think critically about a key idea in the chapter.
3. Activities for the classroom are in each chapter. These give readers tasks to carry out in their fieldwork assignments or in their classroom teaching. These activities help students relate the chapter discussion to actual teaching.
4. A chapter on children with special needs discusses teaching minority children, promoting equity for all boys and girls in the mathematics classroom, and providing appropriate learning experiences for exceptional children—learning disabled, slow learners, and gifted children.
5. Most of a chapter is devoted to teaching mental computation and computational estimation. In our electronic age, elementary school children need to begin to develop competency in these areas in order to evaluate the output of calculators and computers.

6. Calculator activities are found in most chapters. The activities help children learn to use calculators to replace rote memory. This is an important learning since calculators make much in our modern world possible.
7. Useful appendices are provided:
    - Appendix A: National Council of Teachers of Mathematics Curriculum, Evaluation (1–10), and Assessment Standards
    - Appendix B: Interactive Instruction Lesson
    - Appendix C: Answers for Chapter Two Selected Problems
    - Appendix D: Pattern for Clown Suit
    - Appendix E: Names and Addresses of Suppliers of Mathematical Learning Materials
    - Appendix F: Table of Suggested Mathematics Topics and Objectives for Kindergarten and Elementary School Grades. This table will help readers decide on activities appropriate for children in actual classrooms.
    - Appendix G: Masters for Materials to Duplicate. These can be used to make copies of materials for children.

I wish to thank those who contributed to the writing of this book. First, I appreciate the contributions of my students who over many years have given me insights about teaching. In the last few years many used earlier versions of the book and gave me helpful suggestions for improvement. I wish to thank the reviewers who provided valuable feedback for clarifying and improving sections of the manuscript. They are Christine Browning, Western Michigan University; Leroy G. Callahan, State University of New York at Buffalo; Lucy Dechene, Fitchburg State College; Thomas C. Gibney, University of Toledo; Andrea Guillaume, California State University, Fullerton; Barbara Lehman, Mississippi State University; Dorothy Spethman, Dakota State University; William K. Tomhave, Concordia College; and Carmen Zuniga-Hill, California State University, Fullerton. Last, I am very grateful to my husband, Robert T. Holmes, for his help, support, and encouragement, without which I could not have written this book.

EMMA E. HOLMES

CONTENTS

New Directions in Elementary School Mathematics

CHAPTER 1

New Directions in Elementary School Mathematics

To the Reader:

Each chapter begins with an Introductory Problem for you to solve. As you consider the problem's solution, you will overview the chapter. The problems are open-ended; that is, there are different valid solutions. Superior solutions will deal with as many topics and subtopics in a chapter as possible.

A new direction in elementary school mathematics is to connect mathematics to children's lives and to school subjects other than mathematics. Many of the Introductory Problems involve making these connections. Be creative in your solutions to these problems to experience the possibilities of this new direction in teaching elementary school mathematics.

▪ INTRODUCTORY PROBLEM ▪

Recall how you learned mathematics in the elementary school, or review your observations of mathematics teaching in today's schools. As you study this chapter, compare new directions in teaching to your experiences or observations. Note both similarities and differences. Particularly, compare the interactive approach and new assessment practices with teaching methods and assessment procedures with which you are familiar.

INTRODUCTION

Significant changes are occurring in teaching elementary school mathematics so that children will learn the mathematics necessary for living and working in the twenty-first century. The new directions emphasize understanding mathematics and solving problems. Children are helped to realize that mathematics is needed to understand certain aspects of many school subjects and real-world situations. Skills such as mental computation and computational estimation are stressed, and less attention is given to paper-and-pencil computation. Children learn to use calculators and computers and study topics such as data analysis and probability, which will enable them to deal with the vast amount of quantitative information that will be available to them.

New insights regarding how children learn are also influencing teaching. Instruction should help children construct knowledge by experiencing, investigating, solving problems, and thinking critically. Learners should often work in cooperative groups to exchange ideas and learn from one another. Because intrinsic motivation contributes to learning, teachers should help learners develop positive attitudes toward mathematics.

The National Council of Teachers of Mathematics (NCTM) is in the forefront of groups advocating and implementing new directions, and its publication, *Curriculum and Evaluation Standards for School Mathematics* (1989), charts the course for changes in teaching mathematics. *Everybody Counts: A Report to the Nation on the Future of Mathematics Education* (National Research Council, 1989) and *Reshaping School Mathematics: A Philosophy and Framework for Curriculum* (Mathematical Sciences Education Board, National Research Council, 1990) also describe needed changes and how they can be implemented.

The new directions in learning and teaching mathematics are exciting to put into practice and motivating for children, and they enable learners to develop abilities and skills to deal with the modern world. This text describes the changes in objectives and gives resources for understanding and implementing the new directions in mathematics teaching in the elementary school.

This chapter gives an overview of instruction based on the new directions. It discusses goals for teaching elementary school mathematics and how to teach. Thus, both the "what" and "how" of teaching are addressed. The sections are: Goals for Elementary School Mathematics, A Framework for Teaching, New Directions with Calculators and Computers, and Summary. Other chapters deal with teaching and learning specific topics in elementary school mathematics.

GOALS FOR ELEMENTARY SCHOOL MATHEMATICS

Six goals for teaching and learning are discussed in this section:

1. Develop problem-solving abilities.
2. Develop reasoning abilities.
3. Develop conceptual knowledge.
4. Develop procedural knowledge.
5. Develop positive attitudes.
6. Develop abilities to work and communicate with others.

TABLE 1.1 National Council of Teachers of Mathematics Curriculum Standards

Grades K–4	Grades 5–8
Standard 1. Mathematics as Problem Solving	Standard 1. Mathematics as Problem Solving
Standard 2. Mathematics as Communication	Standard 2. Mathematics as Communication
Standard 3. Mathematics as Reasoning	Standard 3. Mathematics as Reasoning
Standard 4. Mathematical Connections	Standard 4. Mathematical Connections
Standard 5. Estimation	Standard 5. Number and Number Relationships
Standard 6. Number Sense and Numeration	Standard 6. Number Systems and Number Theory
Standard 7. Concepts of Whole Number Operations	Standard 7. Computation and Estimation
Standard 8. Whole Number Computation	Standard 8. Patterns and Functions
Standard 9. Geometry and Spatial Sense	Standard 9. Algebra
Standard 10. Measurement	Standard 10. Statistics
Standard 11. Statistics and Probability	Standard 11. Probability
Standard 12. Fractions and Decimals	Standard 12. Geometry
Standard 13. Patterns and Relationships	Standard 13. Measurement

National Council of Teachers of Mathematics. (1989). *Curriculum and Evaluation Standards for School Mathematics*, pp. 15, 65. Reston, VA: Author. Reprinted by permission.

The goals are based on the Standards discussed in *Curriculum and Evaluation Standards for School Mathematics* (NCTM, 1989) (see Table 1.1). Curriculum Standards and Evaluation Standards are provided in Appendix A. Appendix A also gives Assessment Standards (NCTM, 1993). Standards that are relevant to a chapter's content are referred to in that chapter.

The goals reflect contemporary thinking about the purposes for learning elementary school mathematics and the nature of learning. You will find that the goals help explain the new directions.

Develop Problem-Solving Abilities

Problem solving in elementary school mathematics is the process of finding answers to questions embedded in stories, text material, school assignments, and real-life situations. Teachers use interesting problems that relate to children's lives and encourage children to create problems that have significance for them (see Standard 1 in Curriculum Standards for Grades K–4 and 5–8, Appendix A). Problems include topics in geometry and measurement as well as numbers, and many problems involve content from science and the social studies. Problem solving enables learners to see the relevance of mathematics to other subjects and to the real world.

Problems are both a means and an end in elementary school mathematics instruction. As a *means* for teaching mathematics, problems enable students to construct mathematical ideas (Carpenter, Carey, and Kouba, 1990). They lead children to investigate, explore patterns, and think critically. To solve problems, students must observe, relate, question, and infer.

The ability to solve problems should be a major outcome of instruction in mathematics, and hence problem solving can be considered an *end* of learning. Children should be able to solve real-world problems that have mathematical dimensions, as well as textbook or teacher-posed problems. Problems should help learners make connections between mathematics, their lives, and other school subjects (see Standard 4 in Curriculum Standards for Grades K–4 and 5–8, Appendix A). Puzzling situations that involve mathematics should be a challenge to learners, and they should be able to pose problems whose solutions resolve the difficulties.

To make certain students can solve problems, most lessons involve problem solving. Children learn the steps in problem solving, problem-solving strategies, and how to formulate problems. Instruction emphasizes that many problems can be solved in different ways and that some problems have more than one solution (see Standard 1 in Curriculum Standards for Grades K–4 and 5–8, Appendix A). Chapter 2 discusses teaching and learning problem solving, and all chapters emphasize problem solving as an approach to learning.

Develop Reasoning Abilities

To understand mathematics, learners must *reason* about ideas. They must see relations and connections and make sense of mathematics. They must be able to draw conclusions, to induce patterns from examples, and to deduce ideas from other ideas. They must be able to use models and mathematical ideas to explain their thinking (see Standard 3 in Curriculum Standards for Grades K–4 and 5–8, Appendix A).

Children develop reasoning abilities as they answer thought-provoking questions and engage in activities that require reasoning. Examples of questions that require learners to reflect and reason are given throughout the book. Each chapter also gives many activities that require learners to reason about mathematical ideas.

A set of problem cards can be assigned to give students opportunities to reason about numbers and shapes. Written on each card is a problem question; reasoning must be used to answer the question. Teachers can write cards and share them among themselves, or students can write cards for their own or another class. Learners work with the cards individually, in pairs, or in small groups. Sharing answers and the reasoning used to solve a problem should be a part of the activity. An example of a problem question for young learners is: What's My Name? I am an even number. I am less than 30, but greater than 10. The sum of my digits is 10.

Develop Conceptual Knowledge

Conceptual knowledge is knowledge of concepts, relations, and patterns. It enables students to make sense of mathematics. If students have conceptual knowledge, when asked to justify their work, they do not reply as did one of my students, "Mr. Toner told me to do it this way."

Conceptual knowledge is attained by integrating new knowledge with what is already known (Lindquist, 1989; NCTM, 1989). Networks of internal representations are constructed and restructured as learners create conceptual knowledge (Hiebert and Carpenter, 1992; Hiebert and Lefevre, 1986). Higher-level thinking is fundamental to the process. Learners compare, relate, and infer. They resolve inconsistencies and verify their ideas to develop mathematical meanings.

In the elementary school, conceptual knowledge is constructed as problems are solved, investigations carried out, and questions pondered. Meanings and connections among ideas develop as learners work with concrete, pictorial, and symbolic materials, reflect on what they have done, and communicate with others. To develop mathematical meanings, they work together and alone, solving problems in their own way.

The motivation for constructing conceptual knowledge is the need to make sense of experience and expand one's understanding. Awareness of a lack of understanding and unsolved problems give impetus to learning.

Develop Procedural Knowledge

Procedural knowledge is the recognition of symbols and the ability to follow rules to "do" mathematics. It can be thought of as having mathematical skill and carrying out action sequences (Hiebert and Carpenter, 1992). One action leads to another, as when performing a computation.

According to Hiebert and Carpenter, mathematical expertise involves both conceptual and procedural knowledge and an awareness that procedures are based on mathematical principles. Conceptual and procedural knowledge are related to attain mathematical power. Procedures connected to conceptual knowledge give flexibility to mathematical thinking and enable learners to extend the range of both types of knowledge when new problems arise (see Standard 4 in Curriculum Standards for Grades K–4 and 5–8, Appendix A).

If children learn procedures without understanding, procedural knowledge consists of meaningless routines. There are no reasons for rules, and mathematics is mindless. Children do not understand what they are doing, and they do not find the study of mathematics enjoyable or satisfying.

Develop Positive Attitudes

Attitudes are perceptions about ourselves, others, objects, or ideas. They involve either positive or negative feelings and predispose us toward certain behaviors (McLeod, 1992; Reyes, 1984). Positive attitudes about ourselves would involve feelings of competence and self-worth and confidence in our ability to succeed if we are responsible and exert effort. Positive attitudes toward mathematics would include liking mathematics and believing that the study of mathematics is valuable (see Standards 1 in Curriculum Standards for Grades K–4 and 4 in Curriculum Standards for Grades 5–8, Appendix A).

A feeling that one is competent is related more to intrinsic motivation than to extrinsic motivation and is enhanced by challenge (Lepper and Hodell, 1989; Ryan, Connell, and Deci, 1985). *Extrinsic motivation* is directed toward attaining goals set by others. Learners who are extrinsically motivated behave to receive stickers, grades, or similar rewards. *Intrinsic motivation* is directed toward attaining our own goals. We behave to please ourselves. To foster intrinsic motivation, feelings of competence, and positive attitudes toward mathematics, teachers provide challenges appropriate to learners' developmental levels, and they make sure that children will be successful if they exert effort. They help children persevere by giving support and encouragement, and they provide opportunities for choices among assignments to enable children to become autonomous, responsible, and confident learners.

Feedback given to learners also influences motivation and feelings of competency. Feedback can be either controlling or informative. *Controlling feedback* tells a learner how the student's work pleases the teacher or meets certain standards of performance set by others. ("I am proud of what you did today.") Controlling feedback is related to the development of extrinsic motivation (Cohen, 1985; Ryan, Connell, and Deci, 1985). *Informative feedback* tells a learner the nature of his or her strengths and weaknesses and fosters intrinsic motivation. ("Using a table to solve the problem, Manuel, showed creative thinking.") Teachers who use informative feedback give children specific information about their work and help learners focus on how to use the information to become more competent.

Belief in the value of mathematics would relate mathematics to life. Results of the 1986 National Assessment of Educational Progress show that third-grade children generally like mathematics (60%) and think they are good at mathematics (65%) (Dossey, Mullis, Lindquist, and Chambers, 1988). However, fewer children at this level wanted a job involving mathematics (40%). Thus, it would appear that although many third graders like mathematics and are confident about their mathematical ability, they have less positive attitudes about a career involving mathematics. To enable children to realize the importance of mathematics in the work world, learners should often discuss the usefulness of mathematics in real life and its relation to our technological culture.

Develop Abilities to Work and Communicate with Others

Children learn as they carry out activities and discuss their ideas with teachers and peers. Communicating ideas and reacting to others' comments help students form mathematical ideas (see Standard 2 in Curriculum Standards for Grades K–4 and

5–8, Appendix A). Particularly when working with peers, children have many opportunities to explain, question, and reflect. In so doing, they build new knowledge structures or schemata.

If learners are to profit fully from interacting with others, an atmosphere of mutual respect and trust must prevail. Children need to learn to communicate ideas clearly, listen attentively, question courteously, and disagree with ideas, not persons. Of course, children should be cooperative and responsible not only in mathematics classes but at all times. Therefore, children are helped to learn human relations skills that apply to all classroom interactions. Skills that facilitate working and communicating with others are usually emphasized during the first weeks of school and reaffirmed often during the school year. They are taught mainly through discussion and modeling (Holmes, 1991).

A FRAMEWORK FOR TEACHING

A framework for teaching has six components that make up the parts of this section: How Children Learn Mathematics, Knowledge of Mathematics, Instructional Strategies, Instructional Methods, Instructional Planning, and Assessing Learning. Superior teachers have strengths in all these areas. However, each teacher combines these components in his or her own unique way so that children attain mathematical power.

How Children Learn Mathematics

Children learn mathematics by *thinking* about their experiences in and out of school rather than by attending to explanations by a teacher or a textbook. They construct mathematical meanings (Kamii,1990; Labinowicz,1985; Piaget, 1952). School experiences become more important than out-of-school experiences as children mature. School experiences enable learners to construct mathematical knowledge by integrating meanings already acquired with new ideas that develop as they engage in activities that stress problem solving, investigation, and communication with others. Such activities lead children to think about number and space patterns and relations, thereby developing an understanding of mathematics.

Three cognitive processes contribute to the construction of mathematical knowledge: representation, reflection, and automatization (Hiebert, 1990). These processes involve doing, observing, abstracting, relating, inferring, concluding, and developing skill.

Mathematical ideas are *represented* in real-life events through oral and written language and by objects, pictures, graphs, and symbols (Hiebert, 1990). Representing their thinking helps children learn mathematics, but the representations are separate and may be unrelated in the child's mind. For example, representing the fact $7 + 2 = 9$ with counters is showing only one instance of addition. To understand addition, children must think about the similarities and differences among many different facts and different representations.

Reflecting on what has been represented results in an awareness of relations and patterns and enables students to construct mathematical meanings (Hiebert, 1990). Learners engage in critical thinking, make inferences, and develop abstract ideas as they make connections between and within representations. For example, after using objects to solve addition and subtraction problems, showing addition facts with different materials, making records of what they have done, noting what others have done, and comparing and inferring as they complete their work, children form the concept of addition by mentally constructing relations between representations. An example of constructing a relation within representations is: After covering squares and rectangles with triangles, children construct the idea that different geometric figures can be covered completely by smaller figures, and they develop the understanding that any geometric figure can be broken into other geometric figures with the area of the original figure remaining the same.

During the representation and reflection phases of learning, learners share what they have done orally and in writing to clarify their ideas and expand meaning (NCTM, 1989). Whole class discussions provide opportunities for students to explain how they completed their assignments. They also often write reports of their thinking in journals and "write-ups."

Automatization involves automatic or effortless performance. It means acting with minimal thought. Automatization leads to procedural knowledge and develops from practicing to develop skill and reviewing to ensure retention and mastery. It enables learners to attend to analyzing and relating, because almost no mental effort is required to deal with procedures that have been automatized; other thoughts can fill our minds at the same time. Automatization becomes an objective after the conceptual knowledge that underlies a procedure is developed.

Games, puzzles, and problems provide opportunities for students to automatize procedures (Kamii, 1990) and are preferable to drill exercises. However, some practice activities may be needed to attain immediate recall of needed information.

To construct knowledge, children must also be *motivated*. Motivation directs learning. Contemporary theories of motivation emphasize that our thoughts influence our motivation. What we think about the task and ourselves motivates us to learn or not to learn (Ames and Ames, 1984). Problem-solving tasks that provide opportunities for learners to feel autonomous and capable give rise to intrinsic motivation to learn mathematics.

The process of constructing knowledge is a slow one (Hiebert, Wearne, and Taber, 1991). Learning takes time. Meanings are formed over days, weeks, months, and years as students grasp relations among concepts and make the connections and coordinations that are necessary to develop understanding.

Knowledge of Mathematics

No teacher can teach what he or she does not understand. Elementary school teachers must have knowledge of mathematics. The NCTM has developed standards for the mathematical content that should be acquired by all teachers in grades K–4, 5–8, and 9–12 (NCTM, 1991). Their recommendations are useful for considering what mathematical knowledge teachers need to guide children's learning of mathematics. This book is not designed to teach mathematics, but a review of some topics will occur as readers focus on how to teach mathematics to children.

Instructional Strategies

Instructional strategies are procedures for guiding learners to develop mathematical knowledge. Teachers use three strategies: explanation, questioning, and cognitive modeling. They also learn to be effective discussion leaders.

Explanation. Explanation is telling children what to do, observe, and think. Explanations involve descriptions and demonstrations. They are de-emphasized in contemporary approaches to teaching because learners build mathematical meanings through their own representations and reflections rather than by listening and observing. However, explanation is used to present information of an arbitrary nature. For example, teachers demonstrate how to form numerals for the numbers 0 to 9; they show and explain mathematical sentences for basic facts.

Questioning. Questions guide learners in their construction of mathematical knowledge, because to answer questions, children must think mathematically (Burns, 1985). Questions can require immediate recall of information, problem solving, or be open-ended, that is, have more than one answer. Responding to questions can require relational, inductive, or deductive thinking. Answering questions also involves communicating ideas.

Relational thinking ties new information to prior learning. It includes making correspondences, connections, and transformations. It can deal with comparing, ordering, estimating, or evaluating and is needed to analyze and solve problems. Sample questions to stimulate relational thinking are: "How can thinking the tens and ones parts help you?" "How are those ideas alike? different? What is the connection between what you and Ruth said?" "Why does that answer make sense?"

Inductive thinking means inferring from examples. The examples are generated by the teacher or class members. As children solve problems or complete instructional activities, they often use inductive thinking to discover patterns, develop rules, and note relations. Box 1.1 illustrates how a teacher can encourage students to report the thinking that led to their awareness of rules. Such sharing can help all class members gain new knowledge.

At times teachers guide learners to observe characteristics common to several examples. They ask questions requiring learners to compare, classify, and infer. In particular, the question, "What do you notice about . . . ?" helps learners think inductively.

Deductive thinking involves reasoning from prior knowledge. It is the "if . . . , then . . ." type of thinking. Students draw conclusions, give implications, and generate new examples of concepts or rules. An example of teacher–student interaction that involves deductive thinking is given in Box 1.2.

Questions that encourage learners to *communicate mathematical ideas* ask them to explain what they did or how they thought. Explaining the meanings they have acquired helps children refine their thinking and construct knowledge. Students question and react to each other as they work in small groups, and the communication resulting from these interactions enables learners to construct mathematical ideas. A teacher and a student can exchange ideas, or communication can take place between a teacher and all class members during a discussion of work completed or problems solved. Examples of teacher questions that encourage children to communicate their ideas are: "Please tell us how you decided to use a table to solve that problem." "We would like to know how you and Jane decided on that creative solution." "How did you think to solve that problem?"

Questioning is preferable to explanation because it gives students opportunities to organize ideas and engage in higher-level thinking. It is also motivating to learners because it enables them to become aware that they are competent and can think mathematically.

To stimulate higher-level thinking, students must be given time to consider answers to questions. "Wait-time" for questions that require rote or routine responses is 1 to 3 seconds. When questions require higher-level thinking, the time teachers wait until they ask for responses extends to many seconds or even minutes.

Cognitive Modeling. *Cognitive modeling* means "thinking out loud." Cognitive modeling helps learners look at another person's thinking when he or she solves a problem or carries out a procedure. Both teachers and students model their thinking for others (Vetter, 1992). Box 1.3 gives an example of a lesson that incorporates cognitive modeling.

Leading Discussions Effectively. Effective discussion leaders involve all class members in the discussion. They make certain that those who wish to explain their ideas have the opportunity to do so, and they give children time to share their thinking. They solicit ideas from many learners rather than relying on the same children to respond to questions or explain solutions to problems. They encourage children to listen and to respect and respond to others' comments. They guide children to expand their thinking by asking thought-provoking questions and suggesting that learners look at alternative ideas. Effective discussion leaders also help children de-

BOX 1.1 Thinking Inductively

Ms. Lee: For several days we have solved story problems with tens using stick bundles and 10-dot strips. Yesterday several of you started to think the answers. Let's discuss what you learned from solving the problems with materials that helped you find a way to think the answers. On the chalkboard are three of the problems we solved yesterday. Please use the overhead to help us follow your thinking.

1. Mr. Romer's fifth grade was selling school tee shirts to make money for the school library. The first week the class sold 40, and the second week they sold 50. How many did they sell in the two weeks?
2. Leslie saved the money she made baby-sitting to buy some furniture for her room. She bought a desk and a chair after very careful shopping. The desk cost $40 and the chair cost $20. What was the total cost of both pieces of furniture?
3. The kindergarten teacher said the children needed more red and yellow crayons. She asked the principal for 30 red crayons and 30 yellow crayons. How many crayons did she want?

Salvador: (Showing the tens bundles on the overhead as he explains.) When I used the stick bundles to solve the first problem, I noticed I had 4 tens bundles and 5 tens bundles. "Oh," I said to myself, "that is 9 tens, or 90." That made me decide, I could use facts to find how many tens I had and then give the tens answer. I used that plan to solve the other problems.

Alicia: That's about like I figured out a rule. In the third problem, I was counting out 10-dot strips when I figured out that you can add the 10-dot strips just like you can count them. So I thought 3 10-dot strips plus 3 10-dot strips is 6 10-dot strips, which is 60. I tried my rule on the other problems I had solved with the 10-dot strips, and the rule worked.

Ms. Lee: Please write your rules on the chalkboard so that we can all decide if we understand how you thought the answers. Please use the chalkboard so that your rules will be there when the overhead goes off.

> *Salvador's rule:* Add the tens like they were ones, go back to the tens, and make the answer so many tens; then think the ordinary name, like 9 tens is 90.
>
> *Alicia's rule:* To add tens and tens, think a basic fact for the tens numbers, and give the answer with a place-value name, like 60.

Ms. Lee: Thank you, Salvador and Alicia. How are Salvador's rule and Alicia's rule alike or different?

Teresa: They are alike because they both add the tens. They get a tens answer and rename it for a place-value number.

Ms. Lee: Teresa, please write that on the chalkboard.

Teresa writes: Think tens, use a fact to add tens, rename the answer as a place-value number.

Ms. Lee: Thank you, Teresa. Any other ideas?

Ben: There is one rule, like Teresa said, but Salvador and Alicia just gave the rule in different words.

Ms. Lee: Yes. How can we write what Salvador and Alicia were thinking in math sentences? One sentence will use numbers, and the other will have tens words.

Grace: I think I can do that.

Walter: I am not sure, but I'll try.

Ms. Lee: Please write the sentences on the chalkboard.

Grace writes on the chalkboard:
40 + 50
4 tens + 5 tens = 9 tens = 90

Walter looks at Grace's work and says, "I get the idea, but I'll make the sentences equal." He writes: 30 + 30 = 3 tens + 3 tens = 6 tens = 60.

Ms. Lee: Thank you. Please study the math sentences that Grace and Walter have written, and think one way to say the rule that goes with the math sentences. . . . Any questions? . . . No questions. It seems we are ready to use the rule for adding tens. Work with your partner to solve several new problems I'll put on the chalkboard. Either think the answers or write "tens" words in math sentences, but give the answer as a place-value number. Think of a way to check your solutions.

The students then solve several math sentences, such as, $40 + 30 = N$, discuss their solutions, and report they checked solutions using materials or counting.

To study the teacher-student interaction, answer these questions:

1. Why did Ms. Lee have students use materials to solve problems with tens numbers for several days before introducing the rule?
2. Why did she write the previous day's problems on the chalkboard?
3. Why did she have students explain their thinking?
4. Why did she ask students to compare the rules Salvador and Alicia wrote?
5. What would you do if no students chose to write the math sentences? Give the reason(s) for your response.
6. Why did she have students work in pairs to solve several math sentences using the new rule?
7. How did she ensure that the class followed the discussion?
8. How does this lesson episode exemplify inductive thinking?

BOX 1.2 Thinking Deductively

Mr. Ludwig: A few days ago we studied the rule for adding tens mentally. Today we will work with hundreds. In your mathematics groups decide how you would solve the math sentences on the overhead. You can use any method you wish.

$$300 + 400 = N$$

$$500 + 200 = N$$

$$300 + 600 = N$$

$$400 + 200 = N$$

Mr. Ludwig circulates to determine children's progress with the assignment. He decides they have extended their understanding of adding tens to adding hundreds and are ready to discuss their solutions.

Mr. Ludwig: Let's leave our groups and discuss how we found the solutions to these math sentences. Jamie, will you please report for your group. Tell us the solutions and how you found the answers.

Jamie: Our group decided that you can use the tens rule, only think hundreds. The solutions are

$$300 + 400 = 700$$

$$500 + 200 = 700$$

$$300 + 600 = 900$$

$$400 + 200 = 600$$

Mr. Ludwig: Thank you. Did other groups get the same answers?

Spokepersons for the other groups: Yes.

Mr. Ludwig: Did any group write the math sentences using hundreds words?

Stephen: Our group did.

Mr. Ludwig: Please write the first math sentence on the overhead to show the class your group's work, Stephen.

Stephen writes:
3 hundred + 4 hundred = 7 hundred = 700.

Mr. Ludwig: Thank you. Did any group use hundred squares?

Mr. Ludwig: None, it seems. These problems must have been easy for you. Why?

Gloria: We know the facts, and you can use them with hundreds like with tens. You just remember the problem is with hundreds.

Mr. Ludwig: Good reasoning, Gloria. To end our work today, math partners please take turns asking each other addition questions with hundreds like those we studied today.

A short time is given to this follow-up. Mr. Ludwig circulates to assess the questions and answers.

Questions to study the teacher–student interaction:

1. Why did Mr. Ludwig begin with math sentences for groups to solve?
2. Why did he have Stephen put his group's work on the overhead?
3. Why did he not have the class write a rule? Do you think they should have written a rule? Why or why not?
4. Why did he not have the class use hundred squares to verify their thinking? Do you think he should have done so? Why?
5. What deductive thinking took place during this lesson?

velop positive attitudes toward mathematics by guiding them to see the relevance of what they are learning.

Instructional Methods

Teachers choose one of three instructional methods to foster learning: direct instruction, interactive teaching, or cooperative learning. Teachers use all these methods over time. However, interactive teaching and cooperative learning are the methods teachers use to give new directions to mathematics learning in their classroom, and they are emphasized in this text.

Direct Instruction. *Direct instruction* is based on the idea that learners need to be told how to think about mathematics. Explanation is therefore emphasized. Because explanations do not provide for learner construction of ideas, they are deemphasized in interactive approaches for teaching concepts, procedures, and strategies.

BOX 1.3 Cognitive Modeling

Ms. Cromer: When we work with our partners, we can use thinking out loud to help us solve problems. I will solve a problem this way. Then you can ask me questions to make sure you understand how to think out loud when you solve a problem. Next we will try it with our partners. After we have used it for several days, we will talk about its usefulness. The problem I will solve is:

> Jack had $24 to spend on birthday presents for his twin sisters. He planned to spend the same amount on each. How much was that?

Thinking out loud is like talking to myself. This is how I would do it.

"First I must read the problem. (Reads the problem.) Because the problem says twin sisters, I know there are two sisters because twins are two people. Now I will draw a picture for the $24. That is 2 10 dollars and 4 ones.

(Draws on the chalkboard)

Jack buys two presents with that money. That means he divides it by two. The math sentence is: $24 \div 2 = N$. I can do that in my head. He uses $10 for each girl plus $4 \div 2$, which is $2. So he spends $12 on each. I will check by multiplying: $2 \times 12 = 24$. It checks. Now I must decide if the answer makes sense. Yes, because there are two sisters, and he spends a lot less than $24 on each. I can see that the picture of the money could be split in two, and each would get $12. The answer makes sense." Did you understand my thinking out loud as I solved the problem? Are there any questions?

Sharon: Do you always draw a picture when you think out loud?

Ms. Cromer: No. If you understand the problem, you can just set up a math sentence and solve it. But drawing a picture often makes it easier to set up a math sentence.

Ruben: Do you always check when you think out loud?

Ms. Cromer: Yes. Whenever you solve a problem, you should check the computation and think about the sense of the answer. That is true for thinking silently or out loud. Why should you check?

Ruben: I guess to make sure you did it right.

Ms. Cromer: Yes, because careful work pays off in school and out of school. Now let's give in our own words what thinking out loud means.

Kara: It's saying what goes on in your mind as you think about the problem and find the answer.

Ms. Cromer: You've got the meaning of thinking out loud. There are several problems in your textbook on page 35. Please take turns thinking out loud as you solve the problems. Partners listen to each other, and after a problem is solved, talk about what you noticed or learned when thinking out loud. Later the class will discuss your reactions to thinking out loud, and we will talk about why it is useful for learning mathematics.

Questions to study the cognitive modeling strategy:

1. Write your own definition of cognitive modeling.
2. How does cognitive modeling differ from explanation?
3. What do you think are the strengths and weaknesses of this strategy?
4. Select a mathematical procedure to present using cognitive modeling. Demonstrate the strategy to each other, and discuss your reactions to cognitive modeling.

Interactive Teaching. Interactive teaching is based on two major premises: (1) Understanding develops as we mentally process information and construct ideas. Our own thinking enables us to establish relations between what we know and new information. Mathematical knowledge is attained as we think about numerical and spatial concepts. (2) Problem solving is the most important means for stimulating thought. Problem solving is fostered by:

- Open-ended questions that lead to reexamination and rearrangement of what is known.
- Activities that involve thoughtful interpretation of actions; they include investigations and explorations.
- Questions that require deliberation to answer; these are problems in the usual sense.

Interactive teaching enables teachers and students to influence each other's thinking. Teachers make assignments that provoke thinking to enable students to construct concepts, develop rules, and learn problem-solving strategies. They ask children to talk about their work, and they think a great deal about learners' responses. Teachers' reflections enable them to plan instruction so that learners will advance in their learning of mathematics (Fennema, Carpenter, and Peterson, 1989).

Interactive teaching also enables students to influence each other's thinking. As they work cooperatively to solve problems, learners stimulate one another by sharing and questioning. During whole-class discussions, learners are encouraged to react and ask questions when the messages they receive do not make sense. The classroom becomes a forum for the exchange of ideas, and all are expected to be responsible enough to demand meaning. (Appendix B gives an example of an interactive teaching lesson to teach various approaches to regrouping in mental computation.)

An interactive teaching lesson begins with the teacher asking the students an open-ended question or directing them individually, in pairs, or in groups to carry out an activity or solve a problem. Students are given time to think about answers to the question, complete the activity, or solve the problem. Often, they are asked to make records of their work.

An example of an *open-ended question* that begins an interactive teaching lesson is, "What is an average?" (Arlin, 1990). After thinking about the question, students give their answers, react to and question one another, and the teacher asks questions in response to students' ideas. Finally, the class decides on an answer to the question that is meaningful to them and mathematically correct.

An example of a *worksheet activity* for an interactive teaching lesson follows: Each person will be given two long strips of paper by the class monitors. Cut one strip into three short strips. Make as many different triangles as you can from these three short strips. Use the small strips for sides. Jot down your observations on your worksheet. Then take the other long strip, and repeat the task, but make the lengths of the short strips different from the first time you carried out the task. Compare your findings from the two tasks, and discuss them with your study partner. Write your conclusions on your worksheet.

An example of a *problem* is: Reina has four braclets, a white, a blue, a yellow, and a black one. If she wears them two at a time, how many different combinations of bracelets will she have to wear?

While children are working on their assignments, the teacher interacts with individuals or groups, asking questions or making comments about their work. These exchanges enable teachers to become aware of the children's thinking and the meanings they have acquired.

A class discussion of findings follows students' completion of their work. During the discussion, the teacher listens to learners and continues to evaluate children's thinking. Teachers' interpretations of learners' understanding help them guide the discussion, ask thought-provoking questions, and plan follow-up instruction. Examples of teacher questions are: "Tell us more about your idea that. . . ." "Why did you use your counters that way?" "Could we solve that problem another way?" "Is there a pattern in the answers?" "What is it?" "Please explain your thinking to obtain that solution."

As sharing is affected by attitudes, teachers create a class climate that encourages students to express their ideas and helps students feel that their contributions are valued by the teacher and the class. To emphasize the importance of learners and their ideas, teachers use language that focuses on children. They avoid using the pronouns "I" and "me" and phrase their comments to emphasize the words "you" and "your." For example, they say, "Please explain your thinking to the class," rather than, "Tell me how you figured that out." Teachers I work with report that such a change in language changes the class climate. They and their students focus on ideas rather than view discussions as a time for performing for the teacher.

Cooperative Learning. Cooperative learning involves children working together in small groups to complete assignments, solve problems, or carry out projects

(Artzt and Newman, 1990). As noted, cooperative learning is often a phase of interactive teaching.

Two to four children usually comprise a cooperative learning group. They can be at the same or different ability levels depending on the assignment. Usually, children are assigned to groups by the teacher, so that there will be a mix among children of different ability levels, sexes, and ethnic backgrounds. Each child in the group may have a specific role such as leader, recorder, or materials' monitor.

When working cooperatively, children help one another understand ideas, solve problems, or develop proficiency. They learn to continue a discussion until all are convinced that an idea or problem solution arrived at by the group is reasonable. They sometimes work together to master basic skills.

When children are working in cooperative groups, the teacher moves from group to group to evaluate progress or interact with learners. After groups have completed their work, they usually share what they have done.

To make groups effective, children are taught human relations skills, and they evaluate their work in terms of both cooperative and supportive behaviors and the mathematics learned. Johnson and Johnson (1987) report that children achieve more and develop more positive attitudes toward themselves and others when they learn in cooperative groups than when they learn in individual or competitive arrangements.

Instructional Planning

Instructional planning involves using the total environment to teach mathematics and organizing to teach specific content. Using the total environment involves employing real-world experiences and the content of other subjects to teach mathematics. Teachers help children discover that mathematics is everywhere. Suggestions for finding mathematics in children's daily lives are given in Table 1.2.

When planning to teach specific mathematical content, teachers work with units and lessons. To plan effective units and lessons, teachers must have knowledge of many facets of instruction, including how children learn mathematics, mathematical content, appropriate teaching strategies, instructional methods, and assessment procedures. These topics are discussed in other parts of this chapter. Effective planning also involves distinguishing between plans for direct and interactive teaching. A later part of this section discusses lessons plans for these two approaches.

A *unit* deals with a broad area of study, such as learning the meanings of addition and subtraction with fractions. Units give conceptual and procedural knowledge to be attained, problems and activities for students, and suggestions for assessing learning. Units usually take one to six weeks. Units are written by classroom teachers and by local, state, or national groups. Teachers adapt units prepared by others to meet the needs of their own classes. The following chapters discuss the

TABLE 1.2 Suggestions for Using Experiences in Children's Lives to Teach Mathematics

1. Classroom activities such as determining absences, collecting money, dividing the class into groups, taking inventories, or counting days in a month or until a special event
2. Times and length of time for daily events, such as sleeping, eating, brushing one's teeth, riding the bus, watching TV, and playing; distances to school
3. Collections of children (e.g., dolls or toy cars)
4. Sports
5. Vacation trips
6. Class field trips
7. Purchases: Catalogues can be used for making wish lists with costs
8. Investigating a block or square mile of the neighborhood: number of houses, stores, trees, etc.
9. Pets: What kind; size; food for pets: amount and cost

topics that comprise units. The chapter sections will serve as guides in planning units.

Lessons are segments of instruction designed to deal with specific conceptual or procedural learning. Several mathematics periods may be needed for learners to carry out a lesson activity or solve a problem. Aspects of planning lessons include: being aware of lesson structure, formulating objectives, and selecting activities.

Lesson Structure. A lesson episode has three parts: pre-lesson, lesson, and post-lesson. The *pre-lesson* gives children opportunities to participate in interesting, challenging, or skill-developing activities. They motivate learners but often do not relate directly to the objective of the lesson. Examples of such activities are: sharing of examples of the use of mathematics in students' daily life, journal writing, mentally calculating or estimating a solution, practicing a skill, reading or listening to a story that incorporates mathematics, discussing the mathematical ideas in a story (see Gailey, 1993, for bibliography), and solving a novel problem. Five to 10 minutes at the beginning of a mathematics period are usually sufficient for these activities.

If homework has been assigned, the pre-lesson begins or ends with collecting and, possibly, checking homework. Many teachers collect homework, grade papers once or twice a week, and do a random check on the other days. Other teachers have pupils check their own homework to provide immediate feedback.

The *lesson* is devoted to activities designed to attain an instructional objective. For example, an objective could be for learners to understand whole number multiplication as repeated addition. Learners attain a lesson objective as they complete assignments, reflect on their work, and engage in discussions. To attain his or her objective, a teacher chooses an appropriate approach such as interactive teaching, individual or group projects, mathematical games, or computer activities.

Rarely do teachers begin an interactive lesson by telling learners the lesson's content or performance objective. Learners might then focus on what the teacher had said was to be learned without internalizing meanings. The teacher gives an introduction to the lesson by stating what is to be *done* and, if appropriate, by making suggestions or posing a question to guide learners' thinking about the activity. A teacher determines if a lesson objective has been met by questioning learners, listening to them, and observing their work. Students are helped to recognize their own lesson attainments by sharing what they did and thought and frequently summarizing, orally or in writing, the ideas they developed in a lesson.

The teacher can begin a lesson by saying, "We will play a game today." If the game is used to introduce a concept, the teacher may say, "As you play this game, think about. . . . We will talk about your ideas when we finish the game." Many lessons can begin with a statement similar to: "We will be solving problems today. Solve them in your own way. You can use the counters in the bag in your desk or grid paper in the paper folder. When you finish, we will share your solutions and your thinking to solve the problems."

Usually, the entire class is studying the same topic in a unit. However, when studying certain unit topics, some students will need more or less time than other students to attain understanding or skill. Therefore, learners can be grouped and assigned activities that are appropriate to their developmental level. The grouping changes frequently, and many opportunities are provided for children to study in different groups and in a whole-class setting.

Teachers can adapt teaching to individual differences by giving students choices among activities or by assigning different tasks to different groups. Whether chosen by students or assigned by the teacher, different activities can deal with the same type of content but involve different levels of complexity. Box 1.4 gives activities that would enable a teacher to adapt to individual differences. When different students complete different activities, the class discussion focuses on an exchange of ideas that benefits all students. Many suggestions for adapting in-

BOX 1.4 Attending to Individual Differences

The following activities provide different levels of challenge and can be used with students at different levels of mathematical ability. To provide for flexibility, assign some groups activities 1 and 2, other groups, 3 and 4. Assign the most capable students activities 6 and 7. Tell the class that when they finish their work, others may need to study their work to complete the final activity for the day. When all groups have reported their findings, display the students' work so that the results can be used to carry out activities 5 and 8. Groups of students would choose 5, 8, or 9 as a follow-up activity. Their results would be presented to the whole class.

1. The following numbers are called triangular numbers. Find the pattern for making triangular numbers and show the next four triangular numbers.

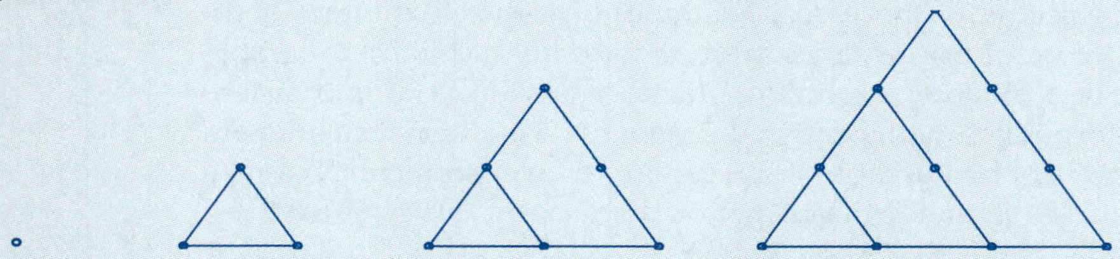

2. List in order the numbers that result when you add the number of dots in each triangular number. What pattern do you notice? Continue the pattern for the next four numbers. (*Hint:* Use a hundred square from the assignment file. Circle the numbers in your list on the chart to help find the pattern.)
3. We can make staircases with squares like the following. Make staircases with four, five, six, and seven steps.

4. List in order the number of squares for each staircase. What is the pattern? Continue the patterns for four more numbers. (Hint: Use a hundred square from the assignment file. Circle the numbers in your list on the chart to help find the pattern.)
5. What is alike and different about the pattern for the number of dots in triangular numbers and blocks in staircases? Think why this pattern occurs.
6. Some numbers are called square numbers. The first three square numbers are:

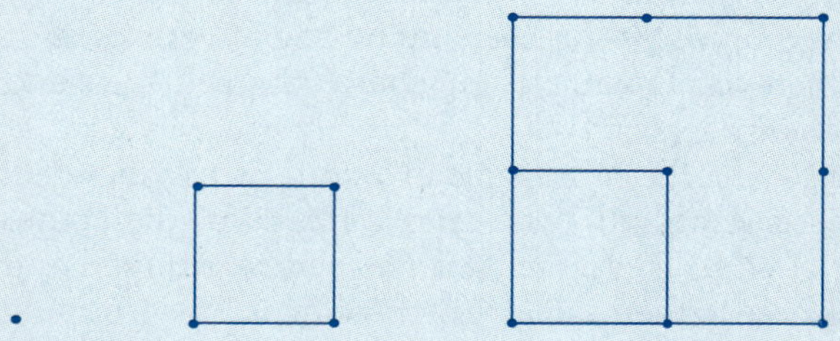

Make the next four square numbers.

7. List the number of dots in the square numbers. Look for a pattern, and keep it going for four more numbers. Look for a reason for the pattern.
8. Add the dots in two successive triangular numbers, and write in order the sums for the pairs. Look for a pattern. What other pattern is it like?
9. Take a square of wallpaper from the assignment box. Paste it in the middle of a sheet of paper you will also find in the assignment file. Use crayons to keep the pattern going until the paper is covered.

struction so that *all* children learn mathematics are given in Chapter 15, "Mathematics for Children with Special Needs."

The *post-lesson* concludes an episode. Activities similar to those used in the pre-lesson are used, and homework, if assigned, is given. Whenever homework is assigned, time should be given to explaining the assignment so that students will understand what is to be done.

Quizzes and tests are given during the time usually devoted to mathematics instruction. They usually take only part of the period. Games or motivating activities are scheduled for the remainder of the period.

Formulating Objectives. Objectives are formulated for the pre-lesson, the lesson, and the post-lesson. Objectives, however, are achieved over time. A single lesson usually does not enable a learner to construct his or her own meaning or develop skill. Teachers know this and give learners time to attain mathematical knowledge.

Objectives for the pre-lesson include those that develop interest in mathematics, relate mathematics to real life, provide for review, or involve skill maintenance. Over time activities for the pre-lesson relate to each of these objectives.

Objectives for the lesson deal with mathematical concepts and procedures and with the thinking processes involved in reaching the conceptual or procedural objective. *Conceptual objectives* state the meanings to be acquired and deal with understanding ideas and their relationships. An example of a conceptual objective is to understand that one meaning of multiplication with fractions is to "take a part." *Procedural objectives* deal with knowledge of the steps to follow in a specific situation or how to do something. Using algorithms to compute with whole numbers or fractions involves procedural knowledge. *Process objectives* deal mainly with mathematical thinking and with using strategies. They help learners see relations and make connections. Teachers decide on process objectives for lessons, as well as conceptual and procedural objectives. Examples are: translate from grouping objects to writing an addition mathematical sentence, compare an estimate to a computed solution, and find number patterns. Problem-solving strategies include drawing a diagram and working backwards.

Objectives for the post-lesson are similar to those for the pre-lesson, or they deal with assigning homework.

Selecting Activities. Activities are selected for the parts of a lesson. There are two main types of activities: responding and constructing activities. A *responding activity* asks children to follow directions, carry out steps, use a strategy or rule, or practice a skill. The student is expected to respond in a prescribed way and therefore does not engage in higher-level thinking.

A *constructing activity* requires learners to be mentally active and creative. There is no formula or rule to follow routinely to complete a constructing activity. A constructing activity is a problem-solving endeavor and involves making decisions. Higher-level thinking skills such as relating and inferring are required to carry out constructing activities. Constructing activities ask learners to produce and evaluate representations of ideas, develop graphs, find patterns, construct examples of concepts, and pose and solve problems. They often relate to real-world situations or contribute to understanding concepts in content areas other than mathematics.

Constructing activities should be used whenever possible, for they provide opportunities for students to create mathematical ideas rather than routinely deal with a set of instructions and questions, as is the case with responding activities. Figure 1.1 gives examples of activities that illustrate differences between responding and constructing activities. All chapters give examples of constructing activities to be used in class or, in some cases, for homework.

Games seem to be responding activities, but they provide opportunities for children to compare, evaluate, and communicate. They are also motivating (Kamii, 1985). Games are recommended as learning and practice activities.

URE 1.1 Responding and Constructing Activities

Both a responding and a constructing activity can use this framed clown.

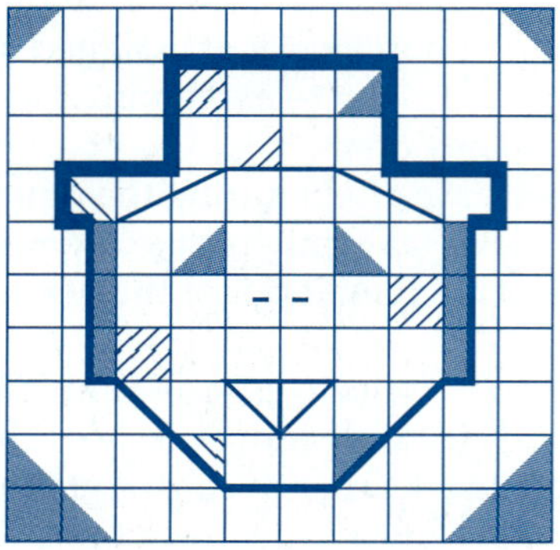

RESPONDING ACTIVITY: Look at the picture — a framed clown drawing. What percent of the picture is the clown? What percent of the clown is dark patches? Light patches? His eyes? His mouth? His hat? The frame?

CONSTRUCTING ACTIVITY: Look at the picture — a clown drawing in a frame. Think about how you could describe the clown using percent of the drawing and frame. Take a piece of grid paper from the paper cabinet. Make a *different* drawing, and write at least 7 descriptions of your work that involve percent of the picture. Your picture should fill a 10×10 grid. (Why that size?) All the drawings will be displayed for the class members to see. We will use the drawings to think about percent.

Activity for the Classroom 1.1. Play a mathematics game with a small group of children (See Chapter 3 for suggestions, or make up a game). Decide what thinking is required to play the game.

Lesson Planning for Direct and Interactive Teaching. The objectives of both direct instruction and an interactive teaching approach are that children will learn concepts, procedures, and strategies. In learning based on *direct instruction* students *receive* information from knowledgeable persons and review, practice, and solve problems to learn mathematics. The role of the teacher is to give clear explanations, usually presenting the material in small steps so that it can be understood by learners, to ask questions to keep students involved, and to check for understanding. Students demonstrate achievement by computing correctly and solving problems (Good, Grouws, and Ebmeier, 1983; Rosenshine and Stevens,1986). The lesson plan in Box 1.5 reflects this concept of teaching.

In *interactive learning,* the students *construct* knowledge by problem solving and investigating, reflecting on their work, and communicating with others. The teacher assigns problems and activities that provide opportunities for learners to develop understanding. Students share their work and discuss the meanings they have developed. To help students clarify thinking, grasp relations, and create knowledge structures, teachers often ask questions that require higher-level thinking. Students demonstrate learning in various ways, for example, writing about mathematics, solving problems, and posing problems. Box 1.6 gives a lesson plan for an interactive lesson.

Reader Activity 1.1

Compare the direct teaching and the interactive teaching lesson plans. Then compare the two lesson plan examples. In what ways are they alike? How do they differ?

Boxes 1.7 and 1.8 show how lesson plans for the two approaches would be written for teaching a particular mathematics lesson. The lesson objective in both examples is for students to learn the extended algorithm for multiplication of a tens-plus-ones number by a ones number.

BOX 1.5 Plan for Direct Teaching Lesson

OBJECTIVE

State learning to be achieved usually in terms of behavior students will demonstrate.

PREPARATION

Assemble material, and write pertinent information on the chalkboard, if required.

PRE-LESSON

1. Students check homework.
2. Review concepts and skills covered in homework.

LESSON

1. Introduction
  a. State objective.
  b. Review prerequisties.
2. Presentation
  a. Explain concept or steps in procedure; break material into small steps for easy comprehension.
  b. Model (use manipulatives as required).
  c. Ask many questions related to your explanation or modeling.
  d. Repeat explanations or modeling, as necessary.
3. Guided practice
  a. Students carry out task or steps in procedure as you observe, question, and reteach until they make correct responses.
4. Independent practice
  a. Students work independently at task for concept development or to practice skill.
  b. Give help to those who are having difficulty attaining objective.
  c. Assess progress.
5. Special reviews
  a. Conduct reviews weekly and monthly of concepts and skills taught in previous period.
  b. Test learners frequently as part of reviews.

POST-LESSON

1. Assign homework.
2. Discuss homework so that students know what is to be done.

Assessing Learning

New directions in assessment are outlined in *Curriculum and Evaluation Standards for School Mathematics* (NCTM, 1989) and *Assessment Standards for School Mathematics*, Working Draft (NCTM, 1993). These publications emphasize that a new assessment system must be developed at local and state levels and that teachers must be involved in the process. The new assessment system will give *performance standards* or statements of expectations of students' performance in mathematics judged to be important in today's world. Some states have adopted the term *outcome-based standards* to refer to the goals of mathematics learning. Whatever the term used to describe the mathematics to be learned, assessment systems should be based on the following criteria:

BOX 1.6 Plan for Interactive Teaching Lesson

OBJECTIVE

State meanings, concept, or procedure to be constructed.

PREPARATION

Assemble material, and write pertinent information on the chalkboard, as required.

PRE-LESSON

1. Students discuss homework, if assigned.
2. Students engage in interesting, challenging, motivating, or skill-building activities.

LESSON

1. *Introduction*
   a. Tell the class the initial organization for the lesson: individual or group work.
   b. Tell the class what they are to do: solve problems, carry out an activity, continue the study of a topic, or work on an ongoing project.
   c. Assign problems or activity. If appropriate, ask students to make records of their work.
2. *Activity/problem-solving phase*
   a. Students engage in mathematical thinking while manipulating, investigating, experimenting, and solving problems. While students work on the assignment, circulate among pupils, observing and listening and sometimes questioning and commenting. Students may be given an open-ended question to think about prior to a class discussion.
3. *Sharing and discussing phase*
   a. Students report their own or group's problem solutions or outcomes of the activity, or they discuss their answers to the open-ended question.
   b. Lead a discussion. Ask what, why, and how questions so students attain lesson objective. Questions should enable students to use higher-level thinking and relate models to symbolic representations, if appropriate for the lesson.
4. *Summarizing phase*
   a. Students in a class setting review what they did or what was learned.
   b. Students demonstrate learning (e.g., create their own problems, solve a problem posed by the teacher, exchange ideas with a partner, or write-up what was learned).
5. *Assessment of learning of unit material*
   a. Before, during, and following instruction use different types of assessment: observations, interviews, student journals or logs, completed assignments, group and class contributions, projects, portfolios, quizzes, and tests.
   b. Stress student self-assessment.

POST-LESSON

1. Use the same type of activity as in the pre-lesson.
2. Assign and explain homework as needed.

1. Every student will achieve mathematical power.
2. All students will have opportunities for learning mathematics.
3. Performance will be judged broadly, in terms of different kinds of mathematical thinking and different mathematical concepts and skills.
4. Evidence for making inferences about students' learning will be collected from many sources.

BOX 1.7 Direct Teaching Lesson Plan Example

OBJECTIVE

To use an extended algorithm for multiplication computation of a tens-plus-ones number by a ones number.

PRE-LESSON

1. Have students check their own homework. (Assignment was: Write multiplication facts with products from 21–30, 31–40, . . . , 81–90.)
2. Have a five-minute multiplication basic fact drill. Use large flash cards for all in the class to see.

LESSON

1. *Introduction*
   a. Tell learners the objective.
   b. Ask learners to study 27 and 38 and to explain the meaning of the number in each place.
2. *Present new learning (explain and model)*
   a. Write on the chalkboard

$$\begin{array}{r} 27 \\ \times\ 3 \\ \hline \end{array} \qquad \begin{array}{r} 38 \\ \times\ 4 \\ \hline \end{array}$$

   b. Tell learners that they multiply parts, the ones by the ones and the tens by the ones. Explain that they learned the multiply-by-parts rule when learning the basic facts. Remind them that they renamed one factor as a sum and multiplied each addend by the other factor. Give the example:
   $5 \times 6 = 5 \times (5 + 1) = 25 + 5 = 30$.

   Ask children what the tens and ones parts are in the two-digit factors in the problems on the chalkboard and the ones in the other factor.

   Model using the extended algorithm, explaining how the multiply-by-parts rule is used as you carry out each step:

$$\begin{array}{r} 27 \\ \times 13 \\ \hline 21 \\ +60 \\ \hline 81 \end{array} \qquad \begin{array}{r} 38 \\ \times\ 4 \\ \hline 32 \\ +120 \\ \hline 152 \end{array}$$

   c. Make a chart showing the first example you have just explained and the steps in the computation:
      1. Multiply the ones by the ones. Write 21 below 3.
      2. Multiply the tens by the ones. Write 60 below 21.
      3. Add the partial products for the solution 81.
      4. Think: Does the solution make sense?

   Have students explain the steps. Ask students to tell you what to write on the chalkboard or overhead to solve two more problems ($6 \times 16 = N$; $8 \times 41 = N$).
3. *Guided practice*
   a. Write a new problem ($5 \times 35 = N$), and ask children to compute the product on a study paper. Have several students use the chalkboard or overhead to show and explain their work. Question other students about the steps in the algorithm.
   b. Repeat Step 3a with different problems until most students attain the objective.
4. *Independent practice*
   a. Write three problems (4×62, 6×25, and 9×84) on the chalkboard or overhead for students to solve independently.
   b. Give individual explanations to those who have not learned the algorithm.
   c. Collect papers for grading.

POST-LESSON

1. Assign and discuss homework: 10 problems on page 61 of your textbook: multiplying a tens-plus-ones number by a ones number.

5. Assessment will focus on a learner's success in meeting expectations.
6. Inferences from the results of assessment will determine what the student can do.
7. The results of assessment will be used to enhance the learning of mathematics.
8. Communication among all those with an interest in the learning of students (i.e., students themselves, parents, caretakers, teachers, school officials, government officials, and the general public) will be facilitated.

Standards are usually written for broad areas of learning. To determine their own mathematics learning objectives, teachers use the performance standards in district curriculum guides, state frameworks, and publications of national groups. The chapters in this book give learning objectives to which teachers may refer in writing their objectives for a unit of study.

Teachers gather and interpret information about students' learning before introducing a unit of study, in the course of teaching a lesson, and after completing instruction to attain one or more objectives. Sources of information for assessment include: observations, interviews, learning logs (journals consisting of words and

Box 1.8 Interactive Teaching Lesson Plan Example

OBJECTIVE

To understand the extended algorithm for multiplying a tens-plus-ones number by a ones number and to use the algorithm.

PREPARATION

1. Before class post the names of learners in each group, and write and duplicate three story problems for students. For example,
   a. The chef at Molly's Restaurant knew that during the long Fourth of July holiday weekend his grilled chicken sandwiches would be very popular. He decided he would need 27 pounds of chicken breasts for each day of the three-day holiday. He placed his order for all the chicken breasts on Wednesday, two days before the holiday. How many pounds of chicken breasts did he order?
   b. Mr. Manowitz noticed that 16-oz sweet potato cans were on sale for a savings of $.20 a can. His family really liked canned sweet potatoes, so he decided to buy 6. As he carried out the sack he thought, "This sack is heavy. How many ounces did I buy?" What is the answer to his question?
   c. The first-grade class was making May baskets for a bulletin board. Ms. Evans, the teacher, planned to give each child 7 half-pieces of colored paper for a basket, flowers, leaves, and stems. There were 28 children in the class. How many half-pieces of colored paper did she need to have ready for the class?

PRE-LESSON

1. Discuss homework write-ups (assignment was: Write up the responses of two adults to the question: When do you need to know how to multiply numbers greater than 10?) Mention that we will soon be learning to multiply large numbers because as they found out, it is a skill we need to know.
2. Three-minute drill on multiplication facts. Each student uses his or her own flash cards.

LESSON

1. *Introduction*
   a. Ask learners to form designated groups.
   b. Give problems to learners; ask them to solve them individually any way they wish, make a record for each, and when most in the group have finished, discuss their work in their groups.
2. *Activity/problem-solving phase*
   a. Students solve problems as indicated.
   b. Circulate to observe work; question and comment as needed.
3. *Sharing and discussing phase*
   a. Have groups report their work. Have one student write the problem on the chalkboard or overhead:

$$\begin{array}{r} 27 \\ \underline{\times 3} \end{array}$$

Say, "Please show your solution on the overhead, and tell how you solved the first problem."
(I made an array:

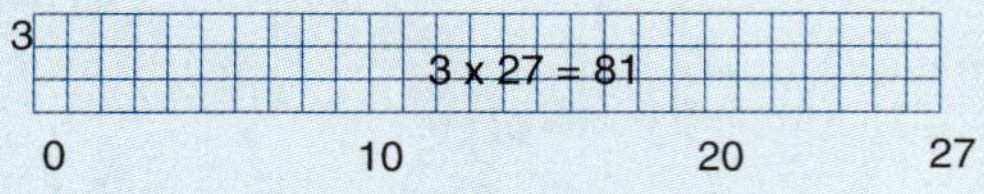

I made an addition problem:

$$\begin{array}{r} 27 \\ +27 \\ \underline{27} \\ 81 \end{array}$$

I multiplied mentally: 3×20 is 60, and 3×7 is 21; $60 + 21 = 81$.) Have each student tell why his or her answer is reasonable.
   b. Question and comment so that students learn to use extended algorithm.
      1a. If a student can explain his or her mental multiplication solution, question him or her to help the class understand the use of the distributive property of multiplication over addition (think-the-parts rule).
      1b. If no student can explain using the distributive property of multiplication over addition to carry out the mental computation, say, "Remember the think-the-parts rule. Recall, you can answer $4 \times 7 = N$ by thinking $(4 \times 5) + (4 \times 2) = 20 + 8 = 28$. How would you use the think-the-parts rule to remember $8 \times 6 = N$? (Possible response: $(8 \times 5) + (8 \times 1) = 40 + 8 = 48$.)
      2. "Let's discuss how to use the think-the-parts rule in writing out a computation. To use the rule, let's write our problem this way:

$$\begin{array}{r} 20 + 7 \\ \underline{\times 3} \end{array}$$

pictures), work products (e.g., problem solutions), projects, and portfolios (Beyer, 1993; Carter, Ogle, and Royer, 1993; Huinker, 1993; Lindquist, 1988; Peck, Jencks, and Connell, 1989). As in the past, teachers use tests in assessment (van den Heuvel-Panhuizen and Gravemeijer, 1993), but tests are designed to give more information about a student's learning than is obtained when a student circles a multiple-choice item, fills in a blank, or gives a computed sum, difference, product, or quotient. For

"How would we multiply the parts? (3 x 7 and 3 x 20). Please show that:

$$\begin{array}{r} 20 + 7 \\ \times 3 \\ \hline 60 \quad 21 \end{array}$$

"Notice there is a plus sign in the first factor. How do we find the final product? What is the product? (Add the two parts, 81.) Please do that:

$$\begin{array}{r} 20 + 7 \\ \times 3 \\ \hline 60 + 21 = 81 \end{array}$$

"We do not need to write our problems in this very long form. You remember the vertical form in addition. How would we write our multiplication problem in the vertical form? (Students show. If no student volunteers to give the extended algorithm, model the extended algorithm.)

$$\begin{array}{r} 27 \\ \times 3 \\ \hline 21 \\ +60 \\ \hline 81 \end{array}$$

"Please explain each step in this form and how it connects with the form we have just talked about. (Students explain their ideas.)

c. "Now, let's look at the repeated addition and arrays that some made to solve the problem. How do they connect with the computation we have shown?" If necessary, continue with questions so that students explain that they multiplied the ones and tens separately and that an array also shows the ones times ones and the ones times tens partial products.

d. Ask several students to give the steps in the paper-and-pencil computation. Write the steps on a chart:

To multiply a tens-plus-ones number by a ones number:
Multiply the ones times ones and record.
Multiply the ones times tens and record.
Add the partial products.
Think: Does the solution make sense?

Have students write the other story problem questions in vertical form on the overhead, and use extended algorithms to find the solutions. The class discusses their work. Ask questions to emphasize multiplying ones by ones and tens by ones and adding the partial products. Stress the sense of the procedure. Also have students refer to the problem to decide if the solution makes sense.

4. *Summarizing phase*
   a. Ask each student to make up two or more number problems for a tens-plus-ones number multiplied by a ones number and use the steps the class developed to solve the problems. Circulate, observe, and provide help as needed.
   b. Groups study members' problems and solutions to determine if everyone knows how to use the algorithm. Circulate and observe. Work with groups if they request help.
   c. Students summarize what they have learned. Help learners state that the ones and tens in one factor are multiplied by the other factor and that the partial products are added.

POST-LESSON

1. Assign and discuss homework.
   a. Write three story problems whose solutions involve multiplying a tens-plus-ones number by a ones number.
   b. Solve the problems using the rule we developed, and decide if each answer makes sense.
   c. For one problem also use another method.
   d. Write up how you thought to solve one problem and decided if the solution made sense.

example, to demonstrate knowledge of the meaning of fractions, a test item could ask students to make diagrams to show $\frac{2}{3}$, $\frac{3}{4}$, and $\frac{1}{6}$ using two of the following: geometric figures, number lines, or grid paper. They could also be asked to write a short essay describing the meaning of one of the fractions.

Student self-assessment is also a component of assessment in contemporary classes (NCTM, 1989, 1993). Students learn to assess themselves and their learning.

They are helped to judge their perseverance and assess each day's work. They learn to use metacognitive strategies to assess their comprehension of mathematical ideas. They develop habits of considering the reasonableness of estimations and problem solutions and of checking mental and paper-and-pencil computations. Students learn self-assessment approaches by listening to others explain how they assessed their work, by explaining their own self-assessments, and by observing the teacher use cognitive modeling to teach self-assessment. Checklists (Table 1.3) are also useful in teaching self-monitoring (Fortunato, Hecht, Tittle, and Alvarez, 1991).

Older students should develop habits of assessing their progress not only daily but also at the end of a unit or term. They are helped to assess their learning by making graphs of achievements, noting progress in a portfolio of completed assignments, or telling what they have learned in journal entries. They are encouraged to give high priority in their self-assessments to understanding mathematical ideas and acquiring problem-solving abilities.

Assessment before Instruction. Before beginning a unit of study, teachers assess children's knowledge of learnings subordinate to what is to be taught to determine if they can profit from instruction. For example, before teaching estimation of products of two-digit factors, teachers would assess students' knowledge of multiplication facts, mental multiplication of multiples of 10 (e.g., $20 \times 30 = \square$), and ability to compare and order large numbers. Observations, interviews, examination of work products, and tests are used to assess prior learning. Records of students' earlier achievement can also be used.

Teachers also assess students' attainment of the new learning before introducing a new topic because children may already know the material. For example, in working with a second-grade teacher, I found that, prior to instruction, over 95% of the class was competent in mental addition with easy examples with multiples of powers of 10 (e.g., $20 + 40 = 60$). The children had probably extended their knowledge of basic facts and tens without instruction. However, the knowledge demonstrated by these children did not extend to harder examples, such as $30 + 80 = 110$. Therefore, instruction began with the harder examples and was based on children's knowledge of easy examples.

Assessment during Instruction. During lessons and at selected points in a unit study, *in-process assessment* (also called feedback or formative evaluation) gives information concerning students' progress. In-process assessment tells teachers and students what objectives have or have not been attained and is used to plan follow-up instruction. Sources of in-process assessment are teachers' observations and interviews and their interpretations of pupils' learning logs, completed assignments, and responses during class discussions and on quizzes.

Performance indicators give criteria for making judgments about students' learning and are used as benchmarks in assessing achievement. In the past, a performance indicator was usually a percent of correct responses on a daily assignment or test used to indicate an acceptable level of mastery (e.g., 90% correct on a assignment of 10 problems or 9 out of the 10 correct). New directions in assessment use descriptive statements of students' attainments as performance indicators more frequently than quantitative results. Performance indicators are usually given for three levels of attainment: (1) Students do not indicate understanding or skill in a major area of learning. (2) Students are developing understanding or skill in a ma-

TABLE 1.3 Suggestions for Self-Evaluation

1. Do I understand this problem?
2. Could I tell someone what this problem is about?
3. Can I check this solution using a different computational procedure?
4. How does this solution compare with my estimate?
5. Does this solution make sense? Why or why not?

jor area of learning and occasionally can apply their knowledge to problem solving. (3) Students have developed understanding or skill in a major area of learning and can apply their knowledge to problem solving (Beyer, 1993). Examples of these levels for three areas of learning follow:

Concept of Multiplication

Has no concept: Cannot model a multiplication situation with materials.

Developing concept: Often solves multiplication story problems with modeling; cannot create multiplication story problems and model them; models multiplication statements (e.g., 3 fours) with different materials and explains his or her work; models some facts ($3 \times 4 = \square$) and explains his or her thinking; sometimes can write a multiplication fact for a representation of multiplication.

Has developed concept: Solves problems using multiplication facts; creates multiplication problems and solves them using facts; can represent his or her problem solutions if asked to do so; can explain his or her thinking in all instances.

Immediate Recall of Multiplication Facts

Has no skill: Is unable to recall any facts.

Developing skill: Recalls facts using a variety of strategies; has immediate recall of most of the facts with factors 1, 2, and 5.

Has developed skill: Has immediate recall of all facts; rarely uses a strategy for recall.

Fraction Concept

Has no concept: Cannot identify or construct a region or a set partitioned into equal-sized parts.

Developing concept: Identifies and constructs regions partitioned into equal-sized parts and explains his or her thinking; identifies and constructs sets partitioned into equal-sized parts; uses words for common unit fractions represented by diagrams showing fractional parts; knows some fraction symbols; does not construct region diagrams for common unit fractions; cannot give fractions for sets partitioned into equal-sized parts.

Has developed concept: Creates region and set diagrams for unit and common nonunit fractions and labels them with the correct symbol; clearly explains his or her thinking.

Records are kept of observations and interviews made during in-process assessment. They can be written on sticky notes and attached to a chart with a section for each child, or they can be attached to a large desk calendar and later dated and filed in children's folders. Some teachers use index cards for records of observations (Box 1.9). These can be kept in a file box with a compartment for each student.

Observation and interview records on a series of sticky notes or index cards are summarized and combined with assessments of work products and with interpretations of responses on quizzes to give information about learners' progress. Students are told what they have achieved and what the next steps in their learning should be. Teachers use information from in-process assessment to plan lessons so learners attain learning objectives.

Assessment after Instruction. At specified times after instruction has taken place, the achievement of learners is communicated to students, parents, school personnel, and other interested persons. This information is called *summative evaluation* (NCTM, 1993). It is a final assessment for a segment of instruction that consists of several units. Summative evaluation determines learners' attainment of instructional objectives that reflect performance standards. Materials on which to base

BOX 1.9 Evaluation Notes

STUDENT'S NAME: Martha Templeton

September 10

After the members of her group had solved the assigned problems individually, there was consternation over the fact they had different answers. Martha assumed the leadership of her group and explained that there could be several answers to the open-ended problems assigned. Asked each member of her team who had a different answer to explain why his or her answer made sense.

October 1

Volunteered to "think out loud" to demonstrate the "draw a diagram" strategy to the class. Solved a two-step problem using both a diagram and a math sentence.

summative evaluation of learning include in-process assessments, work products, individual or group projects (e.g., bulletin board displays and graphs based on student surveys), tests, and portfolios.

Portfolios or collections of work during a given period are superior sources of evidence in summative evaluation (NCTM, 1993). The work collected in portfolios should be selected by students and teachers. It is a representative sample of work or consists of the student's best papers. In either case, the criteria for selection should be clear to students and those to whom the portfolio is shown.

It is suggested that conferences be scheduled with parents or caretakers to communicate children's attainments. In some schools grades are given, communicated to parents or caretakers, and made a part of the student's school record. Different sources of information can be given different weights in assigning grades, for example, 10% observation and interviews, 10% homework, 10% projects, 10% class assignments, 30% tests, and 30% portfolios.

Assessment results have been used to compare students' achievement with that of others (norm-referenced evaluation) or to determine the extent that students have attained the objectives (criterion-referenced evaluation). Norm-referenced evaluation employs results from standardized tests to compare the achievement of a student, class, school, or district with that of others at the local, state, or national level. Criterion-referenced evaluation helps teachers decide the effectiveness of instruction in helping children attain the learning objectives. Often criterion-referenced evaluation is narrow in scope and consists of scores on tests used to measure achievements that are tied to limited knowledge objectives. New directions in learning mathematics rely much less on norm-referenced and criterion-referenced evaluation than on performance standards and teacher objectives that emphasize all children attaining important mathematical knowledge.

What Is Assessed? Assessment includes gathering evidence about students' understanding, reasoning abilities, competency in problem solving, skills, and attitudes (see Evaluation Standards and Assessment Standards, Appendix A). Assessment of *understanding* determines the extent to which children have internalized concepts and generalizations or developed the meanings of computational procedures. Questions to assess understanding often require students to represent an idea with materials or give the reason for a procedure. Table 1.4 gives examples of new directions in assessing understanding. *Reasoning* abilities are often assessed

TABLE 1.4 New Directions in Assessment

1. To assess children's understanding of fractions, ask them to carry out the following task:

   Represent the whole by a hexagon pattern block. Overlay other pattern blocks on your whole to show the following fractional parts of the whole: $\frac{1}{2}$, $\frac{1}{3}$, $\frac{1}{6}$ and $\frac{2}{3}$. Show the fraction in more than one way whenever possible. Trace the blocks to make diagrams to show your work.

   Write a brief statement telling how you solved the problem that asked you to show $\frac{1}{2}$ or $\frac{1}{3}$.

2. To assess their ability to pose a problem and solve it, ask students to write a story problem using this information and solve the problem.

   Donna's time was $\frac{1}{2}$ hour. Gertrude's time was $\frac{1}{3}$ hour.

3. To assess intuitive understanding of the commutative and associative properties of multiplication, ask a student to solve the following problem:

   Without computing, explain why the product of $36 \times 81 = 54 \times 54$. (Students could be asked to write up their replies.)

by asking students to compare, order, relate, or make logical inferences. Examples are given in Table 1.5.

Competency in *problem solving* is assessed by asking students to solve and pose both routine and nonroutine problems. To assess learners' ability to see the interrelatedness of mathematics and other areas, some problems used in assessment should involve other subjects and everyday life events. Problems can include missing or extra information to assess students' ability to sort out relevant information in a problem. When the problem solutions involve computation, students should have access to calculators so that the ability to analyze problems, not to compute, will be assessed.

Basic mathematical *skills* are assessed by means of oral or written tests. Assignments completed by students can also be used to assess skills. Immediate recall of basic facts for the four operations, competency in mental computation with multiples of powers of 10, ability to estimate, and efficient use of frequently used paper-and-pencil computational procedures with whole numbers, fractions, and decimals are evaluated after instruction in these areas and periodically retested to determine if the skill has been maintained. Some test items should require more than application of rules (Table 1.6).

Attitudes are assessed by observing students' interest in mathematics, their enthusiasm for investigating and solving problems, how they pose problems, their eagerness to explore new mathematical topics, and their willingness to work with others and share their ideas.

Assessment should enable students to form positive feelings about themselves and their ability to learn mathematics. As they become aware of their attainments, learners should develop feelings of self-worth and pride.

TABLE 1.5 Evaluating Logical Thinking

1. Sara's teachers asked her to solve $51 - 16 = N$ without renaming 51 as 40 + 11. What could Sara tell her teacher? (One response: Add 4 to each number, and then subtract.)
2. John, Henry, Danny, and Alfredo went fishing. The numbers of fish they caught are 2, 6, 3, and 5. They had been studying averages in school and decided to figure out the average number of fish they caught. Then Alfredo had an idea. He said, "What would the average be if we each caught 1 more fish for each number we caught? Like 3, 7, 4, and 6." After they figured out the answer, Danny thought that was a fun problem and decided to make more problems like it. He asked, "What about if we each caught 3 more or 5 more for each number we caught?" After they figured out these problems, Henry said, "I think there is something fishy here." John said, "There is a pattern!" What was the pattern the boys discovered?
3. How are squares and triangles alike and different?

TABLE 1.6 Evaluating Skill

1. Circle the math sentences that can be solved by regrouping (trading):

   a. $25 + 56 = N$ e. $71 - 24 = N$
   b. $38 + 41 = N$ f. $56 - 33 = N$
   c. $57 + 57 = N$ g. $95 - 38 = N$
   d. $33 + 37 = N$ h. $78 - 43 = N$

2. Write two multiplication math sentences for each of a, b, and c whose solutions would be estimated as: a. 500 b. 700 c. 900

3. Which has the largest quotient? Is it possible to decide without computing? Why or why not? (Write your answer to the question.)

   a. $\frac{5}{6} \div 3 = N$ b. $\frac{5}{6} \div 4 = N$ c. $\frac{5}{6} \div 2 = N$

NEW DIRECTIONS WITH CALCULATORS AND COMPUTERS

The NCTM (1987, 1989) recommends that calculators be used at all grade levels in the classroom, for homework, and for assessment; that calculators be available to learners at all times; and that every student be able to use the computer as a tool for learning and have access to a computer for individual and group work. Their recommendations are timely. Outside of school, today's children live with technology. Many have calculators and computers at home. They see calculators used when they make purchases. They notice the use of computers in stores and offices. Often their parents use computers at work. The school has a responsibility to help children discover the power of calculators and computers and use them to learn and do mathematics in the elementary school. The new directions in elementary school mathematics include the use of calculators and computers. This section gives an overview of the use of calculators and computers in elementary school mathematics. Calculator activities are described elsewhere. Some chapters have a section describing calculator activities; in other chapters, they are listed in sections that deal with activities and games.

Resources for software are given at the end of chapters. The programs listed stress meaning or well-designed practice. Many other superior software packages are available, as high-quality software for learners is found in stores and catalogues with greater and greater frequency. Before purchasing any software for use by students, however, preview it. Most city and county curriculum centers have libraries of software where you can preview and evaluate programs.

Calculators and Elementary School Mathematics

Many fear that the use of calculators will interfere with the learning of mathematics. Just the opposite is true. Calculators can help children develop concepts and engage in problem solving in ways not possible with manipulatives and paper-and-pencils. Calculators can be used to develop skills. They have a role in testing and develop positive attitudes toward mathematics (Hembree and Dessart, 1986, 1992; Suydam, 1987). The following discussion deals with calculators in concept learning, problem solving, skill development, and testing; introducing calculators; and the misuse of calculators.

Calculators in Concept Learning. Calculators enable learners to develop concepts and recognize patterns because students can generate more examples than if they work only on paper-and-pencil problems. Reflecting on many examples enables students to recognize the distinguishing characteristics of a concept or pattern. Children can extend learnings with small numbers to large numbers and hence deepen their understanding. They can experiment and test their hypotheses about number relations using calculators. Number sense in regard to both whole numbers and decimals develops from such experimentation.

Ideas that can be developed or extended using calculators include:

- Counting can be by ones or other numbers.
- There are patterns in counting, the basic facts tables, and number sequences.
- Multiplication is repeated addition, and division is repeated subtraction.
- Place–value notation is based on multiplication or division by 10, 100, 1000, or other powers of 10.
- The commutative and associative properties of addition and multiplication apply to whole and decimal numbers.
- Using a number as a factor a given number of times raises the number to that power.

Calculators in Problem Solving. Problem solving is enhanced by the use of calculators. Research has demonstrated that students' scores on tests of problem solving improve when they use calculators (Hembree and Dessart, 1986, 1992) and that students select and use appropriate problem-solving strategies and are more confident and interested in problem solving when permitted to use calculators in problem solving (Szetela and Super, 1987).

Using calculators to solve problems enables students to explore possible solutions and evaluate their sense. Freed from the tediousness of paper-and-pencil computation, students can try different approaches to understanding a problem and deciding on a method of solution. They can "play around" with problems until meanings are clarified and sensible solutions are determined.

Calculators enable learners to connect problem solving to their world. Students can create and solve large number problems from information that appears in reports of the economy, population, pollution, sports statistics, and governmental activities. Such problems make the world more comprehensible, but the complexity of the computations involved make such problems inaccessible to elementary school students who compute with only paper and pencil.

Calculators make it possible for young children to solve problems with large numbers before they know paper-and-pencil methods. The meanings of the operations that develop as learners study basic facts can be the basis for problem solving with large numbers. When they understand the operations and know how to use a calculator, children can solve school, home, and community problems that involve tens and hundreds. Solving these problems adds interest and usefulness to the study of mathematics.

The benefits of using calculators are so great that children should not be denied the opportunity to use calculators to solve problems. If they are allowed to use calculators, children will find problem solving fascinating and persevere to solve complex and intriguing problems.

Calculators in Skill Development. Calculators can help children master basic facts and develop skill in estimation. To practice basic facts, children can use calculators much like they use flash cards: key in a fact question, give the answer, press "=" to obtain the calculator display, and check the answer shown. Games can also be played with calculators to practice basic facts. Children can develop skill in estimation by checking the closeness of their estimations in whole number and decimal computation with calculator displays and by so doing learn to adjust their estimates. They can also play calculator games to learn computational estimation.

Calculators in Testing. The research of Hembree and Dessart (1986, 1992) showed that if children had instruction in the use of calculators, they achieved higher scores on tests when they were permitted to use calculators than those students who had no instruction with calculators and did not use calculators on the tests. Other studies show that children need to be familiar with calculators if they are to be used as effective tools in a testing situation (Hopkins, 1992; Payne, 1992).

The issue, however, runs deeper than using calculators to teach and test computation. Tests are the "tail that wags the curriculum." Teachers teach to the tests so their students will achieve high scores. If there is to be a restructuring of the curriculum to include greater emphasis on understanding and problem solving, less emphasis on paper-and-pencil computation, and a focus on using calculators to learn mathematics, tests need to be designed that reflect the new directions. Williams (1987) lists three steps to take before calculators are used in testing: (1) Students in all grades will use calculators. (2) A calculator-integrated curriculum will be designed and implemented in the schools. Such a curriculum will deemphasize paper-and-pencil computational methods and stress problem solving and applications rather than computational skills. (3) Students will use calculators on tests designed for calculator use. Such tests would stress understanding of computation rather than correct answers.

There are signs that change is occurring. In December 1985 the Connecticut State Board of Education voted to allow calculators on portions of an eighth-grade state mastery test that was administered in 1986. The test was designed for problem solving and higher-level thinking and is now being extended for use with sixth graders (Leinwand, 1992). Other states and communities are following the lead of Connecticut. For example, the State Boards of Education in Florida, Michigan, and California are in the process of devising tests that permit the use of a calculator for at least some parts of tests (Hopkins, 1992).

Introducing Calculators. Calculators are introduced to young children after they have had opportunities to use manipulatives to construct number ideas. Calculators are introduced to older children at any grade, if they have not yet had the opportunity to use them in mathematics classes. Students should be helped to view calculators as tools for learning, solving problems, and making important mathematical discoveries.

To develop skill in the use of calculators, children need ample time to explore their use. A period of exploration is preceded by a discussion of experiences with calculators, the handling and care of the instrument, and vocabulary words, such as *keyboard* and *display*, that make it possible to communicate about the instrument. If a calculator has a constant arithmetic function, you will probably need to point out this feature: pressing a numeral, operator key, and "=" repeatedly will make the calculator "count." For example, press "1." The calculator displays "1". Press "+" and then press "=" five times. The calculator shows: 1, 2, 3, 4, 5 (*note:* Calculators differ in the keystroking needed to activate the constant arithmetic function).

After a period of experimentation, students can discuss their discoveries, make up problems to solve with calculators, solve the problems, and share how they used the calculators to solve the problems. Thereafter, they should be encouraged to use calculators whenever it seems feasible, and calculator activities and games should be assigned regularly.

Misuse of Calculators. When calculators are used to check paper-and-pencil computation, they are misused (Reys and Reys, 1987). Calculators are for computing and investigating number ideas. Calculators are not used by sensible people to check paper-and-pencil computations and should not be used in this way by children. An estimate should be made to establish the reasonableness of an answer, and checking should involve redoing a calculator computation to verify that the keying was correct.

Calculators should be one of many tools for studying numbers (Berlin and White, 1987). Learners still need to construct number concepts by acting on materials. Calculators cannot replace concrete and graphic materials. Calculators can contribute to learning only when children can use the calculator meaningfully, because they are able to think about numbers.

Computers and Elementary School Mathematics

Computers are becoming commonplace in school as aids to learning. Children can work individually or in pairs at a computer. Some schools place computers in the classroom, others locate the computers in computer labs. They are used in reading, writing, mathematics, science, and social studies instruction. Some programs teach keyboarding. When children use computers to learn mathematics, the computer serves as a tutor, a tool, and a tutee. In this section, each of these functions is described briefly, followed by suggestions for introducing computers.

Computers as Tutors. The computer works as a tutor when it teaches concepts or skills. In most cases, the computer presents information and asks questions. The learner responds; the computer evaluates the response and decides what to present next. This type of teaching is known as Computer-Assisted Instruction (CAI). The types of CAI are tutorials, drill and practice, simulations, and instructional games.

Tutorials present new subject matter. Usually the program explains the material, presents information in small segments, and asks for specific responses, so that the learner will be involved in learning each step of a procedure, such as multiplying two-digit numbers. After this walk-through, the learner is given more leeway in responding. If the learner types a wrong response, the computer usually repeats the information required to give a correct response. Some tutorials have pictures that illustrate the ideas being taught. However, many tutorials for elementary school mathematics do not emphasize meaning, but merely present the steps in a procedure, so that students will learn to respond in a prescribed way.

Drill and practice programs are designed to help students remember material. The computer asks a question, and the learner responds. When responses are correct, the learner is usually reinforced with comments such as "Super" or a smiling face on the screen. If the response is incorrect, the computer will usually tell the learner to "try again."

Repetition is built into drill and practice programs and thus can be boring. Some are in a game format, which increases interest in the drill and practice. The program may be designed to give a record of the student's work to the student and the teacher. To enable children to grasp the meaning of the material they are endeavoring to remember, Clements (1989) recommends that drill and practice programs be used only after understanding has been developed.

Simulations enable learners to step into the real world. Simulation programs are designed to allow students to carry out activities as they would in real life. They stress exploration, decision making, and problem solving. An example is the *Whatsit Corporation* (Sunburst) that enables groups of learners to set up and manage a business that markets one product for six months.

Instructional Games are not drill and practice activities but, rather, motivating activities with an element of competition. The programs are designed to teach concepts or strategies. An example is *How the West Was One + Three × Four* (Sunburst). This game involves a race between a stagecoach and a locomotive along a number trail. Each player is given three randomly generated numbers to use to plan a move that will advance him or her and will interfere with the progress of the opponent. Students can play together, or one student can play with the computer as the opponent.

Computers as Tools. Computers serve as tools when they carry out definite functions, such as graphing, storing and retrieving information, and calculating. Elementary school children should be engaged in many projects that require collecting data, organizing the information, and making graphs to communicate their findings. It is useful to be able quickly to change a graphic representation so as to determine the display that most forcefully conveys the data. *Graphing programs* are therefore useful to learners. A program to learn and explore graphing is *The Graph*

Club (Tom Snyder Productions). When using graphing programs, students need to be aware of the potential of the program and to experiment with different graphic representations.

Data base programs make it possible to collect large amounts of data, formulate questions, and organize and sort the information. Such programs can provide worthwhile learning activities for children; for example, the sorting activity discussed by Wiebe (1990) enables a learner to experience sorting and re-sorting as he or she mentally creates new categories with different attributes.

Spreadsheets are large tables in a row-and-column format in which cell values can be operated on and changed at any time. Spreadsheets can be used with elementary school children. Working with a simple spreadsheet template, students can deal with different variables in a single problem and note the relations among variables as the numbers are changed. Edwards and Bitter (1989) discuss using large numbers in a spreadsheet activity to extend pupils' understanding. For example, the activity for young learners could be: If 30 granola bars cost $20, how much would 60, 90, 120, . . . , 450 cost?

Computers as Tutees. When a student programs the computer, the computer is the object of instruction, that is, serves as a tutee. To program, the child must know a computer language. BASIC (Beginner's All-purpose Symbolic Instruction Code) is one such language introduced to elementary school children. LOGO (Greek for "word") is another. LOGO was developed by Seymour Papert, a mathematician at the Massachusetts Institute of Technology. LOGO enables children to command a trianglelike figure, the turtle, to make lines and shapes on the monitor. A few simple commands, such as RIGHT 90 or FORWARD 30 give the learner great power to make geometric figures and designs. LOGO provides problem-solving experiences, and is interactive in that, over and over again, the learners directs, the computer responds, and the child reacts to the response. When using the LOGO program, the student is creative and engages in higher-level thinking to produce a design that meets certain criteria.

Introducing Computers into the Classroom. Whether you are going to use commercially produced software for instruction or introduce programming using LOGO or BASIC, you will need to prepare a plan for introducing the computer. The steps in the plan follow:

- Decide on the number of minutes each week each student will have at the computer and prepare sign-up sheets. Many teachers have students working at a limited number of computers in the classroom when other learning activities are taking place. Students are responsible for helping each other keep up with the instruction that was missed while working at the computer.
- Write out the directions for using the computer and the programs. Post these near the computer.
- Briefly explain the purpose for using the computer—what will be learned?
- Explain the scheduling plan to the students. Each week have students sign up for times at the computer.
- Point out the posted directions for using the computer.
- Have one or more students demonstrate how to use the program by following your written directions.
- If you have chosen a game, you may decide to use a large-screen television monitor to run through the game so that all understand the rules.
- If one or more students have had experience with computers, you may ask them to handle questions of procedure when you are teaching other students.
- Have students begin to take turns at the computer.
- When all have had a turn at the computer, ask them for reactions. The discussion should include the learning they believe occurred. The meanings students should have acquired are highlighted by your questioning during the discus-

sion. Students need an opportunity to reflect on their computer experiences in order to gain the greatest benefit from them. A discussion provides such an opportunity.

If only one computer is available, the computer should present challenging instruction, not drill and practice. Decide on programs that provide problem-solving experiences.

If students are going to learn to program, explain that a computer will do exactly as told. Some activities in which students act like computers by following directions given by their peers are useful. Such activities teach giving precise directions in the proper order. Wiburg and Rader (1984) give examples of several games to teach giving directions and thinking sequentially.

Computers, like calculators, should be integrated into the mathematics program and complement other approaches. Children still need work with manipulatives and diagrams. You will continue to use interactive teaching with its emphasis on problem solving and communication. Questioning and listening to children remain the hallmarks of quality teaching.

Reader Activity 1.2

Ask two teachers how calculators and computers are used in their classrooms. Compare the responses. Decide if you would use one or both teachers as models for work with calculators and computers in your classroom.

SUMMARY

The new directions in elementary school mathematics instruction emphasize solving problems, making connections, reasoning about mathematics, relating conceptual and procedural knowledge, developing positive attitudes toward mathematics, working cooperatively and communicating, and using calculators and computers. Students construct knowledge as they investigate, make records of their findings, think critically, and share their ideas with others. They become aware that they are competent and can assume responsibility for their own learning. Interactive teaching, a problem-solving approach to instruction, and cooperative learning were described as methods to implement the new directions, and the importance of questioning to enable students to construct knowledge was emphasized. Units, lessons, objectives, activities, and assessment were discussed as aspects of planning and implementing instruction.

The following chapters describe learning experiences and assessment for specific topics in elementary school mathematics. As mathematics is the study of patterns and relations, constructing patterns and relations is emphasized throughout the book.

REFERENCES

Ames, Russell, and Carole Ames. (1984). "Introduction." In *Research on Motivation in Education, Vol 1: Student Motivation*, edited by Russell Ames and Carole Ames, pp. 1–11. New York: Academic Press.

Arlin, Patricia Kennedy. (October 1990). "Teaching as Conversation." *Educational Leadership* 48: 82–84.

Artzt, Alice F., and Claire M. Newman. (1990). *How to Use Cooperative Learning in the Mathematics Class.* Reston, VA: National Council of Teachers of Mathematics.

Berlin, Donna F., and Arthur L. White. (February 1987). "An Instructional Model for Integrating the Calculator." *Arithmetic Teacher* 34: 52–54.

Beyer, Ann. (1993). "Assessing Students' Performance Using Observations, Reflections, and Other Methods." In *Assessment in the Mathematics Classroom*, edited by Norman L. Webb and Arthur F. Coxford, pp. 111–120. Reston, VA: National Council of Teachers of Mathematics.

Burns, Marilyn. (February 1985). "The Role of Questioning." *Arithmetic Teacher* 32: 14–16.

Carpenter, Thomas P., Deborah A. Carey, and Vicky L. Kouba. (1990). "A Problem-Solving Approach to the Operations." In *Mathematics for the Young Child*, edited by Joseph N. Payne, pp. 111–131. Reston, VA: National Council of Teachers of Mathematics.

Carter, Pamela L., Pamela K. Ogle, and Lynn B. Royer. (1993). "Learning Logs: What Are They and How Do We Use Them." In *Assessment in the Mathematics Classroom*, edited by Norman L. Webb and Arthur F. Coxford, pp. 87–96. Reston, VA: National Council of Teachers of Mathematics.

Clements, Douglas H. (1989). *Computers in Elementary Mathematics Education.* Englewood Cliffs, NJ: Prentice-Hall.

Cohen, Margaret W. (1985). "Extrinsic Reinforcers and Intrinsic Motivation." In *Motivation Theory and Practice for Preservice Teachers* (Teacher Education Monograph No. 4), edited by M. Kay Alderman and Margaret W. Cohen, pp. 6–15. Washington, DC: ERIC Clearinghouse on Teacher Education.

Dossey, John A., Ina V. S. Mullis, Mary M. Lindquist, and Donald L. Chambers. (1988). *The Mathematics Report Card: Are We Measuring Up?* Princeton, NJ: Educational Testing Service.

Edwards, Nancy Tanner, and Gary G. Bitter. (October 1989). "Changing Variables Using Spreadsheet Templates." *Arithmetic Teacher* 37: 40–44.

Fennema, Elizabeth, Thomas P. Carpenter, and Penelope L. Peterson. (1989). "Learning Mathematics with Understanding: Cognitively Guided Instruction." In *Advances in Research on Teaching, Vol. 1*, edited by Jere Brophy, pp. 195–221. Greenwich, CN: JAI Press.

Fortunato, Irene, Deborah Hecht, Carol Kehr Tittle, and Laura Alvarez. (December 1991). "Metacognition and Problem Solving." *Arithmetic Teacher* 39: 38–40.

Gailey, Stavroula K. (January 1993). "The Mathematics-Children's Literature Connection." *Arithmetic Teacher* 40: 258–261.

Good, Thomas L., Douglas A. Grouws, and Howard Ebmeier, (1983). *Active Mathematics Teaching.* New York: Longman.

Hembree, Ray, and Donald J. Dessart. (March 1986). "Effects of Hand-Held Calculators in Precollege Mathematics Education: A Meta-Analysis." *Journal for Research in Mathematics Education* 17: 83–99.

Hembree, Ray, and Donald J. Dessart. (1992). "Research on Calculators in Mathematics Education." In *Calculators in Mathematics Education,* edited by James Fey and Christian R. Hirsch, pp. 23–32. Reston , VA: National Council of Teachers of Mathematics.

Hiebert, James. (1990). "The Role of Routine Procedures in the Development of Mathematical Competence." In *Teaching and Learning Mathematics in the 1990s,* edited by Thomas J. Cooney and Christian R. Hirsch, pp. 31–40. Reston, VA: National Council of Teachers of Mathematics.

Hiebert, James, and Thomas P. Carpenter. (1992). "Learning and Teaching with Understanding." In *Handbook of Research on Mathematics Teaching and Learning,* edited by Douglas A. Grouws, pp. 65–97. New York: Macmillan.

Hiebert, James, and Patricia Lefevre. (1986). "Conceptual and Procedural Knowledge in Mathematics: An Introductory Analysis." In *Conceptual and Procedural Knowledge: The Case of Mathematics,* edited by James Hiebert, pp. 1–27. Hillsdale, NJ: Erlbaum.

Hiebert, James, Diana Wearne, and Susan Taber. (March 1991). "Fourth Graders' Gradual Construction of Decimal Fractions during Instruction Using Different Physical Representations." *Elementary School Journal* 91: 321–341.

Holmes, Emma E. (March 1991). "Democracy in Elementary School Classes." *Social Education* 55: 176–178.

Hopkins, Martha H. (1992). "The Use of Calculators in the Assessment of Mathematics Achievement." In *Calculators in Mathematics Education,* edited by James Fey and Christian R. Hirsch, pp. 158–166. Reston, VA: National Council of Teachers of Mathematics.

Huinker, DeAnn M. (1993). "Interviews: A Window to Students' Conceptual Knowledge of the Operations." In *Assessment in the Mathematics Classroom,* edited by Norman L. Webb and Arthur F. Coxford, pp. 80–86. Reston, VA: National Council of Teachers of Mathematics.

Johnson, David W., and Roger T. Johnson. (1987). *Learning Together and Alone: Cooperative, Competitive, and Individualistic Learning,* 2nd ed. Englewood Cliffs, NJ: Prentice-Hall.

Kamii, Constance. (1990). "Constructivism and Beginning Arithmetic (K–2)." In *Teaching and Learning Mathematics in the 1990s,* edited by Thomas J. Cooney and Christian R. Hirsch, pp. 22–30. Reston, VA: National Council of Teachers of Mathematics.

Kamii, Constance Kazuko. (1985). *Young Children Reinvent Arithmetic.* New York: Teachers College Press.

Labinowicz, Ed. (1985). *Learning from Children: New Beginnings for Teaching Numerical Thinking.* Menlo Park, CA: Addison-Wesley.

Leinwand, Steven J. (1992). "Calculators in State Testing: A Case Study." In *Calculators in Mathematics Education,* edited by James Fey and Christian R. Hirsch, pp. 167–176. Reston, VA: National Council of Teachers of Mathematics.

Lepper, Mark R., and Melinda Hodell. (1989). "Intrinsic Motivation in the Classroom." In *Research on Motivation in Education, Vol. 3: Goals and Cognitions,* edited by Carole Ames and Russell Ames, pp. 73–105. New York: Academic Press.

Lindquist, Mary Montgomery. (January 1988). "Assessing through Questioning." *Arithmetic Teacher* 35: 16–18.

Lindquist, Mary Montgomery. (1989). "It's Time to Change." In *New Directions for Elementary School Mathematics,* edited by Paul R. Trafton and Albert P. Shulte, pp. 1–13. Reston, VA: National Council of Teachers of Mathematics.

Mathematical Sciences Education Board, National Research Council. (1990). *Reshaping School Mathematics: A Philosophy and Framework for Curriculum.* Washington, DC: National Academy Press.

McLeod, Douglas B. (1992). "Research on Affect in Mathematics Education: A Reconceptualization." In *Handbook of Research on Mathematics Teaching and Learning,* edited by Douglas A. Grouws, pp. 575–596. New York: Macmillan.

National Council of Teacher of Mathematics. (February 1987). "NCTM Position Statement on Calculators in the Mathematics Classroom." *Arithmetic Teacher* 34: 61.

National Council of Teachers of Mathematics. (1989) *Curriculum and Evaluation Standards for School Mathematics.* Reston, VA: Author.

National Council of Teachers of Mathematics. (1991). *Professional Standards for Teaching Mathematics.* Reston, VA: Author.

National Council of Teachers of Mathematics. (October 1993). *Assessment Standards for School Mathematics: Working Draft.* Reston, VA: Author.

National Research Council. (1989). *Everybody Counts: A Report to the Nation on the Future of Mathematics Education.* Washington, DC: National Academy Press.

Payne, Joseph N. (1992). "The Effects of Calculators on State Objectives and Tests." In *Calculators in Mathematics Education,* edited by James Fey and Christian R. Hirsch, pp. 177–185. Reston, VA: National Council of Teachers of Mathematics.

Peck, Donald M., Stanley M. Jencks, and Michael L. Connell. (November 1989). "Improving Instruction through Brief Interviews." *Arithmetic Teacher* 37: 15–17.

Piaget, Jean. (1952). *The Child's Conception of Number.* London: Routledge & Kegan Paul.

Reyes, Laurie Hart. (May 1984). "Affective Variables and Mathematics Education." *Elementary School Journal* 84: 558–581.

Reys, Barbara J., and Robert W. Reys. (February 1987). "Calculators in the Classroom: How Can We Make It Happen?" *Arithmetic Teacher* 34: 12–14.

Rosenshine, Barak, and Robert Stevens. (1986). "Teaching Functions." In *Handbook of Research on Teaching,* 3rd ed., edited by Merlin C. Wittrock, pp. 376–391. New York: Macmillan.

Ryan, Richard M., James P. Connell, and Edward L. Deci. (1985). "A Motivational Analysis of Self-determination and Self-regulation in Education." In *Research on Motivation in Education, Vol 2: The Classroom Milieu,* edited by Carole Ames and Russell Ames, pp. 13–51. New York: Academic Press.

Suydam, Marilyn N. (February 1987). "Research Report: What Are Calculators Good For?" *Arithmetic Teacher* 34: 22–23.

Szetela, Walter, and Doug Super. (May 1987). "Calculators and Instruction in Problem Solving in Grade 7." *Journal for Research in Mathematics Education* 18: 215–229.

van den Heuvel-Panhuizen, Marja, and Koeno Gravemeijer. (1993). "Tests Aren't All Bad: An Attempt to Change the Face of Written Tests in Primary School Mathematics Instruction." In *Assessment in the Mathematics Classroom,* edited by Norman L. Webb and Arthur F. Coxford, pp. 54–64. Reston, VA: National Council of Teachers of Mathematics.

Vetter, R. Kay. (November 1992). "The Learning Connection: Talk-Throughs." *Arithmetic Teacher* 40: 168.

Wiburg, Karin, and Barbara Rader. (January 1984). "Computers Are Elementary." *Arithmetic Teacher* 31: 18–22.

Wiebe, James H. (January 1990). "Data Base Programs in the Mathematics Classroom." *Arithmetic Teacher* 37: 38–40.

Williams, David E. (October 1987). "Using Calculators in Assessing Mathematics Achievement." *Arithmetic Teacher* 35: 21–23.

SOFTWARE REFERENCES

The Graph Club
Company: Tom Snyder Productions
Computer: Macintosh
Grade level: K–4

How the West Was One + Three × Four
Company: Sunburst
Computer: Apple II, Macintosh, IBM, Tandy
Grade level: 4–adult

Whatsit Corporation
Company: Sunburst
Computer: Apple II, IBM, Tandy
Grade level: 6–adult

CHAPTER 2

Solving Mathematical Problems in the Elementary School

▪ INTRODUCTORY PROBLEM ▪

Decide what strategies you use to solve problems. List them to use with the problems in this chapter. Solve each problem using a strategy on your list or the one suggested in the discussion. Solve five or more problems using both strategies. Evaluate the effectiveness of the problem-solving strategies you used. How does this activity relate to your teaching children problem-solving strategies?

INTRODUCTION

Everyday we face problems when a situation puzzles or perplexes us. We do not know what to do but believe we must do something. To solve problems, we rely on what we know to restructure a problem situation so that it becomes manageable. Although not all problems we solve are mathematical, many have spatial or numerical dimensions.

The idea that problem solving should be central to mathematics instruction at all grade levels permeates the *Agenda for Action* (NCTM, 1980) and the *Curriculum and Evaluation Standards for School Mathematics* (NCTM, 1989) (see Standard 1 in Curriculum Standards for Grades K–4 and 5–8, Appendix A). The rationale for such an approach is that only those who are mathematical problem solvers will be able to live full, productive lives in the twenty-first century. Problem solvers will be able to cope with the demands of their personal lives, be productive workers, and understand the complex issues that come to the attention of the citizens of a world power.

If the focus of learning mathematics is problem solving, instruction must not only enable students to learn strategies for solving problems but also present content in a problem-solving format. Each chapter of this text discusses using problem solving as the vehicle for learning mathematics. This chapter is about helping children learn to solve different kinds of problems. The sections are: Types of Problems, Attitudes and Problem Solving, Teaching Problem Solving, Calculators and Problem Solving, Metacognition and Problem Solving, Assessing Problem Solving, and Summary.

TYPES OF PROBLEMS

There are two types of problems in elementary school mathematics: routine and nonroutine. *Routine problems* can be solved by established methods. To solve routine problems, problem solvers apply procedures they have learned. Routine problems are often called *translation problems* because the situation description can be translated from words to symbols. Translating the problem into an open number sentence and finding the unknown solves the problem. Routine problems can require one, two, or more steps to solve. Examples of routine problems are:

1. May picked some flowers in her garden and used all the flowers to make 3 bouquets with 9 flowers in each bouquet. How many flowers did she pick?
2. Manual bought 3 shirts, each costing $4.79. The sales tax on the purchase was $.75. He gave the clerk $20. What was his change?
3. What number is 4 times greater than 8?
4. What number is 3 less than 7 times 5?

Routine problems have an important place in the curriculum (Charles, 1985). Because life is full of routine problems, a major objective of instruction is for students to learn to solve such problems. However, an examination of the results of the fourth mathematics assessment of the National Assessment of Education Progress (NAEP) shows that learners have difficulties with all but simple one-step routine problems (Kouba, Brown, Carpenter, Lindquist, Silver, and Swafford, 1988).

Although not strictly routine problems, examples for learners are often also called problems (e.g., $5 \times \square = 45$). That terminology is used in this book.

Reader Activity 2.1

In the next week, make a record of the math problems you solve in your daily life. Were the problems routine or nonroutine? How did you decide?

Nonroutine problems are often referred to as *process problems*. They require more than translating the problem into a mathematical sentence and using known procedures (Kouba et al., 1988). They require that the problem solver construct the method of solution. He or she must plan how to arrive at the solution as well as find the solution. Strategies, such as drawing a picture, guessing and checking, or making a table or organized list, are often used. Nonroutine problems can be open-ended, that is, have more than one solution, as in example 2 in the list that follows. They often involve lifelike situations or making connections with other subjects. Examples of nonroutine problems are:

1. There are 6 students in the Stamp Club. Once each month, the students in the club trade stamps. If each student trades one stamp with every other student, how many trades took place at the club meeting? (Answer: 15.)
2. Prices at the school cafeteria are: turkey sandwich, $.90; ham sandwich, $.85; milk, $.40; French fries, $.99; pasta salad, $.75; ice cream, $.50; apple, $.35; banana, $.35. You have $2.00. You decide you will have a healthful lunch and spend as much of your money as you can. What can be purchased for your lunch?
3. What odd numbers less than 60 have the sum of their digits equal to 8? (Answers: 17, 35, 53.)
4. The population of Sunville was 19,000 in 1970, 21,000 in 1980, and 24,000 in 1990. If growth continues at the same rate, what will the population of Sunville be in the year 2000?

Whether a problem is routine or nonroutine depends on the person solving the problem. A routine problem for a sixth grader would probably be a nonroutine problem for a first grader. A nonroutine problem such as Example 1 can be routine if the problem solver has solved other problems of this type and immediately recognizes the method and number sentence to use to solve the problem.

ATTITUDES AND PROBLEM SOLVING

Students not only develop problem-solving skills but also attitudes toward problem solving. Positive attitudes involve confidence in one's ability to solve problems and a willingness to persevere to find a solution to a difficult problem. Negative attitudes involve dislike for problem solving and attempts to avoid solving problems.

Positive attitudes toward problem solving are formed in a classroom in which students' understanding of a problem is valued at least as much as the correct solution and learners are expected to be able to explain the thinking that led to the solution. Cobb, Yackel, Wood, Wheatley, and Merkel (1988) discuss how teachers can create an atmosphere in which children develop attitudes that contribute to problem-solving skills. Their suggestions include: Let children solve problems independently or in groups, and discuss their solutions. Be nonevaluative in your reactions to children's explanations. Convey the expectation that children can discuss their ideas and correct invalid assumptions on their own if given time and support. Do not call attention to those who solve many problems but, rather, help children express satisfaction and pride when they do not give up but persevere to understand the meaning of even one problem in order to solve it. Help children learn to listen to each other, accept viewpoints other than their own, indicate agreement or disagreement with others' ideas, not the students themselves, and resolve conflicts by reasoning and accepting alternatives. Convey your expectations to learners during discussions, and model valued behavior during whole-class and small-group work.

Chisko (1985) points out that when children come to class with negative attitudes toward mathematics and problem solving, they can be helped to develop positive attitudes through discussions that help them examine their attitudes and explore ways to change them. She also reports that lessons stressing involvement help students change attitudes. Such lessons enable learners to articulate and communicate their thinking and to take control of their learning in small-group and whole-class arrangements. To create interest in problem solving, she has students write problems. She reports that stories from which students can generate problems have been very effective in helping learners become active and involved. Such stories involve many variables such as time, temperature, mileage, and costs. The teacher or students can write these stories.

TEACHING PROBLEM SOLVING

Teachers use the interactive method to teach problem solving as well as mathematical content. Children learn problem solving by solving problems and reflecting on the processes they used to find solutions (Cobb and Merkel, 1989; Cobb et al., 1988; Jacobson, Lester, and Stengel, 1980; Lester, 1983). Questions you ask help students examine their thought processes and consider strategies they used to find solutions. Authorities agree that knowledge of strategies aids finding problem solutions (Charles and Lester, 1984; Schoenfeld, 1980; Suydam, 1980). The steps in the interactive method to teach problem-solving strategies are:

- Assign one or more problems for children to solve. Children read each problem silently or orally and ask about the meaning of any word they do not know. They do not discuss how to solve the problem(s). When word meanings are clarified, they solve the problem(s) individually or in groups of two or three students. As they solve the problem(s), circulate to observe their work.
- Lead a class discussion during which students report their solutions and how they thought to find the solutions.
- Ask questions that enable learners to reflect on the processes they used to find solutions. Use their responses to help them become aware of problem-solving strategies. Whenever possible, have students name strategies.
- Provide many opportunities for students to use strategies, and share their thinking about the use of different strategies. Have students do write-ups that describe how they thought as they solved a problem. Help children realize that often more than one strategy can be used to solve a problem.

There are general strategies for solving both routine and nonroutine mathematical problems and specific strategies for solving particular problems. Both kinds of strategies are examined in the next sections. After each strategy is described, a plan for introducing the strategy is discussed.

A General Strategy for Problem Solving

The best known of the general strategies or heuristics is Polya's (1957) four-step plan, useful for both routine and nonroutine problems. The steps are:

1. Understand the problem
2. Devise a plan
3. Carry out the plan
4. Look back

I describe the steps as if they occur sequentially in the process of problem-solving. Often, however, there is some zigzagging back and forth between the steps, particularly in a demanding problem-solving situation.

Understand the Problem. This step is crucial to successful problem solution. It involves grasping the problem situation, determining relevant facts, deciding the relations among facts, and formulating the problem question. Every written problem, except very simple ones, should be read several times, and the information in the problem studied carefully to grasp its meaning. The information in an oral problem should be reviewed so that the problem is understood. Usually one should restate the problem in one's own words. Constructing a mental picture is also an aid to understanding the problem structure.

Devise a Plan. This step is carried out confidently when a problem is understood. A solution plan is constructed that takes into account the structure of the problem and the question to be answered. If the problem is routine, the task is to write an open math sentence , for example, $19 + 228 = \square$. This involves translating the problem into mathematical language. If the problem is nonroutine, a plan is devised. Often a learned strategy is used.

Carry Out the Plan. To find a correct solution, the plan decided upon in Step 2 must be carried out carefully. To begin, an estimate of the solution is made whenever possible. Diagrams, tables, or lists are constructed neatly so the problem solver will not become confused. Labels are used where appropriate. If the solution calls for computation, most individuals use a hand-held calculator to relieve the burden of paper-and-pencil computation and reduce the anxiety often connected with problem solving. If inconsistencies appear while carrying out the plan, the process is reviewed in order to determine the source of the difficulty.

Look Back. During this step the solution is assessed and problem extensions considered. Computation is checked. Checking can involve solving the problem another way or determining the accuracy of the computation by working backward from the solution to a given number by using the inverse of the operation used in the original computation. If an estimate was made, it is compared to the solution. The solution is also matched against the problem to see if it is reasonable. An important part of this step is extension. This involves seeking out alternative ways to solve the problem and considering how the problem could be varied.

Activity for the Classroom 2.1. Ask five children to think out loud while they solve a story problem. Determine the steps they use and their approaches to solving the problem. Make notes of their responses to use in the next Activity for the Classroom.

Teaching Polya's Four-Step Plan

In the primary grades (K–2) the objectives are for children to learn the importance of understanding problems, the use of a few strategies, and how to decide on the sense of solutions. In the middle (3–4) and upper (5–6) grades, teaching the four-step plan has more specific objectives. Children learn the names of the steps and how to carry them out. Children frequently review the steps as they work in a whole-class or small-group setting.

Teaching "Understand the Problem." Many children come to school knowing how to to solve simple addition and subtraction problems by direct modeling using objects or fingers (Carpenter and Moser, 1983, 1984; Fennema, Carpenter, and Peterson, 1989). After young children have solved problems using their own methods, you can help them realize that solving any problem involves understanding it. You guide students to develop this idea by discussing with them how they solved their problems. Questions to ask during the discussion include:

- How did you know what to do?
- How did you decide what to do with your counters?
- Why do we begin by thinking about the meaning of the problem?
- What happens if you begin without understanding the problem?

The discussion can be concluded with a few children summarizing what they learned about problem solving.

In later grades, early in the school year begin a problem-solving lesson by asking if students know the steps in problem solving. If they know the steps, make a chart listing the steps (Figure 2.1). If they do not know the first or other steps, have them solve a relatively easy problem so that they can be successful, and ask them to reflect on what they did. As they talk about what they did, help them focus on the steps in the problem-solving process. They can suggest labels to help them remember the steps. The chart in Figure 2.1 should be made and displayed. Emphasize the importance of the first step by asking the last two questions in the preceding list.

Students may know that they need to understand a problem but not know how to go about getting its sense. After it is established that the first step is *Understand the Problem,* a discussion can stress what it means to understand a problem. Ask students to tell what they do to understand a problem. Use their responses to bring out suggestions for ensuring understanding. These should include:

- Read the problem until you know what it is about.
- Make sure you know the meaning of all the words.
- Ask the teacher for the meaning of unfamiliar words or unclear statements.
- Say the problem in your own words.
- Think what is happening.
- Make a mind picture of the problem situation.
- Draw a diagram to decide what goes with what.
- Review the facts.
- Tell yourself what facts go together.
- Say what you believe is the problem question.
- Ask yourself if that question were answered would the problem be solved.

These suggestions may be written on a chart for student ready reference.

If no students come up with these ways to understand, present them to the class, and have students use the ideas with specific problems in a lesson that focuses on how to understand problems and that does not involve finding solutions.

FIGURE 2.1 Chart of Problem-Solving Steps

PROBLEM – SOLVING STEPS

1. Understand the Problem
2. Devise a Plan
3. Carry Out the Plan
4. Look Back

Students should report on the usefulness of different suggestions after trying them out.

For example, to introduce visualization to primary grade children, you could use the following problem and teaching sequence:

> *Jack makes 10 cents on each paper he delivers. He delivers 32 papers each day. How much does he make in his daily delivery?*

Tell students the problem, ask questions about unfamiliar words or events, and suggest they make mind pictures to visualize the problem situation. They should share their mind pictures in small groups or with the whole class. Some may report seeing 10 cents falling in Jack's pocket when he delivers each paper; others may have seen Jack collecting 10 cents for each of the 32 papers when he returns to the paper pick-up building; still others may have seen Jack adding up how much money he makes each day he delivers papers.

Thereafter, to emphasize the importance of understanding the problem, you can:

1. Assign a problem and before students begin to solve it, have them study the problem and think about the first step for solving it. Ask for volunteers to use cognitive modeling to demonstrate for others how to carry out the first step.

   If students do not know how to use cognitive modeling for *Understand the Problem,* show the class how to model by thinking out loud, ask them to comment on what they observed, talk with them about what needs to be done to understand the problem, and ask for volunteers to think the first step out loud for others to observe.
2. Ask questions after students have solved specific problems and reported their procedures. Examples of questions are:
   - You said you read the problem three times? Why?
   - How did saying the problem in your own words help you?
   - Why did you make a mind picture (drawing) of that problem? What was your mental picture (drawing)?
   - How did you decide what facts were related to one another (or go with one another)?
   - What helped you decide on that question?
   - Did you ever change your mind about the meaning of that problem? Why?

Teaching "Devise and Carry Out a Plan." Steps 2 and 3, *Devise a Plan* and *Carry Out the Plan,* are dealt with informally in the early grades. Because many young children understand using models (representations) for solving problems when they come to school, the major objective is for them to use this strategy and share their knowledge with others. If your students have not developed any strategies for solving simple problems, you introduce *Act It Out* with manipulatives or teach *Draw a Diagram.* These strategies are discussed in the following section.

Before emphasizing the steps *Devise a Plan* and *Carry Out the Plan* with older children, find out what strategies they use. After a discussion of known strategies, help them realize that these strategies come under the *Devise a Plan* and *Carry Out the Plan* steps.

To guide learners to think about devising a plan and carrying it out carefully, ask questions such as:

- What did you say to yourself as you planned a strategy?
- Please explain why you decided to . . . (guess the answer and decide if the guess made sense, draw a diagram, etc.).
- Why is making a plan important?
- What strategy do you use most often? Why?
- Why have groups solved the problem in different ways?

- Sarah reported that her group started to draw a diagram and then changed to making a table. Why did they do that?
- When should you decide to change plans?
- Did you estimate the solution? Why or why not?
- Why did different groups use the same plan and get different answers? (This question should bring out the importance of making neat diagrams, using labels, computing carefully, and ensuring that work is readable.)
- What helped you decide to add (subtract, multiply, or divide)? The meanings of these operations are reviewed as students answer this question.

Students can use cognitive modeling for others to observe different thought patterns when engaging in Steps 2 and 3. Discuss the differences with them, and help them reach the conclusion that students can follow different thought sequences and even use different plans, yet arrive at the same solution.

Teaching "Look Back." *Look back* involves checking a computation for errors, determining if a solution is reasonable, looking for alternate ways to solve the problem, and extending the problem so as to be prepared for solving problems that have similar characteristics. All children should be helped to learn the *Look Back* step. When young children share their solutions, you ask questions such as: "How can we be sure the answer is correct? Does the answer make sense?" You also discuss with them why checking an answer is a good idea. Over time, children will develop the habit of "looking back" and report how they carried out this step when they share their solutions.

With older children who have not developed the looking-back habit, refer to the *Look Back* step on your chart. Ask them what that means. They will probably reply, "Check a solution." Continue by asking why checking is important and what different ways there are to check. Their answers or your comments regarding different ways to check should include the following:

- If possible, use an alternate strategy to find the solution.
- Compare your answer to your estimate.
- Compute the answer a different way to check its accuracy.
- Ask yourself if the answer fits the problem question.
- Change the problem story so that the question becomes a statement with the answer, and see if it makes sense.
- Ask yourself if the answer deals sensibly with the problem.
- Make a mind picture to see if the solution solves the problem.

Thereafter, until they have learned this step, before they begin problem solving, remind them to check their computations and whether their solutions make sense. When they report on their work, make certain that the "look-back" step is discussed.

Look Back by thinking of related problems broadens students' understanding of problems. To learn about related problems, students can be asked to pose new problems by changing the original problem in some way. They can be asked to extend a problem by using one of the possibilities given in the following list. The assignment can also be open-ended, requiring them to pose a new problem while keeping some aspects of the new problem the same as in the original.

Ways To Change a Problem

1. Give the answer, and make a problem fact an unknown.
   - *Problem:* Each student in our class of 29 students needs 2 pounds of clay to make a candle holder for a holiday gift. How many pounds of clay do we need for the students?
   - *Extension:* There are 29 students in our class. The teacher, Ms. Sawada, bought 58 pounds of clay for a holiday project. Each student will get the same amount of clay to make a candle holder. How much will each student get?

2. Use different numbers.

- *Problem:* What number is 4 less than 5?
- *Extension:* What number is 2 less than 9?

3. Change the problem situation, but retain the structure.

- *Problem:* Jan and Dad bought some cookies. She took 1 dozen to Girl Scouts. He took 1 dozen to his office. They gave 6 to Grandmother and had 18 left for themselves. How many did they buy?
- *Extension:* Ernesto and Roger collected rocks. They put 4 large rocks in a green sack to give Ernesto's class and 8 small rocks in a brown sack to give to Roger's class collection. There were enough left for Ernesto and Roger each to have 7. How many did they collect?

4. Give the problem more steps.

- *Problem:* Bob bought 2 cassettes of his favorite recording artist for $4.99 each. What did the two cassettes cost?
- *Extension:* Bob bought 2 cassettes of his favorite recording artist for $4.99 each. He paid 6% sales tax. What was his total cost? If he gave the clerk $15, what was his change?

5. Make the problem more complex.

- *Problem:* Tom has more marbles than Fred. Jim has less marbles than Fred. Who has the most marbles?
- *Extension:* Tom, Fred, and Leon have the same number of marbles. Alex has fewer than Tom. Jim has more than Alex and more than Leon. Who has the most marbles?
- *Problem:* What number is 7 times 4?
- *Extension:* What number is 15 less than 7 times 4?

6. Make the problem more restrictive.

- *Problem:* What numbers less than 50 have the sum of their digits equal to 8?
- *Extension:* What even numbers less than 50 have the sum of their digits equal to 8?

Students demonstrate they remembered to include the *Look Back* step when they report how they checked problems or posed related problems. If during a class discussion, they do not share how they carried out this step, ask how this step could be carried out.

After Polya's four-step plan has been introduced, it is often reviewed before students begin a problem-solving lesson. As noted in this section, students are often asked how they used the steps after they solved problems. They can also be encouraged to include descriptions of how they solved problems when they write in their journals.

Activity for the Classroom 2.2. Use the notes you made for Activity for the Classroom 2.1 to determine what the children you interviewed know about Polya's problem-solving steps. Compare their responses to decide the range of your students' understanding of the problem-solving steps.

Specific Strategies for Problem Solving

Specific strategies are used with both routine and nonroutine problems. For routine problems the most used strategy is *Write an Open Math Sentence.* Some problem solvers may use *Use a Simpler Problem* or *Recall a Similar Problem* before writing the open math sentence for a routine problem.

For nonroutine problems there are a number of strategies: *Act It Out, Draw a Diagram, Guess and Check, Work Backwards, Make an Organized List, Make a Table, Find a Pattern, Use a Simpler Problem, Recall a Similar Problem,* and *Use Logic.* The first four strategies are emphasized in grades K–2. Students will often use the *Draw a Diagram, Guess and Check,* and *Work Backwards* strategies thereafter. The next five are learned in grades 3–5. The final strategy, *Use Logic,* is introduced in grade 5 or 6.

Learners should also become aware that some problems have extra or missing information. Many real-life problems are complex because irrelevant or missing information is part of the problem situation.

In this section, problems are given to illustrate each strategy and to use to teach the strategy. For ready reference, all problems given as examples in this section are numbered consecutively. Answers for selected problems are in Appendix C.

Write an Open Math Sentence. This strategy involves establishing the relations and question in a problem and translating them into mathematical language. Children must understand the concepts of the operations and writing open math sentences if they are to use this strategy.

Problem Examples

1. Mohammed learned to spell 3 words today and 3 words yesterday. How many words did he learn to spell in those two days?
2. Sue bought 4 scarves. She gave one to her friend for her birthday. How many scarves does Sue own now?
3. Desiree went on a two-week vacation. How many days was she on her vacation?
4. Mr. Gates had 24 celery sticks for snacks for the 8 boys in his scout troop. How many did each get if they shared the snacks equally?

Teaching "Write an Open Math Sentence." Later chapters will discuss in detail the procedure for teaching the meaning of the operations and the writing of math sentences. Only an overview of the interactive teaching plan is given here:

- Give one or more story problems.
- Ask children to solve the problem(s) individually or in groups using strategies meaningful to them. After they solve the problem(s), they report their solution(s) and how they thought to solve the problem(s).
- After children have solved many problems using methods of their own choosing, shared their solutions and strategies, and shown that they have constructed the concept of an operation, introduce math sentences.
- Point out how to write an open math sentence using math symbols, numerals, and a placeholder such as □ or *N* to represent the problem relations and question.
- Assign activities that enable boys and girls to extend their understanding and skill.

The use of open math sentences for solving story problems will need to be reviewed in the middle and upper grades. One approach to such a review is to assign groups or individuals several routine and nonroutine problems with the directions to decide only on the solution plan. A discussion of their conclusions is used to highlight the difference between problems that can be solved by using an open math sentence and problems that require other plans for their solution.

Act It Out. Children make sense of a problem situation by acting it out using manipulatives or role playing. Actions help them represent a problem structure in a way meaningful to them. This strategy is very useful when a routine problem, such as Problem 5, is a challenge for young children and can be called nonroutine for them at this time in their schooling.

Problem Examples

5. When Mark was sick he got 3 get-well cards on Friday and 4 on Saturday. How many did he get in those two days?
6. Fran is making a yard for her dog. She bought 40 feet of fence. She wants her dog to have as much room as possible for running. What is the largest enclosure with straight sides she can make? The use of string and paper squares will aid in the solution to this problem before children know how to compute area. Give each group a length of string 40 inches long and paper squares 5 inches × 5 inches. Say, "Forty inches of string can be used to think about 40 feet. The 40 inches of string will help you solve Fran's problem."
7. Fred, Joe, and their Uncle Robert wanted to investigate an island in Townsand Bay together. They had a small canoe, but it could hold only 150 pounds. Fred and Joe each weighed 75 pounds, and their uncle weighed 150 pounds. How could they all get to the island if they used the canoe.

Teaching "Act It Out." As noted, many children come to school using fingers or objects to solve problems. When they work together in groups, children often learn these approaches from one another (Behounek, Rosenbaum, Brown, and Burcalow, 1988). They may also learn to "act out" a problem with manipulatives by observing others share this strategy in whole-class discussions. If children do not invent this strategy or do not learn it from their peers, you model it for them. A discussion of what you did is followed by children showing how to act out a problem using objects.

The Act-It-Out strategy can also involve using the problem situation as the basis for a play. This approach is useful with young children because a play usually mirrors real life and makes a problem meaningful. It should be used occasionally with older children, because children of all ages enjoy and learn from this activity. It can also give insight into a problem such as, for example, Problem 7.

Matz and Leier (1992) describe a playlet approach that involves students writing plays involving mathematical problems and producing them with the audience participating in the problem solution. They report that this approach has many benefits for middle- and upper-grade learners.

Example for Introductory Lesson for Young Children

8. Dhong saw 2 birds on a garden wall. He then noticed that 3 more birds flew to the wall and sat beside the others. How many were on the wall?

Draw a Diagram. The *Draw a Diagram* strategy involves representing a problem situation with a sketch or diagram. It is one of the most important strategies for problem solving because of its wide applicability to routine and nonroutine problems. Hembree (1992) concluded from an analysis of 487 problem-solving studies that students profited more from instruction in the *Draw a Diagram* strategy than from other strategies.

Problem Examples

9. Katrina notices that 4 classmates are in front of her in the cafeteria line and 6 are behind her. How many are in the line?
10. The circus clown, Sam, likes to put on different funny faces. He has a blue rubber nose, two big red ears, a red nose, and two big green ears. How many funny faces can he make by using one of his noses and two ears of the same color?
11. Dad is making a fence 6 meters long. There will be 3 meters between each post. How many posts are needed?
12. A roller coaster takes 10 people every 4 minutes. The people have just gotten on. You say, "I'll get my ride in 12 minutes." Where are you in line? How many people are in front of you?
13. A bug fell into a bottle 8 inches high. It climbed up the side 4 inches each day and fell down 2 inches each night. How many days does it need to reach the top and climb out?

14. There are 30 chairs in the fifth-grade class. The chairs are arranged in a rectangle with 10 chairs in each of 3 rows. If the teacher wanted to arrange the chairs in a different rectangle, how many ways could she do this?

15. It takes Jack 30 minutes to feed 53 cows. If he takes a 15-minute break after every hour's work, how long will it take him to feed the 636 cows in his feed lot and have his breaks? He gets no break after his last hour. Why?

16. A special hen on Granny's farm lays some very peculiar eggs. Every third egg has no yolk. If the hen lays 4 eggs each day, how many eggs with yolks will she lay in 5 days.

17. At a holiday party, every person shook hands with every other person. If there were 6 people at the party, how many handshakes took place?

18. A very unusual insect was found in Kathy's school room. It produces twins each day. The twins also produce twins each day themselves after they are born. How many insects will be in the room in 3 days if the insect found produces twins the first day?

19. A plane carrying 4 people and food and water for a relief effort makes an emergency landing in a remote forest meadow after experiencing engine trouble. The pilot studies the map and decides that 6 days are needed to reach a town for help. If 1 person can carry enough food and water for 1 person to travel 4 days, what is the least number of people that will have to start out in order for one person to reach the town to get help?

Teaching "Draw a Diagram." You help children translate actions into diagrams to become familiar with this strategy. With young children the words "math picture" rather than "diagram" can be used. Some children think that drawing a picture means taking great care and giving enough time to the drawing to include details, such as leaves on trees or buttons on shirts. You help children understand that a math picture means a quick sketch or using shapes or tallies to stand for counters.

To teach children who cannot show what it would mean to draw a picture for a problem, help them translate their work with manipulatives to math pictures. You can say, "Let's make a picture that shows how we used our counters to solve the problem about the teddy bears. Since the counters are still on your desks, you can use them to help you make a math picture. The picture will show what the counters show. What will you draw?"

After children have worked on this assignment, they share and discuss what they have done. If the class has difficulty seeing their peers' drawings, children can be asked to put their math pictures on the overhead for better viewing. Other problems are then solved using drawings. Lessons such as this are continued until most children are able to model a problem with drawings.

Individual attention is given to those children who are usually unable to make diagrams. They are asked questions about how each fact or relation in a problem should be represented, as in the following examples.

Examples with Questions

20. Don wanted to count the pennies in his pockets. He took the 5 pennies he had in one pocket and the 3 pennies in the other pocket and counted them altogether. How many pennies did he have?

The questions for this routine problem could be:

- How do you know what the story is about?
- What did Don want to do?
- How can you show that with counters? Why?
- How would you show that with circles instead of counters?
- What is alike about counters and circles to solve the problem?
- What would you do next? Why?
- How does your drawing tell the story?

To teach making drawings for nonroutine problems, ask questions that help children translate the problem to pictures by considering a way to represent relations. Possible questions for problem 16 are:

- What does the problem tell us about the special hen?
- (If necessary: What kind of eggs does the special hen on Granny's farm lay?)
- What is an egg yolk? What is an egg with no yolk?
- How could a picture show what the hen lays in five days?
- What is the problem question?
- How would the picture help answer the question?

Guess and Check. The *Guess and Check* strategy is most appropriate for those problems in which trial and error as well as reasoning is involved in determining the answer. This strategy helps children realize that good guesses have a place in mathematics and should not be avoided. They learn that for some problems an educated guess is the only way to begin, because no other approach is feasible. They find out that the *Guess and Check* strategy differs from an estimate in that it is a way to solve a problem, whereas an estimate helps judge the sense of a solution that was found by using an estimation strategy.

Problem Examples

21. Place the numbers 1 to 6 in the circles so that no lines connect consecutive numbers (Figure 2.2).

FIGURE 2.2 "Guess and Check" Problem

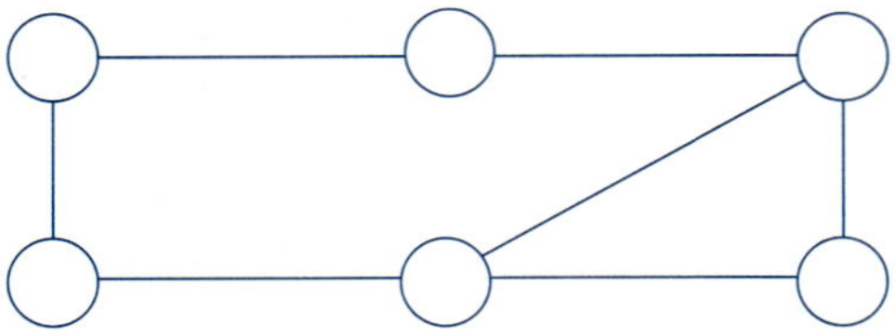

22. Place the numbers 1 to 7 in the boxes so that the sum in each of the rows and the diagonals is 12 (Figure 2.3).

23. Place the number 6 in the center of the wheel. Next, use the numbers 1 to 11 in the boxes on the wheel rim so that each 3 numbers connected by the spokes in a line equals 18 (Figure 2.4). Do not use 6 on the wheel rim.

24. What two consecutive numbers have a sum of 53 and a product of 702?

25. Use the numbers 1 to 6 so that each side of the triangle has the same sum (Figure 2.5).

26. Ms. Lerner bought some posters to use to decorate her sixth-grade class. Some cost $2.50, and some cost $1.75. She spent $8.50. How many of each did she purchase?

27. Write each number 1 to 12 on a card. Arrange the 12 cards in a rectangular shape so that each side equals 26 (Figure 2.6).

Teaching "Guess and Check." The problems used to introduce this strategy must be those that can be solved by some sort of guessing or trial and error. However, inference is also usually involved in finding answers.

Examples for Introductory Lesson

28. Use the numbers 2, 3, 4, or 6 to make these sentences true:

a. ______ + ______ + ______ = 11
b. ______ − ______ − ______ = 0
c. ______ + ______ − ______ = 4
d. ______ + ______ + ______ = 9

29. What two consecutive numbers have a sum of 31?

30. What is the pattern ? 3, 4, 12; 3, 2, 6; 3, 6, 6; 3, 8, 24; 3, 9, 9.

After children solve these problems, they discuss how they thought to find answers. The fact that guessing and checking was a strategy is emphasized. Chil-

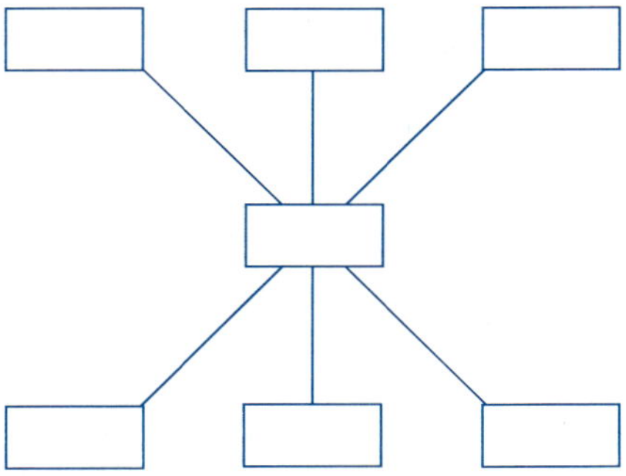

FIGURE 2.3 "Guess and Check" Problem

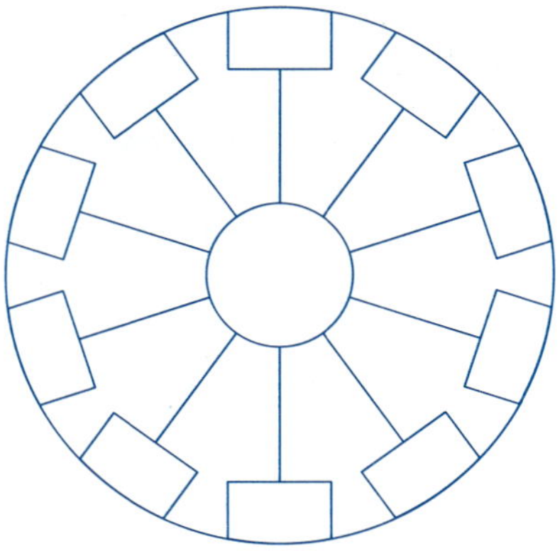

FIGURE 2.4 "Guess and Check" Problem

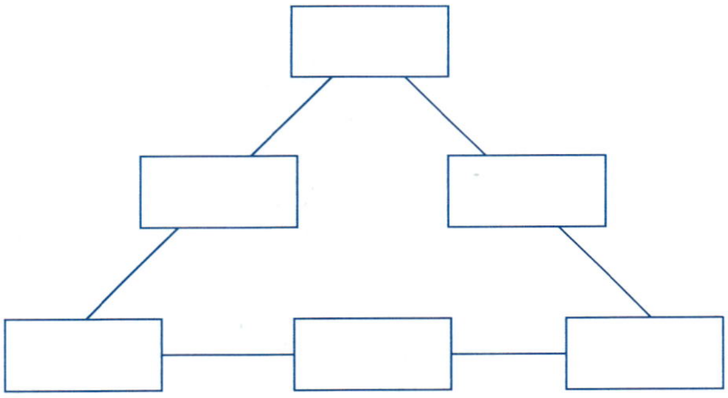

FIGURE 2.5 "Guess and Check" Problem

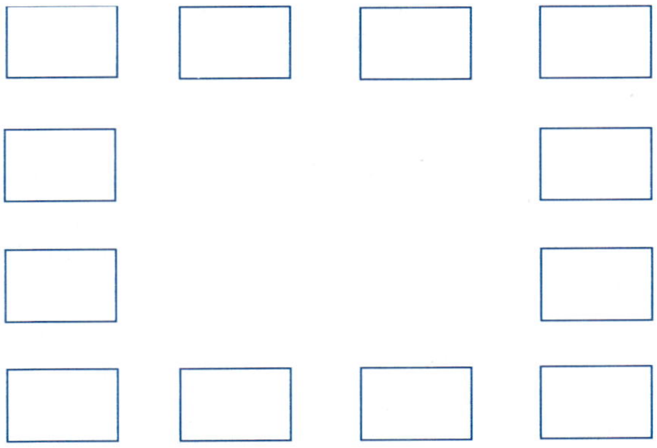

FIGURE 2.6 "Guess and Check" Problem

dren are asked to comment on the merits of guessing. It is decided that for some problems that is the only way to start but that one must check up on the guess. If it isn't the solution, guess and check again.

Work Backwards. At times the ending number is known and the starting number is unknown. Because the strategy is to reverse the operations to find the beginning number, children need to understand inverse operations to solve problems using the *Work Backwards* strategy.

Problem Examples

31. Richard is thinking of a number. If you add 6 to the number, subtract 7, divide by 2, and add 9, the result is 11. What number is Richard thinking of?

32. Mr. Smith's hobby is to bake bread. He baked a number of loaves on his day off and froze three for use next week. He left one in the cupboard and divided the others into two baskets, one for each of his two sisters across town. Each sister got two loaves. How many loaves did he bake?

33. Amanda had a pocket full of coins. She thought she had $1.75. She bought two pencils for 49 cents and an eraser for 25 cents. She counted 98 cents in her pocket after her purchases. Did she know how much she had in her pocket before she bought the school supplies? Why or why not?

Teaching "Work Backwards." Begin with a very easy problem (e.g., number 34) to help children get the notion of beginning with the ending number and using inverse operations to compute the numbers until the starting number is found. Discuss with them how they found the solution, guiding them to realize the "work backwards" process. Increase the difficulty as pupils become competent in working backwards.

Example for Introductory Lesson

34. Martha had some money in her pocket. She spent $.30 for an oatmeal cookie for a snack. She then counted $1.00 in her purse. How much did she have before she got her snack?

If some students report they subtracted the numbers, ask questions such as: "Why did you subtract? (To find what was left.) Do you want to find what was left? What do you want to find?" "What does the problem tell you about $.30 and $1.00?" "What makes up the money she had to begin? What can you do with $.30 and $1.00 to find what she had to begin?" Questions such as these can stimulate discussion that helps students become aware of using "opposite" operations to reach a starting number.

Make an Organized List. A list or companion lists are constructed to keep guesses or calculations orderly and ensure that all possibilities are taken into account and no entries are repeated. Counting is often used to figure out entries. The list or lists are used to make comparisons or discover patterns to determine one or more solutions.

Problem Examples

35. Tim made up a problem for his friend. He said to him, "I have 6 coins, quarters, dimes, and nickels. I have $1.00. What coins do I have?" What would his friend answer?

36. You have 2 dimes, 2 nickels, and 20 pennies. You buy a tablet at the school store that costs 34 cents. How many different ways could you pay for the tablet?

37. Chocolate drops cost 7 cents, and peppermint drops cost 5 cents. How many of each could you have bought if you had 21 cents and have less than 5 cents left?

38. Gayle was sweeping her balcony when she noticed that Maria was sweeping her balcony. They talked about what they were doing. Gayle said she swept her balcony every 3 days, and Maria said that she swept hers every 4 days. When would they both be sweeping their balconies on the same day again?

39. A farmer sold both chickens and pigs to a supermarket. Another farmer wanted to know how many he sold, so he asked. The first farmer answered, "10 heads and 30 legs." How many of each did he sell?

40. A Vehicle Shop sells two-wheelers and three-wheelers. You wonder how many of each type they have, but when you look in the window you can see only wheels. You count 24 wheels. How many of each type could the shop carry?

41. William is making identification tags to sell at the school fair. His machine makes the numerals 1, 2, and 3. If he puts 1, 2, or 3 numerals on a tag and does not use any numeral more than once on a tag, how many different tags can he make for sale?

Teaching "Make an Organized List." Use a problem that has several answers. Have children list the combinations they tried as well as the solutions. Say, "How can we put these possible solutions in order?" Groups or individuals can work on this problem and report their conclusions. You note that such a list is a good way to solve a problem of this type. Have pupils work several more problems using an organized list.

Example for Introductory Lesson

42. Sabina has 8 coins worth a total of 50 cents. What could they be?

Make a Table. Tables consist of rows and columns that show related variables in a problem. Often one column or row lists events in natural order, such as 1, 2, 3. The entries in tables frequently show a repeating sequence, and a study of the entries can lead to a discovery of patterns.

Problem Examples

43. Peter decided to earn some money buying and selling baseball cards. He can buy 3 cards for $5. He decided he will sell 2 cards for $5. How many must he buy and sell to make $25?

44. Hernandez and Tomas are working at the fast-food restaurant to make money for school books. Hernandez has worked longer and makes $2 more an hour. Tomas make $6 an hour, so Hernandez of course makes $8 an hour. How many hours will Hernandez and Tomas each have to work to earn the same amount of money? For Hernandez to have twice as much as Tomas?

45. Two joggers are using the same track, which is 400 meters around. The first jogger runs 200 meters each minute; the other jogger runs 100 meters each minute. If they begin at the same time, when will they meet again at the beginning of the track?

Teaching "Make a Table." To introduce this strategy, use a rather easy problem whose solution will give a row and column arrangement to the numbers in the solution. As students discuss their solutions, you can show them how to draw lines to make the cells in a table. Name the strategy, "Make a Table," and give a few other problems that are solved with the same strategy. Help pupils generalize that tables help us notice how numbers go together or are related.

Example for Introductory Lesson

46. Max decides to get in shape by running. Because his doctor told him to begin slowly, he decides to run 8 minutes the first day and increase the running time 2 minutes each day. He decides to stop increasing his running time when it is 26 minutes. Give the number of minutes he will run each day until he runs 26 minutes, and tell how many days it will be until he runs 26 minutes.

Find a Pattern. Patterns dominate the study of mathematics. Patterns are regularities that enable us to write rules and predict outcomes. Chapter 3 gives activities for helping young children explore patterns in designs. Older children solve problems that require finding patterns in numbers and space figures.

A problem that is solved by looking for a pattern often requires making a table or list or using a *Guess and Check* strategy. Several of the problems in the sections

Make a Table and *Guess and Check* involve pattern discovery. (Did you make a table or a list for any problem in the following list? Did the table or list help you find a pattern?)

Problem Examples

47. Figurate Numbers. Make dots to show triangles as in Box 1.4. (If you keep making triangular shapes in the same way, how many dots will the triangle have if it has 6 rows? 24 rows? *Hint:* To find a pattern, list the number of dots added in each successive triangle. Write *1* for the first triangle at the beginning of your list. Think the pattern as you add the numbers in order.

48. Jonas is using blocks to make staircase (see Box 1.4). How many blocks are in his staircase when it has 5 steps? If he made 15 steps, how many blocks would he need?

49. Complete the following, using your calculator:

2, 5, 11, 23 _______, _______, _______

Teaching "Find a Pattern." To introduce this strategy, give a problem that would seem tedious if a pattern were not found to use in finding a solution. A hint regarding how to make a table may be necessary to help students discover the pattern.

Examples for Introductory Lesson

50. How many squares of different sizes in a 7×7 square (Figure 2.7)? *Hint:* Make a table that shows the number of squares of different sizes in squares of size 1×1, 2×2, etc., to help find the solution.

51. The following is called a Fibonacci sequence, after the medieval mathematician who discovered it. Find the next five numbers in the sequence and give the pattern rule.

1, 1, 2, 3, 5, 8, 13, _______, _______, _______, _______, _______.

Extension: Start with any two numbers and generate a Fibonacci sequence.

Use a Simpler Problem. Problems with large or fractional numbers often seem difficult. Substituting small whole numbers usually enables a problem solver to deal more easily with the problem structure, solve the problem with the substituted numbers, and go back to the original problem knowing a strategy for solution and having the confidence to solve it. Routine problems can often be simplified by this strategy (See problem 52).

Problem Examples

52. The county fair took in $563,625. If 12,525 adults visited the fair, how much was spent on the average by each adult?

53. If 4 is used as a factor 100 times, what is the digit in the ones place?

FIGURE 2.7 "Find a Pattern" Problem

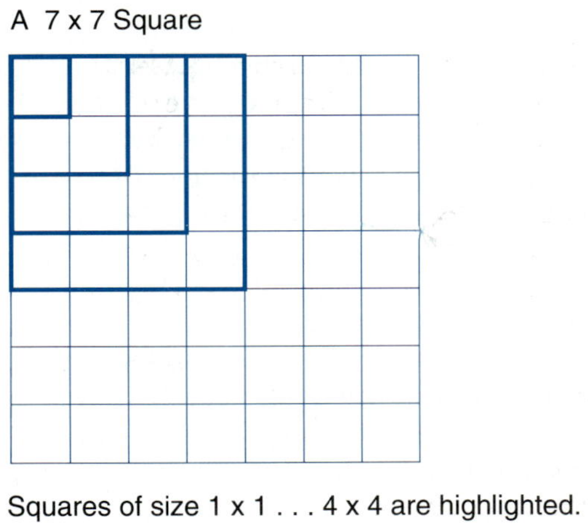

Teaching "Use a Simpler Problem." Give two similar problems, one with small numbers and one with large numbers. When introducing the problems, say, "Think how one problem might help you solve the other." After pupils solve both problems, help them generalize the procedure to other problems, by saying, "How can we use our solutions to these problems to help solve other problems?" When they decide that they can make a problem easier to understand by substituting small numbers, name the strategy, *Use a Simpler Problem,* and ask them when they would want to use this strategy. Help them realize it is useful when they are stumped by large numbers or fractions.

Have each student write a story problem with fractions or large numbers, exchange the problem for one written by another student, and use this strategy if he or she needs to do so to solve the problem. Then have them read their problems and discuss their thinking to find the solutions. If they followed the *Use a Simpler Problem* strategy, have them explain the reasons for their choice.

Examples for Introductory Lesson

54. a. The teacher said the principal bought 50 books for the 2 fifth-grade classes? If they were distributed equally, how many did each class get?

b. The federal government office ordered 3,630,000 sheets of new stamps for the 660 largest post offices. If they were distributed equally, how many sheets did each large post office get?

55. a. Gloria was happy that she had a new baby sister. She told two friends. If each friend repeated Gloria's news to two friends in an hour, each of these friends gave two more friends the news in an hour, and the news spread in the same way every hour, how many people will be told about Gloria's baby sister the 4th hour?

b. Extend the problem to 10 hours. If pupils make a table, they can see the doubling pattern that appears in the simpler problem and use it in Problem 55. b.

Recall a Similar Problem. Many problems have the same structure and are solved using the same plan. Often the language of the problem is enough to remind the problem solver of a similar problem. For example, Problem 56 is similar to Problem 7 and Problem 57 is similar to Problem 17. Note, however, that Problem 57 differs from Problem 17 in one important way. (What is it?)

Problem Examples

56. There were 3 dogs and 3 cats on an island. They all wanted to go to the mainland because of flooding on the island. They had one boat that would take only 2 animals, but when there were more dogs than cats in a group, the dogs tormented the cats. Therefore, the cats would not let themselves be outnumbered by the dogs. How did they all get to the mainland?

57. Ms. Emerson said, "Hello," to every one of the 7 children in her scout troop. Every girl said hello to Ms. Emerson and to every other girl. How many times was "Hello" said?

Teaching "Recall a Similar Problem." Help students learn this strategy by presenting a problem similar to one solved previously, asking students to study it, and discussing their ideas before solving the problem in their groups. Students often remember that it was similar to one they had already solved (Lester, 1983), and they realize that the new problem will be easy because it can be solved like the earlier one. When pupils report on the similar problem and how it helped them, say, "Remembering a similar problem is a very good strategy that you will find useful for solving many problems."

If no student recalls a similar problem during the discussion preceding the group problem solving, say, "In your groups try to remember a problem similar to this one. That could help you find the solution." If some groups still do not recall the similar problem, give a hint to these groups, such as, "Remember the stamp trading problem."

Reader Activity 2.2

Find the problem-solving strategies taught to learners in grades 2, 4, and 6 by studying teachers' manuals for students' mathematics textbooks for these grades. Compare the suggestions in one teacher's manual for teaching two different strategies with the suggested plans here.

Example for Introductory Lesson

58. At a business meeting, every salesperson exchanged names with every other salesperson. If there were 9 people at the meeting, how many name exchanges took place? How many names were exchanged?

Use Logic. Logic problems involve "if . . . , then" reasoning. The strategy is to determine what is known and use this knowledge to establish other relations or connections. A matrix can help a problem solver keep track of decisions in logic problems that involve narrowing possibilities by reasoning. Logic problems involving ordering are often solved using diagrams.

Problem Examples

59. Amy is shorter than Tom. Lee is shorter than Amy. Who is tallest?

60. Patty, Masako, Judy, and Rose have ages between 8 and 13. One is 9; one, 10; one, 11; and one, 12. Masako is older than Judy and younger than Rose. Rose is younger than Patty. What is the age of each person?

61. Fred, Walter, and Duc live next to each other. They are a teacher, a medical doctor, and a salesperson. Walter lives in the middle house. When Duc went on a vacation, the medical doctor kept his dog. The teacher and Fred share a fence. What work does each do?

62. Carol, Bryan, Susan, and Patrick each takes good care of his or her pet. The names of the pets are Curley, Beauty, Spot, and Patches. No pet has a name that begins with the same letter as its owner's name. Susan does not take care of Beauty or Patches. Bryan does not own Patches. What is the name of each owner and his or her pet?

Teaching "Use Logic." To help students become aware of the usefulness of eliminating possibilities by reasoning, have them solve a problem in which possibilities are quickly eliminated. Discuss the process they used. Help them verbalize the notion that it is necessary to eliminate possibilities by reasoning about what is known to occur and therefore what cannot occur.

As a matrix is a useful technique for keeping track of thinking, if no student has devised the method, suggest it as an aid to reasoning, and have students try it to solve the introductory problem. You may need to model this approach. (See Figure 2.8 for matrix solution for Problem 63.) Make certain the students realize that some problem solvers do not use a matrix to solve a logic problem, but that they should know about this approach and use it if it is helpful to them.

Example for Introductory Lesson

63. Myko, Mark, Carlos, and Angel are in the orchestra. One of them plays the trumpet, one the violin, one the viola, and one the drums. Mark plays the trumpet. Myko's classmate plays the viola. Carlos and Angel are not interested in

FIGURE 2.8 Solution Matrix for Problem 63

	Viola	Violin	Trumpet	Drums
Myko	No	Yes	No	No
Mark	No	No	Yes	No
Carlos	No	No	No	Yes
Angel	Yes	No	No	No

playing the violin. Angel doesn't like the drums and would never play them. Who plays each instrument?

Activities for Learning Problem Solving

The activities in this section can supplement lessons in which students are assigned problems. These activities enable students to gain new insights about problem types and strategies for solution.

ACTIVITY 2.1
Lots of Problems.

Name a situation, or have students give a situation of interest to them. Ask students to think of as many mathematics problems as possible that could arise in that situation. Groups may brainstorm to create problems and report their ideas to the class. Examples of situations are:

- A student's birthday party
- The first day of school
- A class trip to the zoo
- Helping take care of the family when Mother is sick
- A family picnic in the park
- The first (last) day of vacation
- A community event, such as a parade

ACTIVITY 2.2
Problems Everywhere.

Have students use social studies, current events, science information, or their everyday experiences to write problems. Students should choose the problems they try to solve. Moses, Bjork, and Goldenberg (1990) state that children will raise more problems than they can solve and that some problems can serve as challenges for a long time. They also suggest naming ideas after the inventor, for example, Harvey's problem or Lisa's method.

Ford (1990) explains how students can write mathematical problems by using the steps in the writing process developed by teachers of English: Prewriting, Writing, Conferencing, Revising and Editing, and Publication.

ACTIVITY 2.3
Vary a Problem.

Students can be asked to vary the problems created in activities 2.1 and 2.2. They can decide to:

- Change the question in a problem, but keep the facts.
- Keep the question and change the facts.
- Write a problem similar to a given problem.
- Write a second step to a problem.

ACTIVITY 2.4
Use your Textbook.

Have students find sets of three problems in their textbook that would be solved using the same strategy. (The assignment may need to specify that the problems must come from different lessons as some textbooks give all the same kind of problem in a lesson.)

ACTIVITY 2.5
Write-ups.

Have students frequently write a report of their thinking while they solved a problem. Students can share these write-ups and compare their thinking processes. They should be able to conclude that different people arrive at solutions by different routes. At times, have them choose the problems to use in their write-ups.

ACTIVITY 2.6
Sorting.

Silver and Smith (1980) suggest this activity as a way to help students develop skill in identifying similar problems. Prepare a set of 10 problems with subsets of related problems. Write (or photocopy) the problems on separate cards. Give each group the 10 problems. Have groups partition the cards into subsets of mathematically related problems. Class discussion of groups' work follows. Such a discussion helps children gain insight into similarities and differences among problems and how problems can be related.

ACTIVITY 2.7
Alike and Different.

Give each of several groups two problems that involve the same operation but different situations. Have the groups think how the problems are alike and different. Have them discuss their conclusions in a whole-class setting.

To teach understanding two-step problems, give students a one-step and a two-step problem that include some of the same information. Their discussion of likenesses and differences in the two problems will help students focus on the characteristics of two-step problems and how they differ from one-step problems.

ACTIVITY 2.8
Extra or Missing Information.

Give students problems such as:

> *Linda was shopping for a bike for her son. He was 7 years old. She bought a bike for $67. How much money did she have left?*
>
> *George liked to play hockey. He played in 15 games. Seven were home games. How many were won?*
>
> *Tara and her friend, Carol, like to bake. They decide to make cupcakes for the school bake sale. The school hoped to raise $250 for math materials. The girls make 8 dozen cookies.*
>
> *Allen wanted to go with his cub scout troop to the Bear Scout Camp in August for a week. It would cost $50. His parents said he could go if he earned the money mowing the grass each week. They would pay him $8 a week to mow the grass. He also remembered he had a birthday in June and would probably get some money from his Aunt Lucy, because she sent him money last year for his birthday. How many weeks did he need to work to make the money he needed?*

Students study the problems in groups and discuss their reactions. Have them write problems with extra or missing information and share them with each other. Often include one or more of their problems in assignments.

CALCULATORS AND PROBLEM SOLVING

Calculators should be available for problem solving (NCTM, 1989). Calculators aid problem solving by freeing students from tedious computation and focusing students' attention on the problem rather than the computation (Duea, Immerzeel, Ockenga, and Tarr, 1980; Reys, 1989). Students who use calculators are more competent, show greater interest, and develop greater confidence in problem solving than when they do not have the opportunities to use calculators in problem solving (Hembree and Dessart, 1992). However, students need to be taught how to use calculators if they are to gain the benefits from their use (Payne, 1992).

Although many computations related to problem solving appear to be less demanding if a calculator is used, problems with large numbers particularly lend themselves to calculator use. These problems can be interesting and entertaining.

Calculator Problem Examples

- How old will you be in 2010, 2020, 2050?
- How many times does your heart beat in an hour? day? week? year?
- How many gallons of gasoline would it take to travel by car across Asia or Europe between cities of your own choice?
- How much water do you drink in a day? week? month? year?
- How many minutes do you spend traveling to school in a day? week? year?
- How long would it take to count to a million?

Students can write calculator problems for others to solve. These problems can be written on 3×5 cards and filed. Class members should choose which problems to solve. Later answers and solution methods are shared.

Activity for the Classroom 2.3. Use information in newspapers, magazines, and government or industry reports to write three problems that would be suitable for the children you are teaching to solve using calculators. Assign these problems, and have groups solve them. Have groups present their problem-solving strategies. *Extension:* Give students numerical information, or ask them to find it in publications, and have learners write problems for classmates to solve using calculators.

METACOGNITION AND PROBLEM SOLVING

Metacognition is the term used to describe the knowledge and control a person has of his or her own mental processes (Garofalo and Lester, 1985). It involves knowledge of oneself, tasks, and strategies. For example, a student can know that he or she is good at problem solving, that taking time to check a computation can lead to greater success than not checking, and that to draw a diagram is a good strategy.

Another aspect of metacognition is monitoring and regulating one's behavior. According to Garofalo (1987), this aspect of metacognition involves deciding *when*, *why*, and *how* one should go about problem solving. He claims that we should help students learn to watch themselves and assess their own behavior to enable them to become strong problem solvers. Lester (1983) points out that metacognitive instruction should emphasize student analysis of their thinking when they solve problems and provide opportunities for students to share their insights.

There are three ways you can help students develop metacognitive awareness (Garofalo, 1987):

1. By having discussions that encourage students to understand themselves and the importance of controlling their thinking and behaving when problem solving. Examples of questions you can use for such discussions are:

- Tell us what you say to yourself to help you solve a problem. What questions do you ask yourself?
- What kind of problems are you particularly good at solving?
- What kind of problems give you trouble?
- What should you do when you think a problem is hard?
- What directions can you give yourself if you start to give up?
- Why is checking (estimating) important?
- How can you remember to check (estimate)?
- What are some things you can think about when your solution plan doesn't work out?
- What can you think when your solution process is different from a friend's, but you both have the same answer?
- How do you extend your understanding of problems by making up related problems?

2. By giving students information about the nature of problem solving. For example, you can tell students;
   - Some problems can take a long time to solve.
   - You get better at problem solving if you solve a lot of problems.
   - My way of solving a problem is often not the only way.
3. By sharing that you can also find problems difficult and need to monitor and regulate your thinking and doing.
   - Report incidents of working with problems you found difficult.
   - Work cooperatively with students on a challenging problem you cannot solve to demonstrate how you monitor your problem-solving behaviors.

ASSESSING PROBLEM SOLVING

What to Assess

Assessment of problem solving involves much more than checking students' answers. It should include assessing their thinking processes when solving and posing problems, their motivations, and their beliefs about problem solving as well as their solutions to problems.

Approaches to Assessment

The approaches to assessment are not different from those used to assess any mathematical learning and include observation, interviews, work products, quizzes, and tests (Charles, Lester, and O'Daffer, 1987). How to score problem solving is discussed in the next subsection.

Observation. Teachers observe children solving problems when students work in small groups or individually and when they make reports of problem solving to the class. The information collected would give evidence pertaining to student characteristics and behaviors such as given in the following list.

Thinking Processes of a Student Engaged in Problem Solving

Understand a Problem

- Gives time to understanding a problem.
- Appears to restate the problem in his or her own words.
- Isolates relevant facts and the problem question.
- Makes notes of information to be remembered.
- Asks for clarification of words or facts that do not have meaning for him or her.
- Uses aids such as drawings or objects to clarify a problem.

Devise a Plan
- Chooses a strategy appropriate for a particular problem.
- Accepts that there are alternate strategies for solving some problems.
- Can explain his or her choice of a strategy to others.
- Demonstrates familiarity with different strategies.

Carry Out a Plan
- Estimates solutions when appropriate.
- Uses a calculator when appropriate.
- Monitors his or her progress, reviewing the problem and rethinking the chosen strategy when it appears that a sensible solution is not forthcoming.
- Keeps useful records of work.
- Is a neat and careful worker.
- Looks for more than one solution in open-ended problems.
- Labels the answer in a meaningful way.

Look Back
- Checks solutions for computational accuracy.
- Examines reasonableness of solution in terms of the problem.
- Considers if there is more than one solution.
- Compares solution to estimate when appropriate.
- Looks for extensions of the problem–generalizes the solution strategy or examines related problems; poses problems.

Learners' Motivations and Beliefs
- Willingness to try to solve a problem
- Perseverance in the face of setbacks when solving problems
- Enthusiasm for problem solving
- Self-confidence in problem solving
- Pleasure and pride in problem-solving accomplishments
- Verbalizing belief that he or she is a good (poor) problem solver

Records are made of observations. These can be anecdotal records or entries on a check sheet that includes the listed statements.

Interviews. Interviews can be conducted with one child or a small group. Children should be given a problem and asked to tell how they would think as they solve the problem. If a small group is being interviewed, a set of problems can be given to the group and each child asked to tell about a different problem. Such an approach helps you deal with individual differences, and it provides a learning experience for others. Questions to ask during interviews include:

Thinking Processes of a Student Engaged in Problem Solving

Understand the Problem
- How do you begin when you have a problem to solve?
- What do you do after you read (or hear) a problem?
- What do you do if you do not know the meaning of a word? Why?
- (With a specific problem) What is happening that makes a problem? What is a good question for this problem?
- If you do not understand the problem at first, what do you do?

Devise a Plan
- Do you talk to yourself about your solution plan? How do you do this?
- What plan do you think you use the most? Why?
- What strategies do you remember that you could try in different problems?
- (With a specific problem) What plan would you use? Why?

Carry Out a Plan
- Did you estimate? Why or why not?
- When would you use a calculator? Why?
- Is neatness important? Why?

- When should you give labels to numbers?
- Is changing your plan ever a good idea? Why or why not?
- (With a specific problem) Please show me how you would carry out your plan?

Look Back

- What is the best thing to do when you have found an answer to the problem question?
- What does it mean to check your answer?
- (With a specific problem) How did you decide if this solution answers the problem question?
- Does this problem bring other problems or solutions to your mind?
- Make up a problem that is similar in some way to this problem.
- Make up a problem that would be solved by a similar strategy.

Learners' Motivations and Belief

- Do you like to solve problems? Why or why not?
- What do you like most about problem solving? The least?

Work Products. Students are frequently asked to write out their thinking to solve a problem as well as to give the problem solution. Often they are asked to pose new problems. These write-ups and problems should be collected in portfolios and used to assess a student's progress in problem solving and creating problems.

If the solution to the problem is open-ended, the creativity and insightfulness of the solution should be assessed together with the reasonableness of the solution. Achievement in problem solving can be assessed by using the three descriptive performance criteria discussed in Chapter One—none, some, and mastery—or on a 5-point scale from least to greatest progress.

Quizzes and Tests. Quizzes and tests are multiple-choice or completion, or they require students to solve one or more problems, show their work, and report the solution(s). Students can also be asked to pose problems. Multiple-choice items can be designed to assess more than correct solutions. Students can be given a set of responses and asked to determine the best question, the most efficient strategy, or to chose the answer that is the most reasonable for a problem. Completion items can ask students to give the problem facts needed to solve the problem, the problem question, or the strategy to be used to solve the problem. Some problems on tests can be open-ended. Students can be asked to pose problems for given information or for a given operation.

Problems should be similar to those studied by students if the objective is to determine if problem-solving strategies have been learned. If the objective is to determine if students can generalize the solution strategies they have learned, the problems can be more difficult, but with the same basic structure as those studied.

TABLE 2.1 Example of Focused Holistic Scoring Point Indicators

0 Points
- Paper is blank.
- Data are recorded, but not used meaningfully.

1 Point
- Some indication of understanding of problem, but no indication of strategy for solution is shown.

2 Points
- Inappropriate strategy, incorrect answer, but problem seems to be understood.
- Appropriate strategy incorrectly implemented.
- Correct answer, but strategy not indicated or work shown is incomplete.

3 Points
- Solution strategy appropriate, but part of the problem was ignored.
- Solution strategy appropriate, but correct answer not labeled or incorrectly labeled.
- Solution strategy appropriate, but computational error led to incorrect answer.

4 Points
- Appropriate strategy and correct answer, correctly labeled.

TABLE 2.2 Analytic Scoring Scale

Understanding the Problem	0: Complete misunderstanding of the problem
	1: Part of the problem misunderstood or misinterpreted
	2: Complete understanding of the problem
Planning a Solution	0: No attempt, or totally inappropriate plan
	1: Partially correct plan based on part of the problem being interpreted correctly
	2: Plan could have led to a correct solution if implemented properly
Getting an Answer	0: No answer, or wrong answer based on an inappropriate plan
	1: Copying error; computational error; partial answer for a problem with multiple answers
	2: Correct answer and correct label for the answer

Randall Charles, Frank Lester, and Phares O'Daffer. (1987). *How to Evaluate Progress in Problem Solving,* p. 30. Reston, VA: National Council of Teachers of Mathematics. Reprinted by permission.

Scoring

A good assessment of a student's work includes both the thinking involved and the final product (Otis and Offerman, 1988). Two approaches to scoring both aspects of assessment are focused holistic and analytical scoring (Charles et al., 1987). *Focused holistic scoring* involves assigning a total score to a student's work. The criteria used to obtain the score is established by the teacher. Table 2.1 gives an example of criteria used for focused holistic scoring based on Charles et al. *Analytical scoring* gives points for different aspects of a student's work; the points are added for a total score. An example of criteria for analytical scoring is shown in Table 2.2.

Scores from either focused holistic scoring or analytical scoring of a pupil's work over time can be summed to give a picture of the student's problem-solving behavior. Trends should also be noticed—do scores decrease, increase, or remain the same?

SUMMARY

Different types of problems and problem-solving strategies were discussed in this chapter, with suggestions for teaching both Polya's four-step strategy and specific problem-solving strategies. Many examples were given of routine and nonroutine problems and of problems that could be solved by the strategies: *Write an Open Math Sentence, Act It Out, Draw a Diagram, Guess and Check, Work Backwards, Make an Organized List, Make a Table, Find a Pattern, Use a Simpler Problem, Recall a Similar Problem,* and *Use Logic.* A section of the chapter dealt with developing positive problem-solving attitudes. Activities for teaching problem solving were given, and suggestions were made for using calculators in problem solving. The relation of metacognition to problem solving was examined. A final section discussed assessing problem solving.

REFERENCES

Behounek, Karla J., Linda J. Rosenbaum, Les Brown, and Janet V. Burcalow. (Decemebr 1988). "Our Class Has Twenty-five Teachers." *Arithmetic Teacher* 36: 10–13.

Carpenter, Thomas P., and James M. Moser. (1983). "The Acquisition of Addition and Subtraction Concepts." In *Acquisition of Mathematics Concepts and Processes,* edited by Richard Lesh and Marsha Landau, pp. 7–44. New York: Academic Press.

Carpenter, Thomas P., and James M. Moser. (May 1984). "The Acquisition of Addition and Subtraction Concepts in Grades One through Three." *Journal for Research in Mathematics Education* 15: 179–202.

Charles, Randall I. (February 1985). "The Role of Problem Solving." *Arithmetic Teacher* 32: 48–50.

Charles, Randall I., and Frank K. Lester, Jr. (January 1984)."An Evaluation of a Process-Oriented Instructional Program in Mathematical Problem Solving in Grades 5 and 7." *Journal for Research in Mathematics Education* 15: 15–34.

Charles, Randall, Frank Lester, and Phares O'Daffer. (1987). *How to Evaluate Progress in Problem Solving.* Reston, VA: National Council of Teachers of Mathematics.

Chisko, Ann M. (November 1985). "Developmental Math: Problem Solving and Survival." *Mathematics Teacher* 78: 592–596.

Cobb, Paul, and Graceann Merkel. (1989). "Thinking Strategies: Teaching Arithmetic Through Problem Solving." In *New Directions for Elementary School Mathematics,* edited by Paul R. Trafton and Albert P. Shulte, pp. 70–81. Reston, VA: National Council of Teachers of Mathematics.

Cobb, Paul, Erna Yackel, Terry Wood, Grayson Wheatley, and Graceann Merkel. (September 1988). "Research into Practice: Creating a Problem-solving Atmosphere." *Arithmetic Teacher* 36: 46–47.

Duea, Joan, George Immerzeel, Earl Ockenga, and John Tarr. (1980). "Problem Solving Using the Calculator." In *Problem Solving in School Mathematics,* edited by Stephen Krulik and Robert E. Reys, pp. 117–126. Reston, VA: National Council of Teachers of Mathematics.

Fennema, Elizabeth, Thomas P. Carpenter, and Penelope L. Peterson. (1989). "Learning Mathematics with Understanding: Cognitively Guided Instruction." In *Advances in Research on Teaching,* Vol 1, edited by Jere Brophy, pp. 195–221. Greenwich CT: JAI Press.

Ford, Margaret. (November 1990). "The Writing Process: A Strategy for Problem Solvers." *Arithmetic Teacher* 38: 35–38.

Garofalo, Joe. (May 1987). "Research Report: Metacognition and School Mathematics." *Arithmetic Teacher* 34: 22–23.

Garofalo, Joe, and Frank K. Lester, Jr. (May 1985). "Metacognition, Cognitive Monitoring, and Mathematical Performance." *Journal for Research in Mathematics Education* 16: 163–176.

Hembree, Ray. (May 1992). "Experiments and Relations Studies in Problem Solving: A Meta-Analysis." *Journal for Research in Mathematics Education* 23: 242–273.

Hembree, Ray, and Donald J. Dessart. (1992). "Research on Calculators in Mathematics Education." In *Calculators in Mathematics Education,* edited by James T. Fey and Christian R. Hirsch, pp. 23–32. Reston, VA: National Council of Teachers of Mathematics.

Jacobson, Marilyn H., Frank K. Lester, Jr., and Arthur Stengel. (1980). "Making Problem Solving Come Alive in the Intermediate Grades." In *Problem Solving in School Mathematics,* edited by Stephen Krulik and Robert E. Reys, pp. 127–135. Reston, VA: National Council of Teachers of Mathematics.

Kouba, Vicky L., Catherine A. Brown, Thomas P. Carpenter, Mary M. Lindquist, Edward A. Silver, and Jane O. Swafford. (April 1988). "Results of the Fourth NAEP Assessment of Mathematics: Number, Operations, and Word Problems." *Arithmetic Teacher* 35: 14–19.

Lester, Frank K., Jr. (1983). "Trends and Issues in Mathematical Problem-Solving Research." In *Acquisition of Mathematics Concepts and Processes,* edited by Richard Lesh and Marsha Landau, pp. 229–261. New York: Academic Press.

Matz, Karl A., and Cynthia Leier. (April 1992). "Word Problems and the Language Connection." *Arithmetic Teacher* 39: 14–17.

Moses, Barbara, Elizabeth Bjork, and E. Paul Goldenberg. (1990). "Beyond Problem Solving: Problem Posing." In *Teaching and Learning Mathematics in the 1990s,* edited by Thomas J. Cooney and Christian R. Hirsch, pp. 82–91. Reston, VA: National Council of Teachers of Mathematics.

National Council of Teachers of Mathematics (NCTM). (1980). *An Agenda for Action: Recommendations for School Mathematics of the 1980s.* Reston VA: Author.

National Council of Teachers of Mathematics (NCTM). (1989). *Curriculum and Evaluation Standards for School Mathematics.* Reston, VA: Author.

Otis, Marlys Johnson, and Theresa Reardon Offerman. (April 1988). "How *Do* You Evaluate Problem Solving?" *Arithmetic Teacher* 35: 49–51.

Payne, Joseph N. (1992). "The Effects of Calculators on State Objectives and Tests." In *Calculators in Mathematics Education,* edited by James T. Fey and Christian R. Hirsch, pp. 177–185. Reston, VA: National Council of Teachers of Mathematics.

Polya, G. (1957). *How to Solve It: A New Aspect of Mathematical Method,* 2nd ed. Garden City, NY: Doubleday.

Reys, Barbara J. (1989). "The Calculator as a Tool for Instruction and Learning." In *New Directions for Elementary School Mathematics,* edited by Paul R. Trafton and Albert P. Shulte, pp. 168–173. Reston, VA: National Council of Teachers of Mathematics.

Schoenfeld, Alan H. (1980). "Heuristics in the Classroom." In *Problem Solving in School Mathematics,* edited by Stephen Krulik and Robert E. Reys, pp. 9–22. Reston, VA: National Council of Teachers of Mathematics.

Silver, Edward A., and Philip J. Smith. (1980). "Think of a Related Problem." In *Problem Solving in School Mathematics,* edited by Stephen Krulik and Robert E. Reys, pp. 146–156. Reston, VA: National Council of Teachers of Mathematics.

Suydam, Marilyn N. (1980). "Untangling Clues from Research on Problem Solving." In *Problem Solving in School Mathematics,* edited by Stephen Krulik and Robert E. Reys, pp. 34–50. Reston, VA: National Council of Teachers of Mathematics.

WHERE TO LOOK FOR PROBLEMS

Krulik, Stephen, and Jesse A. Rudnick. (1984). *A Sourcebook for Teaching Problem Solving.* Boston: Allyn & Bacon.

Sobel, Max A., and Evan M. Maletsky. (1988). *Teaching Mathematics: A Sourcebook of Aids, Activities, and Strategies,* 2nd ed. Englewood Cliffs, NJ: Prentice-Hall.

SOFTWARE RESOURCES

The Factory
Company: Sunburst
Computer: Apple
Grade level: 4–12

Duplicate and design products by punching holes, rotating various degrees, and painting stripes on surfaces of the "product."

The King's Rule
Company: Sunburst
Computer: Apple
Grade level: 4–6

Induce number patterns to gain entrance to rooms in the castle. Patterns range from easy to difficult.

Puzzle Tanks
Company: Sunburst
Computer: Apple
Grade level: 3 and up

Four levels of problems that involve versions of the classic problem: Given two containers of different sizes (e.g., 3 and 7), how can you fill a third container of yet another size (e.g., 5) with water. Adding and subtracting in various ways are required to solve the problems.

CHAPTER 3

Learning Number Concepts in the Early School Years

▪ INTRODUCTORY PROBLEM ▪

A high priority of Ms. Yost, the first-grade teacher, is for the children to work together as a class family. She believes that this will happen only if they know one another, so she began the year by helping children learn one another's names. In the first week of October most children were able to call their classmates by name. They were also beginning to read each other's names. She remembered that last year Diane, one of the students, had said, "Let's learn to spell one another's names," and the most able learners really enjoyed learning to spell the names of their classmates. She would mention spelling names this year and believed that some in the class would find it a challenge. "Reading and writing names involves knowing the letters of the alphabet," she thought, "and so the activity is a valuable learning experience." Then she remembered that in the teacher's room, Jamie, the other first-grade teacher, had said that this year she was putting math into other subjects and had been delighted with the math the children were learning. "Aha," she thought, "We can use our names in math as well as language. There are many opportunities for number readiness and number learning using the letters in children's names. We'll do this tomorrow morning."

As you study this chapter, make a list of the possibilities for learning about numbers as children get acquainted and learn to call one another by name, to examine the letters in each other's names, and to read and write names.

INTRODUCTION

Many children come to school with intuitive ideas about mathematics. Experiences in their lives have enabled them to become aware of counting, numbers, shapes, sizes, and patterns. Experiences in preschool, kindergarten, and first grade help them build on this knowledge. However, some children begin school with a meager background and have not developed beginning number or geometric concepts. They need many school experiences to develop these ideas.

New directions in early school mathematics instruction give attention to all the standards developed by the National Council of Teachers of Mathematics (NCTM, 1989) for K–4, with problem solving, the development of number sense, patterning, and geometry and spatial awareness receiving special attention. Problem solving for young children often involves real-life situations. As they solve problems related to their lives, children think about how to solve problems, as well as find answers to problems. Number sense for young children involves knowledge of numbers, number relations such as "greater than" and "less than," and the relative magnitude of numbers. Young children investigate patterns in numbers, figures, and real life. Geometry and spatial awareness deal with knowledge of shapes and the geometry of one's surroundings (see Chapter Eleven).

This chapter discusses learning number concepts in the first years of school (see Standards 1, 6, and 13, in Curriculum Standards for Grades K–4, Appendix A). The first two sections, Number Readiness and Developing Number Meanings, describe instruction that would be appropriate for preschool, kindergarten, or first-grade children who have little background in mathematics. The topics discussed in Section three, Extending Number Concepts, would be introduced in grades 1 and 2. The fourth section is Assessing Number Learning in the Early School Years. A Summary is the final section of the chapter.

Even with young children, interactive methods are used. Teachers ask open-ended questions, assign exploratory-type activities, and pose problems for children to solve. They provide opportunities for children to discuss mathematics with one another to clarify and integrate ideas. They listen to learners and relate instruction to children's understanding.

Two organizational plans provide the classroom structure for interactive teaching. Over time both arrangements are used.

1. Children work independently or in small groups at learning centers or stations; you move from group to group observing and interacting with learners.
2. The whole class or a small group works under your guidance.

In the first situation, class discussions frequently follow children's completion of work; in the second, discussions are a part of the lesson. During a discussion, you frequently ask questions so that children can refine and justify their ideas. An important question is, "Why?" It is asked in response to correct as well as seemingly incorrect answers (NCTM, 1991).

Children are encouraged to feel pleasure in completing the activities and develop self-pride in achievement. Teachers help children develop feelings of autonomy, competency, and self-worth to enable them to develop positive attitudes toward the study of mathematics.

NUMBER READINESS

Number readiness involves developing thinking abilities such as classifying, comparing, and ordering. These processes are fundamental to the development of number ideas. The number knowledge of young children also includes conservation of number and an understanding of patterning.

Number concepts develop as children investigate and think about the relations between objects and groups of objects. Out of their experiences, children coordinate ideas of order and class inclusion to create number concepts (Kamii and DeVries, 1976; Piaget, 1952). Ordering involves arranging in terms of increasing or decreasing properties. Class inclusion involves mentally including one in two, two in three, three in four, and so forth.

Objects used to help children construct number concepts include tiles, beans, screws, washers, bottle caps, jar lids, and buttons (sometimes referred to as "junk materials"); commercially produced materials such as linking cubes, Cuisenaire rods, pattern blocks, and attribute blocks; and teacher-made materials such as number bars (see Appendix G) or strips (Figure 3.1). Bars for numbers 1 through 10 can be made by cutting tag board covered with a 1-in grid. The grid is printed or pasted on the tag board, which is laminated before the bars are cut. Strips have no divisions.

Before using materials in lessons, children explore the objects, particularly those unfamiliar to them, such as linking cubes. Children need to "play" with objects before using them in ways you suggest. After children play with objects, making "pictures" or designs with them, they are ready to describe the characteristics of objects, called *attributes*. They should be able to recognize the color, size, and shape of objects before using the objects in activities.

Classifying

Classifying is a mental activity that enables us to deal with all aspects of life. We categorize experiences and react to the categories in similar ways. Knowledge grows as we establish relations among categories. For example, we classify sounds and letters and note the relations among them to learn to read. We classify situations as joining or separating in order to decide whether to add or subtract. We often classify objects in order to count. For example, we classify to answer the question, "How many children are wearing sandals?"

Classifying experiences for young children begin with sorting, that is, categorizing objects by perceivable characteristics. Later, children classify by creating categories to use in separating objects into different groups.

Classifying activities should be designed as problem-solving experiences. Children should be given objects and asked to put them into groups that are alike in some way. They should not be told the attribute to use in classifying (e.g., color). They should also be encouraged to make more than one classification. After they complete their work, they explain their classifications to each other. For example, you can give each pair of children a can of screws, bolts, and nuts, and say, "How can these be grouped so that everything in a group is alike in some way? Find as many ways as you can." In one classroom where the children were given this task, the teacher was astonished at the many classifications the children constructed.

Children should have many opportunities to classify junk and commercial materials. Different types of materials can be classified by different groups. Children can move from center to center, working on different days with different materials.

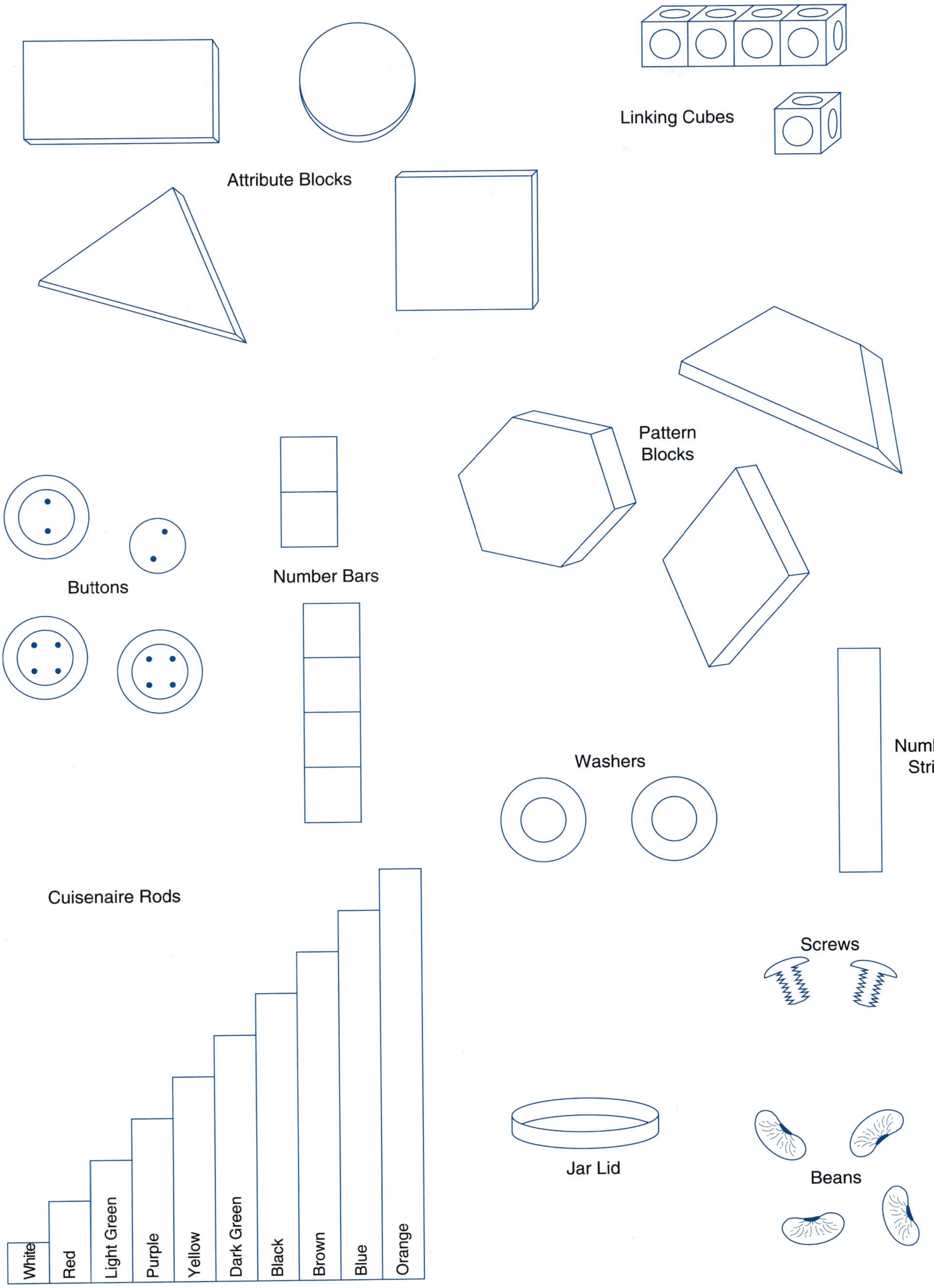

FIGURE 3.1 Materials for Number Learning

ACTIVITY 3.1
Classifying Ourselves.

Ask children to decide how the members of the class could be placed in groups with all in a group having the same attribute, such as eye color. Designate where each group will stand, and have children decide where they belong. Have them move in an orderly manner to the place designated for their category. A variation is for you or a child to ask some children to move to a designated place and the class infers the category.

ACTIVITY 3.2
Classifying Shoes.

Have children sit in a circle. Each takes off one shoe. The class decides how the shoes could be sorted, and each child places his or her shoe in the proper category.

ACTIVITY 3.3
Finding Groups.

Have pupils use catalogues or newspaper advertising sections. Have them choose two categories of pictures to cut out (e.g., cars and trucks, vegetables and fruits, tables and chairs, etc.). They display their work by pasting the pictures on sheets of paper. When they share their work with the class, they describe the categories.

Comparing

Comparing is fundamental to understanding numbers. "Greater than" and "less than" are concepts inherent in number and measurement meanings. As children work with objects, they become aware of concepts such as: longer (shorter) than, larger or bigger (smaller) than, darker (lighter) than, more (less) than, and the same (not the same) number. You introduce the vocabulary words they need to communicate their ideas.

Children examine equivalent and nonequivalent sets to develop ideas of same and not the same number. Equivalent sets are those whose elements can be matched one-to-one. We say there is a one-to-one correspondence between the elements of the two sets. Equivalent sets have the same number. Nonequivalent sets cannot be matched one-to-one; one set has more or fewer elements than the other set, and the sets do not have the same number (Figure 3.2).

Play activities often involve making one-to-one correspondences, such as when setting the table in the play corner. For example, on a table there should be a spoon for every plate and a cup for every saucer. As you talk with children about their play, use the phrase "one-to-one matching." Also ask them if the two sets have the same number and why the sets have or do not have the same number. Several children can give their ideas. If the ideas differ, children should be encouraged to react to one another. Children are often convinced of the error of their thinking when they reason with others.

Instances of one-to-one correspondence that arise in connection with school activities can be used to teach the idea of "same number." Examples are: each child is given a piece of paper for drawing; at library time, each child has a book to look at; and at snack time, each child is served a cracker. Have children pass out supplies or food and explain what they did to help them grasp the idea of one-to-one correspondence. Ask questions such as: "Are the number of children and the number of books the same? Why?"

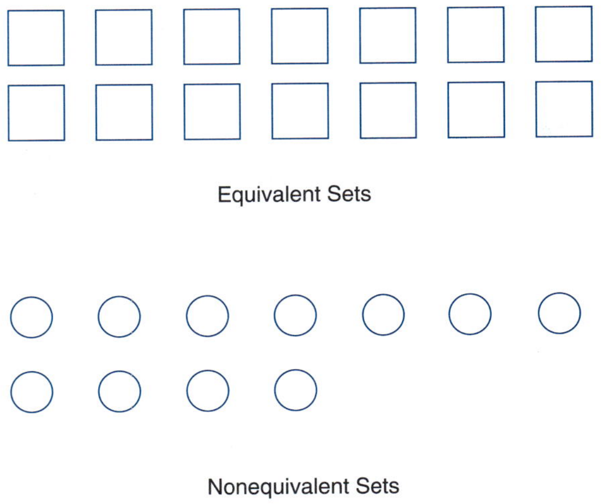

FIGURE 3.2 Comparing Sets

ACTIVITY 3.4
Comparing Classroom Objects.

Have children work in pairs. Ask each child to take a pencil. Say, "I wonder what we can find out about our pencils! Look at the two pencils you and your partner have. Partners tell each other how the pencils are alike and different." Several children tell the class what they noticed about the two pencils. It is expected that children will use words such as longer, shorter, bigger, smaller, and the like. If not, these words are introduced.

After several comparing activities, introduce the word "compare." Say, for example, "When we tell that one pencil is longer than another pencil, we are comparing pencils. To compare we can also say one pencil is shorter than the other. Let's look at our pencils again. Juan, please tell us how your pencil and Ben's pencil compare." Have children ask others in the class, "How does your pencil compare with mine?" When children understand what it means "to compare," ask them to find objects in the classroom that can be compared (e.g., books, teacher's and pupil's desk). They can also think of objects at home that can be compared.

ACTIVITY 3.5
Compare and Move.

Give directions such as take a short step, take a longer step, take the same-length step, take a short hop, take a shorter hop, and so on. After children understand the directions for this activity, a child can be the leader.

ACTIVITY 3.6
Make a Funny Snake.

Children should work in small groups for this activity. Have children use attribute blocks to fill in an outline of a funny snake (Figure 3.3A). Directions for choosing attribute blocks are: Each block must be a color (shape, size) different from the previous block. Before they begin their work, have children give examples, such as the block for the body can be larger than the block for the head. They should show the attribute blocks to illustrate their ideas.

When children can deal with more than one attribute, the directions can be to make the blocks differ by two attributes. With older children, one (or two) and only one (or two) attributes can differ (Figure 3.3B).

FIGURE 3.3 Attribute Activities. A, Outline of a Funny Snake. B, Blocks Differ by One and Only One Attribute. C, Blocks Differ by Two and Only Two Attributes.

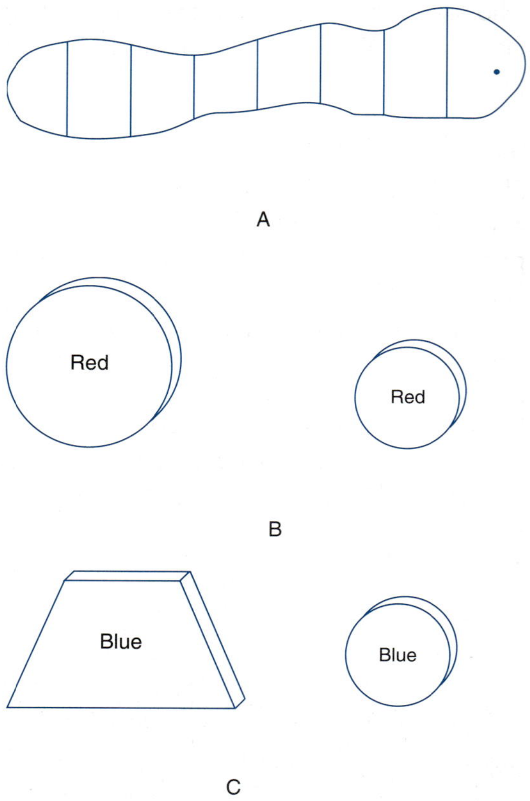

ACTIVITY 3.7
Spin and Compare.

Materials needed are (1) a spinner with sections showing long, short, dark, light, wide, and narrow ribbons; and (2) 10 to 12 ribbons that have attributes like those in the pictures on the spinner. Two children play as a team. Children take turns spinning and choosing a ribbon that is the same (or opposite) from the picture on the spinner. When all the ribbons have been collected, the child with the most different ribbons wins.

ACTIVITY 3.8
Equivalent and Nonequivalent Sets.

This is a small group teacher-guided activity. Each child in the group has eight blue and eight yellow plastic teddy bears and colored disks or counters to make one-to-one correspondences. A story that involves matchings is told to the group. For example, you could say, "The blue teddy bears went for a walk in the woods. Each blue teddy bear took a yellow teddy bear with him because they were friends. With your bear counters, please show the blue teddy bears and their yellow teddy bear friends beside them. After a while each blue and yellow teddy bear found a bunch of red berries to eat. What can we use for the bunch of berries? Please show each bear and his bunch of berries." Other instances that call for one-to-one correspondences would appear throughout the story, and children would make the matchings. Some parts of the story could require children to think about nonequivalent sets. For example, say, "Two blue teddy bears decided to take a rest while the others looked for honey. All the teddy bears that looked found bee hives with honey, but the two who rested did not find any bee hives with honey. How can we show the bears and their honey? Were there more teddy bears or more bee hives? Why?"

ACTIVITY 3.9
Comparing Groups.

Show children boxes of pencils or other objects; one nearly full, the other, nearly empty. Say, "What do you notice about these boxes of pencils?" Guide them to compare the contents of the boxes by using language that involves expressions such as "many more" and "many less."

Direct children's attention to objects in the environment that show large differences in amounts. For example, say, "How do the children and the teachers in this school compare in number?" Ask them to find examples of groups at school or at home whose numbers can be compared. (Hints can be: what can be compared on the school parking lot? the cafeteria and a classroom? the school kitchen and the cafeteria?) Whenever possible, discuss their examples using words that emphasize large differences in amounts.

Ordering

Beginning experiences with ordering involve arranging objects in a series in terms of an increasing or decreasing attribute. Ordering on the basis of qualitative comparisons is often called *seriating*. Objects to order include pencils, bottles filled with water, fine-to-coarse sandpaper, blocks, jars, lids, and tone bells. Kits of objects to order can be made so that different kits are available for groups to order at different learning stations or centers.

To introduce ordering, give each pair of children six pieces of paper cut in graduated sizes. Ask the children to arrange the pieces in order. After the groups have finished their ordering, talk about what they did and why. Introduce the word, "ordering." Most ordering activities require materials that are not available for all the children, but can be in learning centers. Children take turns at the centers. Activity 3.9 is a whole-class activity children will enjoy.

ACTIVITY 3.10
Ordering Hands.

Have each child trace around his or her hand with fingers not spread and cut out the tracing. Groups of four can order their "hands," and a committee can help you order all the hands for a bulletin board display. The activity can be repeated with fingers spread, and a display made as before. Pupils can discuss the similarities and differences in the two displays.

Variation: Have each child trace around his or her shoe and cut out the shape. Small groups can order their shoes. A display can be made of the cutout shoes.

Conservation of Number

Conservation of number is the idea that the number of a set remains the same or invariant even if the elements of the set are rearranged. Piaget (1952) introduced the concept of conservation. It formed the basis for many of his ideas about children's development of number. Many authorities today consider it to be an aspect of number knowledge but also emphasize the importance of classifying, ordering, counting, and immediate recognition of the number of a set in developing number concepts (Moser, 1988).

To determine if a child conserves number, place about 20 counters on the table. Place 8 on the table in a row (Figure 3.4). Ask the child to make a second row so that the counters match one-to-one (Figure 3.5A). (Use at least 8 so that the child must think about the numbers. With numbers smaller than 8, the child may use perceptual clues to respond to your questions.) If a child cannot make a one-to-one correspondence, discontinue the task because knowledge of equality is based on understanding one-to-one correspondence. Ask, "Do the two rows have the same number or does one have more or less? Why do you think that?" If he or she does not tell you that the numbers are the same, discontinue the task, because conservation is based on understanding the concept of equality.

Continue by rearranging the counters in one row. They may be spread out or pushed together (Figure 3.5B). Point to the two groups as you say, "Are there more here, or here, or is the same number in each group?" After the child responds, ask the justification question, "Why do you think that?" Conservers recognize that whatever the arrangement, the groups have the same number and will justify their responses by giving a logical reason, such as, "You did not take any away or add any," or "The counters could be put back so they would match like before."

Activity for the Classroom 3.1. Carry out the conservation task with three children in kindergarten or grade 1. Compare their responses, and assess their knowledge of numbers.

ACTIVITY 3.11
Bean Drop.

This activity is best for a small group. Give each child in your group a paper cup and take one yourself. Say, "Let's find out what happens to numbers when we drop beans in our cups." Give each child and yourself a different number of beans. Ask them about the number of beans they and you have. They should observe that the numbers are different. Everyone drops beans in his or her cup. Then ask, "What do you know about the number of beans in different cups?" You may need to ask, "Do we have the same number of beans in our cups? Why do you think that? How can you prove it?"

Then say, "This time, let's find out what happens if we each drop a bean in our cup at the same time. Let's each drop a bean when I say, 'Drop'." Each drops seven beans in his or her cup, one at a time, when you give the drop direction. Then ask, "What is true about the number of beans in each cup?" If no child says, "The numbers are the same," ask, "Do we all have the same number of beans in our cups?

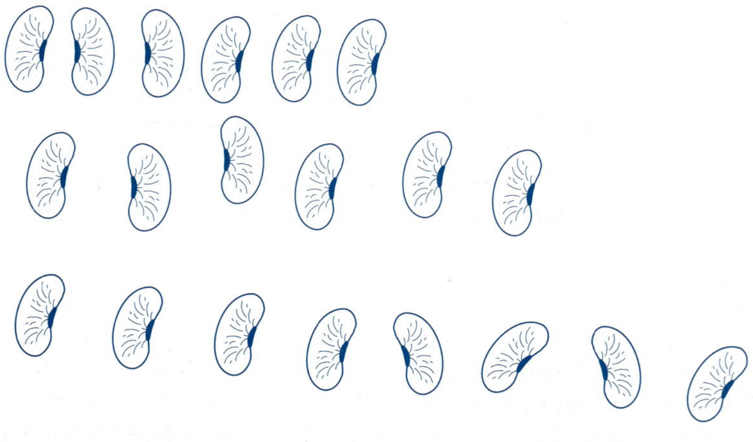

FIGURE 3.4 Eight Beans in a Row from a Set of 20 Beans

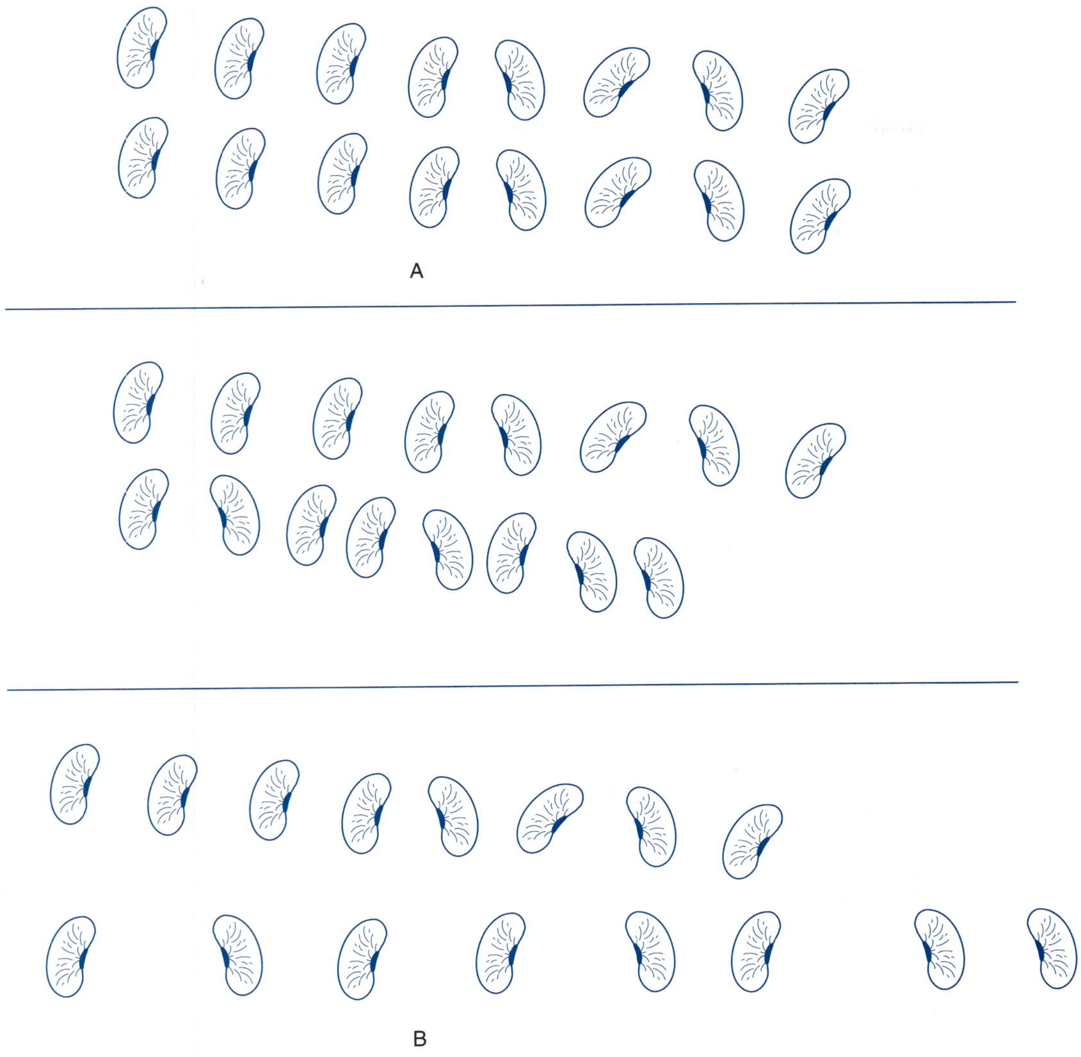

FIGURE 3.5 A, Two Sets of Beans in One-to-One Correspondence. B, Two Different Rearrangements of One Row in Set of Two Rows

Why or why not?" Have children give their reasons, and test them out. If no one suggests matching, say, "What would matching our beans with someone else's beans tell us? . . . Let's do it." (Designate the pairs of children who will match their beans.)

After children have worked in pairs to place their beans in one-to-one-correspondence, ask them to make different arrangements with their beans. Repeat the questions regarding set equivalence, and provide many opportunities for children to share their thinking in response to these questions. Have some children each remove one or two beans from their arrangements, and repeat the questions.

ACTIVITY 3.12
Fists of Beans.

Ask children in a small group each to reach in a bag of beans, take a fistful of beans, and lay them on the table. Designate pairs of children to compare the number of beans they took and to tell one another why they think the number is the same or not the same. Have each pair of children show the others their sets of beans, report if the number of beans in their fistfuls is the same or not the same, and tell why they did or did not have the same number of beans.

Patterning

Patterning involves examining, creating, and extending a pattern or sequence. To a great extent, mathematics is the study of patterns. Observing patterns in numbers and shapes enables us to deal intelligently with the environment and advance in the study of mathematics.

Lessons to introduce patterning can begin by asking pupils to observe patterns occurring in the environment, such as patterns on clothing, or to repeat a pattern of movements. To direct children's attention to a pattern in clothing, you can say, "Look at the flowers on Beverly's blouse. What do you notice about the flowers?" A pattern of movements can be introduced with Activity 3.13. Children discuss what they have noticed or done, and the word "pattern" is introduced. Patterning activities soon involve copying, continuing, and creating patterns.

ACTIVITY 3.13
Rhythmic Hand or Body Movements.

Begin a movement pattern such as clap, clap, snap. Say, "Join in when you can do it." Have children explain the pattern. Other patterns involve clapping over your head, clapping in front of you, turning, bending, and the like.

ACTIVITY 3.14
Follow the Leader.

Children demonstrate movement patterns (e.g., bend to the right, bend to the left, clap), and the class follows. You choose the first leader, and then each leader chooses the next leader. You can use a timer or the second hand on the clock to mark the time allowed for each leader.

ACTIVITY 3.15
Patterns with Objects.

Attribute blocks, pattern blocks, buttons, beads, large and small paper clips, and other common objects can be used in patterning. Children create and repeat patterns using objects, and they sometimes copy their work by tracing the objects or using attribute stickers (Figure 3.6).

ACTIVITY 3.16
Dot, Line, and Curve Patterns.

Children make repeating patterns with dots, lines, and curves as in Figure 3.7. After children make these patterns, they share them with the class, explaining what they did.

ACTIVITY 3.17
Using Patterns.

Patterns can be created to use on functional objects, such as place mats, cloth chair-back covers, or wrapping paper.

FIGURE 3.6 Repeating an Attribute Blocks Pattern

FIGURE 3.7 Repeating a Curves, Line, and Dots Pattern

ACTIVITY 3.18
Reverse a Pattern.

Suggest that children copy a pattern backward. After the reversed pattern is completed, children should explain how it was done.

DEVELOPING NUMBER MEANINGS

According to Fuson and Hall (1983), a mature understanding of number results from the integration of different meanings for number. Children develop number meanings as they use numbers in different contexts, such as counting, cardinal number, ordinal number, measurement, and nonnumerical contexts. Gradually learners coordinate the meanings formed in different settings to develop a mature number concept. This section discusses learning the number word sequence, counting and cardinal number, recognizing the number of a set by sight, using ordinal number, and nonnumerical use of numbers. Activities to foster understanding are described. In carrying out the activities, children manipulate objects or work with pictures. They also think and talk about what they did. Numerals are not introduced until later. Chapter Twelve discusses measurement.

Learning the Number Word Sequence

Knowing the sequence of number words involves saying the counting words in order with no awareness of the number meanings attached to the words (counting by rote). Many children come to school knowing how to count by rote. In some preschools and kindergartens, however, children may not be able to give the counting words in correct sequence. For example, they could say, "One, two, four, seven, six." Fuson and Hall report that most middle-class children can count to 100 by rote by the end of kindergarten if instruction emphasizes such counting.

Rhymes and finger plays are often used to help children learn the counting sequence. Counting activities that arise in connection with school life also help children learn the counting words in order (e.g., counting the number of boys and girls present and absent by counting empty chairs).

ACTIVITY 3.19
Count as the Ball Bounces.

Have children bounce a ball on the counting words in a rhyme, such as the following, and throw the ball on the words following the counting words. The activity can be used as a circle game, or two children can play together, throwing the ball to each other.

One, two, buckle my shoe
Three, four, close the door
Five, six, pick up sticks
Seven, eight, close the gate
Nine, ten, begin again.

Other counting activities are counting jumps, hops, or a combination of jumps and hops.

ACTIVITY 3.20
A Finger Play.

Children make two fists and open their fingers as they say this rhyme:

I see a beehive
(Make two fists)
I see some bees
One bee, bzz (Extend one finger)
Two bees, bzz (Extend one more finger)
. . .
Ten bees, bzz (Extend 10 fingers)

Dutton and Dutton (1991) provide many number finger plays for young children.

Counting and Cardinal Numbers

Counting involves matching the number words to objects. The numerosity of a set, that is, the cardinal number, can be determined by counting. Certain principles govern counting to determine the number of objects in a set: (1) the order of the number words is stable; (2) there must be a one-to-one correspondence between the number words and the items in a set; (3) the items in a set may differ; (4) the order in which the objects are counted is irrelevant; and (5) the last number counted names the cardinal number of the set (Gelman and Meck, 1986).

Many children come to school with an intuitive knowledge of these principles. They can count objects and use counting to give the cardinal number of a set. If children have not developed counting skills, you plan activities to help them learn to give the counting words in order (discussed earlier), to count objects, and to determine the cardinal number of a set.

As they learn to count objects, some children will need to touch the items to keep track of the count, others may keep track of the items by an overt action such as nodding. Permit them to do so as long as the actions are needed, but discuss how to count without touching to help learners become aware of the mature procedure.

Turn as many classroom activities as possible into counting opportunities, and sometimes count for "fun." For example, have children count the boys, the girls, and all the children in the class; those eating in the cafeteria; those that came on the bus; the days that have passed in the current week, month, or school year; the days between children's birthdays; and, for fun, count wrists and elbows while waiting for the dismissal bell to ring or the school bus to arrive.

Frequently ask children to tell how many are in a set after they have counted. If they need to recount, they have not learned or cannot remember that the ending number tells the cardinal number of the set.

Children should be asked both to give the number of a set and produce a set with a given number. Counting a given set is somewhat less demanding than counting to produce a set of a given size. In response to the question, "How many?" children learn that counting gives the answer. However, if asked to make a set of a given size, the child must construct a set with a specified number by taking part of a set with an unspecified number and determine if he or she has produced a set with the given number.

Kamii and DeVries (1976) stress asking children to produce a set that matches another set without giving them the number of the set. Part of the task for a child is to determine the number of the set to be produced. For example, say, "Please get enough books so each child in your group has a picture book," and later, "How many did you get? Why?"

ACTIVITY 3.21
Help the Puppet Count.

Use a hand puppet to count items. Ask children to listen to the hand puppet to determine if it knows how to count. Have the puppet make counting errors (e.g., skip a number, not give the correct sequence, skip items, and the like). When children find an error, ask them to show the puppet how to count the items with no mistakes.

ACTIVITY 3.22
Treasures.

Collect items such as colored paper clips, screws, nuts, bolts, shells, or buttons in small boxes or plastic bags. Counters obtained commercially such as plastic teddy bears are favorites of children. At first the boxes or bags contain up to 10 objects; later more objects are added until 20 are included. Say, "Let's pretend we went to find treasures and each one found the treasures in front of you. How can you find how many treasures you found?" The children should reply, "Count." (Do not tell children what to do; always give them opportunity to tell you how to find the answer. However, if they cannot answer the question, you can give a hint by saying, "Could you count?") After each has counted his or her treasures, the children discuss how many they counted, and some demonstrate what they did. Children can also compare the numbers of their treasures, using gross comparisons such as "more than."

To help children think about beginning the count with any item, ask questions such as: "Why did you begin here? Could you begin somewhere else? Why?"

Give each child a few more treasures, or have each child give you a few of his or her treasures, and repeat the activity.

ACTIVITY 3.23
How Many?

Say, "Another teacher asked me how many window panes, doors, tables, and light fixtures we have in our room? How would I find out what to tell her?" Children can chorus-count the items, or small groups can count different items and report on their count. You can make a record of their counts to show children that symbols are written to remember the results of counting.

ACTIVITY 3.24
Counting Steps.

Say, "It would be fun to know how many steps it takes to go from a table (chair or desk) to the door (office or playground). How would we find out? What would we find out if we started at the door and counted steps to the table rather than count from the table to the door?" Children can also count the steps they take at home such as from the front door to their bed. Let them share what they have counted at home. (Later have children estimate and compare the count to the estimate.)

ACTIVITY 3.25
Follow Me.

You or a child serves as the leader and tells the class to make 10 or less same bodily movements, such as clapping, extending arms, or touching an ear. Children in the class count as they carry out the direction.

Variation: The leader makes a sequence of two or three movements and repeats the sequence once or twice. One or more children then carry out the sequence without the leader's guidance. The other children decide if the sequence and number were the same as the leader's.

ACTIVITY 3.26
Same Number.

Display a picture of toys on the overhead, and give a problem such as: John has these toys. Tom wants the same number. Say, "Show what Tom wants with your counters." Ask children how they knew what to do. Follow with similar questions. Later children can find pictures in story books and pose problems such as yours. Classmates use objects to solve the problems.

ACTIVITY 3.27
Number Pictures.

Children make number pictures with groups of toothpicks. They tell about their pictures using number words (Figure 3.8). For example, a child could say, "My toothpicks show two and one."

ACTIVITY 3.28
Buttons for the Clown Suit.

Duplicate a picture of a clown suit for each child (see Appendix D for pattern). The suit should have no buttons. Give two children about 10 buttons. Have them take turns asking one another to name a number of buttons for the clown suit and select that number. The child who produces the set lays the buttons on his or her clown suit. The two children then count to check the number.

When children can count to tell how many in a set, activities provide opportunities for them to learn to count on and count back.

ACTIVITY 3.29
How Many in All?

To encourage counting on, use a card on the overhead (Figure 3.9). Slide a few objects under the card. Then place a few more objects on the overhead. Tell the class how many are under the card. Ask how many are on the overhead and how the answer was found. Children can discuss their ideas with a partner before one or more children answer the questions.

FIGURE 3.8 Number Pictures with Toothpicks

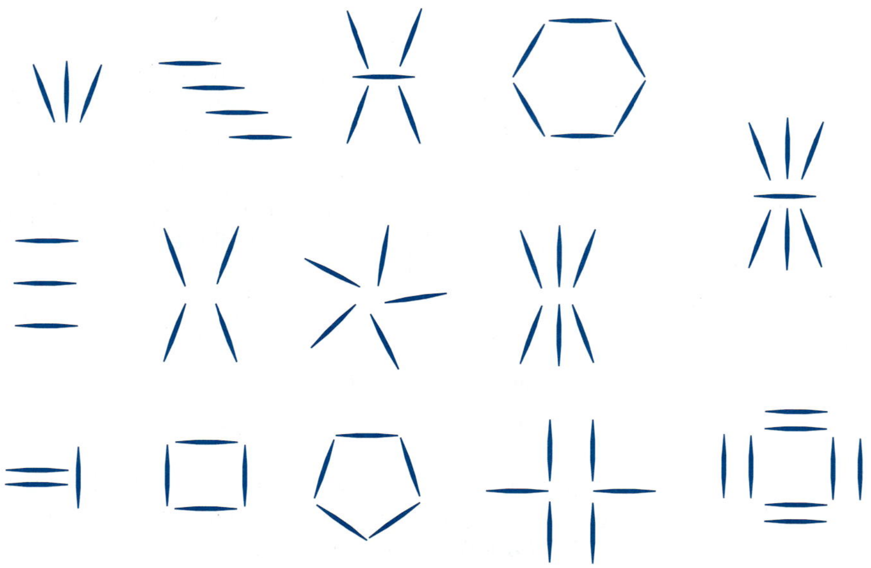

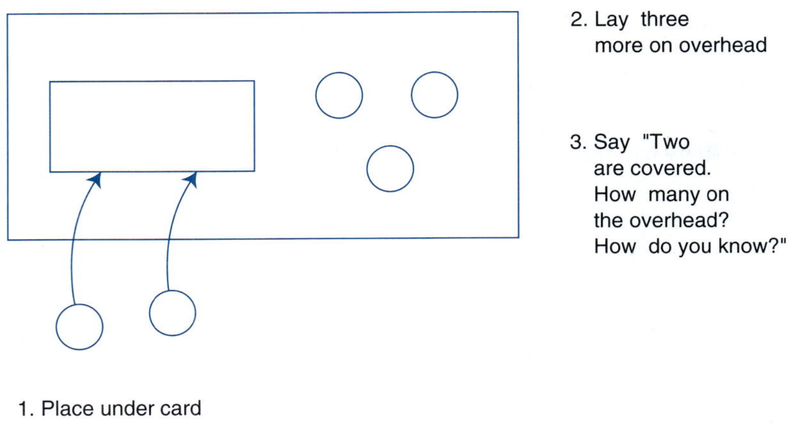

FIGURE 3.9 How Many in All?

ACTIVITY 3.30
Count On.

Show less than 10 objects on the overhead. Have one child count several, and ask the rest of the class to finish the count. When children understand the procedure, have them engage in the *Count On* activity in pairs. Child 1 shows a number of objects less than 10, counts a few, and asks child 2 to finish the count. The children then trade tasks.

ACTIVITY 3.31
Count Back.

Use a card on the overhead. Slide a few objects under the card. Then place a few more objects on the overhead. Tell the class how many altogether are on the overhead. Ask how many are under the card and how the answer was found (Figure 3.10). Again, two can work together to answer the questions before several tell their

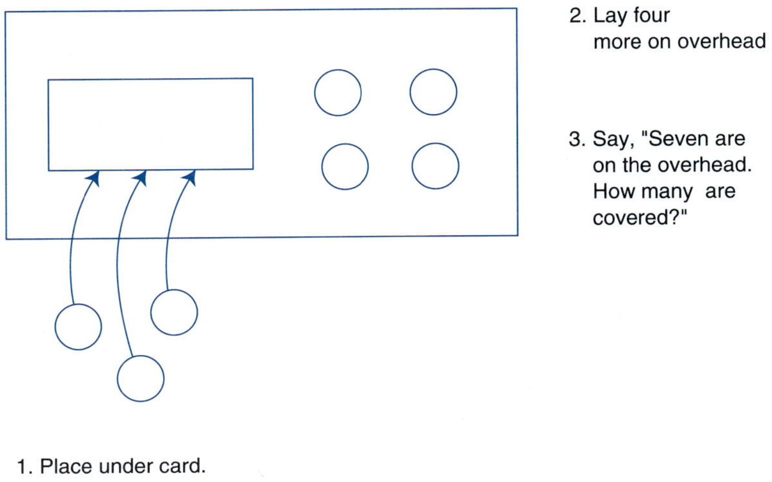

FIGURE 3.10 Count Back

thinking to the class. If no one mentions counting back, ask how they could count back to answer the question, and have some children demonstrate how to do this.

Activity for the Classroom 3.2. Plan and teach a lesson involving counting objects to help children develop the ability to count on and count back. Include counting in lifelike settings. Was counting on or counting back easier to learn or was there no difference? How would you use the answer to the previous question to plan other lessons?

Recognizing the Number of a Set by Sight

Immediate recognition of the number of a set is called *subitizing*. We immediately name the number of a set with four or less objects. Larger sets are broken into smaller sets for number recognition. Noticing a pattern makes it possible for us to give the number of a set without counting.

When children can subitize, they can attend to other aspects of a problem than counting. Relieved of the counting task, they have more space in short-term memory to process information and can therefore advance in their work with numbers (Resnick and Ford, 1981).

Reader Activity 3.1

Toss less than 10 but more than 4 counters on the table two or three times. Decide how you group the objects to give the number of the set.

Activities 3.32 and 3.33 make use of number patterns, or "pictures," to teach subitizing and grouping for number recognition. The activities deal with numbers through 10. Dots, stars, or other small objects can be pasted or drawn on cards or paper plates to make number pictures. The objects should be arranged in patterns for easy number recognition (Figure 3.11).

ACTIVITY 3.32
What Do You See?

Show a number card or plate with 10 or less objects arranged in a pattern. The children give the number in unison. Several children tell how they knew the number of the set.

ACTIVITY 3.33
Tell the Number Game.

A set of 20 cards showing sets of objects arranged in patterns is used by two pupils. It is placed face down in the middle of the activity area. The pupils take turns showing a card drawn from the pile of cards and giving the number of the set. When the number is named, the player gets the card. When the cards are gone, the "winner" has the most cards. Both students can be winners because the number of cards is even.

ACTIVITY 3.34
What Do I See?

Ask children to observe arrangements of objects in the classroom, school, or away from school. Have them notice patterns that enable them to tell a number of objects without counting (e.g., 4 chairs around a table, 4 legs on a chair, 3 wheels on a tricycle, and 6 panes in a window). Pupils share what they have seen. They can draw

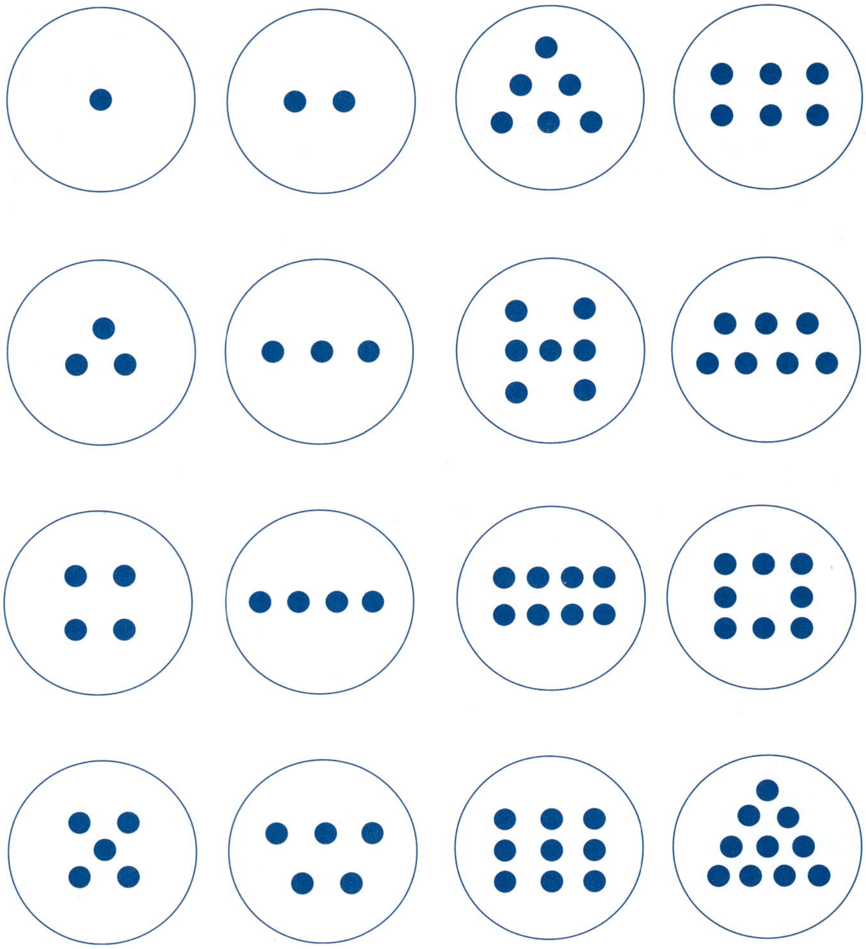

FIGURE 3.11 Plates with Dot Number Pictures

pictures of what they have observed. The pictures can be shared or displayed on the bulletin board.

ACTIVITY 3.35
Dominoes.

Children can play with dominoes in learning centers or during rainy day recess time. Domino-type cards can use standard domino patterns or other patterns useful in subitizing (Figure 3.12). Beginning work with these cards gives children opportunities to match sets with the same number.

ACTIVITY 3.36
Imagine.

Say, "Close your eyes, and imagine as many things as you have eyes." The children then draw in the air what they imagined. One or more children tell what was imagined. Children can take your place and make up directions after the procedure is understood.

FIGURE 3.12 Path with Domino-Type Cards

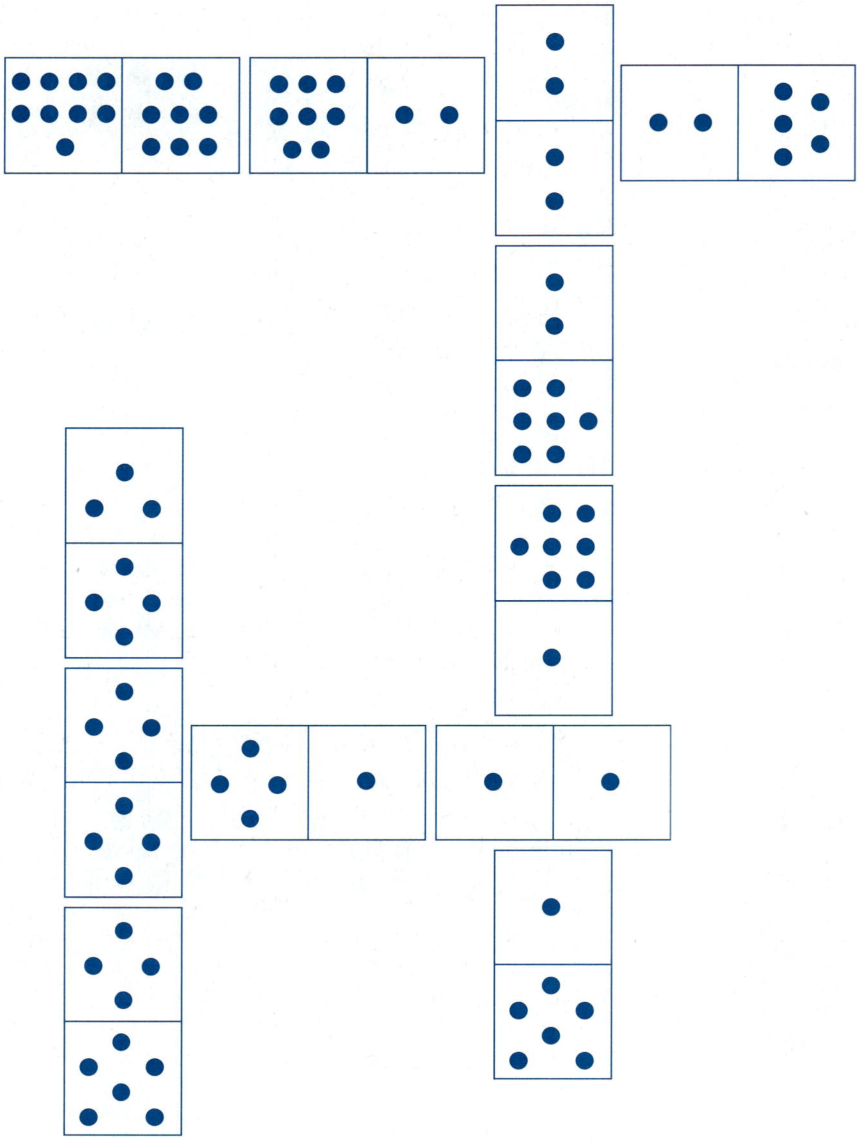

ACTIVITY 3.37
Learning Zero.

To introduce the number "zero," say, "How many cats bark?" Introduce the idea of "not any" and the word "zero" as children give answers to this and similar questions. Children then make up questions that can be answered by "Zero."

Using Ordinal Numbers

Numbers are used in an ordinal sense to give position. Counting words can be used to name a number position. For example, "Table 4 may go to recess." Often, however, ordinal words such as first or second, are used. Pupils need many experiences to learn these words.

Instruction creates classroom situations that involve ordinal numbers. For example, give directions such as: The first child in each row may get in line. This week's birthday child can be the first child in line. Last week's birthday child can be the second person in line. Activity 3.16 is a fun activity to teach ordinal number words and meanings.

ACTIVITY 3.38
Ordinal Number Fun.

Children form several lines with 10 or less children in each line. They count off using the ordinal words. You give directions for fun or silly activities, such as, "The fifth and sixth children can shake hands," or "The third child can rub his or her right elbow."

Nonnumerical Use of Numbers

Numbers are used in street addresses, telephone numbers, license plates, and to indicate football players. In such contexts they are used for identification or coding. Children may be confused by these uses, but little is known about whether or not such confusion interferes with developing number meanings (Fuson and Hall, 1983).

EXTENDING NUMBER CONCEPTS

When children demonstrate that they can count, subitize, produce a number of objects, and know several ordinal numbers, they are helped to extend their number concepts. Instruction involves children in: studying number relations and patterns, learning the anchors five and ten, constructing part–part–whole relations, using numerals to communicate ideas, connecting symbolic and concrete or pictorial representations, and working with calculators. These goals are interrelated and are often pursued simultaneously.

Studying Number Relations and Patterns

Mathematics as the study of relations and patterns is emphasized in contemporary approaches to teaching (Mathematical Sciences Education Board, 1990). Children study equality and inequality relations, with special attention given to the ideas "one or two more" and "one or two less." Skill in counting on or back does not guarantee that the concepts of "more than" and "less than" have been formed, and these ideas must be given special attention (Van de Walle, 1990). Children classify, compare, and order sets by the number of items in the sets as well as count to become aware of relations. When children can count beyond 20, counting can provide opportunities for noting base ten patterns and enables children to construct a mental number line that serves as a basis for comparing numbers.

ACTIVITY 3.39
Games.

The games in Box 3.1 give experience recognizing numbers of equivalent and nonequivalent sets. The objective in the first two games described is to match two cards displaying sets with the same number of objects (Figure 3.13). The games can be varied so that a pair consists of two cards showing sets whose numbers differ by one or two.

BOX 3.1 Games for Number Learning

FISH

Objective: Catch a "fish" by putting together two cards showing equivalent sets.
Materials: Twenty-six or more cards showing sets with numbers 1 to 10 represented by dots or pictures. The objects are displayed in number patterns. Two or more of the playing cards show the same number.
Procedure:

1. The teacher or players decide who will begin the game and how the players will rotate to take their turns.
2. Two to four children play. Each player is given the same number of cards. The number depends on the age of the players. The cards remaining after some are given to players are laid face down in the center of the playing area, the "pond."
3. A player fishes by asking another player for a certain card, which he or she must give if it is being held. When given the card requested, a player lays the two matching cards aside. A fish has been caught.
4. If the request cannot be met, the player "fishes" by taking a card from the pond. If it matches a card in his or her hand, the two cards are laid aside. If it does not match a card in his or her hand, the player keeps the card.
5. If each player has had a turn and none has caught a fish, all players take a card from the pond.
6. When one player is out of cards, the game is over.
7. The player with the most matching pairs of cards wins.

RUMMY

Objective: Match two cards that show the same number.
Materials: Same as for *Fish.*
Procedure:

The same as for *Fish* with the exception that when a player has a turn, he or she draws a card from the pile of cards in the center of the playing area.

WAR

Objective: Collect cards with the greater or lesser number.
Materials: Twenty picture cards showing numbers to 10. There are two cards in the pack for each number 1–10.
Procedure:

1. Lay a pack of number picture cards face down in the center of a playing area.
2. Two players pick a card at the same time.
3. The player holding the card with the greater (lesser) number takes both cards.
4. If players draw cards with the same number, they draw cards twice (have a war).
5. The player holding the card with the greater (lesser) number on the second draw gets all six cards.
6. When all the cards are gone, the player with the most cards wins.

Board games are educational as well as enjoyable for children (Figure 3.14). A die or a spinner is used to determine the spaces to move along a path drawn on a playing board—the same number shown on the spinner or one more or one less spaces. Various themes can be used for board games that you, aides, or parents make. For example, themes can incorporate the circus, zoo, farm, or imaginary creatures.

Number picture cards such as shown in Figure 3.13 (sometimes called *number pattern cards*) are useful in the study of equality and inequality. Activities 3.40–3.42 make use of number picture cards.

FIGURE 3.13 Cards with Sets to 10

ACTIVITY 3.40
Number Sort.

Tell children that you have a box of number picture cards. Show five cards, three of which show the same number. Ask, "How could we play with these cards?" If no one suggests putting the cards that show the same number together, say, "We could put all the cards that show the same number in a pile." If a child gives an idea for an activity, call the game by the name of the child who gives the game rule.

ACTIVITY 3.41
Three Pile Sorting.

Suggest a variation of the above: Say, "Let's pick a card and make a pile of cards that show the same number and a pile of cards that show numbers less than the number on the card we picked. What could we put in a third pile?" (Cards with greater

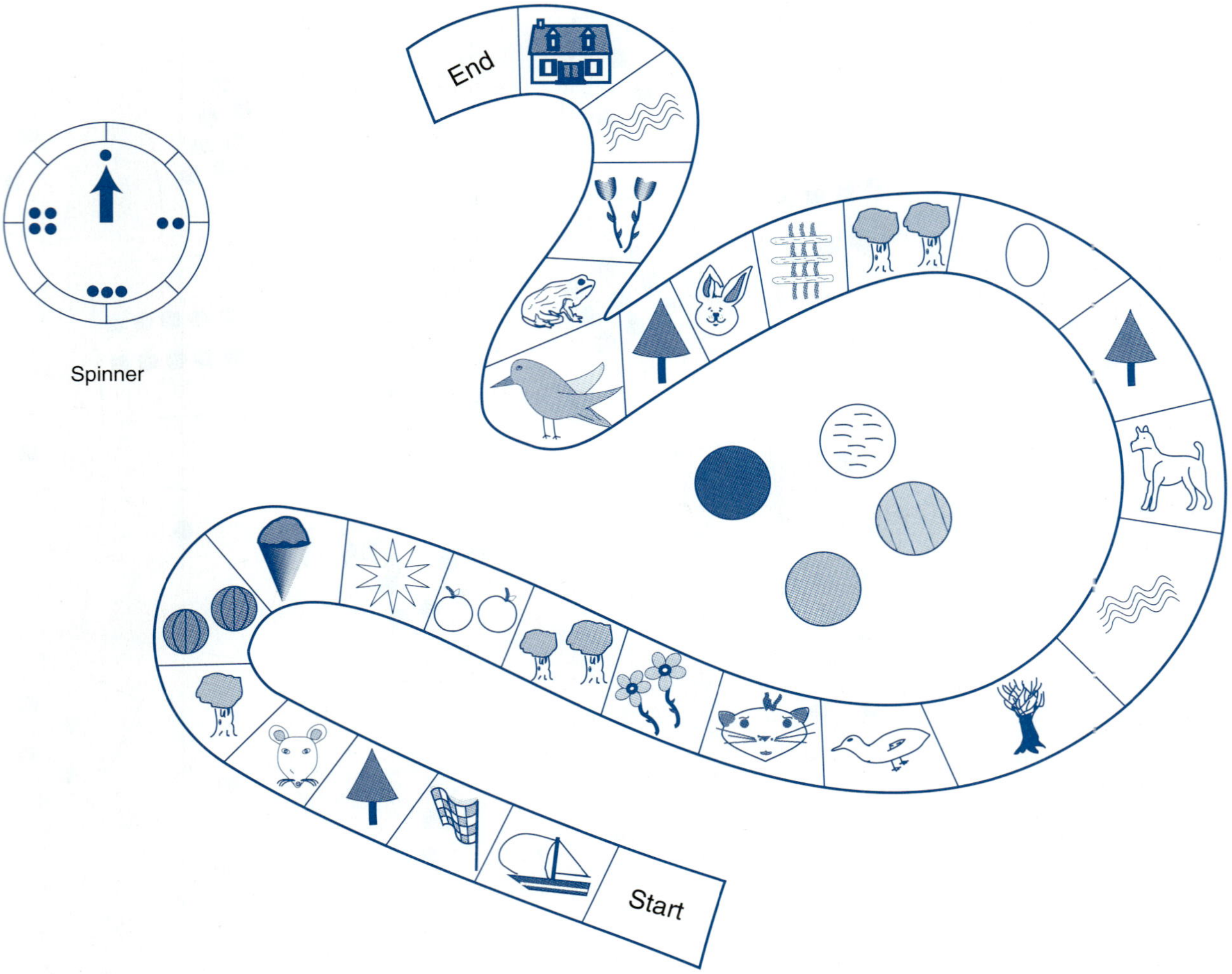

FIGURE 3.14 Board Game

numbers.) If pupils say, "All the cards that are left," reply, "What is true of the number of dots on any of these cards?" (If learners cannot tell, take a remaining card, and ask them to think how its number is different from a number on a card in the first pile.) When pupils have decided what to do, have them name the activity.

ACTIVITY 3.42
Ordering Cards.

Ask children how they could use the cards to show how the numbers go when they count. They should suggest that they could put the cards in order. Ask, "How do you know how to do this?" Continue with probing questions until a child says that each number card in the row should show a number one greater than the number shown on the card before it. Have children order the cards.

ACTIVITY 3.43
Ordering Our Names.

Each child in the class writes his or her name on a strip of large square grid paper (see Appendix G) and cuts off the unused squares. In small groups children find names with the same number of letters and not the same number, and they arrange the names in order from the smallest to the largest number of letters. A committee can work with you to arrange all the names in the class for a bulletin board activity, or the class can work together with each child pinning his or her name on the bulletin board.

ACTIVITY 3.44
Locate.

Use number bars for numbers 10 or less. Each child has five number bars that represent different numbers. Three or four children comprise a group for the activity. One child is the leader and says, "Find a bar that is one (or two) greater (less) than my bar." The other children show bars that meet the description. The leader replies, "Yes, your bars are one (two) greater (less) than my bar." Children take turns being the leader.

ACTIVITY 3.45
Paths.

Children make paths with domino-type cards that show numbers with differences of 1 or 2 (Figure 3.15).

ACTIVITY 3.46
Soft and Loud Counting.

Have children count soft and loud to develop a rhythm that gives emphasis to the multiples of a number. For example, one, two, THREE, four, five, SIX, seven, eight, NINE, . . . , THIRTY. Later, children give only the loud counts to develop an intuitive awareness of multiplication.

ACTIVITY 3.47
Buzz.

This is an old favorite. Children count in round robin fashion, saying "Buzz" on the multiple of the number that is named for that buzz game. For example, one, two, three, four, buzz, six, seven, eight, nine, buzz, . . ., twenty-four, buzz.

Learning the Anchors Five and Ten

Learners develop number sense and comprehension of the base ten system by comparing numbers to 5 and 10 (Thompson and Van de Walle, 1984). Such understanding is fostered by using five- and ten-frames.

Five-frames can represent numbers to 5 or to 10. Ten-frames can represent numbers to 10 or greater than 10 (Figure 3.16).

ACTIVITY 3.48
Look and Tell.

To introduce frames, place counters in a five-frame transparency on the overhead, or use a large flannel board frame with flannel counters. Have children tell the number of counters shown. One or more pupils answer the question, "How did you know what to say?" When necessary, further questioning helps a child relate the number displayed to five. (E.g., a pupil could say, "I can tell it is two more than five, so I know it is seven.") Repeat the activity for ten-frames. When children know how to think about numbers using frames, use the extensions for ten-frames. They can be adapted for five-frames.

Extensions for ten-frames:

1. Labinowicz (1985) suggests having children make different arrangements of counters on ten-frames and discuss the numbers represented (Figure 3.17). Give each

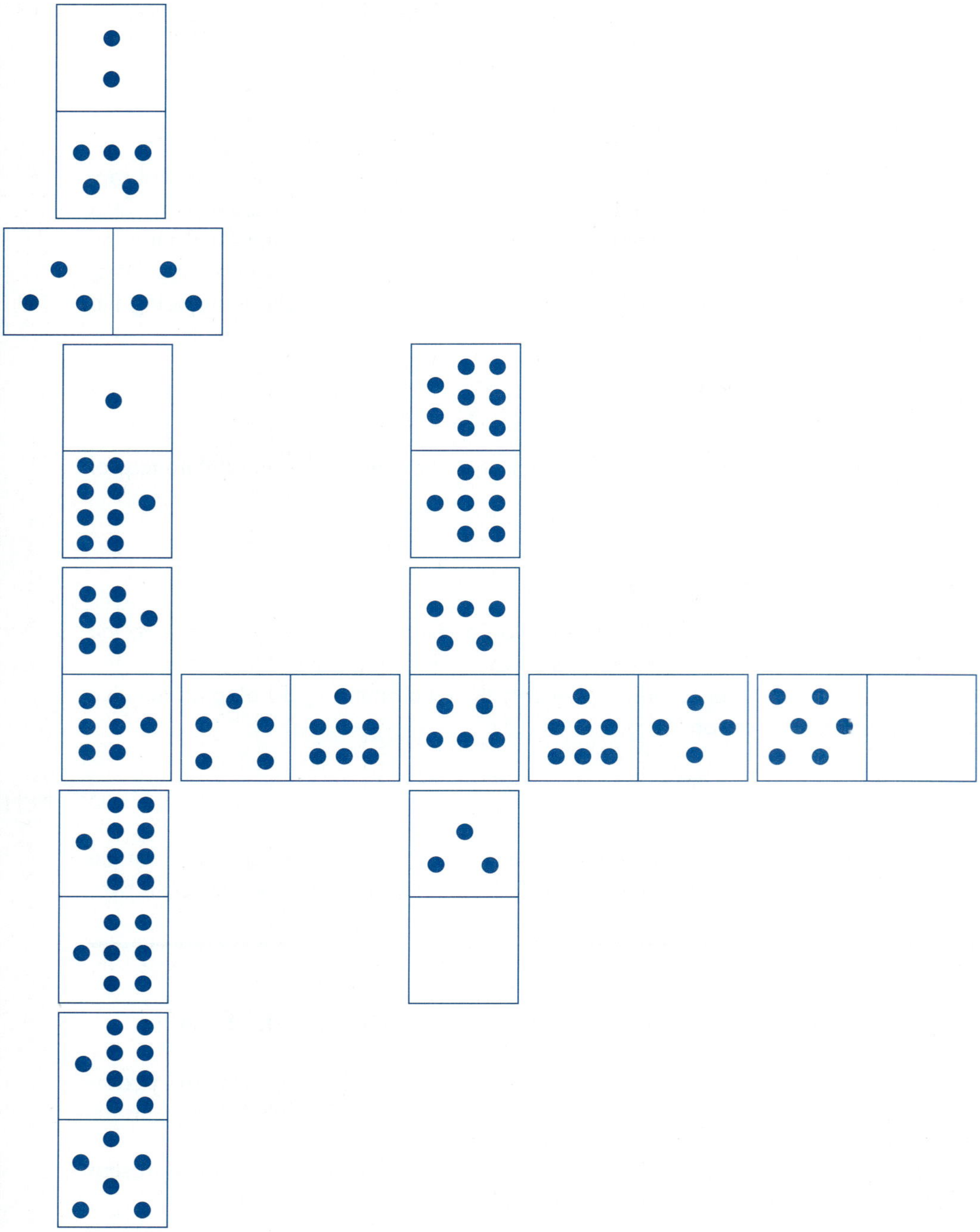

FIGURE 3.15 Paths Showing Numbers with Differences of 2

child a ten-frame. Ask children to work in pairs. Name a number for children to show and think about. Have them use their ten-frames to show the number in different ways. They can tell each other about their different arrangements. One or more children report to the whole class. Encourage them to make as many arrangements as possible. For example, 8 is 3 and 5 more, double 4, or 2 less than 10; 9 is 4 and 5 more, 1 less than 10, or 1 more than double 4.

2. Have pupils tell about a number represented in a ten-frame in two ways. For example, 8 is 3 more than 5 or 2 less than 10.
3. Two children work together using ten-frames and a bag of beans. They take turns showing a number on the frame using the beans and telling how the number relates to 10.

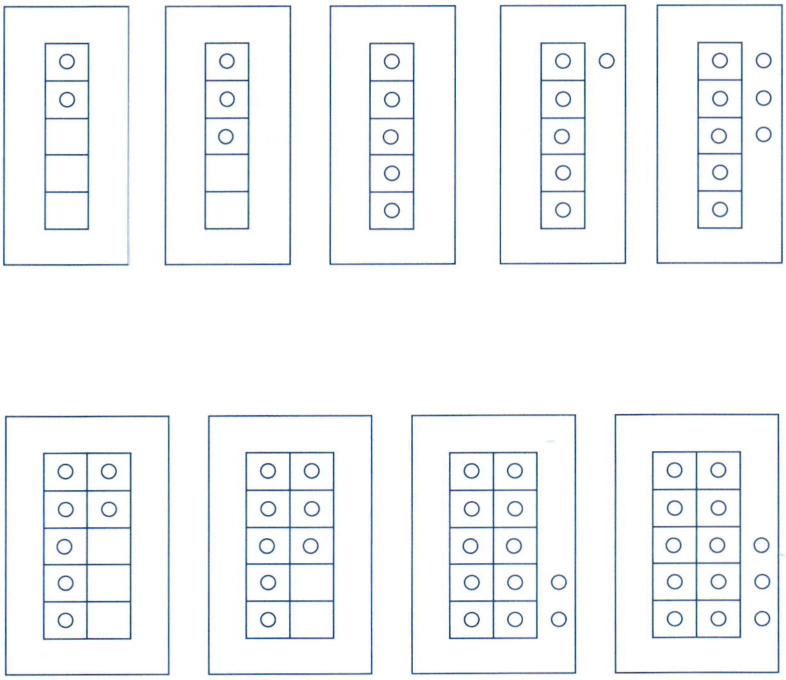

FIGURE 3.16 Ways to Show Numbers with Five- and Ten-Frames

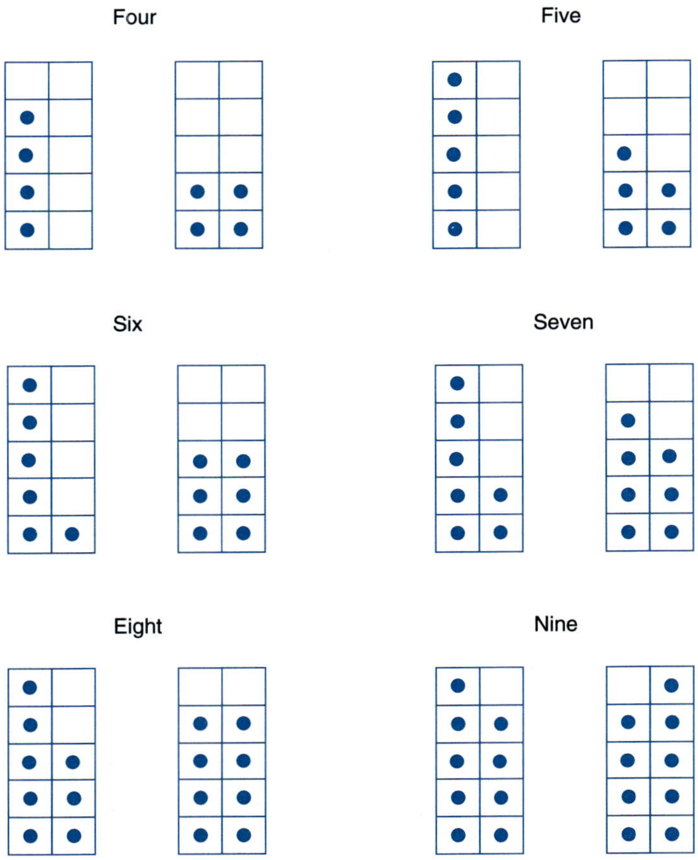

FIGURE 3.17 Numbers Represented on Ten-Frames

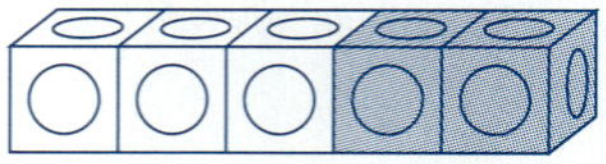

FIGURE 3.18 Interlocking Blocks Showing Additive Structure of Numbers

ACTIVITY 3.49
Say It.

Prepare 10 or 12 cards each showing a number represented with dots on a ten-frame (see Figure 3.17 for examples). The cards are face down between two children. The children take turns picking a card and giving the number represented. When a child tells the number, he or she also tells how the number compares to 5 or to 10.

Constructing Part–Part–Whole Relations

As children subitize, they naturally group objects for quick recognition (Labinowicz, 1985). Resnick (1983) states that knowing that numbers are composed of other numbers is a major intellectual accomplishment that enables children to deal with story problems and mental computation. You help children develop this understanding of part–part–whole relations by providing experiences that foster recognizing sets by means of subsets, and you ask children to explain how they were able to recognize sets by observing the parts of sets.

Experiences highlight both the additive (e.g., $6 = 2 + 4$) and multiplicative (e.g., $6 = 3$ twos) structures of numbers (Van de Walle, 1990). To show the additive structure of a number, manipulatives or drawings are used to represent two addends of a number (Figure 3.18); to show the multiplicative structure, manipulatives or drawings are used to represent two or more equivalent subsets of a number (Figure 3.19). Other experiences give children opportunities to think about a missing subset of a set.

Reader Activity 3.2

Use bars of different colors (or linked cube sets) to show arrangements for numbers to 10. Represent both additive (use only two bars or sets) and multiplicative structures (use two or more bars or sets). Decide how many representations with bars (or sets of linked cubes) are possible for each number to 10. Are there patterns evident in your work?

ACTIVITY 3.50
Using Cubes or Number Bars to Show Part–Part–Whole Relations.

Have children use number bars or linked cubes to show a number and its parts. Two or more bars (linked cubes) are laid against a third bar so that there is a matching (Figure 3.20). The same materials can be used to show that a number can be represented by two or more bars in more than one way. Begin this activity by showing children several examples and ask, "How have I used the bars?" Children explain their ideas. After the discussion, they make their own arrangements.

Variation: One child shows another child one short bar against a long bar (Figure 3.21). The second child decides what short bar is needed to fill the space to make a matching.

ACTIVITY 3.51
Ways to Show Numbers.

To represent part–part–whole relations, have children color the squares in grid paper, or use various objects (paper clips, bread ties, etc.), number bars, or shapes (Figure 3.22). They can work independently or in groups at tables or stations. Make certain they understand the task before they begin. Recalling how they showed a number and its parts with bars or linking cubes can help children decide how to picture a number. A few children can use the overhead to show the class their ideas.

FIGURE 3.19 Interlocking Blocks Showing Multiplicative Structure of Numbers

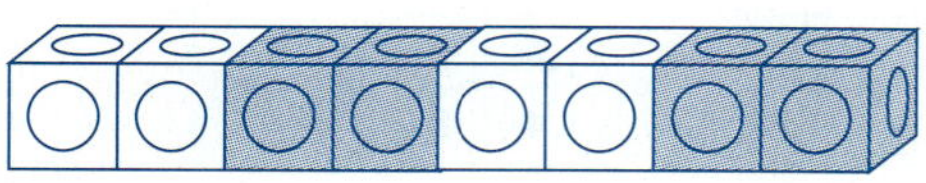

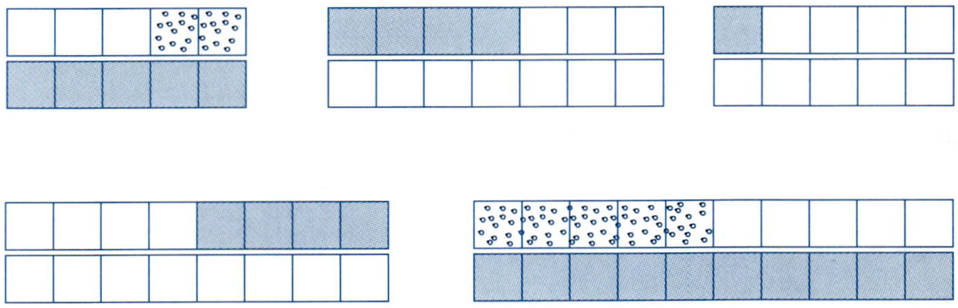

FIGURE 3.20 Using Two Bars to Show a Number

Encourage children to be creative by suggesting they use objects in as many arrangements as they can think of. Have them look at the representations of other children and tell what they see.

Suggest children make books of ways each number from 1 to 10 can be represented using two smaller numbers. The representations in the books can be grid paper diagrams or pictures drawn by the children or cut from magazines. They should share their books, explaining how they have shown numbers.

ACTIVITY 3.52
Screen Game (Baratta-Lorton, 1976).

Pairs of children use 10 or less counters for this game. One player makes a set to represent a number and places a cardboard or transparent screen across his or her set to show two subsets. The other child tells what was done, saying, for example, "You used the screen to show that five counters are the same as three counters and two counters."

ACTIVITY 3.53
Bean Toss.

Children toss beans painted on one side to show a number represented by two numbers (Figure 3.23). Small tiles can also be used. After a few tosses in which the same arrangements are displayed, children can make the arrangements that do not come up with tosses. When working in pairs or groups, children should discuss what the beans show. Records can be made on worksheets (see Appendix G). Children circle sets on the worksheet and color the enclosed beans to record the bean arrangements.

ACTIVITY 3.54
Predict.

Two children play together with a pile of 10 counters. Child 1 names a number less than 5. Child 2 predicts the numbers that can be represented with only sets of that size and uses counters to show the numbers. For example, if 3 counters are named, the player makes sets of 3, 6, and 9 counters. The children evaluate the prediction.

FIGURE 3.21 What Bar Is Missing?

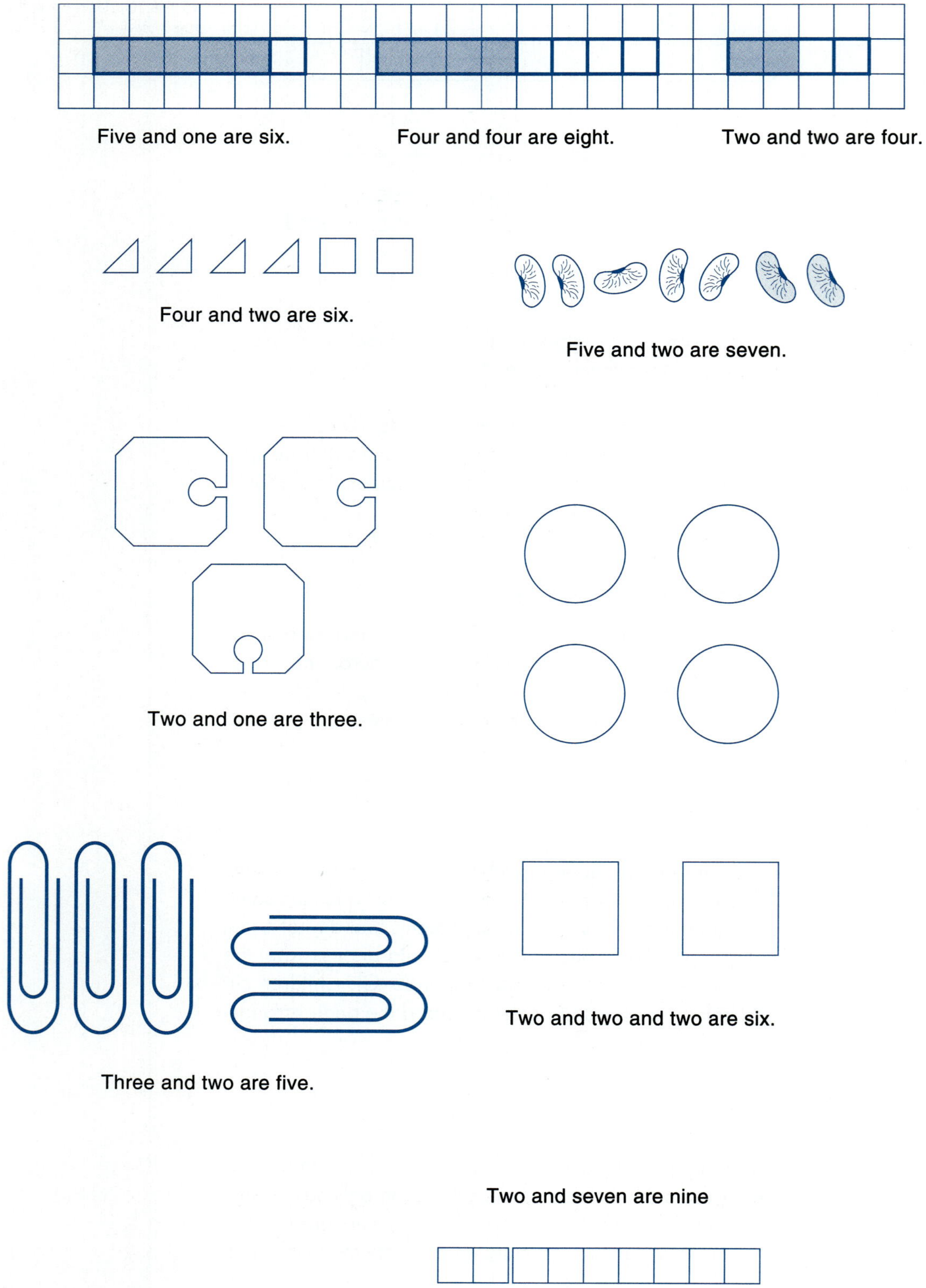

FIGURE 3.22 Ways to Show Numbers

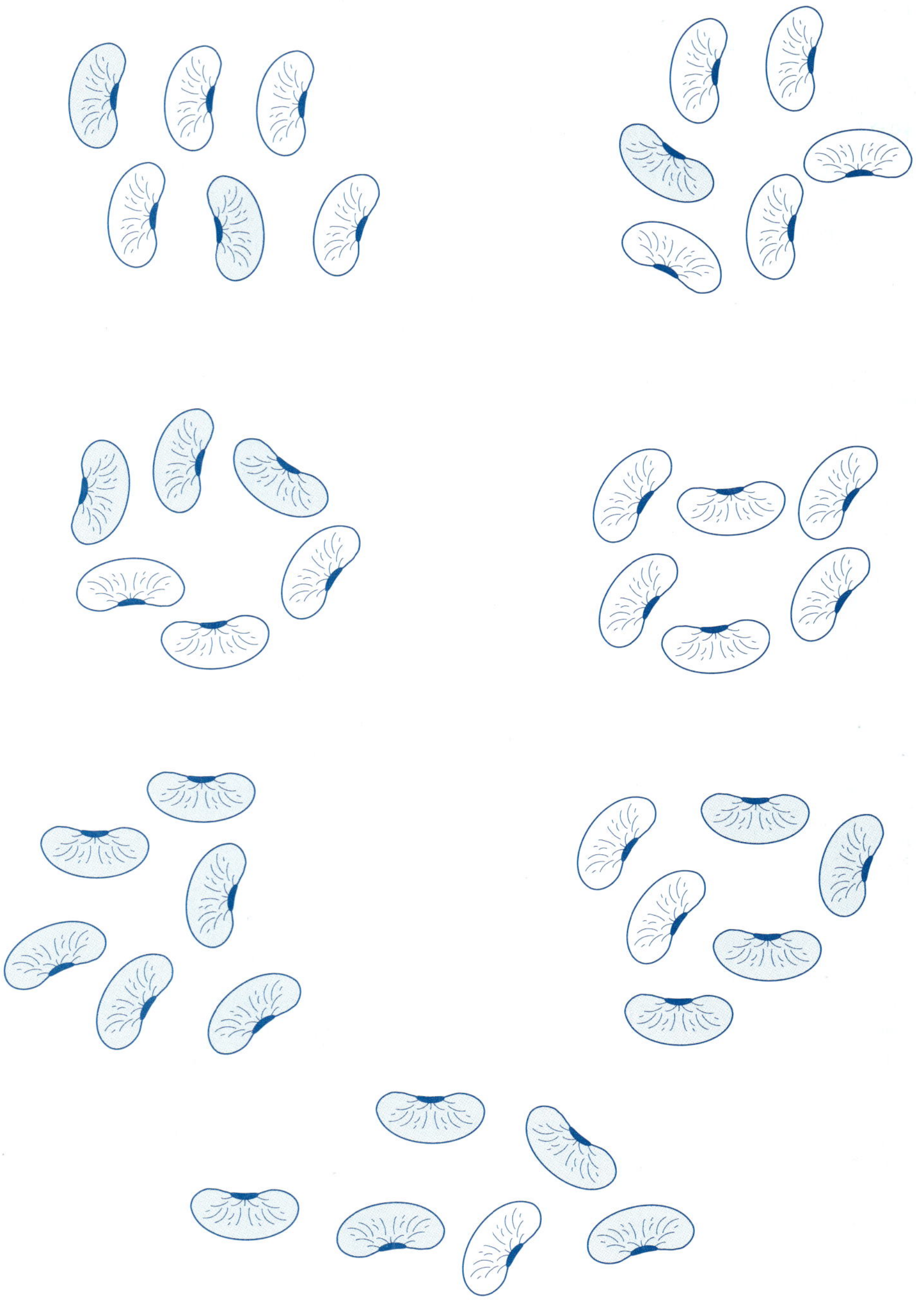

FIGURE 3.23 Beans Painted on One Side Showing Six in Different Ways

The second child then names the number for the first child to use in the next prediction.

ACTIVITY 3.55
Missing Number.

Show a number picture card. Have children give the number. Cover up part of the arrangement. Ask, "How many were covered up? How do you know?" When pupils understand the activity, have them work in pairs, taking turns asking the question and giving the answer.

ACTIVITY 3.56
What Is Needed?

Use any type of counters for this activity. After you introduce the activity, the children work in pairs. Each pair of children takes 10 counters. One child puts down 5 counters (or another number) and says, "What number is needed to make 10 (or another number greater than the first number named)?" The other child uses counters to find the answer to the question. The activity continues with the children taking turns asking and answering the question.

ACTIVITY 3.57
Mystery Numbers.

Ask questions that require students to find a mystery number by thinking and using counters. The questions deal with wholes or missing parts and can be asked in a variety of ways. Examples of questions are:

- If I have three teddy bears and two teddy bears, I have a mystery number of teddy bears. What is the mystery number?
- If I put five counters with the mystery number, I will have seven. What is the mystery number?
- If I begin with four cubes and put a mystery number with them, I will have six. What is the mystery number?
- Janet has six cubes; Joan has three. Janet said, "I have a mystery number of cubes more than Joan." What is the mystery number?

One or more children explain how the mystery number was found. Their explanations are an important part of the activity.

The mystery number can involve joining (separating) sets of equal size or dividing a set into sets of equal size. For example, questions could be:

- If each of three girls has two teddy bears, what is the mystery number of teddy bears there will be if they put their teddy bears together in a line?
- The grocery person had six apples and some plastic bags. She put two apples in each bag. What mystery number of bags did she fill?
- Four boys have eight play trucks altogether. If each has the same number, what mystery number does each have?

ACTIVITY 3.58
Number Words and Pictures.

Have pupils make number pictures using their own drawings or pictures cut from catalogues. Display their work with number words (e.g., two, four) beside the number pictures. Call attention to the words, and have pupils read them. Some learners will be able to write the words and use them to label pictures or diagrams that show numbers and parts of numbers.

ACTIVITY 3.59
Number Word Cards.

Make number word cards (e.g., a card with the number word "five") to use in the following two activities.

1. To learn to read number words, children play games (Box 3.1) that require matching number word cards and number picture cards.

2. Each child takes a card, represents the number on the card using counters of two colors, and tells his or her partner about the number picture.

Using Numerals to Communicate Ideas

When children can count and orally give the number of a set, you introduce teaching the reading and writing of numerals (symbols for numbers). Some may have learned to read numerals incidentally (e.g., when pupils observed you read the numerals on a calendar to give the day or to determine the birthday of each class member), but formal instruction is needed for most children to learn to read numerals.

To introduce *reading numerals,* give pupils opportunities to use what they know to arrive at new knowledge. (With young children, the word "number" is usually used in place of "numeral." The distinction will be made in this book only if the language does not become cumbersome.) To begin say, "We have counted many times. Now we can learn to read the numbers we have been counting. Some may know how to read numbers already. Let's share what we know." Children tell what numbers they can read. Say, "Learning to read numbers on your own was a great thing to do. We can all learn to read numbers."

On the overhead, write, in order, each number to 10 that was mentioned; have the child who said he or she could read it do so. Place that number of objects on the overhead, and ask the class to give the number and read the numeral. Suggest that the children make a bulletin board display for these numbers. Have children draw pictures of sets for the numbers. On the display, beside each set, write the numeral designating the number of the set. (It may take several days to complete this activity.) Introduce the numerals they do not know how to read using the following procedure. If they do not know how to read any numerals, the procedure begins with the number 1.

Place one object on the overhead and write "1." Have the children tell what you have written. Use the same procedure to introduce other numerals. Introduce two or three a day, reviewing those introduced earlier. At the end of the first lesson, start a bulletin board displaying sets of objects and numerals for the number of objects shown. Children draw pictures for the display; you write the numeral for each group of pictures with the same number. Remind the children that they can help themselves learn to read numbers by looking at the bulletin board and reading the numbers when they come into and leave the classroom or if they have a little free time.

Children read numerals to 10 whenever there is an opportunity to do so. Frequently have children study the display of sets and numerals on the bulletin board and read the numerals. Activities 3.60–3.62 will help children learn to read numerals and connect the symbols with their representations.

ACTIVITY 3.60
Game Variations.

The games described in Box 3.1 can be adapted to use with numerals written on one set of cards (called numeral or number cards). A numeral card is matched with a card that gives a set of pictures with that number. Another variation is to match numerals for numbers with a difference of 1 or 2.

ACTIVITY 3.61
Show It.

Each child in a group receives four or five numeral cards. "IT" picks a card from a stack and says, "What is 1 (2) greater (less) than . . . (reading from the chosen card)?

Show It." The child (children) with the numeral card that shows the correct number displays it and reads the number. Children take turns being "IT."

ACTIVITY 3.62
Numerals and Ordering.

Give groups of children number picture cards from 1 to 10 and numeral cards for these numbers. Ask them to order the cards by the numbers on the cards, and place each picture beside the number it represents. Have them discuss their work, the order of the numbers, and the "one more relation."

After children have carried out activities that give them experiences reading numerals and connecting numerals with representations, *writing numerals* is taught. Say, "We know so many things about numbers that we can learn to write them." To help children see the numeral formed correctly (Figure 3.24), model how to write the numeral, and use cognitive modeling (thinking out loud) to emphasize the lines and curves that make up the figures. For some numerals, you may model writing a numeral several times without any verbal communication and ask the children what you did. Before beginning nonverbal modeling, explain the procedure to alert the children to the task of observing your formation of the figures and their characteristics.

Baroody (1987) points out that focusing on the attributes of each numeral is a meaningful approach and enables children to learn to make the numerals more quickly than if numeral characteristics are not emphasized. Grouping numerals that have similar characteristics also helps children learn to form numerals (e.g., 1, 4, and 7 are formed with straight lines).

As children learn to read and write numerals, they should frequently apply what they have learned. Use situations that arise naturally in the classroom, and create situations where reading and writing numerals helps make what is going on comprehensible.

Activity for the Classroom 3.3. Ask students to describe events in their lives that involve reading or writing numerals (e.g., finding a street address). Decide what real-life number awareness your pupils have developed. Ask questions that help them realize the importance of reading and writing numerals.

Connecting Symbolic and Concrete or Pictorial Representations

Many experiences are needed for learners to be able to connect symbolic and concrete or pictorial representations of numbers. These experiences should not be a part of the curriculum until children have developed number concepts (NCTM,

FIGURE 3.24 Writing Numerals

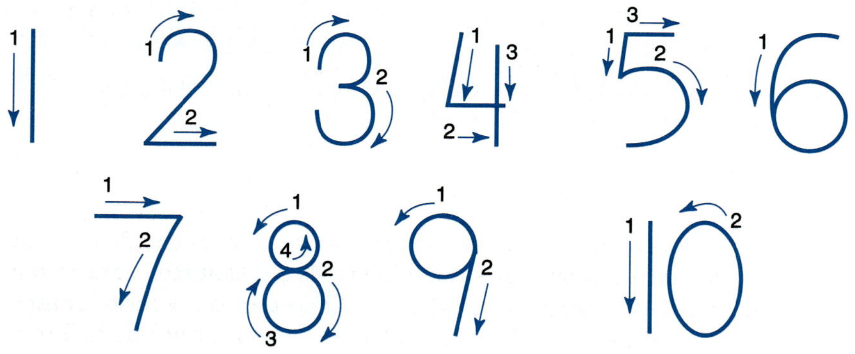

1989). Some activities given earlier for constructing number concepts can be revised to enable children to connect symbolic and concrete or pictorial representations of numbers. Others are described in this section. They involve recognizing numbers of sets and using numerals in experiences that involve comparing, ordering, and relating numbers.

ACTIVITY 3.63
Numbers on Frames.

Give children several worksheets each showing five- and ten-frames (see Appendix G). Model the directions on the overhead: Choose a number from 4 to 10, write it at the top of one sheet, and draw dots to show the number in as many ways as possible on the frames. When finished, repeat the task for other numbers. Have children work with you to complete one worksheet so that they know how to carry out the task. To conclude the lesson, have learners tell one another or the class about their work.

ACTIVITY 3.64
Inventories.

Children can count articles in their desks and make desk inventories. Illustrations that include numerals can be made of the inventory records so that children can compare the numbers of different items in their desks. A child can also compare the number of items in his or her desk with those of another child.

ACTIVITY 3.65
Number Bulletin Board.

Bulletin boards for different topics can be created that require children to draw sets of objects and write a numeral for the number of objects in each set. Topics include: number of persons in my family or number of places I have lived. Although children have not learned to read and write numerals for numbers greater than 10, if sets with numbers greater than 10 are described, you can tell children how to write these numerals.

ACTIVITY 3.66
Make a Number Book.

Children make number books, one page for each number from 1 to 10. Children choose the items to be drawn on each page to represent a number and write the appropriate numeral beside the drawing. Books can also show part–part–whole relations, and children can write descriptions of their representations (e.g., 3 and 2 are 5).

ACTIVITY 3.67
I Know How the Numbers Go.

On wide lined paper, have children write numerals in a column from 1 to 10. Ask them to make tallies or draw pictures beside each numeral to show the meaning of the number. When finished, they share their work and discuss how they knew what to do. Discuss the one-more relation between two numbers.

Working with Calculators

After they learn to read numerals, young children use calculators to relate counting to numerals and to use numerals to develop ideas of counting on and counting back. The constant arithmetic function (see Chapter One) that is a feature of most inexpensive models should be available on the calculators used by young children.

ACTIVITY 3.68
Calculator Count.

Have children watch the calculator count, saying the numbers as the numerals are displayed on the calculator.

ACTIVITY 3.69
Calculator Game.

Two children take turns using a calculator. One child inputs a number 7 or less and gives the direction to go up or down 1, 2, or 3. The second child predicts where the calculator will land when the direction is carried out and uses the calculator to check his or her prediction.

ASSESSING NUMBER LEARNING IN THE EARLY SCHOOL YEARS

Assessment studies children's number readiness, counting and cardinal number ideas, subitizing, ordinal number ideas, and extended number concepts. Evidence of learning is obtained by observing, interviewing, and examining work products. Quizzes and tests, although used, are not a major source of information. As children carry out the readiness activities described in this chapter, notice how children use objects to compare, classify, order, and pattern. Assess aspects of beginning number knowledge by observing children's:

1. Competence in stating the counting words in order.
2. Ability to give the cardinal number of a set after counting. Children should not need to count a second time to answer the question, "How many blocks are on the desk? Why?"
3. Ability to subitize when sets are presented in patterned arrangements.
4. Ability to display the same number of objects as shown in a given set.
5. Use of a count on or count back strategy.
6. Understanding of equality, inequality, and part–part–whole concepts.
7. Use of the anchors five and ten in naming numbers of sets.
8. Reading and writing numerals.
9. Work with calculators.

In an interview children are asked to perform tasks to show the same behaviors you would observe during individual or group instructional activities. You interpret their responses as indicating an understanding or a lack of understanding of numbers.

Work products include children's drawings to show numbers, numerals they have written, and some combinations of drawings and numerals. These should be collected at regular intervals to determine children's progress.

You assess children's progress by studying your dated records of observations and interviews and children's dated work products. The three levels of performance indicators discussed in Chapter One are used to determine children's attainments. On the basis of the assessment, you decide if more activities related to a concept or skill are needed to improve learning, or if new content can be introduced.

A few quizzes or tests may be given to assess children's number learning in a formal way. The tests can be designed as activities in which children write a numeral for each number of a set pictured on worksheets or shown on the overhead. Children can also be asked to draw sets that are equal to or 1 or 2 greater or less than those displayed.

Attitudes toward learning number concepts and skills are assessed mainly by observing children's interest in their work. Children should find activities enjoyable and express pleasure in solving problems, playing games, and engaging in activities that enable them to construct number concepts. They should demonstrate willingness to persevere to complete tasks and demonstrate pride in their accomplishments.

SUMMARY

This chapter has examined new directions in mathematics instruction for young children. Teachers use interactive approaches to help children: develop thinking skills, such as classifying, comparing, and ordering, and understand conservation of number and patterning; develop number meanings as they learn to count, form cardinal number concepts, recognize numbers of sets by sight, and study ordinal numbers; and extend their number knowledge by studying relations and patterns, constructing part–part–whole relations, learning to read and write numerals, connecting numerals to concrete or pictorial representations of numbers, and using calculators. The chapter emphasized that before children are ready to connect number ideas with numerals, they must work with manipulatives and build number concepts by thinking and talking about their actions. A number of activities were described for attaining the goals of beginning mathematics instruction. A section on assessing learning ended the chapter.

One of the themes of the chapter was that teachers do not tell young learners about mathematics but provide opportunities for children to construct concepts by doing, thinking, and communicating. They help children relate what they know to new experiences and encourage them to discuss their ideas. Such instruction helps children learn to trust their thinking and to grow in mathematical power.

REFERENCES

Baratta-Lorton, Mary. (1976). *Mathematics Their Way.* Menlo Park, CA: Addison-Wesley.

Baroody, Arthur J. (1987). *Children's Mathematical Thinking: A Developmental Framework for Preschool, Primary, and Special Education Teachers.* New York: Teachers College Press.

Dutton, Wilber H., and Ann Dutton. (1991). *Mathematics Children Use and Understand: Preschool through Third Grade.* Mountain View, CA: Mayfield.

Fuson, Karen C., and James W. Hall. (1983). "The Acquisition of Early Number Word Meanings: A Conceptual Analysis and Review." In *The Development of Mathematical Thinking,"* edited by Herbert P. Ginsburg, pp. 49–107. New York: Academic Press.

Gelman, Rochel, and Elizabeth Meck. (1986). "The Notion of Principle: The Case of Counting." In *Conceptual and Procedural Knowledge: The Case of Mathematics,* edited by James Hiebert, pp. 29–57. Hillsdale, NJ: Erlbaum.

Kamii, Constance, and Rheta DeVries. (1976). *Piaget, Children, and Number.* Washington, DC: National Association for the Education of Young Children.

Labinowicz, Ed. (1985). *Learning from Children: New Beginnings for Teaching Numerical Thinking.* Menlo Park, CA: Addison-Wesley.

Mathematical Sciences Education Board, National Research Council. (1990). *Reshaping School Mathematics: A Philosophy and Framework for Curriculum.* Washington, DC: National Academy Press.

Moser, James M. (1988). "Arithmetic Operations on Whole Numbers: Addition and Subtraction." In *Teaching Mathematics in Grades K–8: Research Based Methods,* edited by Thomas R. Post, pp. 123–155. Boston: Allyn and Bacon.

National Council of Teachers of Mathematics. (1989). *Curriculum and Evaluation Standards for School Mathematics.* Reston, VA: Author.

National Council of Teachers of Mathematics. (1991). *Professional Standards for Teaching Mathematics.* Reston, VA: Author.

Piaget, Jean. (1952). *The Child's Conception of Number.* London: Routledge & Kegan Paul.

Resnick, Lauren B. (1983). "A Developmental Theory of Number Understanding." In *The Development of Mathematical Thinking,* edited by Herbert P. Ginsburg, pp. 109–151. New York: Academic Press.

Resnick, Lauren B., and Wendy W. Ford. (1981). *The Psychology of Mathematics for Instruction.* Hillsdale, NJ: Erlbaum.

Thompson, Charles S., and John Van de Walle. (November 1984). "The Power of 10." *Arithmetic Teacher* 32: 6–11.

Van de Walle, John. (1990). "Concepts of Number." In *Mathematics for the Young Child,* edited by Joseph N. Payne, pp. 63–87. Reston, VA: National Council of Teachers of Mathematics.

SOFTWARE RESOURCES

Gertrude's Secrets
Company: The Learning Company
Computer: Apple
Grade level: K–3
Basic thinking skills and problem solving. Seven puzzles that involve classifying activities with Gertrude the Goose.

IBM Elementary Mathematics Series
Level 1 Lessons 1–4
Company: IBM/EduQuest
Computer: IBM
Grade Level: K–2

Lessons 1 and 2: comparing and making sets up to 6 (use of a balance pan provides visuals); Lessons 3 and 4: giving numerals, making and ordering sets to 10, and solving related number problems.

Moptown Parade
Company: The Learning Company
Computer: Apple
Grade Level: 1–5

Recognizing patterns in a series of unusual figures, the "moptown parade"; involves reasoning, particularly deduction.

CHAPTER 4

Developing Base Ten and Place-Value Knowledge

▪ INTRODUCTORY PROBLEM ▪

Most children in elementary school are eager to study dinosaurs. They are interested in their characteristics, names, sizes, and when they roamed the earth. Dinosaur facts usually include large numbers. For example, dinosaurs lived during the three periods of the Mesozoic age: the Triassic period (240,000,000 to 205,000,000 years ago), the Jurassic period (205,000,000 to 138,000,000 years ago), and the Cretaceous period (138,000,000 to 63,000,000 years ago). Dinosaurs varied in length from 2.5 to 90 feet. Some weighed as much as 85 tons (World Book Encyclopedia, 1993). Because large numbers about dinosaurs abound, the study of these reptiles provides opportunities to link math and science. As you read this chapter, think of the possibilities for relating dinosaur facts to the study of base ten and place-value concepts at different grade levels.

INTRODUCTION

To work with large numbers in meaningful ways, children must understand the base ten system and place-value notation. The *base ten* system groups by tens and is the basis for counting and place-value notation. A set of objects is counted by groups of tens, hundreds, thousands, and so forth. The rhyme,

> When you get to a ten, start all over again
> And keep track of the tens, ten tens, and so forth,

explains the use of the base ten system quite simply.

The counting words after 20 reflect base ten counting. The number names between 10 and 20 (11, 14) are anomalies; they do not convey the base ten idea. This is unfortunate for it makes learning these number words more difficult than need be. In some languages, such as Japanese, the number words convey more meaning. For example, 14 is said "ten four."

Numeration, the association of a symbol with the number of a set, uses 10 symbols, 0, 1, 2, 3, . . . , 9. These symbols are used in a *place-value scheme,* in which position gives base ten value. The numeral in each position has both a face value and a place value. The face value indicates the number of collections; the place value indicates the size of each collection, which is a power of 10 (1, 10, 10×10, $10 \times 10 \times 10$, . . .). For example, 44 has a face value of "4" in each place, but the place value of each numeral differs—"4" stands for four ones in the right-hand place and four tens in the left-hand place.

Children like to count and learn counting with little difficulty (Kamii, 1985). However, they do not easily learn the place-value system. Ross's (1989) research indicates how confused many children are about the meaning of numerals. As part of her research, she asked 60 children from grades 2 through 5 to count 25 sticks, write the numeral for the number counted, and then tell the meaning of each digit. Twenty-six students gave correct responses. The incorrect responses included that the 2 meant two sticks or to count by 2. When asked to count 26 objects, write the numeral for the number counted, and, before explaining the meaning of each numeral, sort the 26 objects into groups of 4 (2 were left over), almost half of the 30 third graders tested said that the "2" in the numeral meant the 2 left over and the "6" meant the six groups.

Activity for the Classroom 4.1. Replicate Ross's work. Use five students at the same or different grade levels. Write up your results. In your report, include your findings, an objective comparison of different students' responses, and your reaction to the investigation.

Although number names can be a source of confusion, it is children's cognitive structures that lead to a great deal of misunderstanding. Children first use number words in a unitary, not multiunit sense (Baroody, 1990; Fuson, 1990; Kamii, 1989). In counting they use number words initially to refer to single objects or, when used to give the cardinal number of a set, to refer to a collection of single objects (e.g., the number 8 means eight separate objects). A unitary conceptual structure works well enough to study small numbers, including addition and subtraction up to 20, but for work with large numbers, children must be able to think of multiunits, of number words as referring to a collection of entities or a collection of collections (e.g, in counting "one thousand, two thousand, three thousand," one must understand that the number "three thousand" is a collection of three collections of 1000 entities each).

Thinking multiunits is necessary to understand large numbers, numerals, and the operations with large numbers (e.g., addition and subtraction). It takes time to understand multiunits as built up from tens, to grasp the relation between base ten words and place-value numerals, and to learn to compose, decompose, and recompose multiunits in computation. Children need not only time but also many learning activities that enable them to develop multiunit thinking (Baroody, 1990).

Fischer (1990) believes that an understanding of part–part–whole ideas contributes to the development of base ten and place-value concepts. Before beginning work with large numbers, children should have experiences separating small sets into parts, discussing the numbers of the parts in the whole, and writing the numerals. (Teaching and learning part–part–whole relations is discussed in Chapter 3.)

There are two approaches for helping children learn about place value. According to Fuson (1990) learning place-value concepts should be integrated with learning addition and subtraction involving regrouping. She advocates teaching multidigit (more than two places) addition and subtraction in the second grade with regrouping to foster understanding of the meaning of large numbers and place value. The approach connects base ten blocks to numerals on cards displaying single-digit figures to enable learners to understand computational procedures and place-value concepts. Baroody (1990) suggests beginning earlier and teaching place-value concepts in many contexts. According to him, experiences with large numbers and place-value numerals can be a part of many activities in the early primary grades. Often these activities are naturally a part of other experiences, but they can be the focus of instruction. Because I believe that children need a long time and a number of experiences in many contexts to construct and integrate concepts, the approach outlined by Baroody is followed in this book.

During the elementary school years, teachers help children attain nine learnings:

1. A large number of objects can be counted. Counting beyond 10 relies on the base ten system. Both standard names (e.g., 30) and place-value names (e.g., three tens) are used.
2. The number of a set can be represented by grouped materials to show base ten concepts.
3. The number of a set can be represented by numerals employing place-value ideas and using the symbols 0 to 9. It can also be represented by words. We read and write numerals and number words.
4. Place-value numerals can be connected to representations.
5. Numbers can be compared and ordered.
6. Objects can be counted by various groupings (e.g., tens or hundreds) and numbers named by equal expressions (e.g., 230 = 23 tens, 34 hundred = 3400; 46 = 30 + 16).
7. Estimates can be made of large numbers of objects and compared to counts.
8. Large numbers are found in other subjects and real life.
9. The place-value system is a notational scheme in which each place in a place-value numeral represents a value 10 times greater than the value represented by the place to its right.

These learnings involve conceptual and procedural knowledge and relations between the two types of knowledge. To enable children to form concepts and use numerals meaningfully, proportional and nonproportional materials are used (Figure 4.1). Proportional materials show multiplicative relations in base ten by means of size. A collection for ten is 10 times the size of the representation for one; a collection for 100 is 10 times the size of the representation for 10, and so forth. Proportional materials, such as base ten blocks and bars, are pregrouped or they are groupable, such as straws, counters, and linking cubes. Nonproportional materials do not use size to show relations in the base-value system but rely on position, color, or shape to show the relations.

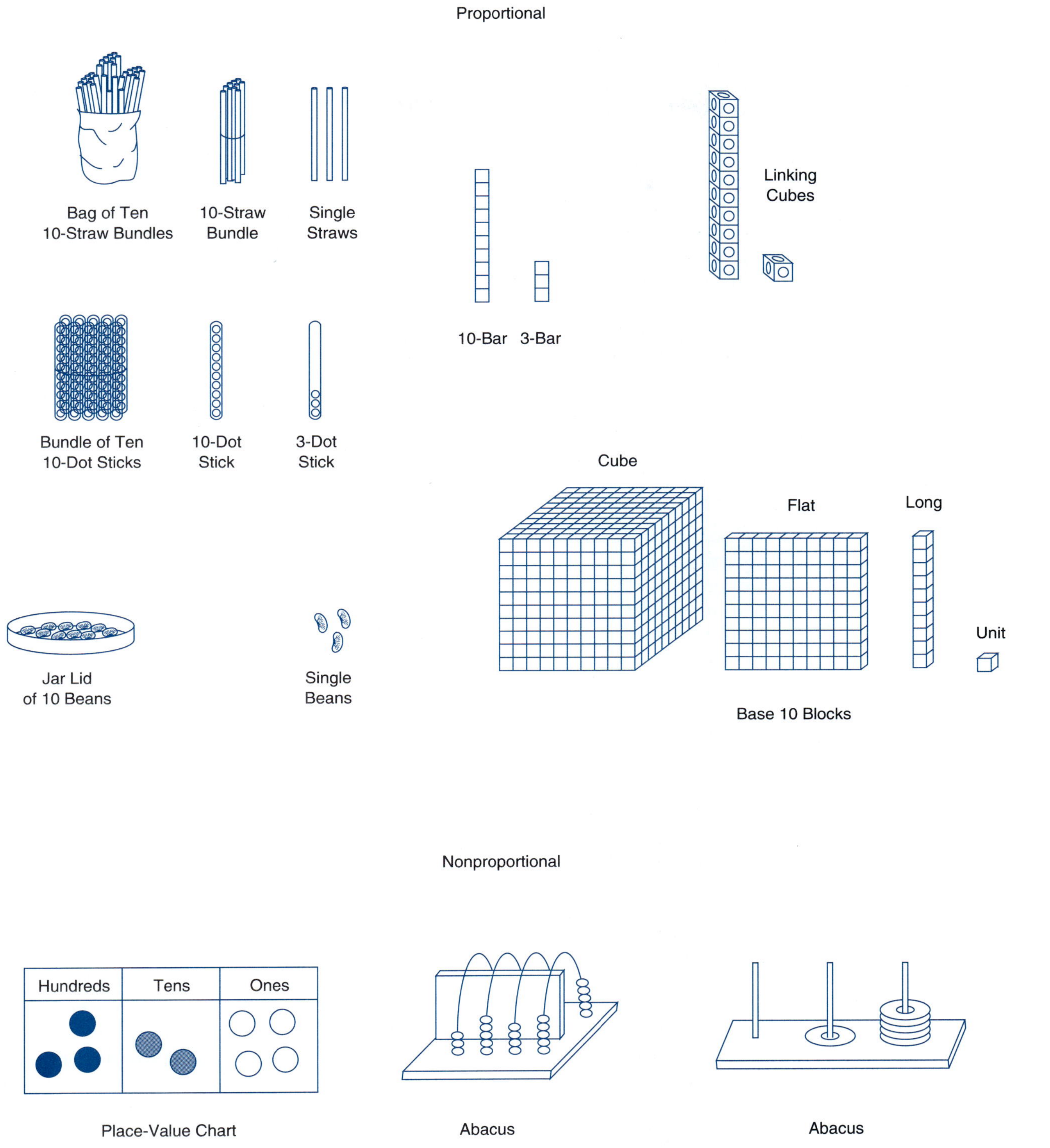

FIGURE 4.1 Materials for Learning Base Ten and Place Value

New directions in elementary school mathematics emphasize that work with materials must be accompanied by thoughtful reflection if children are to internalize base ten and place-value concepts (Baroody, 1989). As they work with materials, children answer questions or solve problems that require higher-level thinking. Often they learn in cooperative settings that enable them to communicate their ideas to others and react to the thinking of their peers.

When you work with groups or the whole class, interactive teaching strategies predominate. Such strategies emphasize problem solving, answering questions in different ways, and justifying answers. These strategies give you knowledge of children's thinking and enable you to guide learning so that children will attain understanding of base ten and place value and use their knowledge in subsequent learning experiences.

There are four sections to this chapter. The first section deals with numbers to 100; the second, with numbers greater than 100. Following the recommendations of the National Council of Teachers of Mathematics (NCTM, 1989), the sections discuss counting, grouping, representing, comparing, and ordering large numbers together with reading, writing, and analyzing place-value numerals (see Standard 6 in Curriculum Standards for Grades K–4, Appendix A). Included in each section are instructional activities that stress pupil problem solving and exploration of relations. A third section gives suggestions for assessment. The final section summarizes the chapter.

NUMBERS TO 100

Counting

Counting is fundamental to understanding numbers to 100. Children count large numbers of objects whenever possible. Chorus counting is an approach frequently used each day to count the number of children present, eating in the cafeteria, or riding the bus. Other counts that can be made are: the number of days until the next class birthday, holiday, or summer vacation; the total number of brothers and sisters of class members; or the number of books in the classroom library.

Estimating frequently precedes counting. Children may make "wild" guesses at first, but their estimating becomes gradually more refined, and the process gives them new insights about numbers.

ACTIVITY 4.1
Deciding What to Count.

To help children begin to look around for sets with many objects, ask them to think of fun things to estimate and count, such as the number of steps from their desks to the door, the number of steps from the room to the cafeteria, the number of windows in the classroom (or building), the number of chairs in the cafeteria, the number of bicycles in the bike rack, or the number of keys on the class computer. After an estimation, chorus counting by class members can be used to count the items named by children. Later children can work individually or in pairs to estimate and count large numbers of objects. If it is obvious that some numbers would be larger than others (e.g., steps to the door versus steps to the cafeteria), children can discuss which number would be larger and the reason for the difference.

ACTIVITY 4.2
Counting Seeds.

Opening fruits and vegetables such as pumpkins, various squashes, green peppers, and melons can be an interesting experience and provide opportunities for estimating and later counting the seeds when they have dried. The seeds can be displayed in plastic bags, and children are encouraged to discuss which food had many, the most, the least, or a few seeds.

ACTIVITY 4.3
How Do We Count?

After children can count to 100, ask them how they remember to count to 100. Through questions, elicit the idea that there is a pattern to the counting. Discuss the pattern of tens (20, 30, . . . , 100) and the meaning of the rhyme, "When you get to a ten, start all over again" (21, 22, 23, 24, . . . , 29). Frequently ask, "How did you remember the words for counting?" or "How would you tell a friend how to count seeds (beans, etc.)."

ACTIVITY 4.4
Counting the Days of School.

On a calendar, keep a count of the days children are in school by marking out the square on the calendar each day of school. Each afternoon before dismissal, count the number of days since school started. (*Note:* This is a counting activity. Numerals are not noted.)

When day 100 is reached, have a special celebration such as a 100 day party, 100 day free time, or 100 day Olympics with competitive events being activities for counting to 100 by ones (the first to count 100 beans by ones from a pile of beans) and tens (the first to hop 10 times while saying "10, 20, 30, . . . , 100"). By the time children have been in school 100 days, they may have learned to read and write numerals to 100. If numerals have been introduced, they can be incorporated into the celebration.

ACTIVITY 4.5
Counting Back.

After children know the counting sequence to 100, have one child take a small handful of beans, place it on the overhead, and ask for estimates of the number. Have the class chorus count backward from the estimate to verify the count, one child removing each bean as it is counted. The children also count the beans left or add beans to determine how the estimate compared to the count.

ACTIVITY 4.6
Let's Estimate.

Several times a week provide jars or displays of objects for children to estimate and then count. Beans of various sizes, marbles, pasta, and the like can be used. After the objects have been counted, ask, "How can we tell if our estimate is too large or too small?" Help children decide to compare the numbers of their estimate and the actual count by adding or removing beans after they count up or down to or from the estimate to the count.

Activity for the Classroom 4.2. Prepare five jars of objects for number estimation. Use numbers of objects that would be appropriate for the grade level in which you are teaching. Ask children to explain their estimation strategies so that all in the class can learn ways to estimate. Then ask the question in Activity 4.6.

Grouping, Representing, Comparing, Ordering, and Estimating

Children need many experiences with grouping objects by tens or tens and ones to understand the base ten system. As children group objects by tens, they learn to count by tens using standard or ordinary names (ten, twenty, thirty, . . .) and by place-value or nonstandard names (one ten, two tens, three tens, . . .). They also represent numbers given orally with various base ten materials, learn to compare and order numbers to 100, and continue to estimate.

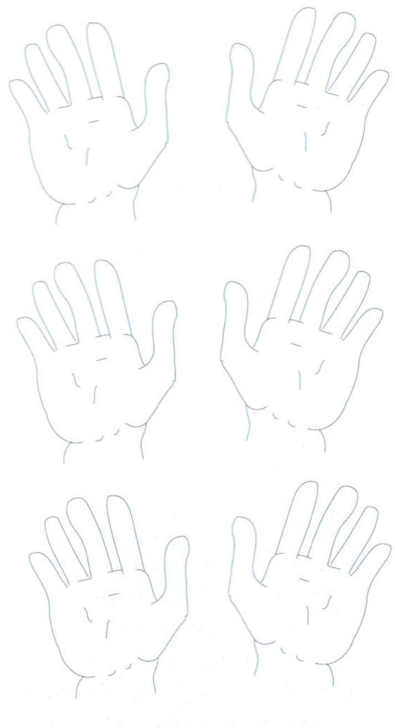

FIGURE 4.2 Hands Picture Showing 30

ACTIVITY 4.7
Showing Groups with Two Hands.

After children have counted the students present, ask them how they could show this number using all the fingers on two hands. Guide to them say, "Ten, twenty, thirty, . . . ," as they extend the fingers on two hands three times to show thirty. They can also use the place-value words one ten, two tens, three tens. If more than 30 children are present, they show the ones on separate fingers. Hands can be used to show other large numbers. Pictures of hands can be used to represent large numbers (Figure 4.2).

ACTIVITY 4.8
Showing a Number with Materials.

Give each child or group a set of pregrouped base ten materials. Ask how the materials could be used to show the number of a set such as the children present. If children focus on the units, say, "Think about counting with two hands. How did we do that?" When children recall counting tens with two hands, ask, "What do you have that would be like counting by tens with two hands?" After they decide how to use the materials to count by tens, children show the number in the class with the base ten materials and handle the materials as they represent the number in the class. Have them say, "One ten, two tens, . . . ," "as well as ten, twenty, ..." You and the class members can suggest other numbers to 100 to represent with pregrouped materials. After the class shows each number, they discuss how they thought to carry out the task.

Later introduce groupable materials. Give each child or group some rubber bands and many objects that are easily grouped by tens, for example, straws cut in halves or thirds or tear strips from computer paper. The latter are free and renewable! My students report that they have had success in helping children grasp the concepts of numbers beyond ten with these 10-dot strips cut from computer tear strips. Say, "We can make our own materials to show tens. How would we do that with the materials on your tables?" If no pupil suggests grouping by tens, say, "How can we make a bundle to show one ten?" or "How can we make a 10-dot strip?" (The 10-dot strips can be pasted on jumbo popsicle sticks to make 10-dot sticks.) If further prompts are needed, show picking up seven straws and putting a rubber band around them or cut a strip of seven dots, and say, "Is this a one ten?" After children answer the question, repeat your earlier questions and have pupils discuss how to use the groupable materials to make tens.

Each child should make a set of 10 tens for him- or herself. When they have done so, they count their sets saying 1 ten, 2 tens, . . . , 10 tens as well as 10, 20, . . . , 100. Each child's materials are stored in a resealable plastic bag for use during mathematics periods.

ACTIVITY 4.9
Grouping the Seeds.

The seeds that were collected for Activity 4.2 should be displayed by groups of tens and ones after children have been introduced to the grouping concept. Place-value mats can be introduced for this activity. These are cardboard, plastic, or 12 x 18 construction paper mats that are divided into two or three sections. The sections may have different colors. Figure 4.3 shows a place-value mat. For display, the seeds can be grouped by tens and ones in plastic bags that are stapled to the mats. You can

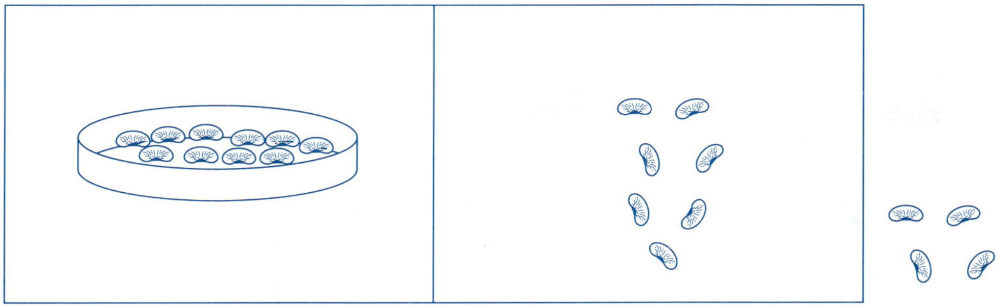

FIGURE 4.3 Place-Value Mat Showing 17

write numerals (e.g., 47) and words (e.g., forty-seven) on the mats for the number of seeds displayed to enable pupils to develop an awareness of symbols and number words. Later children can use their own mats and base ten materials to represent the number of seeds displayed on place-value mats.

Reader Activity 4.1

What in your environment can children count and group that would be enjoyable and give experience to develop the meaning of numbers to 100? List the learnings that should be constructed from activities involving counting and grouping these objects.

ACTIVITY 4.10
What Numbers Shall We Show?

Have children suggest numbers (100 or less) to show on their place-value mats using base ten materials. Vary the materials so that pregrouped and groupable materials are used on different days. Children can work in pairs to carry out this activity.

Variation: Ask children to show a number 10 greater (or less) than the number given.

ACTIVITY 4.11
Making Mats for Objects Counted.

For homework, ask children to choose something to count at home or on the way to school that will be a number more than 10. (Children should discuss what they could count before beginning this homework assignment. Suggestions could include: houses or cars seen on the way to school, number of seats in the school bus, number of keys on a computer, or number of keys on a piano.) Ask them not to tell anyone what they counted. Part of the assignment is to represent the number on a place-value mat by tracing 10-dot strips (pass these out) and drawing dots for units with a pencil or crayon. Collect the mats when they are brought to school. Each pupil tells what kind of objects he or she has counted, and the other children estimate the number of objects recorded on that child's mat. After two estimates, all count the number on the mat. They discuss how they made their estimates.

ACTIVITY 4.12
Grid Paper Records.

Introduce the concept of representing numbers on grid paper by saying, "After we count the students in our class (or the number of the day of the month), let's show the number on grid paper. How would we do this?" Use questions to guide children to the conclusion that each 10 can be shown by outlining 10 squares and ones by outlining 1 through 9 squares (Figure 4.4). Ask children to think of fun numbers to count and show (for a starter, tell children the age of Mickey Mouse—"born" in 1928—to count and show).

FIGURE 4.4 Example of Child's Drawing on Grid Paper

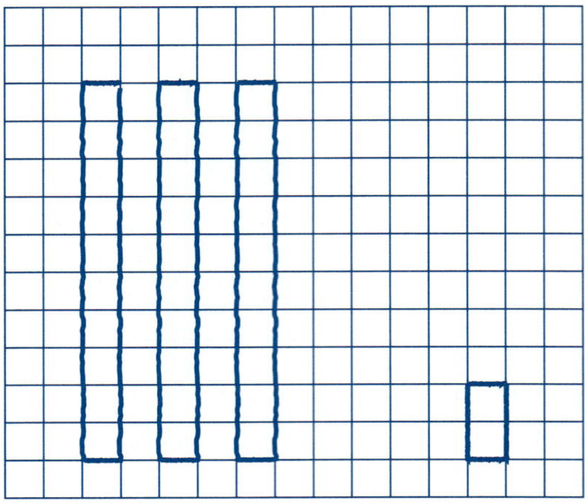

ACTIVITY 4.13
Fishing to 19 Game.

Make 28 cards each showing a number from 10 to 19 with a ten bar and ones bar (Figure 4.5). Five cards are given to each of four players. The remainder are in the center of the playing area face down. Players lay cards in front of them to make a sequence representing the numbers 10 to 19. Players in turn ask the player to their left for a card showing a certain number. If the request cannot be granted, the requesting player takes a card from the pile. If he or she has that card and thus cannot use it, the player returns it to the pile. When one player makes the sequence, he or she is the winner. If one player is out of cards or no cards remain in the center of the table, the player with the most complete sequence wins. (Children can make the cards for this game from squared paper cut in bars and pasted on cards.)

ACTIVITY 4.14
Most Tens Game.

Twenty-four cards showing ten bars or 10-dot strips are needed for this game (Figure 4.6). Four children play the game. To begin the game, the cards are placed in the center of the playing area, face down. Each player takes a card and decides on the number of tens displayed on his or her card. The child with the highest number gets a bean, collects the cards of all the players, and puts them aside. After all the

FIGURE 4.5 Cards for Fishing to 19 Game

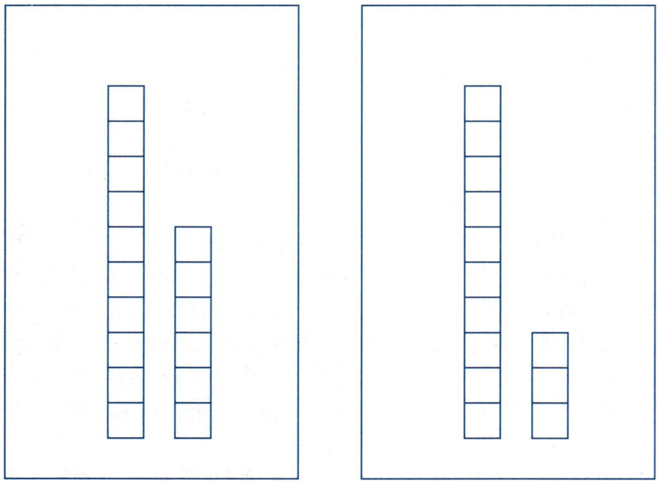

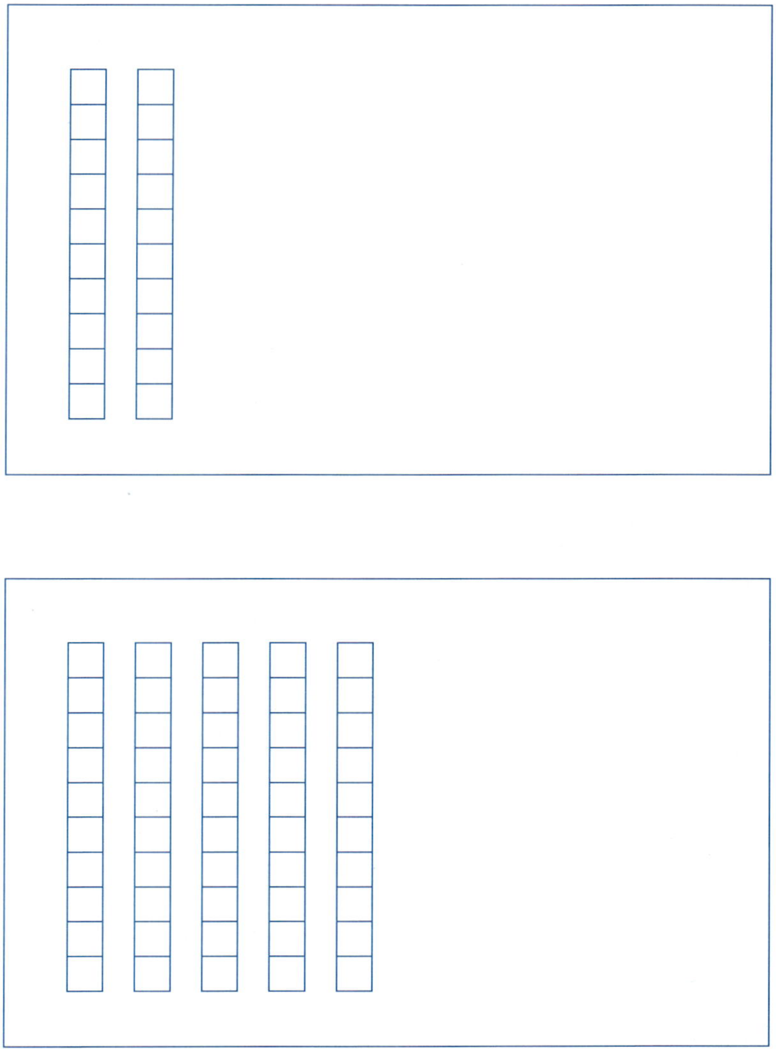

FIGURE 4.6 Cards for the Most Tens Game

cards have been played, the player with the most beans wins. He or she shuffles the cards, places them in the center of the playing area, and another game is played.

Variation: Include tens and ones numbers on the cards.

ACTIVITY 4.15
See the Order.

Give groups of two or three children a packet of 10 cards, each card showing a representation of one of the series of numbers 4–13, 14–23, 24–33, . . . , and 84–93. This sequence is chosen so that the 10 is bridged and several more cards remain to be ordered. (Groups of children could make the cards using grid paper diagrams or 10-dot strips pasted on cards.) Have them order the cards in their packets. When the groups are finished, they place their cards in order around the room, as the class counts. (Use paper clips or clothes pins on a rope hung in the room. Choose a child to order the cards for 1 to 3 and 94 to 100.) The class can count a section of the sequence to begin a math lesson. Both standard names (e.g., 34, read thirty-four) and place-value names (e.g., 34, read 3 tens plus 4 ones) would be used over time. One child should point to the representation as the number is given.

Place-Value Numerals, Representing, Ordering, Comparing, and Estimating

Children have many opportunities to observe numerals for numbers greater than 10 before instruction deals with numerals. The number of children present in the class has been written or displayed with numeral cards each day, and children have read this numeral. The calendar has been referred to each day, with special reference to the dates of children's birthdays. Numerals for large numbers have appeared outside of school where children could view them, such as in stores and on TV. The introduction to reading and writing numerals for numbers to 100 begins with helping children relate what they know to the new learning (see Activity 4.17).

As children learn about numerals and places, the place-value chart is introduced. A place-value chart differs from a place-value mat in that words are used to label the places and place-value materials (e.g., base ten blocks—blocks, flats, longs, units—or tens and ones bars) are not used. Counters or numerals are shown in the places (Figure 4.7). For example, three counters in the tens place indicate 30 (30 in the tens place would indicate 300).

When introducing the place-value chart, help pupils realize that the words in the labels for each place give the place value whereas the counters or numbers give the face value. To introduce the place-value chart, you can display a place-value chart on the overhead and say, "Notice the names of the places. Let's read them together. I will put four counters in the tens place. The counters in the tens place tell what number of tens I am thinking. What number of tens have I shown?" If pupils do not grasp the meaning of place, use cognitive modeling to help them understand the meaning of place, and ask pupils to tell what they learned from your "thinking out loud." Next, write numerals in the places, and have students explain the meaning of the numerals.

The following activities teach concepts related to base ten and place-value numerals. They include reading and writing place-value numerals, representing numerals with place-value materials, and comparing, ordering, estimating, and renaming numbers using numerals.

ACTIVITY 4.16
Go for Blue.

This game develops an intuitive understanding of base ten. It can be played by young children when they can count to 10. The materials for the game are: 2 dice, 1 small blue tagboard square, 35 small red tagboard squares, and 50 small green tagboard squares. Four players take turns tossing the dice, counting or thinking the sum of the numbers represented, and taking that many squares. When 10 green squares are collected, they are exchanged for a red square; 10 red squares are exchanged for the blue square. The winner is the first player to collect the blue square.

Variation: To develop place-value meanings, "Go for Blue" can be played with place-value mats and place-value materials, place-value charts and flip cards, or paper-and-pencil abacuses and beans or washers (Holmes, 1986).

ACTIVITY 4.17
Using What We Know.

The activity begins by asking children to tell what large numbers they know how to read or write. (If they know how to write any numerals, they can write them on the chalkboard.) Show a one hundred square on the overhead (see Appendix G for pattern), and write the numerals for numbers children say they can read or write on this hundred square, saying, for example, "I will write 30 here. Let's read it." As you write a numeral on the chart, have a child tell what it means to him or her. After all the numerals children know how to read and write have been entered in the chart,

FIGURE 4.7 Place-Value Charts Showing 323

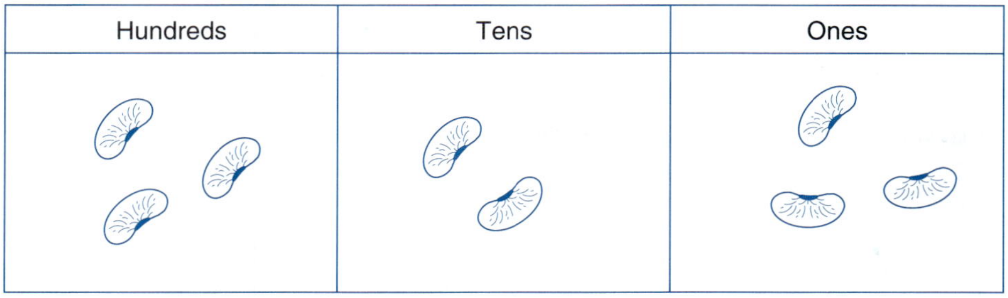

Beans on Place-Value Chart

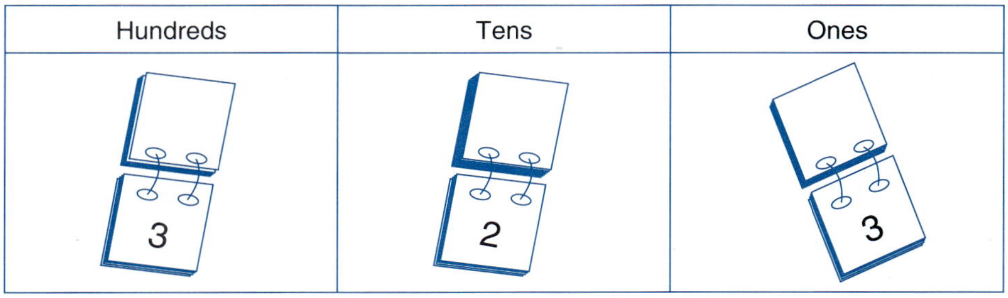

Flip Cards on Place-Value Chart

Hundreds	Tens	Ones
3	2	3

Numerals on Place-Value Chart

ask children to look at the blanks, and solve the problem of deciding how to write the other numerals. (A prompt could be to count to help think of the numbers that are missing.) Have them explain how they decided how the numerals to finish the chart would be written. Write the numerals. Have pupils read the one hundred square. Later, make a chart to display in the classroom (Figure 4.8).

Ask children to explain how to write the numerals to 100 and the pattern that helps them know "how the numbers go." Give each child a sheet of two one hundred squares (see Appendix G for pattern), and have them write the numerals to 100 in each hundred square.

Later have children discuss how to write the words used in reading numerals to 100 (e.g., forty-five). Ask questions that enable them to use what they know to do so. If they can say the words, they should be able to write the words with minimal guidance from you regarding correct spelling and punctuation.

FIGURE 4.8 Chart Showing a One Hundred Square

1	2	3	4	5	6	7	8	9	10
11	12	13	14	15	16	17	18	19	20
21	22	23	24	25	26	27	28	29	30
31	32	33	34	35	36	37	38	39	40
41	42	43	44	45	46	47	48	49	50
51	52	53	54	55	56	57	58	59	60
61	62	63	64	65	66	67	68	69	70
71	72	73	74	75	76	77	78	79	80
81	82	83	84	85	86	87	88	89	90
91	92	93	94	95	96	97	98	99	100

ACTIVITY 4.18
My Book for Numbers to 100.

Each child makes a "Numbers to 100 Book." The book consists of 10 pages with representations of numbers made by a child coloring in small squares of a one hundred square. For each page, a child is given a sheet with two blank one hundred squares (see Appendix G for hundred square pattern). On the first page, 10 squares of a one hundred square are colored by the child; he or she decides what teens number will be represented in the other hundred square. On the second page, 20 squares are colored on one hundred square, and a tens-plus-ones number of the child's choosing in that decade (e.g., 25) is represented in the other hundred square. On the third page, 30 squares are colored on one hundred square, and a tens-plus-ones number of the child's choosing in that decade (e.g., 37) is represented in the other hundred square. This plan continues for nine pages. The tenth page has a hundred square with 100 squares colored. The child writes numerals to 100 in the other hundred square. On each page, the numeral for each number represented is written beside its representation. Each child designs a cover and makes a book of his or her work.

The representations in the book can be used to show numbers to 100. For example, ask children to find 57. They would use the hundred square showing 60. Children can also work in pairs, taking turns asking each other to show numbers. Later children take their books home. Encourage children to read their books to someone at home.

ACTIVITY 4.19
Show and Flip Game.

This game is a variation of an activity introduced by Baratta-Lorton (1976). Two children play the game. The materials needed for the game are: three packets of flip cards, place-value mat, place-value chart, place-value materials, and a die (Figure

4.9). The rules for the game are: Place one flip card packet in each section of the place-value chart. Throw the die, take that number from the materials, place them on the right of the place-value mat, and use the flip card packet on the right side of the place-value chart to record the number of singles you have. Take turns throwing the die and adding material on your place-value mat. Trade for tens when you can. Continue to use the flip card packets to show the numbers on the place-value chart. The first player to reach 100 wins.

The game can be played "backward" with each player beginning with 100 (10 ten bars), removing the number designated by the die, and using the chart to record the play. (The children would have to solve the problem of trading 10 tens for 1 hundred and 10 ones for a tens piece in order to play the game.) The first person to reach exactly no pieces on his or her board—and 0 on each flip card would win.

ACTIVITY 4.20
Flip Game.

This game is identical to *Show and Flip* except that the materials include only a die, a place-value chart, and flip cards. Children count or add to determine the total number they have accumulated and show it on the flip cards.

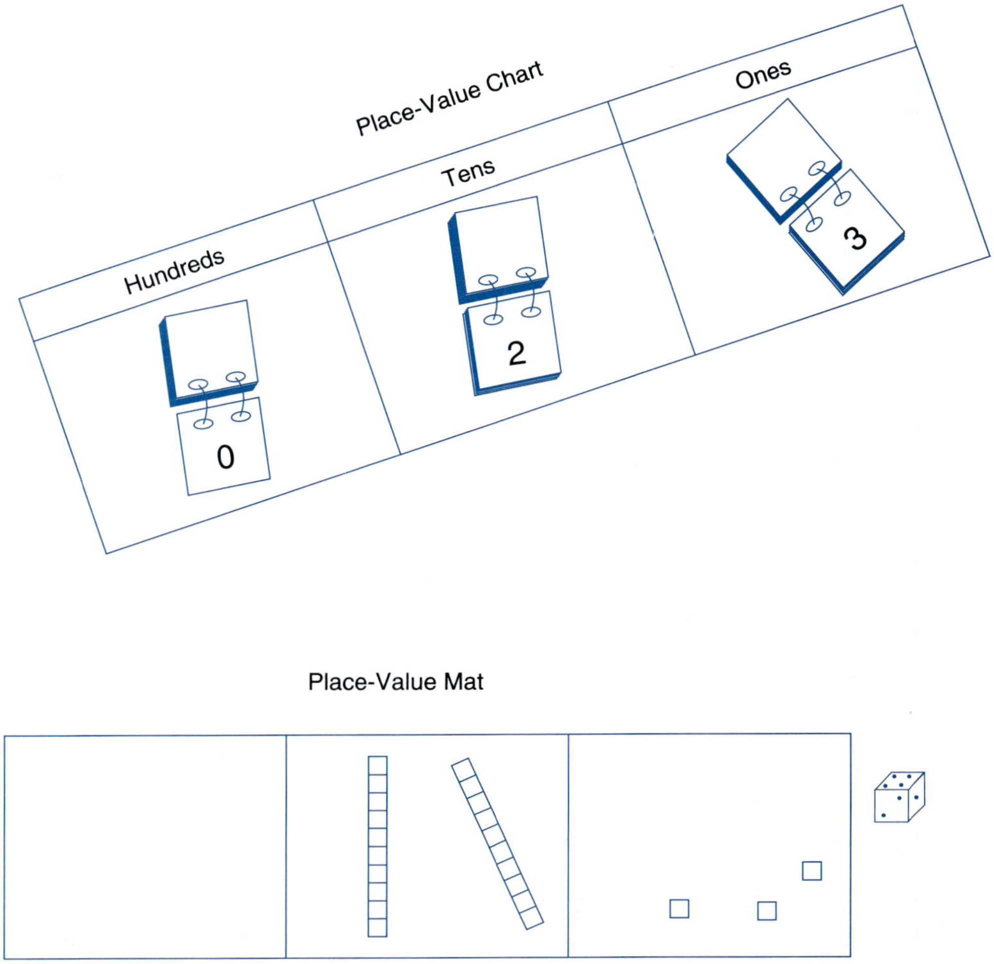

FIGURE 4.9 "Show and Flip" Game

ACTIVITY 4.21
One Hundred War.

You or the children can make cards for *War* with large numbers. The game is played the same way as *War* with small numbers.

ACTIVITY 4.22
Make the Order Game.

You or groups of children make numeral cards for 5 different number sequences of 9 numbers, such as 47 to 55. Each of 4 players receives three cards to begin. Thereafter, they take turns drawing a card from the pile of remaining cards in the middle of the playing area. The objective of the game is to make a complete sequence of 9 cards. The game ends and the winner is declared when he or she has made the sequence or all the cards have been drawn. The winner is the child with the most complete sequence.

ACTIVITY 4.23
Make an Estimation.

Have groups of children make estimating jars for the other children. Each group performs the following tasks: (1) Decide on a group letter such as "L" (make certain groups select different letters); (2) label the jar with the group's letter (a rubber band can hold the label); (3) decide on a number of objects such as beans to put in an estimating jar; (4) select from a pile of objects what is a good estimate of that number; (5) count out the objects, and take more or remove some to equal the number to put in the jar; (6) place the objects in the jar; (7) make a record of the number that is given to you; and (8) place the jar on the Estimating Table. Over about a week, each child in the class estimates the number in each jar, except his or her group's jar, and makes a record of the estimate. The record sheet is given to you so you can decide if the estimates are sensible. The following day the children are given their papers, the groups tell and count out the number of objects in their jars, and the children discuss how they made their estimates and why their estimates were close or not close.

ACTIVITY 4.24
Many Ways to Show.

Pose the problem: How many ways can we show 54 (or any other number) using longs and units (or other base ten material)? Pupils in groups should solve this problem by thinking of representations such as 4 longs and 14 units, 3 longs and 24 units, and 54 units, as well as 5 longs and 4 units. They share their solutions. Continue with other numbers until children understand how to show a number in "ordinary" (standard) and "not ordinary" (nonstandard) ways.

Then children can work in pairs, naming numbers for one another to show in two ways. Numeral cards to 100 can be used by the two children. Students take turns picking a card. Each child shows the number given on the card in two ways, and they compare what they did.

ACTIVITY 4.25
Cover Up.

Each child is given a one hundred square and a blank piece of paper 18 squares long with a strip of 9 squares cut from one side (Figure 4.10). Ask children to show numbers using the materials. Name each number to show using a standard name, a place-value name, or a ten and teen (e.g., 35 = 20 + 15) name. Ask children to give the number another name after they represent it. Say, for example, "How can we

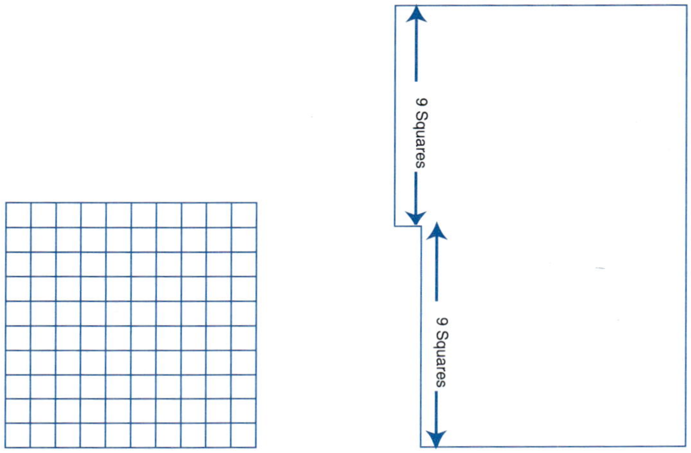

FIGURE 4.10 Cover-Up Activity Materials

show the number 20 + 15 by covering up part of the one hundred square using our long sheet with the cutout piece?" After students show the number, ask, "What are other names for this number?" Have several children show the number on a one hundred square displayed on the overhead by using the cutout piece and tell different names for the number. When children understand how to show numbers named in this way and can give different names for numbers, have them name numbers for others to show. When learners demonstrate they can do this, have them work with each other to show numbers and name them in different ways.

ACTIVITY 4.26
Giving Other Names to Numbers.

Write numbers on the chalkboard or overhead for groups to rename. Have children work in groups to use materials to show nonstandard names for numbers, and then write the nonstandard names (e.g., 34 = 3 tens + 4 ones; 44 = 30 + 14). After they decide the nonstandard names for the given numbers and how to write the math sentences, students report their ideas to the class. They discuss how they knew what to do. If no pupil reports how he or she uses the tens place to rename numbers, question the class so that they understand this process. (*Note:* This activity can accommodate individual differences because some will write more nonstandard names than others. Those writing few nonstandard names should be asked to report first. Why?)

NUMBERS GREATER THAN 100

Numbers to 1000

Children begin their study of numbers to 1000 by discussing what hundred numbers they have heard of and what they mean. The discussion is followed by activities for numbers to 1000: *counting and representing numbers; reading and writing numerals; comparing and ordering numbers; learning to rename numbers; estimating; extending place-value concepts; and using the numbers in other subjects and real life.*

Children count to 1000 by hundreds and by tens. Counting to 1000 by ones is not recommended, but learners can count a sequence of 100 numbers beginning, for example, with 577. Saying the number sequence can be motivated by having children estimate the time it would take and checking the estimate with the clock. After counting, learners should think about the patterns in their counting.

Making a 1000-strip by taping 10 hundred squares together to make a long strip—or stapling 10 hundred squares together to make a packet—enables learners to visualize 1000 and to grasp the notion that 1000 is 10 x 100. The task can begin by saying, "We know how to count to 1000. How can we use these hundred squares to make 1000?" Children explore different arrangements of the hundred squares to make 1000. As they engage in this activity, they develop the idea that 10 hundred squares makes 1000, and the 1000-strip or 1000-packet idea emerges from the exploration. Each child then makes his or her own 1000-strip or packet. If most children decide to make 1000 packets, you should make a 1000-strip so that children can see 1000 squares displayed at one time.

Children extend their knowledge of numerals to reading and writing the numerals for numbers to 1000. Ask the class to solve the problem of writing the hundreds numbers (200, 300, . . . , 1000). When the problem is solved, ask how they thought to do this and particularly how they knew to write "1000." Next, dictate numerals for hundreds and tens numbers and later, hundreds, tens, and ones numbers. Each child writes these numerals, and several pupils share their work by writing the numerals on the chalkboard or overhead. They also tell how they knew what to do. At another time, children work together. Partners take turns dictating numerals from a list you prepare for numbers to 1000. They check their work by referring to the list.

A similar plan can be followed for an activity to teach writing number words (e.g., four hundred) to one thousand.

ACTIVITY 4.27
Make a Hundreds Book.

Making a book of numbers to 1000 is a valuable experience for a child. There are 10 pages in the book, one for each hundred to 1000. Each page of the book shows a multiple of 100 with a sentence about known objects almost to that number (Figure 4.11). The number of objects is marked. One teacher I know reported that when children pasted 4 one hundred squares on a page, they were amazed to find out that 900 could not be shown on even two pages of such a book. After each child has made his or her book, numbers (e.g., 500, 430, 356, or 891) can be found in the book. Children can work in pairs, pointing to numbers given orally or in writing by you or their partners.

FIGURE 4.11 Page from Child's Hundreds Book

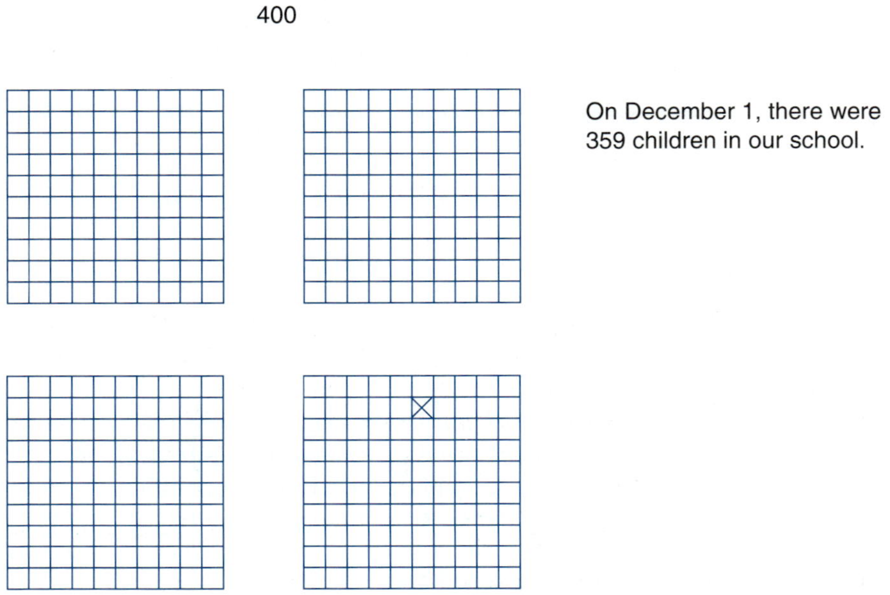

ACTIVITY 4.28
Show and Flip to 1000.

Play the Show and Flip game (Activity 4.19) using cards written with hundreds, tens, or tens-plus-ones numbers (e.g., 300, 60, 45). (Students can make these cards.) The stack of cards is face down. Players take a card in turn, using base ten materials to represent the numbers on the place-value mat and flip cards on the place-value chart (Figure 4.12). The first player to reach an even 1000, not more or less, wins.

ACTIVITY 4.29
All Those Places.

Frequently ask questions such as: How do you know how to read 537? 307? Groups discuss the answers to questions before a class discussion to give many children opportunities to express the meaning they have of place value. Discussions are very important because place value is an abstract idea that children must construct by their own thinking. They do not learn place-value concepts solely by working with materials. They must reflect on their actions. Group and class discussions provide opportunities to reflect.

Children in some classes can do write-ups to answer a question that deals with reading large numbers.

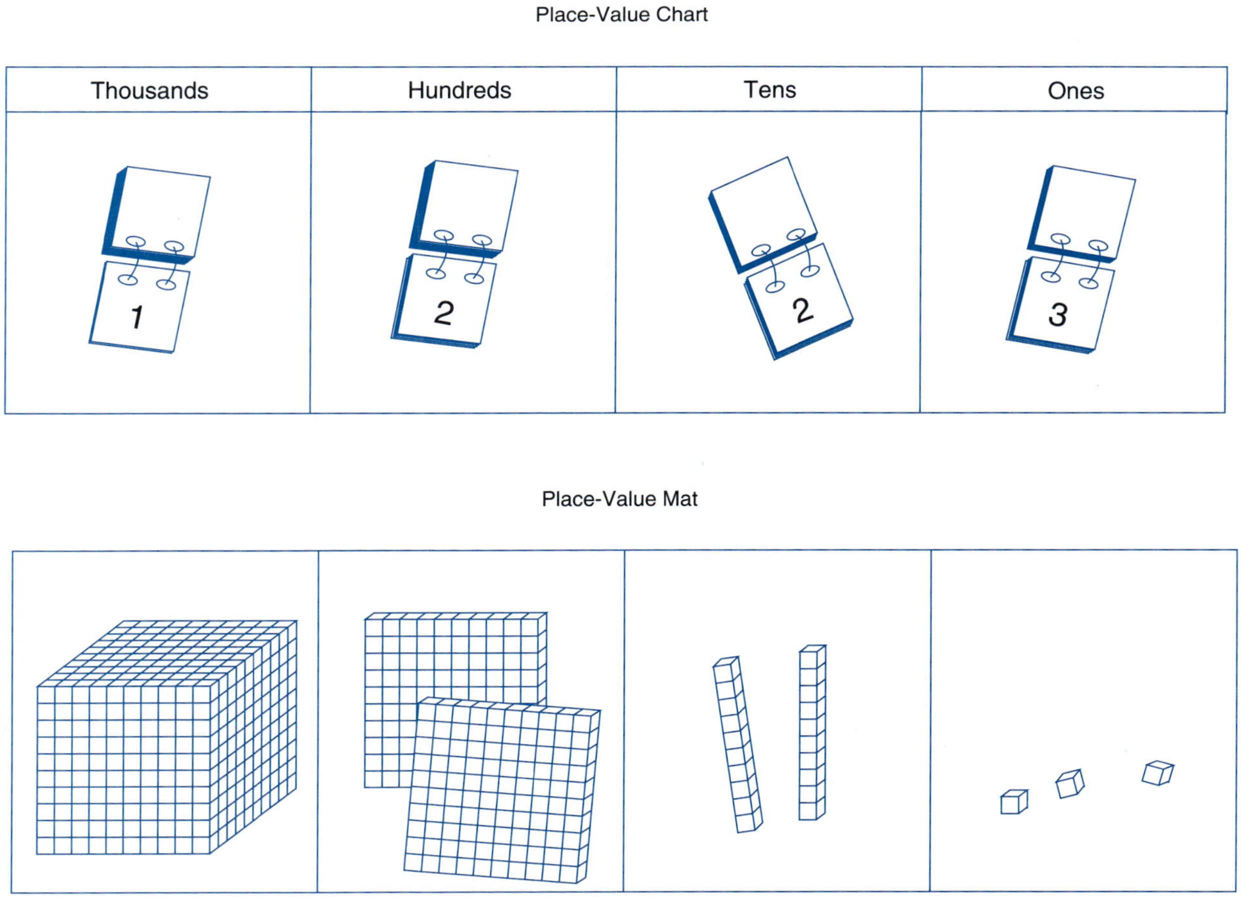

FIGURE 4.12 Materials for "Show and Flip to 1000" Game

ACTIVITY 4.30
Where Is My Number?

Children work in pairs, asking each other to find a number on his or her 1000-strip or packet. After they find a number, they can count the hundreds, tens, and ones to name that number and give other ways to name the number.

ACTIVITY 4.31
Estimation of Objects.

Suggest or ask children to think of large numbers to estimate, such as how many children are in the school, how many lunches are served in the school cafeteria in a week, or how many children are absent in the school district in a week. Have students obtain the reported number from the appropriate school office to compare with their estimates.

ACTIVITY 4.32
Comparing.

Give several problems, such as follow, to pairs of children. Ask each child to write a numeral that solves the problem. After each problem is solved by both partners, they discuss their solutions. A whole-class discussion can complete the activity.

Children can be asked to represent the problem number using materials (hundred squares and tens and units bars, 10-dot strips or sticks and counters, or flats, longs, and units). The class can discuss how the number represented would compare with a representation of the solution for that problem.

1. Name a number a little greater than 345.
2. Name a number greater than 345.
3. Name a number much greater than 345.
4. What number is 10 times greater than 52?
5. What number is 10 times greater than 67?

Variations of this activity are:

1. Change the number described to be less rather than greater.
2. Use two different numbers in a problem; for example, a number less than 220 and greater than 120.

ACTIVITY 4.33
What Are These Numbers?

Write questions such as the following on cards for pairs of learners to answer:

1. Choose five numbers to write in order between 400 and 420.
2. Write these numbers in order: 511, 599, 509, 500, 519. Write up how you knew what to do.
3. Give the number that is between 500 and 600, has a number of tens the same as the number of hundreds, and a number of ones 2 less than the number of tens.

If some learners can write questions such as Number 3, ask them to write them on cards for the use of other children.

ACTIVITY 4.34
Puzzles.

This activity gives experience with renaming numbers to 1000. Pose a puzzle for children in the class to solve with their materials. An example of a puzzle is: What number is 27 tens? Show with 10-dot strips, and write the number on your chalkboard. When children solve problems of this type with no difficulty, they are asked to make up problems for others in the class. Each member of the class solves the problem and represents his or her solution with materials and numerals. One or more children show their solutions on the overhead and explain their thinking to solve the problem.

A variation is to ask groups to write puzzles for one another that involve both renaming and addition or subtraction. Examples are: What number is 32 tens plus 3 ones? What number is 15 tens minus 5? Begin by giving a question and asking children to explain how to think the answer. Continue with other questions. Children can use groupable materials to aid in their solutions. When they understand the process, have groups each make up a puzzle, and ask the class to solve it. Then have the group tell how they thought to make the puzzle. Continue by having groups make puzzles for class use. Explain that the puzzle made by a group must be solved mentally or with materials by that group before it can be used with the class.

ACTIVITY 4.35
War with Large Numbers.

The game is similar to *One Hundred War* (Activity 4.21), except that the numbers named go to 1000. Nonstandard names can be included (e.g., 43 tens plus 4) on the game cards.

Reader Activity 4.2

Choose three activities for learning numbers to 1000. Explain their objectives in terms of the objectives for teaching numbers to 1000 listed in the text.

Numbers Greater than 1000

Objectives for instruction for numbers greater than 1000 parallel those for teaching all large numbers and are:

1. Knowing the meaning of the numbers, including numbers with nonstandard names.
2. Using materials to represent large numbers.
3. Reading and writing numerals for very large numbers.
4. Knowing the meaning of the places in the numerals for very large numbers.
5. Understanding number relations, particularly power-of-10 relations.
6. Comparing and ordering.
7. Estimating.
8. Using very large numbers in other subjects and in real life.

Numbers greater than 1000 are introduced in the upper grades as children observe these numbers in school subjects such as social studies, science, and current events. When a number greater than 1000 appears in learners' study material, ask the class if anyone can read the number. If no one can do so, you read the number. After the number is read by one or more students or you, the class examines the number and thinks about its meaning in the context of the content being studied.

Learners can be asked to find other large numbers in their school studies textbook or in their lives outside of school and report their observations to the class. For example, the population of the state in which the children are living may be reported in a textbook or in the newspaper; city populations are often given on roadway signs. A discussion of students' reports after they complete the assignment can begin the formal study of numbers greater than 1000. Examples of questions and activities for lessons dealing with population that take place over several weeks are given here. Very large numbers that students find in their textbooks in other subjects could be the focus of lessons.

1. Joan reported that the population of our city was 17,650, and she wrote that number on the chalkboard. How did she know to read and write the number? Did she use any number and place-value patterns to help her?

2. How would we use our 1000-strips to show the population of our city? Another city? Can this number be read another way? How?
3. Ask each student to write five numbers greater than 10,000. Math partners will trade, read each other's numbers, and tell what they would mean for the population of a city. To conclude the activity, have children share their work on the chalkboard and explain the meaning of their numbers.
4. (Write the population of the county and of the state on the board) How would we read these numbers? How did you know to read the numbers? Did any patterns help you?
5. About how much less is the population of our city than our county (state)? How did you decide that? About how many times less is the population of our city than our county (state)? How did you solve this problem?
6. Each group please estimate populations for three large or very large cities that you have heard about. Write these on the transparency the monitor will give to each group. Your numbers will be shown on the overhead, and the class will read these populations and think about their meaning in a few minutes. (To help students study the meaning of the numbers, you can say, "Let's think about the meaning of each number to the left of the ones place.") Students can compare their estimates to the reported populations.
7. Each group please write three numbers that are between 100,000 and 1,000,000 on the transparency the monitor will give you. A group member will show them on the overhead, and the class will read these numbers and think about their meaning in a few minutes. (Students discuss the meaning of the numeral in each place and consider how the number can be renamed as an equal number, e.g., 55,600 is 556 hundreds.)

The following activities also deal with one of more of the eight outcome objectives. Some activities are appropriate for only upper-grade children.

ACTIVITY 4.36
Collecting Objects to Show Large Numbers.

Children can collect objects (e.g., pop can tabs) and group them by tens, hundreds, and thousands to develop an awareness of numbers greater than 1000. If each of twenty-five students collects 100 small objects of his or her own choice, the 2500 objects could probably be collected by a class in a short time. Very large numbers, such as a million, can take years to collect. If such a project is undertaken, you and the children should be aware that several classes will probably be involved in the project, you will need to keep it going, and there will need to be a great deal of storage space available for the objects.

Bickerton-Ross (1988) reports on a class project that involved a class in collecting 10,000 objects. After her 15 third graders decided how many each would need to collect, each began collecting 666 small objects at home. (The teacher was asked to collect 10 to reach 10,000.) They decided they needed 4 weeks to complete the collection. When objects were brought to school, displays were made on a large bulletin board in the hall so that all in the school could see the results of the project. Each third-grade student also did a write-up to report on his or her collecting and counting of 666 objects.

The collection of large numbers of objects involves counting. As learners count objects collected, they should become aware of the patterns in counting that enable them to count large numbers. Help them appreciate the power of the repetition of the 1, 2, 3, . . . , 10 sequence in counting and the use of the sequence within a sequence (e.g., one thousand, one thousand one, one thousand two, . . . , one thousand ten, . . . , one thousand fifty, one thousand fifty-one, one thousand fifty-two, . . . , one thousand sixty, . . . , two thousand, . . . , two thousand one, two thousand two, . . . , two thousand ninety, . . . , three thousand, . . . , four thousand, . . . , ten thousand, . . .).

ACTIVITY 4.37
Showing Very Large Numbers.

Groups of 10 children can be asked to show 10,000 small squares by combining their strips or packets. They should be asked how many each student needs to display for the group to show 100,000 and how they solved this problem. The children can predict and then calculate how far 100,000 small squares or 1,000,000 small squares would reach if 1000-strips were used.

ACTIVITY 4.38
What Is a Million?

This activity helps children think about the 1,000,000 small cubes in a 100 x 100 x 100 cube. The cube can be made by groups of children using a frame and hundred squares. Suggest that the class could make a cube 100 squares long, 100 squares wide, and 100 squares high. Have children discuss how to do this and decide on one approach. Harrison (1985) suggests using milk cartons for the frame. Joslyn (1990) used meter sticks. A wooden or cardboard frame could also be used. Large one hundred squares are then attached to the frame. As they discuss their ideas, ask, "If we made such a huge cube, how many small cubes would be in it? Why?"

ACTIVITY 4.39
Charts.

Children in groups use hundred squares to make class charts showing 1000, 2000, . . . , 10,000. Different groups make different charts. The charts are displayed in the classroom. (One of my students had children make such charts to display for Open House to enable parents to understand how children were developing concepts of very large numbers. She reported that the students and their parents profited from the activity.)

The charts can be used to understand equal expressions. For example, have students decide which chart will help them give a hundreds name to 3000, and have them explain how they solved the problem. After a few more examples with multiples of 1000, ask them how to show 33 hundreds on a chart. When they can use charts for problems of this kind, ask questions involving renaming thousands numbers as tens numbers. Students can ask the class other questions to give further experiences with renaming.

After work with charts, have children rename thousands numbers as hundreds or tens numbers. Questions would be similar to: How many hundreds is 4600? How many tens is 3450? How do you know?

As some children report their thinking, help all learners realize that a number can be read as a multiple of different powers of 10 by using different places to name the number. For example, 3500 can be read as three thousand five hundred, thirty-five hundreds, or three hundred-fifty tens. Questions to ask could include: "Can you use any place to name a number? How would you do this? When you rename a number, what happens to its value?" "Let's show these ideas using our charts."

Estimation activities can also be devised for use with the charts. A child can name a large number, show it on the chart, (e.g., 7658), and ask others how the number would be estimated in thousands, hundreds, or tens. One child could then use his or her hand to pass over this number of squares and show how close each estimate would be.

ACTIVITY 4.40
Show a Number on the Calculator.

Have children show the number 11,111 on their calculators, and ask questions such as, "How much greater are the tens than ones, hundreds than tens, thousands than hundreds, ten thousands than thousands? Use your calculator if it will help you answer this question." Use other numbers, and have students discuss their meaning. Ask questions related to the value represented by each place so that students learn that the value represented by each place is 10 times greater than the value represented by the place to its right.

ACTIVITY 4.41
What Is Place Value?

Ask children the open question, "What is place value?" Give time to discuss the question so that they can express their understanding and react to one another to clarify their thinking. During the discussion, ask questions to help them construct the ideas that in a place-value numeral, each place represents a value 10 times greater than the value of the place to its right or 10 times less than the value of the place to its left.

Learners can also write up their responses to this question. The write-ups can be the basis for the discussion. Follow up with Activity 4.42.

ACTIVITY 4.42
Name This Large Number.

Have groups make up questions to ask other groups. The questions must involve multiples of 10 or 100. For example, "What number is 10 times greater than 150?" The groups take turns asking and answering questions. One person from the group that answered correctly explains how the group decided on the answer. Some learners may point out that to multiply a number by 10 (100), you can annex one (two) zeros to the right of the number. Ask how they decided on this rule.

ACTIVITY 4.43
Think About These Numbers.

Ask children to discuss (or write up and discuss) the differences and similarities between two numbers such as 6666 and 6 + 6 + 6 + 6.

ACTIVITY 4.44
Study a Place-Value Table to One Billion (Grade 6).

Give each child a blank place-value table. As the group discusses each power of ten, students write in labels and numerals (Figure 4.13). Help pupils focus on the multiply-by-ten pattern that is the basis of the place-value system. The calculator can

Billions	Hundred Millions	Ten Millions	Millions	Hundred Thousands	Ten Thousands	Thousands	Hundreds	Tens	Ones
1,000,000,000	100,000,000	10,000,000	1,000,000	100,000	10,000	1000	100	10	1

FIGURE 4.13 Place-Value Table

be used to explore this concept. (How?) Have students think how to represent each power of 10 with blocks or squares and how far the materials would extend.

ACTIVITY 4.45
Reading Large Numbers Game.

Children play this game in groups of four or six. The materials are: a die for each group and a place-value chart to one million (or billion) for each player and numeral cards from 1 to 6 for each player. Players take turns rolling the die, and each player places a numeral card for the number rolled in any place on his or her chart. After each place has been filled a round is over, and the player who thinks he or she has the largest number reads the number. The group decides if indeed it is the largest number constructed in the group. If so, the player gets a token. If the player can correctly give another name for the number (e.g., 661,225 = 6612 100s + 25), he or she gets another token. After three rounds, the player with the most tokens is the winner of the game, and another game can be played.

Variations of the game are: (1) receive a token if you build the smallest number in your group; (2) receive a token if you can tell how much larger or smaller your number is than the winner's and the other players agree with you; count this token in the next round; and (3) receive a token if your number is closest to a given number. Sherman (1992) has children use various shapes for places for this game.

ACTIVITY 4.46
Increase or Decrease: A Number Puzzle.

Give children directions as follows, telling them there is no one right answer but that more than one number would solve the puzzle. After groups work on the puzzles, have the class compare their solutions.

1. Increasing this number by 100 does not make the number much greater. Write such a number.
2. Decreasing this number by 546,000 makes this number quite small. Write such a number.

3. Increasing this number by 40,000 makes this number a little larger. Write such a number.

Activity for the Classroom 4.3. Write five puzzles similar to those in *Activity 4.46.* Have children solve them and discuss how they thought to find a solution. Extension: Ask learners to write puzzles of this type for classmates to solve. Students should explain their thinking both to write and solve their puzzles.

ACTIVITY 4.47
Connecting with Other Subjects.

Children make a bulletin board of all references to large numbers they find in their other subjects, hear on TV, or read in the newspaper. Before beginning the bulletin board, ask each child to estimate how many he or she thinks will be found in one week, write his or her name and the number on a card, and give the card to you. At the end of the week, determine the number of references shown on the bulletin board, and return the cards to the children. Decide who had the number nearest to the estimation; have learners tell their reactions to the number found in relation to their estimations.

The activity can be adapted for journal writing. Children keep a journal of all the references to large numbers they find in a week.

The estimation activity (Activity 4.31) in the preceding section of this chapter can be adapted for learning about numbers greater than 1000 and related to the study of other subjects. It can involve estimating numbers such as the number of square miles in various countries, the number of children in school in Third World countries, or the number of different insects in your state. Reported numbers can be found in encyclopedias or obtained from governmental agencies. Estimations can then be compared with the reported numbers. That reported numbers are often best estimates should be discussed by students.

ASSESSING LEARNING OF BASE TEN AND OF PLACE VALUE

Assessment determines the base ten and place-value concepts students have constructed and the skills they have attained that are related to these concepts. Questions assessment should answer include: Do children understand that 10 is used to group when counting objects? Can they represent large numbers? Can they order and compare numbers using numerals and give reasons for what they did? Can they use large numbers in estimation? Is their thinking flexible enough to rename numbers in ways that give their values in powers of 10 but that are different from the standard names? Do they understand the place-value system? Do they understand the large numbers they meet in school subjects other than mathematics and in real life?

Assessment techniques include observations, interviews, assessing pupil work products, and interpreting grades on a few quizzes or tests. You can observe children's work as you circulate among the groups or individuals working on assignments. At this time, you can ask children to explain their work or to answer questions related to the assignment, such as, "Which is larger, 30 + 12 or 42? Prove your answer with the materials on your table" or "How many ways can the number 9400 be read?" These on-the-spot interviews are easier to conduct than individual interviews with pupils in a setting removed from the group. The most important feature of an interview is to ask children to give reasons for their answers. They may be asked to use materials to justify their reasoning. Some interviews can be conducted apart from instruction. You can ask children to count, represent, and rename numbers. A brief record of any interview should be made.

Any work product completed during an activity serves as a piece of work to be assessed to determine children's progress. The books children complete, the diagrams they draw, the records they make, the problems they solve, and the projects they complete give you insights regarding students' understanding. Write-ups and journal entries are especially valuable for assessing learners' understanding.

Quizzes or tests can be given several times a quarter or semester as children study large numbers and place-value concepts. They give more information about a child's understanding if some questions are open-ended and require more than one response. Examples of items are:

Late Primary Grades

1. Draw a picture to show 27. Write a sentence or two to tell what the 2 in 27 means.
2. Match the following by drawing lines. Some numbers may have no matches.

44	five tens plus 12
seventy-three	4 tens + 4
4 tens plus 14	6 tens plus 4
62	38
20 + 18	3 tens + 7
37	60 + 13

3. What is a good estimate of the number of first- and second-grade children in the cafeteria on any one day? Explain how you decided on your estimate.
4. Use grid paper (attached) to show 56. Note whether the child outlines the tens.
5. Write in order any 12 numbers greater than 39 and less than 75.

Upper Grades

1. Prepare a write-up that explains to your parents what 4963 means. Include in your write-up the meaning of 4, 9, 6, and 3.
2. Write two ways to state the number of paper clips in a package that contains 550 paper clips. Do not write 550.
3. Give three thousand-numbers greater than 4701 and three thousand-numbers less than 4701.
4. Explain how you would use blocks, flats, longs, and units to represent 9751.
5. Write out in words: 3056.
6. Complete the following list so that each three numbers in the list are ordered. Any of several numbers can be used in each blank. Choose numbers that make sense to you: 289, ______ , 300; 517, ______ , 571; 400, ______ , 409; 600, ______ , 625.
7. Write up what you would say to a creature from Mars if it said to you, "Tell me what you mean by place value."

SUMMARY

From kindergarten to the end of the elementary grades, children deal with large numbers. This chapter discussed learning numbers to 100, to 1000, and greater than 1000. The learning experiences described enable children to connect large number learning in mathematics to other subjects and real life; understand counting and grouping in base ten; use different materials to represent numbers; read and write numerals; compare and order numbers; discover the patterns in our place-value system; estimate the number of a set with many elements; and learn that numbers can be named in more than one way.

New directions in elementary school mathematics give children opportunities to do, reflect, and communicate to learn large numbers. The activities presented provided for problem solving and individual and cooperative work. Interactive methods were described that would enable students to extend the meaning of large numbers they have developed from life experiences and construct new meanings. Assessing children's learning of base ten and place-value notation was discussed in the final section of the chapter.

REFERENCES

Baratta-Lorton, Mary. (1976). *Mathematics Their Way*. Menlo Park, CA: Addison-Wesley.

Baroody, Arthur J. (October 1989). "Manipulatives Don't Come with Guarantees." *Arithmetic Teacher* 37: 4–5.

Baroody, Arthur J. (July 1990). "How and When Should Place-Value Concepts Be Taught?" *Journal for Research in Mathematics Education* 21: 281–286.

Bickerton-Ross, Linda. (December 1988). "A Practical Experience in Problem Solving: A 10,000 Display." *Arithmetic Teacher* 36: 14–15.

Fischer, Florence E. (May 1990). "A Part–Part–Whole Curriculum for Teaching Number in the Kindergarten." *Journal for Research in Mathematics Education* 21: 207–215.

Fuson, Karen C. (July 1990). "Issues in Place-Value and Multidigit Addition and Subtraction Learning and Teaching." *Journal for Research in Mathematics Education* 21: 273–280.

Harrison, William B. (September 1985). "How to Make a Million." *Arithmetic Teacher* 33: 46–47.

Holmes, Emma E. (February 1986). "Red Bean." *Arithmetic Teacher* 33: 3.

Joslyn, Ruth E. (November 1990). "Using Concrete Models to Teach Large-Number Concepts." *Arithmetic Teacher* 38: 6–9.

Kamii, Constance Kazuko. (1985). *Young Children Reinvent Arithmetic: Implication of Piaget's Theory*. New York: Teachers College Press.

Kamii, Constance. (1989). *Young Children Continue to Reinvent Arithmetic: 2nd Grade: Implication of Piaget's Theory*. New York: Teachers College Press.

National Council of Teachers of Mathematics. (1989). *Curriculum and Evaluation Standards for School Mathematics*. Reston, VA: Author.

Ross, Sharon H. (February 1989). "Parts, Wholes, and Place-Value: A Developmental View." *Arithmetic Teacher* 36: 47–51.

Sherman, Helene J. (November 1992). "Reinforcing Place-Value." *Arithmetic Teacher* 40: 169–171.

World Book Encyclopedia. (1993). S.v. "Dinosaurs." Vol. 5, p. 206. Chicago: World Book, Inc.

SOFTWARE RESOURCES

IBM Elementary Mathematics Series: Math Concepts
Hundreds, tens, and ones:
Level I, Unit 3, Lesson 13; Level I, Unit 4, Lessons 14 and 15; Level I, Unit 5, Lessons 22 and 23; Level II, Unit 1, Lesson 3.
Thousands:
Level II, Unit 3, Lessons 14 and 15; Level III, Unit 1, Lessons 1 and 2
Hundred thousands and millions:
Level II, Unit 6, Lesson 28; Level III, Unit 2, Lesson 6.
Company: IBM/EduQuest
Computer: IBM
Grade level: 2–6

Students work with pictures of proportional materials and number lines to develop meaning and relate meaning and numerals; ordering and comparing included.

CHAPTER 5

Learning the Operations with Whole Numbers

▪ INTRODUCTORY PROBLEM ▪

The traveling library delivered these books to your room a week ago: 10 wild animal books, 7 domestic animal books, 6 reptile books, 8 books on children in foreign countries, 18 fiction books, 2 poetry books, 9 mystery books, and 6 books written in Spanish. The books are to stay a month. There are 26 children in your second-grade class. The record of books read at school or at home after one week was: 5 children read 10 different wild animal books, 3 children each read 4 domestic animal books, 4 children each read 3 different reptile books, 3 children each read 2 different books about children in foreign countries, 9 children read the 18 different fiction books, 2 children read the same poetry book, 5 children read 7 mystery books, and 3 children read the 6 different books written in Spanish. As you study this chapter, list how you could use this information to teach or review the meanings of the operations and the basic facts. Make a record of library books read for another week that could be used in a similar way.

INTRODUCTION

A major objective of new directions in elementary school mathematics is for children to acquire knowledge of the operations with whole numbers. To solve problems and to advance in the study of mathematics, children must understand addition, subtraction, multiplication, and division. They must know whether an operation relates to joining, separating, comparing, or sharing equally. When working with large numbers, they must be able to judge whether to compute mentally, estimate, use paper and pencil, or reach for the calculator to complete the task (NCTM, 1989) (see Standards 7 and 13, in Curriculum Standards for Grades K–4, Appendix A).

It takes time to construct the meanings of the operations, gain immediate recall of the basic facts, and learn the different approaches to computation. Therefore, the mathematics curriculum includes the study of the operations in all grades of the elementary school. More advanced concepts and skills are introduced as children mature and attain earlier objectives, with reviews of topics studied earlier planned for the middle and upper grades.

Initially, children study the operations by learning the basic facts. Four steps are involved in learning the basic facts for an operation:

1. Develop the meanings of the operation.
2. Connect oral and written words and symbols for the operation with meanings.
3. Use strategies to recall basic facts.
4. Attain immediate recall of basic facts.

Constructing the concept of an operation comprises the first two steps; the last two steps pertain to mastery of the basic facts. The first section of this chapter discusses constructing the concepts of addition and subtraction; the second section, multiplication and division. Section three deals with assessment, and the last section is a summary. The following chapter discusses how children attain mastery as they use strategies for recall and work for immediate recall of basic facts. Chapter Seven examines learning the operations with large numbers.

CONSTRUCTING THE CONCEPTS OF ADDITION AND SUBTRACTION

Addition is an operation on two numbers, the addends, to obtain a third number, the sum. Subtraction is the inverse of addition. Addition is related to the joining or combining of sets with no common elements. Subtraction has several interpretations: separating, comparing, and equalizing (Figure 5.1).

Basic facts (or simply, facts) for addition are defined as having addends less than 10, for example, 4 (addend) + 3 (addend) = 7 (sum). The subtraction basic facts are the inverse of the addition facts. The names of the numbers in a subtraction sentence are minuend, subtrahend, and remainder or difference. For example, 7 (minuend) – 3 (subtrahend) = 4 (remainder or difference). Figure 5.2 gives the 100 basic facts for addition and subtraction.

When children can represent a number with materials, can give the number of a set by counting or by instant recognition, and show understanding of part–part–whole relations, they begin their study of addition and subtraction. This usually takes place in grade 1. There are two ways children learn the meanings of

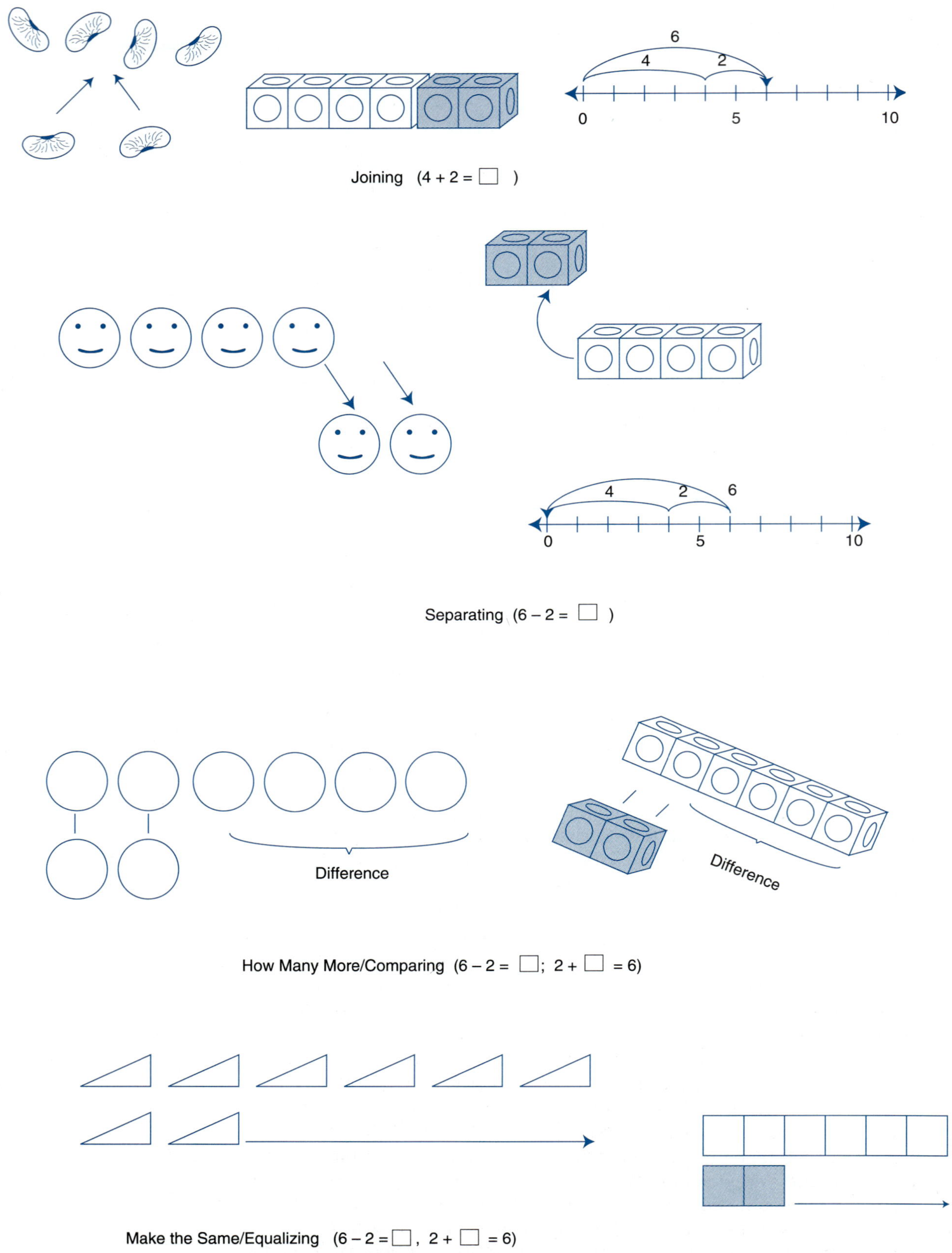

FIGURE 5.1 Models for Addition and Subtraction

+	0	1	2	3	4	5	6	7	8	9
0	0	1	2	3	4	5	6	7	8	9
1	1	2	3	4	5	6	7	8	9	10
2	2	3	4	5	6	7	8	9	10	11
3	3	4	5	6	7	8	9	10	11	12
4	4	5	6	7	8	9	10	11	12	13
5	5	6	7	8	9	10	11	12	13	14
6	6	7	8	9	10	11	12	13	14	15
7	7	8	9	10	11	12	13	14	15	16
8	8	9	10	11	12	13	14	15	16	17
9	9	10	11	12	13	14	15	16	17	18

FIGURE 5.2 Addition Basic Facts

addition and subtraction: (1) solving story problems involving addition and subtraction basic facts (Carpenter, Hiebert, and Moser, 1981; Kamii, 1985); and (2) extending knowledge of part–part–whole relations using sets to represent basic facts (Van de Walle, 1990). Teaching usually involves both approaches to help children construct the meanings of addition and subtraction. One approach is emphasized, however, to introduce addition and subtraction meanings and math sentences.

Solving Story Problems to Learn Addition and Subtraction

Teaching the meanings of addition and subtraction through solving story problems assumes that children will abstract concepts of addition and subtraction from their problem-solving experiences, develop strategies for recall of basic facts, and remember some facts. By beginning with story problems, children learn to consider relationships and construct the meanings of the operations (Fennema, Carpenter, and Peterson, 1989).

Story problems are labeled and classified in different ways, but all classifications are based on similar problems. (See Bebout, 1990; Carpenter and Moser, 1982, 1983; Carpenter, Carey, and Kouba, 1990; Carpenter et al., 1981; and Romberg and Collis, 1987.) Box 5.1 gives a classification of 13 types of story problems useful in teaching children the meanings of addition and subtraction. All the problem types, except comparing and equalizing, involve one set, and the problem solver must deal with the relations among the parts of the set and the whole. In the comparing and equalizing problems, two sets are specified. The problem solver must understand that the key to the solution is to match elements in the two sets and then to deal with the extra elements in the larger set in a manner that solves the problem.

Many children in the early grades have had school and out-of-school experiences that relate to addition and subtraction and have intuitive ideas for solving problems. Teachers help children build on these ideas by assigning different types of story problems (Fennema et al., 1989).

A unit of study emphasizes one or two types of story problems but includes other types children have studied to give them many opportunities to think about number relations in different settings. Problems should be challenging, but children should be able to solve them so that they feel confident about "doing" mathematics. The unit can be taught every day or three or four days a week until children demonstrate that they have constructed the meaning of the problems selected for study. If the problems unit is taught only part of the week, the lessons for the remaining periods in the week deal with other topics, for example, geometry.

After you present a problem, children work in groups or individually, using methods of their own choice to solve the problem. The methods often involve mod-

BOX 5.1 Classification of Story Problems for Addition and Subtraction with Examples

JOINING

1. *Find result*
   Billy had 3 rocks in his collection. Sumiko gave him 4. How many did he have in his collection after he got 4 from Sumiko?
   a. 3 + 4 = □
2. *Find change*
   Billy had 3 rocks in his collection. Sumiko gave him some. Then he had 7. How many did Sumiko give him?
   a. 3 + □ = 7
   b. 7 − 3 = □
3. *Find start*
   Billy had a rock collection. Sumiko gave him 4. Billy then had 7. How many did he have before he got some from Sumiko?
   a. □ + 4 = 7
   b. 7 − 4 = □

COMBINING (PART–PART–WHOLE)

4. *Find whole*
   Billy had 3 rough rocks and 4 smooth rocks. How many rocks did he have?
   a. 3 + 4 = □
5. *Find part*
   Billy had 7 rocks in his collection. Some were rough, and some were smooth. He had 3 rough rocks. How many were smooth?
   a. 3 + □ = 7
   b. 7 − 3 = □

SEPARATING

6. *Find result*
   Billy had 7 rocks in his collection. He gave 3 to Sumiko. How many did he have then?
   a. 7 − 3 = □
7. *Find change*
   Billy had 7 rocks in his collection. He gave some to Sumiko. Then he had 4 How many did he give to Sumiko?
   a. 7 − □ = 4
   b. 7 − 4 = □
8. *Find start*
   Billy gave Sumiko 3 of his rocks. Then he had 4. How many did he have before he gave 3 away?
   a. □ − 3 = 4
   b. 3 + 4 = □

COMPARING

9. *Find difference*
   Billy has 7 rocks in his collection. Sumiko has 3 rocks in her collection. How many more rocks does Billy have than Sumiko?
   a. 7 − 3 = □
10. *Find larger group*
   Billy has 4 more rocks than Sumiko. She has 3. How many does Billy have?
   a. 3 + 4 = □
11. *Find smaller group*
   Billy has 7 rocks. That is 4 more than Sumiko. How many does Sumiko have?
   a. □ + 4 = 7
   b. 7 − 4 = □

EQUALIZING

12. *Find increase*
   Billy has 7 rocks. Sumiko has 3 rocks. How many does she need to have as many as Billy?
   a. 3 + □ = 7
   b. 7 − 3 = □
13. *Find decrease*
   Sumiko has 3 rocks, and Billy has 7. Billy lost some, and now he has the same number as Sumiko. How many did he lose?
   a. 7 − □ = 3
   b. 7 − 3 = □

eling with objects or drawing pictures and counting. After each problem is solved, children discuss their solutions.

When children can solve story problems with objects or pictures and counting, the teacher should introduce math sentences. An open math (or number) sentence has a place holder for the unknown. If the place holder is isolated on the right side of an open math sentence, it is in standard form (e.g., 2 + 6 = □). Math sentences in standard form are introduced first. If the place holder is not isolated on the right side, the open math sentence is in nonstandard form (e.g., □ + 6 = 8). Open math sentences that reflect the structure of a problem are called open direct math sentences. They can be in standard or nonstandard form. Math sentences in nonstandard form can be rewritten in standard form by using knowledge of the meanings of the operations. The "a" category in Box 5.1 gives open direct math sentences; the "b" category gives open math sentences in standard form. I usually refer to any type of math sentence as an "open math sentence" or simply as a "math sentence."

You work with small groups or the whole class to introduce addition (later subtraction) sentences. You say, "There is a way to write math sentences for these problems. They are addition (subtraction) sentences." An example is given, and you model how to write and read the addition (subtraction) sentence. The class does several together. Particular attention is given to the correct reading of the symbols. You note that learners can use math sentences to help solve story problems if they wish. Some use math sentences with objects or counting; others continue solving problems using only counters or drawings and counting. During discussions, those who use math sentences are always given opportunities to explain what they have done, but those using only manipulatives also share their solutions. Discussions that stress connecting solutions reached with the help of manipulatives to solutions using math sentences help children grasp the meaning and usefulness of the latter and encourage them to write math sentences to solve problems.

Direct instruction lessons can also be used to introduce math sentences. Such lessons have been shown to be effective in helping first-grade children learn to use open math sentences that reflect the structure of the problem (Bebout, 1990).

Focus Lesson 5.1 describes a lesson in problem solving with compare problems. Note that in the lesson, the teacher, Ms. Lopez, gives priority to children's descriptions of how they solved the story problems. To internalize mathematical meanings, children need opportunities to communicate their thinking to others and to listen to classmates explain their thinking.

Focus Lesson 5.1. Ms. Lopez has a class of 28 first-grade pupils. She teaches either the whole class or small groups. She chooses children for small groups in order to make better observations than are possible with the total class or to provide challenge or special help. She plans so that different children frequently make up her groups. Today she has a group of 18 children who are able to solve joining and separating (take-away) problems and are ready to study comparing problems. She has asked each one to bring his or her math kit to the study tables at the back of the room. The routine is familiar to the children, so she begins with the first problem. Her problems usually include names of the children in the class, which delights them. The first problem is: Jill's mother bought red and green apples because some in her family like red apples and some like green apples. She bought 6 red apples and 4 green apples. Did she buy more red or more green apples? The children all say, "More red apples," so she asks, "How many more?" The children know they can use any method that will help them get an answer. Most get out counters, but some draw red and green apples using paper and crayons they have found in boxes on the tables. Ms. Lopez walks around and when a child raises his or her hand, Ms. Lopez has the child whisper the answer in her ear. She then gives the child other numbers to use in the apple problem.

When most of the children have finished solving the problem, she begins the discussion. Discussions are important to Ms. Lopez because she believes that children learn from one another, and she therefore stresses that children should listen to their classmates. Today she begins the discussion by asking Jill to tell the group how she figured out the answer. Jill replies that she drew 6 red apples and 4 green apples, but that didn't help much, so she drew a line from each green apple to each red apple, and she found she had 2 red apples left over. Ms. Lopez asks if anyone has a question, and Paul asks Jill why she drew the lines. Jill responds that the lines helped her figure out what it would be if they were the same, and then she could tell how many more were red. Ms. Lopez thanks Jill for her explanation and asks if anyone has a different way. Hiroshi says he used counters. He didn't have red and green buttons, so he used black buttons for the red apples and white buttons for the green apples. He counted out 4 white buttons. He put a black button beside each white button. He knew he had 4 red apples because there were 4 black buttons, and so he counted on—5, 6—to get 6 black buttons for the red apples. He looked, and he saw he had 2 more black buttons, which meant there were 2 more red apples. Ms. Lopez thanks Hiroshi for his report and asks the group if anyone had another way. Karen said she put out 6 buttons for red apples first, then 4 bottle caps for green apples beside the buttons. She then saw there were 2 more red apples. She said that her way was almost like Hiroshi's. Ms. Lopez thanks Karen

Reader Activity 5.1

Tell how Ms. Lopez incorporated the interactive method in her lesson. If possible, discuss your ideas with others.

and moves on to the next word problem, which is similar to the problem that required comparing red and green apples. After children have solved five comparing problems and discussed their solutions, Ms. Lopez concludes the lesson by saying, "You were thoughtful learners today. That makes all of us proud." Ms. Lopez notes that the children in the group modeled the problem with concrete materials and counted the objects. She decides that they need more experiences with comparing problems before they will use more mature problem-solving methods and plans to continue with these problems the next mathematics period.

Extending Problem Solving. Teachers plan their curriculum so that over time children will extend their problem-solving abilities. To achieve this objective, they note when children can solve problems with sums (minuends) to 10 or less by using modeling, and they help children achieve growth in: (1) solving story problems with fact sums (minuends) greater than 10; (2) using mature counting strategies; (3) studying more difficult story problems; and (4) posing story problems.

Solving story problems with sums (minuends) greater than 10. When children solve class problems, such as how many more boys than girls are in our class, they often encounter large numbers and use counting or materials to solve the problems. However, in beginning lessons with basic facts, the sums (minuends) are numbers less than 10. As soon as children are successful solving problems with sums (minuends) to 10, sums (minuends) to 18 are introduced. Facts are chosen at random, not introduced in any order, but all facts are introduced during problem-solving lessons.

Using mature counting strategies. Modeling a story problem with objects and counting all the objects to derive the answer is children's initial approach to solving problems. Later children use the counting word sequence without modeling, but some aids such as fingers may be used to keep tract of the count. Mature strategies for addition are to count on from the first addend and at a more advanced level to count on from the larger addend, even if it is not the first addend (Fennema et al., 1989).

Children who do not develop mature counting strategies independently can be helped to construct them through involvement in experiences you plan (Secada, Fuson, and Hall, 1983). The experiences include observing a classmate or you model the strategy, participating with you in the use of a strategy, or responding to your prompts.

Studying more difficult story problems. The study of addition and subtraction story problems begins with the easiest types, joining and separating with the result unknown and combine with the whole unknown (Box 5.1). Find-change, find-part, and compare or equalize problems are of medium difficulty. Find-start problems are the most difficult (Carpenter et al., 1990). When children can solve the type of problem selected for study, a more difficult type is introduced. Children learn to solve all types of story problems by devising their own strategies when presented with a new problem type, internalizing ideas presented when other children explain their solutions, or participating with others in group problem solving.

Reader Activity 5.2

Write eight story problems, two each for addition find-change and find-start, subtraction compare, and equalize problems.

Posing story problems. Posing story problems for basic facts helps learners think about the meanings of the facts. Children are asked to pose a story problem that would be solved by a fact you provide, for example, $5 + 3 = 8$ or $8 - 5 = 3$. They should share their problems.

Studying Part–Part–Whole Relations Using Sets to Learn Addition and Subtraction

Children who have had experiences with part–part–whole ideas as they worked with sets of objects and engaged in activities to learn part–part–whole relations (Chapter Three) can construct the meanings of addition and subtraction by building on their prior knowledge. They have examined the subsets of many sets, formed sets consisting of two subsets, solved problems involving sets, and by reflecting on their work have attained an intuitive understanding of addition and subtraction. They next learn to use math sentences to communicate addition and subtraction meanings related to the part–part–whole ideas they developed working with sets. If children lack experiences with sets to develop part–part–whole ideas, instruction begins with Chapter Three activities for part–part–whole relations.

This section begins with Focus Lesson 5.2, which describes how Mr. James introduces math sentences for basic facts after learners have had experiences with problems involving sets.

Focus Lesson 5.2. Mr. James has a class of 24 pupils. He thinks that they are all ready to learn about math sentences. He tells the class they will need counters and paper and pencils for their activity this morning. He then explains that to begin he will ask a question and the children can use their counters or think to find the answer. The first question he asks is, "I am thinking of a number that you can show with 3 red counters and 1 blue counter. What is my number?" The children all say, "4," and Mr. James asks them to tell how they found the answer. There are various replies such as: I know 1 up from 3 is 4, I used counters and saw it was 4, and I know 3 and 1 is 4. Mr. James then says to the children, "There is a way to write 3 and 1 is 4 as a math sentence. Numbers tell what we do with counters. Please watch what I am writing. (He writes $3 + 1 = 4$.) We read the math sentence, 3 plus 1 equals 4. Three plus 1 equals 4 is an addition fact. Please read it with me. (Pupils read the fact.) What does an addition fact tell about the counters? Now you are ready to write addition facts. You know how to write the numbers. Watch how I make the plus and equals signs." The class discusses how these symbols are formed before each child writes his or her own sentence, $3 + 1 = 4$. The activity continues with children finding answers to teacher-posed questions, writing the number facts on their individual chalkboards, and showing their work and reading the addition facts. Mr. James uses the words "addition fact" whenever possible and encourages children to do so also.

The next day, after a review of the previous day's lesson, the children are shown how to make "boxes" to stand for missing numbers. Mr. James explains that these math sentences can be called fact or math questions and asks the children to write some math questions with sums 9 or less. He then shows the children how to write fact answers in the boxes. Next they work in pairs, taking turns choosing addition fact questions to write on their individual chalkboards, together finding answers using various strategies, and each writing the answers in the boxes in his or her math sentences.

After an introduction to math sentences, children engage in activities that require representing object arrangements as math sentences and math sentences as object arrangements. The following activities give children experiences relating fact representations to math sentences. Other activities would deal with story problems. After completing the activities, learners discuss their work and the meanings they have constructed.

ACTIVITY 5.1
Subtraction Facts.

Have children work in pairs. Give one child in each pair 5 crayons. Say, "Please give 2 of your crayons to your partner. How many do you have left?" Repeat with 3, 4, and 1 crayon given to the partner. Say, "What happened each time we started with 5 crayons?" (We gave some away.) Continue, "We can make math sentences called subtraction facts that tell about taking away. You just took 1 crayon from 5 crayons. We write the subtraction fact this way, $5 - 1 = 4$, and we read it, "Five minus 1 equals 4. What does this subtraction fact tell us? Let's make other subtraction facts for 5. How would we write a subtraction fact for taking 3 crayons from 5?" The activity continues with pupils modeling subtraction facts for other numbers and reading and writing the math sentences.

ACTIVITY 5.2
See My Fact Picture.

Have children in groups take cards from a bag. On each card is an addition fact or subtraction fact question written on it. Each child draws a picture to find the answer. This procedure continues until children have drawn several cards and made their pictures. The activity ends with children sharing the fact questions and their drawings in a class discussion.

Variation: Ask children to work in pairs, each taking a question card from a bag, drawing a picture to show the fact, and discussing with each other how their pictures give answers to the fact questions.

ACTIVITY 5.3
Many Ways.

Ask children to take 5 counters, some of one shape, the rest of a different shape. Each child shows a fact with the counters and writes the fact represented. Ask several pupils to use materials and write their fact on the overhead to show their work. Ask the class to tell what they notice. Their responses should explain that different counter arrangements and different sentences all tell the facts of 5. Other numbers 9 or less are used, some chosen by the children, and the same procedure is followed. The children summarize the lesson by noting there are different addition facts for numbers to 9.

ACTIVITY 5.4
Facts with Five- and Ten-Frames.

Flexer (1986) stresses the importance of developing the meanings of addition and subtraction facts using five- and ten-frames. She points out that visually relating facts to 5 and 10 enhances both understanding and memory.

For this activity, use an overhead with a five- or a ten-frame transparency. (See Appendix G for patterns for five- and ten-frames.) Arrange disks in the five- or ten-frame (Figure 5.3) to show different facts. Ask children to model your actions using

FIGURE 5.3 Basic Facts with Five- and Ten-Frames

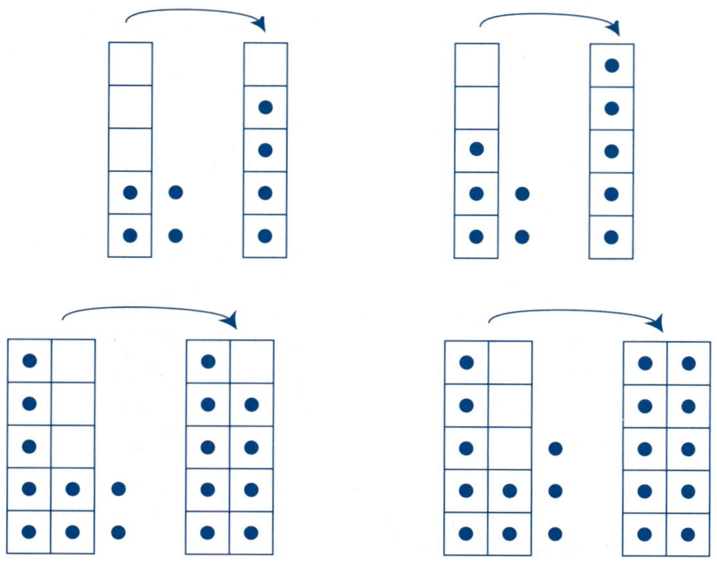

their own frames made of plastic or cardboard. Have children tell what their frames show and write the math sentences that go with the representations. As each fact is discussed, ask questions to help pupils think how the fact compares to 5 or 10. For example, ask, "How does showing 4 + 3 = 7 on the five-frame help to think the fact?"

After writing facts you show in the frames on the overhead, children write facts, often of their own choosing, show their facts with disks on their frames, and explain the meaning of their arrangements using the overhead. Continue to ask questions to emphasize the anchors five and ten.

ACTIVITY 5.5
Addition Fact Books.

Children use number bars to show all the basic facts for a given sum, record what they did with bars on a sheet of grid paper (Figure 5.4), and write the number facts that correspond to their illustrations on the grid paper. (Appendix G gives patterns for grid paper.) They choose the numbers to use, but over time children should use all the sums from 1 to 18. They then arrange the sheets of grid paper in the order of the sums and make a book illustrating the facts. They can tell about their drawings and read their books to one another or to children in another grade. When the books are taken home, children can read them to a parent, caretaker, or sibling.

Variations: Children can make drawings for facts rather than use grid paper. Children can make subtraction fact books.

ACTIVITY 5.6
Number Lines.

Make a walk-on number line by marking a wide strip of heavy cloth with segments 6 inches apart. Write numerals from 0 to 10 at the end of the segments. Fasten the cloth strip to the classroom floor or a surface outdoors. Small groups, working with an aide, take turns walking on the cloth strip to show numbers. For example, they take two steps, from 0 to 2, to show the number 2. Children later can show basic facts on the walk-on number line.

After children understand how to use the walk-on number line, paper-and-pencil number lines are introduced to show facts. (Appendix G gives a pattern for number lines.) Tell them that numbers can be shown on a paper-and-pencil number line by using loops for steps. Model this, and then ask children to think how a fact could be shown on a paper-and-pencil number line. After they report their ideas and the representation is clarified, they show different facts on number lines (Figure 5.5).

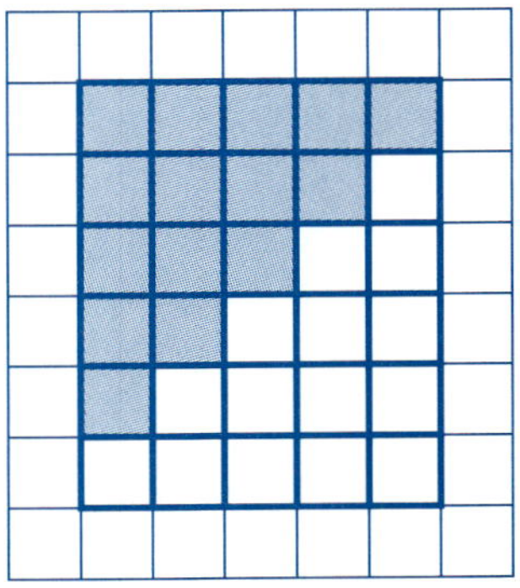

5 + 0 = 5
4 + 1 = 5
3 + 2 = 5
2 + 3 = 5
1 + 4 = 5
0 + 5 = 5

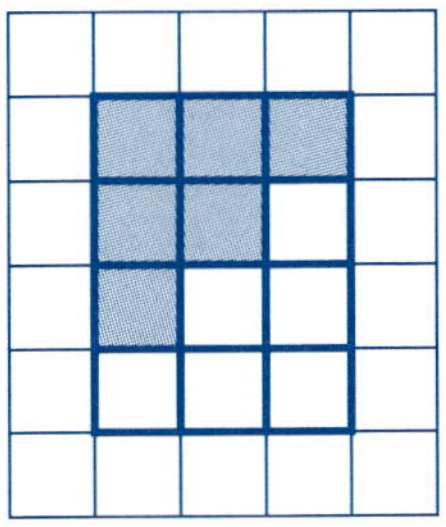

3 + 0 = 3
2 + 1 = 3
1 + 2 = 3
0 + 3 = 3

FIGURE 5.4 Addition Basic Facts Shown on Grid Paper

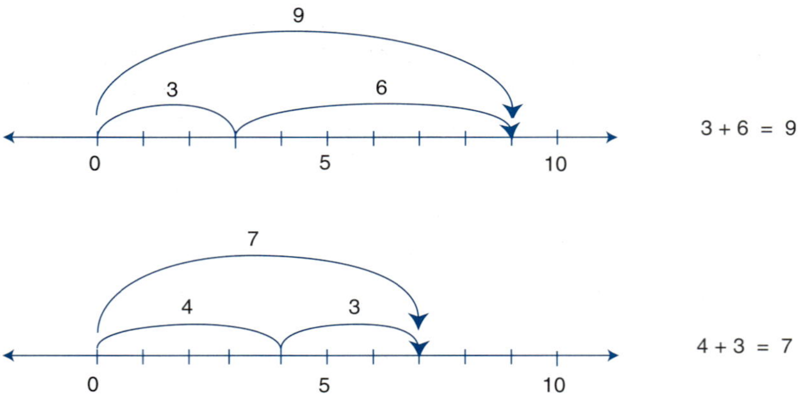

FIGURE 5.5 Addition Basic Facts Shown on Number Lines

Extending Ideas about Addition and Subtraction

Extending activities are used with children who have worked with story problems or with part–part–whole problems to develop ideas of addition and subtraction, can write open math sentences for join and separate problems (find-result) and for combine problems (find-whole), and can use modeling and counting to solve one or more of the other types of problems: find-part, find-change, find-start, compare (three types), and equalize (two types). The first seven activities that follow deal with learning to write open math sentences for find-part, find-change, find-start, compare, or equalize problems. Before introducing open math sentences for these problems, make certain that children can solve the problem by using objects. The last activities introduce relations that help learners remember the facts.

The objective of learning to write open math sentences for all types of problems is to enable learners to connect the structure of a problem to a math sentence that reflects this structure. They continue to solve problems by modeling and counting, counting, or thinking basic facts. In the primary grades, children are not taught to write math sentences in standard form when the structure of the problem would be reflected in a sentence in nonstandard form. On their own, however, some children will write math sentences in standard form (Carpenter et al., 1990). In grades four or above, when children are working with large numbers, rewriting math sentences in standard form can be emphasized to help learners solve math sentences in nonstandard form.

If children are unable to write direct math sentences for change, start, compare, and equalize problems, delay work with the sentences for these problems until children are not frustrated by the task. It may be that children will not be able to write the direct math sentences until they are in a higher grade. Have them continue to use trial and error, counting, and modeling to solve the problems.

The activities that introduce open math sentences in nonstandard form use part–part–whole questions. You should also pose story problems for change, start, compare, and equalize problems. An example of a start story problem is:

I took 7 candies from my bag of candies. Then I had 4 in my bag. How many were in my bag before I took some away?

ACTIVITY 5.7
Missing Number Sentences.

Have children find the mystery numbers in find-change problems any way they wish. Say, "I have 4 cubes. I put a mystery number of cubes with the 4. Now I have 6 cubes. What is my mystery number?" Ask several children to tell how they found that 2 was the mystery number. Then say, "We can write a math sentence for that mystery number question. How could we do that?" Give learners opportunities to answer this question. If no child has an idea, while writing on the overhead or chalkboard, say, "It is: 4 + □ = 6. How do you think we could read it?" Accept any correct reading, but introduce other possibilities as: 4 plus some number equals 6, or 4 plus a missing number equals 6. Continue the activity, and for each question ask pupils how to write the math sentence. Write it as dictated, and have pupils read it. Help pupils recognize any math sentence that does not represent the problem. Children solve each problem using their counters and share their thinking and solution. As soon as children are ready to write their own math sentences, have them do so on their individual chalkboards. Later, ask subtraction questions such as: "I had 7 cubes and dropped some. I had only 5 left. I picked up the cubes I dropped. How many did I pick up?" Introduce math sentences such as 7 − □ = 5.

ACTIVITY 5.8
The Starting Number.

Say, "I am thinking of a starting number of cubes. I put 3 cubes with my starting number. Then I had 7. What is my starting number?" After children find the number and explain their thinking, say, "We can write a math sentence for a starting number question. How would we do that? Yes, it is □ + 3 = 7. How would we read it?" (If no child relates this activity to the *Missing Number Sentences Activity,* ask what comes first and in each position thereafter. It may be necessary to remind children that the starting number is the missing number.) Continue with other start-number questions. Children give the math sentence for each question, and one or more children write it on the chalkboard or overhead. The children read the sentence, use their counters to answer the question, and explain their solutions. When they understand writing math sentences for start-number questions, children write the direct math sentences on their individual chalkboards. If some learners can pose missing number questions for others in the class to solve, have them do so.

Also ask questions such as: "If I take 3 cubes from my mystery number, I will have 6. What is my mystery number?" Learners can be introduced to these math sentences (e.g., □ − 3 = 6), find solutions, and share their work.

ACTIVITY 5.9
Make Equal.

Give a problem such as: There are 7cubes in a red box. There are 4 cubes in a blue box. How many are needed in the blue box so the number of cubes in the two boxes will be the same? After children solve the problem, have them discuss their approaches to find the solution. When children mention joining cubes to the 4 cubes in the blue box to make 7 in that box, ask the class to think about a math sentence that represents the problem (4 + □ = 7). Have them explain how the math sentence connects to the problem. Continue with other equalizing (find increase) problems and related math sentences in this or other lessons. When children understand writing math sentences for equalizing problems, they write their own math sentences before they solve equalizing problems. They find solutions any way they wish and discuss their solutions and the math sentences they have written. Later math sentences for find-decrease equalizing problems can be introduced using a similar approach.

ACTIVITY 5.10
Activity Card Sentences.

Give each child a set of activity cards—numeral cards from 0 to 10, cards for math symbols, and one card displaying a box (□) (Figure 5.6). Ask fact questions with the result, change, or start unknown, and have children use their activity cards to make

FIGURE 5.6 Set of Activity Cards

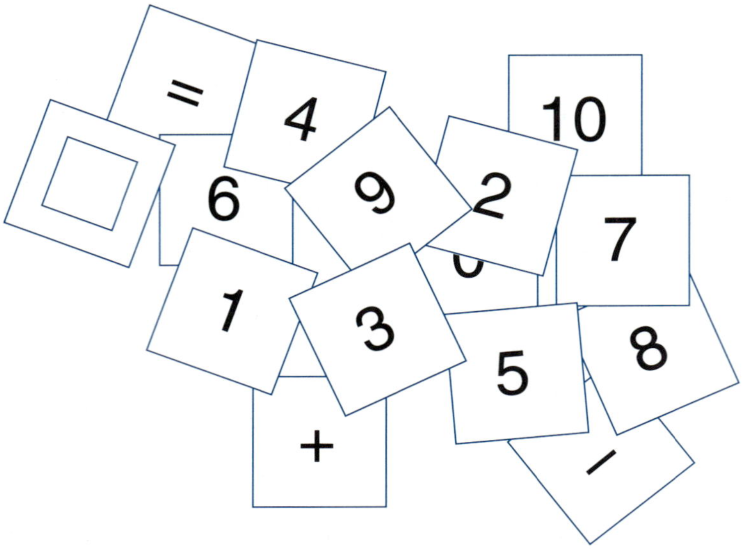

open math sentences for the questions. Children can find answers using counters, counting strategies, or thinking the fact. After each fact question is answered, they discuss their work.

ACTIVITY 5.11
Change One or Two.

This activity helps children write math sentences using the idea of one or two more. Ask questions such as: "How much greater is 7 than 6? Eight is how much greater than 6? What number is 5 less than 7?" Have children find the answers any way they choose and write math sentences for your questions (e.g., 7 = 6 + □). Ask prompting questions, if necessary, such as: "What did you do with your counters? What did you do first? How would we write that? How did you continue? How would we put that idea in a sentence?" When a sentence is written, have several children explain its meaning. Continue with other compare questions, and give time for discussion so that children can communicate how they connect work with counters to math sentences.

ACTIVITY 5.12
Increase or Decrease.

Ask questions such as: "If 9 is increased by 2, what is the new number? If I increase a number by 5 and the result is 11, what is the starting number? What number is 14 decreased by 7?" Children solve the problems in their own ways and are helped to connect their methods to math sentences (e.g., 9 + 2 = □; □ + 5 = 11; 14 – 7 = □).

ACTIVITY 5.13
Hide-a-Number Cards.

Make (or have aides make) sets of Hide-a-Number cards, using the easy subtraction facts with differences to 9, but excluding those with subtrahends 0 or 1 (Figure 5.7). Two children use the cards and a set of activity cards. The two work together, one child finding the number of objects on a card and covering a set (hiding a number).

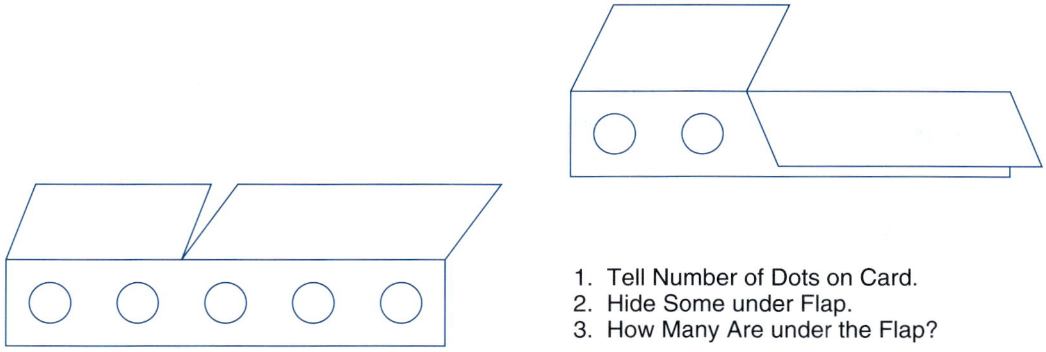

FIGURE 5.7 Hide-a-Number Cards

The other child says the fact represented and shows the fact with the activity cards. The two exchange tasks, continuing to take turns until all Hide-a-Number cards in a set have been used. Later minuends to 18 are used in cards. (If learners have not been introduced to math sentences for such problems, the Hide-a-Number cards can be used without activity cards.)

The remaining activities help learners understand the commutative property of addition, develop an awareness of inverse operations, and develop an intuitive notion of the making-10 strategy to recall facts. Some children become aware of these ideas without your guidance. While working on tasks, if a child tells you about his or her discovery, have the child tell the class what he or she has noticed. All the children test the idea using facts of their own choosing and discuss their findings. You can name the idea in the course of the discussion. If no one makes a discovery, use activities such as the following to bring extending ideas to pupils' attention.

ACTIVITY 5.14
Discover the Addition Order Rule (Commutative Property of Addition).

The addition order rule (commutative property of addition) is: The order of the addends does not affect the sum. Ask children to solve four pairs of math sentences patterned after 3 + 2 = □ and 2 + 3 = □, choosing their own strategies for solution. Suggest that they will make a discovery as they complete the task. When they have completed their work, discuss the discovery. Have children use the overhead to explain the discovery. Call the discovery the "addition order rule." Children then use materials with other facts to learn more about the addition order rule. Ask if they can use the addition order rule with all the addition facts. Have them give the reasons for their replies.

ACTIVITY 5.15
Inverse Operations.

Ask children to write as many math sentences as they can using the numbers 3, 4, and 7 all at a time. Then have them solve the math sentences any way they wish. (The math sentences should be 3 + 4 = 7; 4 + 3 = 7; 7 − 3 = 4; and 7 − 4 = 3.) Have them share their work and how they thought to carry out the task. Have them write their sentences on the overhead as they share them. Ask, "What do you notice about what we have done?" Children will probably first notice examples of the addition order rule. They should then be questioned so that they notice the inverse relation of addition and subtraction and express their ideas by making comments such as: what we did was the opposite; addition and subtraction are backward; or you can get from addition to subtraction and from subtraction to addition. If they do not

Reader Activity 5.3

Use counters to model finding a missing number in addition and subtraction open math sentences in nonstandard form. Do you think that modeling could help children develop an intuitive understanding of transforming open math sentences in nonstandard form to open math sentences in standard form? Why or why not?

make remarks such as these, have them solve 3 + 4 = □ with counters, keep the counters on their desks, and then use the 7 counters to solve 7 – 4 = □. Repeat the "What do you notice?" question. They should notice that they began and ended with 3 counters, and they should be able to explain the idea of inverse operations. If children have not yet grasped this concept, do not continue with the activity. Repeat the lesson after pupils have had more experiences with all types of story problems and part–part–whole questions.

Knowing that addition and subtraction are inverse enables some children to solve open math sentences in nonstandard form. For example, they would reason that to find the missing number, 9, in □ – 4 = 5, you add, because 5 + 4 = □. Similarly to find the missing number, 5, to solve 4 + □ = 9 or □ + 4 = 9, you subtract, because 9 – 4 = 5.

ACTIVITY 5.16
Ten and More.

Use ten-frames for this activity. Ask children to show sums that are greater than 10 on their ten-frames, for example, 8 + 4 = □ (Figure 5.8). (The math sentences to choose from can be posted.) After they complete the task, say, "How did the ten-frame help you find the sums?" During the discussion, question children so that they are aware of thinking parts of the smaller addend, regrouping, and making 10 as steps to find the answer as a sum of 10 plus ones. For example, 8 + 4 = 8 + (2 + 2) = (8 + 2) + 2 = 10 + 2 = 12. The notation is not introduced to children, but by working with frames, they gain an intuitive understanding of the associative property of addition and learn the "making-tens" strategy for finding sums.

The learning experiences described in this section involve children in making translations among models for addition and subtraction basic facts, oral language, and math sentences. They are helped to understand the meanings of addition and subtraction facts in a variety of settings and to develop intuitive understanding of some relations among facts. Work with both story problems and sets enables children to construct concepts of addition and subtraction.

CONSTRUCTING THE CONCEPTS OF MULTIPLICATION AND DIVISION

Multiplication is an operation on two numbers, the factors, to obtain a third number, the product. Multiplication facts involve factors less than 10, for example, 3 (factor) × 2 (factor) = 6 (product). There are 100 multiplication facts (Figure 5.9).

Multiplication is interpreted in four ways: (1) as the joining of sets of equal size; (2) as repeated addition; (3) as a Cartesian product; and (4) as a ratio (Figure

FIGURE 5.8 Ten Frame for Facts with Sums Greater than 10

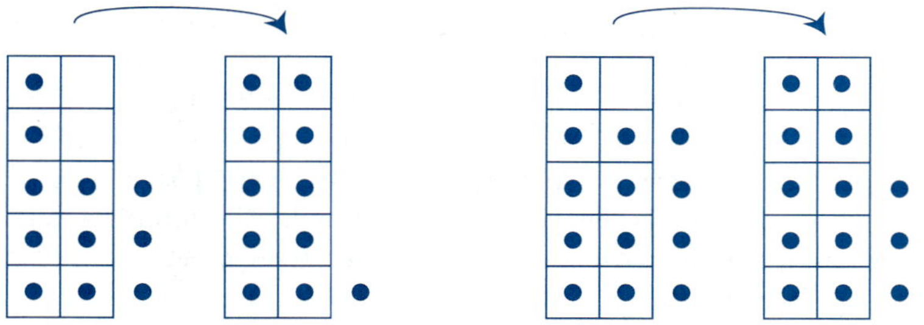

x	0	1	2	3	4	5	6	7	8	9
0	0	0	0	0	0	0	0	0	0	0
1	0	1	2	3	4	5	6	7	8	9
2	0	2	4	6	8	10	12	14	16	18
3	0	3	6	9	12	15	18	21	24	27
4	0	4	8	12	16	20	24	28	32	36
5	0	5	10	15	20	25	30	35	40	45
6	0	6	12	18	24	30	36	42	48	54
7	0	7	14	21	28	35	42	49	56	63
8	0	8	16	24	32	40	48	56	64	72
9	0	9	18	27	36	45	54	63	72	81

FIGURE 5.9 Multiplication Basic Facts

5.10). Story problems for these interpretations are given in Box 5.2. Beginning work emphasizes the first two meanings.

Division is the inverse of multiplication. (If $4 \times 5 = 20$, then $20 \div 5 = 4$ and $20 \div 4 = 5$.) Division can be thought of as finding a missing factor (How many fives equal 20? or How many fours equal 20?). This approach helps many children understand division.

There are 90 division facts because division by zero is not defined (Figure 5.9). The names for the numbers in a division sentence are dividend, divisor, and quotient. For example, 21 (dividend) ÷ 7 (divisor) = 3 (quotient). Division is interpreted in four ways: (1) as a measurement situation; (2) as repeated subtraction; (3) as a partitive situation; and (4) as a ratio (Figure 5.11 on page 144). Story problems for the various interpretations are given in Box 5.2.

Understanding division is more difficult than understanding addition, subtraction, and multiplication partly because situations arise in which the dividend is not a multiple of the divisor, and there is a remainder. Learning about division, therefore, involves understanding the interpretations of division and also how to deal with remainders, particularly in the context of story problems.

Constructing the concepts of multiplication and division involves working with story problems and sets of objects to develop the meaning of the operations, using the language of multiplication and division, and learning to read and write math sentences for multiplication and division facts.

Solving Story Problems to Learn Multiplication and Division

Initial work with story problems in kindergarten and grade 1 includes not only addition and subtraction problems but also multiplication and division story problems. However, most beginning work with multiplication and division story problems is in grades 2 and 3. Children begin solving joining-sets-of-equal-size multiplication problems and measurement- and partitive-type division problems by direct modeling with counting. For multiplication, children use counters or tallies to show the number in a group, continue with the number of groups designated, and then count the total number of objects. For *measurement-type* division problems, children generally lay out the number of objects given, then separate them by size of the group, and finally count the number of groups. However, some children lay out groups of the given size, count the total, and stop when the given total is reached. The number of groups is then counted. For *partitive-type* division problems, children often use a dealing strategy (one to each group specified in the problem). Another strategy is to guess and check, putting what they think will be in each pile and counting the total. Then they adjust until the required total is obtained (Carpenter et al., 1990).

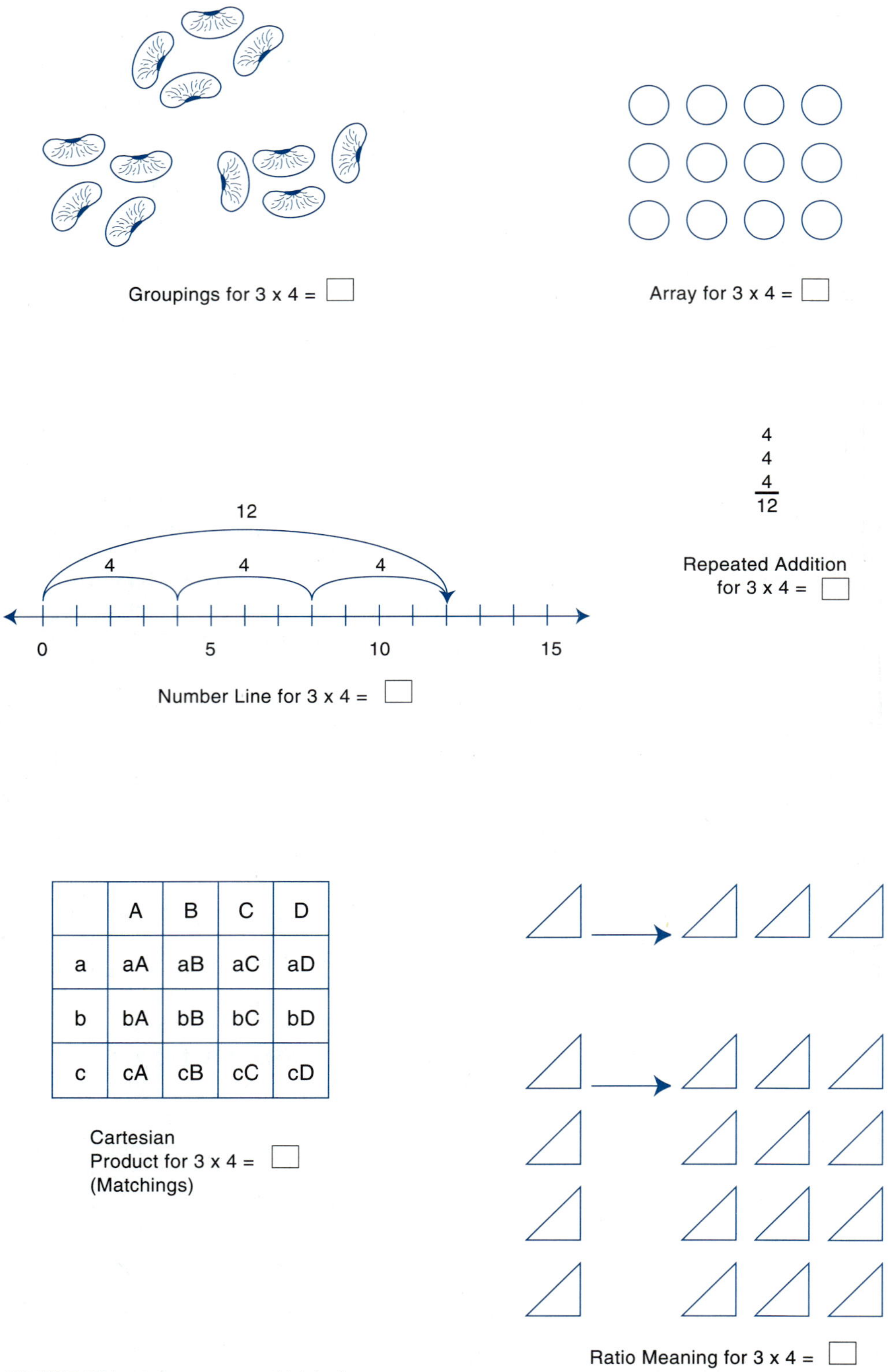

FIGURE 5.10 Interpretations of Multiplication

Multiple or skip-counting often follows direct modeling for multiplication and measurement type division problems. To solve a problem using this strategy, children count by multiples, such as 3, 6, 9 . . . , keeping track of the groups by some means such as using fingers or shaking their head. If children cannot skip-count, they must combine counting by ones with counting the number of groups.

Some children use repeated addition (subtraction) to solve multiplication (division) problems, giving the partial sums (differences) until the solution is reached,

BOX 5.2 Classification of Story Problems for Multiplication and Division with Examples

MULTIPLICATION

1. *Joining-sets-of-equal-size interpretation*
   Jake went rock collecting for 3 days. He found 4 rocks each day. How many rocks did he find? $3 \times 4 = \square$
2. *Repeated addition interpretation*
   (Relates joining sets of equal size to addition.)
   Carmen found 5 rocks each day for 3 days. How many rocks did she collect? $5 + 5 + 5 = \square$
3. *Cartesian product interpretation*
   At the ice cream store Hanna can get 3 flavors, strawberry, vanilla, and chocolate. How many different two-scoop cones can she get? $3 \times 2 = \square$
4. *Ratio (how-many-times comparison) interpretation*
   Papa caught 2 fish. Alfonso caught 4 times as many. How many did Alfonso catch? $4 \times 2 = \square$ $2 / 1 = \square / 4$

DIVISION

1. *Measurement interpretation*
   Leo had 10 pieces of paper to pass out. He was to give 2 pieces to each child. How many children got paper? (How many twos equal 10?) $10 \div 2 = \square$
2. *Repeated subtraction interpretation*
   (Relates measurement interpretation to subtraction.)
   Sally had 16 candies. She gave 8 to each friend. How many friends got candies?
   $$\begin{array}{rl} 16 & \\ -\underline{8} & 1 \\ 8 & \\ -\underline{8} & 2 \\ 0 & \end{array}$$
3. *Partitive interpretation*
   Leo had 10 pieces of paper to give to 5 children. Each child was to get the same number of pieces. How many pieces did each child get? (How many is 10 shared equally among 5?) $10 \div 5 = \square$
4. *Ratio interpretation*
   Fred is 10 years old. Jim is 5. How many times older is Fred than Jim? $10 / 5 = \square / 1$

and finding the total (or number of groups). As this approach does not lend itself to solving partitive-type division problems, children use other methods for these problems.

Children learn to solve problems of all the types described in Box 5.2, beginning with joining-sets-of-equal-size multiplication and measurement- and partitive-type division problems. At first, easy products with factors to 5 are introduced. Later factors to 9 are used in the story problems. A Cartesian product interpretation can be used in some problems to extend pupils' understanding. Ratio problems are introduced in grade 5 or 6, but intuitive experiences with how-many-times comparisons can be introduced earlier.

When children can solve multiplication story problems using counters, tallies, or repeated addition, math sentences are introduced for multiplication facts. You can introduce multiplication math sentences by saying, "We can show what we have done using multiplication math sentences." Have children show a multiplication situation (e.g., 3 fours) with materials. You then model how to write the sentence for the assigned fact ($3 \times 4 = 12$). Introduce the math sentence together with the standard reading of the multiplication fact (e.g., three times four equals twelve, or three fours equals twelve), and ask the children to read and write the fact. Continue the activity with other facts.

When children have had time to develop skill in reading and writing multiplication facts and can solve division story problems, introduce math sentences for division facts in a lesson sequence similar to that for multiplication facts. Emphasize that a division fact can convey the measurement (find number of equal-sized groups) or partitive (share equally) meaning.

Children continue to solve story problems to understand multiplication and division. Lessons include problems involving both multiplication and division facts and sometimes addition and subtraction facts. Learners use materials to find solutions and write math sentences for the problems. They work individually and

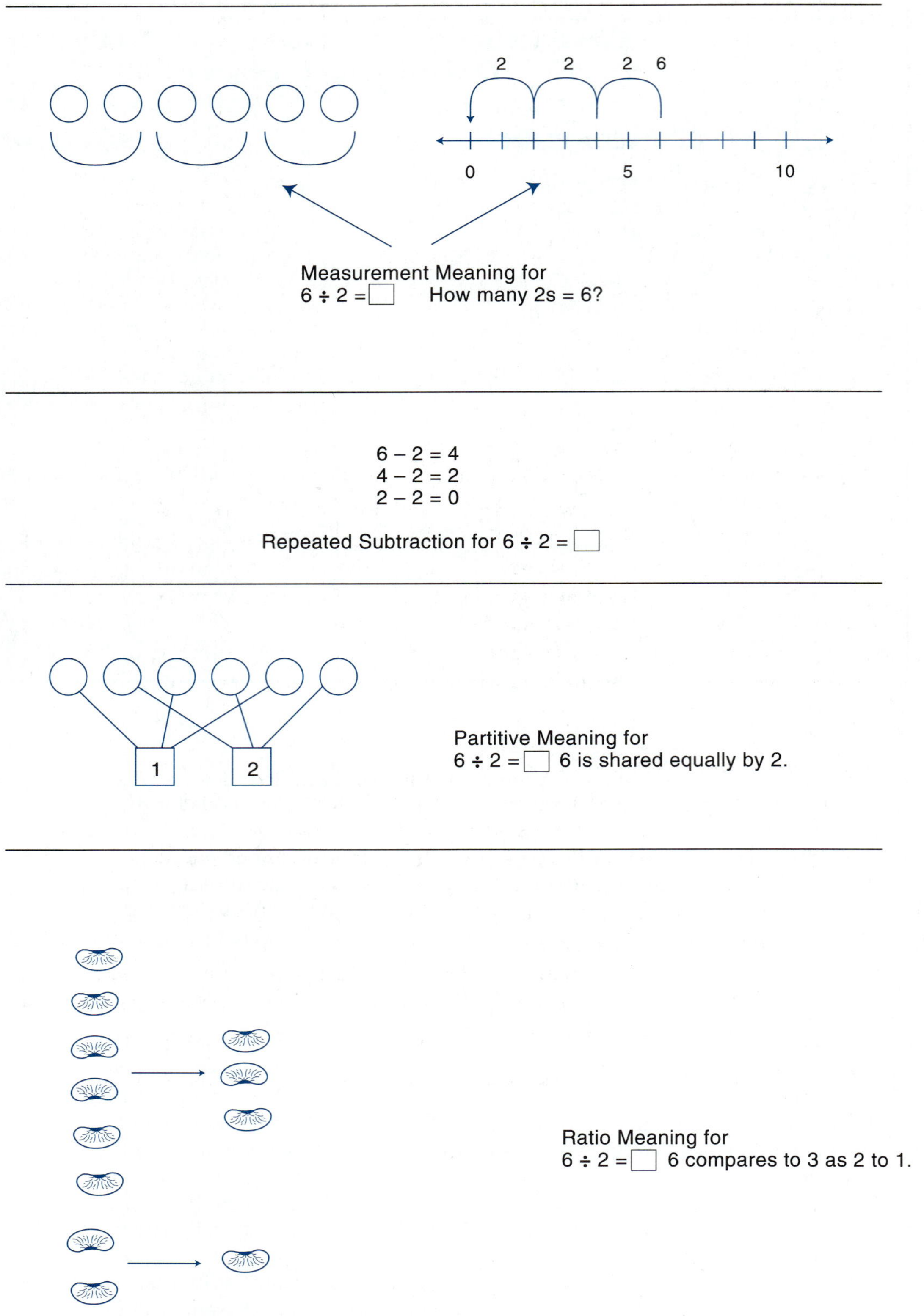

FIGURE 5.11 Interpretations of Division

in groups and frequently share their thinking about the problems and their solutions.

Children are often asked to make up story problems whose solutions are found using multiplication or division facts. You or they can choose multiplication or division facts to use in posing problems. They should share their problems and tell the fact related to each problem.

Using Sets to Learn Multiplication and Division

Assigning activities that make use of sets of objects to study multiplication and division followed by a discussion of the experience is another approach to teaching the meanings of multiplication and division. The activities often involve problem solving.

The activities described here begin with a review of experiences that enable children to use materials to represent the multiplicative structure of a number. (Similar activities with this objective were described in Chapter Three; e.g., Activity 3.51, *Ways to Show Numbers*). Next, activities introduce math sentences. Children should have many opportunities to translate representations with objects or pictures to symbolic representations and symbolic representations to material representations. They also solve multiplication and division story problems and discuss their work to develop the concepts of multiplication and division.

Some activities provide intuitive experiences with the idea that multiplication and division are inverse operations. This is a unifying concept that helps children understand multiplication and division as well as remember facts.

ACTIVITY 5.17
Using Materials to Show Facts.

Give problems for children to solve individually. Problem would be similar to:

1. How many cubes would be in a train made of 4 groups of 2 cubes each?
2. How many blocks are 2 groups of 6 blocks each?
3. How many blocks would be in a tower built from 3 sets of 5 blocks each?
4. If a tower made of 12 linking cubes fell over in 3 equal pieces, how many cubes would be in each piece?
5. If 18 blocks are put in three equal groups, how many are in each group?

Materials available for children's use would include number bars (Figure 5.12), counters, and linking cubes. After children solve the problems, they share their work, explaining how they thought to solve the problems.

ACTIVITY 5.18
Think My Number Game.

Children play in pairs, taking turns giving each other answers to questions you pose to the class. One child gives his or her group's answer. Each player who has an-

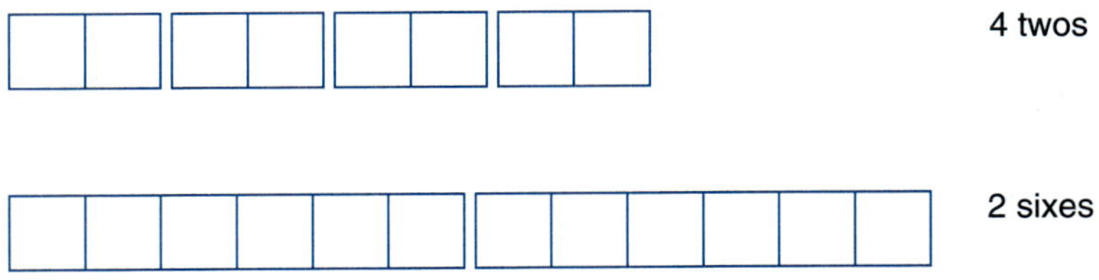

FIGURE 5.12 Number Bar Model for Multiplication

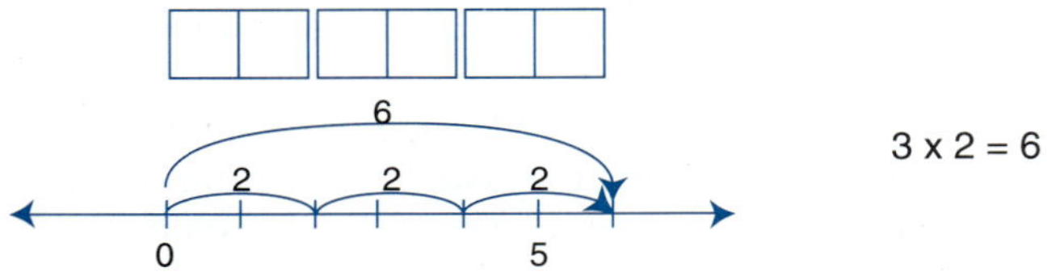

FIGURE 5.13 Multiplication and Number Lines

swered the question correctly makes a tally on his or her player card. (When the game is over, players with the most tallies are the winners.) Ask questions such as: "Add 2 three times. What is the number? How many times can you remove 3 from 6?" At the end of the game, pupils explain how they found answers. They should say that either repeated addition (repeated subtraction) or multiplication (division) can be used to answer the questions.

ACTIVITY 5.19
Multiplication and Number Lines.

After children have used number bars and worked with number lines for addition and subtraction, give each person a sheet of number lines with units the same length as the bars. Say, "We can show multiplication facts on the number line. First, let's show 3 twos with number bars. Now place the bars against the top number line, beginning with 0. Look at the bars, and think, 'If you took the bars away, how would you show 3 twos on the number line?'" Pupils discuss how to represent the fact on the number line and agree on the representation in Figure 5.13. The activity continues with the use of number lines for showing other multiplication facts. Later, number lines are used to show division meanings.

ACTIVITY 5.20
Arrays.

Display arrays (row-and-column arrangements of objects, see Figures 5.10 and 5.14), and ask what they show. Help children use language such as 4 fives to describe what is represented. Tell children that the arrangement is an "array." Then ask children to show multiplication facts by making arrays with counters or by outlining arrays on grid paper. How a completed array shows a division fact can also be examined. First, ask children to look at an array on the overhead and think a division fact. If they cannot do so, say, "How many are in this array? In each row? How many rows? What division fact can we make by looking at this array?" Then continue with other arrays on the overhead.

ACTIVITY 5.21
Sharing Pennies Equally.

Each group of two children has 50 play pennies, 25 for each child. The play pennies are packaged in plastic bags for easy storage and retrieval. Each group of two is also provided with 20 cards with problems, such as: two children shared 8 pennies equally. How many did each get? Use your pennies to show your answer. The cards are face down in the middle of the activity area, and the children take turns drawing the cards. Both children solve the problem and compare their answers (Figure 5.15). An answer sheet with pictures of pennies shared equally by children and keyed to letters on the cards can be provided so that pupils can check their solutions.

This activity should be varied to provide many opportunities to examine the partitive meaning of division. Suggestions for sharing groups equally include apples di-

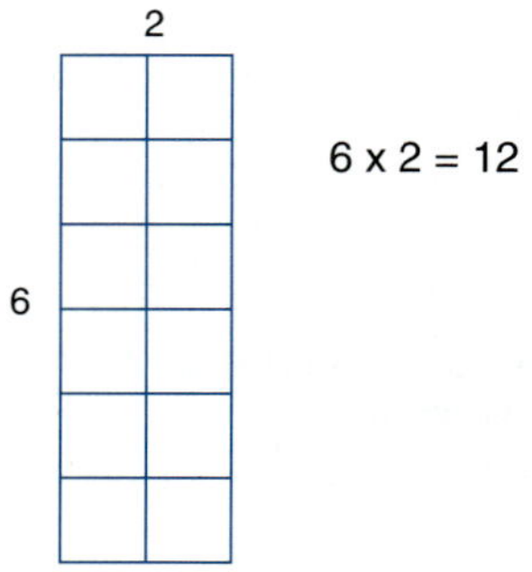

FIGURE 5.14 Multiplication with an Array

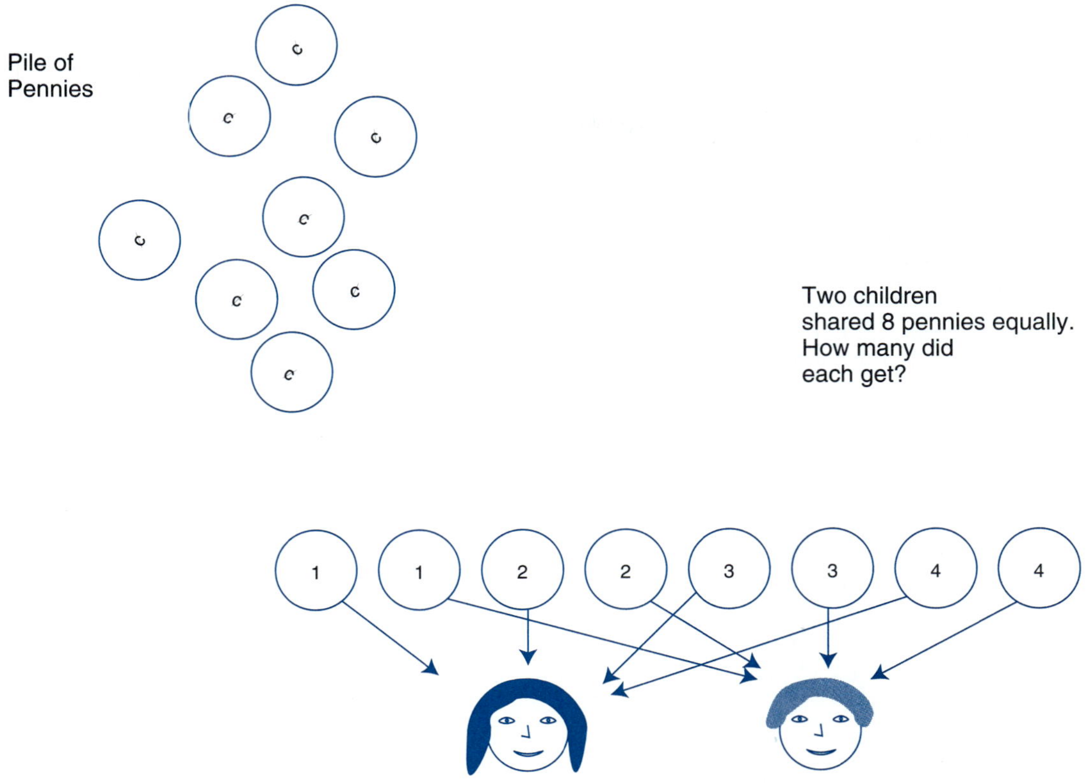

FIGURE 5.15 Sharing Pennies (Partitive Meaning of Division)

vided equally among a given number of bags, candies shared equally among a given number of children, pencils placed equally in boxes, and the same number of books placed on bookcase shelves.

ACTIVITY 5.22
Multiplication Facts on the Hundred Chart.

Supply each children with a sheet of one hundred squares. (At least four can be placed on a sheet.) Assign four multiplication facts, or ask children to choose four facts. Ask, "How can we show multiplication facts on our one hundred squares?" After a discussion clarifies the procedure, children write each fact and represent it on a hundred square by outlining and coloring groups on the square (Figure 5.16). Em-

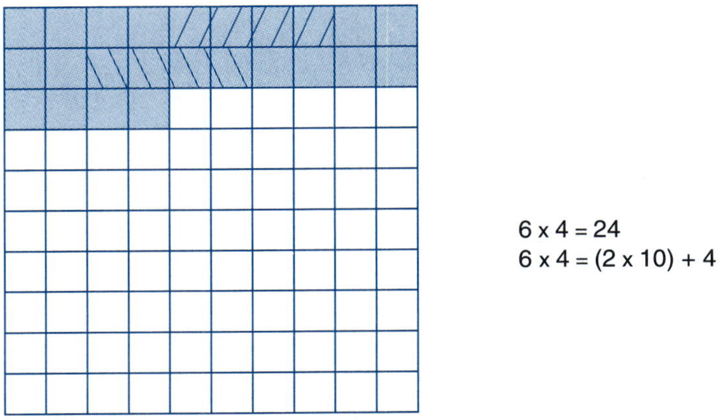

FIGURE 5.16 Multiplication Fact on the Hundred Square

phasize that different colors should be used for adjacent groups. Have children look at the hundred chart and discuss how it shows place-value answers for basic fact questions. For example, 6 fours equals 2 tens plus 4. Children can use the overhead, using colored pens on a hundred-square chart transparency, to explain their work to others.

ACTIVITY 5.23
Facts on the Abacus.

Ask children to use beans with a paper-and-pencil abacus to show multiplication facts. (Figure 5.17). Discuss how they might do this. As they are showing facts, question children so that they notice the renaming in terms of tens and ones. For example, as they show 3 fives, say, "Explain to us how you showed each 5." If necessary, ask. "What did you do when you got to 2 fives? Why?" (Took the 10 beans from the ones post and put 1 bean on the tens post.) "What did you do next? Why?" After showing a fact on the abacus, children should write the math sentence for the fact. They can use the overhead to explain their work, placing beans on a paper-and-pencil abacus drawn on a transparency.

As an extension of this activity, children can use the abacus to show division facts and then write the facts. For example, to show 15 ÷ 5, the child would need to show 15 as 15 ones, removing five three times.

ACTIVITY 5.24
Linking Cubes and Multiplication.

Have pupils show multiplication facts with groups of different colored linking cubes. Ask, "How can we show the place-value name for the product?" They should decide that 10 linking cubes can make a 10. The place-value name would be shown with tens and ones. (Figure 5.18).

ACTIVITY 5.25
Bulletin Board Displays.

Have groups of children make drawings of arrays and write math sentences to show facts whose products correspond to a number in each decade (i.e., facts with products 1–9, 10–19, 20–29, . . . , 70–79, 80–89). Each group will choose (or be assigned) one or more decades. For some numbers there will be more than one

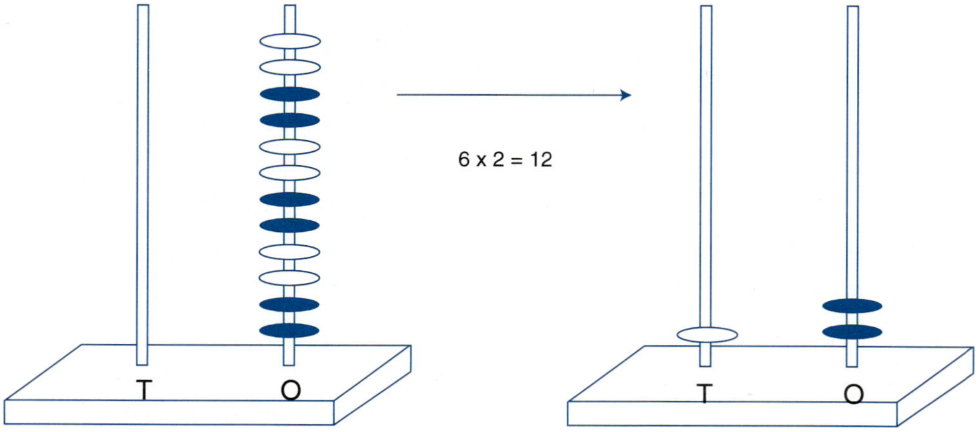

FIGURE 5.17 Multiplication Fact on the Abacus

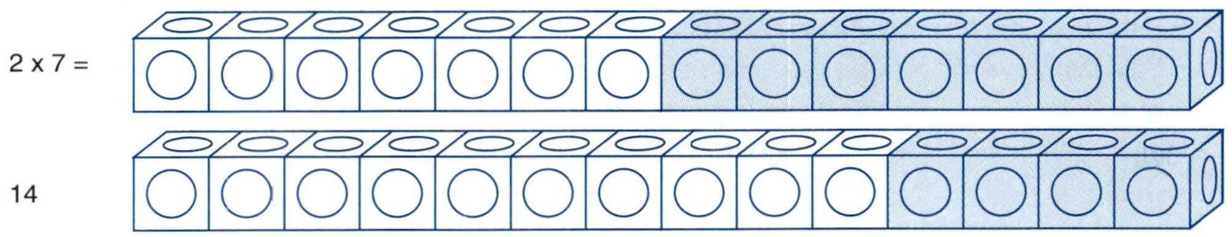

FIGURE 5.18 Multiplication Fact with Linking Cubes

multiplication fact (e.g., 2 × 6 = 12; 3 × 4 = 12). The commuted form for products should be given so that all facts are represented. After children have completed their drawings and math sentences, they can place their work on a bulletin board and discuss the facts in each decade.

ACTIVITY 5.26
Multiplication Fact Books.

Children can work in groups to make multiplication fact books. Groups can use a fact table (see Figure 5.9), or if possible, write their own tables. They write each multiplication fact in the table and represent it with drawings or arrays. (One sheet would be used to represent 5 to 10 facts.) Each group's pages of representations and math sentences are bound into a book. The books are kept in the class's book center or are shared with other classes. In some classes, each child may wish to make a fact book to take home.

Division fact books can be made using the same procedure. Drawings should illustrate both meanings of division. A page can show both the measurement and partitive meanings (e.g., 18 can mean how many threes equal 18 or what is the number in each group if 18 is divided equally among 3 groups).

ACTIVITY 5.27
Facts with Numeral Cards.

Prepare a pack of numeral cards for a group of children at a learning center. A pack for four children should contain 30 cards, 3 for each number 0 to 9. The pack is placed face down on the table. Each child is given a "times" card, an "equals sign" card, and a "box" card. Children work in pairs. Each child in a pair picks two numeral cards from the pack, makes a fact question, puts the cards on the bottom of the pack, and uses materials to show the fact. The two children in a pair then tell each other what they have done and decide if the multiplication fact has been shown correctly.

An extension of the activity is to ask children to give the division fact related to the multiplication fact shown. If they have not learned that division by zero is impossible, tell them they cannot use zero as a divisor. In some classes, a few students may be able to work with you, experimenting and reasoning to arrive at the conclusion that there is no number that, when used as a factor with zero, will give a nonzero number as the product and that therefore division by zero is not allowed.

ACTIVITY 5.28
Multiplication Order Rule (Commutative Property of Multiplication).

The multiplication order rule (commutative property of multiplication) is: The order of the factors does not affect the product. Ask children to give examples of the addition order rule. Then, have them form groups to answer the question, "Is there a multiplication order rule?" Groups should also decide how they can convince the class of the truth of the answer given by their group. After time for groups to complete the assignment, several groups tell how they answered the question and why they believe the answer is correct. Stress using materials to illustrate ideas (Figure 5.19). To conclude, ask how the multiplication order rule is similar to and different from the addition order rule.

ACTIVITY 5.29
Arrays and the Multiplication Order Rule.

Arrays can be used to help children understand the multiplication order rule. Have children use counters to make an array on the surface of a book. Say, "Turn the book carefully so it is sideways. Look at the array, and think what it shows after the turn" (Figure 5.20). Pupils share their ideas, explaining that turning the book sideways shows the multiplication order rule. To provide further examples, have them make arrays for facts of their own choosing to show the multiplication order rule. To begin, ask, "How can we make facts on grid paper to show the multiplication order rule?" (Use two arrays.) Discuss their ideas before they work with the grid paper.

ACTIVITY 5.30
Multiplication and Division Are Inverse Operations.

Ask children to write four math sentences using only the numbers 3, 6, and 18 all three at a time. Have them show the facts on number lines. (The facts will be $3 \times 6 = 18$; $6 \times 3 = 18$; $18 \div 6 = 3$; $18 \div 3 = 6$.) Then, ask, "What do you notice about your facts and how you showed them on the number lines?" Pupils' responses should make reference to the multiplication order rule but also to the inverse relation between multiplication and division, although children will use words such as "opposite" or "backward" rather than "inverse."

Activity 5.30 can build intuitive understanding for changing open math sentences in nonstandard form to math sentences in standard form. If no student discovers how to solve math sentences with missing factors or missing dividends by using inverse operation ideas (e.g., $4 \times \square = 20$ has the same solution as $20 \div 4 = \square$ and $\square \div 4 = 5$ has the same solution as $5 \times 4 = \square$), question them about how they could solve such math sentences. Looking at arrays to think both multiplication and division facts may help them discover the relations between the operations and the math sentences.

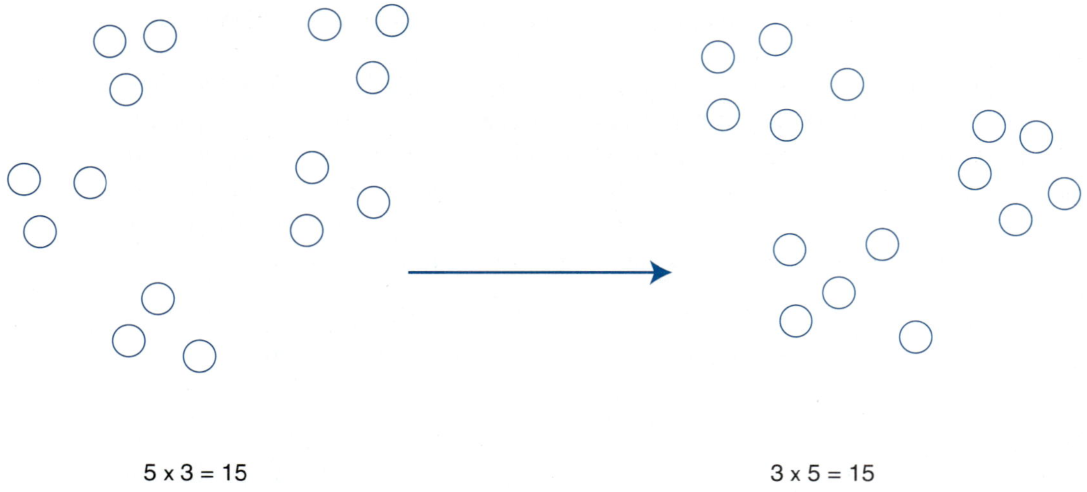

FIGURE 5.19 Counters Showing the Order Rule for Multiplication

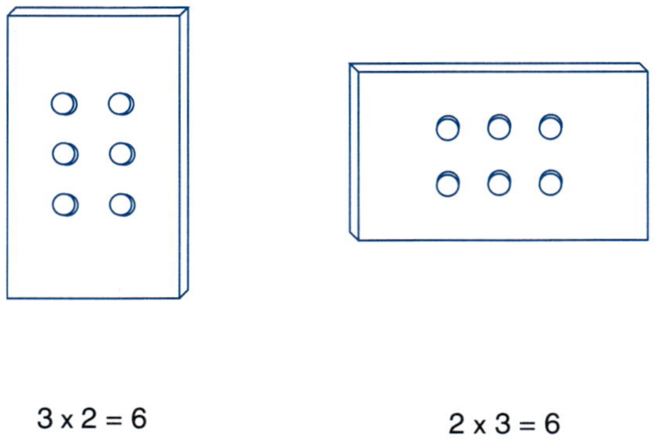

FIGURE 5.20 An Array Showing the Order Rule for Multiplication

ACTIVITY 5.31
Facts and Number Lines.

Children work in pairs. Each child selects a fact from a multiplication fact table and shows it on the number line. The children explain one another's representation, tell the related division fact, and say how it is represented on the number line.

Number lines can also be used to show the multiplication order rule. Children can work in pairs, one showing the fact and the other child its commuted form.

ACTIVITY 5.32
Using Calculators.

Have children give multiplication or division questions. Say, "In what different ways can we use our calculators to find the answers?" Their responses should bring out the use of repeated addition or subtraction on the calculator to find products or quotients.

ACTIVITY 5.33
Even and Odd.

Ask children in pairs to use sets of 2 counters or number-2 bars to show all the numbers they can to 20 (Figure 5.21). Have them save their work. Ask them to write the numerals for the numbers they represented. After individuals or groups have completed the task, discuss what they notice about the numbers they represented. The discussion should bring out that: (1) these are the numbers we say when counting by twos; (2) there is a pattern to the ending numbers (ones): 2, 4, 6, 8, 0; and (3) each number is divisible by 2. Tell them these numbers are called "even" numbers. Have the class decide why they are called even numbers. Give every child a chance to name an even number to 100.

Ask them what numbers they did not show with the counters. Have them use counters to show these numbers, and discuss how the representations differ from the even numbers. They should notice that these representations do not come out "even."

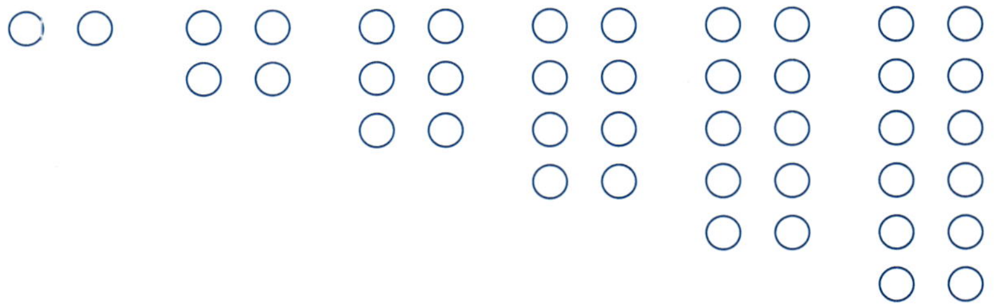

FIGURE 5.21 Counters Showing Even Numbers 2 to 12

Tell the children these are called "odd" numbers. Have children name odd numbers to 100. Ask how they knew what to say.

ACTIVITY 5.34
Even and Odd Numbers on the Calculator.

Have children in groups decide how they would show even and odd numbers on the calculator. Suggest they find more than one way. Have them discuss their solutions to this problem.

ACTIVITY 5.35
Simon Says, "Even Numbers."

Play Simon Says, "Even Numbers" for fun. "IT" names even and odd numbers; players' fingers go up on even numbers. No child should be "out" if he or she puts fingers up on odd numbers. Each child should see whether he or she makes a mistake. The game can also be played with odd numbers.

Extending Ideas about Multiplication and Division

Extending activities enable children to study the distributive property for multiplication over addition, the Cartesian product and ratio meanings of multiplication, and the notion that in some divisions there is a remainder. Many children will have discovered these ideas on their own. For these children, the activities enrich their understanding. For those who have not discovered these relations, the activities develop awareness of the ideas.

ACTIVITY 5.36
Cutting Arrays.

Give a group of children several sheets of grid paper. Ask children individually to make arrays for facts of their own choosing, write the fact, then cut each array into two parts along any top-to-bottom line, and write the facts for the two new arrays formed by cutting the original array. Ask them to look for an interesting discovery (Figure 5.22). Have them discuss their discovery. Help pupils realize that the number of objects in a row of the large array is the sum of the number of objects in corresponding rows of the two smaller arrays. Ask children questions to emphasize the distributive property ($a \times (b + c) = (a \times b) + (a \times c)$). If children do not report in their

FIGURE 5.22 Arrays Showing the Distributive Property of Multiplication over Addition

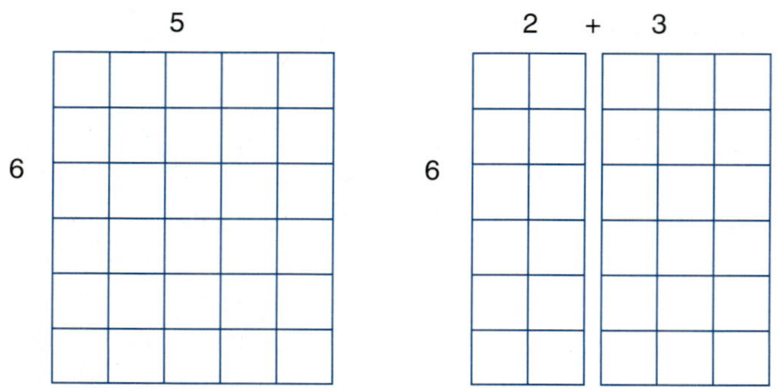

$6 \times 5 = 6\,(2 + 3) = (6 \times 2) + (6 \times 3)$

own words their discovery of the distributive property ("You can think of one factor as a sum and use each addend as a factor with the other factor; add the two sums to get the product"), ask questions that will enable them to grasp this idea. For example, say, "How can you make the multiplication fact in the large array from the two smaller arrays that you had after you cut the large array?" The discovery can be called the think-the-parts rule. Stressing thinking in this activity; do not have pupils write the math sentences.

Continue by having pupils decide how arrays can be used with different multiplication facts to show the think-the-parts rule and then test their ideas by making arrays.

ACTIVITY 5.37 *Combinations.*

Pose a problem that involves the Cartesian product interpretation of multiplication: Ruben likes three ice cream flavors, chocolate, vanilla, and bubble gum. If he can get three toppings at the ice cream store, nuts, candy, and butter crunch, how many sundaes can he get with one favorite flavor of ice cream and one kind of topping (Figure 5.23). Have children solve the problem individually or in groups and report

FIGURE 5.23 Ways to Show Combinations/Cartesian Product Interpretation of Multiplication

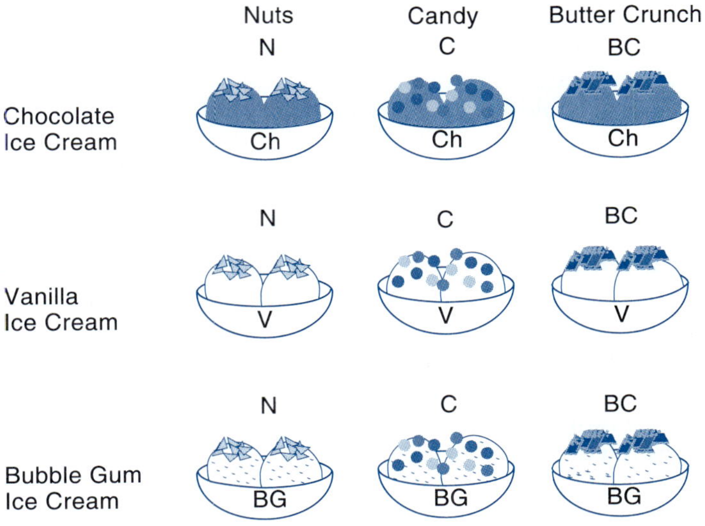

Pictures

	N	C	BC
Ch	Ch-N	Ch-C	Ch-BC
V	V-N	V-C	V-BC
BG	BG-N	BG-C	BG-BC

Matrix

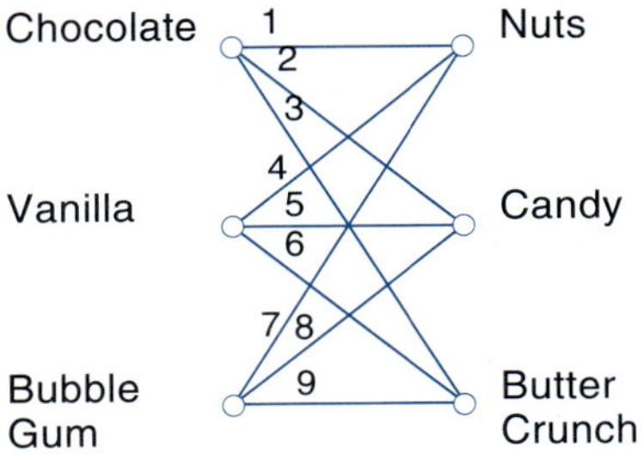

Matchings

their solutions. Ask them what they notice about their solutions. (They are multiplication facts.) Some students can make arrays to show why the solutions to problems of this type are multiplication facts.

Students can pose other combination problems and find the solutions (e.g., meats and vegetables; jeans and sweaters). Children might pose problems involving three categories (e.g., socks, shorts, and tops). Encourage interested learners to solve such problems.

ACTIVITY 5.38
How Many Times as Far?

Each child needs two number lines for this activity and two cutouts that look like insects. (Children can use objects such as beans and pretend they are insects.) Tell this story or one similar to it: There is a speedy insect that can jump three times as far as a slow insect. Pretend your number lines are forest paths. If the slow insect jumps one space on the forest path, how far will the speedy insect go? After children solve this problem, have them discuss their solutions. Then say, "The slow insect jumps two spaces. How far does the speedy insect go?" Continue with other space jumps for the slow insect. Again, have children discuss how they solved the problem. They can show their solutions on a number line transparency on the overhead. Children may enjoy making up problems of this kind.

Activity for the Classroom 5.1. How are the meanings of addition and subtraction or multiplication and division taught in your classroom? Why is this approach used? Do you believe changes should be made? Why or why not?

Division with Remainders (Uneven Division). Problems involving division as well as division computation often involve division with remainders ("uneven division"). Children learn that when the dividend is not a multiple of the divisor, a dividend that is less than the given dividend is used and a remainder not greater than the divisor is found (e.g., to solve $23 \div 4 = \square$, think $20 \div 4 = 5$ with 3 remaining). The introduction to division with remainders involves both work with problems and activities with sets. Problem-solving instruction stresses that the interpretation of the remainder depends on the context of the problem. The following problems and their solutions illustrate how the meaning of a problem determines how the remainder should be interpreted:

> *Eleven people are going on a camping trip. Six people can go in a car. How many cars are needed? Solution: Not 1 car with 5 people remaining! The sensible answer is 2 cars.* (Next higher number *needed for meaningful solution.)*
>
> *Janet has 5 cookies to share evenly with a friend. How many does each get? Solution: Each gets $2\frac{1}{2}$ cookies. (The remainder should be partitioned with each person receiving a fractional part of a cookie.)*
>
> *Don counted 25 mini candy bars in the bag he bought to share equally with 8 children including himself at his party. How many did each get? Solution: Each got 3 candy bars, and Don left the last bar in the bag. (The remainder is a leftover part.)*
>
> *For the spring dance festival, some children will wear ribbon bands around their waists. Three feet of ribbon are needed for each band. Ms. Cole has 28 feet of ribbon. How many bands can be made? Solution: 9 bands with 1 foot of ribbon remaining. (The remainder cannot be used and must be* discarded.)

Children develop an initial understanding of division with remainders by solving problems of these types. Give problems to the class, and have children individually or in groups solve the problems using modeling with counting or recall of facts. Solutions are then discussed. Questions help pupils understand how to interpret remainders in a meaningful way. To develop competency in interpreting remainders in story problems, children can also act out situations or draw pictures representing events in story problems.

Children can also develop an intuitive understanding of division with remainders by carrying out activities such as the following that require solving problems by using objects or number lines. Initially, the numbers 5 and 2 are used in activities as divisors because multiples of 5 and 2 are usually familiar to children.

ACTIVITY 5.39
Rabbit Hops.

Each child has a number line and a rabbit cutout or bean. Ask children to make the rabbit hop by fives (5-hops) to a number that is not a multiple of 5, for example, 16 (Figure 5.24), but before doing so, predict if the rabbit will make it to the destination by taking hops of 5 spaces. After they hop the rabbit, discuss their predictions in the light of their results. Their comments should show that they understand that the rabbit cannot hop by fives to 16, but only to 15 and that to reach 16 the rabbit must make a 1-hop after three 5-hops. Continue with other similar directions. Have children give directions for the rabbit to hop to a number less than 50 by taking 5-hops. Other children predict whether or not the rabbit can reach the destination by 5-hops and explain their reasoning. When children can work with 5-hops, have the rabbit take 2-hops to numbers that are not multiples of 2. Next, use other-size hops, and encourage children to count by multiples as they hop the rabbit.

ACTIVITY 5.40
Where to Start?

Have children make predictions about where to start the rabbit if he is to land on 0. Ask for example, "Where must the rabbit go before starting 5-hops from 32 if he wants to land on 0?" After predictions are made, have children explain how they thought to make their predictions. They then test them.

ACTIVITY 5.41
Bar Arrangements.

Have children work in groups to answer questions written on cards such as:

1. What do you find out when 2 bars are joined to make 15?
2. What do you find out when 4 bars are joined to make 17?
3. What do you find out when 2 bars are joined to make 18?
4. What do you find out when 3 bars are joined to make 13?

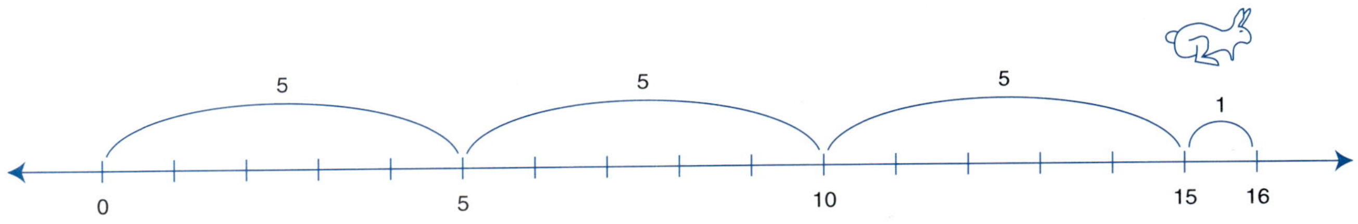

FIGURE 5.24 Division with Remainder Shown by Hopping Rabbit

Children should match same-sized bars to bars showing tens and ones to answer their questions. After time for group work, the class discusses answers and gives reasons for their conclusions. Ask questions such as: "Can you join 2 bars to make 15? Why not? What number a little less than 15 can you make with 2 bars?"

ACTIVITY 5.42
Bean Groupings with Remainders.

Each child needs a supply of beans or other counters. Ask children to show 23 by making groups of 6. After time for working, have them discuss what they noticed. Question children using questions similar to those in Activity 5.41 to enable them to understand that if groups of 6 are made, there will be 3 groups of 6 with 5 left over. Continue with other numbers in which the large group number is not a multiple of the small group number but sometimes include a large group number that is a multiple of the small group number. (Why?) If children are able, have them predict if it is possible to carry out a direction with no leftovers.

ACTIVITY 5.43
Packaging.

All children have counters of some type. They are asked to take a number of counters and decide in how many ways they can package that number into smaller packages with the same number in each package. (They can pretend that they are working in a candy store and that the job is to make candy packages.) For example, if the number given is 20, they will experiment with the counters and find that they can make small packages of 4, 5, 2, or 10. Then ask, "Did anyone try packages of 3 or 6?" (If not, say, "Let's try packages of 3 or 6.") "What happens when you tried packages of 3 (or 6)?" Continue with other numbers such as 12 and 24 objects to be packaged into smaller packages with the same number in each package. A discussion of what has been learned should take place after pupils have worked with several numbers. Questions to ask include: "Did you know before you packaged the candies whether there would be leftovers? Why?"

Children are introduced to using symbols to represent division with remainders in problem-solving lessons or as part of an activity. You introduce the conventional format for writing division with remainders, for example:

$$5\overline{)16}^{\;3\text{ R1}}$$

or an alternative format: 16 = (3 x 5) + 1. The next steps are for children to use modeling and counting or recall to interpret division with remainder sentences and to write division sentences for representations.

Activity for the Classroom 5.2. Plan and teach a lesson that includes your own activity to help children construct the idea of division with remainders. Include questions you would ask during the lesson. Did your group have difficulty with division-with-remainder problems? Why or why not?

ASSESSING LEARNING THE OPERATIONS WITH WHOLE NUMBERS

Assessing children's progress in learning the meanings of addition, subtraction, multiplication, and division basic facts helps you decide what new content children are ready to learn. Assessment procedures include observation, interviewing, examining written work, and testing.

Observation

Observation is invaluable in determining a child's level of understanding for it enables you to assess progress by observing not only a child's completed work but also his or her thinking process and attitudes as the work proceeds. During each lesson, you observe how children solve problems or complete activities. Note particularly the strategies a child uses to solve problems. Knowing whether a child uses direct modeling, a counting strategy, memory, or some combination of these gives more information about a child's level of learning than knowing that he or she obtained the correct answer.

Children's explanations also give important information about their learning because they give evidence of children's mathematical thinking. Questions to answer as you observe children and listen to their discussions include: How do children justify their conclusions? Do they note relationships and give logical reasons for their answers? To obtain such information, you ask questions that require pupils to tell how they thought while working at a task, such as: "How did you think to get that answer?" "Why did you do that?" "Why does that make sense to you?"

To assess attitudes, children's confidence, interest, and cooperation in solving problems and completing activities are observed. Observations answer the following questions: Did the child begin a task promptly and seem to be absorbed in his or her work? Did the child persevere, particularly when difficulties arose? Did the child appear eager to work with the materials to find answers or gain new knowledge? Did the child display social skills necessary to contribute and communicate effectively in a group?

If teachers' observations are to be the basis of judgments about children's achievement, records must be kept. Generally individual records are made. A useful plan is to keep records on index cards or sticky notes and file these under each child's name. Each day as you move from group to group or teach a lesson, you observe three or four children and keep a record of observations of each child. It is wise to note observations on the card at the time of the observation because in a busy day, observations can be forgotten or go unrecorded. Over about two weeks each child is observed. Observation records should include:

- Child's name
- Date
- Problem (if problem is assigned)
  - Story—Operation and type of unknown (e.g., find-start)
  - Part–part–whole and type of unknown (e.g., find-start)
  - Accuracy of solution
- Activity (if activity is assigned)
  - Name of activity
- Strategy for problem solving or to carry out activity
  - Modeling, counting, reasoning, or recall; experimentation
- Explanation of work
  - Evidence of reasoning
- Cooperation
  - Examples: Contributes to group, accepts others' contributions
- Attitudes
- Recommendations

Activity for the Classroom 5.3. Observe children solving story problems or part–part–whole problems for addition and subtraction or multiplication and division. Choose two children who show understanding of the two operations and two who are having difficulty with the meanings of the operations. Ask them to explain how they solved the problems. Write an observation record for each of the four children, using the guide given. Use your write-ups to compare the attainments and attitudes of these children.

Interviewing

Interviews are structured observations. Usually one child at a time is interviewed in a place apart from the distractions of the activities of other children, but you can sometimes include two children in an interview. Each child is given a problem to solve and asked to "think out loud." He or she tells you his or her thoughts as the problem-solving process unfolds. You make an interview record similar to the one for observations, but it usually includes more detail about the child's reasoning. To uncover the child's thinking, you can ask questions such as: "What in the problem told you how to begin?" "Why did you decide to do that?" "How did you figure that out?"

Labinowicz (1985) gives many excellent suggestions for conducting an interview. You should establish rapport before beginning the interview by asking something the child would like to talk about, such as a favorite game. Before giving the child the first task, you should say that you are interested in knowing how the child thinks when working with numbers. The child should be asked to look at and talk about the materials that will be available to him or her. During the interview, you should be encouraging, and your responses to the child's comments should be nonjudgmental. You should make comments such as, "I see," "Go on," or "Uhuh," to encourage the child to tell about his or her thinking and to show the child that you value what he or she says. Comments to avoid are "Good" and "That's right" because they give the impression that you expect certain responses, which is not the case, because your objective is to find out what the child thinks. You should give the child time to think about his or her solution to the problem, waiting in a relaxed manner for the child to respond. Leading questions, such as, "Could you use counters to solve the problem?" should be avoided. Rather, if the pupil need prompts, say, "What on the table can you use to find the answer?"

Interviews are time-consuming and therefore used infrequently. However, if a child seems unable to grasp the meanings of an operation, an interview can reveal the difficulties he or she is having in sensing the relations inherent in the concept of the operation.

Examining Written Work

Even though young children make written records of their work less often than older children, their work products can give clues regarding their understanding of the operations. You study the pictorial representations children make to solve problems. You examine math sentences children write in connection with story problems or number questions to determine their comprehension of problems, and you study these open sentences to determine whether they are in standard or nonstandard form. You examine written work that shows both pictorial and symbolic representations of a situation to determine accuracy of the representation. When reviewing the books children have made, you look for completeness as well as accuracy.

You can keep records of children's written work over a period of time to show growth in expressing mathematical concepts. One plan is to take a work product each month during the school year. Children and their parents are usually pleased to note the progress that has been made in representing ideas.

Testing

Quizzes and tests are used infrequently with young children. However, it may be helpful on some occasions to give quizzes or tests in order to make a formal evaluation of progress. When given, they could include asking questions such as:

- Write a story problem for addition (subtraction) and one for multiplication (division) using any two of the numbers 2, 3, 4, 5, 15, 20, 25, and 30. Solve the problem any way you choose.
- Show the solution to the following story problem in two ways. Kevin got 2 Christmas presents from each of his 2 aunts. How many presents did he receive from his aunts? (*Note:* problems should be given for all operations studied.)
- Give the fact you would think to solve the problem: Ducelia got a piggy bank for her birthday and wanted to put money in it right away. She remembered she had saved $5 from helping her neighbor rake leaves. She found the $5 in her dresser and put it in the bank. She asked her Dad if she could help him do something for a dollar or two. He said he would give her $2 if she washed the car. She got busy at the job and earned the $2. She also put that money in her bank. How much was in her bank now? (*Note:* Problems for other operations could be used.)
- Show 2 more than 5 on the number line or with a picture.
- Draw a picture that shows what is left of a pile of 5 peanuts if a blue jay picks up 4 in its beak.
- Draw a picture to show that 12 balls are 9 balls more than 3 balls.
- Make an array for 3×2.
- Show 3 sevens on this piece of grid paper, using a different color for each 7.

As questions that require children to demonstrate understanding can be answered differently by different children, make every effort to understand the meaning the child is expressing in his or her own way.

SUMMARY

Helping children construct the meanings of addition, subtraction, multiplication, and division as they study basic facts was discussed in this chapter. Two approaches were presented: learning meanings by (1) solving story problems and (2) by engaging in activities that deal with part–part–whole relations. Both approaches foster learning the interpretations of the operations. Instruction to enable children to connect concrete and symbolic representations of facts was stressed.

The chapter emphasized that children need to do, think, and communicate as they construct the meanings of the operations by working with basic facts. *Doing* involves working with concrete, pictorial, and symbolic representations of ideas. *Thinking* involves reflecting on what one is doing or has done and integrating new ideas with prior learning. It includes grasping relations and reasoning as one solves problems or carries out tasks. *Communicating* involves talking to peers and adults about addition, subtraction, multiplication, and division, explaining one's ideas, and reacting to the ideas of others. Communicating also means using pictures, diagrams, and written symbols to represent one's thinking about the operations. Many activities were given that enable children to do, think, and communicate about the meanings of the operations. The design of the activities de-emphasized teacher presentation; learner exploration and discovery were stressed. The importance of teacher questioning in connection with activities was emphasized. Many examples were given of questions to encourage children to construct the meanings of the operations as they study basic facts.

The final section of the chapter discussed assessing children's learning of the meanings of the operations. Suggestions were given for using observations, interviews, written work, and quizzes and tests to determine the nature of children's concept learning and their thinking processes.

REFERENCES

Bebout, Harriett C. (March 1990). "Children's Symbolic Representation of Addition and Subtraction Word Problems." *Journal for Research in Mathematics Education* 21: 123–131.

Carpenter, Thomas P., Deborah A. Carey, and Vicky L. Kouba. (1990). "A Problem-Solving Approach to the Operations." In *Mathematics for the Young Child*, edited by Joseph N. Payne, pp. 111–131. Reston, VA: National Council of Teachers of Mathematics.

Carpenter, Thomas P., James Hiebert, and James M. Moser. (January 1981). "Problem Structure and First-Grade Children's Initial Solution Processes for Simple Addition and Subtraction Problems." *Journal for Research in Mathematics Education* 12: 27–39.

Carpenter, Thomas P., and James M. Moser. (1982). "The Development of Addition and Subtraction Problem-Solving Skills." In *Addition and Subtraction: A Cognitive Perspective*, edited by Thomas P. Carpenter, James M. Moser, and Thomas A. Romberg, pp. 9–23. Hillsdale, NJ: Erlbaum.

Carpenter, Thomas P., and James M. Moser. (1983). "The Acquisition of Addition and Subtraction Concepts." In *Acquisition of Mathematics Concepts and Processes*, edited by Richard Lesh and Marsha Landau, pp. 7–44. New York: Academic Press.

Fennema, Elizabeth, Thomas P. Carpenter, and Penelope L. Peterson. (1989). "Learning Mathematics with Understanding: Cognitively Guided Instruction." In *Advances in Research on Teaching*, Vol. 1, edited by Jere Brophy, pp. 195–219. Greenwich CT: JAI Press.

Flexer, Roberta J. (November 1986). "The Power of Five: The Step before the Power of Ten." *Arithmetic Teacher* 34: 5–9.

Kamii, Constance Kazuko. (1985). *Young Children Reinvent Arithmetic*. New York: Teachers College Press.

Labinowicz, Ed. (1985). *Learning from Children: New Beginnings for Teaching Numerical Thinking*. Menlo Park, CA: Addison-Wesley.

National Council of Teachers of Mathematics. (1989). *Curriculum and Evaluation Standards for School Mathematics*. Reston, VA: Author.

Romberg, Thomas A., and Kevin F. Collis. (1987). *Different Ways Children Learn to Add and Subtract*. Reston, VA: National Council of Teachers of Mathematics.

Secada, Walter G., Karen C. Fuson, and James W. Hall. (January 1983). "The Transition from Counting-All to Counting-On in Addition." *Journal for Research in Mathematics Education* 14: 47–57.

Van de Walle, John. (1990). "Concepts of Number." In *Mathematics for the Young Child*, edited by Joseph N. Payne, pp. 63–87. Reston, VA: National Council of Teachers of Mathematics.

SOFTWARE RESOURCES

Hop To It
Company: Sunburst
Computer: Apple
Grade level: 1–3

Figures such as bunnies and frogs hop along a number line to reach objects. Learner gives facts. Develops meaning of addition and subtraction. Three levels.

IBM Elementary Mathematics Series: Math Concepts
Level 1, Unit 3, Lessons 9 and 10 (addition and subtraction)
Level 1, Unit 6, Lesson 26 (multiplication)
Company: IBM/EduQuest
Computer: IBM
Grade level: 1–3

Meaning developed for operations with word problems and pictures. All interpretations of subtraction. Grouping situations used for multiplication. Problems with missing factors in math sentences are included.

Understanding Multiplication
Company: Tricon
Computer: Apple
Grade level: 2–6

Uses modified domino dot patterns to provide representations of multiplication. Counting is encouraged in the beginning. Also teaches commutative and distributive properties.

CHAPTER 6

Mastering the Basic Facts

▪ INTRODUCTORY PROBLEM ▪

Assume that children have constructed the meanings of the facts for the four operations and have developed some strategies for recalling facts. List 10 facts for each operation you think would be difficult for children to remember. Assuming that children in your class are having problems attaining immediate recall of these facts, what activities would you plan so that learners would master these facts?

INTRODUCTION

Children must master the basic facts if they are to advance in their study of mathematics (Folsom, 1975; Hiebert, 1990; NCTM, 1989). Automatic response is necessary so that thinking can focus on examining relations and analyzing problems rather than dwelling on finding answers to basic fact questions. However, authorities agree that understanding must precede mastery of the basic facts (NCTM, 1989; Suydam and Weaver, 1975; Thornton, 1990).

Children master addition and subtraction facts in grades 1, 2, and 3; multiplication and division facts in grades 3, 4, and 5. Some children memorize a few facts as they solve story problems, play games, and carry out part–part–whole activities. For most children, however, the mastery of facts involves practice, but practice activities should be delayed until children have memorized some facts and can use strategies to recall unknown facts.

Strategies involve thinking number relationships to recall facts (e.g., to solve $5 + 6 = \square$, think $5 + 5 = 10$, $5 + 1 = 6$, $5 + 6 = 5 + 5 + 1 = 10 + 1 = 11$). Thornton and Smith (1988) found that an emphasis on strategies gives children confidence that they can work out unknown facts and leads to greater retention than an emphasis on drill. Instruction in strategies is advocated by many authorities (NCTM, 1989; Suydam, 1984; Thornton, 1990), and new directions in learning elementary school mathematics emphasize learning strategies for the facts before working for mastery (see Standards 8 and 13, in Curriculum Standards for Grades K–4, Appendix A.)

Strategies for recalling facts are most meaningful to children if they figure them out themselves or if they learn strategies by listening to other children explain them. Discussing strategies among themselves also helps children learn strategies. However, learners must be motivated to use strategies. They must believe that learning the basic facts is worthwhile and that they will be successful at recalling facts if they use strategies. Activities discussed in this chapter can only bring the strategies to the attention of learners. They do not ensure they will be used. To develop positive attitudes toward using strategies, you support children in their use of a strategy, for example, by asking them to report on how they used a strategy. You help children reflect on their success when they use a strategy by saying, "You must feel proud that you were able to remember that strategy to recall the fact." In these and other ways you encourage children to be autonomous learners who take responsibility for their own learning.

The preceding chapter discussed instruction to enable children to grasp the meanings of addition, subtraction, multiplication, and division. This chapter discusses helping children learn strategies and achieve mastery of the basic facts after they understand the operations. The main sections of the chapter are: Teaching the Strategies, Introducing Strategies for Recalling Facts, Prerequisites for Learning Strategies, Teaching for Mastery of Basic Facts, and Assessing Mastery of Basic Facts. A summary ends the chapter.

TEACHING THE STRATEGIES

Strategies should be taught so that pupils can help themselves when they do not have immediate recall of a fact. Although some learners discover strategies (they may use the word, "rule") by themselves, others do not. Interactive teaching enables all students to become aware of strategies for recall of the basic facts and the reasons the strategies are sensible and not "tricks."

After you observe that some children can solve problems by thinking the facts, begin the study of strategies by saying, "I have noticed that sometimes you can think a fact answer. You do not use materials and count. Soon we will need to remember all the fact answers. Let's talk about how we can help ourselves remember them. What ideas or strategies do you have for remembering sums (or differences, etc.)." A chart should be made of strategies students report they use (e.g., count up or back, turnarounds, doubles, doubles-plus-one, and think to 10). Tell students that they will study the strategies on the chart over the next few weeks, that other strategies will probably be added to the chart, and that the ideas on the chart can help them when they cannot recall a fact. Encourage them to report any strategy they discover in the future.

Lessons to help all children understand and use the strategies on the chart begin by having those who told about the strategy explain how they use it to help remember facts. Their reports are followed by activities similar to those described in this chapter to introduce strategies.

Lessons to teach strategies not on the chart help children use what they know to develop an awareness of the strategy and when it is useful. Children use materials to explore the sense of the strategy and are asked to think about facts easily recalled if the strategy is used. Explicit directions for using a strategy are not a part of lessons to teach strategies because they do not involve learners in constructing strategies useful to them. Approaches to strategy lessons include:

1. Have children answer fact questions you choose to illustrate a strategy and report how they completed the task. Use their reports to introduce the strategy. Children may then recall fact answers using the strategy or show the meaning of a strategy by using materials. (Activity 6.1 is an example of this approach.)
2. Have students engage in an activity that involves generating facts—often using materials or counting—reflect on their work, and discuss the strategy they used or infer a rule from their reflections. They can use the strategy to find other fact answers. (Activity 6.5 is an example of this approach.)
3. Have students think about how a strategy could be adapted to the same or a different operation. Have them give examples of the adaptation, and discuss them. (Activity 6.7 is an example of this approach.)

During the time children are learning strategies, the vertical form for fact questions should be introduced. You tell children that fact questions can be written in a horizontal or a vertical form. Show the two forms, and ask learners to compare them. Ask them to transform a few math sentences from the horizontal to the vertical form (e.g., 4 + 6 = 10 to $\begin{array}{r} 4 \\ +6 \\ \hline 10 \end{array}$). Thereafter, they should use both forms.

INTRODUCING STRATEGIES FOR RECALLING BASIC FACTS

The strategies for recalling basic facts discussed in this section have been described by a number of authorities (Labinowicz, 1985; Rathmell, 1978; Suydam, 1984; Thornton, 1990). Even though some are more efficient than others, children should be aware of all strategies and choose the ones most useful to them.

Reader Activity 6.1

Decide which facts can be determined by each strategy for an operation. Where there are overlaps, decide which strategy you think pupils would use and why.

The strategies described here are organized by operation: addition, subtraction, multiplication, and division. After a description of the strategies for recalling facts for an operation, activities are presented to introduce the strategy to help children understand and use it. The activities include opportunities for children to explain their thought processes, as well as to use the strategy. As noted, if one or more children have mentioned using a strategy, their reports begin the lesson.

Addition

The strategies for addition are: think turnarounds, think one more, count on two or three, think the rule for zero facts, think doubles, think doubles-plus-one, think five as an anchor, think ten as an anchor, and think compensation.

1. Think Turnarounds. When children understand the addition order rule (commutative property of addition), they are able to use this knowledge to recall unknown addition facts. This strategy can be labeled: think turnarounds. An example is: if 7 + 2 = 9 is known, 2 + 7 = 9 is also known. This strategy is basic to many other strategies discussed in this section.

ACTIVITY 6.1

Ask children to answer three fact questions such as 3 + 4 = □ and think what the facts would be if the numbers were turned around. After they tell about the facts with the numbers "turned around," give them counters and jar lids or lids from yogurt or cottage cheese cartons. Ask them to think of ways to show "turnarounds" with facts of their own choosing and make records of their work (Figure 6.1). After they have finished the task, have them share their ideas. Lead a discussion on the strategy and its usefulness.

2. Think One More. This strategy can be used by children when they are able to *think 1 up* from the larger number when it is either the first or second addend (e.g., 4 + 1 = 5; 1 + 4 = 5). To understand this strategy, children must know the number sequence.

ACTIVITY 6.2

Ask children to name some addition facts with 1 as an addend. Ask, "Is there a way to remember the one facts?" If no child mentions thinking the numbers in counting, say, "We can find a way if we arrange our number bars to show a staircase" (Figure 6.2). When they finish, ask, "How would thinking the staircase help us with the one facts? Does knowing how the numbers go help you remember the one facts? How?" Pupils' responses should help them become aware that each number in counting is 1 greater than the previous number and so the order of numbers in counting is a way to remember the one facts.

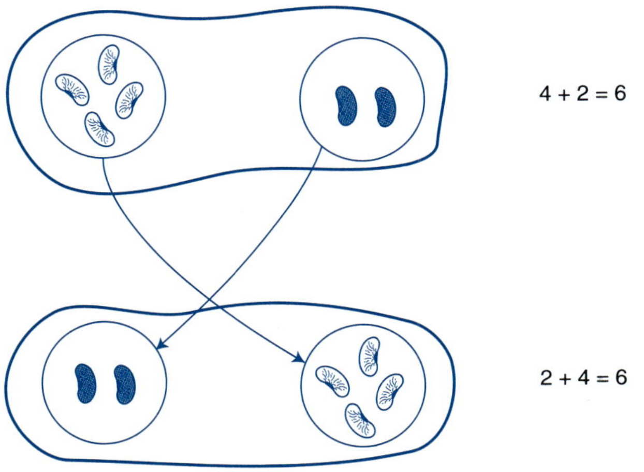

FIGURE 6.1 Counters Showing "Turnaround" Strategy for Addition

FIGURE 6.2 Number Bars Showing "Think One More" Strategy

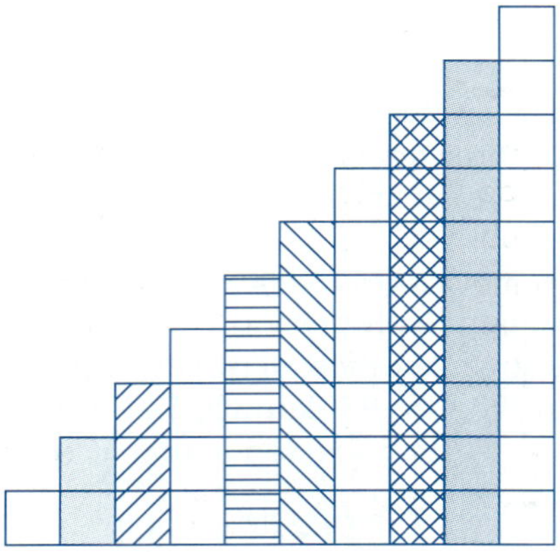

3. Count on Two or Three. This strategy can be used by children when they are able to *count on* from the larger number when it is either the first or second addend (e.g., 5 + 2 = 7 or 2 + 5 = 7). This strategy should be used only with sums in which one addend is 2 or 3 because when counting to add or subtract a number greater than 3, children can easily lose track of what they are doing.

ACTIVITY 6.3

This is a small-group activity. Students use numerals cards showing numerals 1 to 9 (Figure 6.3). One child is "IT," picks a card, shows it, and says, "Tell or count what number is 2 (or 3) more than this number." "IT" calls on a child to answer. The children take turns being "IT."

ACTIVITY 6.4

Have children in small groups take turns drawing fact question cards from a sack. The cards show 2 or 3 as the first or second addend. Each child finds the sum on his or her card by counting on if necessary. After giving the sum, he or she returns the card to the sack.

Conclude either activity 6.3 or 6.4 with a discussion of how to recall the answers to fact questions when 2 or 3 is an addend—by thinking the sum or counting on 2 or 3 from the larger number in the fact question.

4. Think the Zero Fact Rule. The pattern—when one addend is 0, the sum is the other addend (e.g., 6 + 0 = 6)—is the basis for a rule that makes for easy mastery of the zero addition facts.

ACTIVITY 6.5

Talk about zero facts so that pupils know what they are. Ask children in pairs to write three zero fact questions and the answers. Have them share their work, and discuss with them if this was easy or hard to do and why. Conclude by asking them to give a rule for remembering zero facts: the sum is the nonzero number.

5. Think Doubles. Thinking doubles is usually easy for children because they can visualize a doubles pattern or can sense the pattern that each double is two more than the one preceding it (e.g., 4 + 4 = 3 + 3 + 2 = 8). Children are also often interested in doubles. I have heard them saying to each other 1 + 1 = 2; 2 + 2 = 4; 3 + 3 = 6; 4 + 4 = 8, and so on.

FIGURE 6.3 Numeral Cards

ACTIVITY 6.6

Have children look for doubles patterns in real life objects. Give them several days to do this, after discussing the meaning of "doubles" and giving an example of a doubles pattern, such as a carton for a dozen eggs. Suggest they look around their homes, neighborhoods, and stores to find doubles patterns. Examples children could report are: fingers, animal legs, insect legs, and soft drinks in a six-pack (Figure 6.4). Ask children to make drawings of doubles patterns they have observed. Talk about the facts the pictures show and how the pictures can help them remember the "doubles facts." The pictures can be displayed.

6. Think Doubles-Plus-One. When children know the doubles, they are able to use a strategy for recalling facts in which one addend is 1 greater than the other addend (e.g., $3 + 4 = \square$; $3 + 1 = 4$; $3 + 3 + 1 = 6 + 1 = 7$). To use this strategy, children must understand that a number can be thought of in terms of its parts and make use of the think-one-more strategy. They may also use a think-one-less strategy.

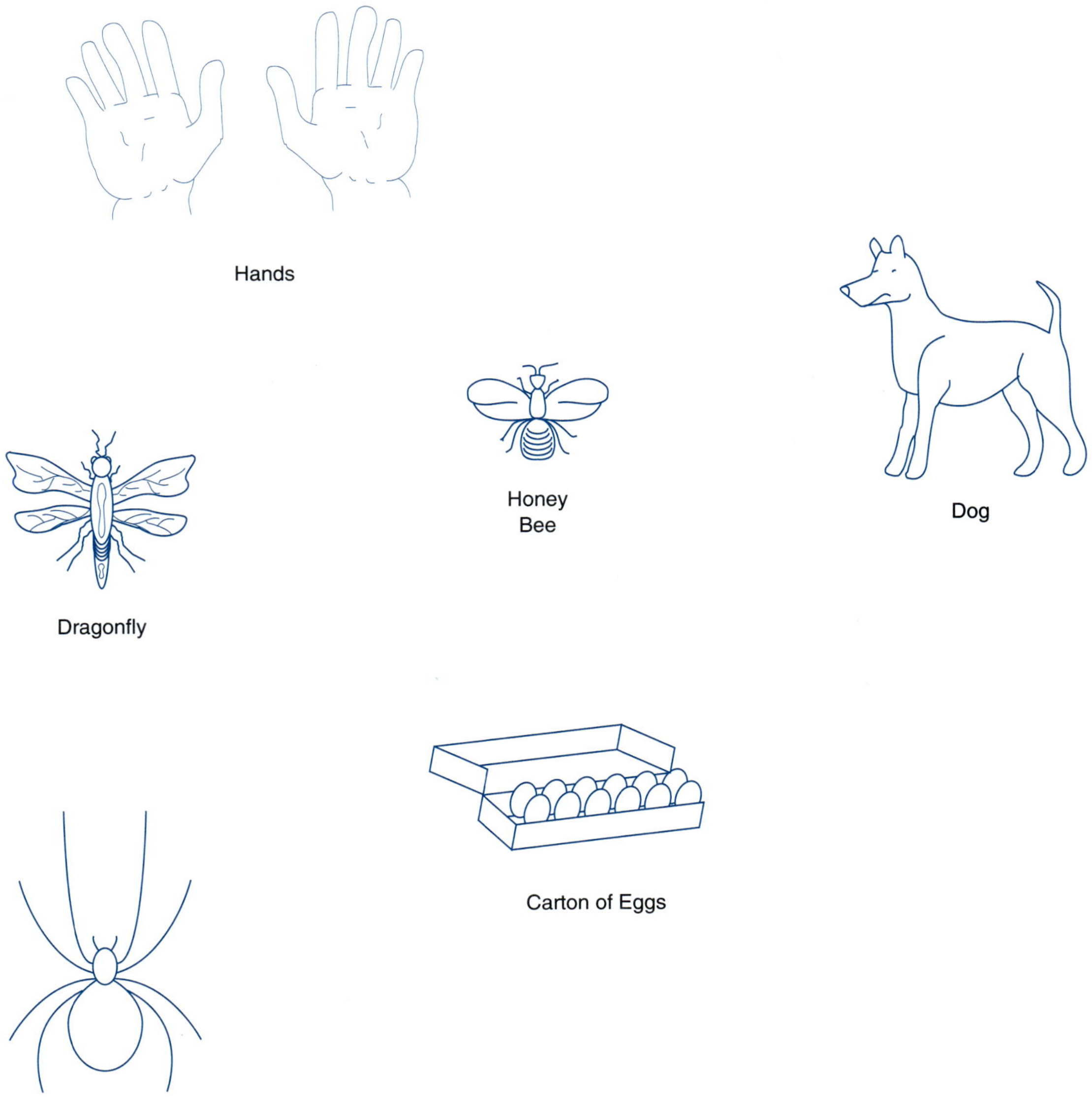

FIGURE 6.4 Double Patterns

ACTIVITY 6.7

Ask children how doubles will help with other facts. If necessary, give an example such as 4 + 4 = 8 and 4 + 5 = 9 for them to discuss. Have children name doubles-plus-one facts and draw pictures of doubles facts and their related doubles-plus-one facts. Have them show their pictures and tell about them. Conclude by listing the doubles-plus-one facts discussed during the lesson and having pupils tell how to remember them.

7. Think Five as an Anchor. Because of their work with the five-frames, many children can visualize a sum that is 10 or less, for example 3 + 2 = 5 and 3 + 4 = 5 + 2 = 7 (Figure 6.5).

ACTIVITY 6.8

Have pupils use their five-frames to find as many facts as possible with sums of 10 or less. Say, "As you are showing the facts, think a mind picture of how they look using the five-frame." Later have pupils close their eyes while one child describes his or her mind picture of a fact on the five-frame. You may need to model this. For example, say, "I am thinking 4 dots in the frame and 3 dots outside. The dots will fill the five-frame, and there are 2 dots outside the frame. 4 + 3 = 5 + 2 = 7." To conclude the activity, have pupils tell about using the five-frame to recall facts.

8. Think Ten as an Anchor. The ten-frame is used to represent facts to 10 and greater than 10 (Figure 6.6). It is especially helpful in learning the "making-ten" strategy: subtract from one number enough to add to the other number to equal 10; add the remainder to the 10 to find the sum. For example, 5 + 7 = □, 7 − 5 = 2, 5 + 5 = 10, 5 + 7 = (5 + 5) + 2 = 10 + 2 = 12.

ACTIVITY 6.9

Ask pupils to experiment with their ten-frames to learn how thinking the ten-frame can help them remember facts. Give them facts to use. Begin with sums less than 10, and follow with sums greater than 10. Suggest that they use counters of two colors. Have them discuss their experiments and show their work on an overhead using a ten-frame transparency and counters of two different shapes. Ask children to list the facts they can recall using the think-ten strategy.

FIGURE 6.5 Five-Frames Showing Addition

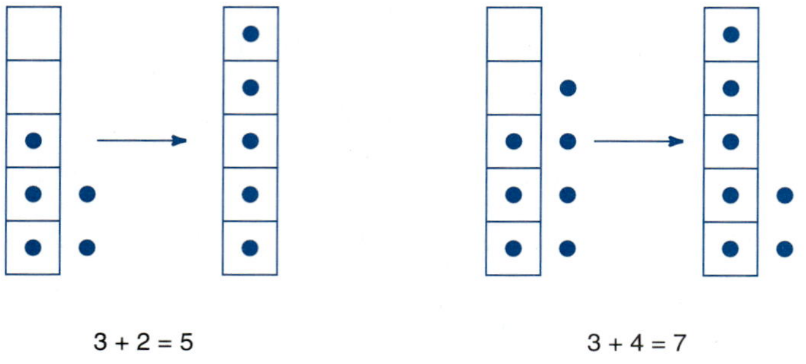

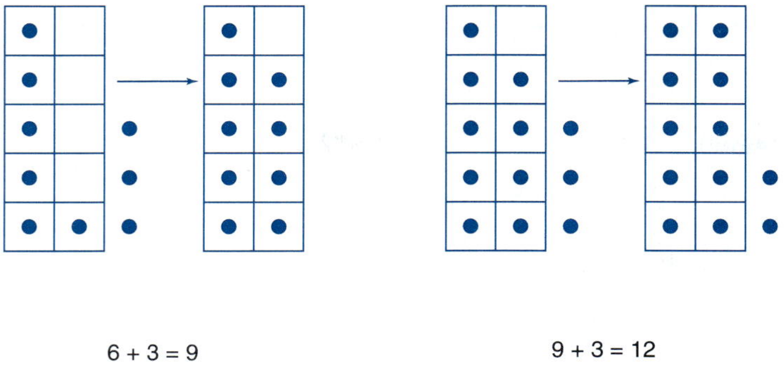

FIGURE 6.6 Ten-Frames Showing Addition

ACTIVITY 6.10

Use of the "making-ten" strategy with facts with 9 as an addend leads to awareness of a pattern: When one addend is 9, the ones in the sum is 1 less than the addend that is not 9; 2 less, when the addend is 8 (e.g., 9 + 5 = 14; 4 is 1 less than 5; 8 + 6 = 14, 4 is 2 less than 6).

If children are capable of forming this rule and using it, have them answer fact questions with 9 as one addend, observe the relation between the addend that is not 9 and the ones in the sum, describe the pattern, and construct the rule. To help them understand why the rule is reasonable, have them represent facts of 9 with diagrams or materials and observe how making 10 decreases the addend that is not 9. Later, they can form a rule for sums with 8 as one addend.

9. Think Compensation (Adjusting). This strategy involves adding to one addend the amount subtracted from the other addend to make a known fact. It is often used to make doubles (e.g., 6 + 8 = 7 + 7 = 14).

ACTIVITY 6.11

Give children counters, and ask them to use the counters to decide how to make "doubles" to answer each of the following: 7 + 5 = □, 6 + 8 = □, and 4 + 6 = □ (Figure 6.7). Ask them to make records of their work. Groups or individuals experiment

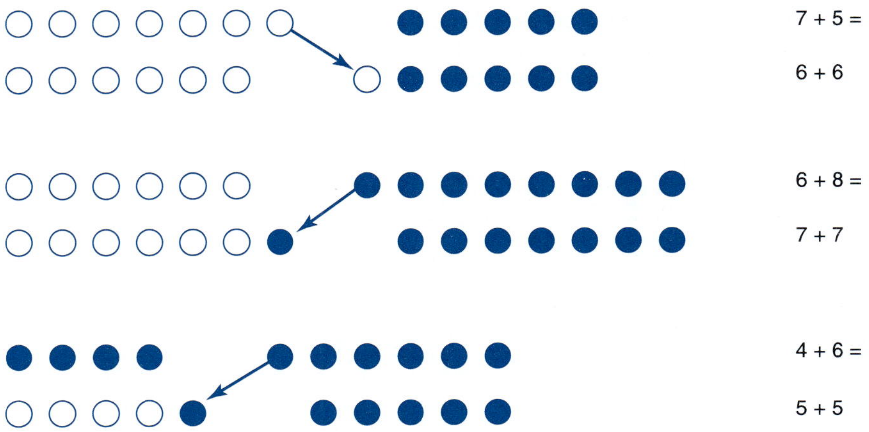

FIGURE 6.7 Counters Showing "Compensation" Strategy

to find the doubles. After time for experimentation, children use their records to share what they did. Help them write a rule: you can subtract an amount from one number and add that amount to the other number to get the same sum. They should test their rule on different facts.

ACTIVITY 6.12

Have pupils decide how to show adjusting with linking cubes (Figure 6.8). Ask pupils to explain what they did and how the cube arrangements can show the rule they made.

Subtraction

The strategies for subtraction are: think one less, count back two or three, count on two or three, think rules for zero facts, think five as an anchor, think ten as an anchor, think compensation (adjusting), and think the related addition fact. The strategies for the subtraction facts are related to the strategies for the addition facts, and the activities for their study are often similar to those for the strategies for recalling addition facts.

1. Think One Less. This strategy can be used by children when they are able to *think 1 back from* the minuend (e.g., 5 – 1 = 4). Activities 6.13 and 6.14 will help children think the number sequence to 9 backward.

ACTIVITY 6.13

Some rhymes give the counting words backward. One such rhyme is, "Ten Red Balloons." Have 10 children stand in the front of the room to be the "balloons." Count the children so each has a number. When his or her number is noted in the rhyme, the child sits down. The words to the rhyme are:

Ten red balloons hanging on the wall
If one red balloon should accidentally fall
There'd be nine red balloons hanging on the wall
Nine red balloons hanging on the wall
If one red balloon should accidentally fall
There'd be eight red balloons hanging on the wall
Eight red balloons hanging on the wall
If one red balloon should accidentally fall
There'd be seven red balloons hanging on the wall
Seven red balloons hanging on the wall . . .
Repeat until there are no red balloons on the wall.

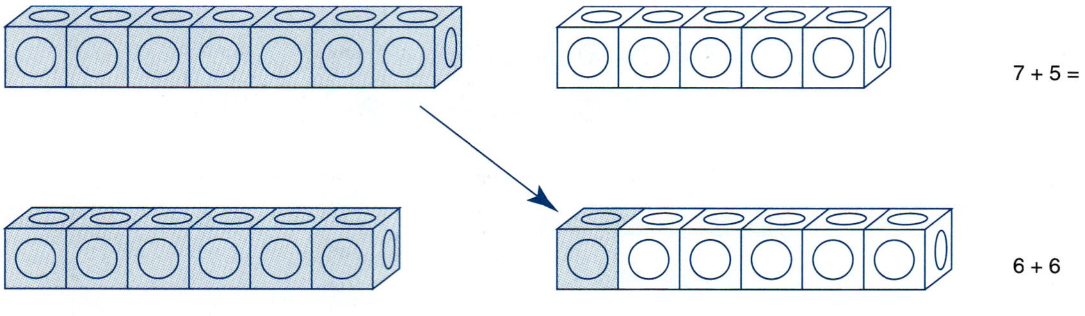

FIGURE 6.8 Linking Cubes Showing "Compensation" Strategy

ACTIVITY 6.14

Use the "blast-off" sequence or backward count (9, 8, 7, ... 1) during the school day. For example, children can blast off for dismissal. Ask what facts can be recalled easily by counting backward. Have children list these facts.

2. Count Back Two or Three. This strategy can be used by children when they are able to *count 2 or 3 back from the minuend* (e.g., 6 – 2 = 4).

ACTIVITY 6.15

To help children learn to count backward for 2 or 3 numbers starting with the minuend, place numeral cards to 10 made of linoleum squares on the floor or playground in the order of the counting numbers. Each pair of children should have a set of cards. The procedure is for one child to stand on a card with a numeral between 2 (or 3) and 10. The second child stands in front of the numeral cards and says, "Tell me where you will be if you step back 2 (or 3). Walk back to the card with that number, and I will come to shake your hand." The children take turns standing on the cards, giving directions, and shaking hands.

ACTIVITY 6.16

Have children use number lines to show facts with subtrahends of 2 or 3 (Figure 6.9). To begin, ask the class to give six subtraction facts with 2 or 3 as the subtrahends. List the facts for children to show on number lines. When they finish, ask them if these facts are easy or hard to remember and why they think so. If they do not think the facts are easy, have them whisper-count back 2 or 3 to give the difference. Have them tell how to count back 2 or 3 to remember facts. Ask if they think they will use the strategy and how they decided to answer the question, "Yes" or "No."

3. Count on Two or Three. This strategy is *count on 2 or 3 from the subtrahend to the minuend* (e.g., 6 – 4 = 2, count on from 4 to obtain the answer 2). To use this strategy, children must sense that the numbers are close enough for counting to be a good strategy and intuitively know that addition and subtraction are inverse.

ACTIVITY 6.17

Pose the problem for groups of two or three children to solve: How can you count on (not back) to solve $7 - 5 = N$ (Figure 6.10)? Suggest that they use materials to think about the problem. Have several children explain their answers to the problem and show with materials how they thought to answer the question. Ask, "Does counting on from the smaller number give the same answer to a fact question as counting back from the larger number? Why? How can you 'prove' it?" Ask which strategy they prefer and why.

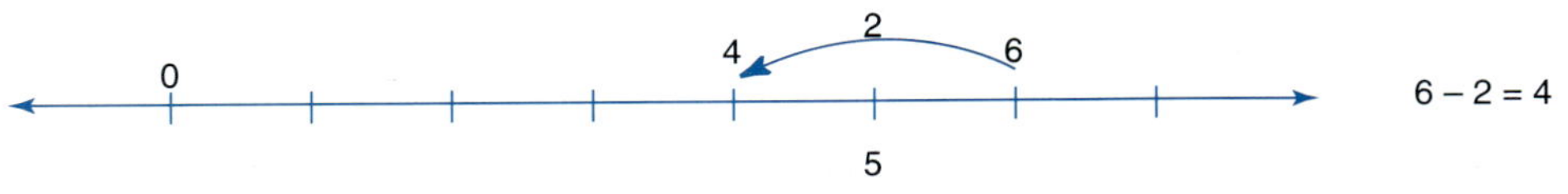

FIGURE 6.9 Number Line Showing "Count-Back" Strategy

FIGURE 6.10 Counters Showing "Count-On" Strategy

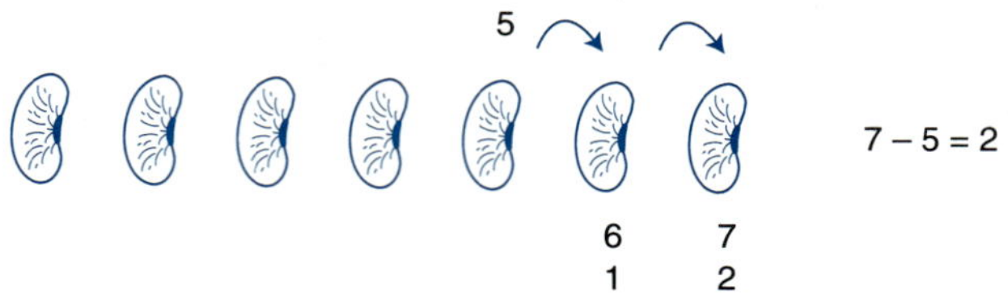

4. Think Rules for Zero Facts. Knowing the rules for the zero subtraction facts makes mastery of those facts easy for learners. The rules are: when the subtrahend is zero, the difference is the other number; when the minuend and the subtrahend are the same number, the difference is zero (e.g., 6 – 0 = 6; 6 – 6 = 0).

ACTIVITY 6.18

Give children five fact questions with zero as the subtrahend. Ask them to solve the fact questions with materials and make a record of their work. Have them look at their records and tell what they notice. Ask how their observations would help them remember the zero facts.

ACTIVITY 6.19

Give children four fact questions in which the minuend and the subtrahend are the same. Have them show the facts with materials, record their work, and talk about the rule they can make on the basis of their experience.

5. Using Five as an Anchor. Because of their work with the five-frame, many children can visualize the difference when five is either the minuend or the subtrahend in a subtraction fact (e.g., 5 – 3 = 2; 6 – 5 = 1).

ACTIVITY 6.20

Ask children to talk about how a fact such as 5 – 2 = 3 looks in a five-frame mind picture (Figure 6.11). Then have them show the fact on their five-frames to check their mind picture. Ask them to draw pictures of five-frames on grid paper for several facts with 5 as one number and explain how five-frames help remember facts.

6. Using Ten as an Anchor. Ten as an anchor can be helpful for recalling facts (a) when the minuend is 10 or (b) and (c) when the minuend is greater than 10. Learners usually prefer one of the two approaches (b or c) for minuends greater than 10.

a. When the Minuend Is 10. Children can *visualize* the ten-frame as two five-frames, think removing counters to subtract and how the ten-frame looks after the

FIGURE 6.11 Five-Frame Showing Subtraction

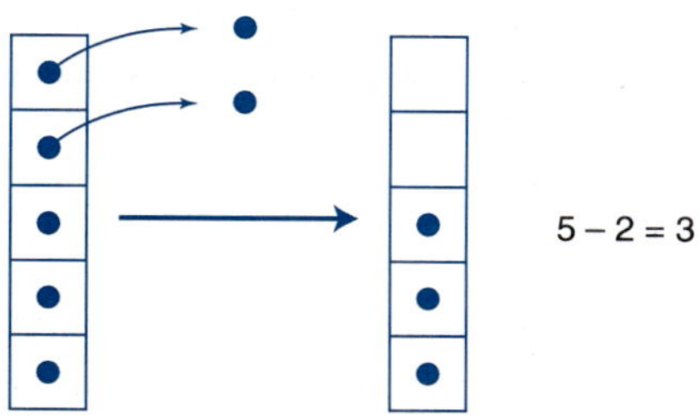

counters are removed. For example, when the fact, 10 – 4 = 6, has been modeled, one five-frame is covered with counters, 4 spaces on the other five-frame are empty, and 1 space is covered with a counter; since 6 spaces are filled with counters, the difference is 6 (Figure 6.12).

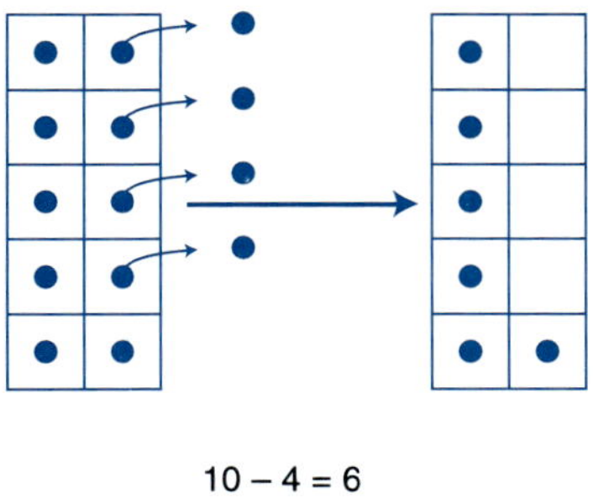

FIGURE 6.12 Ten-Frame Showing Subtraction

ACTIVITY 6.21

Ask children, working in pairs, to show facts with 10 as the minuend on the ten-frame. One child shows a fact, and the other child, after looking at the representation, turns away and tells his or her partner how the fact is shown on the ten-frame. The class discusses how a ten-frame mind picture can help them to remember the subtraction facts for 10.

b. When the Minuend Is Greater than 10 and the Subtrahend Is 8 or 9. Then, a *think-back strategy* can be used: Think how many back to 10 from the minuend and how many back from 10 to the subtrahend. Add the two numbers for the difference. For example, to find 12 – 9 = *N*, think that 12 back to 10 is 2, 10 back to 9 is 1, 2 plus 1 equals 3; so 3 is the difference.

ACTIVITY 6.22

Tell children that they can show 12 – 9 = □ on their ten-frames a new way by following your directions. Ask them to place 10 counters on the ten-frame and 2 outside, remove the 2 outside counters and 1 from those in the ten-frame to "go back to" 9 (2 + 1 = 3; 12 – 9 = 3). Ask them to carry out a similar procedure with the fact questions 14 – 8 = □ and 16 – 9 = □. Ask children to tell what they did in the examples and how this task with the ten-frame could help them remember facts. Have them give facts they could recall using this strategy.

c. When the Minuend Is Greater than 10 and the Subtrahend Is 8 or 9. Then, a *think-up strategy* can also be used. This strategy is an alternative to the think-back strategy: Think the number up from the subtrahend to 10 and the number up from 10 to the minuend. Add the two numbers for the difference. For example, to recall 13 – 8 = *N*, think that 8 up to 10 is 2; 10 up to 13 is 3, 2 + 3 = 5; 5 is the difference.

ACTIVITY 6.23

Adapt Activity 6.22. Use an example such as 14 – 9 = 5. Give directions to lay counters of one color on the ten-frame to show 9. Ask children to use counters of different color to finish making 10 in the ten-frame (1 counter) and to show from 10 to 14 outside the frame with counters of the same color (4 counters). Students explain how they showed the answer to the fact question (5). They use the procedure with a few more facts and discuss how it could help them remember subtraction facts.

Have them compare the think-up and think-back strategies and decide which would help them most to remember facts and why. Different children may have different answers, which will demonstrate that we can think differently but that if our thinking is valid, we will get the same answer as another person.

ACTIVITY 6.24

Ask children to use number lines to model the think-back or think-up strategy (Figure 6.13). Have them share how they used the number lines.

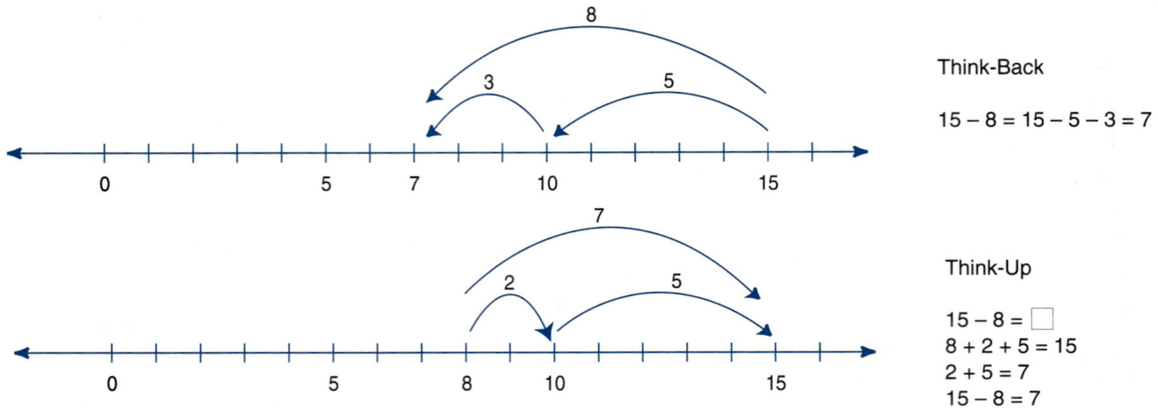

FIGURE 6.13 Number Line Model for "Think-Back" and "Think-Up" to Ten Strategy

Using either the think-back or the think-up strategy, children can also find a useful pattern: When subtracting 9, the difference is always 1 greater than the ones in the minuend (e.g., $15 - 9 = 6$; $6 = 5 + 1$); when subtracting 8, the difference is always 2 greater than the ones in the minuend ($15 - 8 = 7$; $7 = 5 + 2$).

ACTIVITY 6.25

Help children discover the pattern when 9 is the minuend. Ask them to give differences for three fact questions with 9 as the subtrahend, and look for a pattern. If necessary, say, "What is the connection between the ones in each answer and its related minuend (give minuends in your examples)?" Have them share their ideas and how the pattern they found would help remember facts. If the pattern is evident to them, repeat the activity with 8 as the subtrahend.

7. Think Compensation (Adjusting). When using the compensation strategy with subtraction, the same number is added to or subtracted from both minuend and subtrahend to make an easier fact. For example, to find $11 - 3 = N$, thinking 1 less than 11 and 1 less than 3 gives the same difference, or $11 - 3 = 10 - 2 = 8$.

ACTIVITY 6.26

Ask pupils to use linking cubes or number bars to show pairs of facts such as $7 - 3 = \square$ with $8 - 4 = \square$ and $9 - 4 = \square$ with $10 - 5 = \square$. Ask pupils what they noticed as they showed the facts. Have them make a rule from their observations: to make an easier fact, add the same number to both numbers in a subtraction fact and then subtract. When pupils grasp addition compensation in a subtraction fact, repeat the activity so that they understand subtracting the same number from the minuend and the subtrahend in a subtraction fact to obtain an easier fact with the same difference.

8. Think the Related Addition Fact. This strategy is based on the idea that addition and subtraction are *inverse*. Thus, to recall a subtraction fact, think the related addition fact. For example, to recall $9 - 4 = 5$ or $9 - 5 = 4$, think $4 + 5 = 9$. To use this strategy, children must have reversible thought, that is, be able to move back and forth in their thinking and have had experience with "opposite facts."

ACTIVITY 6.27

Ask children how knowing addition helps them remember how to subtract. Have them think how to answer your question by using number bars or linking cubes. In some classes, you will need to give an example, saying, "What subtraction fact questions can you answer if you know 4 + 7 = 11?" Ask them to use the overhead with counters to tell the class their ideas. Next, ask, "What addition fact would you think to solve 12 – 6 = □?" Continue with other similar questions. When they understand how to think a related addition fact to answer a subtraction fact question, ask them to give a subtraction question and the related addition fact that helps them remember the answer to the subtraction question.

Children cannot use the idea of the inverse relation between addition and subtraction if they do not understand the concept. If they need to rethink this idea, Activity 5.15 can be used. If they still cannot use this strategy, reintroduce it later.

Many of these strategies deal with the same facts, and therefore it is not possible to say how many facts can be recalled using certain strategies. The strategy used depends on the student.

Multiplication

The strategies for multiplication are: think turnarounds, think skip-counting by two, think with the clock, think the one facts rule, think the zero facts rule, use the nines pattern, think doubles, use the distributive property of multiplication over addition, and think patterns in endings.

1. Think Turnarounds. Because of their knowledge of the turnaround strategy for recalling addition facts, many children will be able to use the idea of turnarounds to recall multiplication facts. For example, if 4 × 5 = 20 is known, then 5 × 4 = 20 is also known (Figure 6.14).

ACTIVITY 6.28

Children should understand turnarounds because the multiplication order rule (commutative property of multiplication) was introduced when they studied the meaning of multiplication. (See Activities 5.28 and 5.29.) To relate the strategy to earlier work,

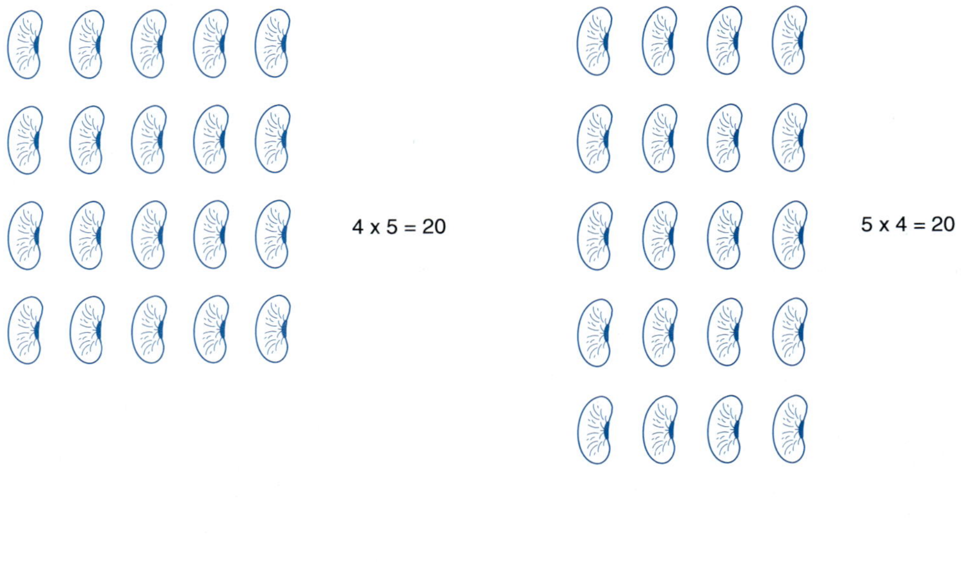

FIGURE 6.14 Counters Showing "Turnarounds" Strategy for Multiplication

say "Remember what we learned when we turned an array for a multiplication array around. (If they do not remember, have them repeat placing counters on a book and turning the book—Activity 5.29.) What does the book-turning experiment tell us about a rule for remembering facts? If you know that 3 × 4 = 12, what other fact is easy to remember by using the turnaround rule? Why? Let's each make a list of five facts and their turnarounds." Have pupils share their lists. You could ask why they choose certain facts.

2. Think Skip-Counting by Twos. If children are able to count by twos, they have access to ten facts and their opposites. For example to find 6 × 2 = *N*, count by twos noting how many times a count is given until 6 counts are determined: 2, 4, 6, 8, 10, 12.

ACTIVITY 6.29

Say, "Let's skip count by twos to find a way to help remember facts. How will it help to recall a fact with 2 as the second factor, such as 4 × 2 = □? What if 2 is the first factor?" Ask pupils to show their thinking with arrays or number lines (Figure 6.15).

3. Think with the Clock. The strategy is: Use the clock for the five facts table, noting the hour numerals for the factor other than 5 and the minute time for the product (e.g., 3 × 5 = 15. Look at the 3 on the face of the clock. Think 15).

ACTIVITY 6.30

Ask children to study the clock for a strategy to remember a particular fact such as 3 × 5 = *N*. If no child discovers the strategy, say, "How many minutes past an hour is it when the little hand points to 3? How will that help with facts?" Continue with other examples, and say, "Close your eyes. Think a mind picture of the clock. What is 4 × 5? Tell us your thinking." To conclude, ask how thinking the clock can help them remember facts.

4. Think the One Facts Rule. The pattern—when one factor is 1, the product is the other factor—gives a rule that makes for easy mastery of the multiplication facts of 1 (e.g., 9 × 1 = 9).

ACTIVITY 6.31

Ask pupils to solve five facts in which 1 is either the first or second factor, using any method they choose. When the work is completed, ask them to look at the results to discover a strategy for remembering facts with 1 as a factor. Ask what other facts can be recalled by this strategy. To help them generalize the rule, ask, what is 26 × 1? 49 × 1? 1 × 237?

FIGURE 6.15 Number Line Model for "Skip-Counting"

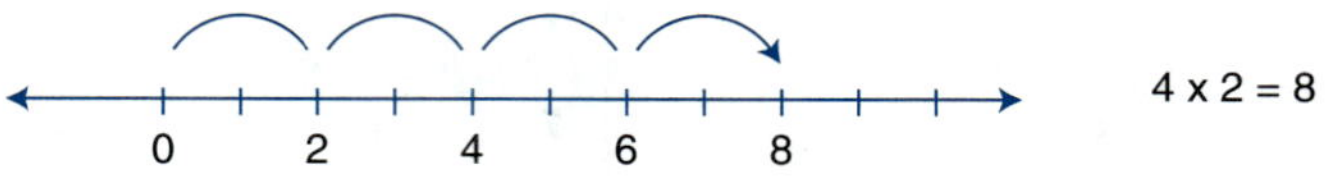

5. Think the Zero Facts Rule. The pattern—when one factor is 0, the product is 0—is the basis for a rule that make for easy mastery of zero multiplication facts (e.g., $4 \times 0 = 0$; $0 \times 7 = 0$).

ACTIVITY 6.32

Say, "Today please solve these three fact questions, $2 \times 0 = \square$, $3 \times 0 = \square$, and $4 \times 0 = \square$, by using repeated addition. What are the sums? Why?" (Someone should say, "If 0 is added 2 times, the answer is 0." Ask, "What is 8×0? 9×0? Why?" Next, have them write several facts of their own choosing when 0 is the second factor. Ask children to give their fact questions and products. Say, "How did you know the products? What is going on here? Is there a pattern? Can we make a rule? What about 0 as the first factor?" After the class decides on a rule that is valid, have them ask each other zero facts.

6. Use the Nines Pattern. Any product with a 9 as a factor has these characteristics: the tens and ones digits of the product have a sum of 9, and the tens digit of the product is 1 less than the factor that is not 9 (or 9 if both factors are 9). For example, $6 \times 9 = 54$ ($5 + 4 = 9$; $6 - 1 = 5$) and $8 \times 9 = 72$ ($7 + 2 = 9$; $8 - 1 = 7$).

ACTIVITY 6.33

Write the fact questions $2 \times 9 = \square$, $3 \times 9 = \square$, $4 \times 9 = \square$, and $5 \times 9 = \square$ on the chalkboard or on the overhead. Ask children to find the answers for these four fact questions and look for a pattern in the products. (You may need to circle the related numbers with colored chalk or pens.) When they discover the pattern, say, "Will this pattern hold for the other 9 facts? How can we find out?" They should decide to study the other facts for 9 to see if the pattern continues.

Activity for the Classroom 6.1. Have students experiment with arrays for the facts of 9 to show the reasonableness of the nines-pattern strategy. (You may need to suggest rearranging the arrays to show tens and ones.) Have them explain the results of their experiments.

7. Think Doubles. There are five doubles (3×3, 4×4, 6×6, 7×7, and 8×8) not covered by the other strategies.

ACTIVITY 6.34

Have children make arrays for these facts, write the facts, and circle the tens and ones with different-color crayons. Discuss features that could be useful to them for recalling the facts (e.g., $6 \times 6 = 36$—the factors are 6, and the product ends in 6).

8. Use the Distributive Property of Multiplication over Addition. There are 10 other multiplication facts and their commuted forms that are not included in the strategies already discussed to total the 100 facts and their commuted forms. The 10 facts are: 3×4, 3×6, 3×7, 3×8, 4×6, 4×7, 4×8, 6×7, 6×8, and 7×8. Often, children use a strategy involving the distributive property of multiplication over addition to recall these facts: when one fact is written as a sum, the product is the sum of each addend with the other factor. For example, $3 \times 4 = 3 \times (2 + 2) = (3 \times 2) + (3 \times 2) = 6 + 6 = 12$; $4 \times 6 = 4 \times (5 + 1) = (4 \times 5) + (4 \times 1) = 20 + 4 = 24$.

ACTIVITY 6.35

This activity helps children use their knowledge of multiplication with 5 to learn the strategy based on the distributive property of multiplication over addition. Ask children to study arrays made with two colors (or different marks) that highlight 5 as a factor (Figure 6.16). Then say, "How does knowing the facts of 5 help with other facts?" Their responses should bring out that a fact such as 7×6 can be thought of as a sum of 7×5 plus 7×1. Children should communicate their thinking about this strategy orally. They do not write the math sentence nor do you introduce the math sentence to record the thinking involved.

To become familiar with thinking how they can use the facts of 5 to remember other facts, children can list some facts they could easily recall if they made a problem with a 5 fact. Have them explain how they decided the facts to list. You can also ask if this "think-the-parts" strategy would help them remember other facts. I have observed children using the strategy by thinking one factor as a sum with no addend a 5 (e.g., $8 \times 3 = (4 \times 3) + (4 \times 3)$).

9. Think Patterns in Endings. There are patterns to the ones in tables of multiplication facts. For example, any fact with 5 as a factor will end in 5 or 0. If children are aware of these patterns, they often use them to recall multiplication facts.

ACTIVITY 6.36

Give children circular regions with 10 subdivisions on the circumference labeled 0 through 9 (Figure 6.17). As children say any multiplication table, they connect the numerals that correspond to the ones in the products. (Model this procedure before asking children to carry it out.) For example, to make the pattern for the 4 table, connect 0, 4, 8, 2, 6, 0, 4, 8, 2, 6, 0. Discuss how this activity can help them remember facts: knowing the endings pattern is an aid to recall.

Variation: Use 100 squares to find patterns instead of circular regions (Figure 6.18).

FIGURE 6.16 Counter Model for Distributive Property of Multiplication over Addition

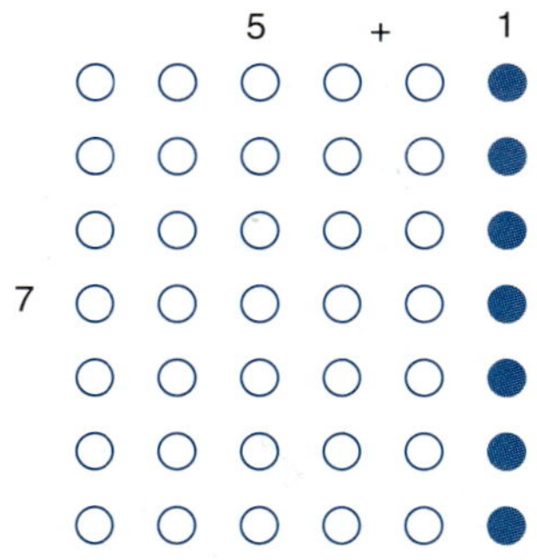

$7 \times 6 = 7 \times (5 + 1) = (7 \times 5) + (7 \times 1) = 35 + 7 = 42$

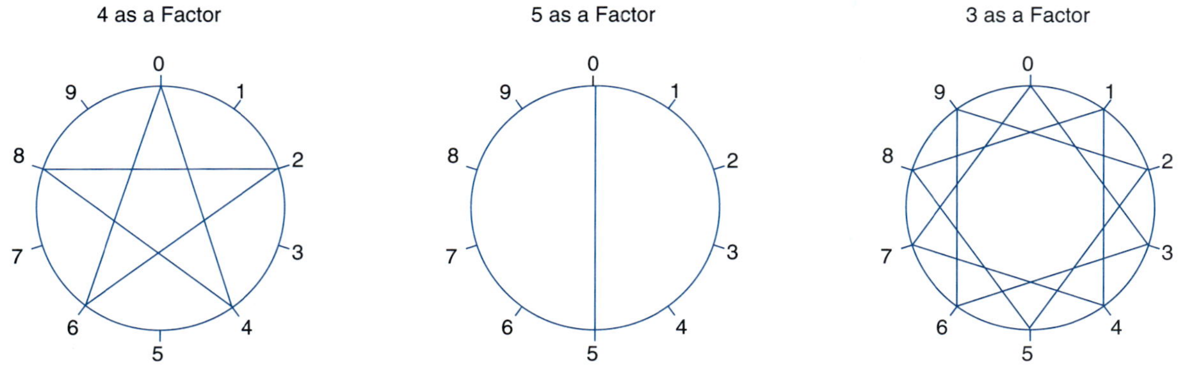

FIGURE 6.17 Multiplication Patterns

Division

The strategies for recalling division facts are: think the related multiplication fact, think skip-counting back by two, think the one facts rule, and think the zero facts rule. In work with division, students also need to develop skill in giving the unseen dividend in division with remainders.

1. Think the Related Multiplication Fact. The inverse relation between multiplication and division provides a basis for this strategy. To think $12 \div 4 = 3$ or $12 \div 3 = 4$, think $3 \times 4 = 12$, or think "What do I multiply 3 by to get 12?" or "3 times what number equals 12?"

ACTIVITY 6.37

Have children make an array for a multiplication fact of their own choosing and discuss how the array shows multiplication. Ask children how the array can also show division. Continue with several more examples, and ask questions so that children express their understanding that multiplication and division are inverse. Then ask how a division fact can be recalled by thinking a multiplication fact. Conclude by having children give division facts that are "opposite" of multiplication facts.

2. Think Skip-Counting by Twos. If children are able to count forward or backward by twos from an even number, they have access to 9 facts for division. For exam-

1	2	3	4	5	6	7	**8**	9	10
11	12	13	14	15	**16**	17	18	19	20
21	22	23	**24**	25	26	27	28	29	30
31	**32**	33	34	35	36	37	38	39	**40**
41	42	43	44	45	46	47	**48**	49	50
51	52	53	54	55	**56**	57	58	59	60
61	62	63	**64**	65	66	67	68	69	70
71	**72**	73	74	75	76	77	78	79	**80**
81	82	83	84	85	86	87	**88**	89	90
91	92	93	94	95	**96**	97	98	99	100

FIGURE 6.18 Chart Showing 8 as a Factor

ple, to find $8 \div 2 = N$, count up or back by twos, noting how many times a count is given until 8 or 0 is reached: 2, 4, 6, 8 or 6, 4, 2, 0.

ACTIVITY 6.38

Ask children to think how, when a dividend is an even number and the divisor is 2, counting on or back by twos will help them recall the fact. After they give their ideas, say, "Your ideas are very sensible. Let's show what you are thinking on number lines. How would we do that?" A few children can use number line transparencies on the overhead to explain their work. When they finish, ask about counting back by twos when the dividend is an odd number. Help them decide if this strategy is useful when the divisor is 2 and the dividend is an odd number.

3. Think the One Facts Rules. Two patterns are the basis for rules that make for easy recall of 17 division facts:

a. When the divisor is 1, the quotient is the dividend.
b. When the divisor and the dividend are the same number, the quotient is 1.

ACTIVITY 6.39

Ask students to write in words the meaning of two division facts with 1 as the divisor. They can choose the facts or you can assign them. (For example, $6 \div 1 = 6$ means, "How many ones equal 6?") Have them discuss how thinking the meaning of these facts gives a strategy for remembering the one facts for division.

ACTIVITY 6.40

Ask children to use repeated subtraction to solve division facts in which the dividend and the divisor are the same number or the divisor is 1. They tell the rules they can make on the basis of their findings.

Have one or more children demonstrate how they use the strategy when both the dividend and the divisor are the same numbers or the divisor is 1.

4. Think the Zero Facts Rule. The pattern—when 0 is the dividend, the quotient is 0—gives a rule for nine division facts (e.g., $0 \div 4 = 0$). Division by 0 is undefined.

ACTIVITY 6.41

Children can verbalize the meaning of several facts when 0 is the dividend to grasp the meaning of the strategy and hence remember it. Ask, for example, "Explain what 0 divided by 5 means." They could answer, "Zero divided by 5 means, how many fives equal 0? Of course, none at all; no zeros will add to 5." Have them form a rule from their work with examples.

Some students may be helped to understand that you cannot divide by 0 by relating division and multiplication. Ask, "What number multiplied by 0 would give 8 (or another number)." Since no number can be found, they may grasp the rationale behind the statement: Division by 0 is undefined.

5. Think the Unseen Dividend. In division computational estimation, it is often necessary to think an unseen dividend that is the largest multiple of the divisor less than the given dividend. For example, to estimate 4929 ÷ 6, one thinks 4800 ÷ 6 = 800, so the estimate for 4929 ÷ 6 is a little more than 800—a good estimate is 815. Recalling the fact to use in such a problem (48 ÷ 6) is a skill elementary school children need to develop.

ACTIVITY 6.42
Thinking the Fact in Division with Remainders.

After children have carried out activities such as Activities 5.39–5.43 in Chapter Five and have developed an intuitive awareness of the need to use a division fact in uneven division, ask them to work in groups or as a class to decide on a plan to use to solve such problems. Give them examples such as 45 ÷ 8 = *N*, 34 ÷ 4 = *N*, and 29 ÷ 3 = *N* to use to develop their plan. You may need to ask questions such as: "What dividend did you use in the first example? Why? Why could we call this an 'unseen dividend?' How did you decide what is the unseen dividend?" Can you use that method in all uneven division involving basic facts? Have students summarize their thinking in a rule or procedure for dealing with uneven division involving basic facts: think the unseen dividend that is the largest multiple of the divisor less than the given dividend (or think the largest number divisible by the divisor), use that dividend in the division to obtain a quotient, and subtract the unseen dividend from the given dividend to determine a remainder. They may not be able to state the rule, but instead give examples. Accept this as their best thinking.

ACTIVITY 6.43
Match-up in Division.

Prepare two lists such as the following, and ask students to match the correct dividend to think when carrying out the division. The list is written so that the same dividend is used in more than one division and there is one dividend not used in any matching. The directions are: Do not compute. Only draw a line from a dividend to the question that can be answered by using that dividend. You may need to use a dividend more than once, and some in the dividend list may not be used.

Division Questions	Dividends
29 ÷ 4 = □	14
61 ÷ 9 = □	30
32 ÷ 5 = □	21
17 ÷ 7 = □	28
23 ÷ 3 = □	54
15 ÷ 2 = □	56

ACTIVITY 6.44
What Is the Leftover?

Learners complete sentences such as the following:

32 = (7 × _______) + _______; 22 = (5 × _______) + _______

55 = (9 × _______) + _______; 19 = (3 × _______) + _______

The directions are: Write the largest number possible on the first line; the smallest number possible on the second line. When you finish the four sentences, write four sentences of your own using the same kind of incomplete sentence. Trade with your math partner. He or she will write numbers in your sentences to make them true. Discuss your work with your partner when you finish. Later, in a class discussion ask pupils to tell what they learned from the activity.

ACTIVITY 6.45
Make Uneven Division Questions.

Assign facts such as 21 ÷ 3 = □, 32 ÷ 8 = □, 16 ÷ 2 = □, and 45 ÷ 9 = □. Ask learners to write as many uneven division questions as possible related to each fact you assigned (e.g., the uneven division questions related to 21 ÷ 3 = □ are 22 ÷ 3 = □ and 23 ÷ 3 = □; uneven division questions related to 32 ÷ 8 are 33 ÷ 8 = □, 34 ÷ 8 = □, 35 ÷ 8 = □, 36 ÷ 8 = □, 37 ÷ 8, 38 ÷ 8, and 39 ÷ 8 = □). When they discuss their work, ask what they noticed about the number of uneven divisions for the different facts (larger divisors have more possibilities for uneven division, and so subtraction to find the remainder may be harder).

Activity for the Classroom 6.2. Select six children with different ability levels, and ask each student how he or she recalls facts. What insights about learners' understanding of basic facts and strategies did you gain from this activity?

PREREQUISITES FOR LEARNING STRATEGIES

Strategies cannot be understood and used to recall facts if children do not have prerequisite knowledge (Thornton, 1990). To learn *strategies for addition and subtraction facts*, children must know the order of numbers, be able to think 1 more or less than a number or count on or back 2 or 3, and realize that the order of addends can be changed (commutative property of addition). Knowing the anchors five and ten is also helpful. Usually children build these prerequisites as they engage in experiences to develop understanding of operations. As you circulate among students when they are working on assignments, ask questions to determine if children have attained the prerequisites for learning strategies for recalling addition and subtraction facts. When working with small groups, you can also ask questions, pose tasks, or give problems to determine if children have prerequisites. Examples are:

- Questions to ask: What number comes after 7? Before 5? How do you know? What number is 2 greater than 6? 2 less than 8? How do you know? Before you compute, tell if any of these number questions has the same answer: $3 + 4 = N$, $4 + 2 = N$, $4 + 3 + N$? Which ones? How do you know?
- Tasks to give: Show as many facts as you can with red rods, light green rods, and yellow rods. Tell about what you did. (Note if the child shows a fact and remarks that it is the opposite of another fact he or she has shown.)
- Problems to ask can require students to focus on relations, for example: Frank and Tom were playing basketball. Frank made 5 baskets in the morning and 3 in the afternoon. How many baskets did Frank make? Then say: "The same day, Tom made 3 in the morning and 5 in the afternoon. What can you say about the number of baskets Tom made?" (Note how quickly the child answers, and be alert to any remarks he or she makes that indicates an understanding that changing the order of numbers in an addition fact does not change the sum.)

Prerequisites for learning *multiplication and division strategies* include skill in skip-counting, knowledge of the multiplication order rule (commutative property of multiplication), finding sums other than basic facts (e.g., 35 + 7 = 42 to solve 6 × 7 = (5 + 1) × 7 = □; see Chapter Seven for discussion of this learning), and an intuitive awareness of the distributive property of multiplication over addition.

Examples of questions are:

- How do you count up to 20 by twos? How do you count down by twos from 20 to 0?
- What do you know about 4×6 and 6×4?
- What is $36 + 6$? (This addition could help a child recall that $6 \times 7 = (6 \times 6) + 6$.)
- What is $40 + 16$? (This addition could help a child recall that $7 \times 8 = (5 + 2) \times 8 = (5 \times 8) + (2 \times 8) = 56$.)
- John did not know 5×6, but he knew 5×5. Would that help him remember 5×6?

It is advisable to keep a record of assessment results so that instruction can be planned to meet the needs of learners. Carrying a pad of sticky notes and a pencil for making records of observations is a good practice to follow when moving among children as they work. The comments or notes can be transferred later to files used for assessment.

TEACHING FOR MASTERY OF BASIC FACTS

Children should be helped to set expectations for mastery. Mastery is answering a fact question in two seconds or less and giving consistent performance over time (Thornton, 1990). Strategies are to be used only temporarily. Mastery of facts is necessary for children if they are to make progress in mathematics (Hiebert, 1990).

To achieve mastery, children play games and engage in practice activities. The game *Bingo,* adapted for any group of facts can help children master the facts. Because of the repetition involved, the games *War, Fish,* and *Rummy* often help children master facts. Kamii (1985) gives many games to help children learn the basic facts.

A number machine activity is another approach to help learners master facts (Figure 6.19). The number machine operates on a number. The activity gives several examples of the machine output, and learners complete a table to show other outputs. Calculator activities such as given in Box 6.1 are motivating to children and also contribute to mastery of the facts.

It is recommended that facts be grouped for study. A set of facts to study should be a small group of the facts pupils need to master. The latter are determined after a test children take to find out what facts they know and which to study. The test would include 75 to 100 (90 for division) facts for the operation being emphasized. Such a test is given infrequently and only for diagnostic purposes or for summative evaluation.

Before practice for mastery begins, remind learners that they know how to find fact answers by using other facts, and tell them they are ready to master the

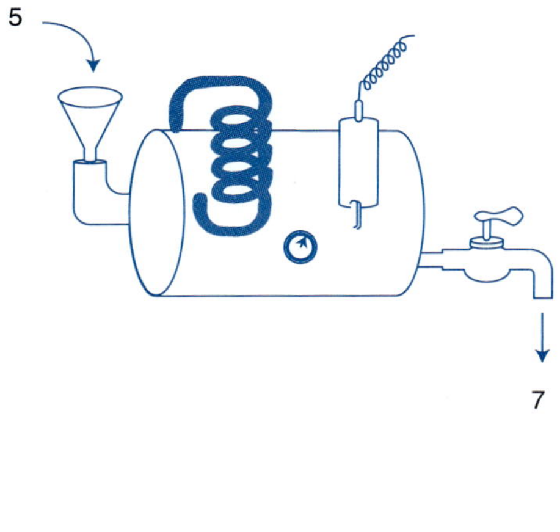

Before	After
5	7
2	4
6	8
3	___
7	___

FIGURE 6.19 Number Machine

BOX 6.1 Calculator Games for Basic Facts

All games are for two players and one calculator.

ADDITION

- Players begin with 0 on the calculator. One player chooses an addition fact sum (or uses a number on a numeral card chosen from a pile). The other player inputs an addition basic fact with that sum. If correct, he or she gets a token.
- The players exchange roles. After each has had 5 turns, the player with the most tokens wins, and the game begins again.
- For example, player 1 says, "14"; player 2 inputs "8 + 6." The calculator display shows "14." Player 2 gets a token.

SUBTRACTION

- One player inputs a basic fact minuend he or she chooses (or uses a number on a numeral card chosen from a pile) and gives the difference in a subtraction fact. The other player inputs a number to reach the difference. If correct, he or she gets a token.
- The players exchange roles. After each has had 5 turns, the player with the most tokens wins the round, and the game begins again.
- For example, player 1 inputs "15" and says, "Show 9"; player 2 inputs "– 6." The calculator display shows "9." Player 2 gets a token.

MULTIPLICATION

- Players begin with 0 on the calculator. One player chooses a multiplication fact product (or uses a number on a numeral card chosen from a pile). The other player inputs a multiplication basic fact with that product. If correct, he or she gets a token.
- The players exchange roles. After each has had 5 turns, the player with the most tokens wins, and the game begins again.
- For example, player 1 says, "14"; player 2 inputs "2 × 7." The calculator display shows "14." Player 2 gets a token.

DIVISION

- One player inputs a basic fact dividend he or she chooses (or uses a number on a numeral card chosen from a pile) and gives the quotient in a division fact. The other player inputs a number to reach the quotient. If correct, he or she gets a token.
- The players exchange roles. After each has had 5 turns, the player with the most tokens wins, and the game begins again.
- For example, player 1 inputs "15" and says, "Show 3"; player 2 inputs "÷ 5." The calculator display shows "3." Player 2 gets a token.

facts. Ask why they think mastery is important. If pupils do not realize the need to recall facts to solve problems outside of school and continue their learning of mathematics, give some examples to demonstrate that mastery is necessary to solve real-world problems, to find out many things about the world in which they live, and to learn more interesting mathematics. Ask them to think of examples in the next few days. Discuss these at a later time.

The procedure based on Thornton (1990) for mastering facts is next explained to the class. You may decide to write some steps in the procedure on a chart so that students will know what they will be doing in the future:

1. A test to find out what they know will be given. Individuals and sometimes the class will spend time learning what they do not know.
2. There will be short practice periods (5 to 10 minutes) during math periods or other times during the day when a few minutes are free.
3. During the practice periods, they will work mostly on groups of facts that need study.
4. There are three types of cards they can use for practice. Each kind is explained and displayed.
   a. Flash cards (Figure 6.20). A flash card gives a fact question on one side, with the fact question and answer on the other side.
   b. Fact family cards (Figure 6.21). A fact family gives a fact, its commuted form, and the inverse of the two facts (e.g., $4 \times 5 = 20$; $5 \times 4 = 20$; $20 \div 4 = 5$; $20 \div 5 = 4$. The card gives one fact on one side; the other side gives the four facts in the family.
   c. Same-answer cards (Figure 6.22). One side of the card gives a sum, difference, product, or quotient. The other side gives all the fact questions with that sum, difference, product, or quotient.
5. Practice periods will involve use of one or more types of cards. During free time, students may use any kind of practice cards for their own study.
6. Learners are to answer the fact question quickly; if they cannot remember the fact answer, they should look at the answer. If they are working with a partner, he or she will give the answer.
7. About once a week, there will be a short quiz (six to eight facts) of the facts studied and some of those studied previously; operations will not be mixed until facts for one operation have been mastered. They should be able to answer the fact questions on the quiz in 12 to 16 seconds. Occasionally, quizzes will include 30 facts to be answered in one minute.
8. The time and length of the quizzes will be announced ahead of time.
9. They should practice at home for several minutes each evening to help themselves learn the facts. They will make flash cards to take home and write a letter to their parent(s) or caretaker to ask for help in studying at home.
10. Some facts will be harder than others, and some children will take longer to learn the hard facts. However, all will succeed if they practice.

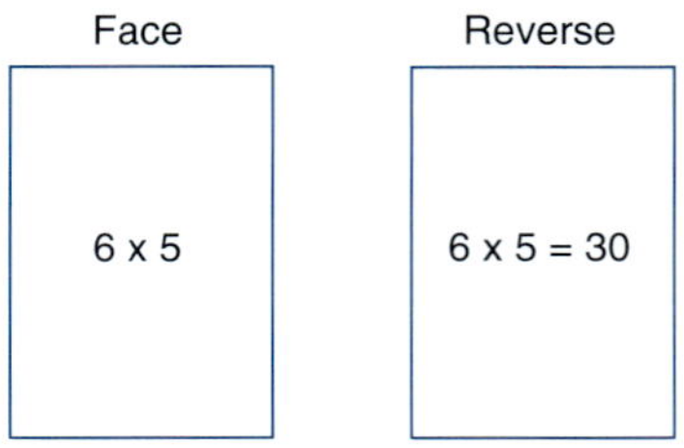

FIGURE 6.20 Flash Card

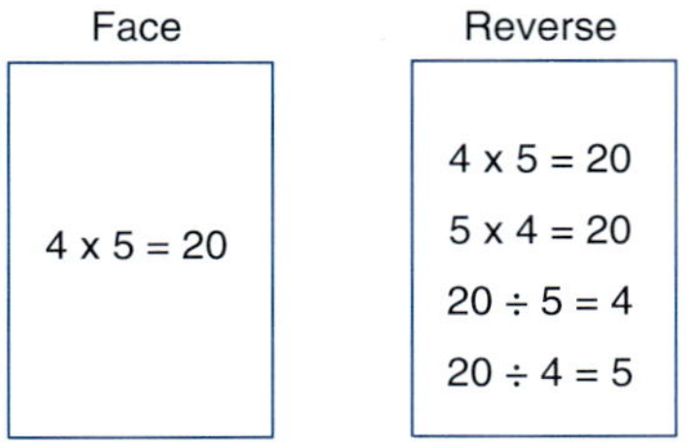

FIGURE 6.21 Fact Family Card

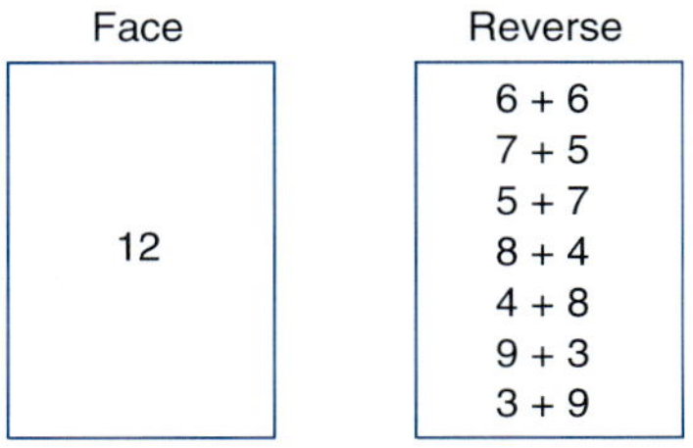

FIGURE 6.22 Same-Answer Card

Reader Activity 6.2

Recall how you learned the basic facts. How does the approach outlined in this and the preceding chapter compare with the approach that was used to teach you the basic facts. React to the similarities and differences in the two approaches.

ASSESSING MASTERY OF BASIC FACTS

Children should be able to answer 30 facts questions correctly in one minute. You keep dated records of a student's scores on quizzes and continue with practice sessions until facts are mastered. Students keep individual records of their progress by shading in the facts mastered on tables of the facts (Figure 6.23). They can also report progress toward mastery in their journals. By grade 5 students should have mastered the facts for all the operations.

Children should be encouraged to feel a sense of accomplishment when a group of facts has been mastered. Because a feeling of competency is intrinsically motivating, practice periods often begin with your reminding students of their progress. Some children will master the facts more quickly than others. Those children who have difficulty with facts can work together, supporting each other as they achieve mastery.

FIGURE 6.23 Child's Record of Multiplication Facts Mastered

X	0	1	2	3	4	5	6	7	8	9
0	0	0	0	0	0	0	0	0	0	0
1	0	1	2	3	4	5	6	7	8	9
2	0	2	4	6	8	10	12	14	16	18
3	0	3	6	9	12	15	18	21	24	27
4	0	4	8	12	16	20	24	28	32	36
5	0	5	10	15	20	25	30	35	40	45
6	0	6	12	18	24	30	36	42	48	54
7	0	7	14	21	28	35	42	49	56	63
8	0	8	16	24	32	40	48	56	64	72
9	0	9	18	27	36	45	54	63	72	81

Fact I Know

SUMMARY

This chapter has discussed strategies for learning the basic facts for addition, subtraction, multiplication, and division. Activities were described for learning and using each strategy. Strategies enable learners to think relations among facts and contribute to pupil's recall. They are introduced when children show understanding of the facts for an operation (see Chapter 5). When children use strategies to recall facts and have memorized some facts, mastery of facts becomes the instructional goal. A plan to enable children to master the basic facts was given. Mastery is stressed because learners cannot experience success in the study of mathematics or cope with the mathematics of daily living if they do not have immediate recall of the facts. Suggestions for helping pupils master the facts and assessing mastery were described.

REFERENCES

Folsom, Mary. (1975). "Operations on Whole Numbers." In *Mathematics Learning in Early Childhood*, edited by Joseph N. Payne, pp. 161–190. Reston, VA: National Council of Teachers of Mathematics.

Hiebert, James. (1990). "The Role of Routine Procedures in the Development of Mathematical Competence." In *Teaching and Learning Mathematics in the 1990s*, edited by Thomas J. Cooney and Christian R. Hirsch, pp. 31–40. Reston, VA: National Council of Teachers of Mathematics.

Kamii, Constance Kazuko. (1985). *Young Children Reinvent Arithmetic*. New York: Teachers College Press.

Labinowicz, Ed. (1985). *Learning from Children: New Beginnings for Teaching Numerical Thinking*. Menlo Park, CA; Addison-Wesley.

National Council of Teachers of Mathematics. (1989). *Curriculum and Evaluation Standards for School Mathematics*. Reston, VA: Author.

Rathmell, Edward C. (1978). "Using Thinking Strategies to Teach the Basic Facts." In *Developing Computational Skills*, edited by Marilyn N. Suydam and Robert E. Reys, pp. 13–38. Reston, VA: National Council of Teachers of Mathematics.

Suydam, Marilyn N. (September 1984)."Learning the Basic Facts." *Arithmetic Teacher* 32: 15.

Suydam, Marilyn N., and J. Fred Weaver. (1975). "Research on Mathematics Learning." In *Mathematics Learning in Early Childhood*, edited by Joseph N. Payne, pp. 43–67. Reston, VA: National Council of Teachers of Mathematics.

Thornton, Carol. (1990). "Strategies for the Basic Facts." In *Mathematics for the Young Child*, edited by Joseph N. Payne, pp. 133–151. Reston, VA: National Council Teacher of Mathematics.

Thornton, Carol, and Smith, Paula J. (April 1988). "Action Research: Strategies for Learning Subtraction Facts." *Arithmetic Teacher* 39: 8–12.

SOFTWARE RESOURCES

Math Blaster
Company: Davidson and Associates
Computer: Apple
Grade level: 1–6

Game format provides practice with basic facts for all operations. Objective is to launch a rocket. Five levels of difficulty. Advanced levels give practice with fractions and decimals.

Speedway Math
Company: Minnesota Educational Computing Corporation (MECC)
Computer: Apple
Grade level: 1–6

Provides practice in basic facts. All operations. Three programs. Programs time and record student's performance.

CHAPTER 7

Computation with Whole Numbers

▪ INTRODUCTORY PROBLEM ▪

Your fifth-grade class is having a paper and plastic recycling drive for 10 weeks beginning in January. The details of the project were reported to all the residents of the school district in the school paper, which is sent to every district household. The plan is: The class will divide itself into teams of four students. Each team will decide on a team name such as the Aces. The residents of the school district will put newspapers or plastic in separate plastic or paper bags at the curb together with their trash. After school, the day the trash is collected the students will pick up the paper and plastic for recycling. A pick-up area of two to four blocks to include the same number of households for each team will be chosen by teams. Each two weeks the students will write an article to be published in the school paper reporting on the paper and plastic collected by each team. How could you include learning mental computation, computational estimation, and paper-and-pencil algorithms in this project?

INTRODUCTION

Computation with whole numbers is finding a place-value solution to an addition, subtraction, multiplication, or division problem when the solution cannot be found by using basic facts alone. In addition computation, at least one addend in the expression must be greater than 10, and in multiplication, at least one factor must be greater than 10. Table 7.1 gives examples of math sentences whose solutions involve computation with whole numbers.

In contemporary society objectives for learning computation are different from those of a generation or so ago. Today's children need to understand various approaches to computation so that they can find solutions appropriate for different problem situations. Sometimes exact answers found mentally are needed, sometimes a computed estimate will do, at other times paper-and-pencil procedures are useful for solving a problem, and often calculators are used to perform the computation. New directions in teaching and learning elementary school mathematics require that students learn all these approaches to computation to cope with the demands of their world (NCTM, 1989). (see Standards 5, 7, and 8 for grades K–4 and Standard 7 for grades 5–8, Appendix A.)

Some suggest that mental computation and computational estimation be taught prior to work with paper-and-pencil computation (Rathmell and Trafton, 1990); others that they be taught concurrently (Hazenkamp, 1986). The plan presented here is to introduce mental computation and computational estimation before paper-and-pencil computation, without expecting that learners will have mastered these approaches before paper-and-pencil methods are introduced.

Paper-and-pencil computation should not be introduced before mental computation and computational estimation. It is believed that if students learn paper-and-pencil methods first, they develop rigid approaches to calculating that interfere with developing alternative strategies for mental computation (Hazenkamp, 1986). Furthermore, knowledge of mental computation and computational estimation enables learners to make sense of written computation and increases their feelings of self-confidence to "do" mathematics (Rathmell and Trafton, 1990).

Instruction in paper-and-pencil algorithms (step-by-step procedures, carried out routinely) stresses the meaning of the algorithms. Pupils begin by solving problems using their own methods, which usually involve the use of materials. To understand the reasons for the steps in algorithms, they connect solutions with materials to paper-and-pencil computation. After they understand the basis for the number manipulations involved in algorithms, children engage in practice activities to achieve mastery (Coburn, 1989).

Calculators are introduced to children in the primary grades to find answers to problems and are used throughout the elementary grades as problem-solving tools. Many calculator activities for learning computation are included in this chapter.

Interactive methods rather than teacher-directed lessons characterize instruction for learning computation (Cobb and Merkel, 1989). Students participate in problem solving, investigations, and discussions that help them understand computational procedures by integrating new information with previously learned concepts and skills. Teachers rarely explain approaches to computation. Instead, they teach computation by assigning relevant activities, listening to learners share their work, and relating their questioning to students' understanding. Learners are

TABLE 7.1 Examples of Computation

24 + 8 = 32	32 − 8 = 24	32 − 24 = 8
30 + 60 = 90	90 − 30 = 60	90 − 60 = 30
24 + 54 = 78	78 − 54 = 24	78 − 24 = 54
6 × 45 = 270	270 ÷ 6 = 45	270 ÷ 45 = 6
26 × 39 = 1014	1014 ÷ 26 = 39	1014 ÷ 39 = 26
50 × 40 = 2000	2000 ÷ 50 = 40	2000 ÷ 40 = 50

then able to construct knowledge by reflecting on their own work, reasoning about numbers, and communicating with others.

There are two parts to this chapter. Part I has three main sections: Foundations of Computation, Beginning Mental Computation, and Strategies for Mental Computation. The main sections in Part 2 discuss Computational Estimation, Paper-and-Pencil Computation, and Choosing a Computational Procedure. Each section includes a discussion of learning objectives, suggestions for teaching, including activities for learners, and an overview of assessment. The final section summarizes the chapter.

Assessment suggestions in each section include those that relate only to assessing computational competency. To avoid being repetitive, assessing attitudes is not discussed in the different sections of the chapter. However, assessment of attitudes toward learning different computational skills is an important instructional task. Attitudes are assessed by determining children's willingness to master various computational procedures and their persistence in achieving competency. Teachers are always alert to children's behaviors that show their attitudes, and they help learners develop positive attitudes toward learning computational skills by helping them realize the value of such skills.

PART I Foundations of Computation and Mental Computation

FOUNDATIONS OF COMPUTATION

Foundations for computation are knowledge of the operations, mastery of the basic facts, understanding the process of thinking parts when working with numbers, and comparing and renaming numbers. These learnings are involved in all computation, and hence the foundations are prerequisites for mental computation, computational estimation, and paper-and-pencil computation. Interactive approaches to teaching and learning the foundations of computation have been discussed in earlier chapters, so they are discussed only briefly here.

Knowledge of the Operations

Knowledge of the operations involves knowing the interpretations of addition, subtraction, multiplication, and division. Mental computation and computational estimation require knowledge of the operations to make sense of what one is doing.

Paper-and-pencil computation becomes routine with practice, but knowledge of the operations is needed to evaluate the reasonableness of solutions. Furthermore, all types of computation are tools for finding answers to real-life problems involving numbers. Deciding how to relate the numbers in a problem requires understanding the operations. A person cannot move to the computational phase of problem solving if he or she lacks an understanding of the operations.

Because the meanings of the operations are learned as children study the basic facts, when children begin the study of computation, they are expected to have knowledge of the operations. To help learners generalize basic fact meanings to the study of large numbers, have them discuss the interpretations of the operations when large numbers are included in story or number problems.

Mastery of Basic Facts

Immediate recall of the basic facts is necessary for the study of computational procedures. If children have not mastered the facts, they have difficulty with computation because most of their working memory's limited capacity is used to figure out the answer to a basic fact question. Too little capacity is left for processing a computational procedure and the task cannot be completed successfully or is completed very slowly. Although it is not necessary for children to have mastered all the basic facts for an operation before studying computation, they must have immediate recall of those facts involved in the computation to be learned. Hazenkamp (1986) suggests that when children know facts such as $2 \times 3 = N$, they can learn mental computation products involving these facts (e.g., $20 \times 30 = N$).

Thinking Parts of Numbers

Thinking parts of numbers, operating on the parts, and combining them to find the solution is a process used in all computation. It is particularly important to understanding paper-and-pencil computation (NCTM, 1989). Two examples are:

1. To mentally compute 35 + 47, one can think 47 is 35 + 10 + 2; 35 + 35 = 70; add 10 (80) and 2 more; the sum is 82. (Do you have a different way?)
2. To mentally compute 41×22, one can think 22 is $(2 \times 10) + 2$; $10 \times 41 = 410$; add another 410, that is 820; add 2×41, which is 80 + 2; 820 + 80 = 900; 900 + 2 = 902. (Do you have a different way?)

To carry out such thought processes, children must have an intuitive understanding of the commutative and associative properties of addition and multiplication, of the distributive property of multiplication over addition (Atweh, 1982), and of renaming numbers (Hazenkamp, 1986). Pupils should have developed an awareness of these ideas when working with basic facts and place-value concepts. If not, several approaches can be used to help them develop an awareness of the properties and think parts of numbers.

1. Ask children to discuss or use materials to review thinking the answers to basic fact questions in different ways. For example, they can make arrays to show $4 \times 7 = 4 \times (5 + 2) = (4 \times 5) + (4 \times 2) = 20 + 8 = 28$. As children talk about different ways to show basic facts, your questioning helps them become aware that they have been "thinking parts."
2. Have children work with place-value materials to study thinking parts. Ask them to show a tens-plus-ones number in as many ways as possible. For example, 24 counters can be rearranged as 2 tens + 4, 1 ten + 14, 1 ten + 2 + 1 ten + 2, 1 ten + 9 + 5, and so on. As children share their ideas, they form ideas of thinking parts of numbers.
3. Review the properties with basic facts for addition and multiplication. Chapter Five has activities that could be used for review as well as initial learning of properties of addition and multiplication.

Comparing and Renaming Numbers

Children must be able to compare large numbers and rename numbers as multiples of different powers of 10 if they are to become competent in computation. Computed solutions must be compared to estimated solutions, and the reasonableness of answers must be determined. Renaming is required in many computational tasks (e.g., $300 \div 6 = 30$ tens $\div 6 = 5$ tens $= 50$). Before beginning computation, you should assess children's ability to compare and rename numbers to 100. When computation involves numbers greater than 100, you determine children's knowledge of these numbers. If students lack knowledge of comparing and renaming large numbers, you reintroduce these concepts. Many activities in Chapter Four deal with comparing and renaming numbers and can be adapted for assessment and review.

Activity for the Classroom 7.1. Write two activities for assessing learners' ability to compare numbers to 1000. Use the tasks in your class. Have students explain how they thought to compare the numbers. Use their explanations to decide what students understand about large numbers.

BEGINNING MENTAL COMPUTATION

Children begin mental computation by developing an understanding of and constructing patterns for computation with multiples of powers of 10, devising rules based on the patterns, and learning higher-decade addition and subtraction. These attainments are necessary for mental computation with hundreds, tens, and tens and ones numbers, for computational estimation, and for paper-and-pencil computation. Attaining these learnings also enables children to make sense of computation.

Computation with Multiples of Powers of 10

Mastery of the operations with multiples of powers of 10 involves using basic facts and giving the solution a correct place value. Examples are:

$$40 + 20 = 4 \text{ tens} + 2 \text{ tens} = (4 + 2) \text{ tens} = 6 \text{ tens} = 60$$
$$80 + 60 = 8 \text{ tens} + 6 \text{ tens} = (8 + 6) \text{ tens} = 14 \text{ tens} = 140$$
$$60 - 20 = 40;\ 6 \text{ tens} - 2 \text{ tens} = (6 - 2) \text{ tens} = 4 \text{ tens} = 40$$
$$140 - 60 = 14 \text{ tens} - 6 \text{ tens} = (14 - 6) \text{ tens} = 8 \text{ tens} = 80$$
$$4 \times 20 = 4 \times 2 \text{ tens} = (4 \times 2) \text{ tens} = 8 \text{ tens} = 80$$
$$40 \times 20 = 4 \text{ tens} \times 2 \text{ tens} = (4 \times 2)(10 \times 10) = 8 \text{ hundreds} = 800$$
$$80 \times 60 = 8 \text{ tens} \times 6 \text{ tens} = (8 \times 6)(10 \times 10) = 48 \text{ hundreds} = 4800$$
$$80 \div 20 = 8 \text{ tens} \div 2 \text{ tens} = (8/2) \times (10/10) = 4 \div 1 = 4$$
$$800 \div 20 = 8 \text{ hundreds} \div 2 \text{ tens} = (8/2) \times (100/10) = 4 \text{ tens} = 40$$
$$4800 \div 60 = 48 \text{ hundreds} \div 6 \text{ tens} = (48/6) \times (100/10) = 8 \text{ tens} = 80$$

To develop understanding and mastery, it is useful to think of patterns (Hazenkamp, 1978, 1986). Useful patterns are:

- *For addition:* Tens plus tens equals tens; hundreds plus hundreds equals hundreds.
- *For subtraction:* Tens minus tens equals tens; hundreds minus hundreds equals hundreds.
- *For multiplication:* Ones times tens equals tens; tens times tens equals hundreds.
- *For division:* Tens divided by ones equals tens; tens divided by tens equals ones; hundreds divided by ones equals hundreds; hundreds divided by hundreds equals ones; hundreds divided by tens equals tens.

The *patterns* for addition and subtraction can be restated as: the sum (difference) has the same place value as the addends (minuend and subtrahend). For multiplication (division) the logic of the place-value system can help some learners recall the patterns: the value represented by any place in a numeral is 10 times greater than that of a place to the right and 10 times less than that of a place to the left.

The *rules* for mental computation are developed from an awareness of the patterns. The rule for addition or subtraction is: Think the numbers as ones, and use a basic fact to find the sum (difference). Give the basic fact sum (or difference) the same place value as that of the numbers in the problem. The rule for multiplication (division) is: Think of the numbers as ones. Use a basic fact to find the product (dividend). Use a pattern to give the product (dividend) a correct place value. Applying these rules often requires renaming numbers, as shown in the examples.

The commutative and associative properties of addition and multiplication and distributive property of multiplication over addition are the bases of the rules. For example, $40 + 50 = 4\ (10) + 5\ (10) = (4 + 5\ )(10) = 9\ (10) = 90$; $20 \times 30 = (2 \times 10) \times (3 \times 10) = (2 \times 3)(10 \times 10) = 6 \times 100 = 600$. (How are the properties used in these examples?)

Learning patterns for the operations with multiples of powers of 10 begins with learners finding solutions to story and number problems using any method or material that is meaningful to them. Children share their thinking and their use of materials. Your questioning enables learners to reflect on their work, extending their knowledge of the meanings of the operations, and constructing computational procedures for work with multiples of powers of 10. Because using place-value words often leads to the discovery of patterns in computation, learners are sometimes asked to rewrite math sentences using place-value words (tens, hundreds, . . .). The patterns constructed in various lessons become the bases for rules for mental computation, and using the rules in various activities and games enables learners to master mental computation with multiples of powers of 10.

The following activities deal first with understanding addition and subtraction and next with understanding multiplication and division with multiples of powers of 10. Games to develop skill are at the end of the section.

Activities for Addition and Subtraction with Multiples of Powers of 10

ACTIVITY 7.1
Story Problems for Addition and Subtraction.

Assign real-life story problems that require adding or subtracting with multiples of powers of 10, with sums less than 100. Suggest to children that they solve the problems using methods that make sense to them. Linking cubes, number lines, 10-dot strips, hundred squares, and counters should be readily available, but you should not direct pupils to use specific materials. Some children will be able to think the solutions. Examples of such problems are:

1. The library was selling old books. In the morning 40 books were sold, and 30 were sold in the afternoon. How many were sold that day?
2. Joseph spent 20 cents for one book and 50 cents for another book. How much did he spend at the book sale?
3. Mary took 60 cents to the book sale. She spent 40 cents for a book. She wanted to buy another book. How much money did she have left for another book?

After each problem is solved, have several children tell what they did and thought to solve the problem, give their solutions, and explain why the solutions are reasonable. Question learners so they understand that the meanings of the operations with large numbers are the same as with basic facts.

- Box 1.1 in Chapter One gives an example of teaching and learning addition of tens using story problems.

ACTIVITY 7.2
Exploring Sums or Differences.

Ask children to find the sums or differences for each of four number questions with sums or minuends less than 100 using their own methods (e.g., What number is 40 + 30? What number is 50 less 30?). Place-value materials should be readily available for children's use, but no directions for the use of the materials are given. It is expected that pupils will use different approaches. Note what approaches were used, and particularly keep a record of any children who do not think in terms of tens and used the ones counters to find sums. After they have finished, pupils report how they found the sums, give their answers, and comment on the reasonableness of their solutions. The use of different materials is illustrated by children. Questions you can use in leading the discussion include: "Please show us how you got that answer. Why did you choose that material to find the sum (difference)? How did you think to find the sums (differences)?"

Many children are able to give sums with little reference to materials. If children show that they are able to do this kind of thinking, say, "Some students found the sums or differences without using materials? Maria, please tell us how you thought when you did this. Let's all try Maria's method. How do we know our thinking was OK?"

ACTIVITY 7.3
Using 10-Dot Strips.

Ask students to use 10-dot strips (Figure 7.1) to solve four open math sentences with sums or minuends less than 100 (e.g., 40 + 20 = □; 70 – 60 = □). After they have completed the task, discuss how the strips show place-value names for the numbers (e.g., 4 tens). Ask students to give place-value names to the numbers in each math sentence, and write the sentences using place-value names for the numbers. Discuss the likenesses and differences between the sentences with the numerals and with the words. (Numbers are the same—have the same value—but the names are different.) Follow with Activity 7.4.

ACTIVITY 7.4
Finding a Pattern for Sums or Differences with Tens and Hundreds.

Ask students to rewrite several open math sentences using place-value words, or use the math sentences with place-value words they wrote for Activity 7.3. After pupils complete the activity, they report what they did. In the course of the discussion, ask questions such as: "What do you notice when we use place-value words to solve

FIGURE 7.1 Ten-Dot Strips Model for Addition with Tens

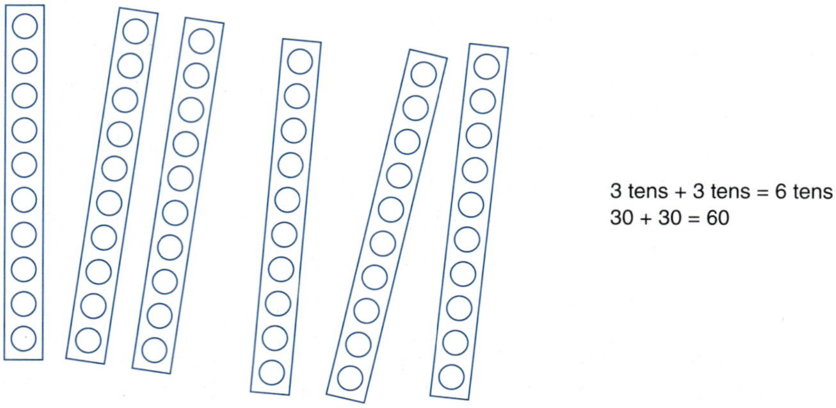

these exercises? Is there a pattern?" "How can we find the sums by thinking the pattern? (Use basic facts in computing, but remember that the sum is tens.)" "Why can we use that rule? (The numbers are all tens.) Let's try it!"

Later, have children work with hundreds and thousands. Children may generalize the pattern to hundreds and thousands. If not, this activity can be adapted to helping children learn patterns for sums and differences for hundreds and thousands and write rules.

- Box 1.2 in Chapter One gives a lesson example of teaching and learning addition of hundreds.

Some students may notice that the sum (difference) has as many zeros as the addends (subtrahend and minuend) and use this pattern to make a rule for finding solutions. Learners should report how they discovered this pattern and the rule they made. Tell them that they can use any rule that is meaningful to them.

ACTIVITY 7.5
Renaming Sums and Minuends.

When learners can use their rules to find sums and differences, introduce story or number problems in which the hundreds plus tens sums or minuends must be renamed as tens (e.g., 7 tens + 7 tens = 14 tens = 140; 140 − 70 = 14 tens − 7 tens = 7 tens = 70). Students should be able to rename the hundreds plus tens numbers as tens numbers because of learning acquired when working with base ten and place value.

To solve the problems, pupils should use any method that makes sense to them. During the discussion ask questions that help children use the mental computation rules they have learned, and rename when necessary. Examples of questions are: "How is that math sentence read if we use tens names for the numbers?" "What is the sum if we use a tens name? A hundred and tens name?" "How do you think to rename a tens number as a place-value number?"

Activities for Multiplication and Division with Multiples of Powers of 10

Mastery of multiplication and division with multiples of powers of 10 involves using basic facts and multiplying the results by the appropriate power of 10 (e.g., $40 \times 60 = (4 \times 6) \times (10 \times 10) = 24 \times 100 = 2400$; $2400 \div 40 = (24 \div 4)\ (100 \div 10) = 6 \times 10 = 60$). This procedure is shortened by using the patterns discussed or the rule: annex the sum (difference) of the zeros in the factors (dividend and divisor).

As noted, Hazenkamp (1986) suggests that patterns with powers of 10 be stressed in teaching multiplication computation. Patterns enable learners to compute quickly because only one step is involved after recalling the basic fact: deciding the power-of-10 name for the number. Following the annex-zeros rule requires two steps after using the basic fact: counting the zeros and then deciding on the name of the number. Either approach, of course, can be used by students. The construction of either rule, however, should develop from the awareness that both are based on the logic of the place-value system—to multiply by 10, annex a zero. The meaning of the place-value system is emphasized throughout the elementary grades, but particular emphasis is given to the multiplicative relationship between the numbers in the places when children study mental multiplication and division.

ACTIVITY 7.6
Story Problems for Multiplication and Division.

Story problems for multiplication with multiples of powers of 10 include those in which (1) one factor is a ones number and the other is a tens number; (2) one factor is 10 and the other is a multiple of 10; and (3) both factors are multiples of powers of 10. Story problems for division have math sentences that are the inverse of those for multiplication problems. Work begins with products less than 1000. Examples are:

1. Mother bought 4 small apples on sale at 20 cents each. How much did the apples cost?
   Mother spent 80 cents buying small apples on sale. She bought 4 apples. What was the sale price of each apple?
2. Mr. Brown gave 10 crayons to each child in the class. There were 20 children in the class. How many crayons did Mr. Brown pass out?
   Mr. Brown gave out 200 crayons to the children in his class. There are 20 children in the class. How many crayons did each child get if each got the same number?
3. New desks have been purchased for the 20 classrooms in the Brewington School building. Each room has 30 desks. How many desks were purchased?
   The principal bought 600 desks for all the rooms in the new Brewington School building. There are to be 30 desks in each room. How many rooms are in the new Brewington school?

Students are assigned problems and choose their own ways for solving them. Solution methods will probably include the use of materials such as base 10 blocks, 10-dot sticks, hundred squares, and repeated addition (Figure 7.2). After they complete the assignment, students discuss the methods they used to arrive at solutions. Your questions help them relate working with materials to mental computation by developing an understanding of the patterns for computation with large numbers.

ACTIVITY 7.7
Arrays.

To learn mental multiplication with multiples of powers of 10, pupils can use arrays to visualize products. Begin this activity with a review of how to make arrays for basic facts. If pupils have not made arrays, model making several arrays for basic facts, have students discuss what they observed, and ask them to make arrays for a few basic facts using grid paper. Students then use arrays to show the solutions to open math sentences with one factor a ones number and the other a tens number (e.g., $2 \times 30 = \square$) or both factors tens numbers (e.g., $20 \times 30 = \square$) (Figure 7.3). After students have completed their work, have several use a grid paper transparency on the overhead projector to show how they approached the task. Discuss what the array shows and why this representation is useful.

ACTIVITY 7.8
Finding Patterns in Multiplication and Division with Multiples of Powers of 10.

Ask children to use place-value words to rewrite three or four open multiplication sentences with tens numbers and to find solutions using their own methods. After solutions are found, the class discusses their work to find a pattern that will enable them to construct a rule to compute mentally. Ask questions such as: "What pattern is seen when we use place-value words to solve these exercises? What rule can we make that uses this pattern?" (Think the basic fact; if one factor is ones, the answer is tens; if both factors are tens, the answer is hundreds.) "Let's check our rule with our calculators. Why has the 'tens times tens equals hundreds' pattern turned up?" The answer to the last question—because that's the place-value system, to multiply by ten,

FIGURE 7.2 Repeated Addition Model for Multiplication with Tens

$$10 \times 20 = 20 + 20 + 20 + 20 + 20 + 20 + 20 + 20 + 20 + 20 = 200$$

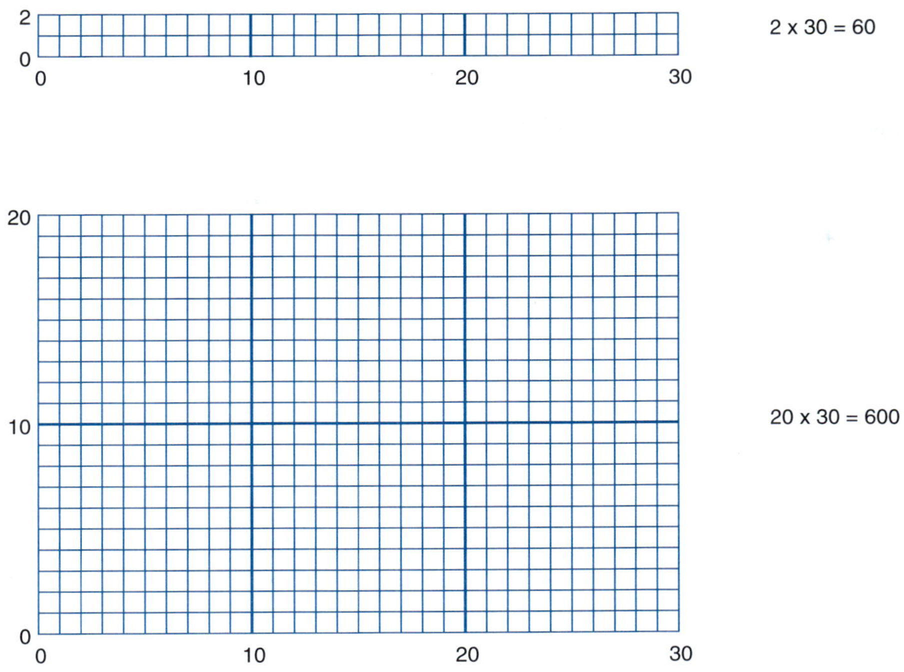

FIGURE 7.3 Array Models for Multiplication with Tens

annex a zero—is emphasized in instruction only if learners understand the concept well enough to explain and use it.

If learners observe the pattern, the number of zeros in the product is the sum (difference) of the zeros in the factors (dividend and divisor), and if they use this pattern to construct a rule, they should explain why their rule makes sense. Suggest that they can use patterns or the "zero rule" to think answers.

Repeat the activity for the pattern tens times hundreds equals thousands. Further work with patterns should include thinking patterns in division. The patterns for division—tens divided by ones equals tens, tens divided by tens equals ones, and hundreds divided by tens equals tens—are introduced in a lesson similar to that for learning patterns and constructing rules for mental multiplication with tens. An alternative approach is for the lesson to begin with the request to think how the multiplication patterns can be used to find division patterns and rules (think the opposite), or it can begin by working with materials to find answers to division questions with multiples of powers of 10.

ACTIVITY 7.9
Broken Calculator Key.

This activity helps students construct the meaning of multiplication and division with large numbers. Pose a problem such as the following for students to solve using the calculator:

The multiplication (or division) key on your calculator is broken. Find these products (or quotients) using your calculator with the broken key. When you are finished, write two or three sentences explaining how you decided to find the solutions and what you learned about mental calculation of products (or quotients).

Multiplication	Division
$2 \times 30 = N$	$60 \div 30 = N$
$10 \times 40 = N$	$400 \div 40 = N$
$20 \times 60 = N$	$1200 \div 60 = N$

ACTIVITY 7.10
Renaming Products and Dividends.

When learners can use rules to find products less than 1000, they study computation with products greater than 1000 and learn to rename hundreds products as thousands plus hundreds (e.g., 60×70 = 42 hundreds = 4 thousand 2 hundred). Story problems or exercises in which the sums are greater than 1000 are assigned to students, and they use any method they wish to find solutions. After they have found the solutions, students discuss their findings. Ask questions to help children use the meanings they have acquired to rename when necessary (e.g., 20×60 = 12 hundreds = 1 thousand + 2 hundred = 1200). Examples of questions are: "What are two names for your solution? How do you know? Please use grid paper to show your thinking (Figure 7.4)." "Make a rule of your idea. When is your rule useful? (When the product is equal to or greater than 10 hundreds.)"

Repeat the activity for teaching division of multiples of powers of 10. Assign pupils three or four math sentences such as $\frac{2700}{90} = N$ or $\frac{3500}{70} = N$. Ask students to find the quotients. If may be helpful to suggest beginning by writing the math sentences using place-value words (e.g., 27 hundreds ÷ 9 tens, 35 hundreds ÷ 7 tens.) If some pupils cannot grasp the concept of renaming, review renaming numbers using the activities in Chapter Four.

Games for the Operations with Multiples of Powers of 10

You may choose to introduce computation with multiples of powers of 10 with one of the games that follow. Then, after children play the game, discussions and activities are used to enable learners to understand patterns and construct rules to use in mental computation. The games are also used to develop skill in computation.

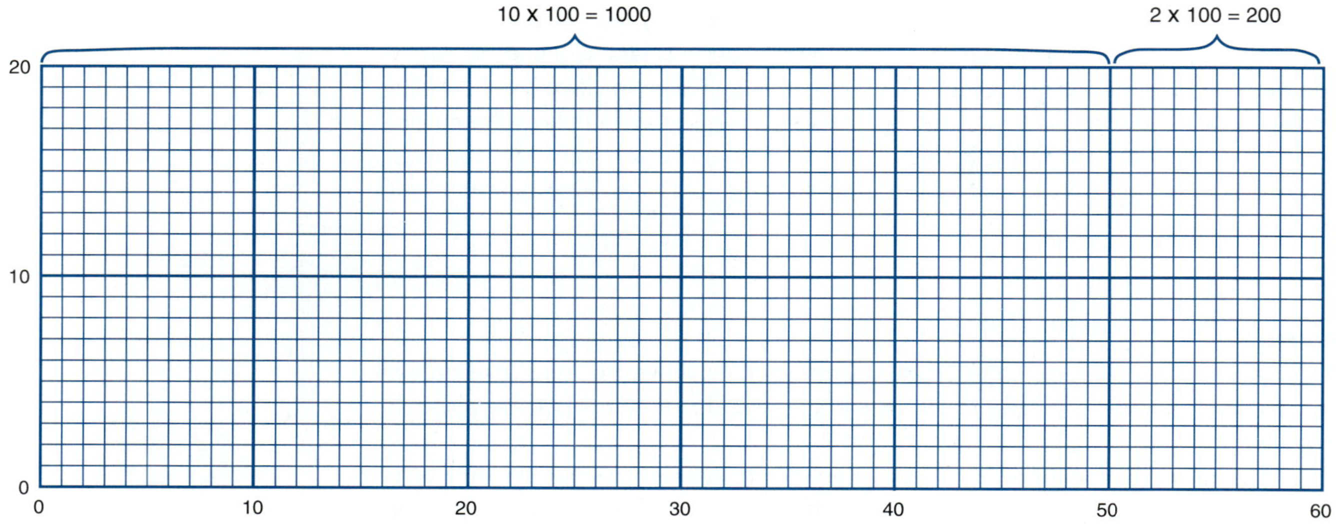

20 x 60 =
2 tens x 6 tens =
12 hundreds =
10 hundreds + 2 hundreds =
1 thousand + 2 hundred = 1200

FIGURE 7.4 Grid Paper Model to Show Renaming a Product

The games are given for addition computation with multiples of powers of 10. Each game can be adapted to subtraction, multiplication, or division.

ACTIVITY 7.11
The Place-Value Chart Game.

Two students each use a place-value chart. Twenty cards with questions for sums less than 200 are face down in the center of the playing area (Figure 7.5). Players take turns picking cards, giving answers, and using numeral cards to show the accumulated total on their own place-value chart. The first player to reach 1000 gets a token, and a round is over. The first player to get five tokens wins.

ACTIVITY 7.12
War with Large Numbers.

The rules for *War* are followed. The cards can be those used for the *Place-Value Chart Game,* or they can have addition questions in which hundreds are used (e.g., 300 + 500 = □).

ACTIVITY 7.13
Take Three Game.

This game is played by two children. Each player takes three cards from a pile of 48 cards. The cards are the cards used in *War*. Each player decides which two numbers from his or her three cards to use to give a sum. He or she shows the three cards, tells the chosen numbers, and gives the sum. The player with the greatest sum gets all the cards. Each player then takes three more cards from the pile. When the pile of cards is gone, the player with the most cards wins.
The game can be played for least sum.

Thousands	Hundreds	Tens	Ones

FIGURE 7.5 Materials for Place-Value Chart Game

ACTIVITY 7.14
I'll Collect Those Cards Game.

This game should be played by four children. Each player gets eight addend cards. The addends are multiples of powers of 10. Players in turn show two addend cards. Other players look for two cards in their hands that give a sum greater than that given on the cards shown by the first player. The player who first lays down two cards with a greater sum collects the four cards. The game (or round) ends when one player is out of cards. The player with the most cards wins that game (or round). Play continues with the winner shuffling the cards and dealing them again.

The game can be played for finding the lesser sum. If it is adapted for division, pupils must find cards that give quotients in multiples of powers of 10 (e.g., 4200 ÷ 50 = □ would be excluded for learners who are beginning the study of mental computation. It would be used when they have developed strategies for dealing with this type of exercise).

The cards for these games can be used for quick drills with partners to begin a math lesson. Pupils can make cards to use in drills with someone at home.

Higher-Decade Addition and Subtraction

Higher-decade computation, which is also called *computing by endings,* refers to mental computation when one addend or minuend is greater than 10 and the other addend, subtrahend, or difference is less than 10 (e.g., 45 + 4 = 49; 46 + 8 = 54; 57 – 3 = 54; 57 – 53 = 4; 54 – 7 = 47; 54 – 47 = 7). Notice that some higher-decade addition and subtraction involves bridging the decade (e.g., 46 + 8 = 54; 54 – 7 = 47; 54 – 47 = 7). Higher-decade computation can also be used in examples with hundreds (e.g., 530 + 60 = 590) or higher powers of 10.

One approach to helping pupils learn higher-decade addition is to assign a series of open math sentences (e.g., 4 + 3 = *N*, 14 + 3 = *N*, 24 + 3 = *N*, . . . , 94 + 3 = *N*; 4 + 8 = *N*, 14 + 8 = *N*, 24 + 8 = *N*, . . . , 84 + 8 = *N*). Pupils may count to determine the solutions to these problems or use materials with counting (Figure 7.6). They are helped to become aware of these patterns: A basic fact is used to find the sum of the ones. When the sum of the ones is less than 10, the tens are not increased; when the sum of the ones is greater than 10, the tens in the sum are increased by 1. Knowing the patterns enables one to compute mentally and to learn higher-decade addition before addition with tens numbers.

Reader Activity 7.1

Write out the patterns useful for finding differences in higher-decade subtraction.

After students find solutions, they discuss them and how they thought to arrive at the solutions. The patterns are emphasized in the discussion.

This approach can also be used for higher-decade subtraction, and patterns can be found for higher-decade subtraction.

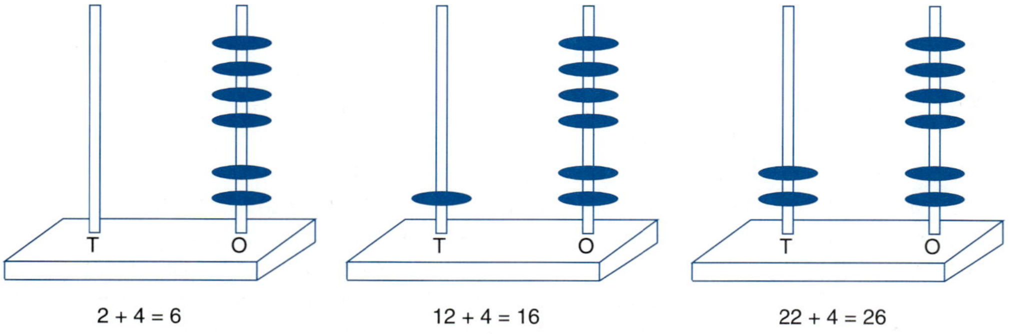

FIGURE 7.6 Abacus Model for Higher-Decade Addition

ACTIVITY 7.15
Showing Higher-Decade Addition Patterns on the Place-Value Mats.

Students use place-value mats with place-value materials to show a series of higher-decade addition combinations and discuss the pattern they observe. The activity can be adapted to subtraction.

ACTIVITY 7.16
Telling the Endings.

Some children grasp the concept of higher-decade addition or subtraction if they say and hear the endings in a series of computations. Have children respond in chorus to a series, such as 4 + 5 = 9, 14 + 5 = 19, 24 + 5 = 29, . . . , 94 + 5 = 99. (Use the related computations for subtraction.) Then ask, "How did you know to give these sums? What helped you?" Students should discuss how knowing the endings helped.

After children understand higher-decade addition and subtraction, they use practice materials to develop skill. Flash cards can be made for problems in different decades and used for practice at school or at home.

Assessing Beginning Mental Computation

Before introducing more difficult mental computation (e.g., 34 + 25; 340 + 53; 40 × 42), you determine if students understand the operations with multiples of powers of 10, can compute mentally with multiples of powers of 10, and have skill in higher-decade addition and subtraction. You observe students solve problems, listen to their explanations during discussions, ask them to tell about their thinking, and give short quizzes that require children to compute mentally with multiples of powers of 10 or give higher-decade sums or differences. The items are given orally or shown on the overhead for a brief time. Records are kept that show the progress children have made in mastering beginning mental computation. Because all computation except calculator computation involves skill in computation with multiples of powers of 10 and often higher-decade addition or subtraction, instruction stresses mastery in these areas.

STRATEGIES FOR MENTAL COMPUTATION

Strategies are used in mental computation to find exact solutions that are more complex than those involving multiples of powers of 10 or higher-decade addition and subtraction. For example, Ms. Mason, the third-grade teacher, would use one of several strategies to compute mentally to solve the following problem as she was going to the laminating machine:

> *I have 8 sheets filled with game pieces for the class. Laminating costs $.22 a sheet. How much will the laminating cost me? Can I really afford it?*

One solution strategy is: think (8 × $.20) + (8 × $.02) = $1.60 + .16 = $1.76. Another is: think 10 × $.22 and subtract 2 × ($.20 + 2), which is $2.20 – .40 – .04 = $1.80 – .04 = $1.76. (Do you have a different strategy for this mental computation?).

You are responsible for determining learners' understanding and skill in mental computation and for planning instruction to enable children to deal with ever-more complex mental computation. This section gives a description of three strategies that you help students develop over time, explains how to introduce strategies to develop understanding, and describes activities to help learners understand the strategies and their use.

Although strategies for mental computation and computational estimation are discussed in separate parts of this chapter, not all strategies for mental computation or computational estimation would be taught before introducing strategies for the other kind of computation. Over time children study both mental computation and computational estimation and learn when to compute mentally to obtain exact answers and when to estimate.

Developing strategies for mental computation takes time. Mastery is not achieved all at once and may take a number of years to achieve. Early instruction is informal and is based on children's own strategies (Rathmell and Trafton, 1990). Later instruction focuses on helping students learn different strategies.

To develop an awareness of strategies for mental computation, before studying the material in this section, the reader should mentally compute the sums, products, differences, and quotients in the following list. Look for alternate strategies, but avoid mentally using a paper-and-pencil algorithm. If possible, share your ideas with others, and discuss the different thinking processes used by different individuals. Then decide which of the following strategies you and others used in your mental computation.

1. $102 - 50 = N$	6. $18 \times 35 = N$
2. $56 + 36 = N$	7. $60 \times 25 = N$
3. $78 - 19 = N$	8. $42 \times 75 = N$
4. $76 + 49 = N$	9. $624 \div 12 = N$
5. $18 + 33 = N$	10. $990 \div 45 = N$

Three Strategies

The strategies for mental computation are front-end, compensation, and compatible numbers. With possibly the exception of the front-end strategy, they often go by different names. As the name is less important than the idea it represents, children should use a label that is meaningful to them. They may name a strategy, or you can suggest a label.

Front-End. Front-end strategies for addition, subtraction, and multiplication begin with the left-hand digit. Examples are

$40 + 58 = N$ Think $(40 + 50) + 8 = 90 + 8 = 98$
$34 + 57 = N$ Think $30 + 50 = 80$, $4 + 7 = 11$, $80 + 11 = 91$
Or think $34 + 50 = 84$, $84 + 7 = 91$
Or think $34 + 50 = 84$, $84 + 6 + 1 = 90 + 1 = 91$
Or think $57 + 30 = 87$, $87 + 4 = 91$
Or think $57 + 30 = 87$, $87 + 3 + 1 = 90 + 1 = 91$
$67 - 54 = N$ Think $60 - 50 = 10$, $7 - 4 = 3$, $10 + 3 = 13$
Or think $67 - 50 = 17$, $17 - 4 = 13$
$400 + 342 = N$ Think $400 + 300 + 42 = 700 + 42 = 742$
$500 - 150 = N$ Think $500 - (100 + 50) = (500 - 100) - 50 = 400 - 50 = 350$
$3 \times 53 = N$ Think $3 \times 50 = 150$, $3 \times 3 = 9$, $150 + 9 = 159$
$70 \times 34 = N$ Think $70 \times 30 = 2100$, $70 \times 4 = 280$, $2100 + 280 = 2380$
$400 \times 61 = N$ Think $400 \times 60 = 24{,}000$, $400 \times 1 = 400$, $24{,}000 + 400 = 24{,}400$

Compensation. The compensation strategy is, in general, to adjust the numbers so that they are easier to process mentally. A variety of compensation strategies are used by those who compute mentally. After compensating, the front-end strategy is often used.

$49 + 21 = 50 + 20 = 70$ (subtract from one addend; add the result to the other addend to obtain an equal expression)

$84 - 19 = 85 - 20 = 65$ (add or subtract the same number to or from both the subtrahend and the minuend to obtain an equal expression)

$25 \times 56 = 50 \times 28 = 100 \times 14 = 1400$ (double one factor and halve the other factor, or halve and double to obtain an equal expression)

$2250 \div 50 = 4500 \div 100 = 45$ (multiply dividend and divisor by the same number to obtain an equal expression)

$25 \times 36 = 100/4 \times 36 = 3600/4 = 900$ (rename 25 as 100/4 to obtain an equal expression)

Compatible Numbers. The compatible numbers strategy selects or adjusts numbers so that they fit together. This strategy can be named "working with friendly numbers." As multiples of powers of 10, multiples of 5, and numbers divisible by 2, 4, or 5 are easy for many students to process, this strategy involves finding and using these numbers.

$$25 + 26 = 25 + (25 + 1) = (25 + 25) + 1 = 50 + 1 = 51$$
$$67 + 34 = 67 + (33 + 1) = (67 + 33) + 1 = 100 + 1 = 101$$
$$125 + 55 = 125 + (50 + 5) = (125 + 50) + 5 = 175 + 5 = 180$$
$$42 \times 125 = (40 + 2) \times 125 = (40 \times 125) + (2 \times 125) = ([40 \times 100] + [40 \times 25]) + (2 \times 125) = 4000 + 1000 + 250 = 5000 + 250 = 5250$$
$$3644 \div 4 = (3600 \div 4) + (44 \div 4) = 900 + 11 = 911$$

Introducing the Strategies to Develop Understanding

Understanding the strategies involves higher-level thinking, such as relating and inferring. Concepts formed by learners during prior learning experiences are the basis for these thought processes. The sequence for teaching a strategy is:

1. Assign story problems, number questions, or open math sentences with the directions: solve by computing mentally; decide on the strategy you used to compute mentally; use materials if the solution cannot be found by mental computation. The problems should be those that would be solved most easily with a particular strategy.
2. Lead a class discussion during which students explain their work to each other. Call attention to the sense of the strategies presented.
3. Have children decide on a good strategy for the problems. Help them recognize the characteristics of the problems that make the strategy useful. If most learners do not use a strategy but solve the problem with materials, use cognitive modeling to introduce the strategy, and point out the number relations involved and why the strategy is appropriate for the problems.
4. Have students use the strategy to solve several problems. Encourage them to check and to consider the reasonableness of their answers. When only one strategy is known, repeating the computation serves as a check. When children have learned several strategies, a computation can often be checked by computing a different way. For example, $42 \times 50 = (42 \times 100) \div 2 = 4200 \div 2 = 2100$ or $42 \times 50 = (40 \times 50) + (2 \times 50) = 2000 + 100 = 2100$. To determine the reasonableness of a solution before they learn estimation strategies, students should think about the sense of the solution in the problem situation.

Real-world situations should be used in introductory lessons and many subsequent lessons (Hazenkamp, 1986). Life-related problems are motivating, and understanding is enhanced when a lesson relates to everyday activities. Moreover, because studies show that mental computation is often used to solve real-life problems (Hope, 1986), learning mental computation to solve real problems prepares children for life and thus has a social value.

Initially, lessons to teach strategies deal with the front-end strategy. When children demonstrate skill in mental computation with multiples of powers of 10, groups or pairs of children are assigned two or three story problems whose solutions require more mental processing than computation with multiples of powers of 10. The first story problems are addition and subtraction problems in which one number in each problem is a tens number and the other a tens-plus-ones number (e.g., 40 + 23 = □; 63 – 20 = □). The lesson follows the four steps.

If some children have difficulties with addition and subtraction mental computation when one addend is a multiple of ten and the other is a tens-plus-ones number, have them use materials to understand the difference between math sentences such as 30 + 20 = □ and 30 + 23 = □. Ask, for example, "When you used materials, what extra step was in the second addition question? How would you carry out that step mentally?" When someone suggests a procedure, have the student explain his or her thinking. If no one can mentally find the sum, use cognitive modeling.

In the upper grades, more difficult addition and subtraction computations that lend themselves to the front-end strategy are assigned (e.g., 33 + 35 = *N*, 36 + 35 = *N*, 67 – 24 = *N*, 62 – 26 = *N*). If learners cannot hold in mind all the separate computations required to complete a more difficult computation, instruction involving these computations is delayed until a later time, possibly the middle school years, and children use paper-and-pencil computation to find solutions to such problems.

After children have mastered the facts for multiplication and can mentally compute products when one factor is a ones number and the other a tens number or both are tens numbers (e.g., 3 × 30 = *N*; 20 × 40 = *N*), some will be able to learn the front-end strategy to compute mentally when one factor is a ones number and the other factor is a tens-plus-ones number (e.g., 2 × 32 = *N*). To develop understanding and skill, some students may relate the distributive property of multiplication over addition, which they used to remember facts, to this mental computation. Work with arrays helps them visualize multiplying the tens and ones of one factor by the ones of the other factor (Figure 7.7). Later, some may extend the front-end strategy to mental computation when both factors are two-digit numbers, one a tens number, the other, a tens-plus-ones number (20 × 32). Not all children can keep in mind the steps required in this mental computation. They will learn to compute these products using paper-and-pencil.

After children have some success using the front-end strategy, the other two strategies are introduced following a similar instructional procedure.

When solving problems arising in the course of class activities or often when engaging in practice activities, students choose their own strategies. As there are usually alternate ways to determine a solution, different children will arrive at answers in different ways. Children should not be expected to use the same strategy when computing mentally, but they should be given opportunities to learn a variety of strategies from which they can choose the one most meaningful to them in a particular situation.

Activity for the Classroom 7.2. Discuss with learners the usefulness of mental computation. Tell them that you are interested in how they think to compute mentally. Give them several examples for each strategy, and ask them to choose three examples and think out loud as they find solutions. Notice if there is a pattern to the problems and strategies they choose to compute mentally.

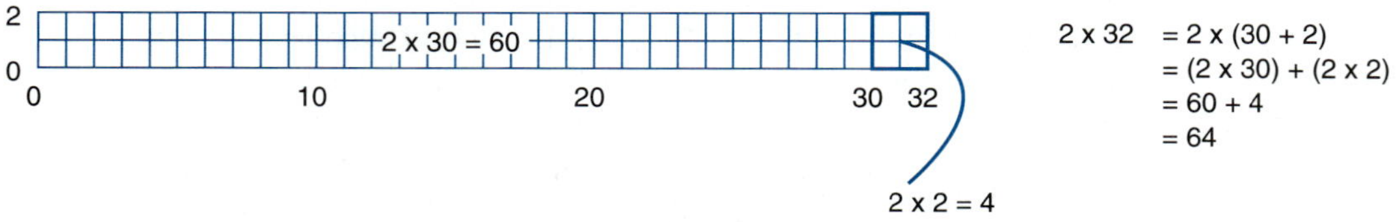

FIGURE 7.7 Array Model Showing Partial Products

Activities to Develop Competency in the Use of Strategies for Mental Computation

The following activities include class and group assignments and games. Some of the activities involve using the calculator.

ACTIVITY 7.17
Skip-Counting.

Ask the class to chorus-count by tens or twenties beginning with a tens-plus-ones number (e.g., 32). This can be done in connection with a hundred-squares chart, with children touching or marking the numbers on their own 1000-strips or packets (see Chapter Four) as they count. Discuss the pattern observed in counting. Ask, "How does this counting help us learn mental computation?"

ACTIVITY 7.18
Skip-Counting Game.

Children play the following game when they can skip-count by nonmultiples of 10: Children play in groups of four. About 10 numbers that are not multiples of 10 (e.g, 34, 59) chosen at random from 10 to 80 are written on cards. The cards are face down in the center of the playing area. Players in turn pick a card and count from that number by 10 (or 20) for three numbers. The next player continues for three numbers, and so on. The first player to reach the nineties (90–99), keeps the card. When all the cards are gone, the player with the most cards wins.

ACTIVITY 7.19
Change in One Input Game.

Two pupils use 20 to 30 game cards with directions that require addition, subtraction, multiplication, or division with a power of 10 and a calculator. Students can make these cards after they study samples you write and understand how the cards are written. Examples of cards for each operation are:

Change 450 to 250 in one input.	Change 875 to 895 in one input.
Change 672 to 642 in one input.	Change 680 to 580 in one input.
Change 760 to 7600 in one input.	Change 55 to 5500 in one input.
Change 9990 to 999 in one input.	Change 340 to 34 in one input.

Pupils take turns picking a card from a stack of game cards that are face down in the playing area. When a player has a turn, he or she reads the task on the card. The other player uses his or her calculator to carry out the task. If the player can perform the task, he or she keeps the card. If not, the card is put aside. The player with the most cards is the winner when all the cards are used. A list of tasks could also be given to a pair of players with the players taking turns reading from the list. The list could be written on a computer and copies made for a number of pairs of players, or different lists could be made for players with different skills. For example, the tasks could deal only with tens, not hundreds as in the examples. If a player carried out the directions on the list correctly, he or she would get a token rather than a card.

A variation is: Two players take turns inputting a number on a calculator and giving directions (e.g., input 653 and say, "Go to 713"—the other player adds 60; input 45 and say, "Go to 450"—the other player multiplies by 10). The directions given cannot involve changing more than two digits and must require adding, subtracting, multiplying, or dividing by a tens number. The player following the directions gets a token for each input needed to reach the given number. After five minutes of play (students watch the clock) and after each has had the same number of turns, the player with the fewest tokens wins.

ACTIVITY 7.20
Replace Game.

Players take turns inputting a three-, four-, or five-digit number on the calculator. The player who inputs the number tells the other player which digit is to be replaced by zero. The player operating on the number must correctly replace with zero in one input and tell what was done. If he or she does so, the player receives a token. At the end of 5 or 10 minutes and after both players have had the same number of turns, the player with the most tokens wins. For example, the first player shows 5467 on the calculator and says, Replace the 4 with 0. The other player subtracts 400 to show 5067 and says, "I subtracted 400."

The game can be adapted for addition. For example, player 1 inputs 864 and says, "Replace the 86 with 94. Keep the other digit." Player 2 would add 80 to follow the direction.

ACTIVITY 7.21
Make 100 Game.

Prepare 40 cards with numbers that are multiples of 5. Pairs of cards in the set show numbers that equal 100 (e.g., 35 on one card, 65 on another card). Four children play the game. Each player gets 6 cards. The objective is to make 100 by summing the numbers on two cards. Players in turn ask players to their left for a card needed to make 100. If a player cannot give the number requested, the asking player chooses a card from the pile of extra cards, uses it to make a pair, or keeps it. The cards making 100 are laid in front of the player who made the pair. The game is over when one player has no cards or no cards remain in the pile. The player with the most pairs is the winner. (Variation: A player is an instant winner if he or she can make 100 [or 100 more than once] with all his or her cards when they are passed out. When this happens, the cards are reshuffled, and another game begins.)

This activity can be adapted for the calculator. Two pupils take turns naming a number for the other player to input. The number is to be a multiple of 5. The player giving the number then challenges the other player to make 100 in one input. If the challenged player can make 100 in one input, he or she gets a token. After each has had eight turns, the player with the most tokens is the winner, and another game begins.

A more difficult game involves using any number as an input and giving the challenge to make 100.

ACTIVITY 7.22
Double It Game.

The game is for two to four players. The cards used are the same as in *Make 100.* Players in turn pick cards from the center pile and each gives the double of the number on the card drawn (doubling is used often in mental computation). If the player gives the correct double, he or she keeps the card. If not, the card is set aside. When all cards are used, the player with the most cards wins. (If needed, the players can have a key to show correct answers.)

ACTIVITY 7.23
The Most Pairs.

Two students should play this game. The cards can be those for Activity 7.21 or can be made so that each shows a number that is an addend in a more difficult combination with a sum of 100 (e.g., 22, 78). A three-minute egg timer is used. Each player gets 20 cards, face down. Players take turns setting the timer and saying, "Turn your cards over. Make sums of 100." At the end of three minutes, the player with the most 100 sums is the winner. (If needed, the players can have a key to show correct answers for this game.)

ACTIVITY 7.24
Balancing.

This activity and Activity 7.25 are adapted from Cobb and Merkel (1989). After children have had experiences with a balance scale, pictures of a balance scale with one 100 card and cards with numbers that sum to 100 are given to a group of children. The group works together to find the number cards that sum to 100 to make the scale balance (Figure 7.8). The activity can be assigned or chosen by one child who needs more practice to learn sums to 100.

ACTIVITY 7.25
What Is Missing?

Individuals or pairs of students can complete a sequence of exercises in which addends or sums (factors or products) are missing. For example: $25 + 75 = N$; $25 + 76 = N$; $N + 77 = 102$; $78 + N = 103, \ldots, N + 80 = 105$; $11 \times 2 = N$, $11 \times 3 = N$, $11 \times N = 44$, $11 \times 5 = N$, $N \times 6 = 66, \ldots, 9 \times 11 = N$.

This activity can readily be planned to teach compensation with addition or subtraction. For example, $34 + 66 = N$, $33 + N = 100$, $N + 68 = 100, \ldots, 30 + 70 = N$. The sums can also be greater than 100.

After students have completed any version of the activity, have them discuss patterns they may have observed. They may like to make sequences for other students to complete.

ACTIVITY 7.26
Division Made Easy.

Ask pairs of students to study equations such as $4956 \div 14 = 4956 \div (7 \times 2) = (4956 \div 7) \div 2 = 708 \div 2 = 354$; $1248 \div 24 = 1248 \div (4 \times 6) = (1248 \div 4) \div 6 = 208 \div 4 = 52$. A discussion follows students' study. During the class discussion, children are helped to understand that the divisor cannot ever be renamed as a sum. Only the dividend can be renamed as a sum (division is right, not left, distributive). However, the divisor can be renamed as a product. The inverse multiplication sen-

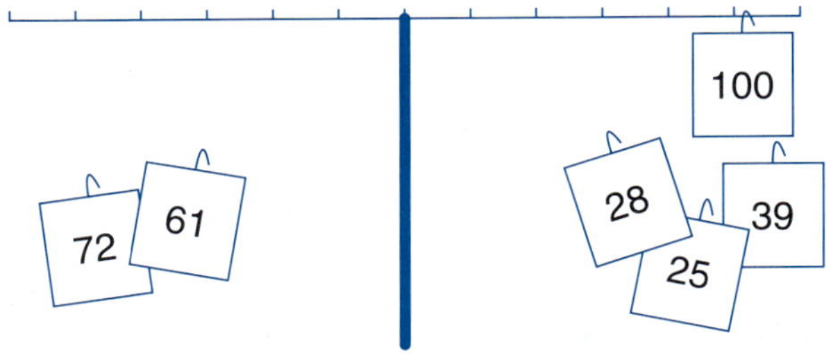

FIGURE 7.8 Materials for "Balancing" Activity

tences can be used to help children understand this concept (e.g., $52 \times 24 = 52 \times (4 \times 6) = 1248$, so 1248 is divisible by 4×6). Students carry out several computations using this strategy (e.g., $7236 \div 18$) and share their thinking.

ACTIVITY 7.27
Halving and Doubling.

For some mental computation, the computation is easy if one factor is halved and the product obtained doubled to find a solution. For example, in the problem $4 \times 16 = N$, think, 2×16 is 32, double 32 is 64. Give problems that can be easily solved by this compensation-type strategy, such as, $4 \times 45 = N$ or $6 \times 35 = N$. Have pupils solve the problems and report their solutions. If a child mentions this strategy, have him or her explain it to the class. If no child reports the "halving and doubling strategy," model it, and ask the class to react to what they observe. Have them try it out on several examples and tell their reactions.

ACTIVITY 7.28
Useful Products.

Two products with both factors tens plus ones are easily computed mentally, (1) those with factor 11 and the other factor any two-digit number (e.g., $11 \times 34 = \square$); and (2) those with both factors in the same decade and ones both 5, or other numbers that sum to 10 (e.g., $25 \times 25 = \square$; $34 \times 36 = \square$). Use problems of either type for the first activity. (Include problems so that there is no trading if one factor is 11—later students can decide how to deal with trading.) Have students use calculators to find the solutions to four problems, and induce the rules. Later, use the other type of problem. Have them study the sense of their rules by examining partial products in extended algorithms when they have learned paper-and-pencil computation.

Reader Activity 7.2

Carry out Activity 7.28, and infer the rules. (See end of chapter for rules.)

Assessing the Use of Strategies for Mental Computation

Assessing the use of strategies in mental computation should include asking children to explain their thinking. Students can write up how they thought to find a solution. Very brief interviews in which a student explains his or her thinking on one or two examples can be conducted with individuals when the class is engaged in group work or in individual study. Children should be informed of the procedure and be excused from group or individual work if they do not have time to complete it. At a previous time they should have discussed how interviews help both you and them assess progress. The results of an interview should be discussed with the student interviewed, so that a plan can be made regarding how to use the information gained to foster further progress.

Observations of children's success in playing games, such as those described in this section, and their work products based on activities can sometimes give information regarding how children think to compute mentally, but more often they only reveal a learner's competency in mental computation. Quizzes in which children write answers computed mentally also give information regarding children's competency. The items can be shown on the overhead for five to ten seconds, depending on the complexity of the computation.

As with all assessment, records must be kept so that instruction can be planned to help children gain greater understanding and skill. Records also give you and your students evidence of progress.

Computational Estimation and Paper-and-Pencil Computation

PART II

Computational estimation is finding a computed solution that is not exact, but close enough to be useful for solving a problem. It requires mental calculation, but is not as precise as mental computation, which provides exact solutions. It is particularly appropriate for many real-life problems where inexact solutions give sufficient information for dealing with the problems. Computational estimation is also taught to serve as a check on computation with paper-and-pencil or a calculator.

Exact solutions for more difficult computations than can be carried out mentally are found using paper-and-pencil computation or a calculator. *Paper-and-pencil computation* involves the use of algorithms, that is: step-by-step procedures that are carried out routinely.

The sections of this part discuss computational estimation and paper-and-pencil computation in turn. New directions in elementary school mathematics based on interactive teaching and learning continue to be emphasized throughout this part of the chapter.

COMPUTATIONAL ESTIMATION

Computational estimation is often resisted by students because they have developed the idea that a mathematical solution must be exact. They need help to develop a mind-set that enables them to accept the need for inexact answers (Trafton, 1986). Real-life problems involving computational estimation help develop such a mind-set because they demonstrate the usefulness of the process. They also give students opportunities to reason about numbers, an essential component of computational estimation.

This section discusses developing the meaning of computational estimation, strategies for computational estimation, learning strategies for computational estimation with activities for learning strategies, and assessment of learning.

Developing the Meaning of Computational Estimation

Learning the meaning of computational estimation begins in the early primary grades with thinking about numbers that are greater than, less than, or about the same as a given number. Children make estimates of quantities (see Chapter Four for activities) and discuss comparisons between the estimated and the counted amount. Later, the study of mental computation gives children tools to use in computational estimation.

Soon after children can compute easy examples mentally, they develop the meaning of computational estimation. Initial activities stress problems that involve thinking about number relations but do not ask for numerical solutions. Problem examples are:

1. You have \$5. The teddy bear you want to buy costs \$4.49. Can you buy it? Why or why not?

2. Sally had \$4. She wanted to buy two books at the book sale. One cost \$3.35 and the other cost \$1.75. Did she have enough money? Why or why not?
3. We have 30 children in our class. The principal gave the teacher 100 pencils for the students to use this semester. The teacher had asked for at least 3 pencils for each child. Did the principal give her as many as she wanted? Why or why not?
4. Tom has \$10. He wanted to buy 3 roses at \$1.95 each for his mother for Mother's Day. Did he need more money? Why or why not?

The focus of the class discussion following individual or group work is that exact answers are not required to solve such problems but only a reasonable estimate. Students are asked to change the problems so that the situation would require an exact solution (e.g., in Problem 1, if the teddy bear is purchased, the buyer would want to know his or her exact change). Using the problems as given and revised, they compare situations that require an exact number solution and those that require an estimated solution. They discuss the type of situation that requires only an estimate.

Further experiences are planned to help children become aware of the practice of reporting estimated numbers. For example, children are asked to decide if the following reports give exact or estimated numbers. After it is decided that the numbers are estimated, the class discusses why estimated numbers would be reported and why they are useful to those who receive the reports.

- The population of our city is 101,600.
- One thousand citizens appeared for the hearing on the proposed new park on the north side of the county.
- Kaiko, a Japanese robot built to explore the ocean depths, cost \$50 million.

Activity for the Classroom 7.3. Have students use their textbooks in other subjects or newspaper articles to find examples of estimated numbers. Ask them to report their findings. When they give their reports, have them reflect on the idea that mathematics gives meaning to other school subjects.

Specific strategies for computational estimations are emphasized after students understand that computational estimation involves inexact solutions and that many problems and reports that occur in real-life settings need only inexact answers.

Strategies for Computational Estimation

There are four main strategies for computational estimation with whole numbers: front-end with adjustment, rounding, compatible numbers, and clustering (Reys, 1986). Students should be taught when it is appropriate to use one of these strategies and when mental computation is more appropriate. For example, Reys (1988) believes that 24 + 31 should be computed mentally.

Front-End with Adjustment. Front-end computational estimation involves using the left most digits to determine an estimate and adjusting the result to obtain a better estimate. Reys (1986) notes that this strategy is most useful for addition. Examples are:

1. 348 + 619. Using a front-end strategy, think: 3 + 6 = 9, 300 + 600 = 900. The estimate should be a number greater than 900, probably about 970 because 48 is close to 50 and 19 is close to 20.
2. 736 + 852. Using a front-end strategy, think: 7 + 8 = 15, 700 + 800 = 1500. The estimate should be a number greater than 1500, because 36 + 52 is greater than 80, so my estimate is 1585.
3. 43 × 62. Using a front-end strategy, think: 4 × 6 = 24. The estimate is a number greater than 24 hundreds or 2400, because (3 × 60) + (2 × 40) would be over 200, so my estimate will be 2600.

Rounding. Rounding is a strategy that changes the numbers to be used in computational estimation so that they are easier to manipulate mentally. For children, rounding rules for tens numbers are: If the ones in the number are less than 5, think the next lower 10; if the ones in the number are 5 or greater, think the next higher 10. A companion rule is: if both numbers are close to 5, round the smaller number up and the larger number down. The rules can be extended to other powers of 10. Examples are:

1. $43 + 32$ rounds to $40 + 30$; $46 + 38$ rounds to $50 + 40$.
2. 52×62 rounds to 50×60; 58×67 rounds to 60×70.
3. 37×66 rounds to 40×60.

Estimations obtained by rounding numbers can be adjusted. For example, the estimation in Problem 1 for $46 + 38$ would be a little less than $50 + 40$.

Compatible Numbers. Compatible numbers fit together. They are multiples of 2, 5, or 10 that are easy to add, subtract, or multiply, or one number is divisible by the other, making division easy. The strategy can also involve determining an equal expression that includes a fraction. The strategy is to look for such numbers and use them in computational estimation. Examples are:

1. $365 + 643 = N$. To estimate, think $350 + 650 = 1000$.
2. $3765 \div 41 = N$. To estimate, think $3600 \div 40 = 360 \div 4 = 90$.
3. $4916 \div 78 = N$. To estimate, think $4800 \div 80 = 480 \div 8 = 60$.
4. $25 \times 335 = N$. To estimate, think $25 \times 320 = (\frac{25}{100}) \times (320 \times 100) = \frac{1}{4} \times 320 \times 100 = 80 \times 100 = 8000$.

Clustering. Clustering is grouping addends so that an average amount is evident. For example, to estimate the attendance each day in Park City Elementary School for which the figures for one week are 35,245 + 41,700 + 32, 449 + 38,275 + 29,654, one could think the attendance clusters around 35,000, so the estimate is 35,000 each day.

Learning Strategies for Computational Estimation

Problem solving can lead to students' understanding of strategies for computational estimation. Examples of problems to introduce each strategy follow.

Front-End with Adjustment

1. Mary had 75 cents to spend at the school fair. She thought she would like to buy a soft drink for 33 cents and a hot dog for 52 cents. Estimate if she could buy the soft drink and hot dog.
2. At his parents' garage sale, Felix helped his parents. They said if he made $75, he could have the money for a bicycle. He sold clothing for $59 and dishes, pots, and pans for $47. Estimate what money he made to decide if he could buy the bicycle.

Rounding. Joan was working at the school fair. The fair profits from candy apple sales were to be used to buy orchestra music. She knew the sales had to be $150 to make enough money to buy orchestra music. In the morning, 68 people bought candy apples from her at 98 cents each. In the afternoon, the man in charge of the fair said that they should reduce the candy apples to 90 cents to sell more. She sold 107 apples in the afternoon. Estimate what her sales totaled to decide if the school could buy orchestra music.

Compatible Numbers

1. Albert's dad flies a lot in his job. He told Albert that the last three months he flew about 8480 miles in 42 days. That seemed like a lot of travel, and they decided

to figure out how many miles he flew each day he was in the air, if he flew the same number of miles each day. Estimate this number of miles.

2. Suzanne's family took a trip last summer to see relatives. They traveled 2452 miles in 8 days of travel coming and going to their relatives' home town. If they traveled the same number of miles each day, about how many miles did they drive each day?
3. Volunteers were working with county personnel to plant trees on an area that had been deforested by fire. A total of 212 people signed up for a weekend project to plant 4500 trees in predug holes. About how many were each expected to plant, if it was thought they would each plant the same number?
4. Three hundred thirteen people worked for six weeks gathering signatures for a school bond issue to be put on the ballot in Falls City. They gathered 9465 signatures, which was more than enough to get the issue on the ballot. Assume each gathered the same amount and estimate about how many signatures each person collected.

Clustering. At Seth's school the number of children in each grade of two classes is: Kindergarten, 52; first, 49; second, 53; third, 47; fourth, 49; fifth, 50; sixth, 51. After Seth's mother read this in the school paper, she asked him to estimate the average number in each grade? What did he tell her?

After they solve problems selected to introduce each strategy, students discuss their thinking. You listen to their ideas and follow up with questions that help students note the characteristics of the problems that make a strategy particularly useful. If children do not use the strategy applicable to the problems, explain that there is another strategy, and use cognitive modeling so that pupils can observe the thinking process involved in using the strategy. Students discuss their observations, the strategy, and where it applies. To develop competency in the use of a strategy, they solve problems or engage in activities such as the following. Reys (1986) suggests practice sessions of five to ten minutes each week.

ACTIVITY 7.29
Greater or Less.

This activity can be used as an activity for two children, or one child could work alone with the activity cards. Each activity card gives an open number sentence and a reasonable estimate. Children draw cards and work in pairs (or alone) to think an estimate for the open sentence, compare their estimate to that given on the card, and decide if it is greater or less than the estimate on the card. They also explain to each other the reasons for their decisions. Then, they use their calculators to find the exact solution, and they decide if their estimate was better because it was closer to the exact solution than the estimate given. In the following list the first two columns give examples for the cards. The examples are illustrative of those that could be used for teaching strategies for estimation with different operations and, except for older students, would not include all the operations. The last column gives the calculator solutions students would use in their comparisons. These numbers would not be on the cards.

The first six examples point out the need to adjust answers when the front-end estimation strategy is used. The next five show the importance of adjusting when using the round-up strategy. The last exercise involves thinking compatible numbers.

Estimate	Is Your Estimate Greater than, Equal to, or Less than this Number?	Calculation for Comparison
647 + 817 = □	1400	1464
532 + 342 = □	800	874
52 × 52 = □	2500	2704

83 × 13 = □	800	1079
31 × 44 = □	1200	1364
762 + 459 = □	1100	1221
761 + 874 = □	1700	1635
821 − 655 = □	100	166
76 × 86 = □	7200	6536
58 × 47 = □	3000	2746
2907 ÷ 17 = □	150	171
2646 ÷ 42 = □	60	63

Students can make cards for this game. Making activity cards for other members of the class requires learners to think about the reasonableness of estimates and could be both educational and challenging for some students.

ACTIVITY 7.30
Using a One Hundred Chart.

Each child has a one hundred square with numerals (see Appendix G for pattern). You give a number, and the students locate the multiple of 10 nearest that number on their square and put a marker on the numeral. In groups of two, students explain to each other why they decided where to put the marker. One child tells the class what his or her group decided. After they understand the procedure, students can work in groups, taking turns giving each other numbers and explaining how they decided where to place the marker.

An adaptation is to carry out the activity using number lines labeled each 10 from 0 to 100 rather than using the hundred square.

ACTIVITY 7.31
Who Counted More Numbers?

Ask questions or give a study sheet with questions that require children to think about the reasons for rounding strategies. Examples are: Sue counted from 62 to 70. Alice counted from 62 to 60. Who counted more numbers? Why? Julian counted from 776 to 780. Martin counted from 776 to 770. Who counted more numbers? Why?

ACTIVITY 7.32
Board and Dice Game.

Two to four players take turns throwing two dice on a playing board (Figure 7.9). Numbers on which the dice land are rounded, and the player throwing the dice adds the rounded numbers and records the result on his or her tally sheet. Each player keeps track of his or her total. The first player to reach 500 wins.

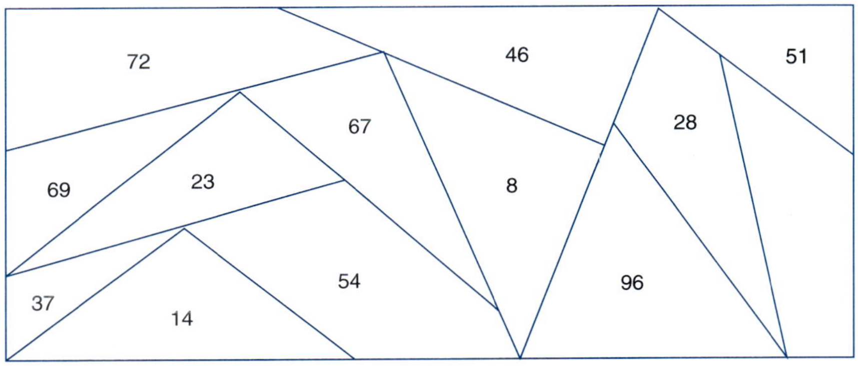

FIGURE 7.9 Playing Board for Rounding Game

The calculator helps children develop skill in estimation because individually or in groups they can evaluate their own estimates by checking them against answers found using the calculator. Thus, it is a self-teaching tool. Three calculator activities follow.

ACTIVITY 7.33
The Range Game (Wheatley and Hersberger, 1986).

Two players take turns finding number sentence solutions that are whole numbers within a given range. Cards or a list of open number sentences each with a range of solutions are provided. The game can be played for any operation. Examples are:

$27 + \square = N$	Range of N is 80 to 90.
$35 - \square = N$	Range of N is 10 to 20.
$45 \times \square = N$	Range of N is 950 to 1000.
$780 \div \square = N$	Range of N is 25 to 50.

Players take turns drawing cards with the problems or uncovering each problem in a list. The players make inputs on the calculator as needed to find a whole number solution in the range. Each input gives the player a token. The objective of the game is to make as few inputs as possible, and therefore, when all the cards have been used, the player with the least tokens is the winner.

This game can be used as an individual activity with a student noting his or her improvements. He or she can make a record of the number of inputs used for each number sentence and work to lower the number of inputs needed.

Some students may enjoy finding all the possible whole number solutions within the range. They may predict the number, jot it down, find the solutions, and compare their prediction with the number determined.

ACTIVITY 7.34
What's Your Estimate? Game.

Each of four players writes a number sentence on a small piece of paper. The solution should be too difficult for most to calculate mentally, for example, $459 + 678 = N$ or $47 \times 73 = N$. All the number sentences are laid in front of the players. Each player makes an estimate of the solution to each number sentence except his or her own and makes a record of the estimate. Players in turn tell their estimates to the player writing the number sentence. He or she then uses a calculator to find the solution and tells it to the players. The person with the best estimate of the solution collects a token. When a player collects six tokens, he or she wins the game, and another game begins.

ACTIVITY 7.35
Pick One.

Learners draw cards, each of which gives an open number sentence and three estimates. Children in groups of two take turns deciding which estimate is the most reasonable and explaining the reasons for that choice. They use calculators to compute the exact solution, and note how close their choice was to the computed solution. Examples of problems for cards follow. Computed solutions (not shown on pupils' cards) are given in parentheses. The examples in the list are designed to encourage students to think rounding, rename the rounded number as a fraction, compute mentally, and adjust if necessary. Thus, in the first example, 49 is close to 50, so think $\frac{50}{100} = \frac{1}{2}$; base the estimate on $\frac{1}{2} \times 36$; do not adjust. The activity can deal with this or another strategy.

Math Sentence	Which is the Most Reasonable Estimate for the Solution?		
49 × 36 = □	1700	1800 (1764)	1900
52 × 44 = □	2300 (2288)	2400	2500
26 × 84 = □	2100	2200 (2184)	2300
88 × 47 = □	4000	4200 (4136)	4400
74 × 44 = □	3100 (3256)	3200	3300

As in Activity 7.29, children can make activity cards for others to use and in so doing reflect on the reasonableness of estimates.

Activity for the Classroom 7.4. Write a *Pick One* activity that involves a different strategy from that used in Activity 7.35, and use it with students. Observe children as they discuss their choices with one another. Write up the results of your observations.

Assessing Computational Estimation

To assess learners' skill in computational estimation, you can use quizzes or tests, observations, interviews, and students' reports. Quizzes and tests should be short and include no more than 10 or 12 items. Each item should be shown on the overhead projector for 10 to 20 seconds (Reys, 1986). Children write their solutions, which you use to determine their progress.

As children discuss their approaches to computational estimation in small groups and whole-class settings, you observe and make notes of their strategies. Short interviews make it possible to interview more than one child. Asking a child to estimate only one computation will keep interviews short and still give you information about his or her thinking.

You also assess children's attainments as you evaluate children's oral and written reports of the strategies and thinking processes they used for computational estimations. You determine the appropriateness of their strategies and the flexibility of their thinking. As with all assessment, dated records are kept so that achievement over time can be determined. Both you and the students should keep records.

PAPER-AND-PENCIL COMPUTATION

Even though children still need to know the algorithms for paper-and-pencil computation (step-by-step procedures performed routinely), many advocate that they be de-emphasized in instruction. The NCTM's *Curriculum and Evaluation Standards* (1989) state that calculators should be used for complex calculations but that paper-and-pencil algorithms can be used for simple computations. Colburn (1989) advises that algorithms to be mastered for addition and subtraction should not involve numbers of more than two or three digits, two digits for multiplication, and one-digit divisors for division.

The number relations that are the basis for the algorithms should be emphasized in instruction (Burns, 1989; Hamrick and McKillip, 1978; Hiebert, 1990). Such knowledge contributes to children's understanding of mathematics and encourages learners to expect mathematics to make sense.

If the study of algorithms is to be meaningful to children, algorithms must also be seen as tools for solving real-life problems. Children should use algorithms to compute to solve problems written by adults, but they should also write problems requiring computation that reflect the context of their own lives, and they should solve problems written by their peers.

The first part of this section gives the algorithms for each operation. The second part describes the steps for teaching algorithms, with an emphasis on helping students understand the reasoning behind the algorithms and their usefulness in problem solving. The third part details activities for teaching algorithms for addition, subtraction, multiplication, and division. The fourth part discusses using the calculator to extend understanding of computation. The final part of this section discusses assessing students' learning of paper-and-pencil algorithms.

Algorithms for the Operations with Whole Numbers

Addition and subtraction algorithms can involve renaming (trading or regrouping) or no renaming. Mathematics educators advocate teaching algorithms that involve renaming and no renaming at the same time (NCTM, 1989). Combinations in which both numbers are tens plus ones and renaming is not involved in the computation can be solved mentally by many learners (e.g., $34 + 55 = N$ or $57 - 14 = N$). However, some children need to use algorithms to find answers to these exercises. Therefore, they are included in paper-and-pencil computation, but children who can compute mentally are encouraged to do so.

Children *do not* use paper-and-pencil algorithms for higher-decade addition and subtraction combinations (e.g., $52 + 7 = 59$; $43 + 9 = 52$; $47 - 46 = 1$; $86 - 8 = 78$) and for sums or differences in which one or both numbers are multiples of powers of 10 (e.g., $60 + 20 = 80$; $40 + 32 = 72$; $300 + 162 = 462$; $70 - 50 = 20$; $46 - 30 = 16$; $764 - 200 = 564$). These combinations should be computed mentally. Using paper-and-pencil procedures for these calculations discourages mental computation. (Why?)

For multiplication, algorithms are learned for products in which one or both factors are tens plus ones. They do not use algorithms for tens times tens (e.g., 40×60). Although some children can mentally compute a product when one factor is a power of 10 (e.g., 62×20), these numbers are included in paper-and-pencil algorithms because such mental multiplication is not easy for some children. If children can compute mentally, they should do so.

The division algorithms studied are those in which the divisor is a one- or two-digit number. Children probably should not be expected to develop accuracy and speed in division with two-digit divisors. They should compute mentally when the divisor is tens and a multiple of the dividend (e.g., $1200 \div 60 = N$).

The exploration of algorithms with large numbers for any operation can contribute to the development of meaning (NCTM, 1989). Children should examine how the same meanings and procedures apply to both large and small numbers.

The study of standard algorithms is made more meaningful if children have opportunities to explore extended algorithms. Extended or developmental algorithms show each step in the procedure and help children grasp the reasoning behind the algorithms (Hiebert, 1990; Stanic and McKillip, 1989). Extended algorithms for each operation are included in the examples.

Examples of Algorithms

Addition

Standard Algorithms

$$\begin{array}{r} {}^{1}27 \\ +45 \\ \hline 72 \end{array} \qquad \begin{array}{r} 67 \\ +32 \\ \hline 99 \end{array}$$

Extended Algorithms

$$\begin{array}{r} 27 \\ +\,45 \\ \hline 12 \\ +\,60 \\ \hline 72 \end{array} \qquad \begin{array}{r} 67 \\ +\,32 \\ \hline 9 \\ +\,90 \\ \hline 99 \end{array}$$

Subtraction

Standard Algorithms

$$\begin{array}{r} {}^{5}\not{6}{}^{1}2 \\ -\,45 \\ \hline 17 \end{array} \qquad \begin{array}{r} 55 \\ -\,32 \\ \hline 23 \end{array}$$

Extended Algorithms

$$\begin{array}{r} {}^{5}\not{6}{}^{1}2 \\ -\,45 \\ \hline 7 \\ +\,10 \\ \hline 17 \end{array} \qquad \begin{array}{r} 67 \\ -\,32 \\ \hline 5 \\ +\,30 \\ \hline 35 \end{array}$$

The extended algorithm for subtraction probably provides less opportunity to develop meaning than the extended algorithm for addition, because the process of renaming must be done before the recording takes place. The following format can help learners understand the procedure:

$$\begin{array}{rcrr} 62 & = & 50 & +\;12 \\ -\,45 & = & -\;40 & -\;\;5 \\ \hline 17 & = & 10 & +\;\;7 \end{array}$$

Multiplication

Standard Algorithms

$$\begin{array}{r} 22 \\ \times\,43 \\ \hline 66 \\ +88 \\ \hline 946 \end{array} \qquad \begin{array}{r} {}^{3\not{1}} \\ 36 \\ \times\,53 \\ \hline 108 \\ +180 \\ \hline 1908 \end{array}$$

Extended Algorithms

$$\begin{array}{r} 22 \\ \times\,43 \\ \hline 6 \\ +\,60 \\ 80 \\ \underline{800} \\ 946 \end{array} \qquad \begin{array}{r} 36 \\ \times\,53 \\ \hline 18 \\ +\,90 \\ 300 \\ \underline{1500} \\ 1908 \end{array}$$

Division

Standard Algorithms

$$\begin{array}{r} 226 \\ 3\overline{)678} \\ \underline{-6} \\ 7 \\ \underline{-6} \\ 18 \\ \underline{-18} \\ 0 \end{array}$$

$$\begin{array}{r} 56 \\ 23\overline{)1288} \\ -\,\underline{115} \\ 138 \\ -\,138 \\ \hline 0 \end{array}$$

Extended Algorithms

a.
```
       226
    3)678
     -600   200
       78
     - 60  + 20
       18
     - 18     6
        0   226
```

b.
```
        56
   23)1288
    -1150    50
      138
    - 138   + 6
        0    56
```

c.
```
        56
   23)1288
    - 230    10
     1058
    - 460    20
      598
    - 460   +20
      138
    - 115     5
       23
     - 23     1
        0    56
```

Learning Algorithms

The learning of paper-and-pencil algorithms is delayed until children are able to compute mentally and estimate solutions, but not until they have a high level of skill in mental computation and computational estimation. Algorithms for addition and subtraction are learned in grade 3, and multiplication and division, in grades 4 or 5.

The foundation components for computation discussed in this chapter enable students to understand the reasons for the steps in algorithms as well as learn to compute mentally and estimate solutions to computation. Therefore, you help students relate their knowledge of the foundation components to algorithms as you guide learners to develop the rationale for these procedures.

Four steps are followed in teaching algorithms:

1. Assign Story Problems for Children to Solve Using Materials. Have children write problems that involve numbers greater than 10. Have children exchange the problems they have written and solve them. Remind learners to think about the reasonableness of their solutions, noting that estimation is a good approach for this. Examples of story problems for which paper-and-pencil computation is appropriate follow.

Addition and Subtraction

1. Martha's mother went shopping to buy a birthday gift for Martha. She spent $29 on the gift. Then she decided to buy a new dress for herself. It cost $48. How much did she spend?
2. Herbert's father had his car at the garage for repairs. The repairman said the cost of a set of spark plugs would be $26 and the labor for the tune-up would be $55. How much money will his father give to the repairman to pay the bill?

3. The principal at Hillside School ordered 65 new mathematics books for the two second-grade classes. Ms. Romano's second grade received 32. How many did the other second grade get?
4. Joanne and Amana were selling tickets for the school fair. Joanne sold 36. Amana was very pleased because she sold 55. How many more than Joanne did she sell?

Multiplication and Division

1. The 27 students in Wendy's sixth-grade class were making wreaths to sell at the school bazaar. They wanted to make money to go to visit the state capital. The class decided that each student should make 8 wreaths. How many wreaths would be made if each person made his or her share?
2. Tonya earned $12 a week taking care of her neighbor's 2-year old daughter when the woman went to an evening computer class at the local high school. She said, "I wonder how much I will earn in this semester of 16 weeks?" What was the answer to her question?"
3. Alfredo was putting napkins on the tables for the scout dinner. There were 12 places at each table. He had a package of 180 napkins. How many tables would get napkins from that box?
4. Don's little league team received a gift of $1200 to buy uniforms. Each uniform cost $75. How many uniforms could they buy?

Children find solutions individually, in pairs, or in groups. Learners are reminded that they can solve the problems any way they choose. Some will invent procedures for computation (Kamii, 1989). They should be encouraged to do so and to share their thinking with their peers. When children invent their own algorithms, they should be helped to examine their reasoning to make certain the procedure is valid.

Addition and subtraction problems are often solved with place-value materials (Figure 7.10). Arrays on grid paper, sometimes place-value materials or repeated addition, are used for finding multiplication problem solutions (Figure 7.11). Division problems can be solved by using place-value materials. Some chil-

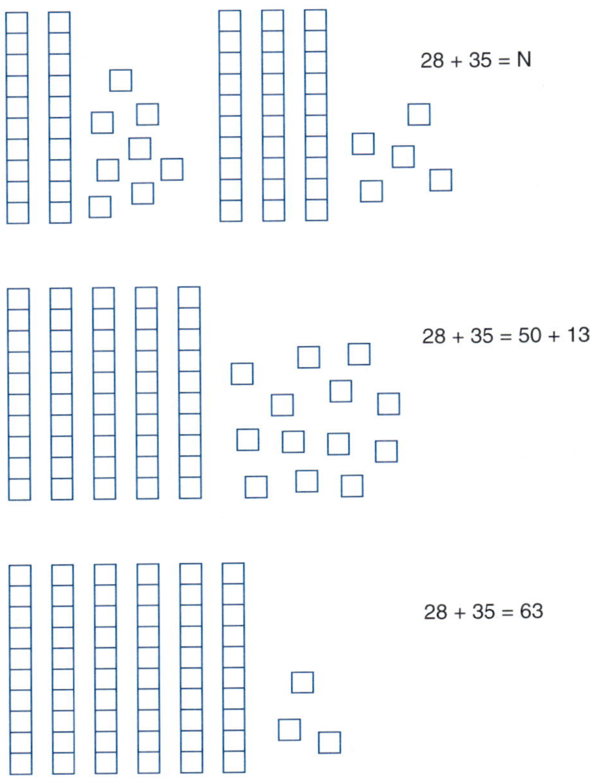

FIGURE 7.10 Place-Value Materials for Solving Addition Computation Problems

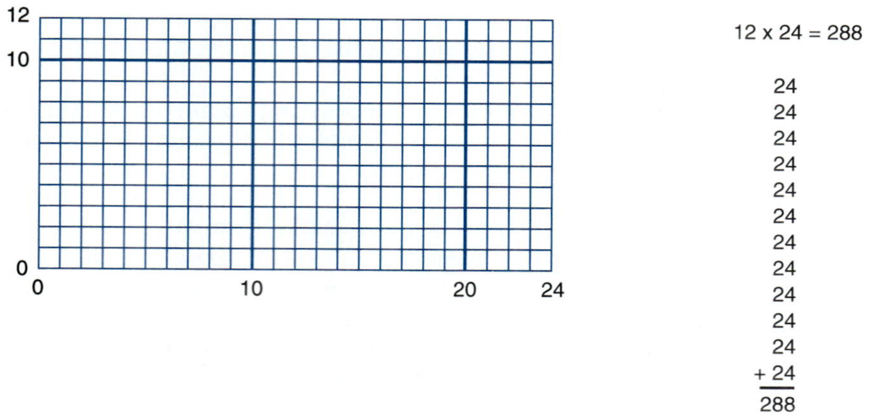

FIGURE 7.11 Array and Repeated Addition Models for Multiplication Computation Problem

dren may use repeated subtraction (Figure 7.12). After children solve the problems, they report how they solved them and why their solutions are reasonable. They may use the overhead projector to show their solutions.

2. Ask Pupils to Use Numerals to Make Records of Their Thinking or of Their Work with Materials. When children can easily solve story problems using materials or thinking, they are asked to make paper-and-pencil records. Figures 7.13 A–C show three different records of thinking addition computation. Discuss how the written records relate to their solutions.

3. Guide Learners to Develop Algorithms by Reflecting on Their Work. Extended algorithms show computations with tens and ones and summing partial computations, which is the way learners often think when reflecting on their work with

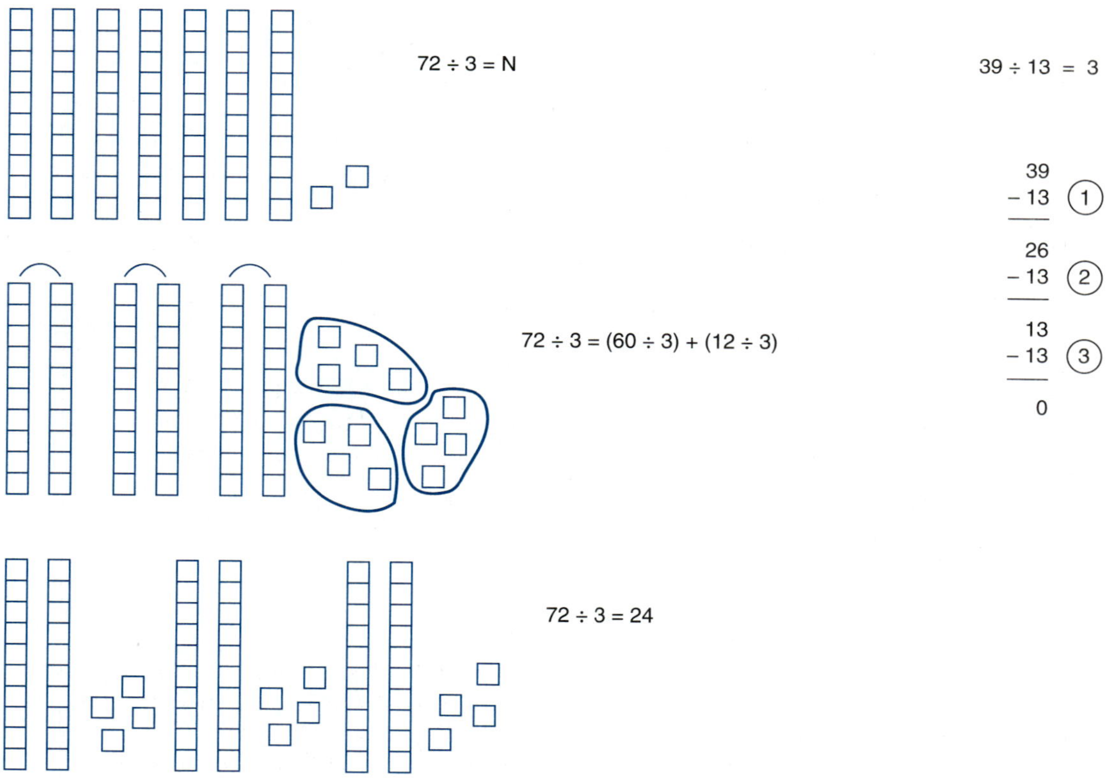

FIGURE 7.12 Place-Value and Repeated Subtraction Models for Division Computation Problems

Records of Children's Thinking			Extended Algorithm
A. 20 + 30 = 50	B. 28 + 2 = 30	C. 28 + 5 = 33	D. $\begin{array}{r} 28 \\ +\,35 \\ \hline 13 \\ +\,50 \\ \hline 63 \end{array}$
8 + 5 = 13	35 − 2 = 33	30 + 33 = 63	
50 + 13 = 63	30 + 33 = 63		

FIGURE 7.13 Thinking Sums and Extended Algorithm for 28 + 35 = □

materials (Figure 7.13A). Therefore, extended algorithms are learned before standard (conventional) algorithms. Extended algorithms also reveal the rationale of algorithms more than the standard procedures do.

To introduce the addition extended algorithm, you guide learners to relate their work with materials (Figure 7.10) and their records of thinking (Figure 7.13A) to the extended algorithm (Figure 7.13D). Have children look at the arrangements of materials or their records. You write the extended algorithm on the overhead or chalkboard and say, "Please look at what I am writing. We can find the sum by making a record of thinking this way. Why did I write '13,' '50,' and '63'? How does your work with place-value materials tell what I have written? What are the steps in using this method? Notice I began with the ones." To make certain students understand the algorithm, have students complete several examples. In groups, have them tell one another what they did. Finally, ask several students to show their work on the chalkboard or overhead and to explain the steps to the class.

To solve subtraction story problems, students use materials and thinking as they did with addition (Figure 7.14 A–F). Extended algorithms (Figures 7.14C and 7.14F) are introduced with discussions that help learners relate work with materials to the extended algorithm. Learners are also encouraged to relate the extended algorithm for addition to the extended algorithm for subtraction. Ask children to think how they could use what they learned about addition computation to help them with paper-and-pencil subtraction. Discuss subtracting ones and tens and making a record of these subtractions. Have them use the chalkboard or overhead to show their ideas. When the format is established, children complete several examples, discuss them in groups, and share ideas with the class before they work independently.

The extended algorithm for multiplication is usually introduced with a story problem whose solution involves multiplication of a two-digit number by a one-digit number (e.g., 5 × 39). Children use repeated addition, arrays, or mental computation to find solutions, and they discuss how they solved the problems. During the discussion, you introduce the extended algorithm. Your questions and comments help students connect their solutions to the extended algorithm and understand how each partial product is found (see Box 1.8).

To introduce the extended algorithm for multiplication of a two-digit number by a two-digit number, ask each child to make an array for 13 × 23 and to draw a dark line across the array to show the products when 10 and 3 are factors and a line up and down the array to show the products when 20 and 3 are factors. When they have made their dark lines, 10 × 20, 10 × 3, 3 × 20, and 3 × 3 will stand out (Figure 7.15A). Have children examine the partial products shown on their arrays and write the appropriate math sentences in the sections of their arrays. Write

$$\begin{array}{r} 23 \\ \times\,\underline{13} \end{array}$$

on the overhead and say, "Look at the product of 3 × 3 on your arrays. How was that partial product found? Remember the form we studied for easier multiplication problems? Where should we write the product of the ones times ones?" You or a learner should write this partial product on the overhead. Continue questioning and recording in this manner until the computation is completed (Figure 7.15B). Learners next make up their own examples, solve them, and share their work.

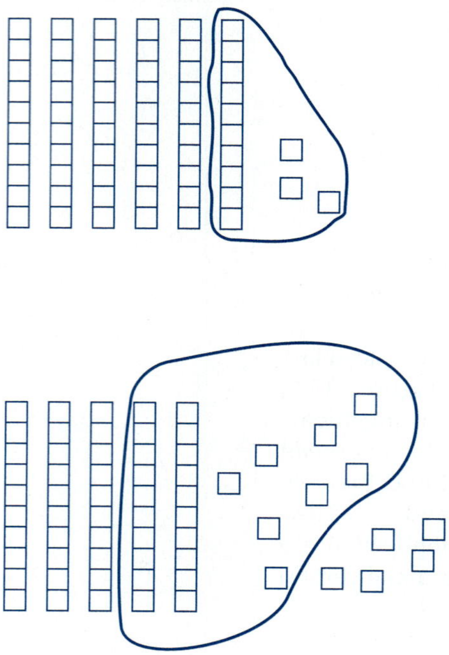

A.

Think:
63 is 50 + 13

1. Subtract 8 from 13.
2. Subtract 20 from 50.
3. Answer is 35.

B.

Extended
Algorithm

```
 5 1
  ~~6~~3
 − 28
    5
 + 30
   35
```

C.

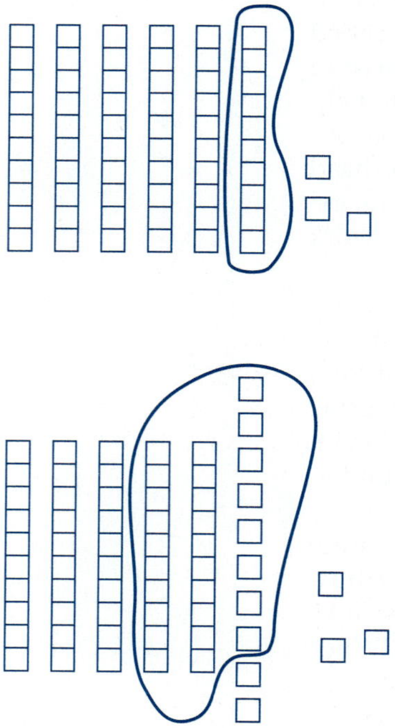

D.

Think:
63 is 50 + 10 + 3

1. Subtract 8 from 10.
2. Subtract 20 from 50.
3. Answer is 35.

E.

Extended
Algorithm

```
5 + 1
  ~~6~~3
 − 28
    5 = (10 − 8) + 3
 + 30
   35
```

F.

FIGURE 7.14 Materials Solutions for Subtraction, Records of Thinking, and Extended Algorithms

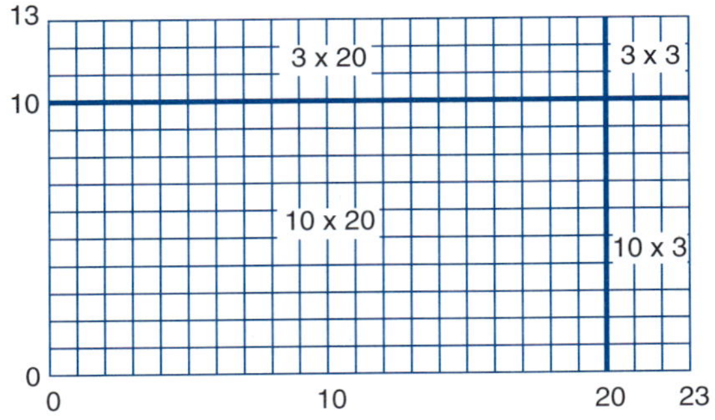

A.

```
  23
 x13
   9   = 3 x 3
  60   = 3 x 20
+ 30   = 10 x 3
 200   = 10 x 20
 299
```

B.

FIGURE 7.15 Array and Related Extended Algorithm Showing Partial Products

For division, learners are asked to use records of repeated subtraction as the basis for the algorithm. You guide them to understand that the algorithm involves subtracting more quickly by using multiples of 10 times the divisor as subtrahends. Examples b and c for division extended algorithms given earlier in this chapter show how this process can be adapted to a learner's ability to estimate partial quotients. (Which example would be easiest for a student? Why?)

Most students can learn extended algorithms when you use questions similar to those in the interactive lesson example (Box 1.8) or suggested in this chapter. However, sometimes you may need to use cognitive modeling to help students understand extended algorithms. Then, students explain what they observe and are given many opportunities to discuss the reasons for the steps in extended algorithms.

To understand the steps in extended algorithms, pupils should use extended algorithms for any operation, at least for a short time before working with standard algorithms. After studying standard algorithms, some children may choose to use extended algorithms. The choice should be theirs.

Introduce standard algorithms by saying, "There is a short paper-and-pencil method used by most people when they do not have a calculator. You should know what it is. Because of what you already know, you can learn it easily." Usually, you will model the standard algorithm for the students, with or without thinking out loud. If you use *silent modeling*, you carry out the standard algorithm without talking. The children observe the process, and by relating what they notice to their understanding of the extended form, they are able to explain the steps. For example, when they see you write "1" and "3" in

$$\begin{array}{r} {}^{1}26 \\ +\underline{57} \\ 3 \end{array}$$

they explain that this shows 13, or the sum of 6 plus 7.

After you complete several examples with silent modeling and children explain the meaning they have of the procedure, they work with you to complete several examples. Each child then completes some examples independently.

If you *think out loud,* note what is being done and why. Also comment on the reasonableness of the solution, referring to the foundation components where appropriate. After the procedure is completed, the children work though several examples with you and discuss the sense of what they are doing. With either modeling approach, children continue to work with you until they develop a knowledge of the steps in a standard algorithm and can give the reasons for the steps.

Children learn that looking back at solutions is the final step in computation. Both paper-and-pencil and calculator computations must be checked for accuracy and reasonableness; in problem solving, solutions must also make sense in the context of the problem. To help learners develop the habit of looking back, children are frequently asked how they checked for accuracy and why their solutions are reasonable. Class discussions that deal with determining reasonableness should bring out the importance of estimating. Learners can also be asked to write up how they thought to decide if their solutions were reasonable.

4. Provide Practice Materials for Children. Children develop skill in the use of algorithms after they understand the procedures. Short practice periods several times a week are scheduled until children develop skill. Thereafter, review of algorithms takes place about once a week to reconsider meanings and maintain skill (Rathmell and Trafton, 1990).

Activities for Algorithms

The first five activities give alternate approaches to computational procedures that give students opportunities to study rationales for different algorithms and to examine number relations in new settings. The next two activities are different approaches to practice. The last two extend learners' knowledge.

ACTIVITY 7.36
Scratch Method of Adding.

The scratch method is an old method. It can help children understand place value. All computation is recorded as in the second step in the following. Begin with the highest power of 10.

1. Add 4 + 7, write 11 as shown in the tens and ones places; scratch out 4 and 7.
2. Add 8 + 9, write 7 in the ones place, add a 10 to the tens, scratch out 1, record 2, scratch out 8 and 9.
The sum is 127.

$$\begin{array}{r} \not{4}\not{8} \\ +\not{7}\not{9} \\ \hline 1\not{1}7 \\ 2 \end{array}$$

Model the scratch method without verbalizing. Ask children what you are doing and why it makes sense. Have children complete several exercises using the scratch method. Discuss how it differs from the standard algorithm.

ACTIVITY 7.37
Using the 10 Facts in Subtraction.

When the number of the ones in the subtrahend is greater than the number of the ones in the minuend, an alternate approach to subtraction uses the 10 facts and does not require regrouping:

1. Think 8 tens less 1 ten is 7 tens; record 7 in the tens place.
2. 10 – 7 = 3; record 3 in the ones place.
3. 70 – 40 = 30; record.
4. Think 1 left; record in the ones place.
5. Add partial differences.

$$\begin{array}{r} {}^{7}\not{8}1 \\ -\,47 \\ \hline 3 \\ +\,30 \\ 1 \\ \hline 34 \end{array}$$

This method parallels what many children do with materials. They trade a ten for 10 ones and remove the ones from the 10 ones. They do not regroup and then remove the ones. Therefore, this algorithm can be introduced when children are working with materials. Children may use the algorithm if it is meaningful to them.

ACTIVITY 7.38
Equal Addition (Compensation) Method.

This algorithm is used when renaming is required. The procedure is to add 10 ones to the ones in the minuend and 1 ten to the tens in the subtrahend (which is subsequently subtracted), in effect adding 10 – 10 = 0. A record is made as in the example:

```
  1
  62
 5̶4̶8
 ---
  14
```

You model the use of this algorithm. To understand the idea of compensation with two-digit number computation, students think about the compensation strategy used when working with basic subtraction facts (e.g., 11 – 5 = 12 – 6 = 6) and discuss how this strategy is used in paper-and-pencil computation. They try this algorithm to see how they like it. Some children will find it easier than the standard algorithm and adopt it for use in all subtraction computation when renaming is needed.

ACTIVITY 7.39
Lattice Method for Multiplication.

Lattice multiplication, also called the *Gelosia method*, makes use of a framework (Figure 7.16). The framework consists of rectangles, each of which is divided by a diagonal line. There are as many rectangles in one row as there are digits in one factor and as many rows as the number of digits in the other factor. The digits of one factor are written above each rectangle along the top; the digits of the other factor beside the rectangles to the right of the framework. Beginning with the ones in both factors, each pair of numbers is multiplied in turn, and the product written in the proper rectangle, one digit to a triangular region. If a product is less than 10, the upper triangular region of a rectangle is empty. Add along the diagonals, beginning at the lower right corner, renaming as necessary. The sums are recorded as shown in the Figure 7.16. The product is read from the top of the left-hand side to the far right at the bottom.

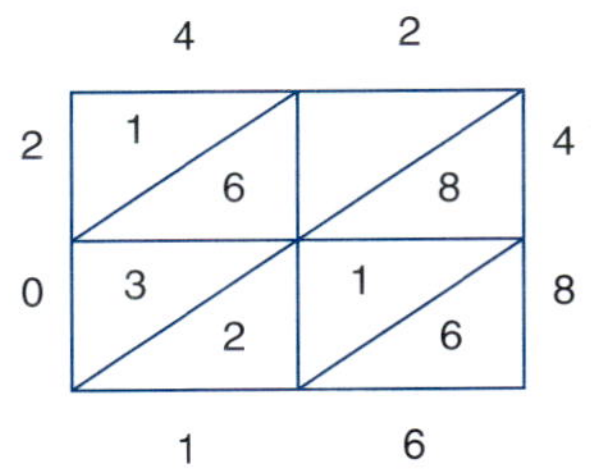


```
  42
x 48
----
2016
```

FIGURE 7.16 Lattice Method for Multiplication

To teach the lattice approach, show both the lattice and the standard form for a computation. Students compare the two forms. They discuss their observations, develop the steps in the lattice method, and try it out. Cognitive modeling is an alternate approach to introducing the method. Some learners find the lattice method easier to use than other approaches and use it for whole-number multiplication computation.

ACTIVITY 7.40
Halving and Doubling Method for Multiplication.

The steps in the halving and doubling method for multiplication are to double one factor and halve the other until the latter is no greater than 1. Any fractions are discarded. The results are written in columns as in Figure 7.17. The results of doubling that are opposite even numbers in the halving column are discarded by crossing out. The results of doubling that are written opposite odd numbers (those not crossed out) in the halving column are added to give the product.

13	x	16
~~6~~		~~32~~
3		64
1		128
		208

FIGURE 7.17 Halving and Doubling Method for Multiplication

Reader Activity 7.3

Write a problem for each of the five alternative algorithms, and solve it using both the standard and alternative algorithms. Compare the two algorithms. What are your reactions to using the alternative algorithms?

ACTIVITY 7.41
A Surprising Result.

Pupils choose any number with an odd number of different digits (no two digits the same). Next, they reverse the digits and subtract the smaller number from the larger number. The difference is divided by 11. Each student follows the procedure four times and looks for a pattern in the quotients. (Each quotient is divisible by 9, or the sum of the digits in the quotient is 9.)

ACTIVITY 7.42
Fill-ins.

Children complete algorithms in which some work has been deleted (Figure 7.18). In a class discussion, children should explain to one another the strategies used to determine fill-ins. That inverse operations must be used to complete the exercises should be highlighted in the discussion.

ACTIVITY 7.43
Prime and Composite Numbers.

(See Standard 6 in Curriculum Standards for Grades 5–8, Appendix A.) Have children make the Sieve of Eratosthenes. (An interested child could find out "who is Eratosthenes.") Each learner uses a hundred square with squares filled in with numerals to 100. The directions are: circle 2 and cross out all the numerals for numbers divisible by 2 except 2, repeat procedure for 3, 5, 7, then the numeral for each remaining number that is divisible only by 1 and the number itself. Note that 1 is neither prime nor composite and so is a separate category (Figure 7.19). Discuss what the sieve shows: circled numerals show prime numbers.

Students in groups can make arrays for numbers to 25 to determine the characteristics of prime and composite numbers. (Factors of a prime number are 1 and the number itself; composite numbers have factors that are prime numbers.)

ACTIVITY 7.44
Factor Trees.

Show students several factor trees (Figure 7.20), and ask them how they were constructed. Groups answer this question and report their responses to the class. After a plan for determining the prime factors of a number using the factor tree is agreed on, have students make factor trees for at least three composite numbers of their own choice. Choices are to be between 24 and 100. As they discuss their work, it should become apparent that there are different factor trees for the same composite number but that all the factor trees for a composite number have prime numbers on the bottom row.

FIGURE 7.18 Algorithms with Missing Numbers

$$\begin{array}{rrr} & \_\_ & 6 \\ + & 7 & \_\_ \\ \hline 1 & 4 & 4 \end{array} \qquad\qquad \begin{array}{rrrr} & & \_\_ & 9 \\ & \times & 6 & 4 \\ \hline & 1 & 1 & \_\_ \\ 1 & \_\_ & 4 & \_\_ \\ \hline \_\_ & 8 & \_\_ & 6 \end{array}$$

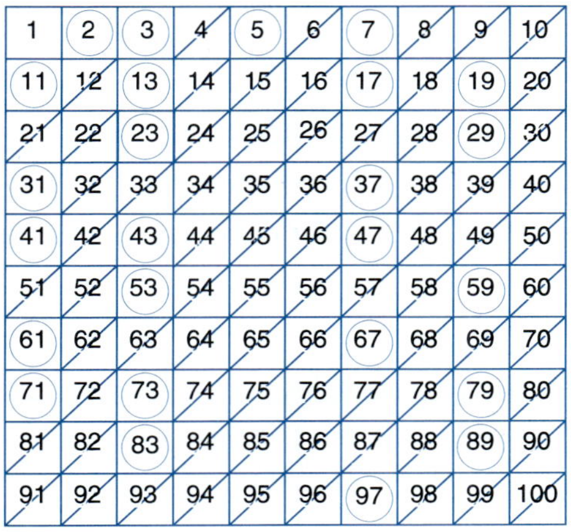

FIGURE 7.19 Sieve of Eratosthenes

Using the Calculator to Extend Understanding

The calculator removes the drudgery from computation and permits experimentation. As learners investigate relations or test hypotheses, they develop new meanings. The activities given can help children become curious about numbers and ask questions that can be answered by using the calculator to carry out investigations.

ACTIVITY 7.45
Rearranging.

Students write four two-digit numbers, find the sum, rearrange the numbers in four or more ways, and find the sums of the rearranged numbers (e.g., 46 + 34 + 78 + 14 = 172; some rearrangements: 14 + 78 + 34 + 46 = 172; 46 + 78 + 34 + 14 = 172; 14 + 34 + 46 + 78 = 172; 46 + 14 + 34 + 78 = 172; 78 + 34 + 46 + 14 = 172). They follow this procedure three times and then write several sentences telling their conclusions. Their written work should explain that the numbers can be arranged in any way but that the sum remains the same. Students can also carry out this activity for multiplication.

ACTIVITY 7.46
How Many Ways?

Ask learners to use their calculators to find the product of $36 \times 81 = N$ in as many ways as they can by using their knowledge of the meaning of numbers and multiplication. Possible responses are:

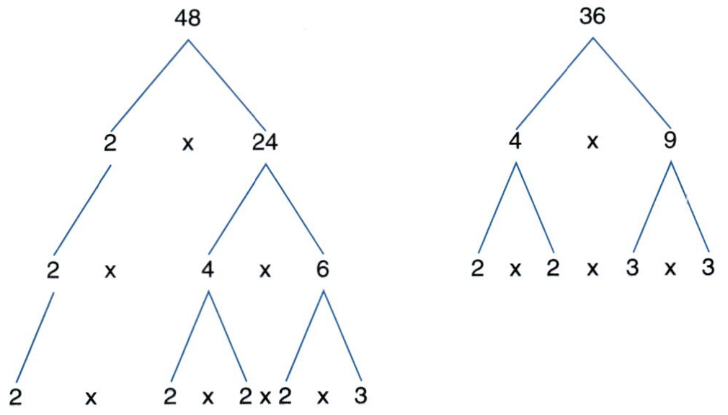

FIGURE 7.20 Factor Trees

$$(30 + 6) \times (80 + 1) = (30 \times 80) + (30 \times 1) + (6 \times 80) + (6 \times 1) =$$
$$2400 + 30 + 480 + 6 = 2916$$
$$(6 \times 6) \times (9 \times 9) = (6 \times 9) \times (6 \times 9) = 54 \times 54 = 2916$$
$$(4 \times 9) \times (9 \times 9) = 4 \times (9 \times 9 \times 9) = 4 \times 729 = 2916$$
$$(2 \times 18) \times 81 = 2 \times (18 \times 81) = 2 \times 1458 = 2916$$

Other products to investigate are 24×48, 12×54, and 45×25. They discuss their work and their reactions to the activity.

ACTIVITY 7.47
Multiplying Even and Odd Numbers.

Students should make hypotheses regarding results of multiplication of even by even numbers, odd by odd numbers, and odd by even numbers. They use their calculators to test their hypotheses and revise them when necessary. They should discuss the reasons for the rules that result from their work. The activity can be extended to division.

ACTIVITY 7.48
More on Prime Numbers.

Ask children to find as many prime numbers as possible for homework for a week. List these on the bulletin board, with students initials displayed beside the prime numbers they report. When they make their reports, ask, "How did you find prime numbers?" Discuss their responses.

Suggest that a group investigate the latest research on finding prime numbers with computers. Another group could research Goldbach's conjecture. Christian Goldbach (1690–1764) determined that even numbers greater than 4 can be found by adding two odd primes: $3 + 3 = 6$; $3 + 5 = 8$; $5 + 5 = 10$; $5 + 7 = 12$. Since no proof for this has yet been found, it is still a conjecture.

ACTIVITY 7.49
Find the Pattern.

Assign learners a sequence of problems such as the following: $9 \times 9 = N$; $8 \times 10 = N$; $7 \times 11 = N$; $6 \times 12 = N$; $5 \times 13 = N$; $4 \times 14 = N$; $3 \times 15 = N$; $2 \times 16 = N$; and $1 \times 17 = N$. They can use calculators or paper-and-pencil computation to find the products. Ask them to find the pattern in the products.

Extension: As you noticed, there is a pattern to the math sentences. Students can find the pattern, write other sequences, find the products, and decide if the pattern they discovered in the first activity is found in the new products.

ACTIVITY 7.50
Rewriting Math Sentences.

Give students pairs of related open math sentences and ask them to find the solutions (e.g., $N - 4 = 6$ and $6 + 4 = N$; $4 + N = 10$ and $10 - 4 = N$). They share their work, explaining that each pair of math sentences has the same solution because addition and subtraction are opposite (inverse). Assign pairs of math sentences with large numbers, such as $N + 45 = 82$ and $82 - 45 = N$; $N - 39 = 15$ and $15 + 39 = N$, and say, "Use your calculator, if you wish, to find solutions." When finished, students share their solutions and how they thought to solve the problems. They should tell why the solution for each pair of math sentences is the same and again discuss the concept of inverse operations. Your questions help them decide how and why they can rewrite nonstandard math sentences in standard form so that they know whether to add or subtract. Make a chart of their ideas. Give students a few sentences in nonstandard form to rewrite in standard form. Have them explain how they completed the task.

Finally, assign a few large number story problems that would be translated into math sentences in nonstandard form. Have students find solutions. Ask them to share their solutions and how they thought to solve the problems. They should tell how they wrote math sentences in nonstandard form and rewrote the sentences in standard form so they would know whether to add or subtract.

Some students will probably mention that they did not write a math sentence in nonstandard form to solve a problem but knew what operation to use. Have them explain how they thought to do this. The ensuing discussion should bring out when to add (to find a total) and when to subtract (to find a part that is left, to find a difference, or to make equal). Tell students that they do not need to write and rewrite a math sentence if they can think the operation to use to solve a problem. Say that it is good thinking to decide how the problem facts are related and what operation to use to solve the problem; they can then write the sentence in vertical form and compute to find the solution.

At a later time, when students need to solve problems such as $15\ N = 345$, adapt the activity for rewriting nonstandard multiplication and division math sentences in standard form.

Assessment of Paper-and-Pencil Computation

The assessment of paper-and-pencil computation is generally in the form of short quizzes or tests, that include only simple computations. Pupils should be able to complete six to eight problems with no errors in an amount of time that is reasonable for that operation and the complexity of the exercises (e.g., two-digit multiplication will take more time than two-digit addition). Time yourself, and adapt for the age group you teach to determine the amount of time needed that is reasonable. Quizzes and tests should be given after pupils demonstrate skill, not when learning the algorithm. They can be administered several times a semester. Some items in a quiz should check for understanding. Examples of such items follow.

1. Draw a picture to show the meaning of 3×21.
2. Tomas lost his calculator and forgot how to multiply. How could he solve the open math sentence, $14 \times 21 = N$? Only write one or two sentences to answer the question. Do not find the product.
3. Write either less than (<) or greater than (>) in the space to show the relation.
   a. $56 + 75\ \ 125$
   b. $99 - 40\ \ 50$
   c. $34 \times 45\ \ 1200$
   d. $650 \div 30\ \ 22$
4. In the following computation, how is 160 found?

$$\begin{array}{r} 24 \\ \times\ \underline{45} \\ 20 \\ +100 \\ 160 \\ \underline{800} \\ 1080 \end{array}$$

   Write out your answer.
5. How would you check your computation to ensure that the problem $39 + 62 = 101$ is correct?
6. Write at least three math sentences with the sum 546. (An example is: $421 + 125 = 546$; do not use this math sentence.) Each math sentence is to have addends different from those in the other sentences. The addends are to be tens or hundreds numbers.

If children are accurate, but work very slowly, you can check their knowledge of basic facts. As in all assessment of learning, knowing how the learner is thinking is invaluable in planning for remediation. Therefore, endeavor to interview learners who have difficulties.

CHOOSING A COMPUTATIONAL PROCEDURE

After studying different computational approaches, students need to learn how to decide which computational approach—mental computation, computational estimation, paper-and-pencil computation, or calculator usage—is appropriate for dealing with a particular problem. To help children think about making choices, some lessons emphasize how to decide what procedure to choose for a certain problem. Examples of problems to use in these lessons are:

1. Jane is saving money to go to camp for 2 weeks. It will cost her $169. Her father gives her $5 each week to mow the grass and $8 each week to clean the house. How many weeks will it take her to earn the money she needs for camp?
2. We have 26 children in our class. There are 45 books in the class library. Are there enough books for each child to have a book to read in school and a book to take home for a week?
3. Mike knows he spends on the average 10 hours each week completing homework assignments. He asked himself how many hours he spends on homework in a school year of 36 weeks. What is the answer to his question?
4. Marie read that the daily circulation of the city newspaper, Martinville News was 35,453. She said to herself, "If each paper costs $.25, how much money is collected each day? I can compute to find out." What was the answer to her question?

ACTIVITY 7.51
Which Computational Procedure?

Ask each student to write four problems to use in lessons related to the topic, "How to Decide Which Computational Approach to Use." They can use newspaper articles, TV or radio reports, and events in their lives as the sources for their problems. Each problem is to require a different computational approach. They do not need to solve their problems. Each problem is to be written on a separate sheet of paper.

When the problems are submitted, they are shared equally among groups of students. Each group studies the problems, decides on the computational approach to use to solve each problem, selects one problem for each computational approach to share with the class, and presents its report to the class. In the follow-up lesson, the class writes guidelines for deciding which approach to use to solve a problem. Guidelines students could suggest are:

- Compute mentally, if possible.
- Use paper and pencil for easy problems.
- Estimate if you do not need an exact solution.
- When the computations are long and you could easily make a mistake, use your calculator.
- Estimate to make sure your computations are correct.

SUMMARY

The first section of Part 1 of the chapter described learning the foundations for computation—knowledge of the operations, mastery of basic facts, thinking parts of numbers, and comparing and renaming numbers. It was noted that learning mental computation, computational estimation, and paper-and-pencil computation depend on knowing the foundations. Beginning mental computation was discussed in the second section of Part 1. Children first learn to compute mentally with multiples of powers of 10 and become skillful in higher-decade addition and subtraction. They then learn strategies for mental computation. These strategies, discussed in the third section of Part 1, are front-end, compensation, and compatible numbers.

Part 2 of the chapter dealt with computational estimation and paper-and-pencil computation. Four strategies for computational estimation were presented: front-end with adjustment, rounding, compatible numbers, and clustering. Learning both extended and standard algorithms was described in the second section of Part 2. Learning to choose a computational procedure was also discussed in Part 2.

The sections in each part included an overview of each approach, using interactive approaches to teach computational procedures, and activities to enable students to construct meanings and develop skill. The activities stressed problem solving and work with materials to promote understanding, and they included games to develop skill. Assessment of learning that emphasized determining how children think about computation was discussed in connection with each topic.

REFERENCES

Atweh, Bill. (1982). "Developing Mental Arithmetic." In *Mathematics for the Middle Grades (5–9),* edited by Linda Silvey and James R. Smart, pp. 50–58. Reston, VA: National Council of Teachers of Mathematics.

Burns, Marilyn. (1989). "Teaching for Understanding: A Focus on Multiplication." In *New Directions for Elementary School Mathematics,* edited by Paul R. Trafton and Albert P. Shulte, pp. 123–133. Reston, VA: National Council of Teachers of Mathematics.

Cobb, Paul, and Graceann Merkel. (1989). "Thinking Strategies: Teaching Arithmetic Through Problem Solving." In *New Directions for Elementary School Mathematics,* edited by Paul R. Trafton and Albert P. Shulte, pp. 70–81. Reston, VA: National Council of Teachers of Mathematics.

Coburn, Terrence G. (1989). "The Role of Computation in the Changing Mathematics Curriculum." In *New Directions for Elementary School Mathematics,* edited by Paul R. Trafton and Albert P. Shulte, pp. 43–56. Reston, VA: National Council of Teachers of Mathematics.

Hamrick, Katherine B., and William D. McKillip. (1978). "How Computational Skills Contribute to the Meaningful Learning of Arithmetic." In *Developing Computational Skills,* edited by Marilyn N. Suydam and Robert E. Reys, pp. 1–12. Reston, VA: National Council of Teachers of Mathematics.

Hazenkamp, Donald W. (1978). "Teaching Multiplication and Division Algorithms." In *Developing Computational Skills,* edited by Marilyn N. Suydam and Robert E. Reys, pp. 78–95. Reston, VA: National Council of Teachers of Mathematics.

Hazenkamp, Donald W. (1986). "Components of Mental Multiplying." In *Estimation and Mental Computation,* edited by Harold L. Schoen and Marilyn J. Zweng, pp. 116–126. Reston, VA: National Council of Teachers of Mathematics.

Hiebert, James. (1990). "The Role of Routine Procedures in the Development of Mathematical Competence." In *Teaching and Learning Mathematics in the 1990s,* edited by Thomas J. Cooney and Christian R. Hirsch, pp. 31–40. Reston, VA: National Council of Teachers of Mathematics.

Hope, John A. (1986). "Mental Calculation: Anachronism or Basic Skill?" In *Estimation and Mental Computation,* edited by Harold L. Schoen and Marilyn J. Zweng, pp. 45–54. Reston, VA: National Council of Teachers of Mathematics.

Kamii, Constance. (1989). *Young Children Continue to Reinvent Arithmetic: 2nd Grade: Implications of Piaget's Theory.* New York: Teachers College Press.

National Council of Teachers of Mathematics. (1989). *Curriculum and Evaluation Standards for School Mathematics.* Reston, VA: Author.

Rathmell, Edward C., and Paul R. Trafton. (1990). "Whole Number Computation." In *Mathematics for the Young Child,* edited by Joseph N. Payne, pp. 153–172. Reston, VA: National Council of Teachers of Mathematics.

Reys, Barbara J. (1986). "Teaching Computational Estimation: Concepts and Strategies." In *Estimation and Mental Computation,* edited by Harold L. Schoen and Marilyn J. Zweng, pp. 31–44. Reston, VA: National Council of Teachers of Mathematics.

Reys, Barbara J. (1988). "Estimation." In *Teaching Mathematics in Grades K–8: Research Based Methods,* edited by Thomas R. Post, pp. 279–302. Boston: Allyn & Bacon.

Stanic, George M. A., and William D. McKillip. (January, 1989). "Developmental Algorithms Have a Place In Elementary School Mathematics Instruction." *Arithmetic Teacher* 36: 14–16.

Trafton, Paul R. (1986). "Teaching Computational Estimation: Establishing an Estimation Mind-Set." In *Estimation and Mental Computation,* edited by Harold L. Schoen and Marilyn J. Zweng, pp. 16–30. Reston, VA: National Council of Teachers of Mathematics.

Wheatley, Grayson H., and James Hersberger. (1986). "A Calculator Estimation Activity." In *Estimation and Mental Computation,* edited by Harold L. Schoen and Marilyn J. Zweng, pp. 182–185. Reston, VA: National Council of Teachers of Mathematics.

SOFTWARE RESOURCES

Digitosaurus:
Company: Sunburst
Computer: Apple
Grade level: 2–6

Practice with operations and estimation. Teacher can decide on problem difficulty and operation.

Five in a Row
Company: Critical Thinking Press and Software
Computer: Apple, IBM, Macintosh
Grade level: 2 and up

Game to teach mental computation and thinking skills. Involves using a calculator with given numbers to decide on computations to obtain numbers that are placed on a board. Goal is to get five in a row on the board before one's opponent.

What Do You Do with a Broken Calculator?
Company: Sunburst
Computer: Apple, IBM, Macintosh
Grade level: 4 and up

Find solutions to problems in different ways; program gives calculator to use, but calculator has some keys broken. Student can review steps taken. Problems from easy to hard.

Rules for Activity 7.28

Rule for Multiplication by 11

- The ones number in the product is the ones number in the factor that is not 11.
- The tens number in the product is the sum of the numbers in the factor that is not 11.
- The hundreds number in the product is the tens number in the factor that is not 11.
- Trading can add 1 to the tens number. For example, $11 \times 23 = 253$; $11 \times 39 = 429$.

Rule for Multiplication when the Factors are in the Same Decade and the Ones Numbers in the Factors Sum to 10

- The tens and ones in the product are the product of the ones in the factors.
- The hundreds or hundreds and thousands in the product are the product of the tens number in one factor times (the tens number plus 1 in the other factor). For example, $25 \times 25 = 625$; $35 \times 35 = 1225$; $34 \times 36 = 1224$. (Do you have another rule? Prove that it is the same as the rule given here.)

Reader Activity 7.4

Examine paper-and-pencil computations to find the rationale for these rules.

CHAPTER 8

Learning about Fractions*

▪ INTRODUCTORY PROBLEM ▪

Tracy, Sara, Jeff, and Luis are the members of a committee to write a district *Introduction to Fractions Curriculum.* Jeff opened the first meeting of the committee saying, "I am unsure of what the district office has in mind. They told us we were not to deal with computation with fractions. How can we write a K–4 curriculum for introducing fractions, when there is so little to learn?"

Sara responded by saying, "That's what I think. In my third grade we use the pie diagrams, and children learn to read and write fractions quickly. The unit takes only a few days."

Tracy then said, "I was unsure of what we were to do, too. So when I went to the math conference last week, I attended the session on fractions. I was surprised to find out what children need to learn to understand fractions. They need to know a lot to be able to grasp the meaning of computation with fractions in the upper grades. The speaker gave me some great ideas and suggested readings that I found in the district curriculum center."

Jeff was obviously pleased to hear what Tracy said and responded, "Nice work, Tracy! Tell us what you learned."

Luis spoke up and said, "I'll outline your ideas as you tell us about them so that we will have something written down to get us started."

"Good idea, Luis," said Jeff.

As you study this chapter, decide what fraction learnings would be on Luis's outline. Think about the fraction curriculum for K–4 the committee would write.

*The term *fraction* technically refers to the numeral and *rational number* refers to the concept. The word *fraction* is used in this book to mean both the number and the numeral because it is commonly used in the elementary school.

INTRODUCTION

The study of fractions in the elementary school ranks in importance with the study of whole numbers. Understanding fractions enables children to deal with real-world problems, to develop mental structures that contribute to further learning, and to develop meanings that become the foundation for the study of algebra in the post elementary years (Post, Behr, and Lesh, 1982).

However, children have had difficulty learning fraction concepts, and they have not performed well on the National Assessment of Educational Progress (NAEP) tests. For example, on the fourth assessment of the NAEP, only 25% of the third graders knew that four fourths make a whole, and fewer than 50% of the seventh graders replied that $5\frac{1}{4}$ was the same as $5 + \frac{1}{4}$ (Kouba, Brown, Carpenter, Lindquist, Silver, and Swafford, 1988). Research studies also document the lack of understanding of fractions among children (Behr, Lesh, Post, and Silver, 1983).

One source of children's difficulty is that many of the whole-number ideas of order, which children have constructed in the primary grades do not always apply to fractions, and these whole-number ideas interfere with developing an understanding of fractions (Behr, Wachsmuth, Post, and Lesh, 1984; Post, Wachsmuth, Lesh, and Behr, 1985). For example, when the numerators are the same and the denominators differ, the fractions are compared by comparing denominators using order ideas that are the inverse of those for whole numbers; for example, 5 is less than 6, but $\frac{1}{5}$ is larger than $\frac{1}{6}$. When the denominators are the same, fractions are compared by comparing numerators using whole-number ideas; for example, $\frac{5}{6}$ is greater than $\frac{3}{6}$.

The different interpretations of fractions can also cause children problems. Elementary school children learn three interpretations of fractions: part–whole, indicated division, and ratio.

The *part–whole* interpretation refers to the concept of dividing a unit into equal-sized parts and comparing a part or parts to the unit. It is the basis for children's work with area, length, and volume models. Area models include circular and rectangular regions; length models, number lines; volume models, cups and real objects such as apples and pies. The part–whole interpretation can also refer to the idea of partitioning a set of discrete (separate) objects into equal-sized parts and comparing a part or parts to the whole set. It is illustrated in problems such as: Jake had a granola bar. He cut it into four same-sized pieces and gave one piece to Don. What fractional part of the bar did he give to Don? Don had three cherries. He gave Jake one. What fractional part of the cherries did he give to Jake (Figure 8.1A).

The *indicated division* meaning involves the division operation to solve problems such as: Rita has three pizzas to serve to her guests and herself at a dinner party. Eight people will share the pizzas. If each receives the same amount, how much of the pizzas will each person receive (Figure 8.1B)? The part–whole and indicated division meanings are discussed in this chapter.

The *ratio* meaning refers to a relative comparison, such as in the problem: Jack caught 6 fish; his father caught 8 (Figure 8.1C). What is the relation between the number of fish Jack caught and the number his father caught? Teaching and learning the ratio interpretation of fractions is discussed in Chapter 13.

Reader Activity 8.1

Write two story problems for each of the three interpretations of fractions.

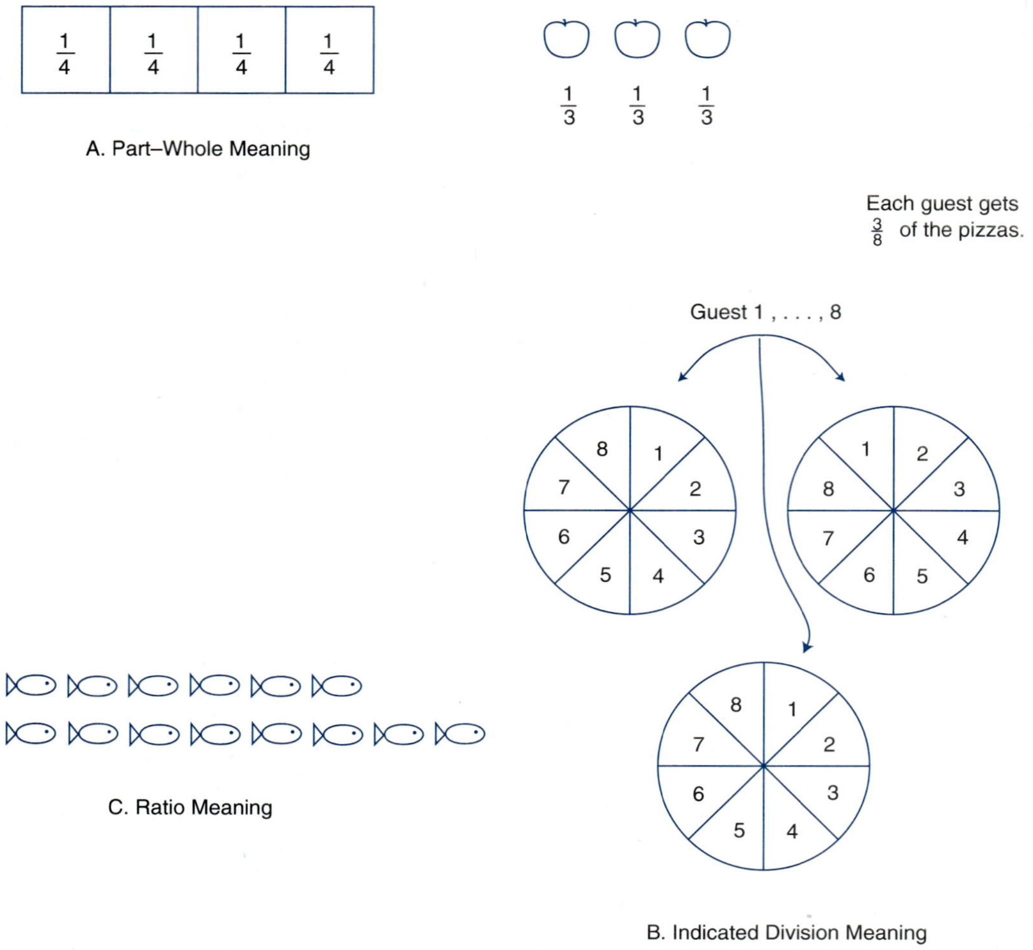

FIGURE 8.1 Models for Fraction Meanings. A, Part–Whole Meaning. B, Indicated Division Meaning. C, Ratio Meaning

Authorities stress that children can understand fraction concepts if (1) learning experiences are based on children's informal knowledge; (2) problem solving involves various representations of fraction concepts; (3) opportunities are provided for learners to discuss ideas; (4) the curriculum is paced to reflect children's intellectual development; and (5) the introduction of symbols is delayed until children can use fraction words, orally and in writing (Kieren, 1984; Mack, 1990; NCTM, 1989; Payne, 1984; Payne, Towsley, and Huinker, 1990; Post and Cramer, 1987). (See Standard 12 in Curriculum Standards for Grades K–4, and Standards 5 and 6 for Grades 5–8, Appendix A.)

New directions in teaching and learning elementary school mathematics emphasize introducing fraction concepts based on these principles. This chapter discusses how to implement these principles in the initial work with fractions using interactive approaches to instruction. There are six sections: Introduction to the Partitioning Concept, Developing the Language of Fractions, Beginning Experiences with Relations among Fractions, Learning Fraction Symbols, Extending Understanding of Fractions, and Assessing Fraction Learning. A summary ends the chapter.

Each section describes activities designed to help children construct fraction concepts and relations by working with materials. The activities also provide opportunities for informal reasoning and making connections. To carry out the activities discussed in this chapter, each child should have a set of fraction disks made from circular regions. A set of fraction disks includes a circular region that represents one whole and enough separate unit fraction pieces (halves, thirds, fourths, sixths, eighths, tenths, and twelfths) to make a whole. Each group of equal-sized fraction pieces should be a different color. There are no symbols on the fraction pieces (Figure 8.2).

Sets of fraction bars made from rectangular regions should also be provided for each child (Figure 8.3). Two sets of fraction bars are needed by each learner in the elementary grades. One set consists of a bar representing one and other bars of the same length, marked off in halves, thirds, fourths, sixths, eighths, tenths, or twelfths. The second set will be the same as the first set except the marked bars will be cut into separate pieces that can be manipulated. Both the wholes and the pieces are called "fraction bars." Symbols are not used on the bars. Each subset is a different color (e.g., whole is white, halves are yellow). Appendix G has patterns for fraction disks and bars. Other area models can be constructed on grid or dot paper. Pattern blocks can also be used as area models (Figure 8.4). Discrete materials, such as counters, are needed for some activities.

INTRODUCTION TO THE PARTITIONING CONCEPT

Comprehending fractions and fraction computation depends on grasping the idea that a quantity can be partitioned into equal-sized parts and one or more parts compared to the whole. The concept of partitioning a quantity into equal-sized parts underlies the three fraction interpretations children study and is central to understanding fractions (Behr et al., 1983).

However, partitioning into equal-sized parts is a complex idea and develops slowly. Its gradual development has been documented by Pothier and Sawada (1983) with children from kindergarten to grade 3. They report that children learn about sharing from life experiences but that initially "sharing fairly" means that each receives the same number of pieces, not that the pieces are the same size. Gradually children learn that one-half means two equal-sized parts, and they develop an awareness of other fractions whose denominators are found by halving (e.g., one-fourth and one-eighth), are even numbers (e.g., one-sixth), or are small odd numbers (e.g., one-third and one-fifth). Later other fractions are understood.

The objective of beginning instruction is for children to learn (1) even sharing means that the parts are the same size or that all parts contain the same number of objects; (2) the number of parts corresponds to the number of even shares; and (3) the parts equal the whole. To develop these ideas, children first partition into two or four equal-sized parts. As children develop the concept of partitioning into equal-sized parts, activities incorporate partitioning into more than two or four equal-sized parts.

Teachers should not delay introducing fractions with denominators other than 2 and 4. Using fractions whose denominators are only 2 and 4 limits children's opportunities to grasp the general nature of the part–whole concept. By grade 3 or 4, fractions with denominators to 10 should be used in learning activities (Payne, 1984). By grade 6, fractions to twelfths will have been introduced (Bezuk and Cramer, 1989).

Fraction names, such as one-fourth, are not used in initial work with fractions (Behr and Post, 1988). As they carry out the activities, children are encouraged to think and talk about their work using phrases such as "two same-size parts," "four equal-size" pieces (or *equal-sized*, the technically correct term), or "four beads in each part." Fraction names are introduced after children grasp the notion of partitioning into equal-sized parts.

Later children learn fraction symbols. Children should have a firm grasp of the meaning of a fraction and use its oral name to show understanding of the con-

FIGURE 8.2 A Set of Fraction Disks

cept before they are introduced to the symbol that represents the fraction (Bezuk, 1988). Payne, Towsley, and Huinker (1990) would not introduce symbols until children can name, count, and compare fractions, and they note that symbol introduction can be delayed until grade 3. Payne (1984) advises that the introduction of written symbols for even unit fractions (fractions with numerators of one) be delayed until grade 2.

FIGURE 8.3 Fraction Bars

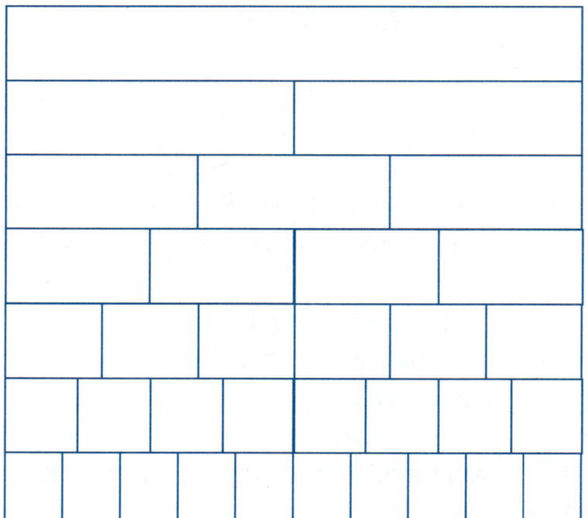

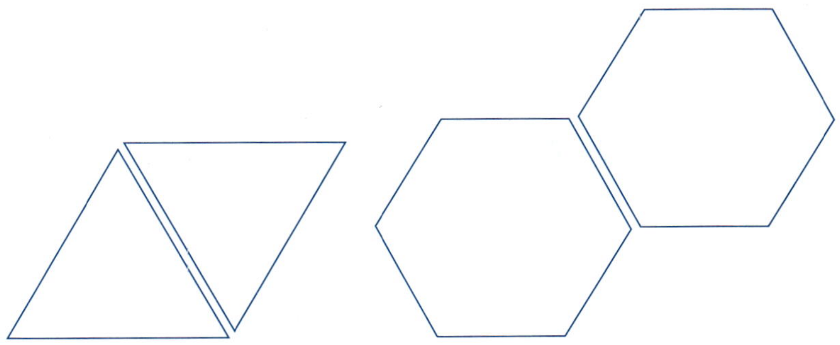

FIGURE 8.4 Pattern Block Models for Fractions

Activities for Introducing the Concept of Partitioning into Equal-Sized Parts

ACTIVITY 8.1
Play Activities.

When children are at play, opportunities arise for discussing partitioning into equal-sized parts. For example, when children are playing house, they may divide play food so that each gets a "fair share." Discuss how they know what is fair.

Play with pattern blocks provides opportunities to ask children about a design made with four blue diamonds. Questions to ask are: "How many diamond pieces are in your design? Are the pieces the same size? How do you know?"

Ask children to arrange dolls, trucks, or other toys on shelves or the four corners of a box so that each place has the same number of toys. After the task is completed, ask questions such as: "How did you think to follow the direction? Tell what you did." (You will need to limit the number of toys used for this activity.)

ACTIVITY 8.2
Paper Folding.

Often children fold paper in two or four equal-sized pieces for use in illustrating the parts and sequence of stories they read, hear, or create. They fold paper for art activities such as making snowflakes. Teachers use such activities to teach ideas of partitioning or have children engage in a paper-folding activity "to find out what happens when you fold paper." Questions asked are: "How does your paper look after you folded the corners together? How did it look before you folded it? What has changed? What is true about the two parts?" After a second or third fold, ask questions that focus children's attention on the number of equal-sized parts before and after the fold. Talk about doubling when children can grasp this concept. Include predicting the number of parts resulting from folding after children have had sufficient experience with paper folding to anticipate what happens when paper is folded in half more than one time.

ACTIVITY 8.3
Using Class Situations.

Whenever a set is to be shared evenly by a group or groups, note the event. For example, if each child in a group is to receive three cups of finger paint, say, "I have this tray of finger paint cups for the finger paint group. Each child will get three cups. Is that sharing fairly? Why?"

ACTIVITY 8.4
Even Sharing.

Activities can be devised to focus on even sharing. Several examples are given here.

1. Have children work in pairs. One should make a big play dough cookie, the other a big play dough candy bar. (Paper cookies and candy bars can be distributed for this activity.) Each child cuts his or her play dough goody to share it with the other child in the pair. Have the children talk about how they shared. For the initial task, do not mention fair share. This idea should surface in the discussion. If not, ask questions such as: "Sally, do you think you got a fair share? Why do you think that? Who got a fair share? Why do you think so?" After the discussion, ask children to remake the play dough cookie or candy bar so they can cut it again. Tell them to cut the cookie or candy bar a different way so each gets a fair share. Follow up with a discussion of the activity. During the class discussion, use the words "same-sized piece" or "equal-sized piece." Note if children use these words. If not, repeat the activity at a later time, using several expressions to designate parts that are equal in size. Continue to observe children's use of words that indicate an understanding of partitioning into equal-sized parts.
2. Again have one child in a pair make a big play dough cookie, the other a big candy bar. Give each pair two to four paper dolls or plastic teddy bears. Ask the children to think how to cut their treats so each doll or teddy bear gets the same amount and then to make the cuts (whenever possible, mention thinking ahead or planning, which is an important aspect of problem solving). Have them discuss with their partners how they cut the play dough food; then conduct a class discussion in which children explain how they shared their cookie or candy bar and why they decided each toy got the same amount. You can ask children to comment on others' remarks by saying, "What was especially good about how Jose cut his candy bar for the four teddy bears?" Also ask, "What would happen if the pieces were put back together?"

   Over time, vary this activity, using other pretend food (e.g., pizzas, pies) and other toys. Gradually change the number of those sharing to 8, 6, 3, and 5. The Pothier and Sawada's (1983) investigation mentioned previously concluded that children develop notions of fractions with denominators in this order. Often ask questions such as: "If three children share a big cookie, how many equal-sized pieces will there be?" "If a large candy bar is cut into five equal-sized pieces, how many children can share the candy bar equally?"
3. Have children in pairs or groups of four share countable materials (Figure 8.5). Give time to discussing how to share the objects fairly. They should communicate the fact that sharing is fair if each child receives the same number of objects. Use questions, if necessary, to bring out this idea.

   Children can share plastic eggs in egg cartons so that each of two or three children gets the same number or an even share.
4. Have pairs or groups of children share materials evenly, such as counters or crayons, before beginning an activity that involves the use of the materials. Briefly discuss how they decided what was an even share.

Activity for the Classroom 8.1. If you are teaching in a primary classroom, list at least four classroom situations that could involve partitioning into equal-sized parts. During the next few days, emphasize partitioning into equal-sized parts in these situations. Assess children's understanding of the concept by noting their use of language and their behavior as they solve a sharing-evenly problem.

ACTIVITY 8.5
Introducing Fraction Materials.

Give each child two halves from a fraction kit and a whole disk. Say, "Please look at these materials. What can you tell about them?" Their responses should indicate

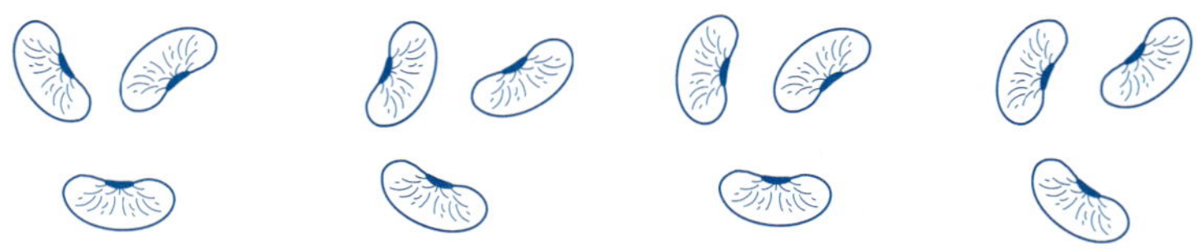

FIGURE 8.5 Counter Model for Even Sharing

that they know the unit piece is a whole, the two pieces are the same size, and together they make a whole. Also ask children to tell what they did or thought to find out about the materials. They should say they matched pieces to show they are the same size. (Ask about the size of the pieces if pupils notice only color or shape.) Continue with other same-sized fraction pieces.

Use the same procedure when fraction bars are introduced. Have children examine the materials and discuss their observations. Children should be aware that some bar pieces are the same size and shape and a given number cover a whole.

ACTIVITY 8.6
Match Fraction Bars.

Use fraction bars for this activity. Ask children to match shorter pieces the same length with longer bars. The children can pretend the long bar is a candy bar and the shorter bars show the pieces shared equally among friends. Discuss different ways to match different long bars with shorter bars of the same length. Children discuss their explorations by saying, for example, "I matched two yellow bars with a white bar," or "Four blue pieces match a white bar."

Reader Activity 8.2

Use the patterns in Appendix G to make a set of fraction disks and two sets of fraction bars. Experiment showing fractions with your materials to determine their value for learners.

DEVELOPING THE LANGUAGE OF FRACTIONS

When children demonstrate that they grasp the notion of partitioning into equal-sized parts, they learn to use fraction names in their discussions. In general, this is in grade 1. Words denoting fractions are also used in written work, not fraction symbols. During this phase of instruction, both unit and nonunit fractions are studied.

A sequence for introducing unit fraction names and activities for reviewing unit fractions and introducing nonunit fractions follow.

Sequence for Introducing Unit Fraction Names

1. Distribute pictures of fraction bars for halves. Discuss that this fraction bar shows dividing into two equal-sized parts. Ask if someone can tell the class the name of each part. If no child knows, tell the class that each part is called one-half. Have children point to each one-half of their fraction bars and say its fraction name. You may decide to have children cut the fraction bar into halves.
2. On the overhead show pictures of objects cut in half and a few pictures in which objects are not cut in half. Have children discuss each picture, naming the one-half parts if the object pictured is partitioned into two equal-sized parts.
3. Give children activity sheets such as in Figure 8.6, and ask them to look at each picture and circle it if the picture shows two one-halves. (Point out that *halves* is the word for more than one half.) After they have completed the task, discuss each figure. Question children so that in the course of the discussion they review that cutting in half means there will be two equal-sized parts.

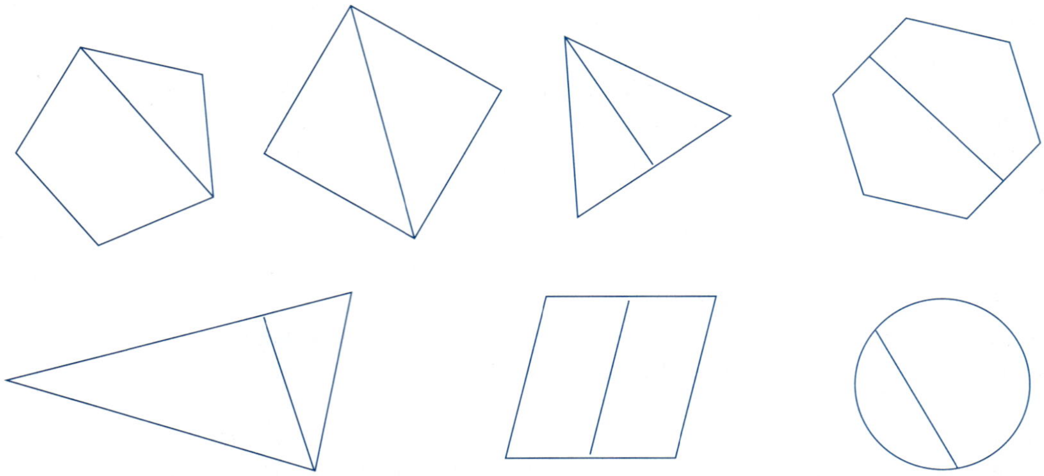

FIGURE 8.6 Activity Sheet for Halves

4. In following lessons use fraction bars to introduce the names of fractions with other denominators, using a sequence similar to that for halves. Help children learn to say the names of the parts by telling them that the names, beginning with thirds, are the same as the words they know for being third, fourth, and so on, in line. Always ask children if they know the names before giving the names yourself. (Why?) After introducing names for thirds and fourths, when introducing names for other fractions, have children study their fraction bars and predict the names of the fractions represented. Discuss how they knew the names.
5. Write the name of a unit fraction after the name is given orally. Make a fraction chart, showing a representation of the fraction and its name. Begin with one-half; when another fraction name is introduced, add it to the display.
6. In the course of the lessons to introduce unit fraction names, frequently discuss how the number of equal-sized pieces relates to the name of each part. During the discussion ask questions such as: "If your mother said, 'You can have one-fourth of the pie,' into how many equal-sized pieces did she cut the pie? How do you know?" Help children to generalize by asking questions such as: "If a big pie was divided into seven (nine, eleven) equal-sized pieces, what would be the name of each piece of the pie?"

Activities for Introducing Fraction Names

ACTIVITY 8.7
Fold and Name.

Repeat the paper-folding activity (8.2), and have pupils name the fractions shown by the foldings.

ACTIVITY 8.8
A Bulletin Board for Reading and Writing Unit Fraction Names.

Have the class make a bulletin board to learn unit fraction names. To ensure well-formed representations, give children circular regions or fraction bars partitioned into halves, thirds, fourths, sixths, and eighths. Have them color one part to represent a unit fraction for display on a bulletin board entitled, "Where is the Fraction's Name?" You write the word *one-half*, and so on, on cards to use in the display on the bulletin board. Groups of children are asked to tack yarn from a fraction name to its representation. At the end of the day, the yarn is untacked so that others can engage in the activity the next day.

Later, have children use cards to write the names of the fractions on the bulletin board. Remove the yarn and place the children's cards in a pocket behind the fraction disk named on the card.

ACTIVITY 8.9
Fraction Bingo.

The bingo cards show pictures of unit fractions. The rules for *Bingo* apply, with the caller giving the names of unit fractions and players finding that fraction model on their cards.

After children learn to read the words that give fraction names, *Bingo* can be played with the caller displaying fraction pictures on the overhead or showing large fraction bars or regions with one part shaded. The bingo cards give the names of unit fractions, and children find the fraction names on their cards.

ACTIVITY 8.10
Counting Fractions.

When the names for unit fractions are known, children can count fractions. Three activities help children learn to count fractions.

1. Fraction bars and fraction disks are used for this activity. To begin the activity, have children predict how many fourths are in a whole bar. Then say, "How can we check our prediction?" After children suggest counting, distribute fraction materials. Have children lay all the bars except fourths upside down. (Color-coding will help them do this quickly.) Count the fourths on the fourths bar to check the prediction. (Four fourth pieces can also be laid on one whole). Ask, "How did you know to predict fourths?" Follow the same procedure for counting other fractions represented with bars. Repeat the task with fraction disks.
2. Put fraction pieces on a unit circular region on the overhead. Have children decide on the name for each fraction shown. Ask, "How did you know?" When they respond that they counted the pieces, have them verify their idea by counting the pieces as you or a child removes them from the unit circular region on the overhead.
3. Have pairs of children "Play Teacher." One child says, "Please find the thirds (or other fraction pieces) in your set of fraction disks. Count them as you place them on the whole piece." The children take turns giving and following the directions.

ACTIVITY 8.11
Naming Nonunit Fractions.

When children understand counting fractions, give groups of children fraction activity sheets. Each sheet shows these nonunit fractions represented by shaded parts of circular regions: two-thirds, three-fourths, and five-sixths. For the discussion, the circular regions can be pies. Ask each group to decide on the name of the part shaded. After time for them to discuss and decide on the names of the three fractions represented, have the groups report to the class. The reports include how they decided on the names, as well as the names. If no group reports counting to determine fraction names, ask, "How could counting help us find the names of these pieces?" After children grasp the notion of counting to find the names of nonunit fractions, distribute activity sheets showing different nonunit fractions, and ask groups of children to decide on the fraction names. After time for them to determine the fraction names, conduct a class discussion during which children give the fraction names and explain how they determined these names.

When children are competent in naming nonunit fractions, give groups activity sheets with unit and nonunit fractions with the same denominators (Figure 8.7). Ask them to write the names of the unit fractions and predict how to write the names of the nonunit fractions. After time for them to solve this problem, have groups report how they solved the problem and the thinking that led to the solution. If no group solves the problem correctly, help them relate oral counting and naming with the written forms. During the discussion help children realize that the number of equal-sized pieces is the first part of the fraction name and the size of the pieces, the second part. Tell them that a hyphen is used between the words.

ACTIVITY 8.12
Making Designs.

Have children use pattern blocks to make designs that show different unit or nonunit fractions. They can also make repeating patterns from their designs. In small groups, have them share their work.

ACTIVITY 8.13
Geoboard Representations.

Geoboards are useful for representing fractions (Figure 8.8). Introduce geoboards in a whole-class activity. Ask children to study the geoboard. Ask how one whole could be shown on the geoboard using rubber bands. After they decide that a square or rectangular region could be one whole, discuss how to use rubber bands with geoboards. Next, have children make units of different sizes. Then have them show various fractions, name them, and share what they have done with others in their group. Stress showing fractions in different ways. This activity can be adapted for dot paper (Figure 8.9).

BEGINNING EXPERIENCES WITH RELATIONS AMONG FRACTIONS

When children can use fraction names, they study concepts that express relations among fractions. They compare and order fractions, investigate equivalent fractions, and make connections between the size of a fraction and the number of equal-sized pieces in a whole (Bezuk and Cramer, 1989). Initial activities to construct these ideas employ words, not fraction symbols. However, the activities may be used after symbols have been introduced.

Manipulative materials are used to carry out each activity. As mentioned, each child must have his or her own sets of materials to be able to relate thinking to action.

Activities for Beginning Study of Fraction Relations

ACTIVITY 8.14
Exploring Fractions with Materials.

After children know fraction names, have them match same-sized pieces in fraction kits to wholes and discuss their observations. They should observe that two halves make a whole, four fourths make a whole, and so on. When pupils appear to grasp the concept of parts that make a whole, to determine if they can generalize, ask questions such as: "How many ninths (tenths, twelfths) make a whole?"

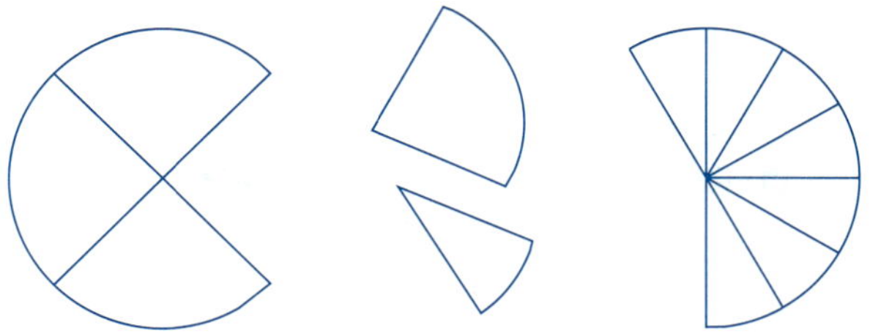

FIGURE 8.7 Activity Sheet for Nonunit Fractions

ACTIVITY 8.15
How to Compare Fraction Pieces.

Comparing the size of two fractions is introduced with unit fractions. Ask each child to take a one-third piece and a one-fourth piece from his or her fraction kit. Say, "Which piece shows the greater fraction? How do you know?" Have several children demonstrate matching pieces to determine which shows the greater fraction. Next, question children about which piece shows the lesser fraction, and repeat the matching.

A related activity is to use fraction bars for comparing fractions. Ask children to use bars to decide if one-half is greater or less than one-third. Let them experiment with the bars to determine that the bars must be placed together at one end to compare them. You may need to question children for them to understand how the bars must be placed for comparing.

ACTIVITY 8.16
Is the Fraction Greater or Less?

Children work in pairs for this activity. One child chooses a fraction piece from his or her fraction kit and names it. The other child chooses a different fraction piece, names it, and tells whether it shows a fraction greater or less than the piece chosen by the first child. The children should match their pieces to check the second child's comparison. The children then switch tasks, continuing to take turns using different fraction pieces until you call the class together and have several children tell about their fraction comparisons.

A related activity is to compare nonunit fractions with like denominators. Prepare an activity sheet showing different fractions with like denominators (Figure 8.10). Children can work individually or in pairs. Have a class discussion of com-

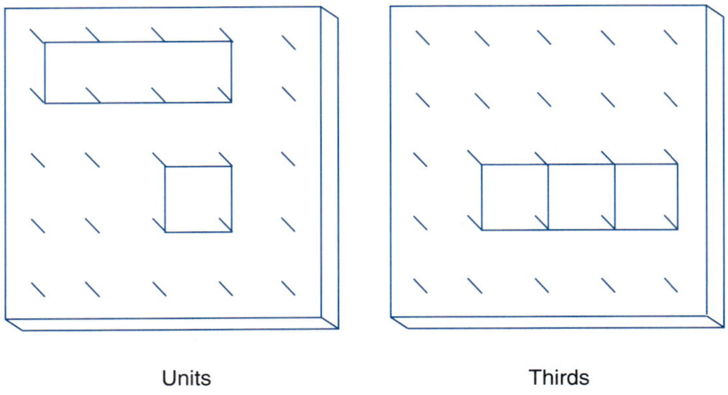

FIGURE 8.8 Geoboards Showing Fractions

FIGURE 8.9 Showing One-Half on Dot Paper

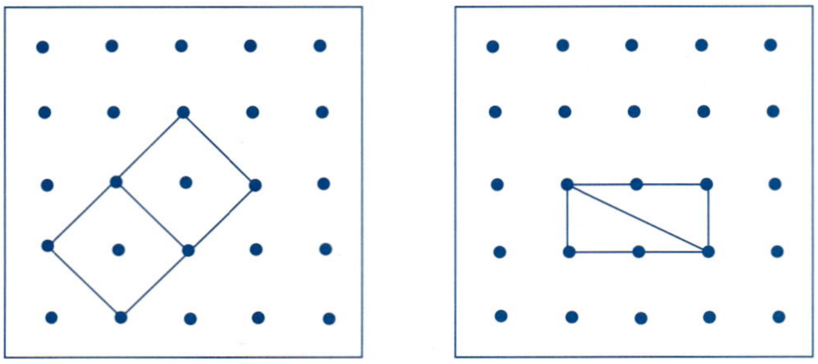

pleted work, stressing the thinking process used to decide on the answer. Counting to compare fractions should be noted in the course of the discussion.

ACTIVITY 8.17
Fractions with Fraction Disks, Fraction Bars, and Counters.

This activity helps children develop flexible thinking with regard to fractions. Because it requires higher-level thinking, if children cannot understand the task, do not continue with the activity. Use the names of the colors you have chosen for your sets of fraction materials, rather than the fraction word, which is given here. Ask questions such as: "If the one-half (e.g., yellow) piece is a whole, what is one-half? If the one-half piece is one-fourth, what is the whole?"

Some questions are answered by using counters. Examples of such questions are: "If two counters are one-half, what is the whole? If two counters are one-third, what is the whole?" These questions can be stated as problems, which could be more motivating to children. Examples are: You have two pencils. That is one-half of the number Jim has. How many does Jim have? For lunch, you ate two cookies from a cookie package in your lunch box. That was one-fourth of the cookies in the package. How many were in the package? Counters should be readily available for children to use to solve these problems. When they finish their work, they should demonstrate to each other the procedures they used to find the answers. They can lay counters on an overhead to show their solutions.

ACTIVITY 8.18
Ordering.

Have children choose three fraction pieces of different colors from their fraction manipulatives. Ask them to put the fractions in order, beginning with the smallest-sized fraction. After they finish the ordering, children tell the fractions they choose and how they decided on the order of the fractions. They can use an overhead to share their work. Repeat for other sets of three fractions.

ACTIVITY 8.19
Noting Relations.

The purposes of this activity is for children to become aware that the more equal-sized pieces in a whole, the smaller the pieces. Ask children to cover one whole with fourths and another with halves. Have them pretend the wholes are small pies. Discuss how many pieces are in each pie. Then ask, "If you like pie and are very hungry, would you ask for a piece from the pie with the four or two same-sized pieces? Why?" Continue by asking children to show two "pies" at the same time; name the number of pieces into which each pie is cut. Repeat the kind of question used for halves and fourths, but use fraction names as well as number of pieces in your ques-

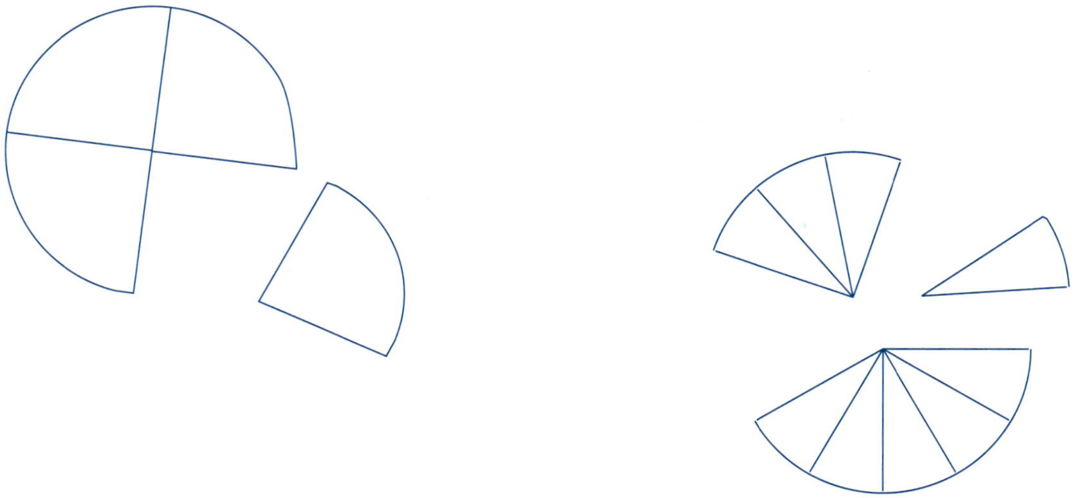

1. Name the fractions
2. Ring the greatest in each set
3. Use your fraction disks to check

FIGURE 8.10 Comparing Fractions

tions. For example, ask, "If you are hungry, would you ask for a third or a sixth of a pie? Why?" As children discuss the answers to these questions, help them express the idea that the more equal-sized pieces in a whole, the smaller each piece will be. Conclude the discussion by asking children to think the answers to questions such as: "Is one-sixth of a candy bar larger or smaller than one-eighth? Why?" As children need many opportunities to explore ideas with materials, use fraction bars as well as fraction disks to develop this concept.

Follow this activity with an activity sheet such as shown in Box 8.1. Use the activity sheet for whole-class work.

ACTIVITY 8.20
Introducing Equivalent Fractions.

Begin by saying, "We have covered whole circular pieces with many small equal-sized pieces to find out how many covered the disk completely. Today let's cover a one-half piece with smaller pieces of the same size to find out how many will cover it. With your partner, find the different ways you can cover a one-half piece with smaller same-sized pieces. Use as many of your one-half pieces as you can. Keep each covering so we can talk about what you have done." After children have found several fractions equivalent to one-half, discuss their work. Children can show the small equal-sized pieces that cover the one-half on the overhead and explain their discovery. For example, a child would say, "I covered one-half with three one-sixths."

ACTIVITY 8.21
Problem Solving.

When these problems are assigned, stress using materials to find the answers. After children have had time to find the answers, discuss the process they used as well as their answers. Examples of problems for children to solve are:

1. If Mother divides a pizza evenly among the four people in your family, will you get more or less than one-half?
2. Fred hoped he would get one-fourth of the apple pie his Dad bought at the market. His Dad cut the pie into six same-sized pieces and said Fred could have one of the pieces. Did Fred get his wish?

BOX 8.1 Activity Sheet for Fraction Relations (Whole-Class Activity)

- Ask children to cover each whole of the first two indicated colors with bars of the same color. Colors of fraction bars for activity are: One whole: white; $\frac{1}{2}$: yellow; $\frac{1}{3}$: green; $\frac{1}{4}$: blue; $\frac{1}{6}$: red; $\frac{1}{8}$: purple; $\frac{1}{10}$: pink; $\frac{1}{12}$; orange.
- For each pair of colors, read each question in turn.
- Have them place an X on a line to indicate the correct answer.
- Have them explain their answers before asking them to use the next pair of fraction bars.

Color	Which whole takes less bars to cover it?	Which whole takes larger bars to cover it?	Which whole takes more bars to cover it?	Which whole takes smaller bars to cover it?
Green				
Blue				
Red				
Purple				
Pink				
Purple				

3. Edward bought a giant candy bar. He said, "I will eat one-sixth each day after lunch." His big sister said, "I think you should eat one-eighth each day." Whose plan would give him a smaller piece each day?

LEARNING FRACTION SYMBOLS

When children can represent fractions with materials and use words to discuss fractions, they are ready to learn symbols for fractions. This usually happens in grade 2.

Procedure for Introducing Symbols for Fractions

1. Remind children that they know how to write fraction names with words. Ask children if they know another way. If they do, give time to discussing what they know. If not, tell children that fractions can be written with numbers as well as words.

Ask children to take a whole fraction disk and a one-half piece from their fraction kits. Give children paper to use to write fraction symbols. Ask them to place the one-half piece on the whole and name the fraction. On an overhead or tack board, display a fraction disk with one-half shaded, and ask the name of the shaded part. Write "one-half" next to the representation. If they have indicated they know how to write fractions, ask one or more children to show the class how to write one-half using numbers instead of words. If no child knows, write $\frac{1}{2}$ on the overhead or tack board beside the word *one-half*. Ask children what they notice about this way to write one-half. Help children recognize that the bottom number tells how many equal-sized parts in the whole and the top number tells how many to think about. Have children point to their one-half piece and write the symbol $\frac{1}{2}$ on their paper next to the one-half piece.

Have each child complete an activity sheet that requires writing $\frac{1}{2}$ next to representations of one-half. Include diagrams that do not show one-half; ask children to write "$\frac{1}{2}$" only beside the pictures that show one-half. Also include whole regions with the direction to show one-half, and write the fraction.

2. Later, use a similar sequence to introduce the symbols for one-third ($\frac{1}{3}$) and one-fourth ($\frac{1}{4}$). During the discussion ask what is different about the names and fraction symbols for one-half and one-third. Help them decide that the word *third* helps us know that there are three equal parts in the whole, and we write 3 below the bar, but the word *half* doesn't give any help. We must remember to write 2 below the bar when we are thinking "halves." Repeat the question for halves and fourths. Use some activity sheets that include representations of $\frac{1}{2}$, $\frac{1}{3}$, and $\frac{1}{4}$ for children to label. The activity sheets should also show whole regions and give the direction: Show one-half, one-third, and one-fourth on different wholes and label each drawing with the fraction you have shown. (Their drawings will give an indication that they understand a concept, but of course not show equal-sized pieces precisely because they will not measure to complete this task.)
3. When children grasp the idea of relating the words for fractions to the written symbols, ask them to show one-sixth with materials, predict how to write the fraction, think the reasons for their prediction, and write the symbol on a piece of paper. They discuss how they completed the task. During the discussion, review the meaning of the top and the bottom number, and introduce the words *numerator* and *denominator*. Continue with other unit fractions. You can also ask children to write and explain the symbols for fractions such as one-seventh. I have found children enjoy showing that they understand a concept and can use it to construct interesting examples.
4. Some time later introduce symbols for nonunit fractions by giving groups of two or three children an activity sheet showing two-thirds, three-fourths, and three-eighths and asking them to predict how to write the symbol for these fractions. Have them write their predictions beside the illustration. When the groups have finished their work, ask a pupil from each group to show the class their group's prediction and explain how they decided to write the fractions. During the discussion, children review the meaning of the top and bottom numbers in fractions and express the idea that the whole is divided into equal-sized parts. Continue by asking children to write symbols for other nonunit fractions you show on the overhead. Have them explain the meaning of the symbols they write.

Activities for Initial Work with Fraction Symbols

ACTIVITY 8.22
Matching Games.

Use games in which children must relate words, symbols, and representations to teach recognition of symbols and their meaning. Matching games, such as *Fish* and *Rummy* (see Box 3.1), are ideal for this purpose. Include words, symbols, and representations on cards used in the games. The objective is to get two cards, at least one of which must be the fraction word or symbol.

ACTIVITY 8.23
Using Symbols.

Distribute activity sheets showing circular or rectangular regions; tell students that each region is a whole. Give fractions for them to represent on the regions. Later, students use transparencies of wholes on an overhead to show how they represented the fractions on their activity sheets. They also discuss how they thought to complete the assignment.

ACTIVITY 8.24
Recording Counting Fractions.

Give each of two children an activity sheet showing six or eight halves and a similar number of thirds. Ask them to count the fraction pieces and write down the fraction symbols as they count. One child writes for halves, one for thirds. (Any group that finishes before the discussion can write the fractions for counting fourths and sixths to two wholes, although no pieces are displayed.) Have children use the chalk board to show how they wrote these fractions for the fraction pieces displayed and ask them to explain the meaning of the fractions. If some have written fractions for counting by fourths or sixths, have them explain their work.

EXTENDING UNDERSTANDING OF FRACTIONS

Learners extend their understanding when they represent fractions with different types of grid paper, use number lines, work with equivalent fractions, study new interpretations of fractions, use reference fractions in estimation, study mixed numbers, and solve real-life problems involving fractions. The activities in this section help children acquire these fraction ideas and develop strategies for solving fraction number problems and problems related to real-life. They also give prerequisite understanding for fraction computation. Materials are used in most activities as the objective is to develop visual images and intuitive understanding so that learners will be ready for more demanding work on a symbolic level (Post and Cramer, 1987). The activities can be used with some learners in grade 3 but may be more appropriate for children in grades 4, 5, and 6.

Activities for Extending Understanding of Fractions

ACTIVITY 8.25
Constructing Representations.

Children use triangle or square grid paper for this activity (patterns are in Appendix G). Begin by asking children how many triangles or squares would be needed if you wanted to show a whole divided into halves. When they decide it is two, ask them to show a whole and color $\frac{1}{2}$ (Figure 8.11). Continue by asking them to think of other fractional parts of a unit to show on triangle or square grid paper and label their work. The work with halves or other fractions can be incorporated into making patterns (Figure 8.12).

FIGURE 8.11 Grid Paper Models for Fractions

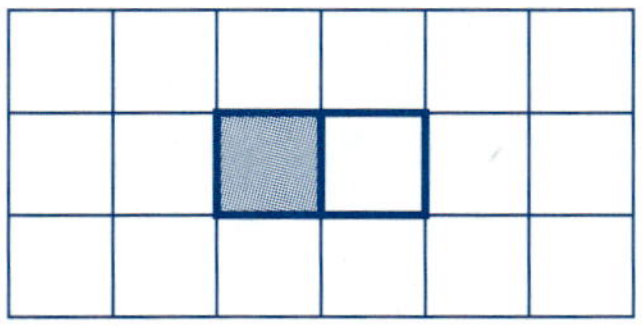

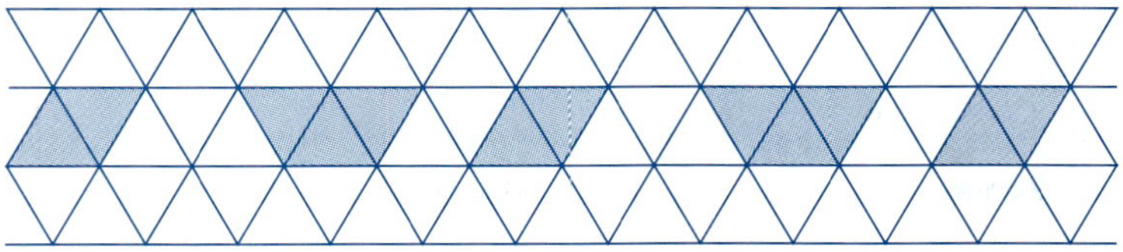

FIGURE 8.12 Grid Paper Pattern Showing Halves and Thirds

ACTIVITY 8.26
Introducing Number Lines.

Payne et al. (1990) advocate delaying the introduction of linear models until after initial learning of addition and subtraction. Behr and Post (1988) claim that although children appear to have difficulties with number lines, if teachers use them appropriately and recognize that children can experience difficulties, number lines help children clarify concepts of order and equivalence of fractions, and they are also useful for representing addition and subtraction of fractions. Therefore, I suggest introducing fraction number lines before work with addition and subtraction.

When fraction number lines are introduced, students should be helped to understand that a fraction such as $\frac{1}{4}$ on a number line represents a length of $\frac{1}{4}$ of a unit and a unit is the length from 0 to 1. The fractions $\frac{2}{4}$ and $\frac{3}{4}$ show how many $\frac{1}{4}$ lengths are being considered.

When introducing fraction number lines to children, explain that number lines help us understand fractions. Give each child a number line for fourths to place underneath a fraction bar for fourths (Figure 8.13). Ask, "How are the fraction bar and the number line alike and different?" Their answers or your comments should bring out: "Both show a whole partitioned into equal-sized parts with the same lengths. The number line shows one unit of length partitioned into four equal-sized parts, and the fraction bar shows four equal-sized parts of an area." Children should be asked to observe where the fractions are written on a number line and should notice that they are written at the end points of fractional parts. Continue the activity by having children examine number lines showing halves and other fractions. Have them discuss what they notice about these number lines. Students should then label fraction number lines of one unit for different fractions. The line segments on the number lines should be marked for pupils to label. (Why?)

ACTIVITY 8.27
Working with Fractions for Wholes.

Have pairs of children take turns arranging halves and thirds to make units. After they have completed the task, have the class count the pieces in unison. Then ask, "What do you notice about $\frac{2}{2}$? About $\frac{3}{3}$? What other name can we give to $\frac{2}{2}$? To $\frac{3}{3}$? How could we write that in a math sentence ($\frac{2}{2} = 1$; $\frac{3}{3} = 1$)?" Have several children show the class their ideas for math sentences. Have each child write a math sentence for $\frac{4}{4}$. Discuss their math sentences and their thinking to complete the task. Have them make up other examples.

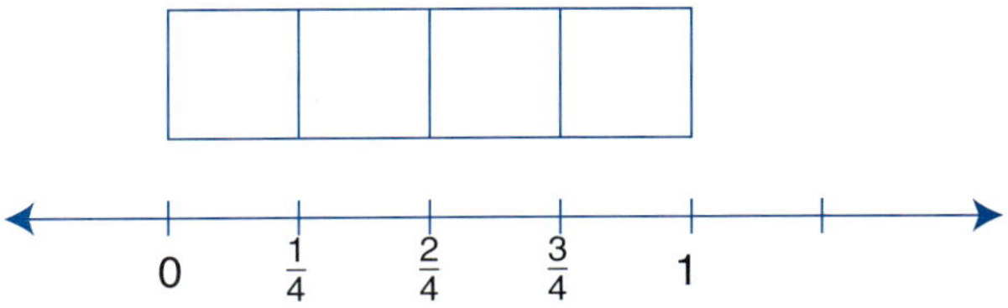

FIGURE 8.13 Number Line and Number Bar

ACTIVITY 8.28
Math Sentences for Equivalent Fractions.

Begin with an activity similar to Activity 8.20. After children have shared their work, ask them to write math sentences telling what fractions equal one-half. After time for group work, have children share their ideas using the overhead or chalkboard. They should have decided that the math sentences are $\frac{2}{4} = \frac{1}{2}$, $\frac{3}{6} = \frac{1}{2}$, $\frac{4}{8} = \frac{1}{2}$, and $\frac{5}{10} = \frac{1}{2}$. Math sentences for other equivalent fractions can also be developed from work with materials. A chart can be made by learners that show all equivalent fractions learned by working with materials.

ACTIVITY 8.29
Equivalent Fraction Investigations.

Box 8.2 gives an activity sheet to help children grasp the meaning of equivalent fractions. They use their fraction pieces to complete the activity.

BOX 8.2 Activity Sheet for Equivalent Fractions

1. Name 1 yellow piece in as many ways as you can.
2. Name 2 blue pieces in as many ways as you can.
3. Name 4 orange pieces in as many ways as you can.
4. What equivalent fractions can you name by using the fraction disks on this activity sheet or your fraction disks with the same colors?

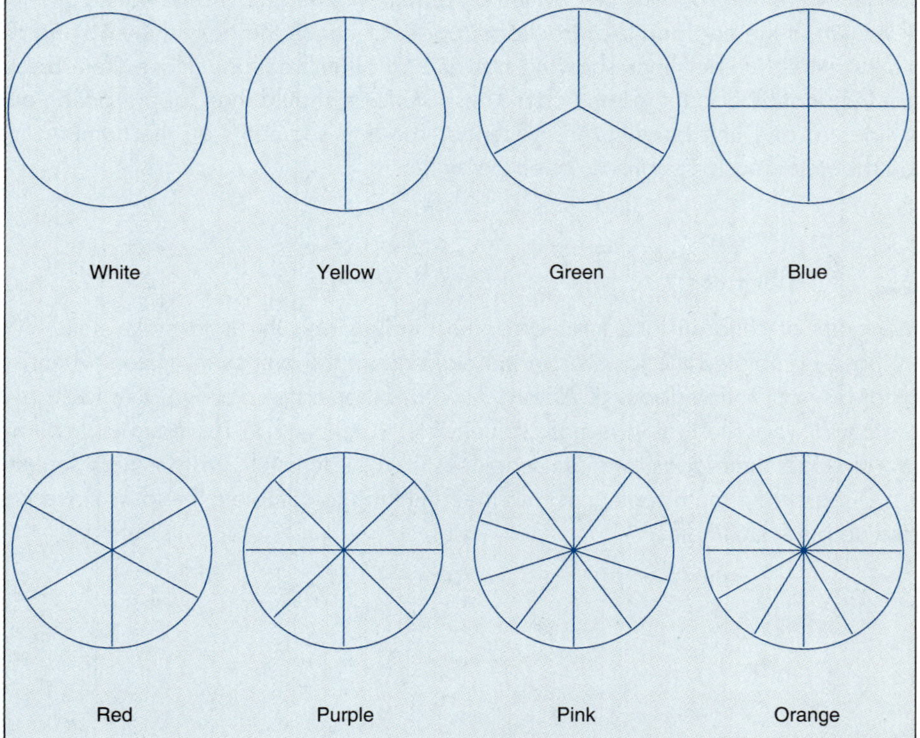

ACTIVITY 8.30
Equivalent Fraction Games.

Matching games for equivalent fractions (*Rummy* and *Fish* with new names) will help children gain immediate recall of common equivalent fractions. One-half of the cards show symbols for equivalent fractions (e.g., $\frac{1}{2} = \frac{2}{4}$), the other half show pictures of equivalent fractions. The game *War* can be played with the same cards.

ACTIVITY 8.31
Equivalent Fractions Designs.

Using pattern blocks, children can make designs that show equivalent fractions. To begin, give each child green (sixths) and red (halves) pattern blocks. Say, "Decide how to use both green and red blocks to make a design that shows one-half. Then make the design." After learners work out their designs, have them tell about their work (Figure 8.14). Discuss why the design shows $\frac{3}{6} = \frac{1}{2}$. Continue by asking children to use blocks to show other equivalent fractions of their own choice and tell each other how they completed the task. During the discussion, children name the fractions represented.

Related activities ask learner to use crayons to color triangle or square grid paper to make design showing equivalent fractions (Figure 8.15). Paper folding also can give insight into equivalent fractions. (How?)

ACTIVITY 8.32
How Does the Fraction Compare to One Whole?

This activity requires children to determine the difference between each of the following fractions and 1. The problem is phrased as: "What is the difference between each piece, $\frac{2}{3}$, $\frac{3}{4}$, $\frac{5}{6}$, $\frac{7}{8}$, and one whole?" Use your materials to help you decide. (Note that in all the examples the difference is a unit fraction.) Number lines should be used in this activity as well as fraction disks and fraction bars. This activity gives prerequisite understanding for dealing with the questions in number 2 in the following activity. It also lays the foundation for estimation in computation with fractions.

ACTIVITY 8.33
Comparing to a Reference Fraction.

The first few times this type of activity is used, children should use materials to answer the following questions. The questions would be the focus of different problem-solving lessons. They would not all be used at the same time.

1. Which is closer to your $\frac{1}{2}$ piece? (*Note:* Only unit fractions are used.) $\frac{1}{3}$ or $\frac{1}{4}$? $\frac{1}{6}$ or $\frac{1}{4}$? $\frac{1}{6}$ or $\frac{1}{3}$? $\frac{1}{8}$ or $\frac{1}{6}$?
2. Which is closer to 1 whole? (*Note:* Only fractions with the same numerator differences from a whole are used so that their difference from 1 will be easily com-

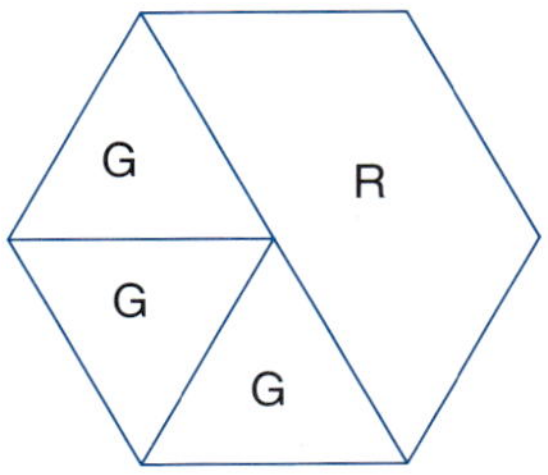

FIGURE 8.14 Pattern Block Equivalent Fraction Design

FIGURE 8.15 Grid Paper Equivalent Fraction Designs

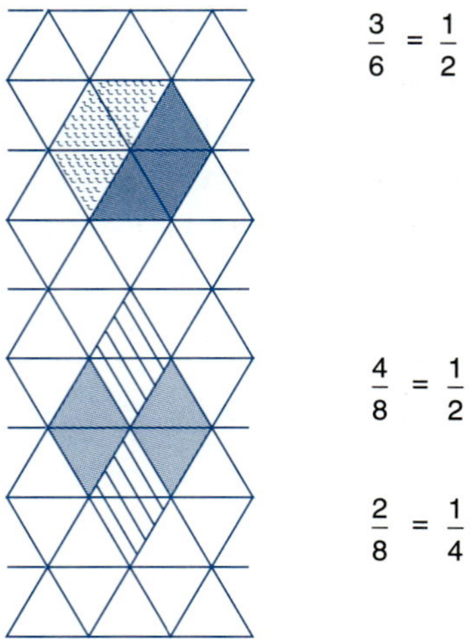

parable. To begin, this difference from 1 should be a unit fraction.) $\frac{3}{4}$ or $\frac{2}{3}$? $\frac{7}{8}$ or $\frac{5}{6}$? $\frac{3}{4}$or $\frac{5}{6}$?

3. Which is closer to 0? (*Note:* Only unit fractions are used.) $\frac{1}{2}$ or $\frac{1}{4}$? $\frac{1}{3}$ or $\frac{1}{4}$? $\frac{1}{8}$ or $\frac{1}{6}$?

After children have had many opportunities to solve these problems using materials, you can ask them to think the answers and share their strategies. A useful strategy that could be reported by a student for the first group of questions is: Think which fraction is larger. This tells you which fraction is closer to one-half; one way to know which fraction is larger is to remember that the fewer the number of equal-sized pieces, the larger each piece and the larger the fraction. The denominator tells the number of pieces. To answer the second group of questions, a useful strategy is: For each fraction given, think the fraction needed to make a whole. Then decide which of the fractions needed to make the whole is smaller. That tells you which fraction is closer to one whole. For the last question, the strategy is the same as the strategy for the first questions except that you think which fraction is smaller.

Children who explain their strategies should be given adequate opportunities (perhaps demonstrating with materials) to explain how they arrived at their conclusions. This may help other children learn to use a reference point. However, even upper grade learners often cannot process information at only a symbolic and abstract level. To foster learning, students should be provided with opportunities to study ideas by working with materials and symbols (Harrison, Brindley, and Bye, 1989).

ACTIVITY 8.34
Name a Fraction Close (or Not Close) to a Reference Fraction.

Have children solve the problem of finding two or three fractions pieces close (or not close) to $\frac{1}{2}$ and 1 whole. They should use their fraction bars or fraction disks. A discussion of the solutions to the problem and some demonstrations indicating how they obtained their answers should follow the problem-solving experience.

ACTIVITY 8.35
Find Fractions between Two Fractions.

Ask children to use fractions disks or bars to find fraction pieces between $\frac{1}{4}$ and $\frac{1}{2}$, $\frac{1}{2}$ and $\frac{3}{4}$, $\frac{3}{4}$ and 1. Children should discuss their work.

ACTIVITY 8.36
Comparing Fractions with Different Numerators and Denominators.

This activity asks students to compare fractions such as $\frac{3}{4}$ and $\frac{1}{2}$, $\frac{1}{2}$ and $\frac{4}{6}$, and $\frac{7}{8}$ and $\frac{3}{6}$, by naming which is the larger. Tell children they can use materials to solve these problems, but suggest that any children who want to think the answers should do so. Have children write up how they solved the problems. They should also share their strategies. Some children will be able to apply the ideas gained from work with Activities 8.33 and 8.34. During the discussion bring up the idea of using a reference of $\frac{1}{2}$ or 1 if no child reports using this strategy. A question to ask is: "How can comparing to $\frac{1}{2}$ or 1 help with this task?"

ACTIVITY 8.37
More Comparing.

Fractions to be compared include unit fractions with different denominators and nonunit fractions with the same numerators and different denominators or different numerators and denominators. (Examples are: Which is greater? $\frac{1}{3}$ or $\frac{1}{4}$, $\frac{6}{10}$ or $\frac{6}{8}$, $\frac{5}{6}$ or $\frac{1}{3}$, $\frac{8}{12}$ or $\frac{2}{10}$. *Note*: When pairs have unlike numerators and denominators, their differences are large.) Have students use materials if they wish and also give reasons for their selections. For example, students would say $\frac{5}{6}$ is closer to 1 than $\frac{1}{3}$, so it is greater.

ACTIVITY 8.38
Ordering Fractions.

In this activity, children order fractions represented by drawings (Figure 8.16). Ask students to study the drawings, decide how to order the fractions represented, and write the fractions in order. After student complete their work, ask, "How did you solve this problem of ordering fractions? Where did you place $\frac{3}{12}$ and $\frac{1}{4}$? Why?"

In a later lesson, ask students to order fractions designated by symbols. Examples include those that can be solved by using reference points: $\frac{1}{4}$, $\frac{5}{6}$, $\frac{1}{2}$; $\frac{1}{2}$, $\frac{7}{8}$, $\frac{2}{3}$; and $\frac{5}{12}$, $\frac{5}{6}$, $\frac{6}{10}$. Tell students that they can use materials or thinking to solve the problem in this activity. Have them share their solutions and strategies.

ACTIVITY 8.39
Estimation with Fractions.

Ask children to decide if a fraction is close to 0, $\frac{1}{2}$, or 1. The statements can be posed as true or false, with pupils giving reasons for their responses. For example, True or False: $\frac{3}{8}$ is close to $\frac{1}{2}$. True, because $\frac{3}{8}$ is close to $\frac{4}{8}$, which is one-half.

Activity for the Classroom 8.2. Write six true or false statements that give pupils experience estimating with fractions, and use them with students in your class. Have them work in pairs and explain why the statement is true or false. Extension: Ask learners to write the same kind of questions to ask each other.

ACTIVITY 8.40
Indicated Division.

Indicated division is best introduced with problems. Two problems are:

1. Ms. Ho wants to make 4 hair ribbons, each the same length, for her cousin's daughters. She has 3 yards of ribbon. How long will each be?

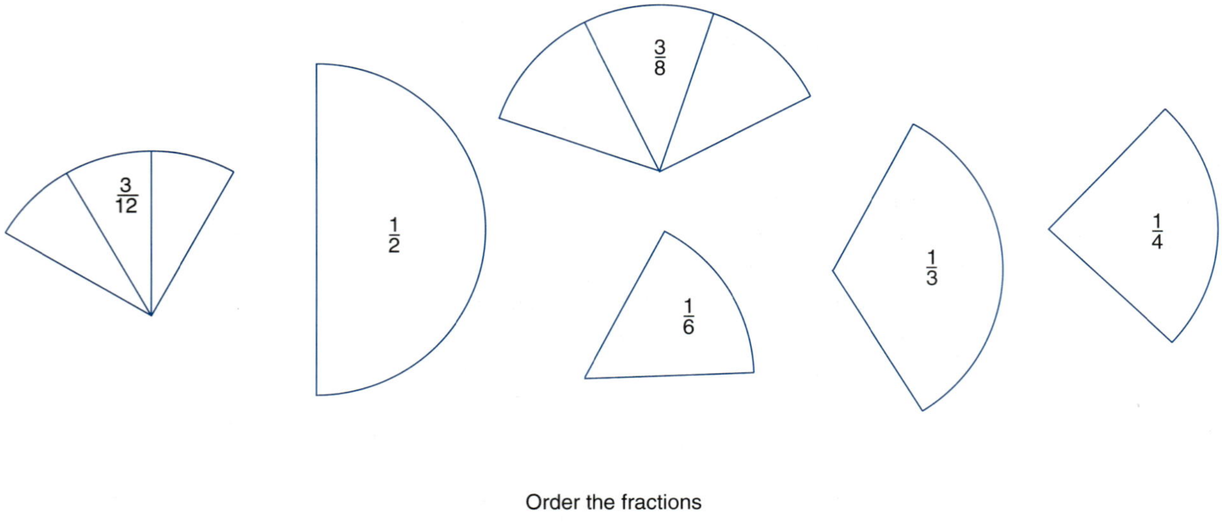

FIGURE 8.16 Activity for Ordering Fractions

2. Our family of 6 is going to share 4 pizzas for tonight's supper. If we share them equally, how much will each get?

After students solve the problems, they discuss this fraction meaning. The focus of the discussion should be that a number of wholes is divided evenly but the result is not wholes, but a fraction. The indicated division interpretation will be more readily understood if students are asked to use pictures or paper folding to aid in understanding the problems.

ACTIVITY 8.41
Finding Part of a Set.

Ellerbruch and Payne (1978) suggest that students should not be given activities that require finding part of a set. They advise relating situations such as $\frac{1}{4}$ of 8 to whole-number division ($\frac{1}{4}$ of 8 is $8 \div 4$). (The problem, $\frac{1}{4}$ of 8, can be thought of as a multiplication situation involving the "of" interpretation of multiplication of fractions—see Chapter Nine.) If such problems are assigned, real-life situations will help children deal with this topic. They should use materials to solve the problems and later discuss how division by a whole number can be used to solve problems involving part of a set. Examples of problems are:

1. Beverly had 16 flowers to put in vases on the tables for the Girl Scout banquet. The troop leader said, "Put $\frac{1}{8}$ of your flowers in each vase." How many flowers should Beverly put in each vase?
2. The teacher said, "One-third of our class of 24 students will practice for the May Day Dance Festival each morning until May 1." Pat said to himself, "I know how many that is." What number was he thinking?

ACTIVITY 8.42
Agree or Disagree?

Students in pairs or small groups can prepare reactions to statements in the format of agree or disagree. Reactions are to include answers and reasons for agreement or disagreement. Students can be asked to write their reactions. Examples of statements for students to discuss are:

1. $\frac{3}{4}$ is greater than $\frac{6}{10}$.
2. $\frac{1}{2}$ is closer to $\frac{5}{6}$ than to $\frac{9}{10}$.

3. $\frac{4}{8}$ and $\frac{5}{10}$ are not equivalent fractions.
4. $\frac{3}{10}$, $\frac{3}{6}$, and $\frac{2}{3}$ are ordered from smallest to largest.

ACTIVITY 8.43
Mixed Numbers.

Show a representation for three-halves on the overhead. Say, "After the Jones family finished dinner, this much pizza was left. Mother asked Sue to tell her how many halves were left. What did Sue say? Why?" As children discuss their answers, stress counting the number of fractional parts. Have them count the fractional parts shown on the overhead. Ask how the pieces could be rearranged to show a whole and a part. (Place two pieces together to make a whole.) Discuss how many wholes and halves are shown. Help children understand that three halves is one plus one-half. Remark that this kind of number is called a "mixed number." Repeat for other mixed numbers.

Continue by asking children in groups of three to count five halves, five fourths, and five thirds and then use wholes and fraction pieces to decide how to name the fractions as mixed numbers. After they agree how this is done, give the assignment: Show three to seven fraction pieces that together cover more than one whole, but less than two. Name the mixed numbers you have shown. Have students share their work. Repeat the assignment using different numbers of fraction pieces. Also change the range to more than two but less than three wholes.

After children can name mixed numbers, introduce the symbols by asking how they think the symbols would be written. Point out that the plus sign is omitted in the symbols for mixed numbers. Work with mixed numbers can include labeling fraction number lines (Figure 8.17) and renaming the fractions as mixed numbers.

ACTIVITY 8.44
Making a Fraction Book.

Have each child make a fraction book in which they use square or triangle grid paper to illustrate six or more unit fractions of their choice and six or more nonunit fractions of their choice. Beside each representation they write the word and the symbol for the fraction illustrated. They can include a short essay that tells what they think is most important to know about fractions.

ACTIVITY 8.45
Real-Life Problems.

Many activities should be composed of real-life problems. Some teachers also give a problem at the beginning of some mathematics periods for students to solve in groups before the lesson begins. Another approach is to have a problem on the chalkboard for children to study when they arrive for class in the morning. These can be related or unrelated to the topic being studied during the mathematics period. Students work on the problem until class begins or during free moments during the day.

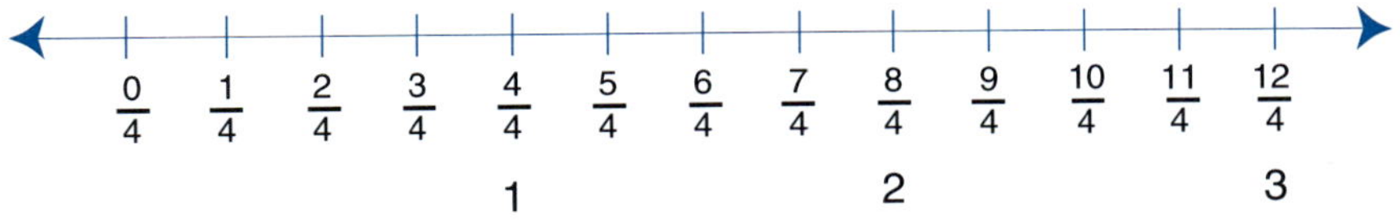

FIGURE 8.17 Number Line Model for Mixed-Numbers Activity

The answer is discussed before children are dismissed or at a designated time another day. Children should also be asked to write problems to share with others. Examples of problems for understanding fractions are:

1. The Schmidt family was having a pizza party for their aunts, uncles, and cousins. But they had a problem. The small pizzas that were delivered from Pizza Place were really cut up! Some were cut in halves, some in fourths, some in sixths, and some in eighths. Mother said each person could have a half. What fractional part of each pizza that was delivered did each person get?
2. Aunt Barbara's hobby is to make doll clothes for her doll collection. She had a lovely one-yard piece of pink satin. She said, "I need one-fourth of a yard for the small doll dress, one-third for the medium-size doll, and one-half yard for the large doll. I wonder if a yard is enough to make all these doll dresses." Was it?
3. Two actors in a class play had headbands. John's was one-half of a yard long; Willie's was three-eighths of a yard long. Which child had the longer band?
4. In a running contest, Karl finished in $\frac{1}{2}$ of a minute, Steve in $\frac{4}{6}$ of a minute, and Bud in $\frac{5}{12}$ of a minute. In what order did they finish the race?
5. Sarah can finish a division example in $\frac{5}{6}$ of a minute. Desiree takes $\frac{11}{12}$ of a minute. How do they compare?

ASSESSING FRACTION LEARNING

Assessment of children's learning of the fraction concepts discussed in this chapter focuses on the meanings students have developed and their interest in activities dealing with fractions. You assess comprehension of partitioning into equal-sized parts, ability to compare and order fractions, understanding of equivalent fractions, knowledge of fraction names and symbols, knowledge of reference fractions, and success in problem solving. You also observe children's willingness to participate in fraction activities and discussions.

Knowledge of a child's level of understanding enables you to plan activities that help the child develop new concepts and extend prior learning. For example, children who show understanding of partitioning into equal-sized pieces are ready to learn fraction names. Those who do not understand sharing evenly need more experience, such as with folding and sharing paper (pretend) pies, pizzas, and candy bars.

Assessment in the primary grades relies heavily on observation and questioning of students while they are working individually or in groups. Records of these observations and mini-interviews are kept so that a profile of student learning is maintained. Samples of a student's work filed regularly in his or her folder also contribute to the learning profile.

In the upper grades, assessment continues to include observation and interviewing. Children's written reports of how they solved a problem are also used. Because such reports give valuable insights into children's understanding of fraction ideas, children should often be assigned write-ups as part of an activity.

Quizzes and tests are used more frequently in the upper grades but can also be a part of assessment in the primary grades. Some items should ask students to make a drawing to show a fraction. Examples of items to assess learning follow. The first two would be appropriate for primary grade pupils.

1. Divide the round paper cake (shown on the test) so that you can give 4 children each the same-sized piece.
2. After you take some for yourself, you have 8 sticks of gum left. You plan to share the 8 pieces equally among four friends. What fractional part of the gum will each get? How many pieces will each friend get?

3. Use a circular region to show $\frac{3}{8}$. Write how you thought to carry out this task. (Circular region is supplied.)
4. Write a story problem that asks children to share objects equally. Each child should get the same number with none left over.
5. Use the number line attached to this sheet to show $\frac{1}{4}$. Label your number line to show you understand how to represent the fraction.
6. Use grid paper to show $\frac{2}{3}$. Label your diagram so that your work is meaningful (grid paper is supplied).
7. Use grid paper to make a rectangular region divided into 4 parts of equal size. Shade $\frac{1}{2}$ of the region. Write how you thought to complete this task.

Items for ordering and comparing fractions or thinking reference fractions can be patterned after tasks or questions given for the activities in this chapter (e.g., Activities 8.32, 8.33, and 8.42).

Activity for the Classroom 8.3. Write four questions to ask students to determine if they can compare and order fractions or use reference fractions. Ask the questions to each of six children. Ask them to tell how they thought to answer your questions. Using the three levels discussed for performance indicators (Chapter One), decide each child's level of understanding and achievement on the basis of his or her work and explanation.

SUMMARY

This chapter discusses the fraction meanings that form the foundation for studying fractions in the upper grades and beyond. New directions in mathematics teaching and learning enable children to think about fraction concepts and relations before symbols are introduced. Initially, children learn about partitioning into equal-sized parts, use fraction words orally and in writing, compare and order fractions, and develop an intuitive understanding of equivalent fractions. When children have constructed the meaning of fractions, fraction symbols are introduced. After learning about fraction symbols, children extend their understanding by engaging in activities that involve using number lines, dealing with ideas such as comparing fractions to the reference numbers 1, $\frac{1}{2}$, or 0, and finding part of a set.

Problems were included in many activities. The use of manipulative materials and diagrams was stressed throughout the chapter to help children form visual images and relate abstract ideas to concrete experiences. Children not only label diagrams of fractions but also make drawings to show the fractional parts of regions. Discussion was emphasized as a part of activities to enable learners to reflect on their actions and share their thinking. The section on assessment focused on assessment strategies that enable teachers to gather information about children's knowledge and thinking processes so that they can plan instruction that promotes further learning of fraction concepts.

REFERENCES

Behr, Merlyn J., Richard Lesh, Thomas R. Post, and Edward A. Silver. (1983). "Rational Number Concepts." In *Acquisition of Mathematics Concepts and Processes,* edited by Richard Lesh and Marsha Landau, pp. 91–126. New York: Academic Press.

Behr, Merlyn J., and Post, Thomas R. (1988). "Teaching Rational Number and Decimal Concepts." In *Teaching Mathematics in Grades K–8: Research Based Methods,* edited by Thomas R. Post, pp. 201–248. Boston: Allyn and Bacon.

Behr, Merlyn J., Ipke Wachsmuth, Thomas R. Post, and Richard Lesh. (November 1984). "Order and Equivalence of Rational Numbers: A Clinical Teaching Experiment." *Journal for Research in Mathematics Education* 15: 323–341.

Bezuk, Nadine S. (February 1988). "Fractions in the Early Childhood Mathematics Curriculum." *Arithmetic Teacher* 35: 56–60.

Bezuk, Nadine, and Kathleen Cramer. (1989). "Teaching about Fractions: What, When, and How." In *New Directions for Elementary*

School Mathematics, edited by Paul R. Trafton and Albert P. Shulte, pp. 156–167. Reston, VA: National Council of Teachers of Mathematics.

Ellerbruch, Larry W., and Joseph N. Payne. (1978). "A Teaching Sequence from Initial Fraction Concepts through the Addition of Unlike Fractions." In *Developing Computational Skills,* edited by Marilyn N. Suydam and Robert T. Reys, pp. 129–147. Reston, VA: National Council of Teachers of Mathematics.

Harrison, Bruce, Selwyn Brindley, and Marshall P. Bye. (May 1989). "Allowing for Student Cognitive Levels in the Teaching of Fractions and Ratios." *Journal for Research in Mathematics Education* 3: 288–308.

Kieren, Thomas E. (February 1984). "Helping Children Understand Rational Numbers." *Arithmetic Teacher* 31: 3.

Kouba, Vicky L., Catherine A. Brown, Thomas P. Carpenter, Mary M. Lindquist, Edward A. Silver, and Jane O. Swafford. (April 1988). "Results of the Fourth NAEP Assessment of Mathematics: Number, Operations, and Word Problems." *Arithmetic Teacher* 35: 14–19.

Mack, Nancy K. (January 1990). "Learning Fractions with Understanding: Building on Informal Knowledge." *Journal for Research in Mathematics Education* 21: 16–32.

National Council of Teachers of Mathematics. (1989) *Curriculum and Evaluation Standards for School Mathematics.* Reston, VA: Author.

Payne, Joseph N. (February 1984). "Curricular Issues: Teaching Rational Numbers." *Arithmetic Teacher* 31: 14–17.

Payne, Joseph N., Anne E. Towsley, and DeAnne M. Huinker. (1990). "Fractions and Decimals." In *Mathematics for the Young Child,* edited by Joseph N. Payne, pp. 174–200. Reston, VA: National Council of Teachers of Mathematics.

Post, Thomas, and Kathleen Cramer. (October 1987). "Children's Strategies in Ordering Rational Numbers." *Arithmetic Teacher* 35: 35–37.

Post, Thomas R., Merlyn J. Behr, and Richard Lesh. (1982). "Interpretations of Rational Number Concepts." In *Mathematics for the Middle Grades (5–9),* edited by Linda Silvey and James R. Smart, pp. 59–72. Reston, VA: National Council of Teachers of Mathematics.

Post, Thomas R., Ipke Wachsmuth, Richard Lesh, and Merlyn J. Behr. (January 1985). "Order and Equivalence of Rational Numbers: A Cognitive Analysis." *Journal for Research in Mathematics Education* 16: 18–36.

Pothier, Yvonne, and Sawada, Daiyo. (November 1983). "Partitioning: The Emergence of Rational Number Ideas in Young Children." *Journal for Research in Mathematics Education* 14: 307–317.

SOFTWARE RESOURCES

Adventures with Fractions
Company: MECC
Computer: Apple
Grade level: 5–8

Practice in ordering fractions; tutorial and game.

IBM Elementary Mathematics Series: Math Concepts
Level 1, Unit 5, Lesson 20 (fractions to fifths), Lesson 24 (fractions to tenths)
Company: IBM/EduQuest
Computer: IBM
Grade level: 2–4

Constructing with fraction strips, estimating, and comparing fractions. Related word problems included.

IBM Elementary Mathematics Series: Math Concepts
Level 11, Unit 4, Lesson 19 (comparison of fractions), Lesson 20 (mixed numbers), Lesson 21 (equivalent fractions)
Company: IBM/EduQuest
Computer: IBM
Grade level: 3–6

Shade fraction strips and use number line. Construct and identify to order, compare, and estimate fractions. Includes related word problems.

Partial Fractions
Company: Sunburst
Computer: Apple
Grade level: 4–8

Teaches fraction size with problems that have one fraction missing. Readiness for multiplication and division of fractions.

CHAPTER 9

Computing with Fractions

▪ INTRODUCTORY PROBLEM ▪

Your class is preparing a May Day Coffee for Parents and Friends. The children have decided to bake cookies, muffins, and coffee cake. There are 23 children in your class, and the class decided that each child could invite 2 guests. The problem is that students found a cookbook for large numbers but the recipes make enough for 100 people. In other cookbooks they located, the recipes are usually for 2 dozen cookies, 8 or 12 muffins, and coffee cakes for 6 persons. As you study this chapter, decide what computations with fractions can be incorporated into this cooking project or other preparations for the May Day Coffee.

INTRODUCTION

In most classrooms computing with fractions has meant manipulating numbers by following rules. Children have not been expected to understand what they were doing. The results of a curriculum that de-emphasizes understanding are evident in children's performance on tests designed to measure their knowledge of computation with fractions. On the second National Assessment of Educational Progress (NAEP), when given the choices of 1, 2, 19, 21, and "I don't know," only 24% of the 13-year-old students were able correctly to estimate the sum of $\frac{12}{13}$ and $\frac{7}{8}$. The most frequent responses were 19 and 21 (Post, 1981). Even with the schools' emphasis on computation, on the fourth NAEP, only 56% of seventh graders could compute $4 \times 2\frac{1}{4}$ (Kouba, Brown, Carpenter, Lindquist, Silver, and Swafford, 1988).

Clearly, learning only procedures does not lead to knowledge of computation with fractions. If children are to develop competence, they must grasp the meaning of the operations with fractions and make sense of the algorithms. However, such learnings are not easily attained. Children often experience difficulties because what they have learned about the operations with whole numbers does not necessarily relate to fractions. The rule for addition often makes no sense to them, and they add both the numerators and the denominators (Mack, 1990). However, the interpretations of addition and subtraction with fractions are usually not difficult for children because the interpretations are the same as for whole numbers. Children can usually remember the rule for multiplication with fractions because it relates to whole-number multiplication, but the meanings of multiplication with fractions cause them difficulty, because they do not understand that multiplication with fractions can often be interpreted as finding one or more parts and is not always interpreted as repeated addition.

To understand the meanings of the operations with fractions, children must have attained certain prerequisite knowledge (Behr and Post, 1988). They should have constructed the partitioning concept, know the meaning of the numerator and denominator and their relation, understand that a fraction is made up of the sum of unit fractions (e.g., $\frac{3}{4} = \frac{1}{4} + \frac{1}{4} + \frac{1}{4}$), be able to use materials to represent fractions, and understand comparing and ordering fractions. Before introducing operations with fractions, children's knowledge of fractions is assessed to determine if they have the prior learning necessary to profit from instruction.

New directions in instruction enable learners to develop the meanings of the operations with fractions. Problem solving with fractions is emphasized. Students use a variety of materials to solve problems and represent sums, differences, products, and quotients (NCTM, 1989). (See Standards 6 and 7 in Curriculum Standards for Grades 5–8, Appendix A.) They compare the meanings of an operation with fractions to its meanings with whole numbers (Reys, Suydam, and Lindquist, 1992) and estimate in order to consider the reasonableness of their solutions (Bezuk and Cramer, 1989; Coburn, 1989). Learners talk about their work and engage in higher-level thinking as they respond to teacher questions; in so doing, they reflect on their actions.

Some children may be able to compute mentally with fractions. Others may develop alternative rules and use them effectively (Mack, 1990). However, all children should be introduced to standard algorithms for fraction computation. To construct a standard algorithm, learners solve story or number problems using materials or thinking, make records of their work, discover patterns, and use the patterns to state the rule (Steiner, 1987). When children have developed the algorithm, they are assigned maintenance activities and they solve and write story problems that involve fraction computation.

Activities for understanding addition and subtraction with fractions are usually part of the fourth-grade curriculum. The algorithms are learned in grades 4 and 5. The meanings of multiplication and division with fractions are learned in grade 5, and algorithms learned in grades 5 and 6. It has been suggested that the study of fraction computation should begin later than has been the practice in elementary schools (Bezuk and Cramer, 1989; Trafton and Zawojewski, 1984).

Some advocate teaching multiplication before addition with fractions, but Behr and Post (1988) point out that because children can relate their knowledge of addition and subtraction with whole numbers to addition and subtraction with fractions, addition and subtraction with fractions should be taught first. The sequence in this chapter reflects their recommendation.

The main sections of this chapter are: Learning Addition and Subtraction with Fractions, Learning Multiplication and Division with Fractions, and Assessing Fraction Computation Learning. The first two sections discuss instruction and give activities to enable children to understand computation with fractions and use algorithms meaningfully. Interactive teaching characterized by problem solving and discussion in small student groups and whole-class arrangements is illustrated. The last section describes assessment procedures and gives examples of assessment questions. A summary ends the chapter.

LEARNING ADDITION AND SUBTRACTION WITH FRACTIONS

Understanding addition and subtraction with fractions is developed before learning the algorithms. Constructing meanings is the topic of the first part of this section. The other parts deal with helping children learn the algorithms for addition and subtraction with fractions and extending understanding. In this section the two operations are discussed together.

Learning the Meanings of Addition and Subtraction with Fractions

Meaning is constructed by learners as they use materials to solve problems and reflect on their experience. Each child must have materials for solving problems, and assignments should involve only fractions that can be represented with the materials available to learners. Materials used to develop meanings are circular and rectangular regions, fraction disks, fraction bars, and number lines (Figure 9.1).

From their work with materials, children construct concepts and develop skills connected to meanings. The learnings are:

1. Addition and subtraction with fractions have the same interpretations as these operations with whole numbers. Children learn that addition with fractions involves joining or combining ideas and subtraction with fractions can mean separating, comparing, or equalizing.
2. Fractions that are added or subtracted must have the same name; sometimes one or both fractions must be renamed. Materials help with renaming.
3. Sums and differences involving like fractions can be mentally computed.
4. Sums and differences can be estimated. Reference points such as $0, \frac{1}{2}, 1$, or 2 are usually used in estimating. Estimates help in judging the reasonableness of solutions.

To construct concepts of the operations, children complete problems individually or in small groups. They use materials to find solutions. A discussion follows pupils' work. During the discussion, children demonstrate how they used materials. Fraction disks and bars can be used on the overhead. Overhead transparencies of fraction bars and number lines are also useful for demonstrations.

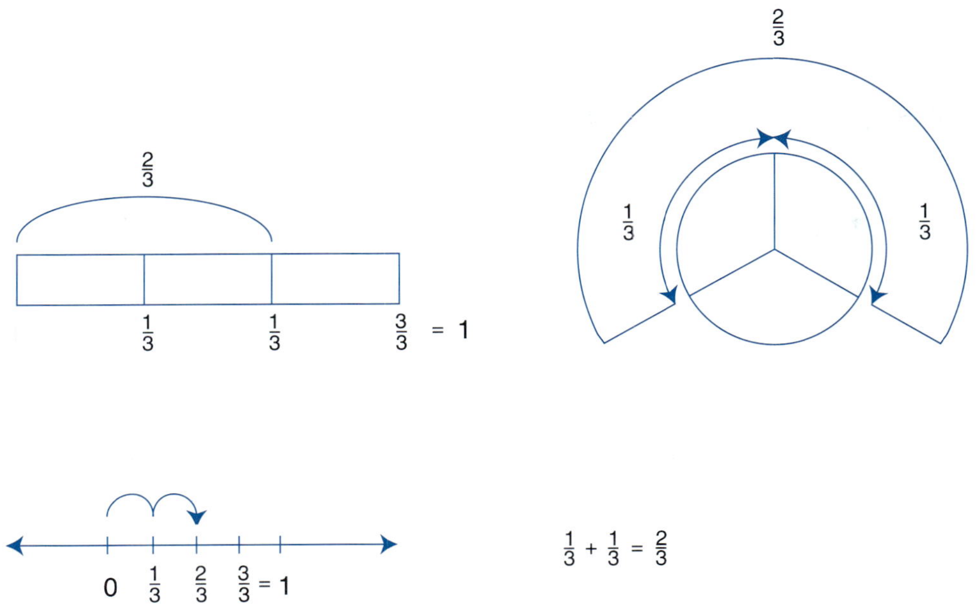

FIGURE 9.1 Models for Addition with Like Fractions

Activities for Learning the Meanings of Addition and Subtraction with Fractions

ACTIVITY 9.1
Solving Story Problems to Learn the Interpretations of Addition and Subtraction with Fractions.

To help students understand that the meanings of addition and subtraction with fractions are the same as with whole numbers, assign problems for students to solve individually or in groups. Give directions to solve the problems with materials or by thinking the solutions and to decide if answers are reasonable. When students finish their work, they share their solutions, how they used materials to arrive at their solutions, and their thinking to decide if their answers made sense. The discussion should bring out the idea that thinking how an answer compares to 0, $\frac{1}{2}$, or 1 makes it possible to decide if the answer is reasonable.

The first problems assigned should be with like fractions. Later problems with unlike fractions are assigned. Problems with unlike fractions may be delayed until children have constructed the algorithms for addition and subtraction with like fractions.

The examples that follow give problems for like fractions followed by problems for unlike fractions. They include only some types of problems for addition and subtraction with fractions.

Reader Activity 9.1

Refer to Box 5.1 in Chapter 5 for types of addition and subtraction problems. Write five fraction story problems for types of problems not included in the following list. Use materials to solve the problems.

Problems with Like Fractions.

1. Sandra took $\frac{1}{6}$ of an apple pie to school for her lunch dessert. She gave her sister $\frac{1}{6}$ of the pie for her school lunch. How much of the pie did they take to school? (Joining: Find result.)
2. Brandon ate $\frac{1}{8}$ of a pizza for a snack and $\frac{5}{8}$ for lunch. How much of the pizza did he eat? (Joining: Find result.)
3. Keri had $\frac{11}{12}$ of a yard of ribbon for wrapping a birthday gift for her sister. She used $\frac{8}{12}$ of a yard for around the box. How much ribbon was left to make the bow? (Separating: Find result.)

4. Maria's recipe for peanut butter cookies takes $\frac{3}{4}$ cup of peanut butter. Marsha's takes $\frac{2}{4}$ cup of peanut butter. Which recipe takes the most and how much more? (Comparing: Find difference.)
5. George rides his bike $\frac{7}{10}$ of a mile to school. That is $\frac{5}{10}$ of a mile farther than his friend, Dong. How far does Dong ride? (Comparing: Find smaller part.)

Problems with Unlike Fractions. The first problems assigned should involve pairs of fractions such that the denominator of one fraction is a multiple of the other, for example $\frac{1}{4}$ and $\frac{1}{2}$ or $\frac{1}{6}$ and $\frac{2}{3}$. When children can use materials to represent sums and differences with such pairs, fractions are used in which one denominator is not a multiple of the other denominator.

To solve problems with unlike fractions, children use trial and error to find materials that can be used to name both fractions (Figure 9.2). If they experiment to determine which fraction bar or disk pieces gives the fractions and their sum the same name, children will develop an intuitive understanding of common denominators (Post, 1981). If children need guidance, ask, "What fraction bar or pieces can you use to name the fractions to find the sum (difference)?"

Examples of problems are:

1. Teresa baked two recipes of holiday cookies last weekend. She used $\frac{1}{4}$ of a cup of sugar in one recipe, and she had no more sugar. She needed $\frac{1}{2}$ cup in another recipe. She asked her neighbor if she could borrow some sugar for the second recipe. Her neighbor gave it to her. How much sugar did she use altogether? (Joining: Find result.)
2. Mike takes a shortcut to school in the morning and walks $\frac{1}{4}$ of a mile. He likes to take the long way home after school, although he knows it is $\frac{5}{8}$ of a mile. How much farther is the trip at the end of the school day? (Comparing: Find difference.)
3. Saturday morning Sabina rode her bike $\frac{1}{3}$ of a mile to Liza's house, and then together they rode $\frac{1}{2}$ of a mile to the park for the school picnic. How far did Sabina ride to the picnic? (Joining: Find result.)
4. Jack put $\frac{1}{3}$ of his little box of raisins on a piece of paper to eat for a snack. He then gave some in the box to his friend and realized that the box was empty. How much of the box did he give to his friend? (Separating: Find remainder.)

ACTIVITY 9.2
Learning to Use Different Materials to Represent Addition and Subtraction with Fractions.

This activity will be used in different lessons to enable children to use different materials to represent addition and subtraction fraction problems. Different materials are introduced because representing operations in different ways can improve comprehension, even if the material causes pupils some disequilibrium at first (Behr, Lesh, Post, and Silver, 1983). Students learn to use circular and rectangular regions, fraction disks, fraction bars, geoboards, dot paper, and number lines.

To begin instruction in the use of a particular material that students have not used previously in computing with fractions, pass out the materials, and ask students how this material could be used to solve a problem you write on the overhead. When they have decided how to use the material, ask a student to demonstrate his or her ideas. If no one volunteers, you model the use of the material, for example, the use of dot paper (Figure 9.3). Say, "Watch what I am doing on the overhead. This is how dot paper could be used to solve the problem." Then, model the solution of a problem with dot paper, and have children explain what you did in your demonstration. Their comments and your questions should bring out how to use the dot pa-

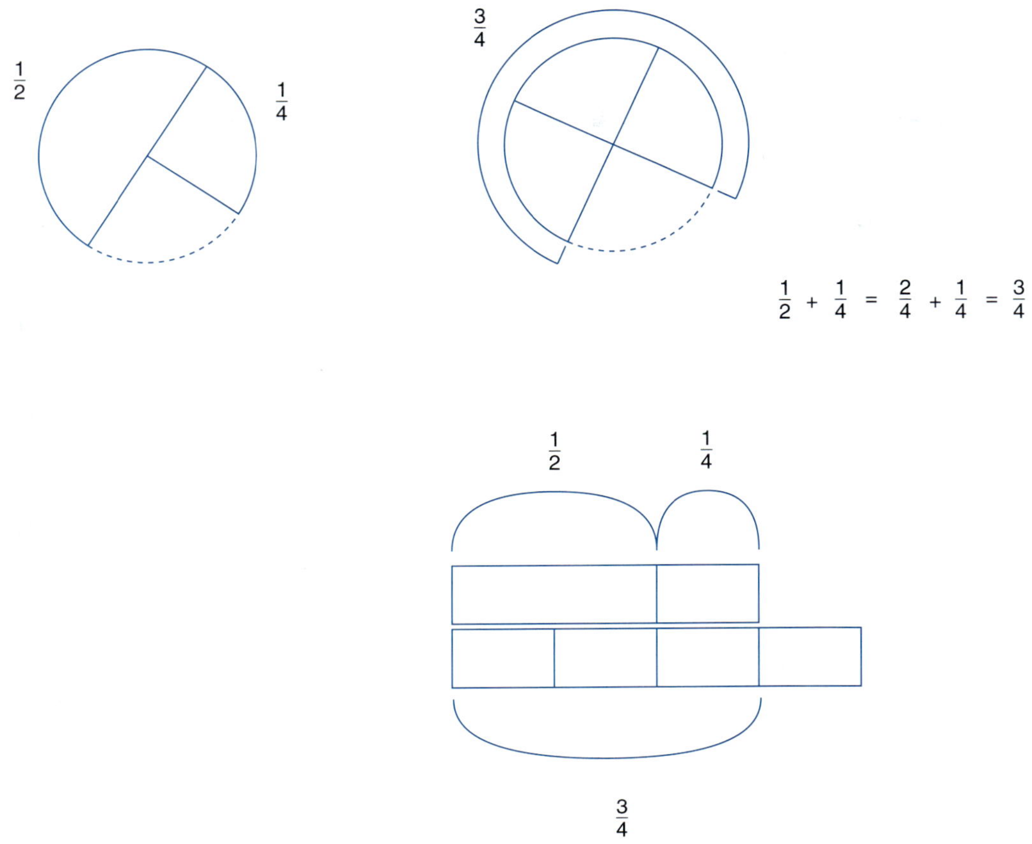

FIGURE 9.2 Models for Addition with Unlike Fractions

per. Have children use their dot paper to solve several problems and discuss how they did it. Later, ask children how to use dot paper to show the solution to a separating or comparing problem.

When children use fraction bars to represent addition or subtraction with unlike fractions, they discover that with like fractions, only one bar needs to be used. With unlike fractions, three bars are used (Figure 9.4). Number lines are used similarly, with one line used to represent addition and subtraction with like fractions, and three number lines to represent addition or subtraction with unlike fractions (Figure 9.5). The placement of the number lines for addition and subtraction with unlike fractions is difficult for most children, and number lines are not recommended as a material to use to represent addition and subtraction with unlike fractions.

ACTIVITY 9.3
Thinking about Addition and Subtraction.

After children have used different materials to solve addition and subtraction problems with fractions, ask them to solve problems, decide if the solutions were reason-

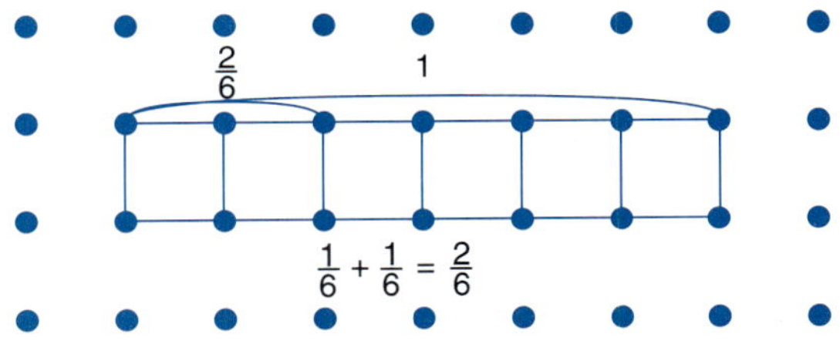

FIGURE 9.3 Dot Paper Model for Addition with Like Fractions

FIGURE 9.4 Fraction Bar Models for Addition with Fractions

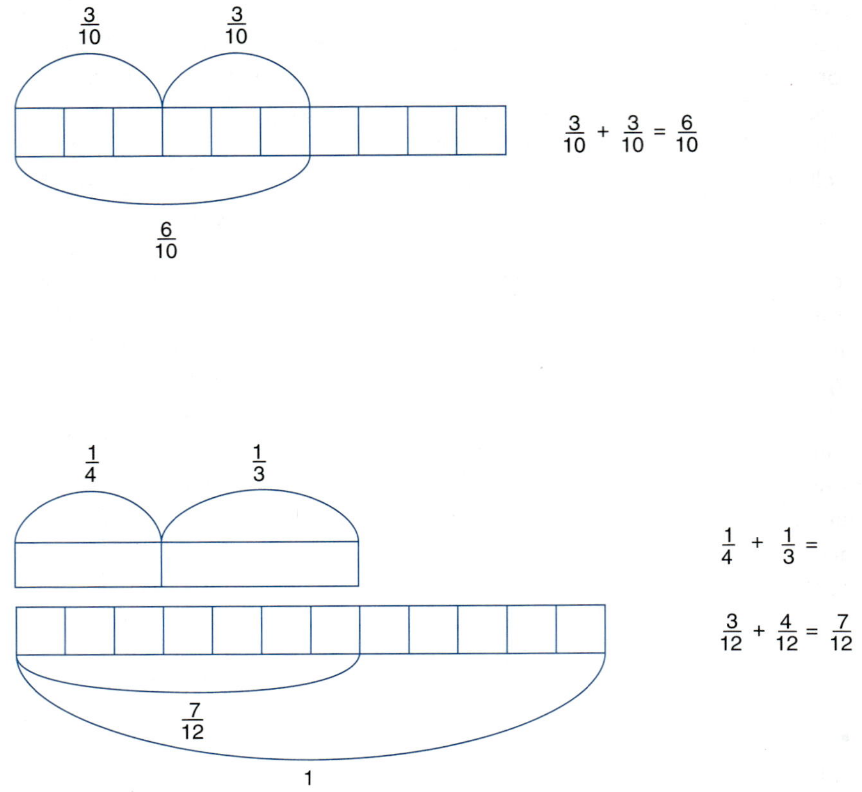

FIGURE 9.5 Number Line Models for Addition with Fractions

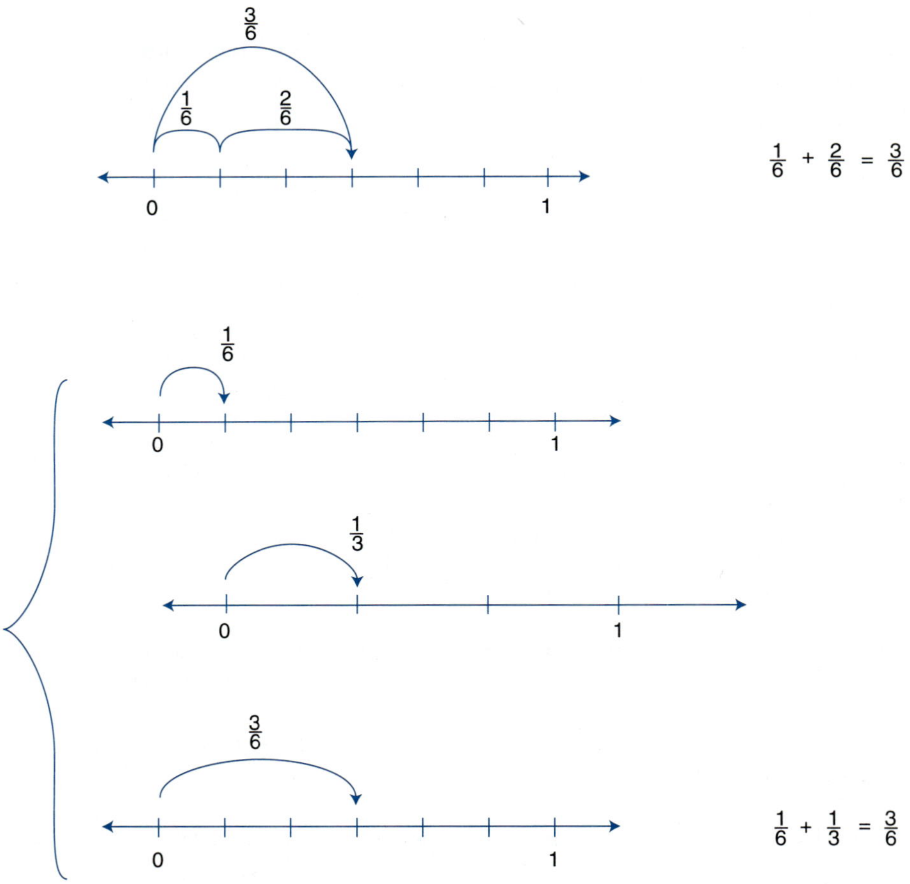

able, and if possible, write math sentences for the problems. They share their work in a class discussion. During the discussion, refer to the math sentences, and ask questions such as: "Why did you decide to add (subtract)?" "How is the meaning of addition (subtraction) with fractions like or unlike the meaning of addition (subtraction) with whole numbers? How do you know?" Their responses to these questions should include the ideas that when a problem involves joining or combining parts, you add, and when a problem involves separating, comparing, or making equal, you subtract.

If students show an intuitive awareness of these meanings by solving problems correctly but are unable to verbalize the ideas, continue to assign problems and provide opportunities for them to talk about their work. Whole-number problems as well as fraction problems should be assigned. The problems can sometimes be the same type so that students' reflections will focus on one method of solution. During a discussion of their work, ask "How?", "Why?", and "What does that tell you?" questions so that learners will analyze how they thought to solve the problems and infer new meanings. Writing problems for different types of story or part–part–whole problems may also help learners express their understanding of addition and subtration and encourage them to form their own valid rules for when to add and when to subtract. In time, they will be able to state the relations orally and in writing.

ACTIVITY 9.4
Think the Sum (Difference).

Students can compute sums and differences mentally after they have worked with materials and understand the meaning of addition and subtraction with like fractions. Because only numerators are added or subtracted and the denominator of the solution is the same as that of the addends or minuend and subtrahend in the problem, many students will have no difficulty mentally computing sums and differences with like fractions. They should be encouraged to do so and to explain their thinking to others. Some lessons can begin by asking learners mentally to compute a few sums or differences with like fractions.

ACTIVITY 9.5
Estimation Activities.

Two different types of estimation activities provide experiences for learning estimation. Because good estimates are based on having an awareness of the relative size of fractions, that idea is emphasized as learners report to the class or each other how they thought to complete these activities.

1. An activity sheet with questions such as the following teach using a reference fraction in estimation:

a. When two of the fractions in this list are added, the sum is less than $\frac{1}{2}$. How many different pairs can be found? $\frac{3}{4}$, $\frac{1}{4}$, $\frac{2}{3}$, $\frac{1}{6}$, $\frac{9}{11}$, $\frac{1}{7}$.

b. Make a drawing to show that the sum of $\frac{3}{4}$ and $\frac{5}{8}$ is greater than 1. Hint: Use paper foldings of two strips of paper before you make your drawing.

c. If two fractions each a little less than 1 are added, what would you estimate their sum to be? Why?

d. Each of these fractions is less than 1. Which two would you estimate have the greatest sum? $\frac{3}{4}$, $\frac{6}{7}$, $\frac{11}{12}$, $\frac{2}{3}$, $\frac{7}{8}$, $\frac{10}{11}$? Why? The least sum? Why?

2. Students make decisions about estimates in this kind of activity. Examples of estimates to judge are:

Problem	Estimate		Your Judgment	
$\frac{2}{3} + \frac{4}{9}$	1	Too low	Too high	OK
$\frac{6}{7} + \frac{9}{10}$	1	Too low	Too high	OK
$\frac{1}{4} + \frac{1}{8}$	$\frac{1}{2}$	Too low	Too high	OK
$\frac{4}{6} + \frac{5}{8}$	$\frac{1}{2}$	Too low	Too high	OK
$\frac{5}{12} + \frac{3}{5}$	2	Too low	Too high	OK

Students can complete the task individually, and explain in groups their choices to one another.

Activity for the Classroom 9.1. Write an addition-with-fractions estimation activity. You may adapt one of the ideas in Activity 9.5 for this assignment. Assign your activity to a group of middle-grade children. As they explain the thinking behind their answers, notice their use of reference fractions, and decide if they understand how to compare sums by using reference fractions.

ACTIVITY 9.6
Equivalent Fractions and Renaming.

This activity helps children develop an intuitive awareness of equivalent fractions and renaming fractions in addition and subtraction. It can be carried out in a whole-class lesson, or groups can work on the problems. Begin with easy problems in which one denominator is a multiple of the other. For example, ask children to find a fraction piece or pieces that cover $\frac{1}{2}$ and $\frac{1}{4}$ placed side by side. One child should then demonstrate on the overhead what he or she has done. When students can solve the easy problems, use more difficult ones, such as $\frac{1}{3} + \frac{1}{2}$ or $\frac{1}{3} + \frac{1}{4}$. Use the "cover side by side" phrasing in the assignment. The activity can be adapted for fractions bars. Children should have the opportunity to "discover" the piece or pieces that match two pieces joined together. Trial and error is an important strategy for developing depth of understanding (Post, 1981).

ACTIVITY 9.7
Showing a New Partition.

The activity example shown in Figure 9.6 gives students opportunities to think about representing equivalent fractions. After they complete the activity, they share their written responses with others in the class.

ACTIVITY 9.8
Designing Tiles.

The activity in Figure 9.7 gives students opportunities to think about equivalent fractions and addition with fractions.

ACTIVITY 9.9
Sums with Pattern Blocks.

Have children use pattern blocks to show sums (Figure 9.8). Triangle or square grid paper can also be used. Designs can be displayed with the sum written in words or symbols.

Please write answers to the questions below. On each diagram draw one line to show your thinking.

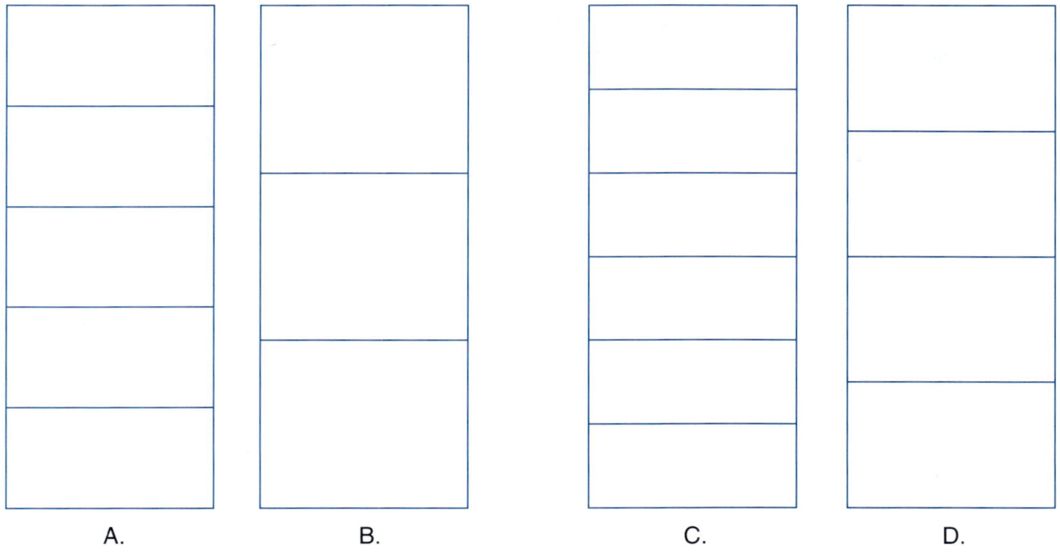

Which would show tenths more easily? Why?

What two fractions would the other region show easily? Why?

Which would show eighths more easily? Why?

What two fractions would the other region show easily? Why?

FIGURE 9.6 Activity Sheet for Equivalent Fractions

ACTIVITY 9.10
Mixed-Number Problems on the Number Line.

This activity gives learners a concrete experience with renaming mixed numbers. It begins with number words to help learners focus on parts of a whole. An activity sheet (Figure 9.9) asks children to find 5 fourths, 7 halves, and 8 thirds, or other improper fractions on number lines and to write the whole-plus-fraction number name in words, as well as to write their own problems. (The number lines are labeled for students.) When the activity sheet is discussed, help learners decide how the numbers could be written with symbols (e.g., 5 fourths = $\frac{5}{4}$ = 1 + $\frac{1}{4}$ = $1\frac{1}{4}$). Ask for the name of these numbers. If they cannot remember, tell them that these numbers are usually called mixed numbers and that the plus sign is omitted in mixed numbers. Ask if they think that "mixed numbers" is a good label. Also give students the label "improper fraction" for a fraction that has the numerator equal to or greater than the denominator.

An adaptation could give children mixed numbers written in words (e.g., one plus three-fourths) and ask them to use number lines to show the halves, fourths, and so on that name the numbers as improper fractions.

ACTIVITY 9.11
Mixed-Number Problems with Rectangular Regions on a Grid.

This activity also gives learners a concrete experience with mixed numbers. The activity sheet tells children to call one box a unit fraction, for example, $\frac{1}{4}$. They show improper fractions, for example $\frac{7}{4}$, and write the mixed numbers (Figure 9.10).

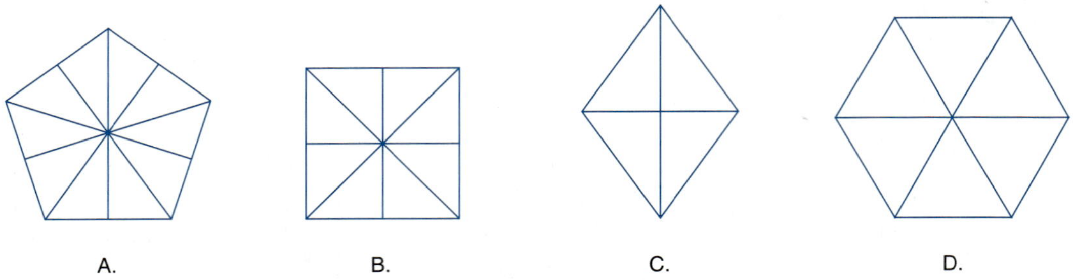

You are a tile designer. Decorate one tile so that it would be attractive one-half yellow and one-half blue. Then decorate the others using two colors for each and your own creative design. Please write the fractional parts colored in math sentences.

Math Sentences

A. ______________________

B. ______________________

C. ______________________

D. ______________________

FIGURE 9.7 Activity Sheet for *Designing Tiles*

Learning the Algorithms for Addition and Subtraction with Fractions

After meanings are developed, algorithms are learned. The algorithm for addition or subtraction with fractions is: If the fractions do not have a common denominator, find a common denominator, and use that denominator to rename the fractions. Add or subtract the numerators for the numerator of the sum or difference; use the common denominator for the denominator of the sum or difference.

The algorithms for addition and subtraction can be learned separately or at the same time to emphasize the inverse nature of the procedure. The first lessons deal only with like fractions with sums less than 1. Later lessons introduce addition and subtraction with unlike fractions and problems with sums greater than 1.

FIGURE 9.8 Pattern Block Models for Addition with Fractions

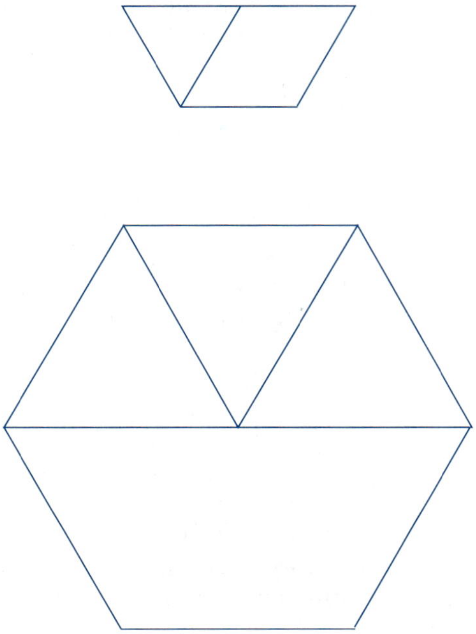

$\frac{1}{3} + \frac{2}{3} = 1$

$\frac{3}{6} + \frac{1}{2} = 1$

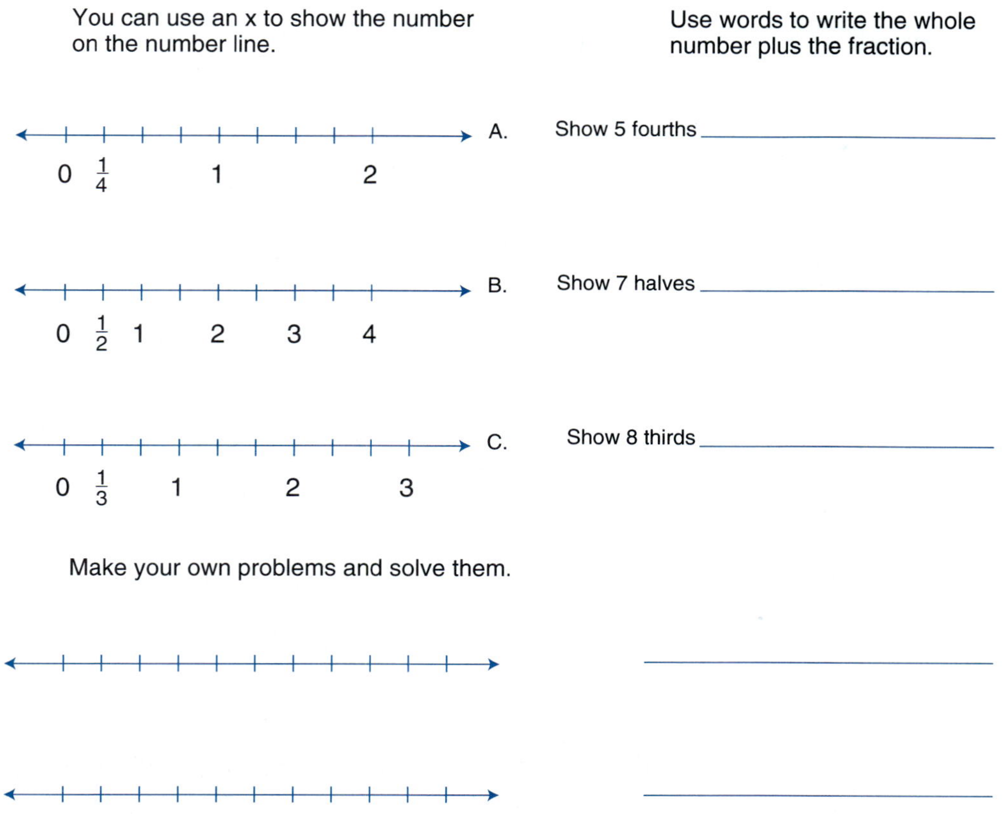

FIGURE 9.9 Activity Sheet for Renaming Improper Fractions using Number Lines

Sequence of Instruction for Algorithms for Addition and Subtraction with Like Fractions

Develop the Rule. Distribute the records students made of their solutions to addition or subtraction problems during an earlier lesson, or begin the lesson with problem solving, and have students use these records of solutions. Explain that the class will be able to figure out a rule because they understand how to solve fraction problems with materials.

Arrange children in groups of three or four. Ask each group to look for patterns in their records that will enable them to write a rule. Circulate and confer with each group. If guidance is needed, ask, "What do you notice about the numerators and denominators in the records of your solutions?"

After most groups have found patterns, conduct a whole-class discussion. Have students give reports of the patterns discovered when they worked in groups. Ask children to make a rule from the patterns they discovered: To add or subtract like fractions, add or subtract the numerators and give the sum or difference the same denominator as the fractions added or subtracted. Ask, "Does this rule always work? How can you tell?" Students should decide to make up new problems to use to test their rule.

Examine and Use the Rule. Continue by asking questions that require students to consider the reasonableness of this rule. For example ask, "What does the denominator tell us about the fraction?" (Its size.) "How does that help us understand why we add or subtract only the numerators?"

The following day distribute a worksheet with five exercises in which denominators are written in words, for example 1 sixth + 4 sixths = N or 7 eighths – 3 eighths = N. Say, "Finding these sums or differences will make it even clearer why we add or subtract only the numerators. As you write your answers, think how us-

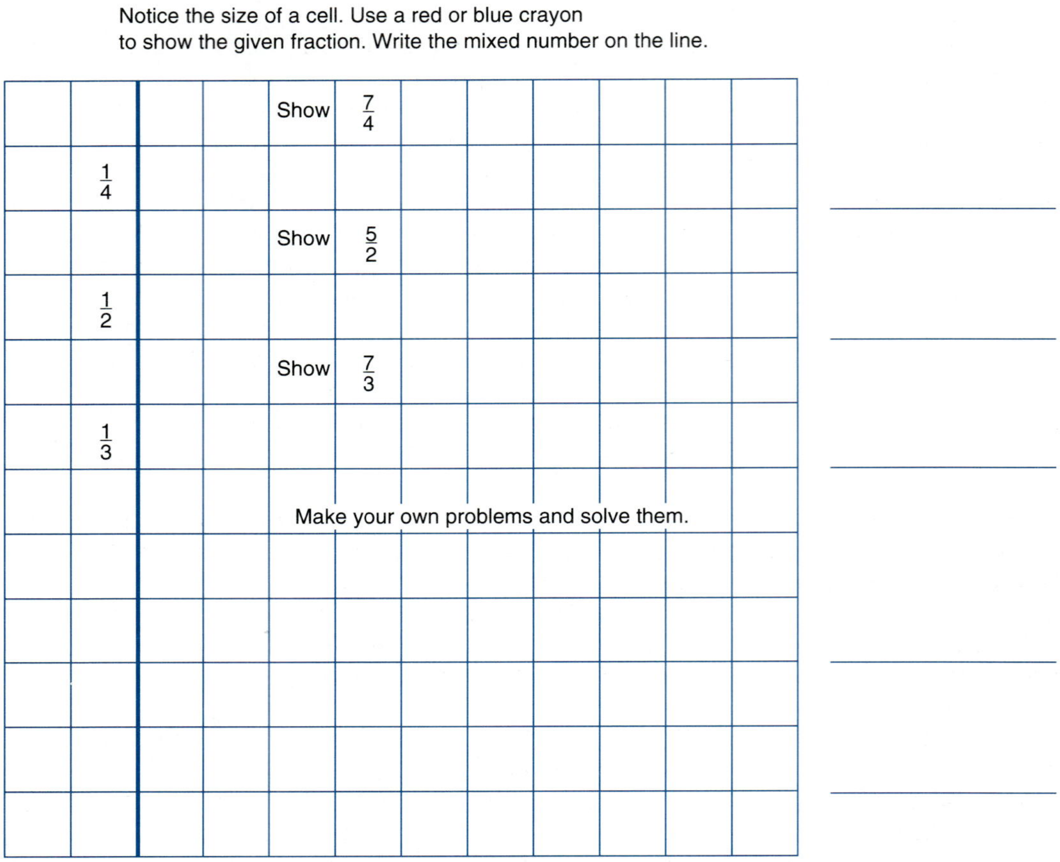

FIGURE 9.10 Activity Sheet for Renaming Improper Fractions using Grid Paper

ing fraction words helps to understand our rule. Write a few sentences to explain your thinking."

A class discussion follows students' completion of the worksheet. The discussion gives students opportunities to explain why denominator words can help understand the rule. To emphasize that words or symbols can be used in addition or subtraction with fractions, each example can be rewritten with symbols and the similarities between the two forms discussed.

Assign practice activities. These should include story and number problems. The story problems should involve different types of problems (see Box 5.1 for types of problems). Encourage students to estimate. After solving problems, students discuss their solutions and the reasonableness of their answers.

Sequence of Instruction for Algorithms for Addition and Subtraction with Unlike Fractions

Addition and subtraction with unlike fractions are introduced when children can add and subtract like fractions and explain in their own words the reasons for the rule. (The numerators are added because they give the number of parts; the denominators are not added because they give the size of the parts.) The instructional sequence assumes that learners have such knowledge.

Introduce the Idea of a Least Common Denominator. Give children a worksheet with problems such as $\frac{1}{2} + \frac{1}{4} = N$, $\frac{3}{4} - \frac{1}{8} = N$, and $\frac{1}{6} + \frac{2}{3} = N$. (Note that examples have sums less than 1 and that the denominator of one fraction is a multiple of the other.) Say, "Study these problems for a few minutes. Think what you know that could help you find the solutions. Choose one or more problems to solve. You can think the answers or use materials." After children have had time to study the problems and solve at least one problem, have them report their solutions and discuss their ideas about how to solve them. During the discussion, students should express the idea that the denominators must be the same to add or subtract the fractions. If students do not indicate that they realize the denominators must be the same to add or subtract fractions, ask, "What did we learn about adding like fractions that should help us with unlike fractions?" Tell students that when denominators are the same, they are called *common denominators* and the smallest common denominators possible are called *least common denominators.* Give learners examples of common and least common denominators, have them discuss the differences, and ask them to give examples. Tell children that in a few days they will study finding least common denominators so that they can easily add and subtract unlike fractions.

Develop the Rule for Finding Equivalent Fractions. The study of common denominators involves knowing how to determine equivalent fractions. Use the records learners made when studying equivalent fractions with materials (Activities 8.28 and 9.7), or assign a similar activity. Ask learners to observe a pattern in the items in the activity and induce the rule for finding equivalent fractions. Have them write up their observations. Have the class discuss their write-ups.

An alternate procedure is for students to fold paper to show halves, fourths, and eighths and look for a pattern useful for finding equivalent fractions. Help students recognize that both the numerator and denominator of a fraction are doubled or increased the same number of times to give an equivalent fraction.

If pupils do not recognize the pattern, say, "Look at $\frac{1}{2}$ and $\frac{2}{4}$. How are they related? What can you do to rename $\frac{1}{2}$ as $\frac{2}{4}$?" Repeat with other pairs of fractions. Also include examples of renaming from higher to lower terms. Continue the discussion until the pattern is evident and students state the rule: multiply (or divide) the numerator and denominator of a fraction by the same number to obtain an equivalent fraction. (Avoid use of the word "reduce" as it carries the connotation of "make smaller." Teach the word "rename" or the phrase "find an equivalent fraction.")

After children write the rule, have them use it to find equivalent fractions. They can share their completed work with a partner, discussing how they arrived at their answers.

To help children understand the mathematics underlying the rule, say, "What is the whole-number name for $\frac{4}{4}$, $\frac{2}{2}$, and $\frac{3}{3}$? Why can you multiply a fraction by $\frac{4}{4}$ to get an equivalent fraction?" (Multiplying a fraction by $\frac{4}{4}$ is to multiply by 1, which does not change its value.) If students cannot carry out this reasoning, use cognitive modeling to help them understand the sense of the rule.

Learn to Find Missing Terms in Expressions. Give children problems such as $\frac{1}{2} = \frac{N}{6}$ and $\frac{2}{3} = \frac{N}{6}$. Tell them to use what they know to find the answers and think of a rule. Some will have memorized equivalent fractions and can readily fill in missing terms. However, they also need to learn the rule: To find the missing numerator, divide the given denominators. Use the quotient as a factor with the given numerator to find the missing term.

Students may be helped to construct the rule by making a record of their thinking as they solve the problem of finding a missing term. Or they may discover the rule as they answer questions such as: "What part of the equivalent fraction is given?" "How was the denominator found? How can you think to find that number? Would that number help find the missing numerator? Why?" Their answers to questions such as these should help students examine the sense of the rule as well as to state it.

If no one finds a pattern in response to your questioning, use cognitive modeling, that is, say your thoughts out loud. Say with the example $\frac{1}{2} = \frac{N}{6}$, "To find the missing number, I need to know what to multiply 1 by; oh, that's the same as what I multiply 2 by to get 6. Divide 6 by 2 to get 3. Now, I can find 3×1 to get the missing term." Children then explain what they observed, model finding a missing term for one another, explain the sense of the steps, and state the rule. Post the rule on a chart. After they construct the rule, students use practice worksheets. They can explain how they thought as they used the rule to find missing numerators.

Later problems with missing denominators are introduced, such as $\frac{4}{5} = \frac{8}{N}$, $\frac{2}{3} = \frac{4}{N}$. Pupils may be able to solve these problems by adapting the rule for finding missing numerators. If not, use questions to help them see the connection between finding missing numerators and finding missing denominators, or use cognitive modeling to help them learn to find missing denominators.

Develop Rules to Find a Least Common Denominator for Two Fractions. Give students an activity sheet with pairs of fractions such as $\frac{1}{2}, \frac{1}{6}; \frac{1}{4}, \frac{3}{8}; \frac{1}{5}, \frac{2}{10}; \frac{1}{3}, \frac{5}{12}$, one of which has a denominator that is a multiple of the other. Ask them to study the problems and to decide how to rename one fraction so that both fractions will have the same denominator. As they exchange ideas regarding how to do this, questions to be asked can include: "How did you decide to multiply 2 by 3? What made you think of 3?" Work with the examples and your questions should help them state the rule: Notice if one denominator is a multiple of the other. If so, divide the larger denominator by the smaller denominator to find the number to use as a factor with the smaller denominator to obtain the least common denominator of the two fractions. Begin a chart of rules for finding common denominators. Follow up with practice using the rule.

The next lesson in the sequence teaches another rule: If the larger denominator is not divisible by the smaller denominator, multiply the larger denominator by 2, 3, 4, . . . , until a product is found that is divisible by both denominators. This is the least common denominator. This rule can probably best be taught by cognitive modeling. As you complete an example, tell what is in your mind. For example, say, when modeling to find the least common denominator for $\frac{5}{8}$ and $\frac{1}{6}$, "I am supposed to find the least common denominator. Oh, I can't divide 8 by 6. I'll multiply 8 by 2 to find out if 16 is divisible by 6. No. Well, I'll try 3 x 8. Yes, 24 is divisible by 6 and by 8." Ask students to discuss what you did to find the least common denominator. Repeat cognitive modeling with other examples. As they explain what they noticed, write important steps they observed on the chart made earlier. Soon, have children volunteer to model talking their thoughts when finding a least common denominator. Next, have children in pairs tell each other how to find least common denominators. Circulate to help those who have difficulty. A few practice worksheets follow the introduction to finding least common denominators.

An alternate rule is to multiply the denominators to find a common denominator. Some children will find this rule easy to use and should be encouraged to use it. It can be introduced by saying, "Think about multiplying the denominators to find a common denominator. In your groups try out this plan on yesterday's problems, decide if it is useful, and if so, make a rule." Later, learners think about when the rule gives a least common denominator. (When the numbers have no common factors.)

Rename Two Fractions So They Have a Least Common Denominator.

1. Review finding least common denominators when one fraction is a multiple of the other or when a least common multiple must be found. Have students find least common denominators for a few pairs of fractions.
2. Ask learners to recall how to find missing terms. Help students use this learning to rename a fraction in a pair after a least common denominator is found. As a class they complete items such as (answers are in parentheses):

   $\frac{1}{2}, \frac{1}{4}$ $\quad$ $(\frac{N}{4}, \frac{1}{4})$ $\quad$ $(\frac{2}{4}, \frac{1}{4})$

   With some learners, instruction can begin with "3."

3. Give problems with the directions to find equivalent fractions with least common denominators for pairs of numbers, saying, "Use what you know to give equivalent fractions so that the fractions in each pair have least common denominators: $\frac{2}{3}$, $\frac{1}{6}$; $\frac{2}{5}$, $\frac{3}{10}$; $\frac{1}{3}$, $\frac{1}{2}$." When they finish, have students share their solutions and their thinking to find the solutions. Ask them to solve a few more while you monitor their work. (Model if no student solves the problems.)
4. Follow up with practice and a discussion of how pupils thought as they completed worksheets.

Use Knowledge of Least Common Denominators to Add or Subtract Unlike Fractions. Give children story or number problems with unlike fractions that can be solved by addition or subtraction. Have them work in groups to solve the problems. Then, discuss their work. If they experience difficulties that cannot be overcome by small-group discussion, call the class together, and write on the overhead or chalkboard: "To help you solve these problems, think about (1) our rule for adding or subtracting fractions with like denominators; and (2) what we learned about renaming fractions so that they have least common denominators." Point out the rules posted earlier. Then students return to their groups and the task of solving the problems.

When children have solved the problems, they discuss solutions and procedures. The steps in the procedure are recorded and posted for students' use:

To Add or Subtract Unlike Fractions:

1. Find least common denominators.
2. Rename fractions so they have least common denominators.
3. Add or subtract the fractions.
4. Check the reasonableness of your answer. Does it make sense?

At this time renaming in lowest terms is not introduced. Because they have had experience with equivalent fractions, renaming in lowest terms can be introduced when children have developed skill in using the algorithms for addition and subtraction with fractions.

Develop Algorithms for Mixed Numbers in Sums or Minuends. Give addition problems that involve sums that are improper fractions, for example, $\frac{5}{6} + \frac{3}{4} = N$. When they finish, if any child has renamed the improper fraction as a mixed number, have him or her explain the procedure to the class. Use the explanation as the basis for the development of the rule. Otherwise, say, "Many times we rename an improper fraction as a mixed number. Let's figure out how to do this." (Activities gave children experiences with renaming, but not with renaming procedures.)

To enable them to develop procedures for renaming improper fractions as mixed numbers, have them examine their records from earlier work (Activity 9.10 or Activity 9.11). Ask them to use their records to construct the rule for renaming an improper fraction as a mixed number: Divide the numbers, and write the remainder as a fraction (e.g., $\frac{9}{2} = 4\frac{1}{2}$). They can verify their rule using number lines or counting. (It is best to use the partitive interpretation of division for this activity.) They can also reason that division is a sensible approach. If they are unable to develop the rule, model the procedure, and have students explain your modeling to develop the rule.

Children will probably have no difficulty with subtraction problems, such as $4\frac{2}{3} - \frac{1}{3} = N$, and can solve them in groups and report on their work with no difficulties. The discussion will emphasize the standard algorithm.

Begin instruction of subtraction problems with renaming (for example, $3\frac{1}{4} - 1\frac{1}{2} = N$) by assigning story problems for children to solve using materials. When they complete their work, have children share their solutions and procedures for solution. The discussion should stress the reasonableness of the solutions.

Children often invent alternative algorithms (Mack, 1990) for such subtraction problems and prefer them to the standard algorithm. If they invent alternative procedures, give children opportunities to explain their alternative approaches and why they make sense. Students need to learn that they can use an alternate procedure only if it is established that it is valid. You help the inventor determine its validity. (An example of one alternative algorithm for $3\frac{1}{4} - 1\frac{1}{2} = N$ is $3 - 1 = 2$; subtract $\frac{1}{2}$ from 2, that is, $1\frac{1}{2}$; $1\frac{1}{2} + \frac{1}{4} = 1\frac{3}{4}$.)

As children should also have knowledge of the renaming procedure, if no group solves the problem using renaming, use cognitive modeling followed by discussion to introduce the standard algorithm: In subtraction with mixed numbers, when the fraction in the minuend is less than the fraction in the subtrahend, rename the minuend by subtracting 1 from the whole number, rename the 1 as an equivalent fraction with the same denominator as the minuend fraction, add it to the fraction in the minuend, find the least common denominator, and subtract. For example,

$$\begin{array}{rcrcr} 3\frac{1}{4} & = & 2+\frac{4}{4}+\frac{1}{4} & = & 2\frac{5}{4} \\ -1\frac{1}{2} & = & -1\frac{1}{2} & = & -1\frac{2}{4} \\ \hline & & & & 1\frac{3}{4} \end{array}$$

(Do you prefer this algorithm or the alternative one?)

Children should use the standard algorithm in a few examples to understand the procedure. They can talk through the procedure to understand it. Help them examine the similarities and differences between subtraction with fractions and with whole numbers. Emphasize the difference between renaming in base ten with whole numbers and renaming fractions as equivalent fractions. In later problem solving, learners should use whichever algorithm makes sense to them—the standard or valid invented algorithm.

Both story and number problems are used in activity sheets. Remind children to think about the reasonableness of each solution by estimating as they solve the problem and to check each solution with the meaning of the problem.

Extending Understanding of Addition and Subtraction Algorithms

When children can solve problems involving addition and subtraction with like and unlike fractions, activities that challenge them to think creatively about the operations can be used. Six such activities are described here.

ACTIVITY 9.12
Make a Sum ***(Behr, Wachsmuth, and Post, 1985).***

The activity sheet's directions are: Write two addition number problems for each of the following: (1) answers less than $\frac{1}{2}$; (2) answers less than 1; and (3) answers between 1 and 2.

ACTIVITY 9.13
Numbers for Sums.

This activity is similar to 9.12, except that children are given fractions to use. The directions are: Use these fractions: $\frac{1}{2}, \frac{1}{3}, \frac{1}{4}, \frac{1}{5}, \frac{1}{6}, \frac{1}{8}, \frac{2}{3}, \frac{3}{4}, \frac{4}{5}, \frac{5}{6}$, and $\frac{7}{8}$. (1) Write a number problem for addition or subtraction with two fractions you choose so that the answer is between $\frac{1}{2}$ and 1; (2) choose other fractions and write another problem so that the answer is between 1 and 2; (3) choose other fractions to use to write one more problem for each of (1) and (2).

ACTIVITY 9.14
Commutative Property for Addition.

Write a list of problems that contain sums and their commuted forms. For example:

$$\tfrac{2}{3} + \tfrac{1}{2} = N \qquad \tfrac{2}{5} + \tfrac{1}{2} = N$$
$$\tfrac{1}{6} + \tfrac{1}{3} = N \qquad \tfrac{1}{3} + \tfrac{1}{6} = N$$
$$\tfrac{1}{2} + \tfrac{2}{3} = N \qquad \tfrac{1}{2} + \tfrac{2}{5} = N$$

Ask children to solve the problems and find a pattern in the math sentences. Discuss the pattern. Question learners so that they realize that the order rule applies to addition with fractions.

ACTIVITY 9.15
Write Problems.

Ask children to write story problems for addition and subtraction with fractions. They can write these problems on cards with answers on answer cards. Make a card file of the problems, and give several problem cards to different children or groups. The name of the writer of the problem should be on the card.

ACTIVITY 9.16
Fraction Magic Squares.

Magic squares require children to use both addition and subtraction to complete the square (Figure 9.11). Some children will enjoy making fraction magic squares.

ACTIVITY 9.17
Designs for Addition.

This activity enables students to write addition sentences for designs. The directions are: Use dots to outline a square region. Use more than four dots to outline the region. The square region represents a unit. Use the unit with two different colored crayons to show an addition sentence with fractions. Then write an addition sentence that describes your work (Figure 9.12). Have children share their work and repeat the activity two or three times, looking for as many different ways as possible to show addition sentences. Have them read the designs as subtraction sentences also. The activity can be adapted for triangle grid paper.

LEARNING MULTIPLICATION AND DIVISION WITH FRACTIONS

Multiplication and division are discussed in separate parts of this section because one meaning of multiplication with fractions differs from the meaning of multiplication with whole numbers and therefore needs special emphasis in instruction.

$1\frac{1}{4}$		$\frac{3}{4}$
	$1\frac{1}{2}$	
$2\frac{1}{4}$		$1\frac{3}{4}$

$1\frac{1}{2}$		$\frac{1}{2}$
	$1\frac{1}{4}$	
2		1

FIGURE 9.11 Fraction Magic Squares

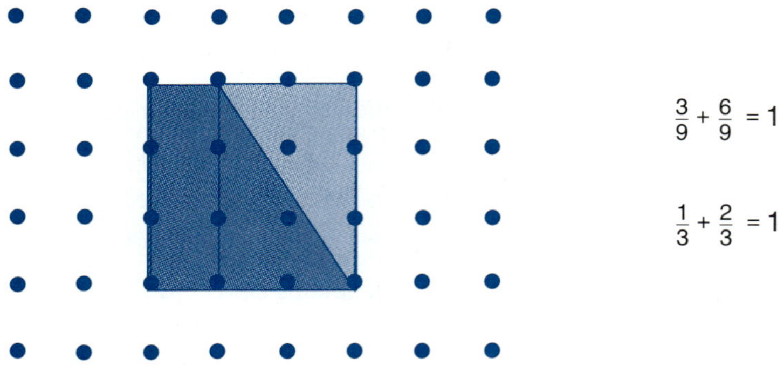

FIGURE 9.12 Dot Paper Model for Addition with Fractions

Multiplication with Fractions

Multiplication with fractions has two meanings: repeated addition as with whole numbers (e.g., $4 \times \frac{1}{2}$, or 4 one-halves) and the "of" meaning (e.g., $\frac{1}{2} \times \frac{1}{4}$, or one-half of one-fourth). The first meaning is not difficult for children to understand because of its similarity to multiplication with whole numbers. It is introduced first, and the algorithm is developed from work with this meaning. The second meaning often causes confusion because the concept involves dividing and multiplying ($\frac{1}{3} \times \frac{1}{4}$ means $(\frac{1}{4} \div 3) \times 1$; $\frac{2}{3} \times \frac{1}{4}$ means $(\frac{1}{4} \div 3) \times 2$.

The sequence of instruction begins with teaching the meaning and algorithm for the repeated addition interpretation and continues with teaching the finding-one-or-more-parts meaning and relating the algorithm to this meaning (Kroll and Yabe, 1987). Both meanings are introduced with story problems and number problems written with words. Children solve these problems with diagrams, materials, or repeated addition and consider the reasonableness of their solutions. When they can solve problems with materials, they write math sentences and consider how multiplication with fractions is like or unlike multiplication with whole numbers. In subsequent lessons they develop the algorithm for multiplication with fractions.

Activities for Learning Multiplication with Fractions: Repeated Addition Interpretation

ACTIVITY 9.18
Solving Multiplication Story Problems.

Story and number problems for the repeated addition interpretation of multiplication with fractions give children an intuitive knowledge of multiplication with fractions (Figure 9.13). Three examples of such problems are:

1. The 4 boys in the Jacobs family each ate $\frac{1}{4}$ of a pie. How much pie was eaten?
2. Jane eats $\frac{1}{2}$ a grapefruit each morning. How many grapefruit does she eat in the 7 days of a week?
3. Sung drinks $\frac{1}{4}$ quart of milk each meal. How much does he drink in his three daily meals?

In another lesson number problems written in words are used. Problem examples are:

1. What number equals four one-halves (Figure 9.14)?
2. What number equals two two-fifths?
3. Five one-halves equals what number?

The procedure is similar to that for beginning work with addition and subtraction with fractions: Problems are assigned and directions given to find solutions using any method useful for finding solutions and to think if the answers are sensible.

John walks $\frac{3}{4}$ of a mile to school each morning. He gets a ride back at the end of the school day. He decided to figure out how far he walked in the 5 school days each week.

$$\frac{3}{4} + \frac{3}{4} + \frac{3}{4} + \frac{3}{4} + \frac{3}{4} = \frac{15}{4} = 3\frac{3}{4} \text{ miles}$$

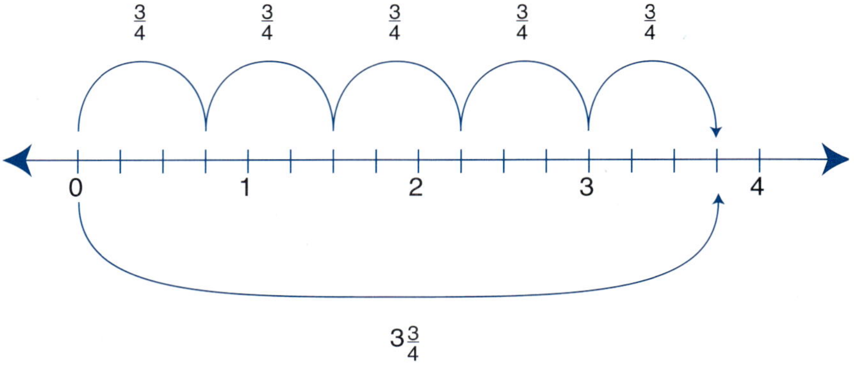

FIGURE 9.13 Story Problem with Solutions for Repeated Addition Interpretation of Multiplication with Fractions

Individuals or groups find solutions, and the class discusses the groups' solutions. In subsequent lessons, other problems are assigned and children are introduced to the use of different materials to represent solutions.

ACTIVITY 9.19
Solving Multiplication Problems Using Different Materials or Approaches.

Children are asked to use materials different from those they chose to use previously to find solutions to story or number problems. For example, if they used fraction disks, they could be asked to use number lines. They experiment with these materials and share their work. If children do not succeed in using the material you suggest, you can use cognitive modeling to introduce using the material to solve problems.

ACTIVITY 9.20
Understanding that the Operation Is Multiplication.

When children can use different materials to solve multiplication problems that involve the repeated addition interpretation, they relate the meaning of multiplication with fractions to multiplication with whole numbers. They use the records they made when completing earlier assignments, or they use the solutions for problems assigned for the lesson. When they have reported their solutions, learners are asked to write the math sentences that would go with the problems. If they use the multiplication sign in their math sentences, ask why they decided that the problems were multiplication. The class then discusses how multiplication with fractions is like multiplication with whole numbers (repeated addition).

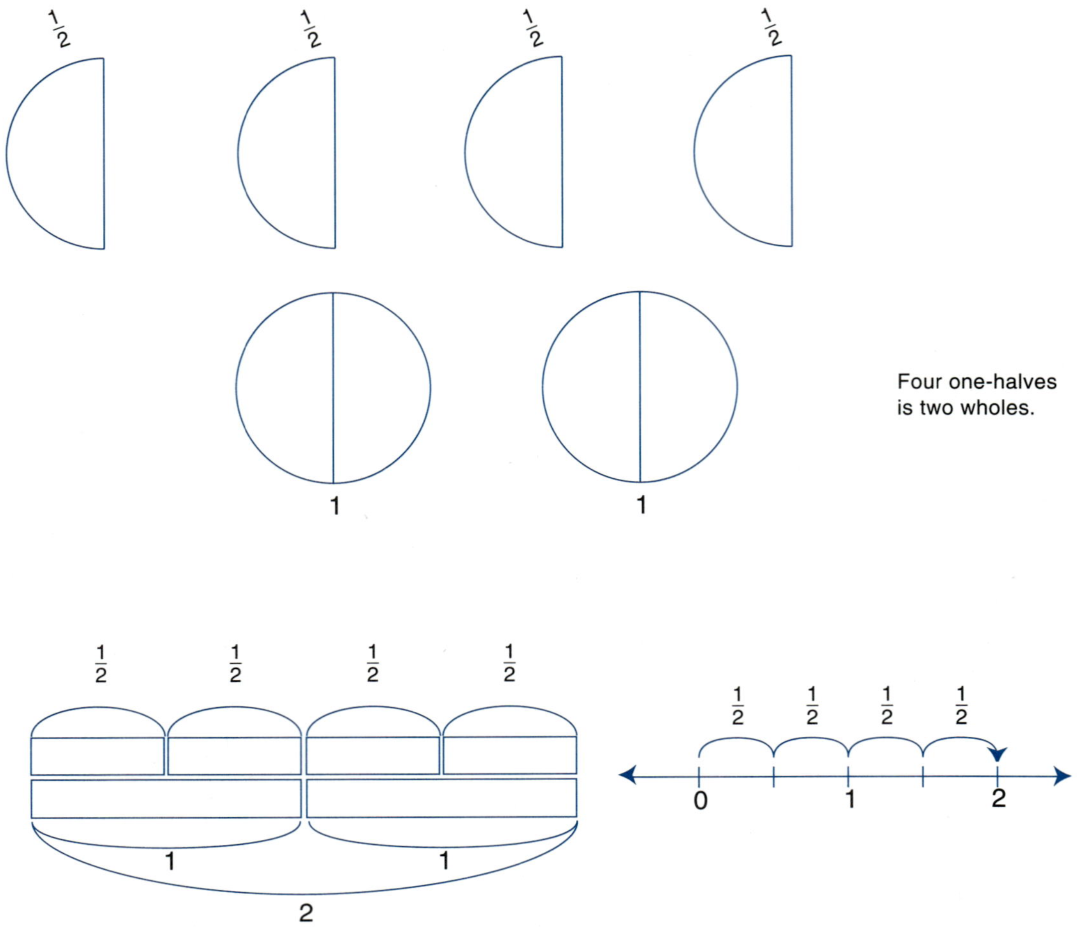

FIGURE 9.14 Models for Repeated Addition Interpretation of Multiplication with Fractions

Reader Activity 9.2

Write four story problems. One factor in the math sentences for solving these problems is a fraction and the other a fraction or a whole number. Draw diagrams to show the solutions.

If they used repeated addition in their math sentences (e.g., $\frac{1}{4} + \frac{1}{4} + \frac{1}{4} = \frac{3}{4}$), say, "Think about 3 + 3 + 3 + 3 = 12. What other operation can you use to think about 4 threes?" Continue with questions to help pupils relate multiplication with whole numbers to multiplication with fractions using the repeated addition idea.

Next, on the overhead write math sentences for multiplication with fractions using the repeated addition meaning. (*Note:* In multiplication with fractions interpreted as repeated addition, the first factor is always a whole number.) Ask children to read the sentences and tell what each means.

ACTIVITY 9.21
Estimation Decision Making.

Use an activity sheet with statements such as the following for children to consider. After time for decision making, members of the class give reasons for agreeing or disagreeing with the answers. Learning is enhanced if children disagree and need to convince their peers of the reasonableness of their answers.

1. Five one-fourths is less than one. Agree or Disagree
2. Seven one-halves is more than three. Agree or Disagree

3. Nine three-fourths is about seven. Agree or Disagree
4. Eleven one-sixths is more than three. Agree or Disagree

ACTIVITY 9.22
Developing the Algorithm for Multiplication with Fractions.

Assign four problems such as:

1. $3 \times \frac{1}{4} = N$
2. $2 \times \frac{1}{3} = N$
3. $3 \times \frac{2}{8} = N$
4. $2 \times \frac{2}{6} = N$

Have children solve the problems using methods of their choice. Have them share their solutions, making records on the overhead or chalkboard. Then, have them work in groups or individually and study their solutions to find patterns that would help them write a rule. In my experience, this is not difficult for children, and they quickly see the pattern and make the rule: multiply the numerators and multiply the denominators of the fractions to find their product.

When children agree on the rule, have them use it to solve problems they previously solved using materials. Compare the solutions using the rule and materials.

Some practice solving number problems with the rule will be necessary. However, this rule seems to be learned easily (Cramer and Bezuk, 1991). Children can write problems to grasp the meaning of multiplication with fractions interpreted as repeated addition.

Extending Understanding of Multiplication with Fractions

When children understand multiplication with fractions using the repeated addition interpretation and the algorithm for solving fraction multiplication problems, they extend their understanding by studying the "of" interpretation of multiplication with fractions. After they demonstrate success in using materials to solve such problems, they relate the algorithm to this interpretation. They also learn multiplication with mixed numbers, estimate products, relate some multiplication with fraction problems to whole-number division problems, and solve two-step problems. The activities in this part are examples of activities for these learnings.

ACTIVITY 9.23
Problems for the "of" Interpretation of Multiplication with Fractions.

Assign problems that initially involve part or parts of a part and later a part or parts of a set. Learners should think about the reasonableness of their solutions. Figure 9.15 shows solutions for the following problems.

1. Mother had $\frac{1}{2}$ of a pizza left after supper. She ate $\frac{1}{4}$ of what was left before she went to bed. How much of the pizza did she eat? (Part of a part.)
2. Aunt May and Aunt Julie are making doll clothes to sell at the School Bazaar. Aunt May has $\frac{3}{4}$ of a yard of lace to use for trim. She gave Aunt Julie $\frac{1}{2}$ of her lace. How much of a yard did she give Aunt Julie? (Part of a part.)
3. Mr. Haskell has $\frac{1}{4}$ of an acre for his garden. He plants $\frac{2}{3}$ of his garden in tomatoes. How much of an acre is in tomatoes? (Parts of a part.)

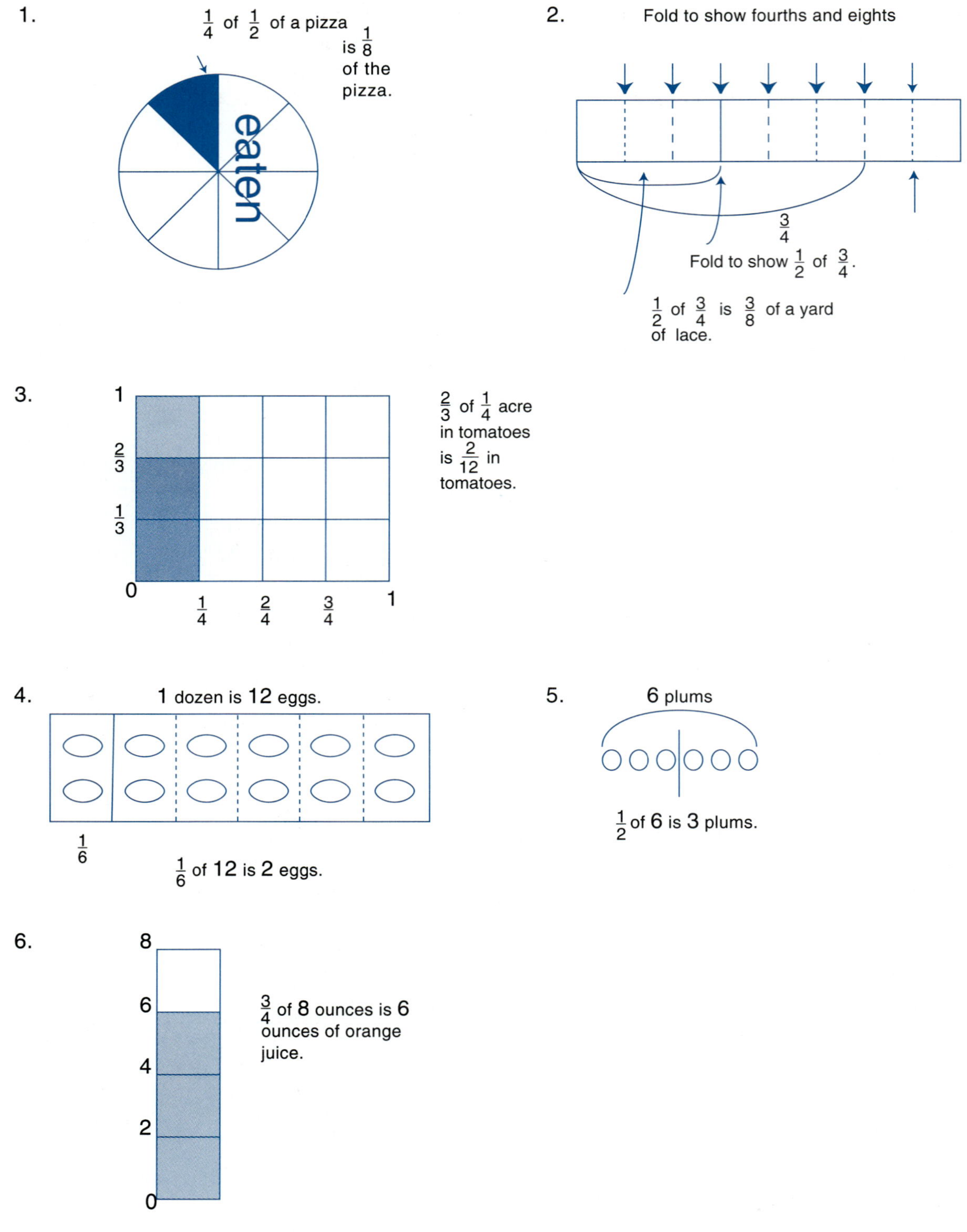

FIGURE 9.15 Solutions for "of" Interpretation of Multiplication-with-Fractions Problems

4. Marc's recipe for custard calls for $\frac{1}{6}$ of a dozen eggs. How many eggs will he need? (Part of a set.)

5. Gina has eaten $\frac{1}{2}$ of the six plums she brought for her lunch. How many has she eaten? (Part of a set.)

6. Sarah drank $\frac{3}{4}$ of her 8-ounce can of orange juice. How many ounces did she drink? (Parts of a set.)

Students solve the problems individually or in groups. Then, they share their strategies and solutions, explaining how they used materials to find solutions. Circular and rectangular regions, grid paper, and paper-folding models are used to find part(s) of a part, and counters or rectangular regions are used to find part(s) of a set. Cognitive modeling is used to introduce a model if pupils do not use it as they solve problems. In all work with the "of" interpretation of multiplication with fractions, students must show the whole because the product is named in terms of parts of a whole.

For some lessons, number problems on activity sheets should be written in words. The use of words can help students understand fraction multiplication problems. Examples of problems given in words are:

1. What number equals one-fifth of one-half? (Part of a part.)
2. What number equals three-fourths of one-half? (Parts of a part.)
3. What number equals one-half of eight? (Part of a set.)
4. What number equals two-thirds of twelve? (Parts of a set.)

ACTIVITY 9.24
Using the Multiplication with Fractions Rule.

When children can solve problems involving the "of" interpretation of multiplication using materials, they learn to use the rule for multiplication with fractions that they developed when studying the repeated addition interpretation of fraction multiplication. Assign four number problems with both factors fractions, but some using words and some symbols (e.g., two-thirds of one-fourth or $\frac{2}{3}$ of $\frac{1}{4}$). Have them estimate the product as less or greater than 1 and find solutions any way they wish. Tell them to study the solutions, look for patterns in the solutions, and think how to write math sentences for the problems using fractions. (*Note:* In a math sentence used to solve an "of" interpretation of multiplication with fractions problem, the first factor is a fraction.)

As they study the solutions, it is expected that some learners will notice that: (1) each solution requires multiplying the numerators and denominators to find the product; (2) this procedure is the rule for multiplication with fractions; (3) therefore, these must be multiplication problems; and (4) "of" in sentences with fractions means to multiply.

Give groups plenty of time to think about how to write and interpret the assigned math sentences. As you circulate, if pupils need guidance, ask questions related to the four ideas noted. For example, ask, "How did you get your solution? What operation could you use? Is that like a rule you know? Why? What does the word 'of' tell you?" When one or more groups reach the conclusion that these are multiplication problems, have them share their thinking.

In follow-up lessons, ask children to write math sentences for problems, estimate solutions, solve the problems, and think about the reasonableness of their solutions. Discuss their solutions and thinking to solve the problems. Guide students to understand that both division and multiplication are involved in "of" multiplication with fractions. Examining the first factor in a fraction multiplication math sentence and recalling that the bar means divide can help students realize that they are dividing as well as multiplying (e.g., $\frac{2}{5} \times 10 = (10 \div 5) \times 2$).

In later lessons include multiplication problems involving both interpretations. Question learners so that they develop the idea that repeatedly adding a fraction or taking a part or parts gives a product smaller than one or both factors. This idea develops slowly, and students should study many situations involving multiplication with fractions. Continue to have pupils use materials and diagrams, and express how their solutions relate to the meanings of multiplication with fractions.

ACTIVITY 9.25
Multiplication Involving Mixed Numbers.

To solve multiplication problems involving mixed numbers when only one factor is a mixed number, the computation can be carried out with a whole number and a fraction (e.g., $\frac{1}{3} \times 3\frac{1}{2} = (\frac{1}{3} \times 3) + (\frac{1}{3} \times \frac{1}{2}) = 1 + \frac{1}{6} = 1\frac{1}{6}$). Learners should relate what they know about multiplication with whole numbers and fractions to solve problems of this type.

When both factors are mixed numbers, the mixed numbers are renamed as improper fractions (e.g., $2\frac{2}{3} \times 4\frac{1}{2} = \frac{8}{3} \times \frac{9}{2} = \frac{72}{6} = 12$). Renaming improper fractions is introduced before multiplication with both factors mixed numbers. Work with materials enables students to develop solutions to use to develop a rule for renaming an improper fraction as a mixed number. (See activity sheet in Figure 9.16 and possible learner solution.)

If groups cannot find a pattern from examining their solutions, use cognitive modeling to introduce the rule: Add the product of the denominator times the whole number to the numerator of the fraction to obtain the numerator of the improper fraction and retain the denominator of the given fraction. Students should then explain why the rule makes sense (for example, they could explain, "It is a shortcut for making and solving an addition problem. You can rename the whole number and add the whole number and the fraction in one step"). Children should practice renaming mixed numbers as improper fractions before beginning multiplication with both factors mixed numbers.

When beginning work with multiplication when both factors are mixed numbers, both story and number problems are used. Examples are:

1. Molly bought a grass mat for her patio. It was $1\frac{1}{2}$ meters by $2\frac{1}{2}$ meters. How many square meters did it cover?
2. June noticed that Sunny Drug Store developed her film into prints $3\frac{3}{4}$ by $4\frac{1}{2}$ inches and Hill Top Super Market's prints were $3\frac{1}{2}$ by $4\frac{3}{4}$ inches. Which prints were larger?
3. What number equals $5\frac{1}{2} \times 6\frac{2}{3}$?
4. What number equals $8\frac{1}{4} \times 2\frac{1}{6}$?

As you circulate while students are working on the problems, you can give guidance by saying, "What is the fraction name for $1\frac{1}{2}$? For $2\frac{1}{2}$? How does knowing about improper fractions help you use your rule for multiplication with fractions? Does your solution make sense? How could you show a solution on grid paper (Figure 9.17)?" When some have solved the problems, have them share their ideas.

If the groups have difficulties getting started, use cognitive modeling to teach multiplying mixed numbers by using improper fractions for the mixed numbers. Children should then model the procedure themselves.

Students in grade 6 or in middle school use algorithms for multiplication with fractions and mixed numbers. However, even in these grades students should work with materials at some time to solve or check multiplication problems, because work with materials helps extend understanding.

ACTIVITY 9.26
Match Estimates Game.

Make 35 problem cards for four players. The cards give problems such as $\frac{1}{2} \times 3$, $\frac{3}{4} \times 8$, $\frac{4}{5} \times 2$, or $\frac{1}{3} \times 9$. Each player gets 7 cards and in turn draws a card from a stack of cards in the middle of the playing area. The objective of the game is to match two cards, each with an estimated solution less than 2 or greater than 2. Pairs are laid aside. When a player is out of cards, the player with the most pairs is the winner. He or she then states which of his or her pairs gives an estimate less than 2 and which

Solve using number lines, grid paper, fraction disks, or fraction bars, or think the solution.

$2\frac{1}{2} = \frac{N}{2}$ $3\frac{1}{3} = \frac{N}{3}$

$6\frac{1}{2} = \frac{N}{2}$ $4\frac{1}{6} = \frac{N}{6}$

Possible Solutions of Learners

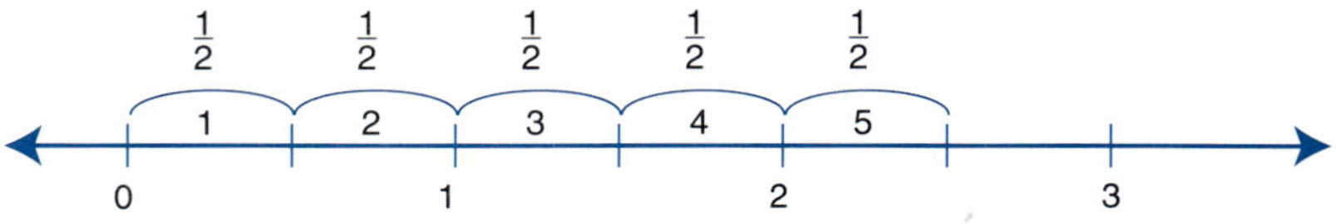

$2\frac{1}{2} = \frac{5}{2}$

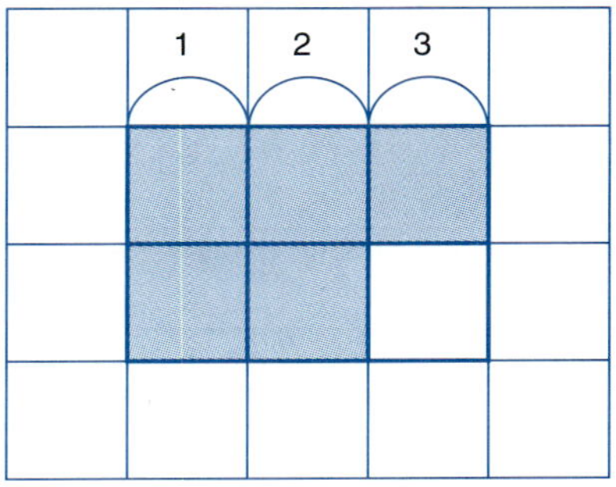

$1 = \frac{2}{2}$

$2\frac{1}{2} = \frac{5}{2}$

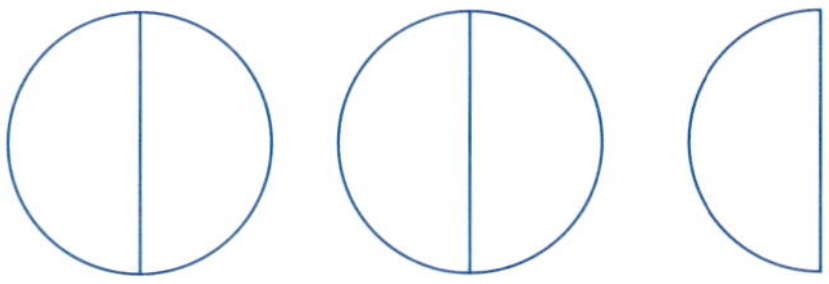

$2\frac{1}{2} = \frac{5}{2}$

Thinking: 1 whole is 2 halves; 2 wholes is 4 halves; 1 more half is $\frac{5}{2}$. $2\frac{1}{2} = \frac{5}{2}$

FIGURE 9.16 Activity Sheet for Renaming Mixed Numbers with Possible Student Solutions

gives an estimate greater than 2. The other players must agree. If they do not, and someone "proves" the winner is wrong, there is no winner.

ACTIVITY 9.27
Thinking about "of" Multiplication Problems.

This activity sheet helps children review the "of" language and develop meaning to use to relate multiplication and division in later lessons. Students are to find pairs of

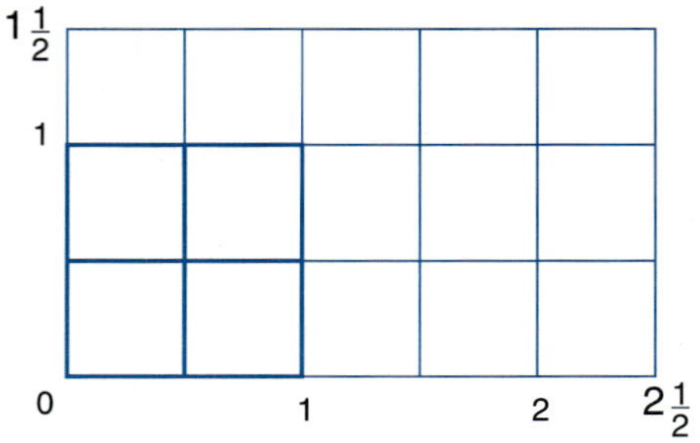

FIGURE 9.17 Grid Paper Solution for Mixed Number Multiplication

$1 = \frac{4}{4}$

$1\frac{1}{2} \times 2\frac{1}{2} = \frac{15}{4} = 3\frac{3}{4}$ Square meters

phrases in the following list that mean the same. The directions can suggest using materials to find the phrases that go together.

1. One-half of four
2. Nine divided by three
3. One-sixth of twelve
4. One-third of nine
5. Twelve divided by six
6. Eight divided by four
7. One-fourth of eight
8. Four divided by two

In a following lesson, children can be asked to write math sentences for the pairs that go together. They share the thinking they used to complete the task.

ACTIVITY 9.28
Estimating Challenge.

A worksheet for problems such as the following will provide challenge for children who can think creatively and flexibly.

1. Give the math sentences for three products that are each less than $\frac{1}{2}$.
2. Give the math sentences for three products that are greater than 1 but less than 4. Use at least one fraction in each sentence.
3. Write a math sentence for a product that is about 1, about 2, about 3, and about 4. (You will have four sentences.) Use at least one fraction in each sentence.

Reader Activity 9.3

Write two math sentences for each of (1) and (2) and four for (3) in Activity 9.28. React to the activity for children in terms of your work.

ACTIVITY 9.29
Practice with More than One Operation.

Practice now includes story problems involving addition, subtraction, and multiplication with fractions. Children write math sentences and estimate to determine the reasonableness of solutions.

ACTIVITY 9.30
The Commutative Property.

Children can learn about the commutative property for multiplication with fractions (e.g., $\frac{2}{3} \times \frac{3}{4} = \frac{3}{4} \times \frac{2}{3}$) by engaging in different activities. Two examples of activities are:

1. Have children find answers to six number problems such that in the assignment one-half of the problems are the commuted form of the other half. During the discussion ask children what they notice about the problems, and help them relate changing the order of factors in multiplication with whole numbers to changing the order of factors in multiplication with fractions.
2. Assign one-half of the class six number problems and the other half of the class the commuted form of these problems. Have them share their work on the overhead. Ask, "What do you notice about these answers? Why are some the same? What does that tell you?"

ACTIVITY 9.31
Two-Step Problems.

These problems involve both multiplication and addition with fractions. For example:

1. An introductory box of chocolates has 8 pieces. Jim bought two boxes of candy, one of light chocolates and one of dark chocolates. He ate $\frac{1}{4}$ of the light chocolate pieces on Saturday and $\frac{1}{2}$ of the dark chocolate box on Sunday. How many pieces of candy did he eat that weekend? Did he eat too much candy? Why?
2. Linda was baking cup cakes for the school bake sale. She used $\frac{3}{4}$ dozen eggs for chocolate cup cakes and $\frac{2}{3}$ dozen eggs for banana cup cakes. How many eggs did she use for the cup cakes?

Have students discuss their solutions. Make sure children understand why two computations are needed to solve these problems.

Division with Fractions

The study of division with fractions in the elementary school involves learning two interpretations of the operations and one or two algorithms for solving division problems. The measurement (or repeated subtraction) interpretation involves the question "How many times is x in y?" The partitive interpretation involves an equal-sharing situation. These interpretations for division with fractions are the same as for division with whole numbers.

The measurement interpretation can be used to introduce division with fractions and be stressed throughout instruction (Steiner, 1987; Trafton and Zawojewski, 1984), or the partitive interpretation can be given emphasis (Ott, Snook, and Gibson, 1991). As students should understand both interpretations in order to solve all types of fraction division in real-world problems, this section deals with both interpretations. The sequence for instruction with either interpretation is: (1) develop the algorithm from pupils' work with that interpretation; (2) teach the other interpretation; and (3) help students apply the algorithm to problems involving the second interpretation. Until research demonstrates the superiority of one approach, teachers must choose which interpretation to use in beginning instruction.

The two algorithms for division with fractions are: invert the divisor and multiply ($\frac{1}{2} \div \frac{1}{8} = \frac{1}{2} \times \frac{8}{1} = \frac{8}{2} = 4$) and the common denominator algorithm ($\frac{1}{2} \div \frac{1}{8} = \frac{4}{8} \div \frac{1}{8} = \frac{\frac{4}{1}}{\frac{1}{1}} = 4$). Children usually learn the former. The common denominator algorithm can be taught as an alternative procedure.

The rationale for the invert-and-multiply rule is based on the simplification of complex fractions. For example:

$$\frac{\frac{1}{2}}{\frac{1}{8}} = \frac{\frac{1}{2} \times 8}{\frac{1}{8} \times 8} = \frac{\frac{1}{2} \times 8}{1} = \frac{4}{1} = 4$$

Most children cannot deal with the logic of the simplification of complex fractions and, therefore, instruction stresses a plausible explanation of the rule based on work with materials (Trafton and Zawojewski, 1984).

The common denominator algorithm is the inverse of the algorithm for multiplication, but common denominators are used to obtain a denominator of 1 in the quotient. This algorithm seems reasonable to some learners because of its similarity to the algorithm for multiplication with fractions. However, the extra step, finding a common denominator, makes the invert-and-multiply algorithm easier to use for most children.

Instruction in division with fractions follows a sequence similar to that for multiplication with fractions:

1. Children use materials or diagrams to solve story and number problems to develop an awareness of the meaning of one interpretation of division (measure-

ment or partitive) with fractions. This interpretation is used in Steps 2, 3, and 4. Learners continue to estimate solutions.

2. Children compare division with fractions to division with whole numbers as they examine the number relations in the problems. Discussion questions enable them to state that division with both whole numbers and fractions is used in repeated subtraction situations (How many xs equal y?) and when a part or a set is to be shared equally. When they understand that division with whole numbers and division with fractions have the same meanings, they write math sentences for problems.
3. Children examine records of solutions to find patterns and use these patterns to construct a rule for division with fractions.
4. They examine the reasonableness of the rule and practice its use.
5. When children can use the algorithm to solve problems involving one interpretation, the other interpretation is introduced. Steps 1 and 2 are repeated.
6. Children decide that the rule learned previously can be used to solve problems involving the new interpretation.
7. Some practice activities are assigned for using the rule for division with fractions with the new interpretation.
8. Children solve problems involving both interpretations of division with fractions. Worksheets include fraction addition, subtraction, multiplication, and division problems.

Activities for Learning Division with Fractions

The following activities give ideas for carrying out the sequence for teaching division with fractions.

ACTIVITY 9.32
Problems for the Measurement Interpretation.

To develop an intuitive awareness of the measurement interpretation of division with fractions, students solve problems such as the following which involve thinking how many of a given number "are in" another number. Repeated subtraction as well as materials can be used to solve these problems (Figure 9.18).

1. Joseph bought 3 packages of candy to put into paper cups for people at his party. He used $\frac{1}{4}$ a package for each paper cup. How many cups did he fill?
2. The teacher, Ms. Fredrick, had $\frac{3}{4}$ yard of ribbon. How many pieces of $\frac{1}{8}$ yard each could she cut to make bows to decorate a bulletin board?
3. The grocery store had 4 dozen chocolate Easter eggs left after Easter. The manager decided to sell them in $\frac{1}{2}$ dozen packages. How many packages would she have then?

ACTIVITY 9.33
Problems for the Partitive Interpretation.

When a problem calls for a part or a set to be shared equally, the problem involves the partitive interpretation of division. To understand this meaning, children solve problems using materials (Figure 9.19). Examples are:

1. One-fourth of a pizza was left after dinner. Mother said it was ok for the two children in the family to eat it before going to bed if they shared it equally. How much did each get?
2. Tom and Jack were not home for lunch, so mother saved $\frac{1}{2}$ of a lemon pie for them to eat when they came home. How much of the pie did each get if they shared it equally?

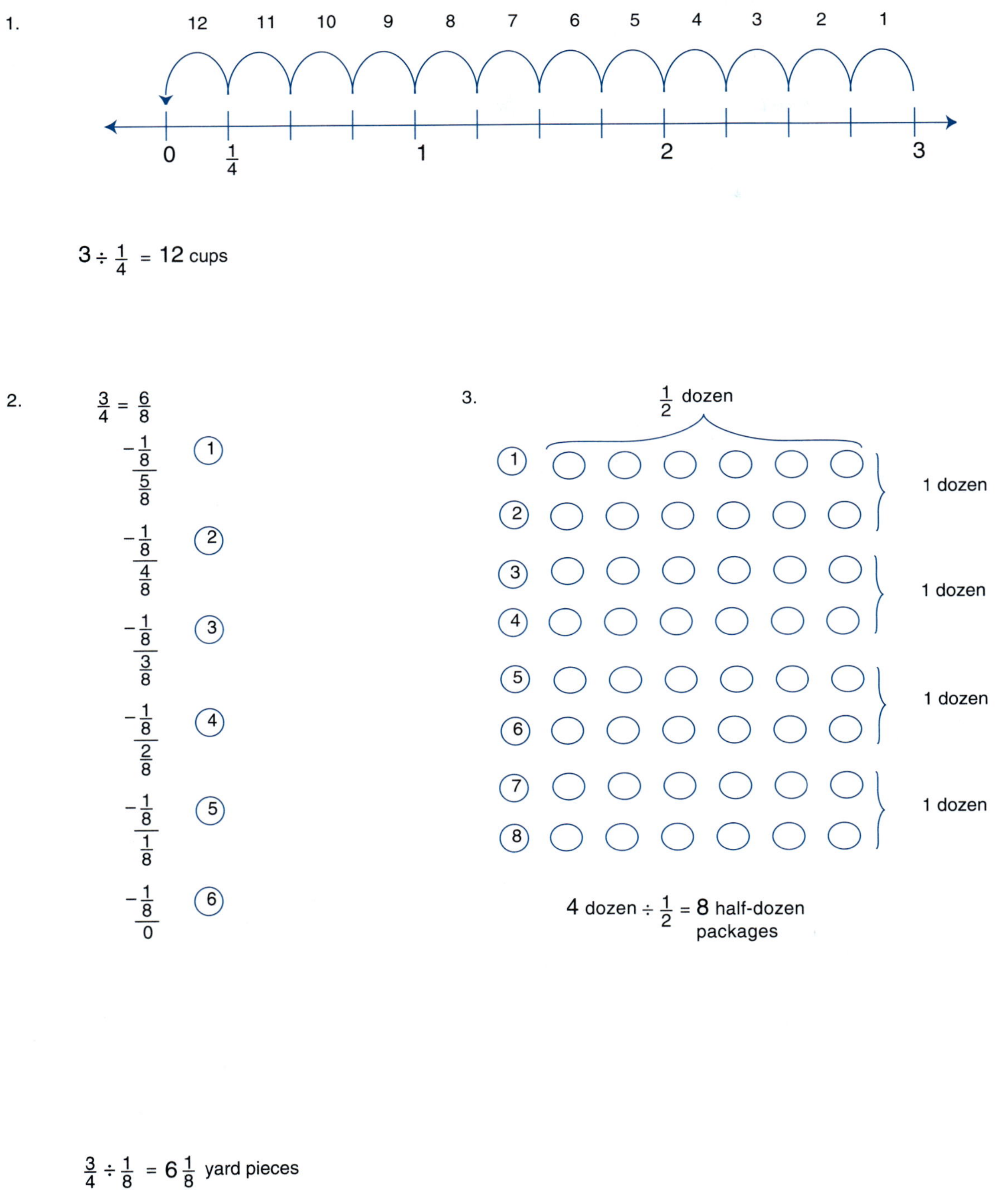

FIGURE 9.18 Solutions for Measurement Interpretation of Division-with-Fractions Problems

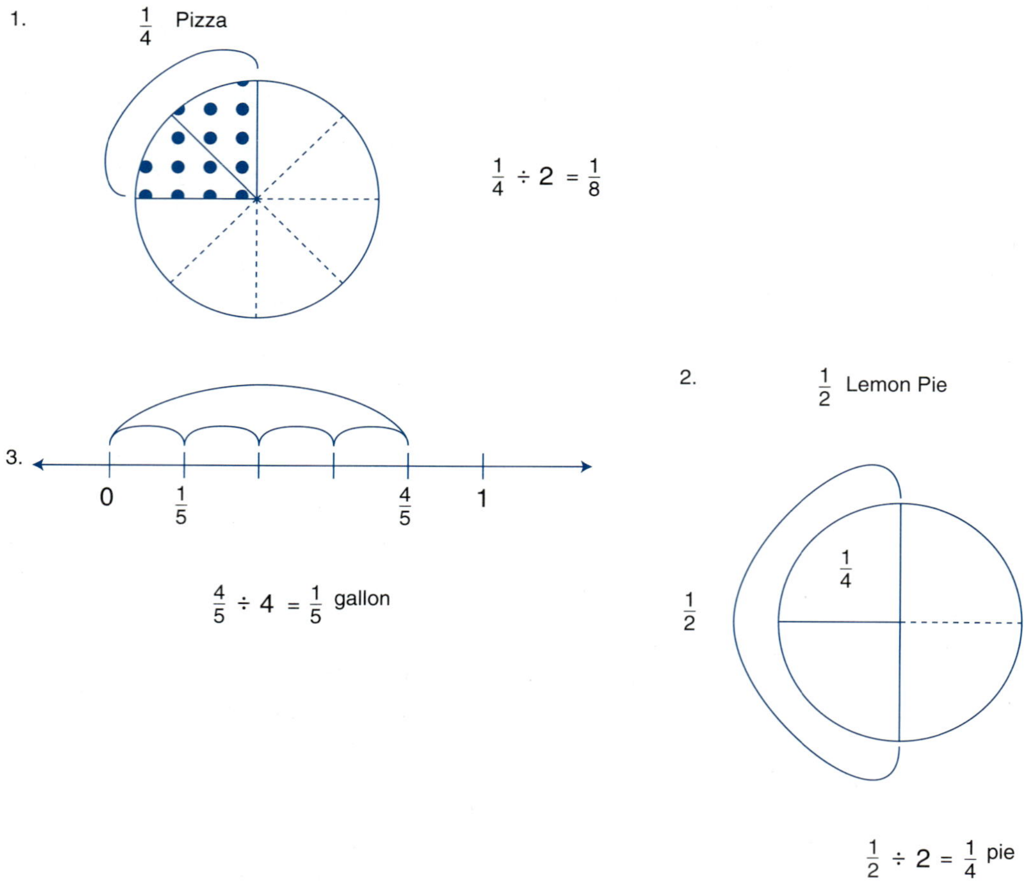

FIGURE 9.19 Solutions for Partitive Interpretation of Division with Fractions Problems

3. Roberto had a $\frac{4}{5}$ of a gallon of lemonade to share equally with 4 people including himself. How much did each get?

ACTIVITY 9.34
Understanding that the Operation Is Division.

To begin lessons that involve deciding that division is the operation to use to solve problems such as those in either Activity 9.32 or 9.33, ask children to examine their solutions to problems solved previously, think what operation could be used in place of materials to find solutions, and write math sentences. Ask questions that help students review that division answers two different questions, "How many *x*s equal *y*?" and "How many is *y* divided equally into *x* groups?" Further questioning helps students to decide the meaning of division in the assigned problems—repeated subtraction or sharing equally. If children have difficulty responding to your questions and writing math sentences for division with fractions problems, ask learners to substitute whole numbers in fraction problems and decide what the operation would be used to solve the whole-number problems. Recalling when division is used in whole-number problems can help children to think the meanings of division with fractions.

Over time, children should solve a number of problems to internalize the use of division in fraction problems. Activity sheets with such problems should also have a few addition, subtraction, or multiplication problems to help children make decisions about the operation to use in different problems. Otherwise, they use division as the operation without giving thought to the meaning of the problem.

This plan is followed for whichever type problem is introduced first, measurement or partitive. When the other interpretation is introduced, this activity is repeated.

ACTIVITY 9.35
Estimation in Division with Fractions.

Several estimation activities are given for estimation in division with fractions.

1. *Estimation War* can be played with cards giving division problems in words. Both the measurement (e.g., "How many three-eighths equal five?") and the partitive interpretations of division (e.g., "Two-thirds divided by six is what number?") would be used. Children should be helped to use a strategy of estimating the solution to be less than $\frac{1}{2}$ or 1 or greater than 1 or another whole number.
2. A study sheet can ask pupils to decide which examples such as the following have solutions (1) less than 1; (2) between 1 and 2; or (3) greater than 2. The directions can be to write (1), (2), or, (3) beside the problem to indicate the estimate:

$\frac{3}{5} \div 7 = N$	_____	$2 \div \frac{1}{4} = N$	_____
$\frac{3}{8} \div 4 = N$	_____	$5\frac{1}{4} \div 4 = N$	_____
$2 \div \frac{2}{3} = N$	_____	$\frac{3}{5} \div 2 = N$	_____
$2\frac{1}{2} \div 2 = N$	_____	$3 \div \frac{7}{8} = N$	_____

After students complete the study sheet, they should discuss the reasoning they used to arrive at the estimate.

3. Students can be asked to write math sentences that have a quotient less than 2, between 1 and 2, or greater than 2. Later, two students can exchange problems. Each should give estimates for the problems written by his or her partner and explain how each estimate was made. A follow-up discussion can deal with how students thought to write the problems.

ACTIVITY 9.36
Constructing the Algorithm Using Measurement Interpretation Problems.

Measurement interpretation problems used to introduce the algorithm for division with fractions should have a whole number divided by a unit fraction:

$$\frac{4}{1} \div \frac{1}{2} = N$$
$$\frac{3}{1} \div \frac{1}{4} = N$$
$$\frac{2}{1} \div \frac{1}{3} = N$$

Students use number lines, fraction disks, or fraction bars to find solutions. Their solutions show that a computed solution involves multiplying the whole number by the denominator of the fraction (Figure 9.20). Pupils should notice this pattern and discuss how to rewrite the math sentence to show the solution (e.g., $\frac{4}{1} \times \frac{2}{1} = 8$). They are told that the inverted fraction is called the *reciprocal* of the given fraction. The class writes the rule: To multiply by a fraction, invert (or use the reciprocal of) the divisor (the second number) and multiply.

If pupils do not discover the pattern, ask questions such as, "Notice the quotient 8. Look at the dividend and the divisor. How could 8 be found? Look at the quotient 12. What is the pattern?"

Using the rule, other problems are solved that involve both unit and nonunit fractions as divisors. The activity includes directions to make estimates to determine the reasonableness of solutions and to use materials to check one or more solutions. When pupils finish, the sense of several problems (How many xs equal *y*?) is discussed.

Later, students solve division problems in which both numbers are fractions. A discussion of the meaning of each problem helps pupils understand the meaning of the problem as well as of the rule.

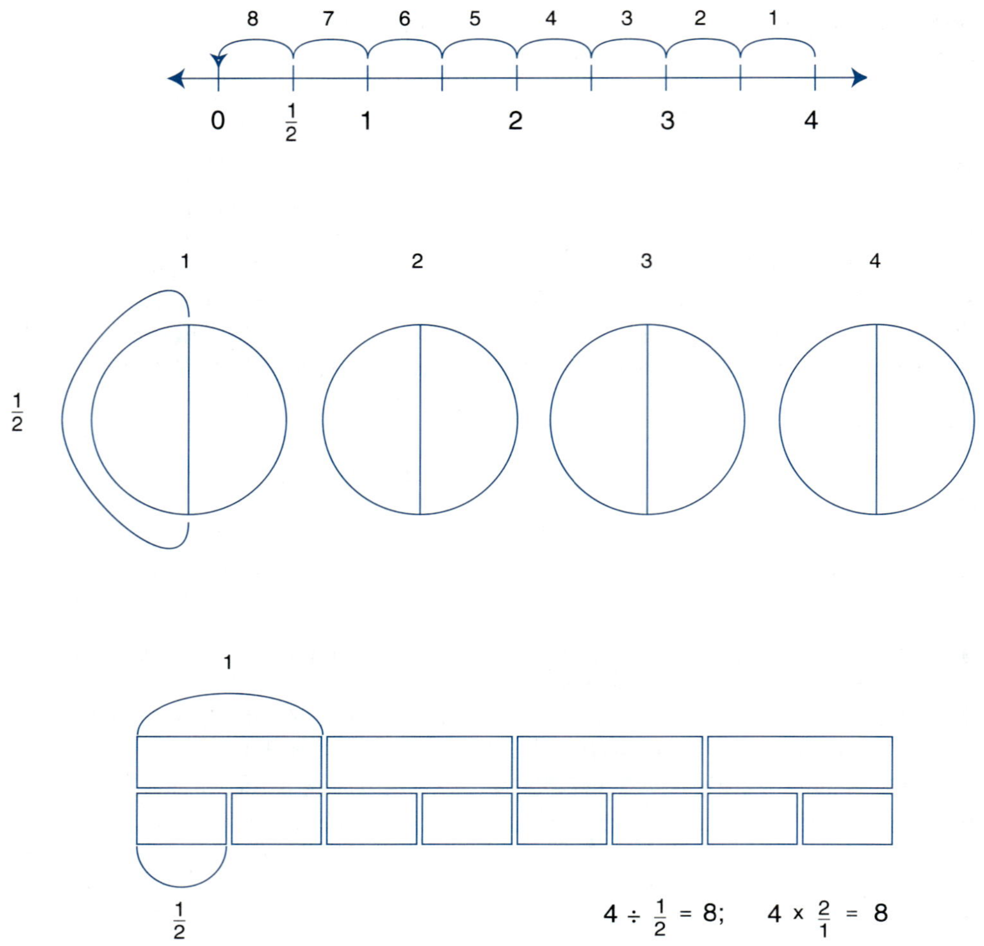

FIGURE 9.20 Finding a Pattern in Fraction Division Solutions

ACTIVITY 9.37
Constructing the Algorithm Using Partitive Interpretation Problems.

The procedure for this activity is similar to that for Activity 9.36 except that the problems reflect the partitive interpretation. Problems have a whole number as divisor, such as:

1. $\frac{1}{4} \div \frac{2}{1} = N$
2. $\frac{1}{2} \div \frac{2}{1} = N$
3. $\frac{3}{4} \div \frac{2}{1} = N$

The pattern–use the reciprocal of the divisor and multiply–should be evident to students from their work with materials (Figure 9.19), and they will be able to write the rule: To divide by a fraction, invert (or use the reciprocal of) the divisor (the second number) and multiply. If the pattern is not evident, ask questions that help them notice the pattern. For example, "Notice the 8 in the denominator of the quotient? How could that 8 be found? . . . What seems to be the pattern?"

Discussion after pupils complete their work should help them look at the meaning of the problems they solved and realize that to divide by a number is to multiply by the reciprocal of that number. For example, to divide a number by 3, find $\frac{1}{3}$ of the number. Noting this relation gives more sense to the rule. Real-life situations can help clarify this idea and should be stressed in the class discussion. For example, if three people share $\frac{1}{2}$ a pizza ($\frac{1}{2} \div 3$), each gets $\frac{1}{3}$ of $\frac{1}{2}$ ($\frac{1}{3} \times \frac{1}{2}$) of the pizza. Students should think of examples to help internalize the idea.

ACTIVITY 9.38
Examining the Sense of the Algorithm for a New Interpretation of Division with Fractions.

After pupils construct the rule using problems that illustrate one interpretation of division, they are helped to generalize the rule to the other interpretation. Problems are assigned to groups with the direction to estimate each solution and think how to solve the problem using a rule, if possible. When children discuss how they used the rule learned previously for the problems assigned, questions help learners infer that the rule makes sense in the new situation. Students' estimates are useful in this discussion because they are based on the sense of problem solutions.

ACTIVITY 9.39
Using Mixed Numbers in Fraction Division.

Assign groups problems that involve mixed numbers in real-life situations. Examples are:

1. A serving of cat food is $5\frac{1}{2}$ ounces. How many servings can be made from 22 ounces? (Measurement interpretation.)
2. Mike has $2\frac{2}{3}$ cups of liquid fertilizer to distribute evenly among 4 plants. How much should he put on each plant? (Partitive interpretation.)

You can ask children what they know about renaming mixed numbers and fraction computation rules to help them solve the problems before they begin their work. When they finish the assignment, discuss their solutions, stressing the renaming of mixed numbers as improper fractions.

ACTIVITY 9.40
Problem Writing.

Students should write problems and give solutions for computation with fractions for all the operations and share their problems. Problem writing enables learners to examine the meaning of situations in terms of mathematical operations.

ASSESSING FRACTION COMPUTATION LEARNING

In assessing learning of fraction computation, you assess four main abilities:

1. Ability to determine relations implicit in fraction story and number problems and use materials to represent those relations.
2. Ability to write math sentences for story problems involving fractions and find solutions.
3. Ability to estimate solutions for computation with fractions and use the estimates to judge the reasonableness of solutions.
4. Ability to compute using the algorithms for the operations with fractions.

Teachers also assess children's motivation to learn and the perseverance they exhibit in completing activities.

Assessment techniques include observations and interviews, examination of students' work products collected in portfolios, and quizzes and tests. Teachers keep records of their assessment of children's progress, and they use their records to revise instruction when they determine that children have not attained learning objectives.

Observations and Interviews

Observe children's work as they complete assignments individually and in groups and when they share their work in a class discussion. Notice interest, perseverance, and the level of work produced. In regard to the latter, observe whether children can use a variety of materials to represent ideas, can express ideas orally and symbolically, and can give reasonable explanations for their solutions.

Most teachers do not have time for lengthy interviews, but short interviews can be carried out while children work on assigned tasks. During these short interviews, you can ask a child questions to assess specific achievements. For example, you can ask a learner to explain how he or she estimated the solution to a number problem. Questions that require students to explain the process they used to obtain an answer are often more valuable than the answer because they reveal children's thinking. Also ask children how they feel about learning computation with fractions. Dated records of observations and interviews, often in the form of anecdotal reports, are kept. Over time you would interview all children in the class and have records that show the growth that has occurred.

Examination of Children's Work Products

Samples of children's work should be kept on a regular basis, such as during the first week of every month or at the middle and end of a unit of instruction. Some of these papers give estimates of solutions or write-ups of how problems were solved. Worksheets that deal with the meaning of an algorithm for an operation should also be included in the portfolio. At times children should choose which papers to include in the portfolio. You and your student should examine his or her portfolio to note evidence of growth. Children in the middle grades are capable of more objective self-evaluation than in the primary grades and should be given the opportunity to work with you to assess their own learning. They are often surprised at how much they have learned, and the resulting sense of achievement contributes to the development of intrinsic motivation.

Quizzes and Tests

Quizzes that consist of about five questions should be given once every week or two. They should be used to assess instruction so that teaching and assignments can be adapted to children's learning needs. Quizzes give progress reports to you and your students. They pinpoint what needs to be done to ensure achievement of fraction computation. By the time children study computation with fractions, they are able to take some responsibility for their own learning. Quizzes give them feedback regarding what areas to emphasize in study. Homework can be adapted so that students have choices of assignments and can concentrate on areas of weakness. For example, if children are having difficulty adding with fractions because they cannot find least common denominators, they should be able to choose homework assignments that give guidance and practice in finding least common denominators. Some of such homework would deal with reporting on the use of materials to show understanding of least common denominators.

Tests are given less often than quizzes and form the basis for summative evaluation. They are longer and are used to assess learning at the end of a topic of instruction, such as multiplication with fractions. If instruction has been adapted to meet pupils' needs as revealed by the quizzes, learners are expected to do well on tests (Bloom, Hastings, and Madaus, 1971).

Story problems similar to those given in this chapter should be used in quizzes and tests, and some of the activities described can be adapted for paper-and-pencil evaluation. Other quiz and test items are similar to:

1. Write a mathematical sentence for these word sentences:
   a. What number is equal to 9 three-fourths?
   b. 8 is how many one-halves?
   c. How much greater is $\frac{4}{5}$ than $\frac{3}{10}$?
   d. What number is $\frac{1}{2}$ and $\frac{1}{3}$?
   e. What is $\frac{1}{2}$ of 5?
   f. What is the fractional part if $\frac{3}{4}$ of a cake is cut into 4 equal pieces.
2. Show the solution to these problems on the number line:
   a. $\frac{1}{2} + \frac{1}{3} = N$
   b. $4 \times \frac{2}{3} = N$
3. Shade one-fourth of the pie (show pie divided into $\frac{8}{8}$).
4. Place an X in the column that gives your estimate:

Less than $\frac{1}{2}$	Between $\frac{1}{2}$ and 1	Greater than 1
$\frac{3}{10} + \frac{1}{5} = N$		
$\frac{1}{2} + \frac{4}{5} = N$		
$3\frac{1}{5} \times \frac{1}{10} = N$		
$\frac{1}{2} \times \frac{1}{8} = N$		
$6 \div \frac{2}{5} = N$		
$\frac{3}{4} \div 3 = N$		

Students should be asked to write out their thinking for a few items on a quiz and on a test.

Activity for the Classroom 9.2. Write and administer a quiz to upper-grade students to determine their attainment of this outcome objective: learners have constructed the different meanings of multiplication with fractions. Have them include a write-up of their thinking for some items in your quiz. Use their answers to your questions and their write-ups to decide if they have constructed the different meanings of multiplication with fractions or if they need more experiences to construct the concepts and solve problems involving the concepts.

The various types of assessment give you different kinds of evidence to use in assessing progress. Interviews, observations, students' write-ups, certain work products, and some quiz or test items help you understand how children think about computation with fractions. Other work products and most items on quizzes and tests give information about children's performance. Both kinds of information about students' learning enable you to plan instruction that takes into account children's areas of strengths and weaknesses.

SUMMARY

New directions in elementary school mathematic stress teaching fraction computation for understanding. Children are not introduced to an algorithm for an operation with fractions until they have constructed the meanings of that operation with fractions. To develop these meanings, they solve problems using different materials and diagrams. They relate the meanings of the operation with whole numbers to the meanings for fractions. They discover that addition, subtraction, and division with fractions have the same meanings as with whole numbers, but that multiplication with fractions has two meanings, one that is the same as multiplication with whole numbers and one that is different from the meaning of multiplication with whole numbers. Important to the development of understanding is estimating solutions using reference points such as 0, $\frac{1}{2}$, 1, or whole numbers greater than 1, and explaining how estimates are used to examine the reasonableness of solutions. Discussing their work with each other and with you enables learners to internalize ideas.

After learners demonstrate understanding by solving story and number problems using materials and diagrams, by estimating, and by writing math sentences for problems, they develop algorithms by examining patterns in their solutions. The sense of these algorithms is established by informal reasoning, not formal logic. The algorithms are seen as plausible because the solutions they generate are reasonable. Last, children practice the use of the algorithms and use them to solve problems.

Many activities that provide opportunities for exploration and reflection were described in this chapter. Class discussions in connection with activities were stressed to enable children to communicate ideas and to confirm or revise their thinking after they have worked individually or in groups.

Assessment was outlined as a means for determining progress and revising instruction as well as a tool to measure children's achievement in fraction computation. Examples of assessment procedures to determine both the meanings and skill children have acquired were also given.

REFERENCES

Behr, Merlyn J., Richard Lesh, Thomas R. Post, and Edward A. Silver. (1983). "Rational Number Concepts." In *Acquisition of Mathematics Concepts and Processes,* edited by Richard Lesh and Marsha Landau, pp. 91–126. New York: Academic Press.

Behr, Merlyn J., and Post, Thomas R. (1988). "Teaching Rational Number and Decimal Concepts." In *Teaching Mathematics in Grades K–8: Research Based Methods,* edited by Thomas R. Post. pp. 190–231. Boston: Allyn & Bacon.

Behr, Merlyn J., Ipke Wachsmuth, and Thomas R. Post. (March 1985). "Construct a Sum: A Measure of Children's Understanding of Fraction Size." *Journal for Research in Mathematics Education* 16: 120–131.

Bezuk, Nadine, and Kathleen Cramer. (1989). "Teaching about Fractions: What, When, and How?" In *New Directions for Elementary School Mathematics,* edited by Paul R. Trafton and Albert P. Schulte, pp. 156–67. Reston, VA: National Council of Teachers of Mathematics.

Bloom, Benjamin S., and J. Thomas Hastings, and George F. Madaus. (1971). *Handbook on Formative and Summative Evaluation of Student Learning.* New York: McGraw-Hill.

Coburn, Terrence G. (1989). "The Role of Computation in the Changing Mathematics Curriculum." In *New Directions for Elementary School Mathematics,* edited by Paul R. Trafton and Albert P. Schulte, pp. 43–56. Reston, VA: National Council of Teachers of Mathematics.

Cramer, Kathleen, and Nadine Bezuk. (November 1991). "Multiplication with Fractions: Teaching for Understanding." *Arithmetic Teacher* 39: 34–37.

Kouba, Vicky L., Catherine A. Brown, Thomas P. Carpenter, Mary M. Lindquist, Edward A Silver, and Jane O. Swafford. (April 1988). "Results of the Fourth NAEP Assessment of Mathematics: Num-ber, Operations, and Word Problems." *Arithmetic Teacher* 35: pp. 14–19.

Kroll, Diana Lambdin, and Toshiaki Yabe. (October 1987). "A Japanese Educator's Perspective on Teaching Mathematics in the Elementary School." *Arithmetic Teacher* 35: 36–43.

Mack, Nancy K. (January 1990). "Learning Fractions with Understanding: Building on Informal Knowledge." *Journal for Research in Mathematics Education,* 21: 16–32.

National Council of Teachers of Mathematics. (1989). *Curriculum and Evaluation Standards for School Mathematics.* Reston, VA: Author.

Ott, Jack M., Daniel L. Snook, and Diana L. Gibson. (October 1991). "Understanding Partitive Division with Fractions." *Arithmetic Teacher* 39: 7–11.

Post, Thomas R. (May 1981). "Fractions: Results and Implications from National Assessment." *Arithmetic Teacher* 28: 26–31.

Reys, Robert E., Marilyn N. Suydam, and Mary Montgomery Lindquist. (1992). *Helping Children Learn Mathematics, 3rd ed.* Englewood Cliffs, NJ: Prentice Hall.

Steiner, Evelyn E. (May 1987). "Division with Fractions: Developing Conceptual Sense with Dollars and Sense." *Arithmetic Teacher* 34: 36–42.

Trafton, Paul R., and Judith S. Zawojewski. (February 1984). "Teaching Rational Number Division: A Special Problem." *Arithmetic Teacher* 31: 20–22.

SOFTWARE RESOURCES

(in Common) Arithmetic
Company: Sunburst
Computer: Apple, IBM
Grade level: 4–6

Game format that involves thinking skills. Includes addition and subtraction with simple fractions.

IBM Elementary Mathematics Series: Math Concepts
Company: IBM/EduQuest
Computer: IBM
Grade level: 3–8
Level III, Unit 3, Lesson 8 (mixed numbers)

Representing, estimating, and converting mixed numbers to improper fractions and improper fractions to mixed numbers.

Level III, Unit 3, Lesson 11 (fraction addition and subtraction), Lesson 12 (fraction multiplication and division), and Lesson 13 (mixed number operations).

Work with identifying, finding, and writing number sentences for sums, differences, products, and quotients. Includes related word problems.

CHAPTER 10

Understanding and Computing with Decimals

▪ INTRODUCTORY PROBLEM ▪

You are Kris's sixth grade teacher. The week before winter break, Kris told you that she was going to be the accountant on her family's trip to visit her grandparents over the holidays. She, her parents, and sister would be on the road five days. She would keep track of the mileage, the number of gallons of gas purchased at different prices, and the cost of meals and lodging. Each of two nights they would have two rooms in a motel; the other nights they would stay with friends. She said she would like to tell the class about her work when she returned. As you read this chapter, think how you would make use of her report in teaching a unit on decimals.

INTRODUCTION

Decimals are fractions whose denominators are powers of 10, but unlike common fractions, they are written in place-value notation. The study of decimals enables children to extend their knowledge of base ten and place value and deal meaningfully with life outside of school. For example, information related to sports events, our money system, government statistics, and metric measurements will make sense to students when they understand decimals. Students' use of calculators is also enhanced when they understand decimals. A knowledge of decimals enables students to evaluate calculator computations and recognize errors made when keying in numbers.

The second National Assessment of Educational Progress (NAEP) shows that American school children have difficulty with decimals. The results for 13-year-old students show that only 34% were able to estimate a decimal between two decimals shown on a number line, and only 38% knew that .2 equals $\frac{1}{5}$. Only 58% could add .70 + .40 + 20. About 50% could multiply decimals, and about 37% were able to divide by a decimal (Carpenter, Corbitt, Kepner, Lindquist, and Reys, 1981). Similar results in decimal computation were found for seventh-grade students in the fourth NAEP (Kouba, Brown, Carpenter, Lindquist, Silver, and Swafford, 1988). Hiebert (1987) states that confusion about decimals is common in high school and beyond. Comparing decimals appears to be difficult even for adult students (Grossman, 1983).

Carpenter et al. (1981) point out that students' source of difficulty with decimals stems largely from their poor conceptual understanding. Students do not know what the symbols mean, and they often overgeneralize their whole-number knowledge to decimals. They believe for example, that 1.326 is greater than 1.4 because they have learned that more numbers mean greater value (Hiebert and Wearne, 1986). Because they do not grasp the sense of the symbols, computational rules make no sense either, and some students make up their own rules (Hiebert, 1987).

Meager understanding appears related to the fact that decimal concepts are complex and take time to develop. Learning does not proceed all at once but is built up gradually as students connect and coordinate external and internal representations (Hiebert, Wearne, and Tabor, 1991). Presumably, not enough time is allotted to developing meaning.

Instruction for meaning begins students' work so that they will become competent in the use of decimals. Work with different models enables students to understand decimals and relations among them and provides opportunities for the development of both oral and written language (CTM, 1989). Later symbols are introduced, and activities are planned that enable learners to connect meanings developed from work with models, oral language, and written words to symbolic representations (see Standard 12, in Curriculum Standards for Grades K–4, and Standard 6 for Grades 5–8, Appendix A).

Instruction for learning the operations with decimals emphasizes the use of models to represent the operations and stresses learning mental computation and estimation. The development of rules is undertaken only when students understand the operations with decimals (Hiebert, 1987). Students study rules so that the algorithms make sense to them, but they only use them for simple calculations. They do not practice for speed and accuracy with lengthy computations. They use the calculator for these computations (Behr and Post, 1988).

The first main section of this chapter, Understanding Decimals, describes new directions in instruction to help learners develop understanding of decimals and construct base ten and place-value relations among decimals. The second main section, Learning Computation with Decimals, deals with interactive approaches to teaching the operations with decimals. The third main section is Assessing Decimal Learning. A summary section ends the chapter.

UNDERSTANDING DECIMALS

Instruction for understanding decimals is designed so that learners will attain nine objectives:

1. Understand partitioning into tenths, hundredths, and other powers of ten; recognize base ten relations among decimals.
2. Develop the language of decimals, and use decimal words in oral and written work.
3. Know that decimals have the same meaning as common fractions whose denominators are powers of 10.
4. Compare and order decimals using words.
5. Know the symbols for decimals.
6. Observe decimals used in real life.
7. Understand the place-value notational system for decimals.
8. Compare, order, and estimate decimals using place-value symbols.
9. Know common fraction and decimal equivalents.

Helping students acquire these learnings is discussed in the five parts of this section: Introduction to Decimal Concepts and Relations, Learning Place-Value Symbols for Decimals, Studying Place-Value Relations for Decimals, Comparing, Ordering, and Estimating Decimals, and Learning Common Fraction Equivalents for Decimals.

Introduction to Decimal Concepts and Relations

Children work with tenths when studying common fractions, but other fractions with denominators to twelfths are also included in learning experiences. Now children study only fractions whose denominators are powers of 10. Hundredths and thousandths are studied as well as tenths.

Students work with a variety of materials to understand that decimals involve partitioning a whole into 10 (10×10 . . .) equal-sized parts and that decimal relations involve base ten concepts. Base ten blocks (cubes, flats, longs, and units), grid paper, base ten or decimal cards (proportional materials that include a big square divided into 100 equal-sized squares, 10 strips each one-tenth of the big square (some are divided into 10 equal-sized squares), and 10 equal-sized squares each one-hundredth the size of the big square), number lines, and decimal wheels are used (Figure 10.1). The cards are made from duplicated materials glued to cardboard. The decimal wheels are made in the same way. (See Appendix G for patterns.) Each child or, at times, each pair of children must have materials if they are to construct ideas from their actions.

ACTIVITIES 10.1a–e
Introducing Partitioning Involving Decimals and Base Ten Relations.

Six different activities that involve the use of materials are described to introduce partitioning involving tenths and hundredths. Activities you devise can be adaptations of these activities. Oral language is used in these tasks, and decimal words (not sym-

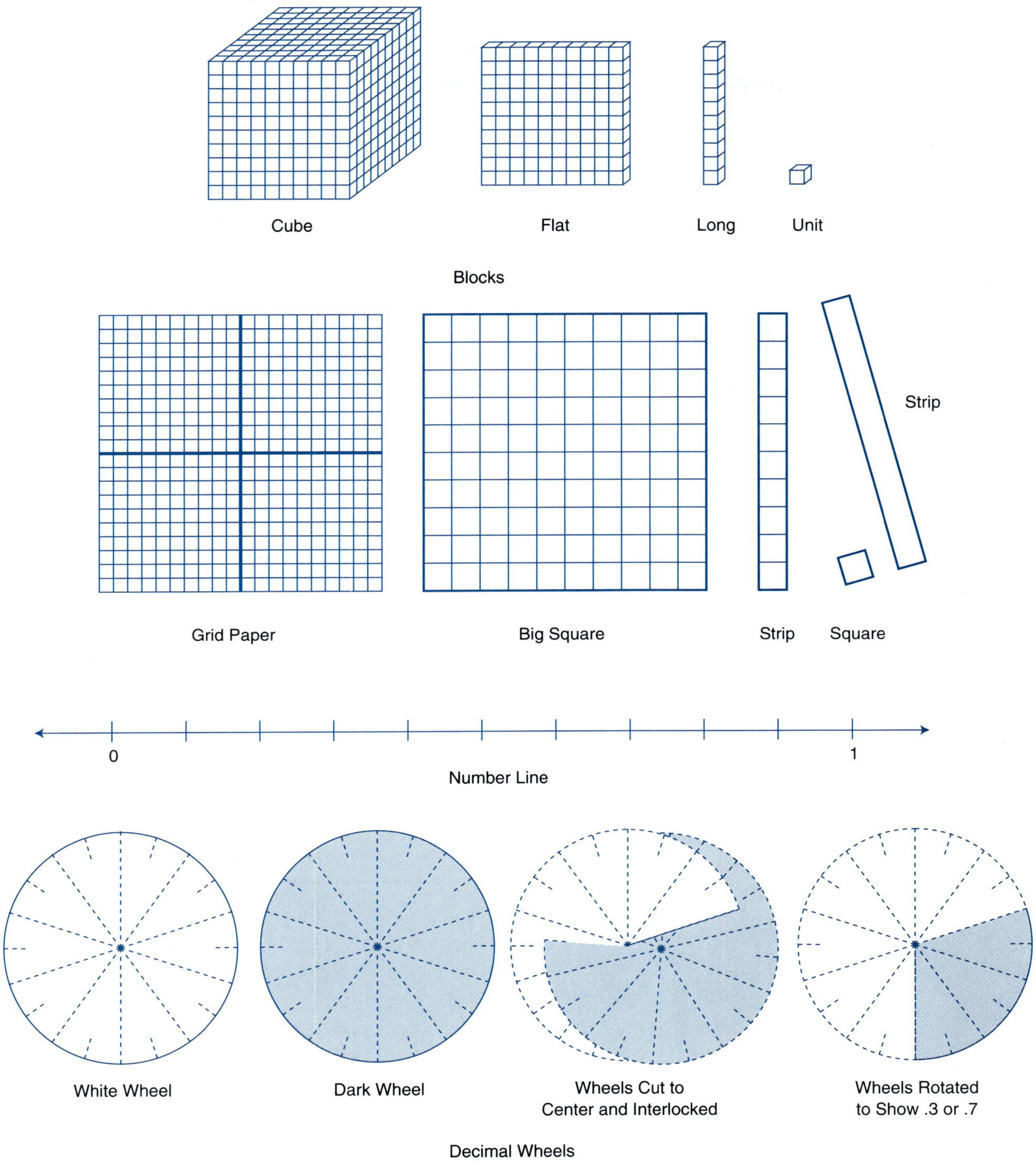

FIGURE 10.1 Materials for Studying Decimals

bols) are written on the overhead or the chalkboard for children to read. In both oral and written work, the "-ths" suffix is emphasized.

a. Each child or two children working together will investigate base ten blocks or decimal cards. Before beginning their work, they are told that the big square and the flat are each one whole and are asked to experiment to find out what fractions the pieces show and how they are related. They share their discoveries. The class

Reader Activity 10.1

Make one set of decimal wheels using the patterns in Appendix G. Make the wheels different colors. slit both wheels to the center so that they can interlock with each other (see Figure 10.1). Experiment with the wheels, and evaluate their use with learners.

discussion should bring out the notions that (1) the big square, flat, strip, and long are divided into equal-sized parts; (2) the words "tenths" and "hundredths" can be used to describe the parts of the large pieces; (3) the big square is 100 times greater than the small square, the small square is one-hundredth of the big square, the same relations exist for the flat and the unit; (4) the big square is 10 times greater than the strip; the strip is one-tenth of the big square, the same relations exist for the flat and the long. A poster showing large diagrams with the labels "10 tenths = 1" and "100 hundredths = 1" beside the appropriate diagram can be displayed (Figure 10.2). Students explain to each other the meanings conveyed by the diagrams.

b. Each child has two decimal wheels of different colors. They are told that each wheel represents 1. Children investigate what can be shown by interlocking the wheels. Children present their ideas and justify them. They decide that the interlocking wheels can show tenths and hundredths. The equal-sized parts of the wheels and the base ten relations are emphasized with the wheels as with the blocks and cards. Children show decimals you or your students name, or they work in pairs asking each other to represent decimals on the wheels.

c. Students may notice equivalent decimals such as 20 hundredths equals 2 tenths when they worked with the decimal wheels. If not, introduce this concept by asking students to show 20 hundredths and 2 tenths. Ask several students what they noticed. When they remark that they both are represented by the same fractional part, ask why this has happened. Their explanations should include the idea that a tenth is 10 hundredths. Ask them to make predictions about other equivalent decimals of their own choosing, to use their wheels to verify their ideas, and to share what they observed with the class.

d. Distribute a study sheet with at least 10 number lines on each sheet. Each line should be partitioned into 10 segments of equal length. Discuss how to label the line in tenths using common fractions. Have one student demonstrate this on a number line displayed on the overhead. All students then label their lines to show tenths. Next, ask them to use one line for each decimal in the following assignment:
Mark with an X

1. Five different tenths numbers of your own choosing at correct points on the number lines.
2. Five different hundredths numbers of your own choosing at points to indicate the hundredths numbers. (Discuss with learners that some hundredths numbers they choose can be marked at estimated points, e.g., 42 hundredths.)
3. Below the mark on the number line, write the common fraction and the decimal word that tells what you have represented.

Have learners tell how decimal words and common fractions are alike and different.

e. Have children work in pairs taking turns at these tasks: (1) writing a common fraction of his or her own choosing; (2) reading the common fraction the partner wrote, representing it on his or her decimal wheel (or tracing with a finger its representation on his or her big square), and (3) explaining the representation. Remind learners to include both tenths and hundredths.

ACTIVITIES 10.2a–d
Comparing and Ordering Decimals

a. Give each child a study sheet that shows 6 of the hundred squares, numbered 1 to 6 (use top 6 diagrams on the base ten paper in Appendix G). Ask students to (1) label each hundred square "1"; (2) show 6 different decimals of their own choosing by shading a portion of each of the 6 squares; and (3) write the decimal part above each diagram, using both decimal words and common fractions.

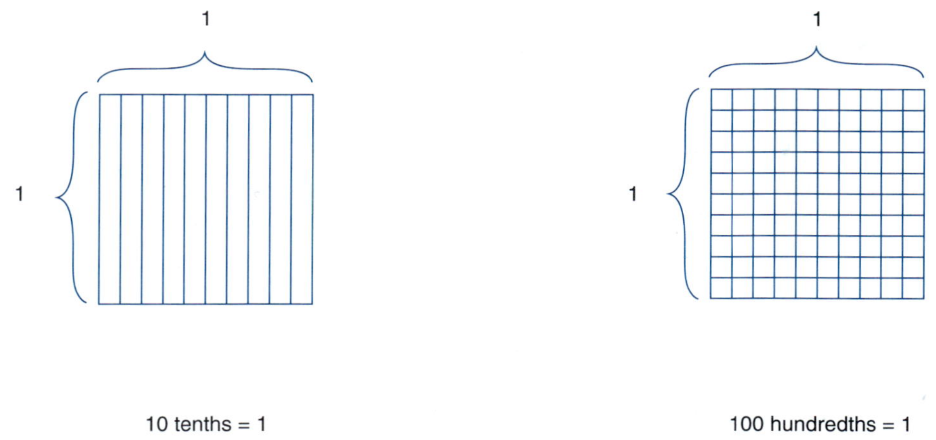

FIGURE 10.2 Poster to Show Decimals

Two children exchange papers, verifying that the labels represent what was shaded. Next, the two children study the first diagrams on their papers and decide which shows the greater fraction and why. They continue by comparing the second, third, . . . , sixth diagrams on their papers. The final task is to compare the decimal words and common fractions for each two diagrams. The activity ends with a class discussion that deals with the question, "How did you decide which was the greater decimal?"

b. Students form groups of four. Designate one student to be the chairperson. Each student is given a sheet of 6 number lines marked in equal lengths. Students number the lines from 1 to 6 and label them in tenths using common fractions. Ask the students to write beside each number line two different decimals (in words) that could be represented on the number line and think which is the greater decimal. The chairperson notices when the members of the group are finished and tells them to exchange papers and mark the point on each number line that represents the greater decimal. Each reads his or her choices and justifies them if another student asks him or her to do so. For extension, they can decide which two decimals in their group have the greatest and which, the least difference. They can report these during a class discussion.

c. Students again form groups of four, and one student is designated the chairperson. Each student shows a decimal on his or her decimal wheel and lays it down. The chairperson calls on one student to order the four decimals represented on the wheels. The wheels are returned to their owners, and the task is repeated four times, each student having a turn to order the decimal wheels.

d. The activity format in (c) is followed, but each student writes a decimal word on a sticky note rather than show a decimal on his or her decimal wheel.

Learning Place-Value Symbols for Decimals

When children can use materials to show tenths and hundredths, explain why a part is a tenth or a hundredth, and use words and common fractions to label their diagrams, place-value symbols for decimals are introduced. Distribute the worksheets completed in Activity 10.1*d*. Have several students show their work on the overhead and explain how they knew the words and common fractions to write.

Then, ask if any student knows how to write the decimal fractions. (Some may transfer ideas about writing cents to writing decimals.) Have them write the decimals beside the common fractions written on the overhead, and ask them to read the decimals. If no student knows how to write decimal fractions, write them yourself, and say, "Notice what I am writing beside these common fractions. What I am writing are called decimals. They have the same meaning as the tenths and hundredths fractions we have studied and are read the same way. The difference is how we write decimal fractions." Have children notice similarities and differences between decimals and common fractions. Help students understand that the decimal point shows the ones place, tenths are the first place to right of the ones, and hundredths, the second.

Children should not use the word "point" when reading decimals. To develop meaning, they must state the place-value designation. For example, .56 is read "fifty-six hundredths," not "point fifty-six" or "point five, six."

Show diagrams on the overhead with tenths and hundredths shaded. Ask children to write both a decimal and a common fraction that tells what part of the square is shaded. Have one child write the decimal and common fraction on the overhead and read the decimal. Discuss how the child knew what to write. Some children may recognize that one zero in a common fraction denominator means one place in a decimal fraction.

In subsequent lessons, activities involve the use of decimal words, common fractions, and decimal fractions to enable learners to make connections among these labels and understand that they are different representations for the same concept.

ACTIVITY 10.3
Game: The Same Decimal.

Tell the class they will make the materials for a game and play the game according to their own rules. Cards for this game are made by the students following this procedure: Cut index cards in half. Give each student two half-index cards. Ask each student to write a decimal of his or her own choosing on one half-card. Designate one-half the class to write the same decimal in common fraction form on their other card; ask the other half of the class to write the decimal in words on the other card. Repeat the task. Collect the cards by matched pairs and sort them into four "games."

Divide the class into four groups. Each group receives one set of game cards. The group is given five minutes to decide the rules for a game, *The Same Decimal,* in which cards giving different representations for decimals are matched. If they cannot make up a game in the time allotted, they play a version of *Rummy* (see Box 3.1). Each group plays the game according to its rules.

ACTIVITY 10.4
Olympic Times.

Ask one or more groups to research times in Olympic events and write two facts about the events that include decimals. When they share their reports, have the class write the decimals for the oral words given. When the reports are finished, ask several children to write the decimals on the chalkboard. The reports are read again and the oral language and decimals compared.

ACTIVITY 10.5
Questions with Decimals.

Pose problems for groups of two or three to solve that require thinking how to partition a whole into 10 equal-sized parts and estimate. Examples of problems are:

1. Estimate .2 across the classroom floor. How did you do it? Would $\frac{4}{10}$ be farther or less far? Estimate how far it would be.

2. Estimate five tenths of the width of your desktop. Would .45 be as wide or less wide? Why?
3. If you read .70 of a good book of 100 pages, how far would you read? If your friend read 82 pages of another copy of the book, did he read more or less than you?

Groups next write similar questions for other groups to answer. Remind the students that the questions should give common fractions, decimals, or words and require thinking tenths or hundredths. Arrange for the groups to exchange questions so that each group will answer another group's questions. During a class discussion, each group shares its best question. A student you name decides what question will be shared if the group cannot agree on the best question.

ACTIVITY 10.6*a and b*
Mixed Decimals.

a. When students have an understanding of decimal fractions, ask them to show mixed numbers such as 2.3 with materials (Figure 10.3). Tell them that the decimal point is read "and" (e.g., 2.3 is read "two and three tenths"). When they finish their work, students discuss their representations.

b. After students have studied metric measures, they can use centimeter rulers in a decimal activity. Children study rulers showing tenths, hundredths, and thousandths. Ask them to use the rulers to draw distances they think different insects would jump or crawl in 10 or more seconds. (Later some learners could verify their ideas by library or field research.) The lines can be labeled in decimeters, centimeters, and millimeters (e.g., .22 decimeter, 2.2 centimeters, and 22 millimeters). A few students can use the overhead to make drawings that correspond to what they did with paper and pencil. Have them explain the base ten relations between different labels.

ACTIVITY 10.7
Design with a Decimal.

Students use a whole such as a 10×10 square or a 5×20 rectangle for this activity. They decide what hundredths they will use to make a design by coloring in the squares. Figure 10.4 shows a design with .24 of the square shaded.

Decimals in Life

Decimals play a major role in activities outside of school and in information reported in the media. They also are used in textbooks children study in social studies and science. Relating these uses of decimals to mathematics enables students to see the connections mathematics has with the other facets of their lives. Call attention to the use of decimals in life inside and outside of school whenever possible.

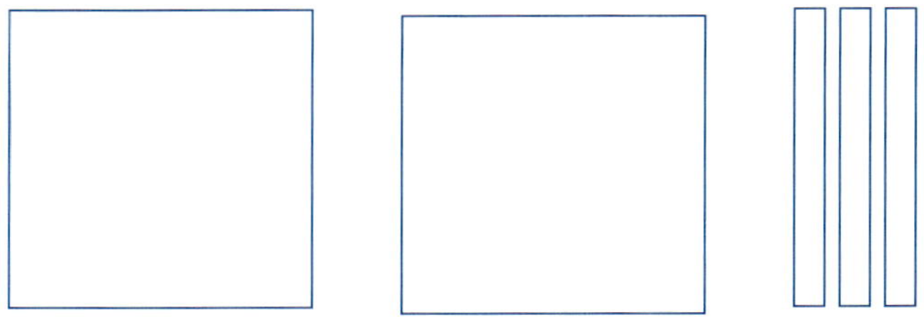

FIGURE 10.3 Model for Mixed Decimal, 2.3

FIGURE 10.4 Decimal Design

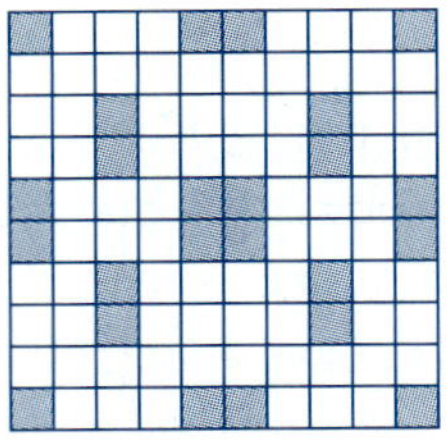

ACTIVITY 10.8
Decimal Hunt.

Have students find decimals in life outside of school and write short descriptions of their discoveries to place on the Decimal Hunt bulletin board. (Items reported would include rainfall, situations involving money, time in sport events, metric measurements related to automobiles, contents of cans and bottles, and others.) Discuss the meaning and usefulness of the decimals students observe.

Studying Place-Value Relations for Decimals

Children know that places to the left of the ones place represent whole numbers and places to the right of the ones place represent decimals. They also know that the value of each place to the left of the ones place is 10 times greater than the value of the place to its right. Now, through their investigations, observations, and reflections, students construct the idea that each decimal place has a value 10 times less than the value of the place to its left and 10 times greater than the value of the place to its right. This concept is not easy to understand. To help learners construct the concept, you use a variety of activities that provide opportunities to relate models to symbols and to explore the relations among the values of places to the right of the ones place. The tasks described in this section are examples of such activities.

ACTIVITY 10.9
Studying Tenths and Hundredths Places.

Children use their decimal wheels and work in pairs; one shows .2 and the other .02. Have them write the decimals and the common fraction forms on a slip of paper that is placed beside the materials. Ask children in groups to study their work and to make as many observations as they can. After time for their group work, a class discussion takes place. During the discussion, questions are asked to help children reflect on relations between the two numbers. For example:

1. How many times greater is .2 than .02?
2. What is the difference between how these fractions are written in common and in decimal form? How is the value of the fraction shown in each form?
3. How is the ones place shown in a decimal fraction? (A decimal point shows the ones place.)
4. What is the value of the first place to the right of the ones place, the second place?

Other examples are used and questions asked to help children focus on the relation between tenths and hundredths and discover how this relation is shown in a decimal and in a common fraction. To end the activity, students can explain to partners what they learned about decimal place values.

ACTIVITY 10.10
Exploring Place-Value Relations.

Give each student a sheet of one hundred squares each labeled "1." On the overhead show diagrams for decimals such as .6, and ask pupils to show on the first square a number one-tenth that size; show a diagram for .06 and ask children to show on the next square a number 10 times greater. They should also write the decimal they show. Continue with other examples to help construct base ten relations with decimals. Have them tell about their diagrams and the decimals they have written. They should say that the value of each place to the right of the ones place is 10 times greater than the place to its right.

Extension: Ask learners how they would show a number 10 times greater than .1 and .6, and how they would show a number 100 times greater than .01 and .06. Have them explain their responses. Repeat for other decimals.

Prepare a study sheet with diagrams similar to those shown on the overhead and directions like those given orally (Figure 10.5).

ACTIVITY 10.11
Introducing Thousandths.

Two activities are useful for introducing thousandths. One can be used initially and the other as a follow-up activity.

1. Give each child 10 hundred squares. Tell them that the squares are pieces of one whole and that they will use them to study decimals. Say, "Please arrange your pieces in a strip to show a whole." Have children tape the pieces together (Figure 10.6). Call the piece a "one whole strip." Have students decide the decimal that names each 100 squares of the one whole strip (one tenth), each 10 squares (one hundredth), and each small square (one thousandth). Have them explain why the small square is called one thousandth of the one whole strip. (They may need to be helped to differentiate between the relation of a small square to a big square and to a one whole strip. Ask questions that help them realize that the size of an part depends on its relation to the whole.) If students do not infer that each small square is one thousandth, use questions such as: How many small squares are in the whole strip? How do you know? If there are 1000 small squares in the whole, what would each small square be called? What part of the whole is each small square?

   Have children count parts of the strip by tenths. Ask them to point to each tenth as they count. Next count by hundredths. As it would take a long time to count the thousandths, ask them to count 10 thousandths at a time. Begin by saying, "What part of the whole is 10 thousandths? How do you know?" (Have children notice that 10 thousandths is 1 hundredth.) They should point to each 10 thousandths as they count 10 thousandths, 20 thousandths, . . . , 100 thousandths, . . . , 1000 thousandths.

   Have a student write the decimals .1 and .01. Then ask, "How do you think we would write the decimal for one-thousandth? Why?" Discuss that it makes sense to use the next place to the right for thousandths.
2. Give each pair of children a meter stick. Ask them to find .1, .01, and .001 of the meter stick (write these decimals on the chalkboard or overhead). Have children explain their choices to the class. Then have them write other decimals for the class to show.

   Note: You will need a number of meter sticks for this and other activities. Perhaps the sticks could be borrowed from other classes for the lesson.

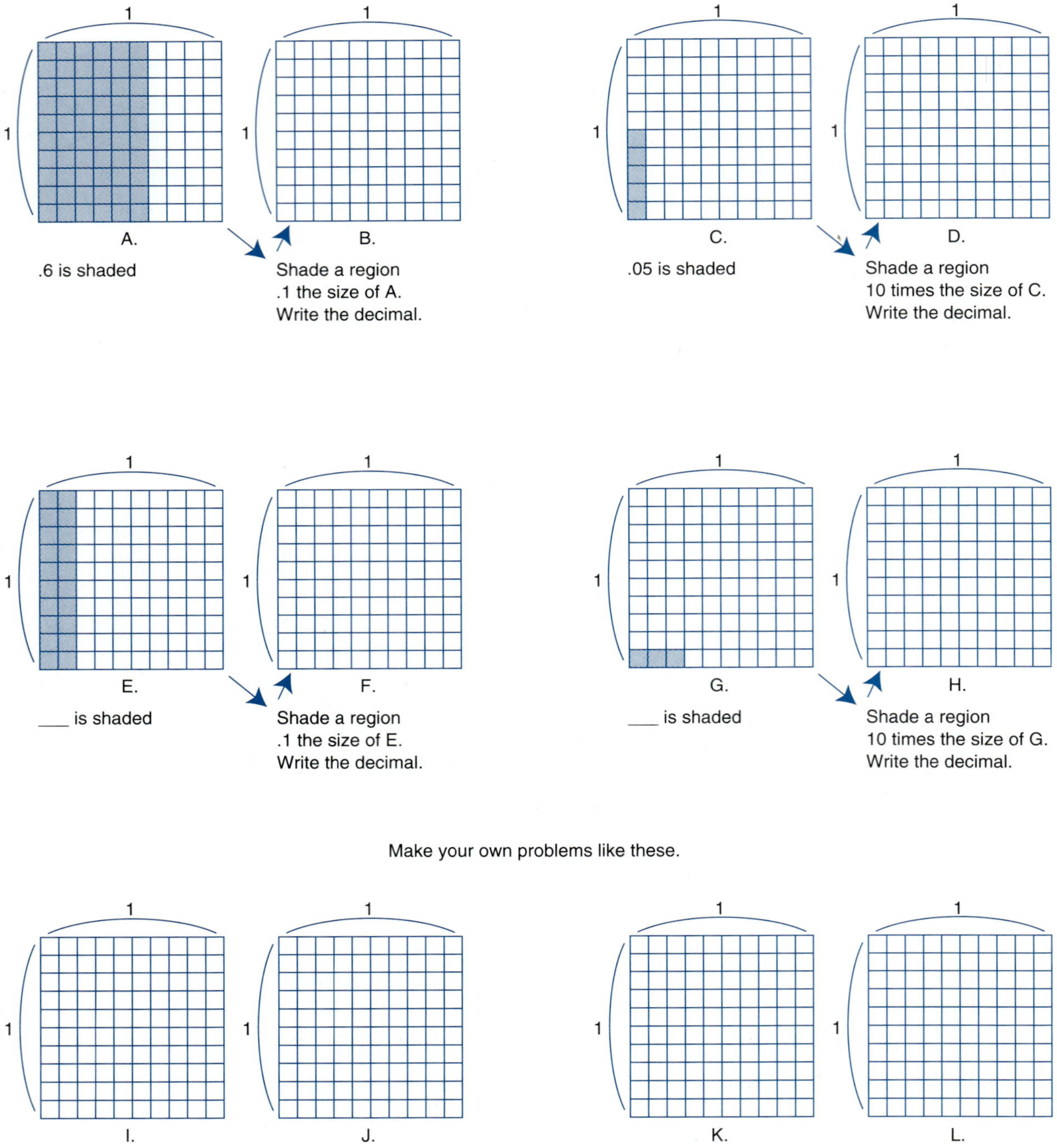

FIGURE 10.5 Study Sheet for Decimal Relations

After children are familiar with thousandths, introduce the idea that the ones place is the center of the place-value system. A table such as in Figure 10.7 can be used to help them grasp this idea. Ask students to study the table to learn more about the place-value system. Questions to ask as students examine the table include: "What number names are related in the place-value system?" "How does the ones place help us see these relationships?" "What does the decimal point tell us?" "Why can we say the ones place is the center of the place-value system?"

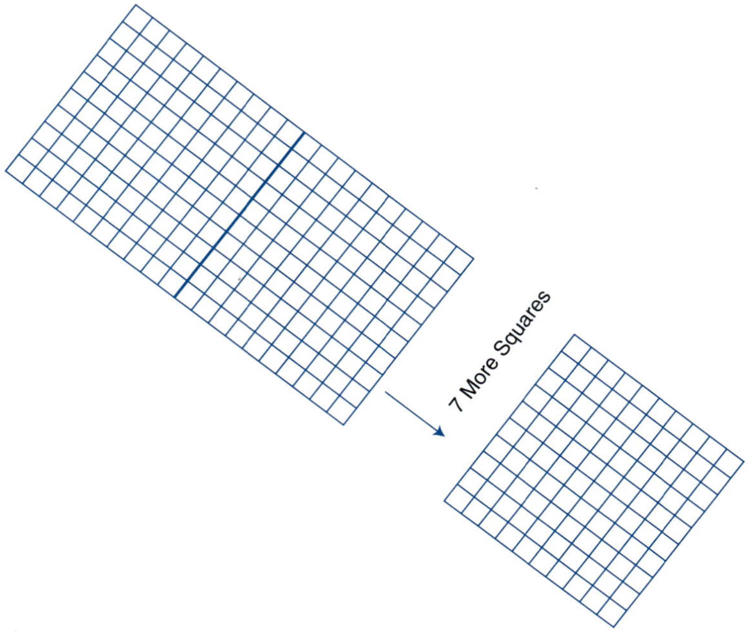

FIGURE 10.6 A One Whole Strip

Comparing, Ordering, and Estimating Decimals

Comparing, ordering, and estimating are related to understanding equivalent decimals. Knowing that annexing or removing a zero to the right of a decimal gives an equivalent decimal (.5 = .50 = .500) is a powerful learning that makes comparing, ordering, and in some cases, estimating almost routine procedures. However, the notion of equivalent decimals is a new idea that is unrelated to children's knowledge of whole numbers and must be built up from meaningful activities.

Activities 10.12–10.20 teach comparing, ordering, and estimating with decimals.

ACTIVITY 10.12
Equivalent Decimals.

Have children use their one whole strips for this activity. Begin with thousandths. Have children decide what part of the strip shows .600. Next, ask them to give a decimal equivalent to .600 by studying the strip. If they are unable to solve this problem, have them count by hundredths and tenths until .600 is reached. Continue with other thousandths. Later, have students give equivalent decimals for examples such as .630, .45, and .3. Have students explain their responses and use the one whole strip to help others understand how they solved the problem of finding equivalent decimals. For examples such as .45, students should express orally that .45 is the same as .450, .40 + .05 and, .4 + .05. Have them use the one whole strip to investigate these ideas.

A related activity is to have children write decimals as common fractions and explain finding equivalent common fractions by multiplying (dividing) the numerator and denominator by 10 (e.g., $\frac{5}{10} = \frac{50}{100} = \frac{500}{1000}$; $\frac{600}{1000} = \frac{60}{100} = \frac{6}{10}$). The concept of equivalent decimals will be meaningful to most students if they explore these relationships with materials as well as find equivalent common fractions.

Students should also show decimal equivalents for mixed numbers (Figure 10.8). Representing mixed numbers as decimals with materials can help students understand how to rename mixed numbers as decimals.

10,000	1000	100	10	1	$\frac{1}{10}$	$\frac{1}{100}$	$\frac{1}{1000}$	$\frac{1}{10,000}$
ten-thousands	thousands	hundreds	tens	ones	tenths	hundredths	thousandths	ten-thousandths
10,000	1000	100	10	1	.1	.01	.001	.0001

FIGURE 10.7 A Place-Value System Chart

ACTIVITY 10.13
Decimals and Math Sentences.

When children can give equivalent decimals, ask groups of students to solve problems that involve writing equivalent decimals; for example, .3 = ______ = ______ or 3.5 = ______ tenths. When they understand the task, each student should write his or her own examples and discuss them with his or her group. Groups can share their work with the class.

ACTIVITY 10.14
Game: Decimal Equivalents.

Twenty-four cards give decimals, and 24 give equivalent decimals in different place-value notation (e.g, .35, .350, .3 + .05). After the cards are shuffled, each of four players is dealt 7 cards. The remainder are in a stack in the middle of the playing area. The game is played like *Rummy* or a similar matching game invented by the students.

FIGURE 10.8 Models for Mixed Numbers

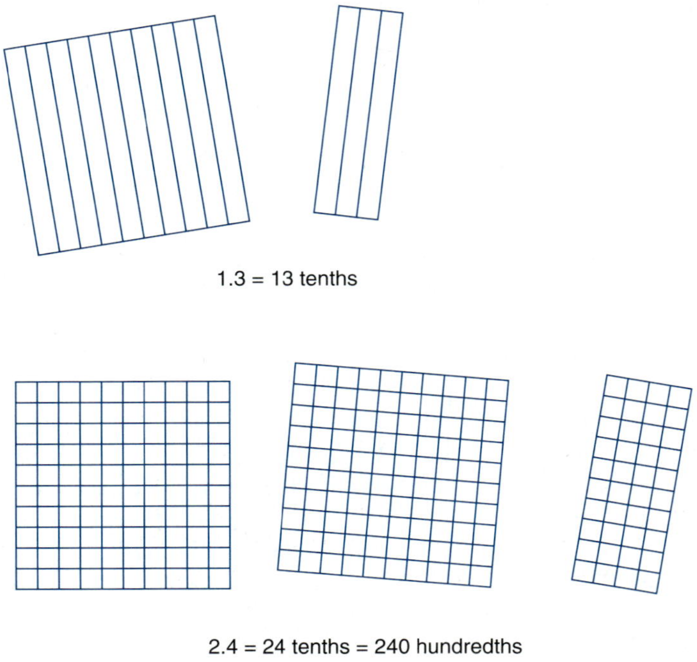

ACTIVITY 10.15
Reading Decimals May Be Confusing.

Lichtenberg and Lichtenberg (1982) point out that because the 3 in .3, .35, and .347 are read differently, students do not realize that it has the same value in each number. With whole numbers, a numeral is always read the same way if it has the same value (e.g., 34, 134, 8134).

To help children recognize that whole-number learnings do not always apply to decimals and that it is the place of a decimal that gives the number its value, have them explore the differences between reading whole numbers and decimals. Begin by asking them to read numbers (e.g, .5, .53, .543, 53, 153, 4253), and decide what are the similarities and differences in the first three and the last three. Questions to ask include: "You said we read the decimals differently. Is the value of .5 the same in each number? Why?" "How would you use materials to show the ".5" in each number?" "What are some other ways to read the decimals?"

ACTIVITY 10.16
A Rule for Equivalent Decimals.

After many experiences using materials and common fractions to find equivalent decimals, have children use an activity sheet similar to:

Show on the Meter Stick (1)

.5 .50 .500 .2 .20 .200 .7 .70 .700

1. What do you notice about these lengths?
2. What do you notice about the symbols? What rule can you develop from your observations?
3. Give these numbers a hundredths name: .3, .6, .9.
4. Give these numbers a thousandths name: .8, .40, .1.

Students discuss their work and decide that annexing a zero to a decimal does not change its value. During the discussion students should note the difference between annexing a zero to the right of a whole number and a decimal. They need to realize that annexing a zero to the right of a whole number changes the place (and the value) of each digit but that annexing a zero to the right of a decimal while changing its name does not change the place (or value) of each digit. To help them construct this idea, groups can consider the questions: "What is the difference between the values of the 5 in (1) and the values in (2)? What does this tell you? How do you know?"

1. .5, .50, .500
2. 5, 50, 500

The discussion following the groups' deliberations helps students understand why zero annexed to the right of a decimal does not change its value.

ACTIVITY 10.17
Comparing Decimals.

Have two or three children work with a meter stick. Display on the overhead or chalkboard four sets of two decimals each (e.g., a set is .34, .325). The children in each group use the meter stick to determine which decimal in a set is greater, or they may first decide which decimal is greater and then check with the meter stick. After time for group work, the class states which decimal is greater and why.

This activity can be adapted for use with decimal wheels. Each child in a pair can show one decimal in a set. Students take turns deciding which decimal is greater and giving reasons for their choice. They should also have opportunities to make up their own examples; make certain they know that a tenths and a hundredths number are to be included in each example.

Comparing decimals can be a problem for some children because they think that .42 is greater than .6. Work with materials can help them. Learner discussions are also useful if they emphasize that decimals are easier to compare if they both have the same place value and that zeros can be annexed to one decimal to give it the same place value as the other decimal.

ACTIVITY 10.18
Game: Up It.

Thirty-six cards show tenths, hundredths, or thousandths (e.g., .7, .07, .620). Eighteen cards display decimals greater than the decimals given on the other 18 cards. Each of four players receives 9 cards. Players in turn display one of their cards to the group and say, "Up it." The first player to show a card greater than the one displayed takes both cards and places them in front of him- or herself. If no one shows a card with a decimal greater than the one displayed, the player keeps his or her card. The game ends when one player has no cards. The winner is the player with the most cards.

ACTIVITY 10.19
Ordering Decimals.

When students can give the greater of two decimals, they order decimals by size. Examples of decimals to order are:

1. .3, .18, .46, .9, .6.
2. .8, .76, .222, .64, .09.

Students can work in groups or individually to order the decimals. After they complete their work, they discuss how they ordered the decimals. A useful procedure is to find equivalent decimals, so that all the decimals to be ordered have the same number of places and are therefore easier to compare. If this idea is not expressed during the discussion, to remind children of the process, ask a question similar to, "How can you use what you know about equivalent decimals to help you order decimals?"

For some children, the first problem should include only three decimals to order. Later more decimals are included in the ordering problem.

ACTIVITY 10.20
Estimating Decimals.

Ask children to decide if each decimal in a list (e.g., .8, .19, .44, .3, .05) is closer to 0, .25, .5, or 1. Children can locate the decimals on decimal wheels or number lines to help decide on the estimate. Discussion should help children think about strategies for estimating decimals. Ask how knowledge of whole number relations can help to estimate with decimals.

Learning Common Fraction Equivalents for Decimals

Common fraction equivalents for decimals should involve activities similar to Activities 10.21–10.23. Later, children can use the calculator to find decimal equivalents for fractions. Initially, however, children need visual experiences to develop intuitive understanding of the equivalents. Over time have children learn common fraction equivalents for .2 ($\frac{1}{5}$), .25 ($\frac{1}{4}$), .33, or .34 (about $\frac{1}{3}$), .5 ($\frac{1}{2}$), .75 ($\frac{3}{4}$), and .66 or .67 (about $\frac{2}{3}$).

ACTIVITY 10.21
Using Decimal Wheels to Find Equivalents.

Decimal wheels are superior materials for learning about frequently used common fraction equivalents for decimals (Van de Walle, 1990). Pass out both decimal wheels and fraction disks. Ask children to choose several fraction disk pieces and to find decimal equivalents for these pieces, using any method they choose (Figure 10.9). Discuss their responses and how they found the decimal equivalents for the fraction disk pieces. Have students each make a list of at least four fraction and decimal equivalents they think would be important to know. Have them explain their choices for the list.

ACTIVITY 10.22
Game: Decimal Equivalents for Common Fractions (DECF Game).

Twelve cards showing shaded regions to indicate common fractions and twelve showing regions to indicate their decimal equivalents are used in the game. The game is played like *Memory*. The rules for *Memory* are: all the cards are laid face down on a playing surface. Two players take turns turning over two cards. If the cards show a common fraction and its decimal equivalent, the player keeps the cards. If not, the cards are laid face down in their original places to be turned over again. When all the cards are gone, the player with the most cards wins.

ACTIVITY 10.23
Asking Preferences.

Have groups of children write three or more questions such as: Which is your preference, $\frac{1}{2}$ a pizza or .6 of a pizza? Why? Which is your preference, $\frac{3}{4}$ of a dollar or .79 cents? Why? Groups trade questions and write answers to the questions. Questions and answers are shared with the class.

Activity for the Classroom 10.1. Write five tasks for sixth-grade students to determine if they can represent decimals on grid paper, give equivalent decimals, and compare and order decimals. Some tasks should require students to tell how they arrived at their answers so that you can assess their understanding as well as their response (e.g., explain how you would decide which is greater, .67 or .8). Administer the tasks to four students. Write a brief report that summarizes your assessment of their understanding and achievement.

LEARNING COMPUTATION WITH DECIMALS

As with whole numbers, children study the meaning of the operations with decimals, mental computation, and computational estimation before they study paper-and-pencil decimal computation (see Standard 7 in Curriculum Standards for Grades 5–8, Appendix A). These learnings are discussed in each of the two parts of this section: Addition and Subtraction Computation, and Multiplication and Division Computation.

In their study of computation with decimals, children are helped to realize that they first think the computation with whole numbers and then give the solu-

FIGURE 10.9 Decimal Wheels Showing Common Fractions and Decimal Equivalents

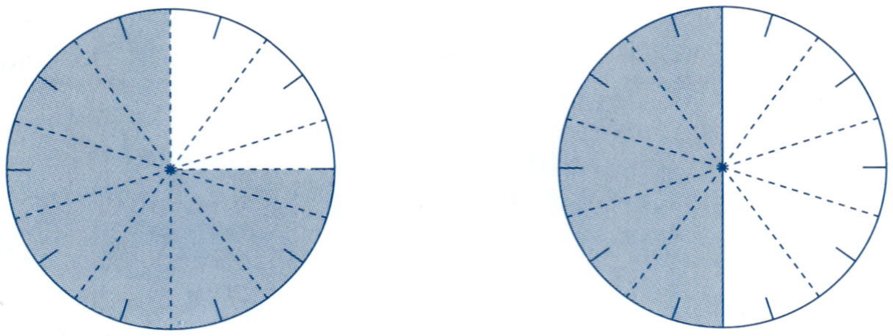

tion its decimal value. The following equations illustrate the rationale for this procedure:

$$.3 + .3 = (3 \times .1) + (3 \times .1) = (3 + 3)(.1) = 6\ (.1) = .6$$

$$.3 \times .3 = 3 \times .1 \times 3 \times .1 = (3 \times 3) \times (.1 \times .1) = 9 \times .01 = .09$$

Addition and Subtraction Computation

Objectives for teaching addition and subtraction computation with decimals are for children to learn that: (1) the meanings of addition and subtraction with decimals are the same as for common fractions; (2) only decimals with like decimal values are added or subtracted; (3) some answers can be computed mentally; (4) estimation of sums and differences should be the first step in computation and the sense of solutions should be checked; and (5) paper-and-pencil algorithms are based on place-value concepts. Problem-solving activities that involve the use of materials begin the study of computation to enable children to focus on the first four objectives. Later, children learn to compute. However, the time devoted to practice is minimal, because hand-held calculators are used for most decimal computations that are not easily computed mentally.

Developing Meanings from Problem Solving. Story and number problems are used to help students understand decimal addition and subtraction. Problem solving helps develop the meanings of addition and subtraction with decimals, the concepts of adding and subtracting decimals with like decimal values, and an awareness of regrouping. When problems are assigned, students are reminded to think about the sense of their solutions. Examples of problems are:

1. Monday it rained .45 inch. Tuesday it rained .75 inches. How much did it rain those two days? How much more did it rain Tuesday? (Joining: Find Result; Comparing: Find Difference.)
2. Denise walks .5 of a mile from school to her house; Joseph walks .25 of a mile. Who walks farther? How much farther? (Comparing: Find Difference.)
3. What number is 9 tenths plus 3 tenths?
4. What is the difference between 8 tenths and 55 hundredths?
5. What is the sum of 6 tenths and 29 hundredths?

As learners use materials and common fractions to solve the problems, they study the meaning of addition and subtraction with decimals and develop the idea of adding or subtracting decimals with like decimal values, such as, .3 + .6 = .9; .5 + .03 = .50 + .03 = .53 (Behr and Post, 1988; Hiebert, 1987). Materials also help students explain why their solutions are reasonable.

Students use base ten blocks, grid paper, decimal cards, number lines, and decimal wheels to find solutions to story and number problems (Figure 10.10 gives grid paper solutions). After solving problems with materials, they are asked to write math sentences to represent the problem situation. As they explain their work, your questions help students express the idea that the *meanings* of addition and subtraction with decimals are the same as for whole numbers and fractions. They should know that addition is used in joining or combining situations and subtraction is used in separating, comparing, or making equal situations.

Manipulative aids help children focus on the idea that because only equal-sized pieces can be combined and counted, only *decimals with the same decimal value can be added or subtracted.* Students can use both common and decimal fractions in some problems to clarify this idea. Thinking about using like denominators when adding or subtracting common fractions enables some learners to understand that when adding and subtracting decimals, the numbers must also have the same decimal values (e.g., tenths). Opportunities to discuss ideas help learners clarify their understanding that only decimals with like decimal values can be added or subtracted and that a solution has the same decimal value as the numbers in the problem. Discussion questions to ask include: "What blocks (cards) did you use to solve that problem? Why?" Children should explain that to count the number of decimal pieces that show the solution, the pieces must be the same size. Further questioning helps them state:

1. When you add tenths to tenths, the sum is tenths, which may be renamed a whole number plus tenths.
2. When you add hundredths to hundredths, the sum is hundredths, which may be renamed tenths plus hundredths.

Regrouping is necessary to find solutions to some of the problems students are assigned. Children should discuss why they traded 10 units for 1 long. Although when computing, the whole-number algorithm is used and the decimal value determined as the last step in finding a solution, their discussion of renaming (e.g., 10 hundredths as 1 tenth in addition and 1 tenth as 10 hundredths in subtraction) helps children grasp the meaning of the process.

Many students will be able to compute the answers mentally, because the assigned computations are easy and learners relate their knowledge of whole numbers and common fractions to decimals. Ask students to solve at least one problem with materials to make certain they understand that to solve a problem, they must think the same decimal value for the numbers.

After children use materials to grasp the idea of adding or subtracting decimals with like place values and regrouping when necessary, they often do write-ups to explain their work. It is expected that they would tell about using equivalent decimals. Students should also be asked to write the math sentences for addition and subtraction problems that show equivalent decimals (e.g., .6 + .29 = .60 + .29 = .89). Class discussion of completed work helps children understand the need to think equivalent decimals in some addition and subtraction problems and write equivalent decimals in math sentences for these problems.

Mental Computation and Computational Estimation. After students understand that in decimal addition and subtraction computation the numbers must have the same decimal value, they are asked to *compute mentally* to find solutions to story and number problems that involve decimals. Examples of problems are:

1. Kelly learned that hamburgers at one restaurant have .3 pound of meat. At an other restaurant, they have .25 pound of meat. What is the difference in the amount of meat in the hamburgers. Which would you buy? Why?
2. Heidi usually runs 1.5 miles in the morning and 1.25 miles in the afternoon. How many miles does she run in a day?
3. Today it rained .3 inches. Yesterday we had .05 inches. How much rain did we have in the two days?

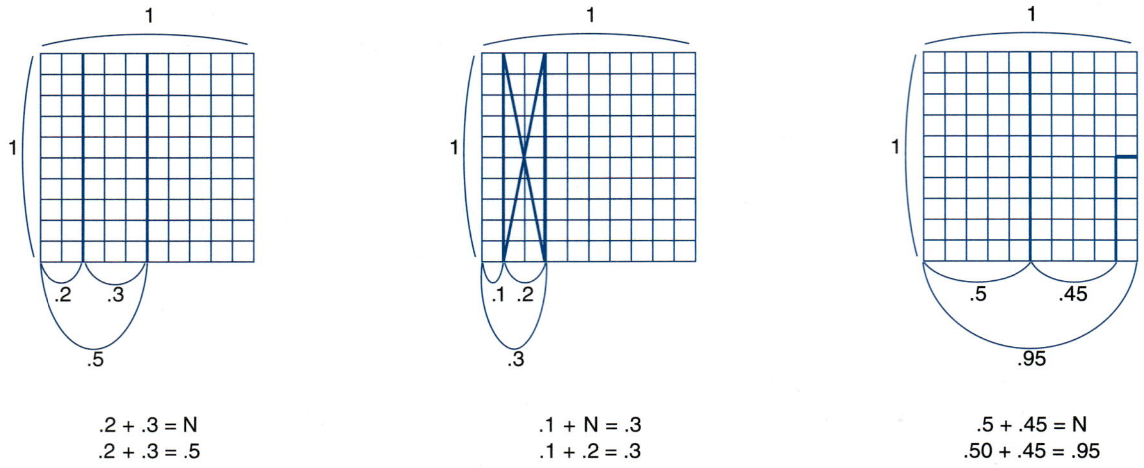

FIGURE 10.10 Grid Paper Solutions for Addition-with-Decimals Problems

4. What is the difference between 6 tenths and 3 tenths?
5. What number is .5 + .04?
6. What number is 3 tenths plus 67 hundredths?

After several solutions are found, students are asked how they knew to compute mentally. The focus of the discussion in response to this and other questions is that mental addition or subtraction (1) often involves thinking equivalent decimals, (2) always makes use of basic facts, (3) always requires giving a solution a correct decimal value, which is the same decimal value as that of the addends or minuend and subtrahend, and (4) involves checking solutions for accuracy and reasonableness.

Writing math sentences with words can help some children construct these ideas. If problems are given with words, students may write the math sentences with words, for example, 6 tenths − 3 tenths = *N*. If they do not use words, say, "Using words in the math sentence can help us learn to compute mentally. Let's try it." During the discussion, students also conclude that strategies for mental computation with decimals are the same as whole-number mental computation: front-end, compensation, and compatible numbers.

Computational estimation problems are introduced about the same time as mental computation. Students are asked to make an estimate of a solution that would be reasonable for a problem. Problems for estimating solutions are:

1. George's record in the broad jump is 1.9 meters. His goal is 3 meters. About how far off is he now?
2. Sara had $50.00. She looked at a coat for $35.99 and shoes for $22.45. Did she have enough money for the two items?
3. Huan lives 2.12 miles from downtown. Dick lives 2.95 miles from downtown. Estimate the difference between the distances of the two boys from downtown.

After students have completed their work, they discuss their estimates and strategies. They decide that the strategies are the same as for whole numbers: front-end with adjusting, rounding, compatible numbers, and clustering. During the exchange of ideas, pupils are guided to observe that the procedure is: Think equivalent decimals, estimate as in whole-number estimation, and give the answer the same decimal value as the numbers in the problem.

Kindig (1986) suggests introducing decimal addition and subtraction estimation with all examples involving numbers greater than 1 and telling students to round to the nearest whole number and then use strategies for working with whole numbers. She also tells students to put their knowledge of money to work in estimating sums and differences. Students learn how to transform their decimal problems into money problems. For example, to estimate 3.466 + 5.481, students think \$3.47 + \$5.48, which for estimation purposes is \$3.50 + \$5.50; the estimate is 9.

Paper-and-Pencil Computation. Algorithms are rote procedures but must be understood if they are to be recalled and followed to obtain correct solutions. If children have had experiences with models, common fractions, mental computation, and computational estimation, paper-and-pencil addition and subtraction algorithms should be easily understood and mastered.

Ask learners in groups to solve decimal problems too complex to do mentally (e.g., 3.45 + 5.63), to use any procedure for solution they wish, to think about the reasonableness of their solutions, to make a record of their work, and to think about a rule for computation that involves placing the decimal point. Have children report on their solutions, written records, and rules. After they reflect on their work in response to your questions, students conclude the rule is: Line up the decimal points to add like values; annex zeros as needed to indicate equivalent decimals; add as with whole numbers; and give the sum (difference) the same number of places as the addends (minuend and subtrahend) to show the place value of the number in the solution (Figure 10.11). The rule should also include a reference to deciding if a solution is reasonable. To verify their rule, pupils can use common fractions (Figure 10.12).

The sense of the rule should be discussed often, particularly the reasons for lining up the decimal points and giving the solution the same number of decimal places as the numbers in the problem (tenths added to tenths is tenths, hundredths added to hundredths is hundredths, and so forth). Once again using decimal words can help learners grasp the sense of the rule. For example,

42	hundredths
+ 83	hundredths
125	hundredths = 1.25

Although some time is given to practice with the rule, the thrust of instruction is for children to understand the rule and be able to judge the sense of a solution. Students are expected to be able to do calculations involving two or three places (whole numbers and decimals) so that they become confident in their ability to deal with easy computations. Speed is not an objective, however. Calculators are used for most computations because they are speedy and accurate.

Multiplication and Division Computation

The objectives for multiplication and division with decimals are the same as those for addition and subtraction: constructing meaning and developing skill. Initially, instruction is planned to help learners understand the meanings of multiplication and division with decimals. Later, they learn mental computation and estimation, and finally, paper-and-pencil computation. Children also learn to use calculators for tedious computations.

The instructional sequence for learning multiplication and division with decimals is similar to that for addition and subtraction. Students first use materials to solve problems. Working with materials helps them discover that the meanings of multiplication and division with decimals are the same as for common fractions

3.45	.5	→	.50	.75
+ 5.63	+ .35		+ .35	+ .93
9.08			.85	1.68

FIGURE 10.11 Paper-and-Pencil Solutions for Addition-with-Decimals Problems

$$\begin{array}{r} 3\frac{45}{100} \\ +\ 5\frac{63}{100} \\ \hline 8\frac{108}{100} \end{array} = 9\frac{8}{100} = 9.08$$

$$\begin{array}{rcr} \frac{5}{10} & = & \frac{50}{100} \\ +\ \frac{35}{100} & = & \frac{35}{100} \\ \hline & & \frac{85}{100} \end{array} = .85$$

$$\begin{array}{r} \frac{75}{100} \\ +\ \frac{93}{100} \\ \hline \frac{168}{100} \end{array} = 1\frac{68}{100} = 1.68$$

FIGURE 10.12 Common Fraction Solutions for Addition-with-Decimals Problems.

and that they can write math sentences using what they know. Using concrete representations to solve problems also gives learners a sense of the size of reasonable solutions for multiplication and division decimal problems and enables them to construct patterns for determining decimal places in products and quotients. The next steps are to mentally compute products and quotients and estimate solutions. The last step is to develop the paper-and-pencil algorithms for multiplication and division with decimals by using patterns. While students are studying paper-and-pencil algorithms, they continue to use calculators in problem solving and learn that calculators should frequently be used for decimal computation.

Developing Meanings from Problem Solving. Conceptual understanding develops as students *solve problems* using models and common fractions. Problems enable students to learn all the meanings of multiplication and division with decimal fractions. The following sample story and number word problems illustrate these meanings:

1. Jack's garden was .4 of his parents' plot. His parents' plot was .6 of an acre. How much of the acre was Jack's garden? (Multiplication: "Of" interpretation.)
2. At the deli they made sandwiches with .25 pound of sliced chicken in a sandwich. Carmen bought 3 sandwiches. How much chicken was in the three sandwiches? (Multiplication: Repeated addition interpretation.)
3. Fritz bought .8 pound of sliced chicken at the deli to make his own sandwiches. He divided the chicken evenly for 4 sandwiches. How much chicken was in each of Fritz's sandwiches? (Division: Partitive interpretation.)
4. Mother is taking medicine for a cold. The prescription is .8 of an ounce. She takes a teaspoon or .2 of an ounce each night. How many times can she take the medicine before it is all gone? (Division: Measurement interpretation.)
5. What number is one tenth of eight hundredths? (Multiplication: "Of" interpretation.)
6. What is seven 3 tenths? (Multiplication: Repeated addition interpretation.)
7. Six hundredths divided into 3 equal parts is what number? (Division: Partitive interpretation.)
8. How many four tenths equal 8 tenths? (Division: Measurement interpretation.)
9. How many 5 tenths equal 2? (Division: Measurement interpretation.)

To introduce decimal multiplication and division, problems such as the preceeding ones are assigned. The students are asked to use any method for solution that seems helpful to them and think about the sense of the solution (Figure 10.13). Beginning lessons will include only one interpretation of an operation, and multiplication and division are studied separately. Soon, both meanings of each operation are studied in the same lesson, and both multiplication and division problems are included. In some lessons, students write a few sentences describing how they thought as they solved one or more problems.

After children find solutions working together or alone, children share their methods of solution. When they can solve problems using materials, they *write math sentences*. They discuss why multiplication or division math sentences fit the problems, and in so doing they examine the meanings of these operations with deci-

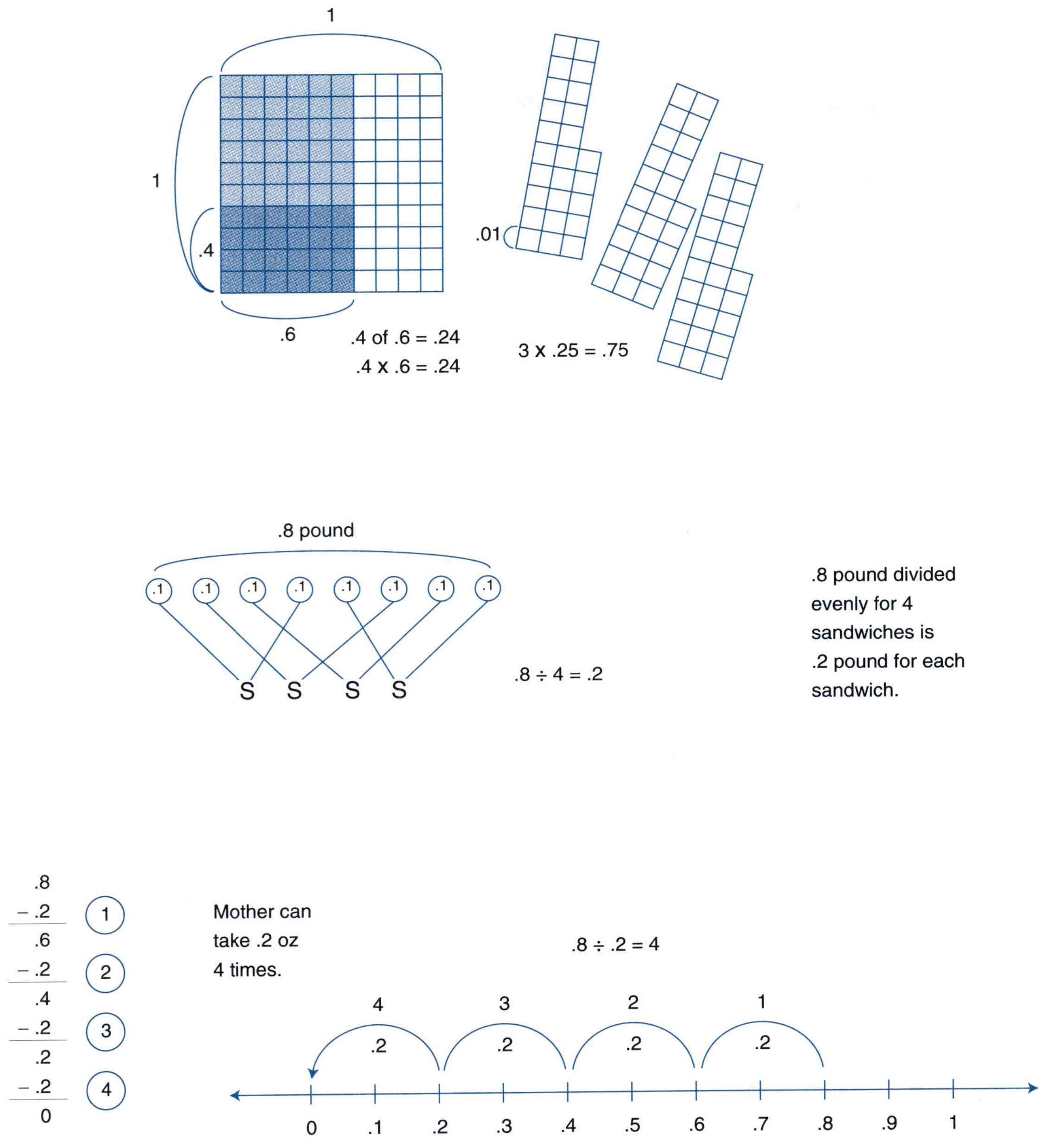

FIGURE 10.13 Solutions for Multiplication- and Division-with-Decimals Problems

mals. They compare the interpretations of these operations with decimals with those for common fractions and whole numbers by substituting common fractions and then whole numbers for decimals in the problems. They decide that the "of" meaning for multiplication with decimals applies to common fractions, but not to whole numbers. Common fraction or whole-number meanings make sense in the other problems. Learners explain that multiplication can be like repeated addition and division means repeated subtraction or sharing equally.

Activity for the Classroom 10.2. Write four problems, each one of which illustrates a different meaning of multiplication or division with decimals. Have learners substitute common fractions and then whole numbers in your problems, and ask them to note the meaning of the operation associated with each problem. They discuss their ideas to help them extend the meanings of multiplication and division with decimals.

Special attention is given to evaluating the *sense of solutions*, and children are encouraged to reason to evaluate the sense of the answer. For example, in Problem

1, children would reason that their answer, .24, found by using grid paper, would be sensible because Jack had only .4 of .6 of an acre and that is not a very big piece.

After finding problem solutions using methods of their own choice, students examine their work to *find patterns* useful for mental computation and estimation. These patterns relate the decimal values of factors to the decimal values of products and the decimal values of dividends and divisors to the decimal values of quotients. The patterns they construct include:

Ones times tenths equals tenths.

Tenths times tenths equals hundredths.

Tenths divided by ones equals tenths.

Hundredths divided by ones equals hundredths.

Tenths divided by tenths equals ones.

Hundredths divided by tenths equals tenths.

Children test these patterns by solving a few new problems with materials or common fractions. They may notice that it seems a pattern does not apply in some problems. However, in those cases one number is renamed (trading occurs) to find the solution (e.g., $7 \times .3 = 21$ tenths $= 2.1$; $2 \div .5 = 20$ tenths $\div$ 5 tenths $= 4$), and it turns out that the patterns are valid. Materials can be used again as a follow-up to demonstrate this renaming. The patterns are then posted and used in the next phase of instruction.

Mental Computation and Computational Estimation. If students have solved problems with materials or common fractions, evaluated the sense of their solutions, and have an understanding of the patterns used to determine the place value of products and quotients, they have the knowledge needed for mental computation and computational estimation with decimals.

A lesson to introduce *mental computation* begins with a review of what they have learned about multiplication and division with decimals and strategies for mental computation. Students are then assigned problems involving multiplication and division with decimals that are simple enough to compute mentally, and they are asked to find solutions without paper and pencil. For example,

1. Teresa bought a candy bar for each of the 6 people, including herself, at her birthday party. Each bar was .6 oz. How many ounces of candy did she buy?
2. Yetta noticed that tapes of her favorite rock star were on sale for 3 for $9.99. She did not have that much money, and so she bought only one. What did it cost without tax?
3. Reuben was selling hot dogs at a school football game. They cost $1.50 with tax. One Mom ordered 4. What would she pay Reuben?
4. Lewis makes $5.25 a hour working at the grocery store as a stock person. He works 10 hours a week? What does he make each week?
5. What number equals 5 tenths times 5 tenths?
6. What number equals $.75 \div .25$?

Learners work in groups or individually, record their solutions, and discuss their solutions and strategies after they have had time to complete the work. They note that the multiplication and division mental computation with decimals is like mentally computing with whole numbers, except, that the solutions are given decimal values. The patterns developed previously enable them to give decimal values to each solution.

Of particular importance is learning multiplication by 10 and 100. Metric measurement involves such multiplication and understanding the algorithm for division also requires knowledge of multiplication by powers of 10. The following activity introduces the rule.

ACTIVITY 10.24
Multiplying Decimals by 10 and 100.

Assign an activity sheet with directions such as the following:

1. Use grid paper or any other material you wish, common fractions, or thinking to answer the following:

a. $10 \times .3 = N$; $10 \times .4 = N$; $10 \times .12 = N$.

b. $100 \times .3 = N$; $100 \times .4 = N$; $100 \times .12 = N$.

2. Write a few sentences to explain why the first answer in (a) and in (b) are sensible.

After students complete their work, they discuss their solutions and explanations. Then, they are asked to find patterns in their answers. From a study of the patterns, some students will be able to state the rule: To multiply a number by 10, move the decimal point one place to the right; to multiply by 100, move the decimal point two places to the right. Annex zeros to the decimals, if necessary. They can test the rule on the calculator. They should also discuss that this rule is based on the meaning of place value—adjacent places are related by multiplication or division by 10.

Computational Estimation is introduced about the same time as mental computation. An interactive lesson introduces the topic. Learners are asked to estimate to solve problems, evaluate their solutions, and think about the strategies they used. After solving the problems, they discuss their work. Questions asked during the discussion help students realize that three computational strategies for whole numbers, front-end with adjusting, rounding, and compatible numbers, are often used in decimal computational estimation, while clustering is used less often. Questions also help learners understand the importance of thinking the decimal value of the numbers in problems and using patterns to determine the decimal value of solutions. The lesson begins with story problems such as:

1. Fanchon's Mom divided a can of cherries weighing 15.5 ounces evenly for dessert for her family of 4. About how many ounces did each person get?
2. Carlos's Dad uses a pedometer to determine how far he walks. He walked 16.5 kilometers in 5 days. If he walked the same amount each day, about how far did he go each of the 5 days?
3. The fifth-grade sold popcorn at the school fair. It cost \$.79 for a small bucket. The members of the class took turns at the booth selling popcorn. They sold 69 buckets. About how much did they make? The sixth-grade sold candy apples for \$.89 each. They sold 52. About how much did they make? Estimate which class made more money.

Kindig (1986) suggests using the repeated addition interpretation of multiplication with decimals for estimation work (e.g., to estimate $42.12 \times .12$, think $42 \times .10 = 4.20$; the estimate is a little more, about 4.50). Initially, students make gross estimates by deciding if the product will be greater or less than one of the factors. Gradually more refined estimates are made using the strategies learned with whole numbers. The money analogy she introduced with estimation of sums and differences continues to be emphasized.

Kindig uses the measurement interpretation for learning estimation of decimal quotients, and the money analogy continues to be stressed. Again, students begin with rough estimates and decide if the quotient will be greater or less than 1. Gradually the estimates improve. For example, to estimate $6.781 \div .132$, students think, "How many 10 cents can I take out of 7 dollars? 7×10 cents is 70 cents. That's too few! 70×10 cents is 700 cents or 7 dollars; 70 is the estimate."

Recognizing common fraction equivalents of decimals enables children to use fractions, when appropriate, to estimate (Vance, 1986). For example, for purposes of estimation 45.36 ÷ .25 can be thought of as $\frac{1}{4} \times 44$.

ACTIVITY 10.25
Decimals to Fractions for Estimation.

To help children learn to use common fractions for certain decimals as an estimation strategy, ask questions such as the following;

1. If you want to find .25 of a number, what fractional part could you think?
2. If you want to find .23 of a number, what fractional part could you think for an estimation?
3. How would you use fractions to estimate solutions to these:

$$.48 \times 52 = N$$
$$.34 \times .74 = N$$
$$.21 \times .68 = N$$

After they have worked on the activity, students discuss their solutions and how thinking fraction parts can often help with estimation. Practice to gain skill in mental computation and computational estimation is necessary for most students. Short practice sessions several times a week are scheduled. The problems involve mostly tenths and hundredths. They can be written by the teacher or the students.

Paper-and-Pencil Computation. Algorithms are shortcuts for finding solutions that can be found by lengthy, but meaningful procedures. Students need to be aware that when they develop algorithms for decimal computation, they are setting up procedures that mask the meaning of what they are doing but that are efficient. (In the case of decimal multiplication, for example, it is possible to think the face value and place value of each partial product, but it is a time-consuming process and requires keeping the decimal points lined up.

For example:

```
   1.24
 ×   .3
 ------
   .012
 + .060
   .300
 ------
   .372)
```

Reader Activity 10.2

Write a multiplication open math sentence with decimals in both factors, and solve. Compute with decimals for each partial product before summing to find the final product. Give reasons why or why not this should be an activity to deepen the understanding of some learners.

Children induce the rule for multiplication with decimals from the solutions for problems they solved earlier and the patterns they formulated for giving the decimal value of products. The rule they develop is: Compute as with whole numbers; count the number of decimal places in the factors to determine the number of decimal places in the product. They can verify this rule using common fractions, but unless they have developed a way to visualize $\frac{1}{10} \times \frac{1}{10} = \frac{1}{100}$, this is also a rote procedure. To review the sense of the rule, students should occasionally be asked to examine its meaning by thinking the size of a piece .1 of .1 and recalling diagrams made earlier.

The rule for placing the decimal point in a quotient is less plausible. It requires reasoning that (1) if the divisor is a whole number, the quotient has the same decimal value as the dividend; and (2) if the divisor is not a whole number, the computation can be carried out with an equal expression that has a whole number divisor found by multiplying the divisor and dividend by the same power of 10. For example,

$$.08 \div .4 = (10 \times .08) \div (10 \times .4) = .8 \div 4 = .2$$

or

$$\tfrac{8}{100} \div \tfrac{4}{10} = (10 \times [\tfrac{8}{100}]) \div (10 \times [\tfrac{4}{10}]) = \tfrac{8}{10} \div 4 = \tfrac{2}{10}$$

To develop the rule for placing the decimal point in quotients, students study the patterns for dividing a decimal number by a whole number that they developed from problem solutions at a previous time. They determine that the quotient has the same decimal value as the dividend when the divisor is a whole number. When they discover that it is easy to find the placement of the decimal point in the quotient when the divisor is a whole number, give problems with decimal divisors (e.g., $5.5 \div .5 = N$). Ask questions such as: "What is the meaning of this problem? Will the quotient be less or greater than 1?" "What do we know about dividing a decimal by a whole number that will help us? How can we make this problem easy by finding an equal expression that has a whole-number divisor?" (Multiply the dividend and divisor by 10—e.g., $5.5 \div .5 = (10 \times 5.5) \div (10 \times .5) = 55 \div 5 = 11$.) Using common fractions can help students realize that multiplying the dividend and divisor by the same power of 10 gives a problem with the same solution.

The next step, probably in a later lesson, is for learners to develop a rule for computation. Assign students several open math sentences whose solutions involve multiplying both the dividend and divisor by 10. Ask them to notice what happens to the decimal points in the numbers when they multiply both the dividend and divisor by 10, and have them discuss their observations. Show the use of arrows to place decimal points in the divisor and dividend (e.g., $.5\overline{)5.5}$). Make certain students understand that using arrows is a shortcut for multiplying the dividend and divisor by the same number.

An alternative rule is: To find the number of decimal places in the quotient, subtract the number of decimal places in the divisor from the number of decimal places in the dividend (e.g., $.25 \div .5 = .5$; 2 minus 1 is 1 place). If the dividend has less decimal places than the divisor, give the dividend the same number of decimal places as the divisor before computing (e.g., $9 \div .03 = 9.00 \div .03 = 300$). This rule is related to the rule for multiplication with decimals. To understand the rule, learners can also consider the sense of math sentences and decimal division patterns.

The emphasis in instruction is for children to understand the algorithms for multiplication and division. They do simple computations, but do not practice for speed and accuracy. Most computations are carried out with calculators, and students should be able to estimate and judge the sense of their answers. These abilities require understanding multiplication and division with decimals.

ASSESSING DECIMAL LEARNING

Assessing decimal learning involves determining students' understanding of decimals and of computation, skill in computation, and attitudes. You observe and interview children, examine their work products, and give quizzes and tests. You will use the three levels of performance indicators described in Chapter 1 (What are they?). Records are kept of observations and interviews to give evidence of progress. Portfolios of children's work products are used by you and with students and interested adults to give information about the ideas and skills learners have developed.

Understanding Decimals

To assess understanding, you observe students' progress in attaining the nine objectives listed at the beginning of this chapter. Observations are made as students work individually, in groups, and participate in class discussions. Questions to ask during interviews or on quizzes or tests can be adapted from the chapter activities or from the following questions. A few items should ask students to write several sentences to tell how they thought to answer a certain question. Such write-ups give valuable information about a student's understanding.

1. Let's look at this one whole strip. Each small square represents a thousandths. Please point to the area that shows 10 thousandths. What is another name for 10 thousandths?
2. Use the number line or a big square to show which decimal is greater, .6 or .52?
3. Use your decimal strips or a big square to show which are equivalent: 2.3, .2, .23, .20.
4. Which decimal is closest in value to 1: .5, .05, .005. How did you decide?
5. Use your decimal wheel to show .25. What common fraction have you shown? How do you know?
6. Please read .2, .23, .234. You gave the 2 a different name in each decimal. Does it have a different value in each? Why do you think that?
7. Give two decimals greater than .8. How did you decide what decimals are greater than .8?
8. Give two hundredths numbers less than five tenths. How did you think to answer the question?

Understanding Computation

1. Please show $.5 - .29 = N$ on this grid paper. (Does the learner know how to begin with a one whole?)
2. Please show $.6 \div .2 = N$ on this number line? (Can the learner interpret this as a measurement division problem?)
3. If a student in another grade asked you, "Why does 4 tenths times 2 tenths equal 8 hundredths?" how would you use grid paper to explain the answer to his or her question?
4. What is a good estimate for $.45 + .62 = N$? Please explain how you arrived at your answer.
5. Is $.894 \div 5$ greater or less than 1? Why? Is $.894 \div .5$ greater or less than 1? Why?

Skill in Decimal Computation

Calculators are used more than paper and pencils in computation involving decimals, and assessment should include only easy computations to be completed with paper and pencil. Calculators should be allowed for most calculations involving story or number problems.

When students' problem solutions are incorrect, it can be due to their not grasping the problem relations. If you determine that it is not the case, but rather it is related to the use of a calculator or a paper-and-pencil algorithm, talking through their procedure often helps students find that they have been careless or have invented an invalid algorithm. Often, errors in using algorithms follow a pattern. If you notice an error pattern, helping the student discover it can help him or her eliminate many errors. Working with place-value materials can also be beneficial to students (Ashlock, 1994).

Estimating answers is necessary when using calculators to make certain that inputs were correct. Some quiz or test items ask students to use computational estimation. An example is:

Joan's estimations for the four problems below are: a. .26, b. .125, c. .5, d. .52

a. $.45 \times .6 = \square$

b. $.78 + .39 = \square$

c. $.63 \div .11 = \square$

d. $.55 - .03 = \square$

Do you agree with each of her estimations? Why or why not?

Attitudes

Attitudes are assessed as you observe and interview students and examine write-ups that ask them to tell how they feel about learning decimals. Questions to guide your assessment include: "Do students show an interest in decimals found in real-life situations?" "Do they participate in discussions involving decimals?" "Do they report using strategies and patterns in mental computation and computational estimation?" "Do they voluntarily tell why their solutions are reasonable?" "Do they demonstrate high expectations for learning to compute with decimals?" If many students seem disinterested in work with decimals, the importance of decimals in the real world can be reintroduced, and learners can be involved in researching the importance of decimals in the lives of children and adults.

SUMMARY

The chapter sections described interactive teaching approaches to enable children to construct decimal concepts and relations, learn decimal notation, understand the meanings of the operations with decimals, become aware of the logic of the algorithms for decimals, and use algorithms or calculators for solving problems involving decimals. Assessment of decimal learning was discussed in the final section.

Several models for studying the meaning of decimals were presented. Activities were described to develop understanding of decimals, learn to read and write decimals, and extend knowledge of the place-value system to numbers less than 1. Instruction for comparing, ordering, and estimating decimals, determining equivalent decimals, knowing decimal equivalents for common fractions, and developing awareness of decimals in real life was discussed.

The parts of the chapter dealing with computation stressed developing the meanings of the operations with decimals, developing skill in mental computation and computational estimation, using calculators to solve problems, and checking solutions. Teaching algorithms was discussed so that children will be able to compute when the computation is not difficult or a calculator is not readily available.

Interactive teaching and learning such as described in this chapter develop confidence in one's ability to "do" mathematics because mathematics makes sense. New directions in mathematics teaching and learning also contribute toward the development of intrinsic motivation and pleasure in studying mathematics.

REFERENCES

Ashlock, Robert B. (1994). *Error Patterns in Computation,* 6th ed. New York: Merrill.

Behr, Merlyn J., and Post, Thomas R. (1988). "Teaching Rational Number and Decimal Concepts." In *Teaching Mathematics in Grades K–8: Research Based Methods,* edited by Thomas R. Post, pp. 201–248. Boston: Allyn & Bacon.

Carpenter, Thomas P., Mary Kay Corbitt, Henry S. Kepner, Jr., Mary Montgomery Lindquist, and Robert E. Reys. (April 1981). "Decimals: Results and Implications from National Assessment." *Arithmetic Teacher* 28: 34–37.

Grossman, Anne S. (May 1983). "Decimal Notation: An Important Research Finding." *Arithmetic Teacher* 30: 32–33.

Hiebert, James. (March 1987). "Research Report: Decimal Fractions." *Arithmetic Teacher* 34: 22–23.

Hiebert, James, and Diana Wearne. (1986). "Procedures over Concepts: The Acquisition of Decimal Number Knowledge." In *Conceptual and Procedural Knowledge: The Case of Mathematics,* edited by James Hiebert, pp. 199–223. Hillsdale NJ: Erlbaum.

Hiebert, James, Diana Wearne, and Susan Tabor. (March 1991). "Fourth Graders Gradual Construction of Decimal Fractions during Instruction Using Different Physical Representations." *Elementary School Journal* 91: 321–334.

Kindig, Ann C. (1986). "Using Money to Develop Estimation Skills with Decimals." In *Estimation and Mental Computation,* edited by Harold L. Schoen and Marilyn J. Zweng, pp. 135–140. Reston, VA: National Council Teacher of Mathematics.

Kouba, Vicky L., Catherine A. Brown, Thomas P. Carpenter, Mary M. Lindquist, Edward A. Silver, and Jane O. Swafford. (April 1988). "Results of the Fourth NAEP Assessment of Mathematics: Number, Operations, and Word Problems." *Arithmetic Teacher* 35: 14–19.

Lichtenberg, Betty K., and Donovan R. Lichtenberg. (1982). "Decimals Deserve Distinction." In *Mathematics for the Middle Grades (5–9),* edited by Linda Silvey and James R. Smart, pp. 142–152. Reston, VA: National Council of Teachers of Mathematics.

National Council of Teachers of Mathematics. (1989). *Curriculum and Evaluation Standards for School Mathematics.* Reston, VA: Author.

Van de Walle, John A. (1990). *Elementary School Mathematics: Teaching Developmentally.* New York: Longman.

Vance, James H. (1986). "Estimating Decimal Products: An Instructional Sequence." In *Estimation and Mental Computation,* edited by Harold L. Schoen and Marilyn J. Zweng, pp. 127–134. Reston, VA: National Council of Teachers of Mathematics.

SOFTWARE RESOURCES

Get to the Point
Company: Sunburst
Computer: Apple, IBM, Tandy
Grade level: 5–9

Provides practice ordering, estimating, and computing (four operations) with decimals. Game format involves problem solving.

IBM Elementary Mathematics Series: Math Concepts
Company: IBM/EduQuest
Computer: IBM
Grade level: 4–6
Level II, Unit 5, Lessons 24 and 25

Express, identify, and order tenths and hundredths as decimals. Use of blocks, number lines, and common fractions to develop meaning. Solve word problems.

IBM Elementary Mathematics Series: Math Concepts
Company: IBM/EduQuest
Computer: IBM
Grade level: 5–8
Level II, Unit 5, Lesson 26

Add and subtracting with decimals.

Level III, Unit 5, Lesson 19

Multiplying and dividing with decimals.

CHAPTER 11

Exploring Geometry and Developing Spatial Sense

▪ INTRODUCTORY PROBLEM ▪

Solve the stick puzzles in Figure 11.1 and decide if they could be used with elementary school students. State why or why not. If you would use them with your students, explain what van Hiele level of thinking students would need to demonstrate to profit from work with the puzzles. (Solutions are in Figure 11.38 at the end of this chapter.)

INTRODUCTION

Geometry involves the recognition of figures, knowledge of their properties, and an awareness of their relationships. Spatial sense is often referred to as spatial visualization or spatial perception; it involves having images of objects. Wheatley (1990) suggests thinking of spatial sense as consisting of three components: construction of images, re-presenting or recalling images, and transforming or mentally manipulating images to deal with a situation or problem. Geometry and spatial sense are interdependent, and learning in one area leads to learning in the other (Del Grande, 1990). The discussion and activities described in this chapter illustrate the interrelationship of geometry and spatial sense.

Knowledge of geometry gives mathematical power (National Research Council, 1989). It makes possible further study of mathematics and provides entrance into the world of science and engineering. As natural and man-made objects exhibit geometric ideas, the study of geometry also contributes to an appreciation and understanding of the real world.

1. Take away 2 toothpicks, and leave 2 squares of the same size.

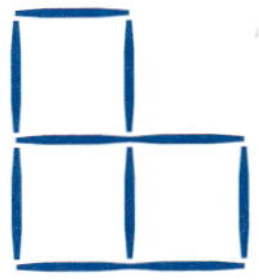

2. Take away 1 toothpick, and leave 3 squares of the same size.

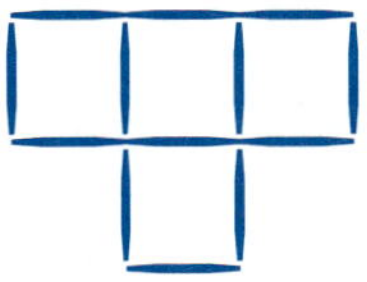

3. Take away 8 toothpicks to change 9 squares to 2 squares.

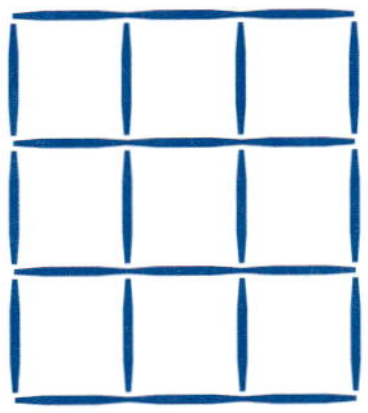

4. Take away 2 toothpicks, and leave 2 squares.

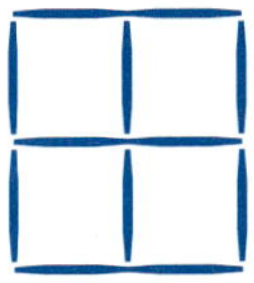

5. Rearrange 3 toothpicks to form a figure that consists of 3 squares the same size.

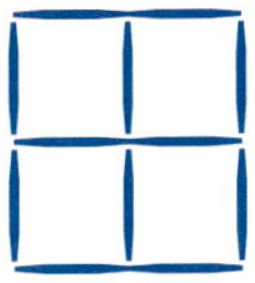

6. Rearrange 3 toothpicks to form a figure that consists of 5 squares the same size.

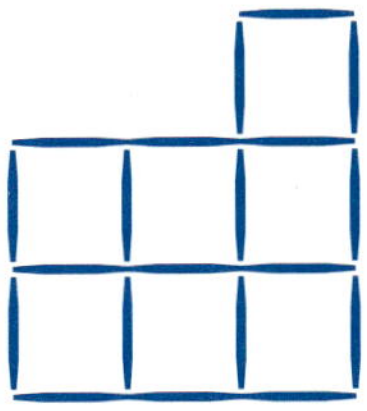

FIGURE 11.1 Toothpick Puzzles

The research of Dina van Hiele-Geldof and her husband, Pierre Marie van Hiele, two Dutch educators, resulted in their model of the development of geometric thought (Crowley, 1987). There are five levels to the model. The first section of this chapter describes these levels and their characteristics. The next section discusses using the model to teach geometry. The following three sections give activities for the first three levels. The sixth section deals with assessing the learning of geometry and spatial sense. A summary ends the chapter.

THE VAN HIELE MODEL OF GEOMETRIC THOUGHT

Five levels comprise the van Hiele model of geometric thought; certain characteristics distinguish the levels (Burger and Shaughnessy, 1986; Crowley, 1987; Hoffer, 1983; Hoffer and Hoffer, 1992).

Levels

Level 0: Visualization. Students recognize figures but not their properties such as right angles. They perceive a figure by its shape as a whole and can identify many figures. Students are able to copy shapes using paper-and-pencil or a geoboard. However, irrelevant attributes such as the orientation of a figure can mislead young children, and they would not think that all the shapes in Figure 11.2 are triangles. Students in the elementary school often exhibit this level in responding to questions that involve thinking about geometric figures (Burger, 1985).

Level 1: Analysis. Students begin to analyze geometric figures. They notice attributes of figures and develop concepts of figures by internalizing the properties they have observed. For example, they say that a triangle has three sides. They can describe figures, knowing, for example, that a parallelogram is a four-sided figure with equal opposite sides and equal opposite angles. However, they have not constructed relationships among figures. They would not know, for example, that rectangles are parallelograms. In defining figures, they often include redundancies, saying, for example, that a rectangle has two pairs of opposite sides that are equal, four right angles, and parallel sides. At this level, children can memorize definitions, but they do not understand them and discard textbook definitions in favor of their own meaningful descriptions. Therefore, they should not be asked to memorize definitions. Some students in the elementary school show indications of Level 1 thought (Burger, 1985).

Level 2: Informal Deduction. Precise definitions are understood and accepted by students at this level, and they can refer to definitions in their study of figures. They understand the relation of properties within and among figures. For example, they reason that in a parallelogram because the opposite sides are parallel, the opposite angles are equal, and they understand that because a square has all the properties

FIGURE 11.2 Triangles with Different Orientations

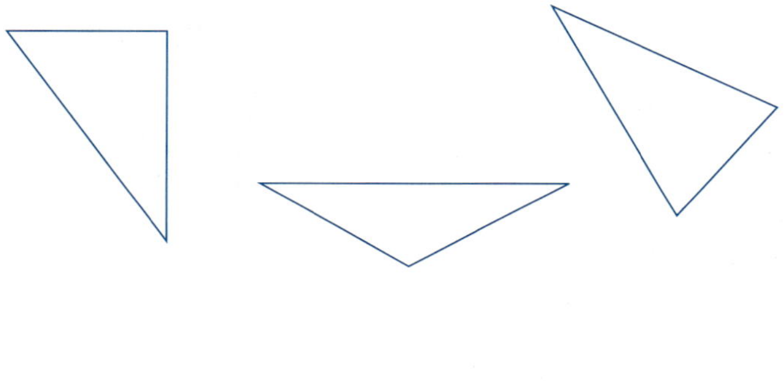

of a rectangle, it is also a rectangle. They have constructed the concept of class inclusion and recognize that a square is a rectangle, which is a parallelogram, which is a quadrilateral. They are capable of "if . . . , then" thinking but cannot construct proofs.

Level 3: Formal Deduction. At this level students can construct proofs, and they rely on proofs to determine the truth of mathematical statements. This level of thought is required to succeed in high school geometry courses.

Level 4: Rigor. This is the level of thought of mathematicians. It is a highly abstract form of geometric thought.

Characteristics of the Model

1. The levels are *sequential*, and learners must move through them in order. When a student has developed the understandings at one level, it is possible for him or her to proceed to the next level. The concepts developed at one level are integrated and extended to develop thought at the next level.
2. *Advancement* from one level to the next depends more on instruction than on age. Experience with appropriate activities enables students to advance to higher levels. Primary-grade children are usually at Level 0, and upper elementary children at Level 1. However, it is possible for both a first-grade child and a sixth grader to be at Level 0.
3. *Attaining* higher levels of geometric thought requires many opportunities to engage in activities that reveal the content and relations of a particular level, to discuss the ideas represented in the activities, to solve problems, and to integrate ideas through review and summarization. Learners can memorize statements involving formulas and generalizations (e.g., a square is a rhombus) but lack an understanding of what they have learned.
4. Learning does not occur if there is a *mismatch* between the level of instruction and a student's level of development. Teachers who employ content, materials, and vocabulary at a higher level of thought than learners are capable of understanding impede the learning of the students who may then become frustrated and anxious.

TEACHING GEOMETRY IN THE ELEMENTARY SCHOOL

Elementary school instruction in geometry concentrates on Levels 0 and 1, with some activities designed for Level 2. The activities to be described for these levels follow guidelines based on Crowley's (1987) analysis of levels, the recommendations of the NCTM (1989), and the characteristics of interactive teaching (see Standard 9, in Curriculum Standards for Grades K–4, and Standard 12 for Grades 5–8, Appendix A).

Guidelines

At Level 0 Students Should

1. Manipulate and identify geometric shapes.
2. Sort and arrange shapes.
3. Draw and construct shapes.
4. Describe shapes in their own words.
5. Solve problems involving shapes.

At Level 1 Students Should

1. Engage in activities similar to those of Level 0, but the focus of the activities should be on properties of shapes, not identification and general form as at Level 0.
2. Classify shapes by properties.
3. Derive generalizations inductively, that is, by studying examples.
4. Use appropriate vocabulary.

At Level 2 Students Should

1. Understand inclusions.
2. Reason.
3. Develop and use definitions.

Activity for the Classroom 11.1. Interview three children at different achievement levels, asking them questions in order to determine their level of geometric thinking. Your questions should be derived from the guidelines.

Organizing for Teaching

Activities are the vehicle for teaching geometric concepts and helping learners advance in thinking about space. Initial activities involve inquiry, information gathering, and vocabulary development; subsequent activities are structured and sequenced, and they orient students to specific ideas and relations; finally activities provide for further exploration, reviewing, and summarizing (Crowley, 1987). Insofar as possible, directions should be given so that students will approach the activity as a problem to be solved. After activities are completed, students discuss their work to clarify and refine their thinking. During the discussion, you ask many questions to help students express ideas and reason about their discoveries. Your questions ask students to describe their observations, explain how they carried out an activity, share solutions, and, when appropriate, to make inferences and summarize learning.

The activities can be used in centers, assigned to groups or individuals working within a whole-class setting, or in some cases assigned as homework if the school policy is to give homework. Some activities require materials that will probably not be available for all children to manipulate. Such activities can be planned over several days; each day a group engages in a different activity and uses different materials.

ACTIVITIES FOR LEVEL 0 (VISUALIZATION) LEARNING

The activities described in this section stress noticing shapes as wholes. They help children become intuitively aware of the properties of shapes. The activities are organized by the objectives manipulating and identifying, sorting and arranging, and drawing and constructing.

Manipulating and Identifying

ACTIVITY 11.1
Making Patterns.

To introduce (or reintroduce) patterns, you can say, "What is special about the stripes on Tom's shirt?" The class then discusses patterns in clothing or in articles that you have brought to class or that are in the classroom.

When it is apparent that children understand the concept of pattern, ask them to make patterns using pattern blocks. (See Figure 3.1 for drawings of pattern blocks.) If necessary, suggest using same-shape blocks or same-shape and different-shape blocks. When the patterns have been made, children describe their patterns, giving the names of the shapes they used. If children have difficulty understanding the characteristics of a pattern, have them copy or continue patterns you have made until they are ready to create patterns. A section in Chapter Three deals with helping children develop patterning concepts.

ACTIVITY 11.2
Shapes in Different Positions.

Have children use pattern blocks or shapes cut from cardboard. Working with a partner, have them show different ways in which the shape can be placed on a piece of paper (e.g., at a 30°, 45°, or 90° angle). Have them show their ideas on the overhead projector and discuss how the shape looks when placed in different positions.

ACTIVITY 11.3
Pictures.

Using pattern blocks, children can make pictures of cats, dogs, houses, or other objects of their own choosing. They can trace the shapes to make records of their work. When sharing their pictures, they should name the shapes. Help them decide to place shapes in different positions to make their pictures.

ACTIVITY 11.4
Figures Game.

Make cards of figures in different orientations (Figure 11.3) for use in games such as *Fish, Rummy* (see Box 3.1), or *Memory* (see Activity 10.22).

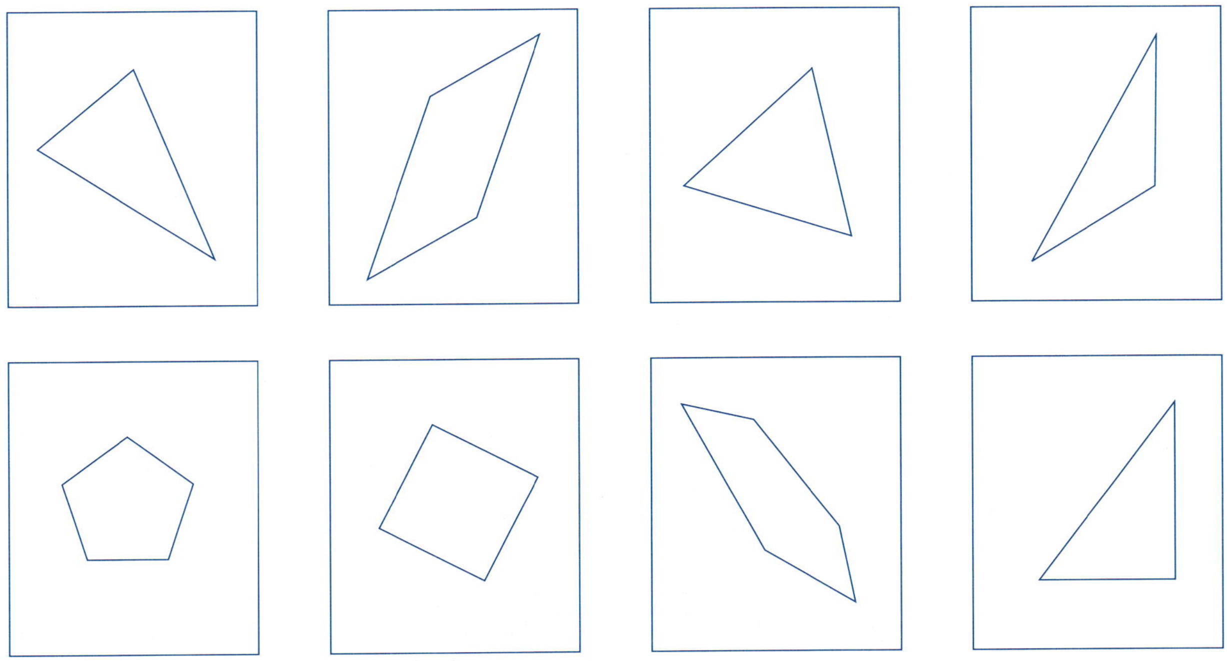

FIGURE 11.3 Figure Cards for Games

ACTIVITY 11.5
Identifying a Partner's Shapes.

Have two children work together. First, each chooses six pattern blocks, some of which are the same shapes, and places them so that both can see the blocks. Suggest placing the blocks in different positions to make the activity more fun. (Model this, if necessary.) Children take turns touching and naming the same-shape blocks their partner selected.

ACTIVITY 11.6
Making Discoveries with Folding.

Give each child several paper squares. Ask children to examine the squares and tell about the shapes. Next, ask them to fold each square in half in a different way, and report what happened to each square (folding made two different shapes). Paper rectangles are then distributed for children to use in half-folding, and the resulting figures are described. Finally, children experiment with folding different paper shapes to make discoveries about how shapes can be constructed from other shapes (Figure 11.4).

A follow-up to this activity is to have children construct shapes using more than one pattern block. They can use the ideas gained from folding to construct the new shapes.

ACTIVITY 11.7
Shape Search.

Ask children to look for shapes in and out of school. Ask them to search for different shapes each of several days or weeks. Examples should include both two- and three-dimensional shapes such as squares, rectangles, ovals, circles, cubes, prisms, and cylinders. They can draw pictures to use in the reports about their "discoveries." (This is an excellent homework activity.)

ACTIVITY 11.8
Collecting Shapes.

Ask students to contribute to a collection of three-dimensional shapes. Cereal boxes, odd-shape tins, balls, bottles, and other objects can be collected. Have children describe the various shapes that have been collected using words such as round, curved, flat, and straight.

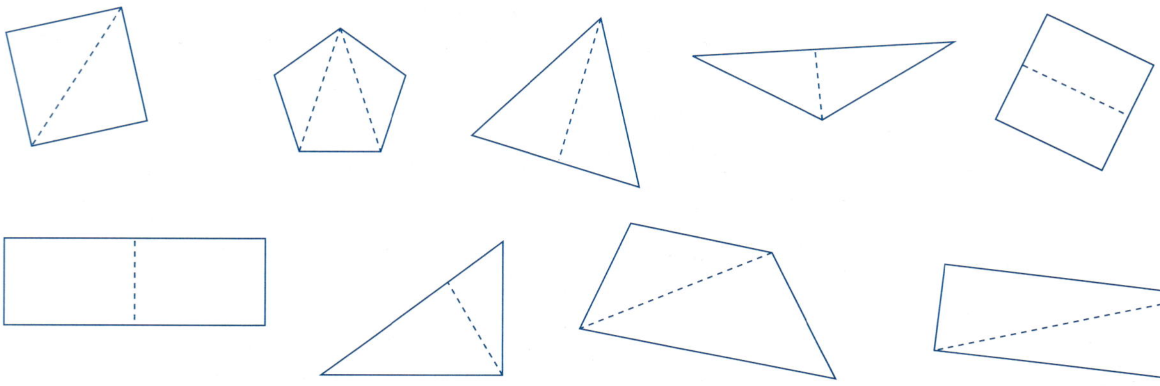

FIGURE 11.4 Folding Shapes to Show Other Shapes

ACTIVITY 11.9
How Do I Look?

Have children examine solids (Figure 11.5) and decide the shapes they see on the flat surfaces. For example, a pyramid will have triangles outlining its faces, a triangle may outline its base; a prism will have rectangles or squares outlining its faces, its bases may be triangles.

ACTIVITY 11.10
Counting Shapes.

Children can solve puzzles that involve counting the number of triangles, rectangles, and other shapes within another shape (Figure 11.6).

ACTIVITY 11.11
Feel It Game.

Objects are placed in a box to which a large sock has been attached. A chart of pictures of the objects is also prepared. Children reach in the box, feel an object, look at a chart of objects in the box, and point to the object they are feeling. They may also name or draw the object selected. To verify their identification, they should take the object out of the box. Common objects, such as spoons, as well as geometric shapes can be used in the activity.

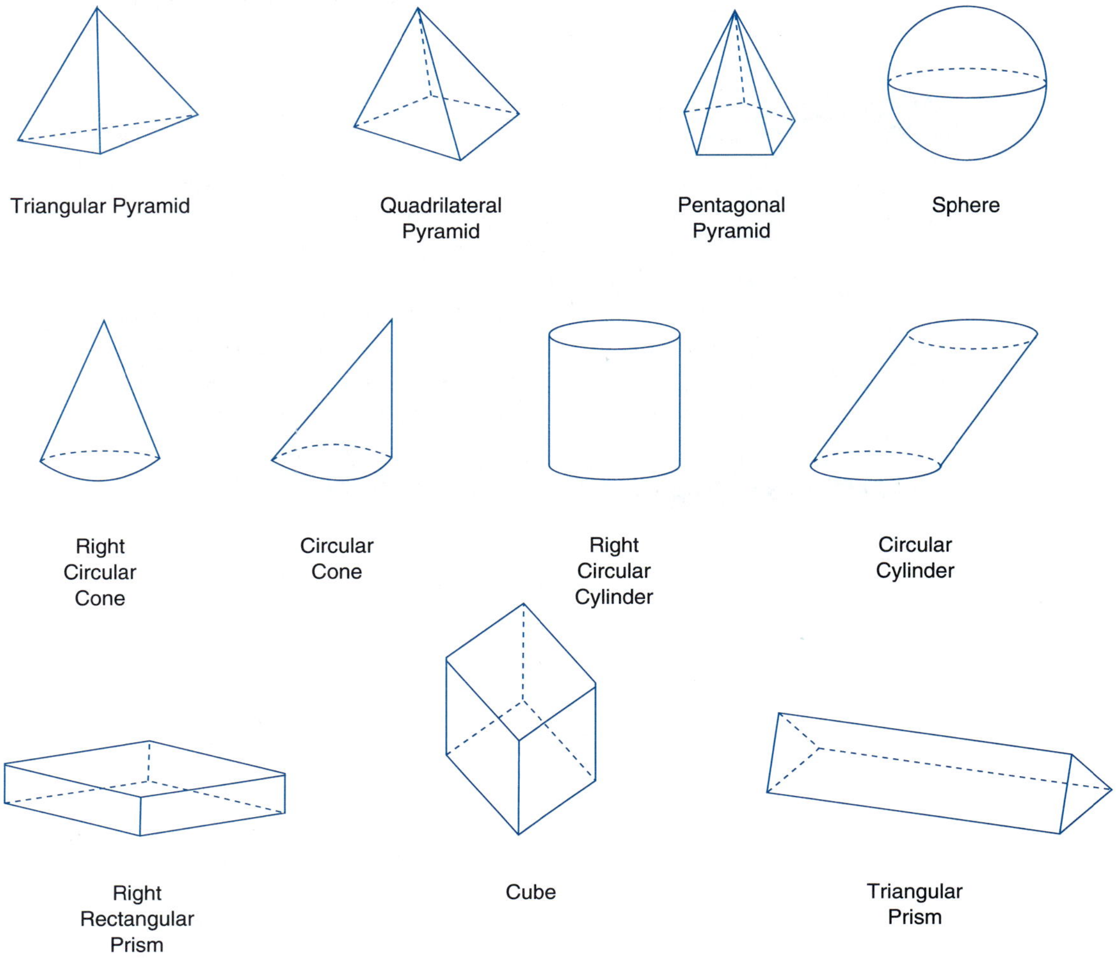

FIGURE 11.5 Geometric Solids

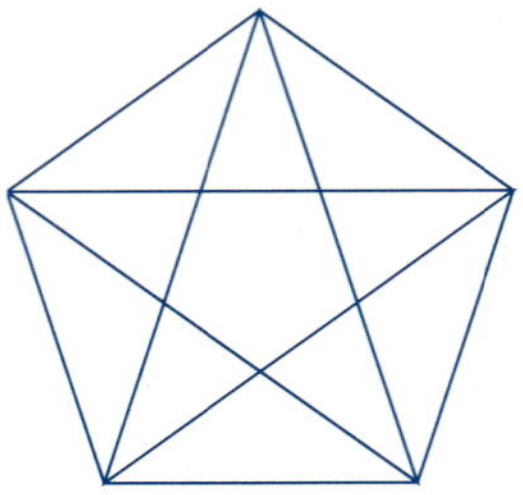

FIGURE 11.6 How Many Triangles?

Sorting and Arranging

ACTIVITY 11.12
Sorting Pattern Blocks.

Have the class work in pairs to sort pattern blocks. Each two children should have about 10 pattern blocks that include two or three shapes. The directions should be, "Put together the blocks that go together in some way." They should not be told how to sort the objects. (Why?) If two children sort by color, ask them to make another sorting in another way. When most in the class have finished, have different children explain how they sorted their pattern blocks. If they do not use the names of the shapes, tell them how to name the shapes.

ACTIVITY 11.13
Tangrams.

Tangram pieces (seven pieces cut from a square as shown in Figure 11.7) can be used in a variety of ways, using two or more pieces. Constructions include making larger shapes from smaller shapes and building pictures (Figure 11.8). Tangrams can be placed in plastic bags for small-group or individual use.

When introducing tangrams, have children name the pieces. Give them the names of the pieces they do not know, such as parallelogram, so that they can discuss their work.

Dunkels (1990) gives directions for making a tangram from a rectangular piece of paper by cutting and folding. Children can make their own tangrams if each step in the process is explained. For sturdy tangrams, cover cardboard (tablet backs will do) with contact paper. Have children trace tangram pieces on the decorated cardboard, and cut out the pieces.

ACTIVITY 11.14
Tessellations.

Tessellating is covering or tiling an area completely with one or more shapes (Figure 11.9). Show children some tessellations, and ask them to look for tessellations or tilings in and outside of school. (Floors are good examples.) Discuss their findings. Have children make tessellations with pattern blocks and show their work to others. (Children can make a follow-the-leader line and walk past the different tessellations.) Ask them to think about a tessellation, other than their own, that they like to look at or would make a beautiful floor. A bulletin board or class book of tessellations constructed on grid paper can also be made for all to enjoy.

Reader Activity 11.1

Make a tessellation. What learning did you gain from the activity?

FIGURE 11.7 Seven Tangram Pieces Make a Square

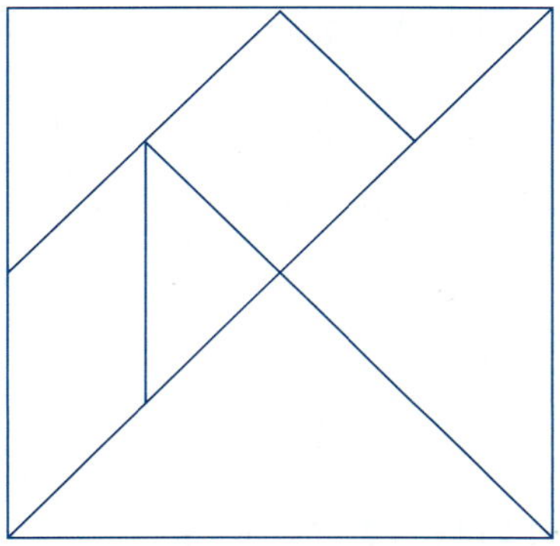

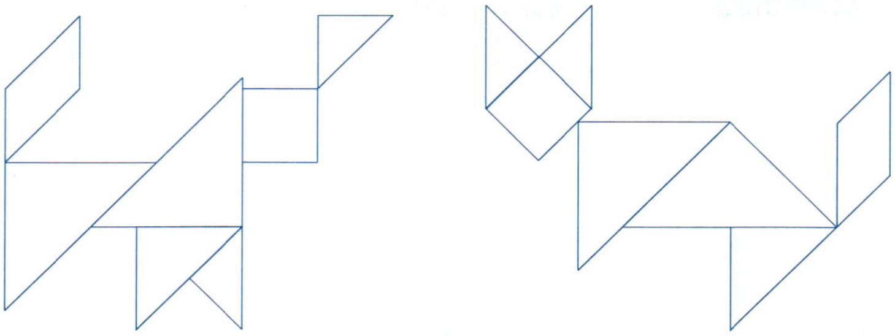

FIGURE 11.8 Tangram "Pictures"

ACTIVITY 11.15
Pentominoes.

A pentomino is a set of five squares connected along their edges. There are 12 possible pentominoes (Figure 11.10). Give children 5 squares, show 1 pentomino to illustrate what connecting along the edges means, and have them solve the problem of finding the 11 remaining pentominoes.

Pentominoes are a kind of polyomino, a set of squares connected along their edges. Children can experiment with different polyominoes: They should discover there are: 1 monomino, 1 domino, 2 triominoes, 5 tetrominoes, 12 pentominoes, and 35 hexominoes.

Drawing and Constructing

ACTIVITY 11.16
Geoboards.

Geoboards enable children to make shapes of various sizes and with various orientations. To begin, let children experiment and make shapes of their own choosing. Later, the directions are to make triangles (rectangles, squares) of different sizes and in different positions (Figure 11.11). When children have finished, they share their work. Encourage those who have positioned their shapes in different ways to explain what they thought as they made their shapes.

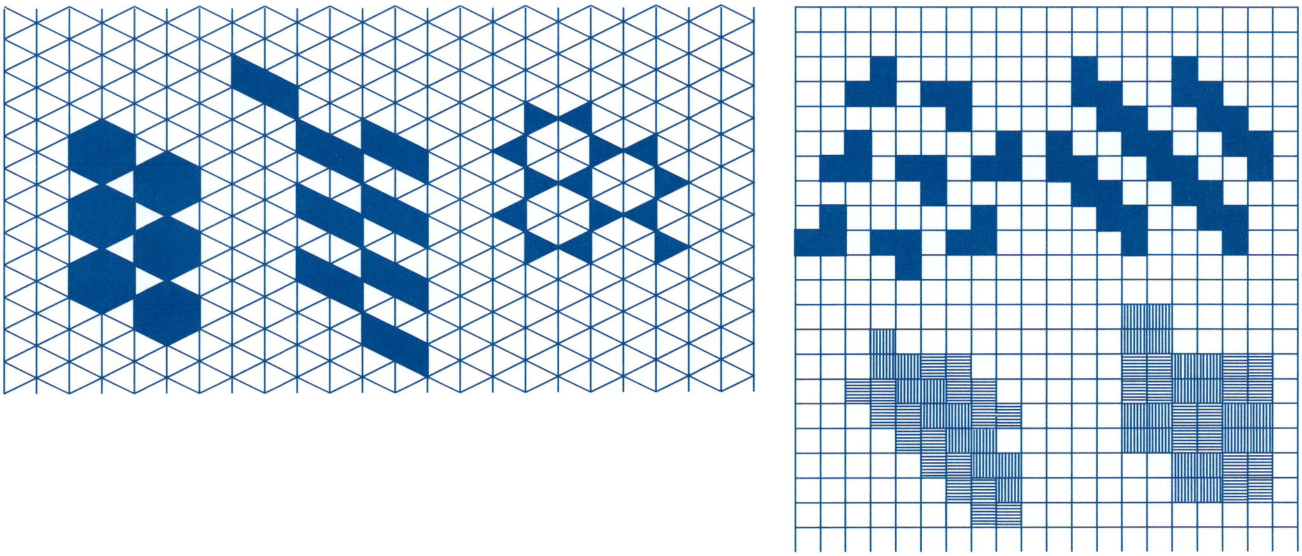

FIGURE 11.9 Tessellations

FIGURE 11.10 Pentominoes

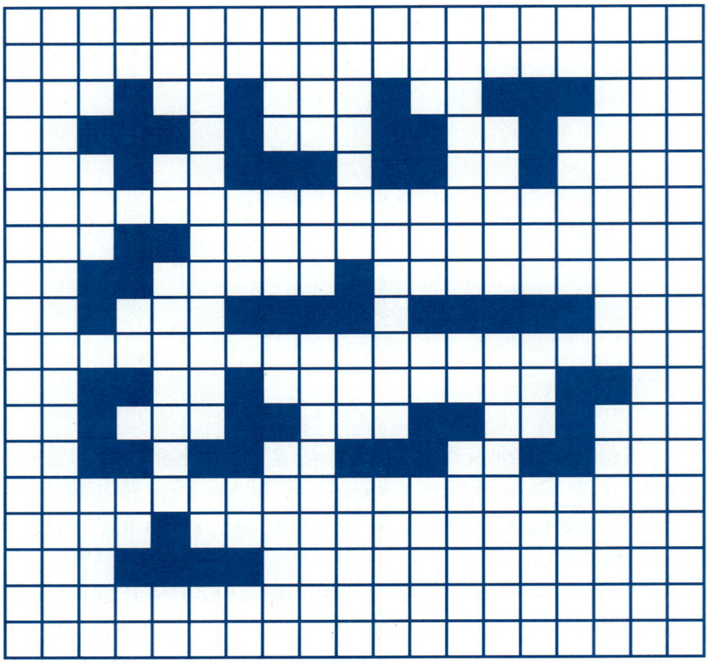

Other activities include:

1. Make as many bigger shapes from smaller shapes as you can (Figure 11.12).
2. Make as many smaller shapes from bigger shapes as you can.
3. Make as many different shapes as you can that have 0 (3, 4, 5) pegs inside.
4. Make as many different shapes as you can that go around 3 (4, 5) pegs.

While children are working on these tasks, circulate and ask pupils to explain how they thought to carry out an activity.

ACTIVITY 11.17
Shape Books.

Suggest that children make *Shape Books* so that they have a record of the shapes they constructed on their geoboards. Have them use straight edges with dot paper to copy the shapes they made on the geoboards or use pictures of geoboards for their copies. (See Appendix G for geoboard pattern.) Shape drawings can also be made by tracing pattern blocks. Have children show many sizes and orientations of

FIGURE 11.11 Geoboard Shapes

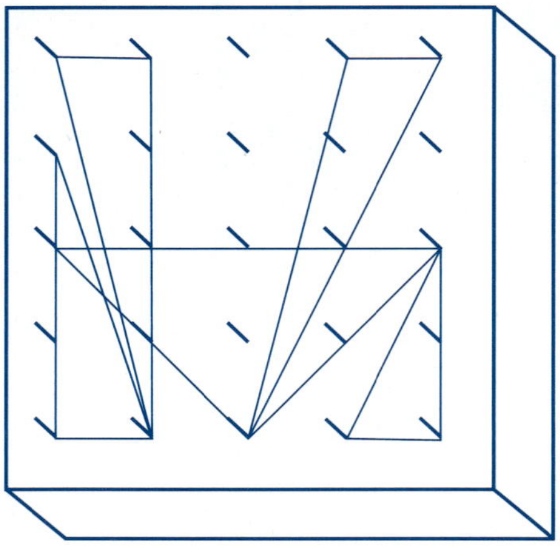

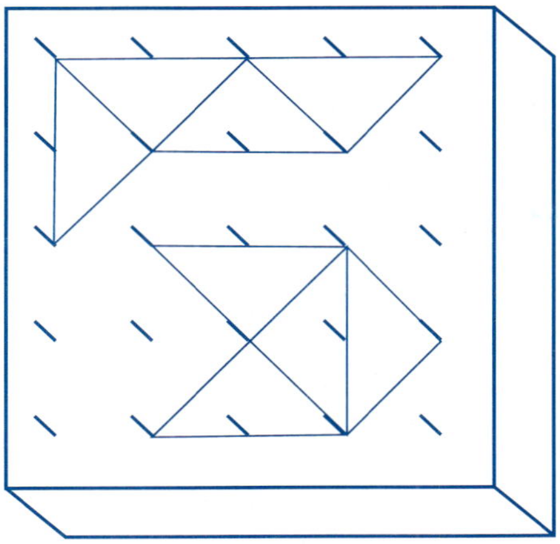

FIGURE 11.12 Shapes from Other Shapes on a Geoboard

the same shape on a page. Collect their work into *Shape Books* for them to take home and share with family members.

Pages for *Shape Books* can also be made from objects cut from newspaper ads or advertisement booklets. Plates, tables, beds, and the like can be used to illustrate shapes.

ACTIVITY 11.18
Copying Shapes (Yackel and Wheatley, 1990).

The objective of this activity is for students to copy drawings, one at a time, shown on the overhead for three seconds. After students have worked for one minute, the drawing is shown on the overhead a second time for three seconds. If students are not finished after another minute, the drawing is shown a third time and left in view so that pupils can complete or revise their drawings. When students are finished, they discuss how they decided what to draw. You can ask questions, such as: "What did you see in the drawing?" "What did you notice first? What part did you draw first?" "Why?"

Variation: Children view a drawing of two or more tangram pieces and arrange tangram pieces on an outline of the drawing. After experiences using an outline, they copy the figure without the outline (Figure 11.13).

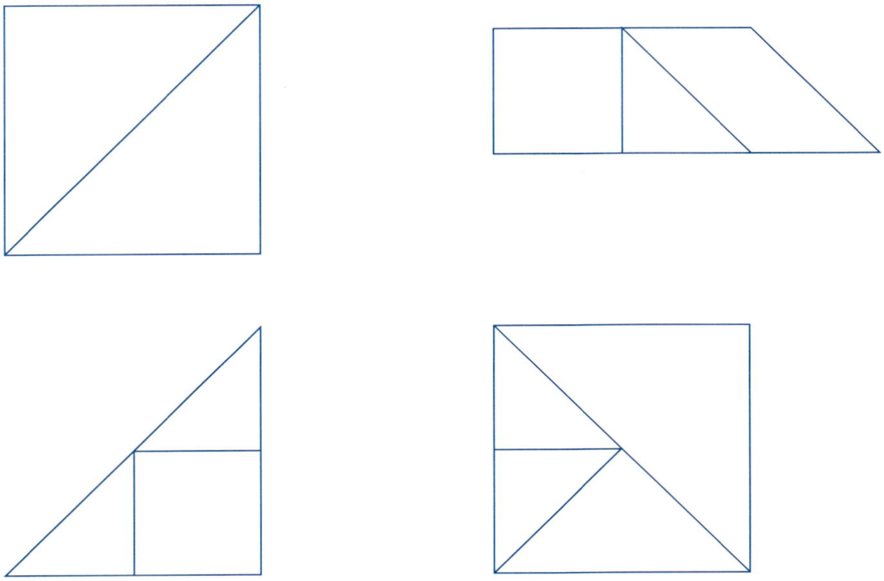

FIGURE 11.13 Shapes on Overhead for Copying Activity

ACTIVITY 11.19
Making Shapes (Prentice, 1989).

Have children make shapes from flexible straws or pipe cleaners. Flexible straws are easy to use because they have built-in fasteners. Make a short slit along the length of the shorter end of a flexible straw, pinch it to a smaller diameter, and insert it in the longer section of another straw to form the side of a two-dimensional shape. (Figure 11.14). Three-dimensional shapes can be made by using twist ties to join faces made from flexible straws. Children can also make models of three-dimensional figures from clay.

ACTIVITY 11.20
Fun in Three Dimensions (Izard, 1990).

This activity helps children visualize three-dimensional objects from different vantage points. Different arrangements of cubes are shown to a group (Figure 11.15). Pictures of the objects can also be shown. Pupils construct the solid displayed by selecting pieces from a collection of pieces (cubes or joined cubes) supplied to them. They work individually or in pairs to construct the solid.

Variations: (1) Students investigate how many buildings can be constructed from 10 (or another number of) cubes; (2) older students can use square or triangle dot grid paper (see Appendix G) to picture three-dimensional arrangements of cubes.

Activity for the Classroom 11.2. Arrange ten cubes and make a two-dimensional drawing of the arrangement from each of two different perspectives. Ask middle- or upper-grade learners to use square dot grid paper to make a two-dimensional drawing of your cube arrangement. Discuss with them what they learned from this activity. Compare their drawings to yours. What have you learned?

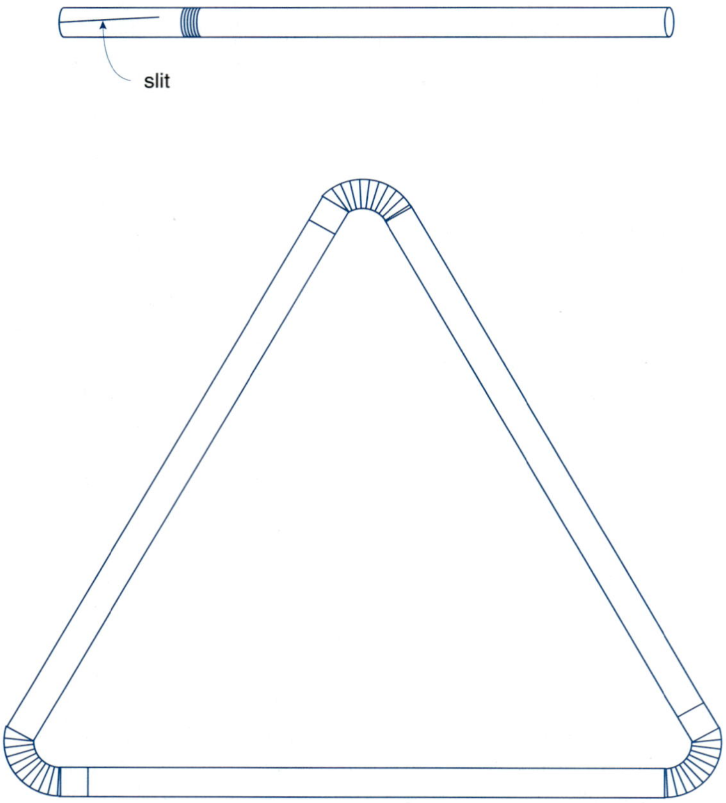

FIGURE 11.14 Shape from Flexible Straws

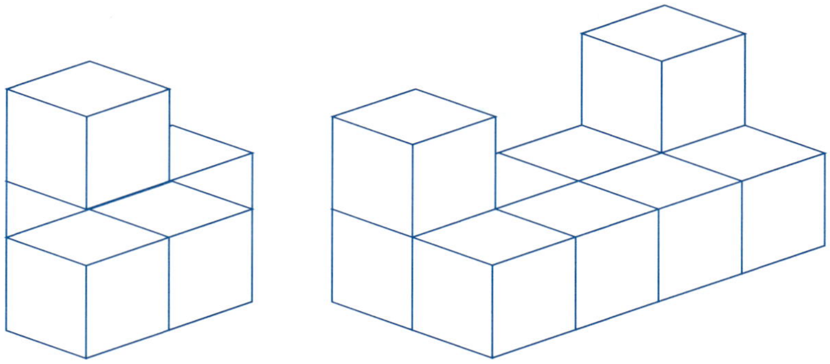

FIGURE 11.15 Three-Dimensional Activity

ACTIVITY 11.21
Using Grid Paper.

Square, dot, or triangle grid paper can be used by children to construct shapes and investigate how larger shapes can be made from smaller shapes (Figure 11.16). The activity can begin with a display of a grid on the overhead and the question asked, "How can we use this paper to show shapes made from other shapes:?" Children can explain their ideas by pointing or outlining sections of the grid on the overhead before the class begins to work with the grid paper. The assignment can be open in the sense that whenever free time (at school or home) is available, children can make shapes on grid paper.

Children's completed work should be placed on the bulletin board and different shapes noted by the class. *Our Book of Shapes* can be made from the work of students and be available for students to enjoy during library time.

ACTIVITIES FOR LEVEL 1 (ANALYSIS) LEARNING

At this level, students are able to focus on the properties of shapes. They pass beyond knowing figures only by their form. The following discussion gives informal definitions of shapes that highlight their properties. However, learners do not study definitions until the next level of geometric thought.

A *simple closed curve* is a path that does not cross itself and returns to its beginning point. It does or does not have *symmetry.* A simple closed curve and its interior is called a *region* (Figure 11.17).

A *polygon* is a simple closed curve whose sides are straight lines. A polygon is named by the number of its sides. For example, three sides, triangle; four sides, quadrilateral; five sides, pentagon; six sides, hexagon; eight sides, octagon; ten sides; decagon. A polygon is regular or irregular. All the sides and angles of a *regular polygon* (Figure 11.18) are equal in measure (congruent). If the sides or the angles of a polygon are not congruent the polygon is *irregular* (Figure 11.19).

A *triangle* can have no, two, or three sides congruent (Figure 11.20). A triangle with no sides congruent is a *scalene triangle;* a triangle with two sides congruent is an *isosceles triangle;* a triangle with three sides congruent is an *equilateral triangle.* Triangles are also named by the size of their angles. A *right triangle* has a right angle (90°). An *acute triangle* has three acute angles (angles less than 90°). An *obtuse triangle* has one obtuse angle (an angle greater than 90° but less than 180°).

Quadrilaterals, like triangles, are classified by the size of their angles and sides (Figure 11.21). A *square* is a quadrilateral with four congruent sides and angles, that is, right angles. A *rectangle* is a quadrilateral with opposite sides congruent and four congruent angles, that is, right angles. A *parallelogram* is a quadrilateral in which both pairs of opposite sides are parallel. A *rhombus* is a quadrilateral with all sides con-

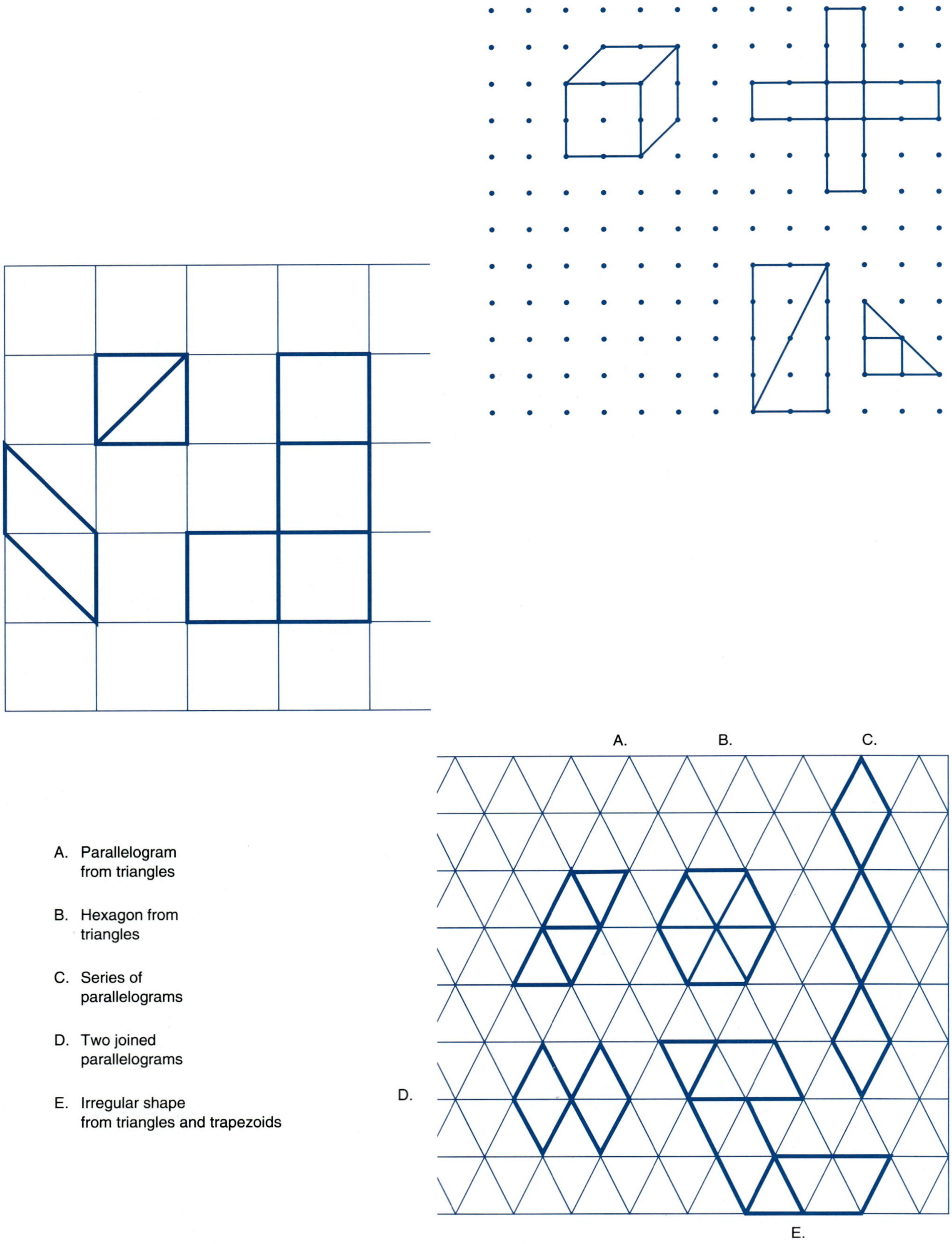

FIGURE 11.16 Constructing Shapes from Other Shapes on Grid Paper

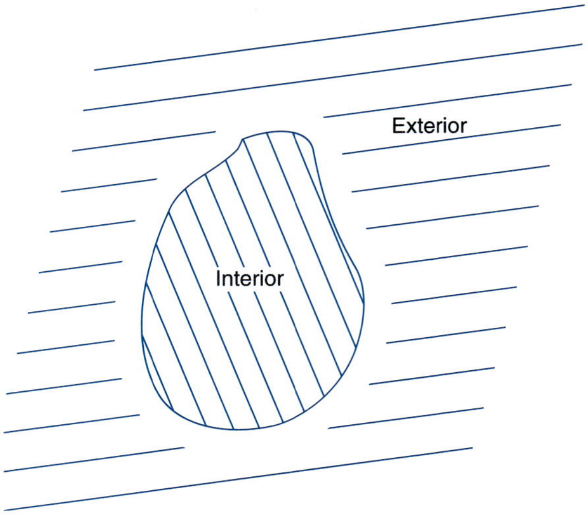

FIGURE 11.17 Simple Closed Curve

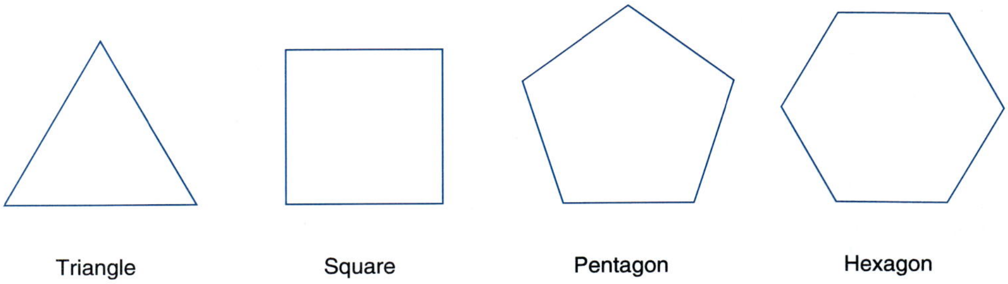

FIGURE 11.18 Regular Polygons

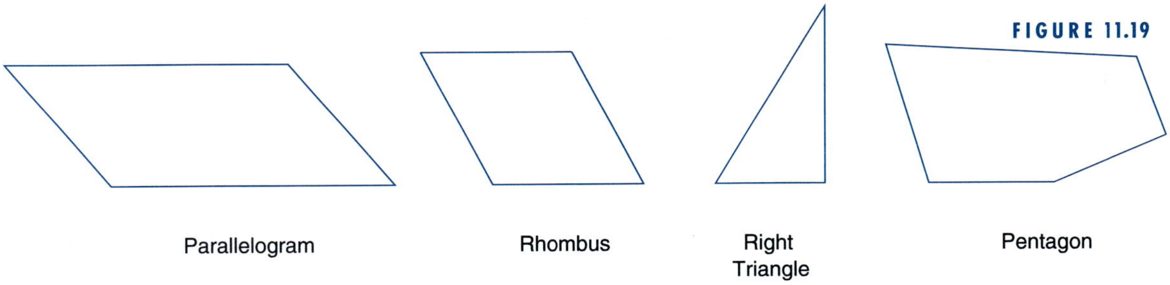

FIGURE 11.19 Irregular Polygons

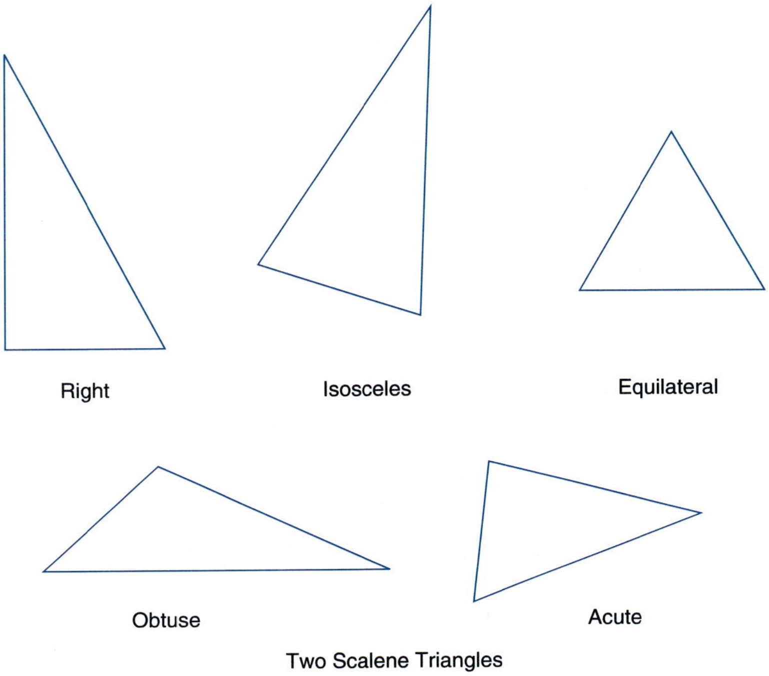

FIGURE 11.20 Triangles

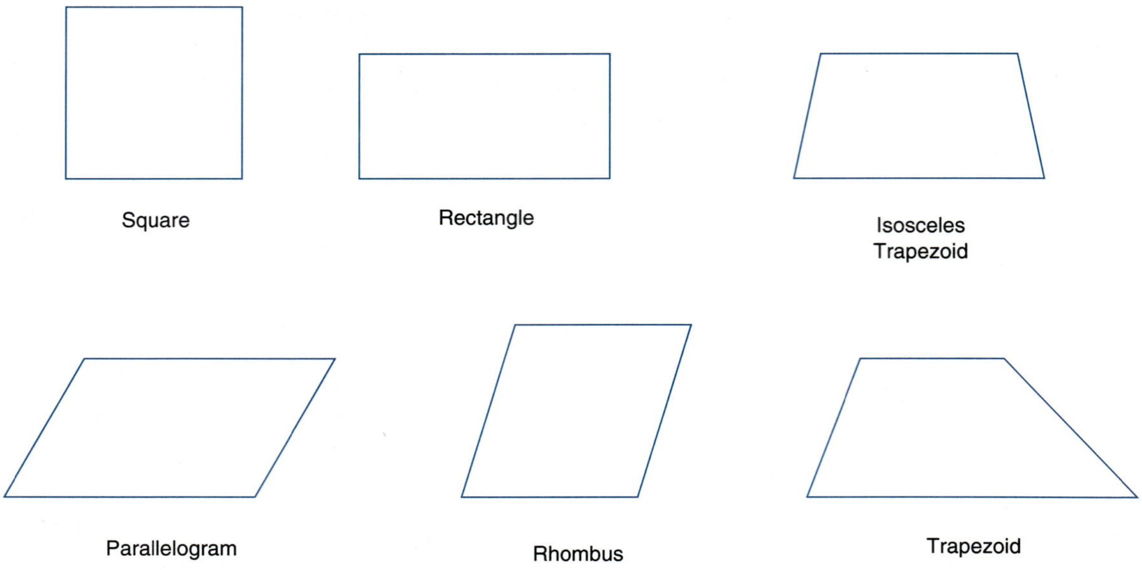

FIGURE 11.21 Quadrilaterals

gruent. A *trapezoid* is a quadrilateral with one and only one pair of opposite sides parallel. A *vertex* is the point where sides meet. A *diagonal* joins two opposite vertices.

A *circle* is a simple closed curve in which every point on the curve is the same distance from a given point, called the center. The *circumference* is the distance around the circle. A line extending from the center to a point on the circle is called a *radius*. A line connecting two points on the circle and passing through the center is called a *diameter*.

Solid figures children study include prisms, pyramids, cylinders, cones, and spheres (see Figure 11.5). A *prism* is a simple closed surface formed by two congruent polygonal regions (they cover each other exactly) in parallel planes, called the bases, and three or more quadrilateral regions that join the bases so as completely to enclose the space. A *pyramid* is a simple closed surface formed by a polygonal region, called the base, and triangular regions joining the polygon and a point outside the base called the vertex so as completely to enclose the space. A *cylinder* is a simple closed surface formed by two congruent simple closed regions, not polygonal, in parallel planes (called bases) and a curved surface that joins the simple closed regions so as completely to enclose the space. The bases of a circular cylinder are *circular regions*. A *cone* is a simple closed surface with a base that is not a polygonal region and one or more lateral surfaces, at least one of which is curved, that join the base and a point not on the base, called the vertex, so as completely to enclose the space. The base of a *circular cone* is a circular region. A *sphere* is a simple closed surface formed by all the points in space equidistant from a point called the center.

The activities for Level 1 thinking deal with identifying properties of geometric shapes, classifying and describing shapes by properties, drawing and constructing shapes using properties, and generalizing.

Identifying Properties of Geometric Shapes

ACTIVITY 11.22
Noticing Properties.

Ask children to use dot paper to make three or more shapes with three, four, five, six, seven, or eight sides. Have them make as many different shapes as they can think of with four to eight sides. Display their work on a bulletin board with a title such as, "How Many Sides to My Shape?" Use the bulletin board for a class discussion, helping children to notice properties or characteristics of shapes. If children do not contribute shapes with properties to be included in subsequent learning experiences, add your own shapes to the display so that examples of such properties as parallel lines, right angles, acute angles, obtuse angles, and congruent sides are shown.

ACTIVITY 11.23
Labeling.

Ask children in groups to decide what names they know for shapes and properties of shapes. Have them share their ideas. Include two- and three-dimensional figures. Those names that children do not know should be introduced. For example, they may not know the words *prism, isosceles triangle,* or *face* (Figure 11.22). Prepare a chart with labeled drawings of shapes so that students have a ready reference for words that will be used in the activities.

ACTIVITY 11.24
Game: What Am I?

Prepare 36 cards with descriptions of geometric shapes and a key for determining the correct names of the figures described on the cards. Include two- and three-dimensional figures and their properties. Students can also write the cards. (Examples of cards: I am a solid figure with six faces, all faces are square regions; I am lines going in the same direction, never meeting.) The cards are shuffled, and each player (4 or 6) receives 9 or 6 cards. Players take turns reading their cards and naming the figures described on their cards. When a player names a figure, he or she lays the card in the middle of the playing area. If he or she cannot name the figure, the player looks at the key, tells the group the name of the figure, gives the card to the player on his or her left or right, and draws a card from that player's hand. The next player then has his or her turn. The first player out of cards wins.

ACTIVITY 11.25
Labeling a Display.

Have students observe shapes in the real world and make drawings of them. Display the drawings on a bulletin board. Students form committees to make labels for the drawings.

ACTIVITY 11.26
Investigating Symmetry.

Show children a folded piece of paper cut to show symmetry (Figure 11.23). Ask them to describe what they see and what they notice about the figure (two parts

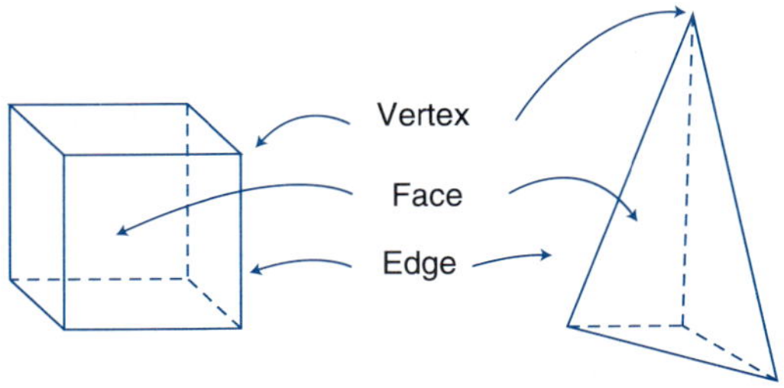

FIGURE 11.22 Labels for Properties of Three-Dimensional Figures

FIGURE 11.23 Fold and Cut a Figure to Show Symmetry

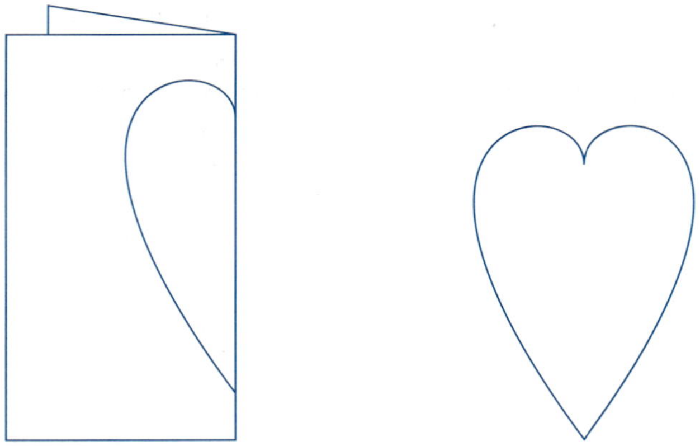

match one to one). As they describe what they see, ask questions that help them realize that the paper was folded before the cutting. For example, if they do not notice the fold say, "Look at the sides and the middle of the paper, and tell everything you see." Give them squares or rectangles, and ask them to solve the problem of how to make a figure with two parts that match one to one. Ask them to share their figures, tell how they made the figure, and what it shows. Introduce the word *symmetry*. Children can then make other figures that have symmetry.

ACTIVITY 11.27
Tracing and Symmetry.

Have children make shapes with symmetry and cut them on the line of symmetry. Collect the half pieces, and a few days later, give each child a half-shape piece. Ask the class to think how they could use the pieces to make pictures that have symmetry. Children can work in pairs or small groups to solve this problem. Have them demonstrate their solutions on the overhead, tracing, flipping, and tracing their pattern again on a transparency (Figure 11.24).

ACTIVITY 11.28
Symmetry around Us.

Ask children to look for examples of symmetry in nature and in the world made by people. Some fruits (e.g., apple, orange) and vegetables (e.g., squash) show symmetry when cut in half. Flowers and leaves can also exhibit symmetry. Flowers, however, can show point instead of line symmetry (Figure 11.25). The letters of the alphabet, written in manuscript, can also be investigated for symmetry.

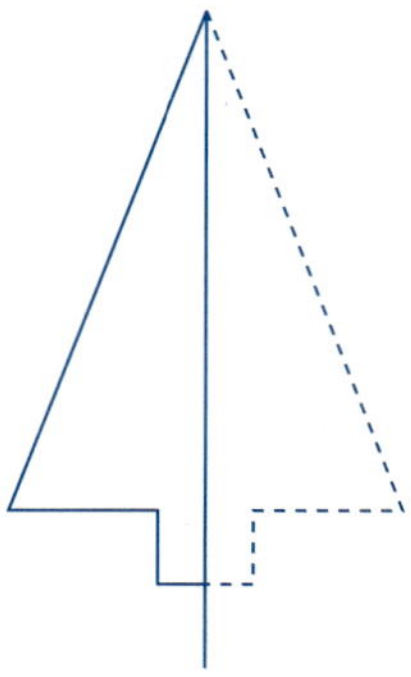

FIGURE 11.24 Draw a Figure, Then Flip It over the Line of Symmetry and Trace

ACTIVITY 11.29
Exploring Angles.

Wilson and Adams (1992) suggest introducing the notion of angle as a turn or rotation. Have children turn their bodies a full-turn, a half-turn and a quarter-turn. Ask them to decide how many half-turns make a full-turn, how many quarter-turns make a half-turn or a full-turn. Discuss things that turn, such as doorknobs and the hands on a clock. Introduce the words *straight angle* for a half-turn and *right angle* for a quarter-turn. Children can also make angles by moving and positioning their arms in different ways.

One pupil can look for a "treasure" in the classroom by following the directions given by other class members that include directions to make turns.

Have children notice angles in the classroom, such as the angle made by opening a door (place tape on the floor to represent the angle made when opening a door far enough for a person to go through, for a cat to go through, etc.); the angle made by turning a chair; the angle made at the corner of a desk.

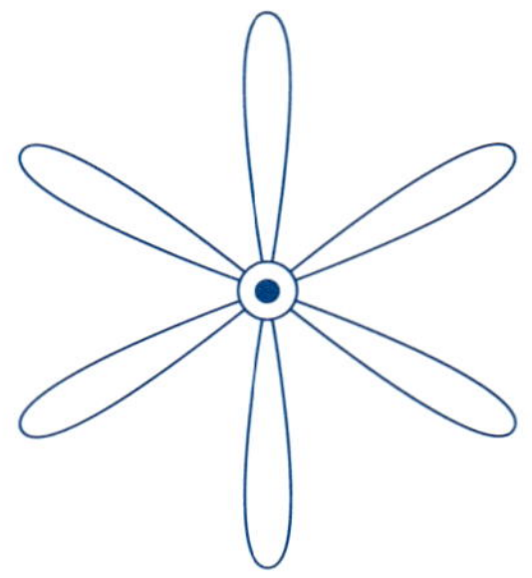

FIGURE 11.25 Point Symmetry in a Flower

Classifying and Describing Shapes by Properties

ACTIVITY 11.30
What Is Common?

Give groups of students sets of shapes or sets of pictures of shapes. Include both two- and three-dimensional shapes in some sets. Ask them to classify the shapes in each set by properties in as many ways as possible. (You can say, "Put together the shapes that go together in some way as many times as you can.") For example, a classification could be: right triangles and no right triangles. Have groups share their classifications.

ACTIVITY 11.31
How Were These Classified?

Show several classifications of figures on the overhead. Each classification can have four or five items. Have children study the classifications to determine the properties used in each classification, and ask them to explain the basis for each classification.

ACTIVITY 11.32
What's My Shape?

Have students write descriptions of shapes for others in the class to read and identify.

ACTIVITY 11.33
For Those in Space.

Have each student write descriptions of two or three geometric figures for someone who has never seen the figures, such as a space being, to use in drawing the figures. Have each student read one description to a small group. The description can be reread once. Each member of the group will draw a figure according to the description given. After all have finished, they compare their drawings. The procedure can be repeated.

Drawing and Constructing Shapes Using Properties

ACTIVITY 11.34
Building Shapes.

Give students a worksheet showing a grid and 4 (or more) isosceles right triangles (Figure 11.26). Two triangles should fit on one grid square. Ask students to cut out the shapes and build new shapes on the grid paper using 2, 3, or 4 (or more) triangles. Have them trace the figures to keep a record of their work. Using combinations of 2,

FIGURE 11.26 Activity Sheet for "Building Shapes"

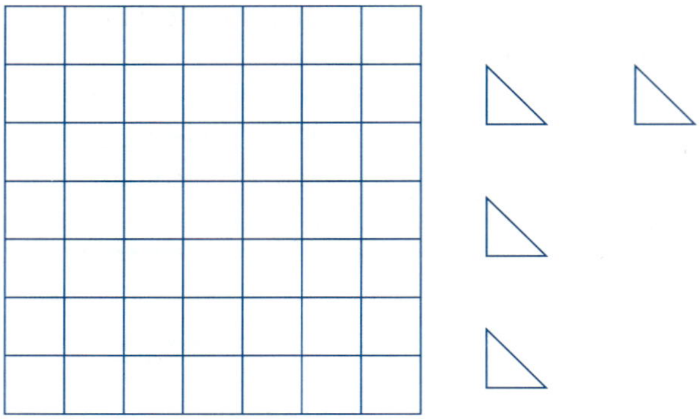

3, or 4 isosceles triangles, 19 shapes can be constructed (Silverman, 1990). Students may work in small groups to build as many shapes as possible. Display their work for sharing. If not all 19 shapes are made, suggest that they work individually or in pairs in free time to make all 19 shapes. Do not give them the answers. Let them work on the task for some time to construct the shapes. Such a problem enables students to develop spatial sense as they ponder the possibilities for all the shapes.

The activity can be repeated using four parallelograms. The parallelogram should be constructed from 2 of the right isosceles triangles so as to fit on the grid (Figure 11.27). More than 14 shapes can be made from combining 2, 3, or 4 of these parallelograms (Silverman, 1990).

Reader Activity 11.2

Use square grid paper to make figures with 2, 3, or 4 parallelograms different from those in Figure 11.27. Should you ask middle- or upper-grade learners to do this? Why or why not?

ACTIVITY 11.35
Observing Our Shapes.

Ask the students to classify the shapes they created from isosceles triangles in Activity 11.34. Help them find shapes that are regular or irregular and symmetrical or not symmetrical if they do not use these categories in classifying. Introduce the vocabulary words *regular* and *irregular.*

ACTIVITY 11.36
Property Card Sort Game.

Property cards and shape-name cards are needed for this game. (Pupils can help make these cards.) Make 36 property cards, including duplicates, and four sets of

FIGURE 11.27 Shapes Constructed from Two or Three Parallelograms

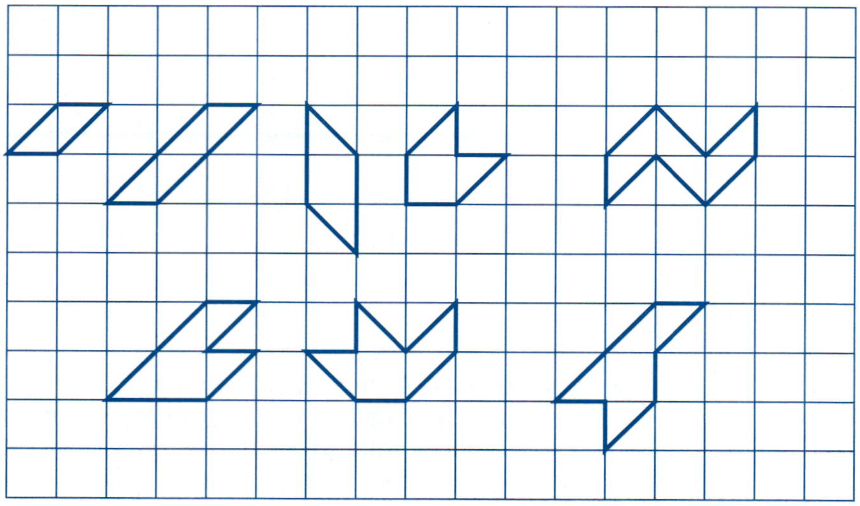

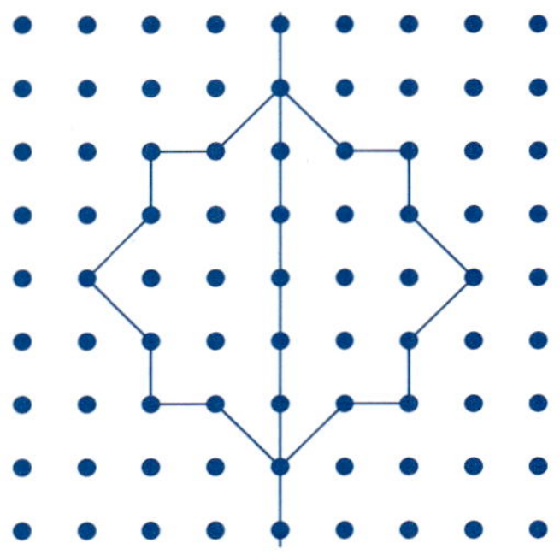

FIGURE 11.28 Symmetry on Dot Paper

shape-name cards, one set for each player. To make both types of cards, cut strips 1″ × 4″, or cut 3″ × 5″ index cards in half. For property cards, write a property on each card. Some examples of properties are: all sides equal, 2 sides equal, 4 right angles, 3 sides, 1 line of symmetry, 2 lines of symmetry, only 1 pair of opposite sides parallel, both pairs of opposite sides parallel. To make shape cards write the name of a shape on a card. Six shape-name cards make a set, for example, triangle, rectangle, square, parallelogram, trapezoid, quadrilateral. *Note:* The property cards should include properties that describe each shape on a shape-name card.

The objective of the game is to have placed enough property cards with a shape-name card so that the shape is well described. To play the game, the stack of property cards is placed face down in the center of the playing area; each of the four players gets a set of shape-name cards. Players place their shape-name cards in front of them and take turns taking a property card from the stack. They place their property cards describing the shape under the shape-name cards. When all the shape-name cards have been drawn, the winner has the most shapes well described and will be able to justify his or her choice of a property card if asked to do so.

ACTIVITY 11.37
Symmetry with Dot Paper.

Have pupils use dot paper to show symmetry in shapes they create. First, have them draw a line on the dot paper, next make a creative shape on one side of the line, and last, using the dots as guides, make a mirror image of the shape on the other side of the line (Figure 11.28). (They may need you to model the procedure.) Have children explain how they thought to make their examples of line symmetry. Pupils may wish to color their designs to show the symmetry. Display the examples of symmetry students have created.

ACTIVITY 11.38
Using a Mira.

A Mira is a see-through mirror made of red plastic (Figure 11.29). It enables children to find symmetry lines and to draw figures. Miras can be purchased at supply houses that sell mathematics materials.

Each child in a small group will need a Mira. First, let children experiment using a Mira with shapes that are symmetrical and some that are not symmetrical. After all children in the class have had an opportunity to work with Miras, ask them to share their discoveries. Later, ask them to solve the problem of using Miras to make figures with line symmetry. Say, "How can we use the Mira to make a shape

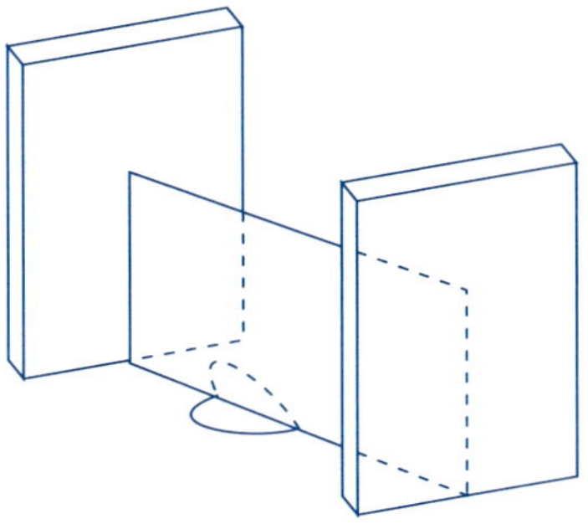

FIGURE 11.29 A Mira

that is symmetrical?" After children solve the problem and make drawings, have them discuss how they thought to do it. Display the drawings for all to see. Woodward and Buckner (1987) report using Miras successfully with second and third graders.

ACTIVITY 11.39
Cutting (Ranucci, 1987).

Have pupils fold a square or rectangle into halves or fourths and make cuts such as shown in Figure 11.30. Before they open the folded paper, ask them to predict what the open shape will look like. Questions about the cuts can also be asked. For example, "If you fold once, what cuts will give you an equilateral triangle? A square?" "If you fold the paper in fourths and make one cut at the intersection of the folds, what shapes can you make, and what shapes are not possible to make?" Students can also solve the problem of determining which capital letters can be cut using folded paper.

ACTIVITY 11.40
Making Nets.

Nets are two-dimensional shapes that fold into three-dimensional figures. Children decide which shapes in Figure 11.31 are nets, and they cut and fold to test their predictions. Some children may be challenged to make nets that are different from those on the activity sheet you supply. Prentice (1989) suggests taking apart three-dimensional figures made with flexible straws to show nets of the figures.

ACTIVITY 11.41
Slicing Solids.

Clay solids can be used to investigate the shapes that result from slicing a solid at different angles (Figure 11.32). Carroll (1988) suggests that oil-based clay, the "modeling clay" used by young children, is best because it will not dry out as water-based clay is likely to do. A piano wire or clay slicer, purchased at art supply stores,

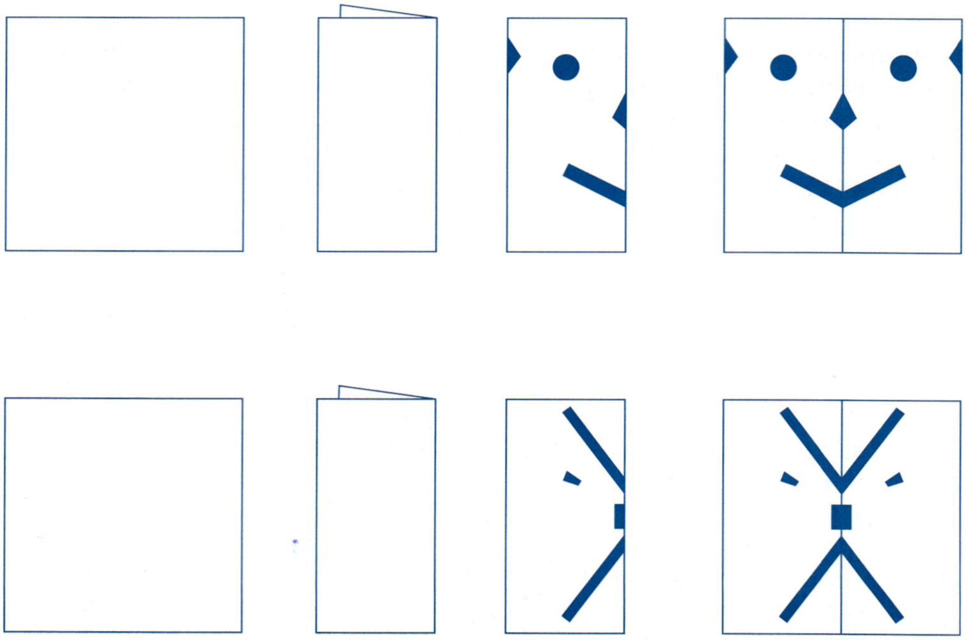

FIGURE 11.30 Cutting Folded Paper to Show Symmetry

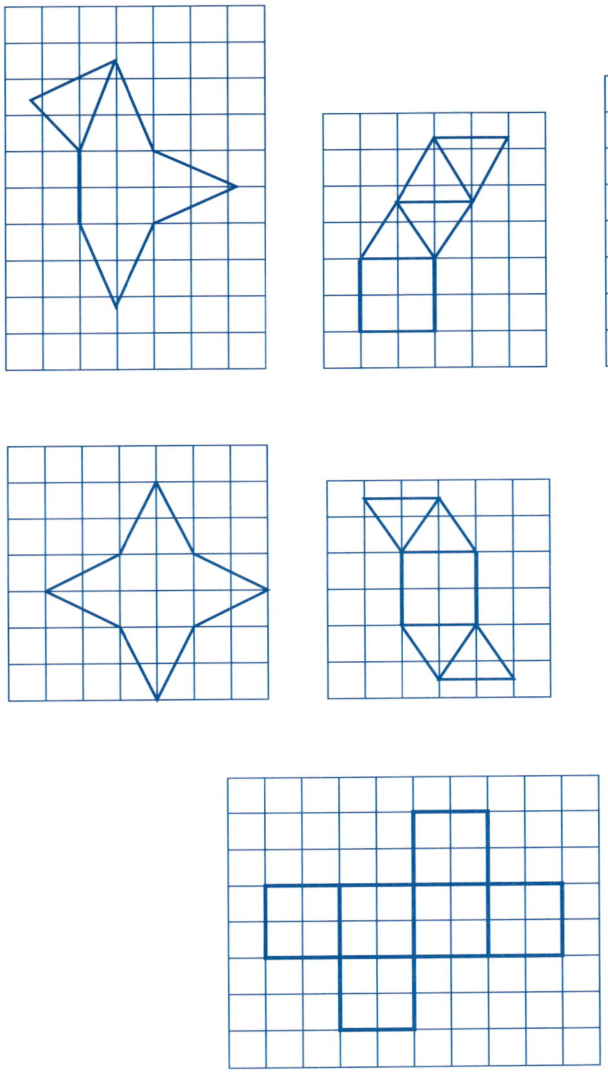

FIGURE 11.31 Which Are Nets?

should be used to give a clean cut. Before making the cut, have students predict the shape of the cross section. A table can be made giving a picture of the solid, a picture of the predicted cross section, the cross section found by cutting, and the name of the cross sectional shape.

Generalizing

ACTIVITY 11.42
Examining Radii.

Give students each an activity sheet showing different-sized circles. A dot is in the center of each circle. Have each student draw several lines from the center of each of his or her circles to the circumference, and ask, "How do you think the lengths of these lines, called *radii*, in each of your circles compare?" After several students have given their answers to this question, ask students to decide how to check their predictions. They should decide to cut a strip of paper the length of the radius of a circle and use the strip to determine the length of other radii in the circle. Discuss the findings for the different circles students used in the activity, and have students generalize their conclusions to any circle.

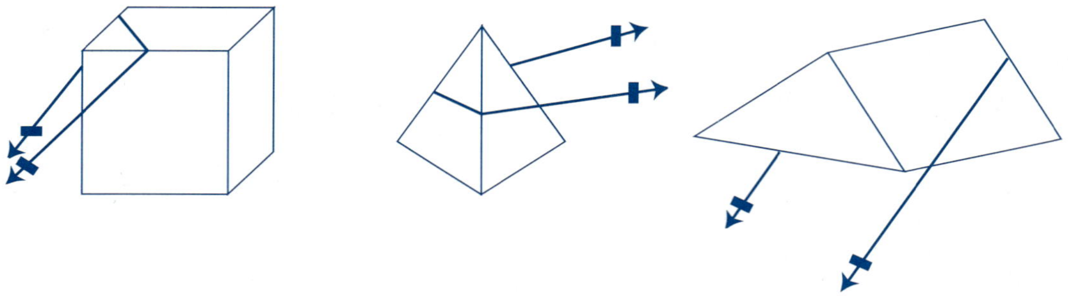

FIGURE 11.32 What Will the Slice Look Like?

ACTIVITY 11.43
The Sum of the Angles of a Triangle.

Have children draw triangles with straight edges. Each pupil tears his or her triangle so that the three angles can be placed side by side (Figure 11.33). Ask, "What do you notice about all the triangles?" Have pupils write up what they did and what they discovered.

ACTIVITY 11.44
The Sum of the Angles of any Figure.

Have students draw all possible diagonals from one vertex of a figure (11.34). Pose the problem: How many straight angles can be counted in the triangles formed by the diagonals in a rectangle, a quadrilateral, a pentagon, and a hexagon? Is there a pattern? What is the sum of the angles of these figures? Have students work in pairs or threes to solve this problem.

ACTIVITY 11.45
Exploring Diagonals of Quadrilaterals.

Exploring the diagonals of quadrilaterals gives the students opportunities to observe many relations. Diagonals are equal or not, perpendicular or not, joined at the center of each diagonal or not, joined at the center of only one diagonal, or at the center of neither (Figure 11.35). Ask students to experiment to see what they can find out about the diagonals of various quadrilaterals they know. Ask, "What do you notice about diagonals that are always true for a particular kind of quadrilateral?"

FIGURE 11.33 Tearing a Paper Triangle to Show a Straight Angle Formed from Angles of a Triangle

ACTIVITY 11.46
Draw and Discover.

Ask students to make some observations from the results of carrying out the following directions:

1. Draw a four-sided figure with only one right angle. Name the figure. Draw another if possible, and name the figure.
2. Draw a four-sided figure with opposite sides parallel and at least one right angle. Name the figure. Draw another if possible, and name the figure.
3. Draw a four-sided figure with all sides equal in length. Name the figure. Draw another if possible, and name the figure.
4. Draw a four-sided figure with all sides equal in length and at least one right angle. Name the figure. Draw another if possible, and name the figure.

Their observations should include statements about the properties of these figures and their thought process while carrying out the activity.

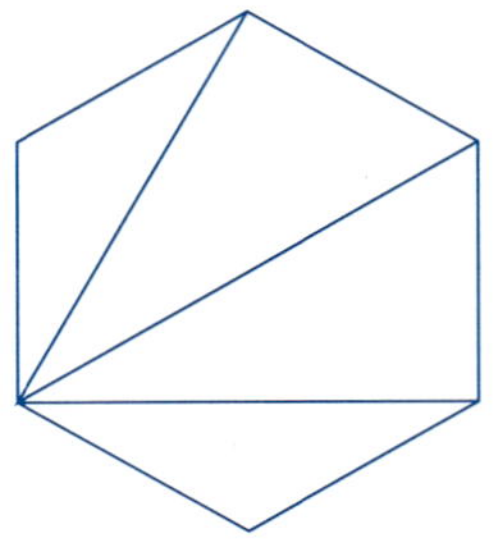

FIGURE 11.34 Drawing to Explore the Sum of the Angles of a Figure

ACTIVITY 11.47
Three Straws.

Have pupils cut strips of about 50 cm into three smaller strips and form triangles with the strips. Have pupils work in groups to get a variety of triangles and nontriangles that show that three strips will not always make a triangle.

Variation: Ask students to experiment to determine what kind of triangle(s) can be formed (if any) from 3, 4, 5, . . . , 12 toothpicks (Figure 11.36). Ask students to complete the table shown in Table 11.1, writing Y (yes) or N (no) in each cell. If two or more triangles of a kind are possible, Y is written two or more times in the cell. A few students can display their triangles on the overhead. The class should discuss the implications of their work (e.g., to make an equilateral triangle, the number of toothpicks must be divisible by 3).

Reader Activity 11.3

Draw the figures in Activity 11.46. What do you notice about the properties of the figures?

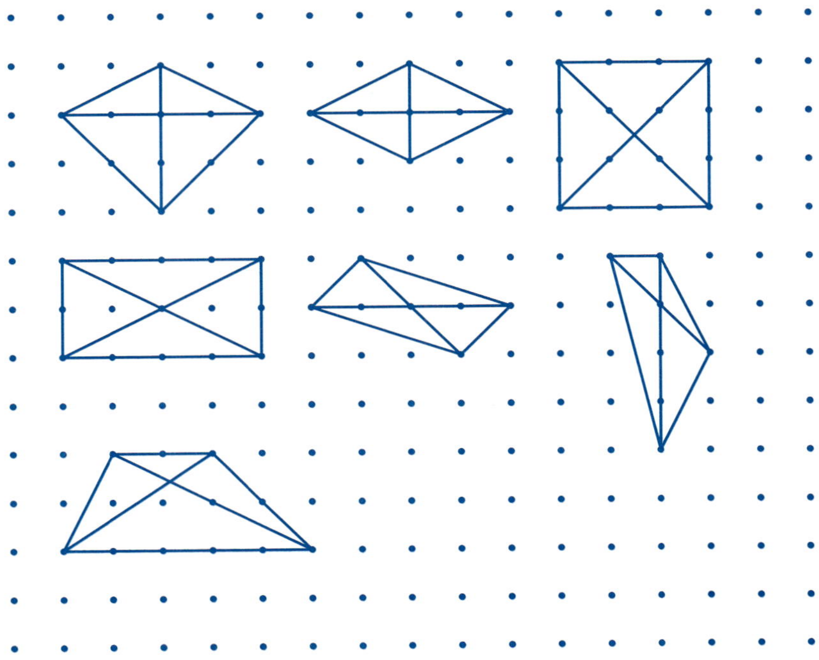

FIGURE 11.35 Exploring Properties of Diagonals

FIGURE 11.36 Toothpick Triangles

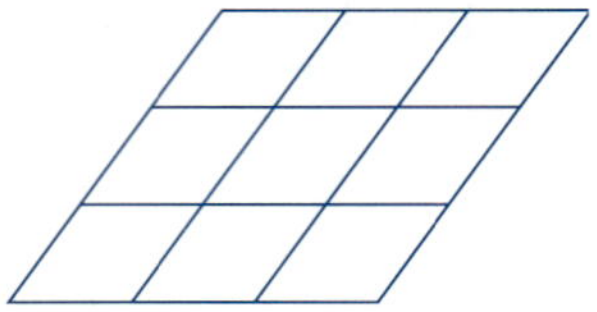

FIGURE 11.37 Diagram for Investigating Equal Angles in a Parallelogram

ACTIVITY 11.48 *Congruent Shapes.*

Ask students to draw five or six triangles or rectangles, at least three of which have the same size and shape, and to cut them out. Introduce the word *congruent.* Ask them to decide what they notice about the shapes that have the same size and shape. (The sides and angles are equal.) Suggest that they trade shapes and make a figure (e.g., robot) with the shapes they receive. They can look at one another's shapes. Several students should tell about the shapes. Encourage them to use the word *congruent* in their descriptions.

ACTIVITY 11.49 *Equal Angles.*

Distribute a diagram such as in Figure 11.37 to each pupil. Ask students to decide which angles are equal and color the equal angles with the same color. Then have them cut out these angles to test their predictions. Help them to conclude that the opposite angles of a parallelogram are equal.

ACTIVITIES FOR LEVEL 2 (INFORMAL DEDUCTION) LEARNING

Development of Level 2 thinking is characterized by understanding the inclusion relation (e.g., a rectangle is a parallelogram), formation of complete definitions, and use of "if . . . , then" statements. Research indicates that elementary school students do not exhibit Level 2 thinking (Burger and Shaughnessy, 1986). However, because advancement to a higher level depends on instruction, it is possible that with quality instruction, some learners will begin to think at this level. The following activities should be used with those few learners who show the logical reasoning characteristic of Level 2. As noted, if there is a mismatch between a learner's level of geometric thought and instruction, students will not profit from the instruction and can experience frustration and discouragement. Level 2 thinking cannot be forced.

ACTIVITY 11.50 *Change and Discover.*

Tell students that this activity will lead to an interesting discovery. There are two possibilities for the activity:

TABLE 11.1 Triangles from Toothpicks

	Equilateral	Isosceles	Right
Number of toothpicks			
3			
4			
5			
6			
7			
8			
9			
10			
11			
12			

1. Ask students to make an irregular quadrilateral on their geoboards and then to:
   a. Change the quadrilateral to a parallelogram.
   b. Change the parallelogram to a rectangle.
   c. Change the rectangle to a square.

   Discuss the meanings implicit in what was done.

2. Ask students to make a square on their geoboards and then to:
   a. Change the square to a rectangle.
   b. Change the rectangle to a parallelogram.
   c. Change the parallelogram to an irregular quadrilateral.

   Discuss the implications of the transformations.

ACTIVITY 11.51
Sides and Angles.

Have students make a table listing various polygons with the number of sides and the number of angles of each polygon. Have them study the chart to make a discovery. (The number of sides and angles is the same.) Question learners to help them discover that quadrilaterals, rectangles, squares, parallelograms, and trapezoids all have four sides and angles. After they make this discovery, say, "Let's think about how these figures are related." Discuss the inclusions.

Reader Activity 11.4

Carry out Activity 11.51, and decide what students would learn from the activity.

ACTIVITY 11.52
Puzzles.

Prepare puzzles such as the following for students to solve. When they understand the reasoning involved in solving the puzzles, ask them to write puzzles.

1. A ____________ is a rectangular that has ____________.
2. All rectangles are ____________.
3. If a shape is a square, it is also a ____________.
4. All quadrilaterals are not ____________.

ACTIVITY 11.53
Definitions.

Ask groups of students to write more than one definition for a shape using in each definition the least number of properties. An example is: A parallelogram is a quadrilateral with both pairs of opposite sides parallel, or a parallelogram is a four-sided shape with both pairs of opposite sides parallel. Have them discuss the thinking involved in writing the definitions.

ASSESSING LEARNING OF GEOMETRY AND SPATIAL SENSE

Assessing the learning of geometry and the development of spatial sense deals with determining the child's level of geometric thought. When the level of children's thinking is known, appropriate activities can be assigned. Children advance from one level to another if the instruction they receive enables them to engage in meaningful activities to develop concepts, express their ideas orally and in writing, exchange their views with others, and solve problems based on the concepts they have constructed (Crowley, 1987). The process takes time. It appears that long periods of time and meaningful instruction are needed for students to form geometric concepts (Burger and Shaughnessy, 1986).

Assessing the level of geometric thought of elementary school children will help you decide whether children are at Level 0 or Level 1. Very few learners will be moving to Level 2 thought. Most assessment questions thus determine whether children focus on the form of a shape or examine its properties. Assessment activities, based on the work of Burger and Shaughnessy (1986) include the following:

1. Draw as many different triangles as you can. (Do children draw right, equilateral, isosceles, and scalene triangles? If so, they are focusing on properties–Level 1 thinking; if not, they would be aware of the form of a triangle–Level 0 thinking.)
2. Ask pupils to put together triangles that are alike in some way. Have them repeat the task in as many different ways as possible and explain what they did (e.g., they could show right, equilateral, isosceles, and scalene triangles, and tell why they made these classifications). Notice if they can sort in many ways, using the properties of sides and angles. If so, they show Level 1 thinking; if not, they show Level 0 thinking.
3. Show children many different shapes with different dimensions and orientations. Ask children to name the shapes and explain why they gave the shape that name. Then, ask them to point to all the rectangles and squares (parallelograms and rhombuses, if they have studied these shapes) and to tell why they are rectangles, and so on. Note their use of properties to explain their selections, which indicates Level 1 thinking. Children who refer to inclusions are showing Level 2 thinking.

Assessment Questions 1 and 3 can be adapted for paper-and-pencil work. In Question 3, for example, children could write "R" on the rectangles, "S" on the squares, and so forth. Suggest to pupils that they write more than one letter on the figure if it is possible to do so. Their responses can help you decide if students are beginning to understand inclusions. However, paper-and-pencil assessment does not determine a student's development of geometric thought as fully as his or her responses to questions posed orally.

On the basis of the assessment, choose activities at the appropriate level so there is a match between instruction and children's thinking. If there is not a match between the level of thinking and instruction, students will not learn geometry and may learn to dislike the subject.

Most children are interested in activities that involve learning geometry. They usually express pleasure when engaged in work with space figures and related topics. Observation determines if children in your class find the activities you plan challenging and enjoyable. You watch their facial expressions and listen to their comments when studying topics in geometry. If they seem interested in some activities and not in others, study the features of the activities they like and endeavor to make these a part of many geometry activities.

SUMMARY

The van Hiele model of the development of geometric thought was used in this chapter as the basis for the discussion of geometry instruction in the elementary school. The levels of the model were described, and it was noted that generally the thinking of elementary school children is at Levels 0 and 1. Only a very few students will be at Level 2 thought. However, if instruction emphasizes constructing geometric concepts, more children in the elementary school could exhibit Level 2 thinking. Children at Level 0 focus on the form of shapes, and children at Level 1 understand the properties of shapes. Level 2 thinkers understand inclusion and can reason informally.

Guidelines for activities at the first three levels were given, and a number of activities relating to the guidelines described. Activities were described for children at Level 0 to help them visualize both two- and three-dimensional shapes. Activities described for learners who think at Level 1 stressed the properties of two- and three-dimensional shapes, and Level 2 activities dealt with inclusions and reasoning. Instruction and activities outlined in the chapter reflected interactive teaching approaches. Such an approach enables learners to construct concepts from their actions and reflections and to clarify and refine ideas by communicating with others about the outcomes of their work.

Assessment activities were provided in the last section of the chapter. Such activities enable teachers to determine children's level of geometric thought and plan instruction that will enable learners over time to move to higher levels of thinking. Assessment of attitudes was also discussed in this section.

REFERENCES

Burger, William F. (February 1985). "Geometry." *Arithmetic Teacher* 32: 52–56.

Burger, William F., and J. Michael Shaughnessy. (January 1986). "Characterizing the van Hiele Levels of Development in Geometry." *Journal for Research in Mathematics Education* 17: 31–48.

Carroll, William M. (March 1988). "Cross Sections of Clay Solids." *Arithmetic Teacher* 35: 6–11.

Crowley, Mary L. (1987). "The van Hiele Model of the Development of Geometric Thought." In *Learning and Teaching Geometry, K–12,* edited by Mary Montgomery Lindquist and Albert P. Shulte, pp. 1–16. Reston, VA: National Council of Teachers of Mathematics.

Del Grande, John. (February 1990). "Spatial Sense." *Arithmetic Teacher* 37: 14–20.

Dunkels, Andrejs. (February 1990). "Making and Exploring Tangrams." *Arithmetic Teacher* 37: 38–42.

Hoffer, Alan R. (1983). "Van Hiele-Based Research." In *Acquisition of Mathematics Concepts and Processes,* edited by Richard Lesh and Marsha Landau, pp. 205–227. New York: Academic Press.

Hoffer, Alan R., and Shirley Ann K. Hoffer. (1992). "Geometry and Visual Thinking." In *Teaching Mathematics in Grades K–8: Research Based Methods,* 2nd ed., edited by Thomas R. Post, pp. 249–277. Boston: Allyn & Bacon.

Izard, John. (Febryary 1990). "Developing Spatial Skills with Three-Dimensional Puzzles." *Arithmetic Teacher* 37: 44–51.

National Council of Teachers of Mathematics. (1989). *Curriculum and Evaluation Standards for School Mathematics.* Reston, VA: Author.

National Research Council. (1989). *Everybody Counts.* Washington, DC: National Academy Press.

Prentice, Gerald. (November 1989). "Flexible Straws." *Arithmetic Teacher* 37: 4–5.

Ranucci, Ernest R. (1987). "Snipshots." In *Geometry for Grades K–6: Readings from the Arithmetic Teacher,* edited by Jane M. Hill, pp. 88–89. Reston, VA: National Council of Teachers of Mathematics.

Silverman, Helene. (February 1990). "Ideas: Spatial Sense." *Arithmetic Teacher* 37: 29–42.

Wheatley, Grayson H. (February 1990). "One Point of View: Spatial Sense and Mathematics Learning." *Arithmetic Teacher* 37: 10–11.

Wilson, Patricia S., and Verna M. Adams. (January 1992). "A Dynamic way to Teach Angle and Angle Measure." *Arithmetic Teacher* 39: 6–13.

Woodward, Ernest, and Patsy G. Buckner. (October 1987). "Reflections and Symmetry—a Second-Grade Miniunit." *Arithmetic Teacher* 35: 8–10.

Yackel, Erna, and Grayson H. Wheatley. (February 1990). "Promoting Visual Imagery in Young Pupils." *Arithmetic Teacher* 37: 52–58.

SOFTWARE RESOURCES

Elastic Lines
Company: Sunburst
Computer: Apple, IBM, Tandy
Grade level: 4—8

Explore shapes and patterns by stretching "electronic" bands over pegs on geoboards of different sizes and types. Manipulate the shapes on a drawing board.

Logo Plus
Company: Terrapin Software, Inc.
Computer: Apple II family
Grade level: 1 and up

Provides opportunities to program the computer to make figures and designs using a triangular figure, the turtle. Gives intuitive experiences with angles, lines, and shapes.

Terrapin Logo for the Macintosh
Company: Terrapin Software, Inc.
Computer: Macintosh
Grade level: 1 and up

Same as *Logo Plus.*

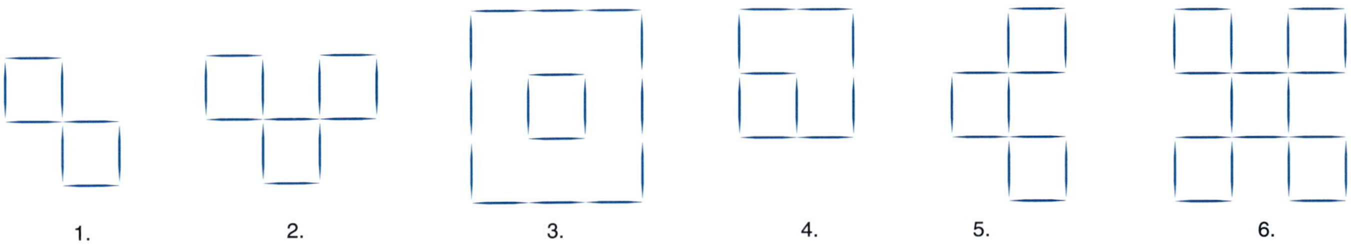

FIGURE 11.38 Solutions for Toothpick Puzzles in Figure 11.1

CHAPTER 12

Measurement Learning: Understanding and Skill

▪ INTRODUCTORY PROBLEM ▪

The PTA is sponsoring a contest to beautify the campus of the Hallack Street School. The contest rules specify that the fifth and sixth grades may enter plans for landscaping, together with the approximate cost, after they consult with the lower grades. The landscaping plans must include how the children in all the grades will assist in the planting. The landscaping can include trees, shrubs, and flowers. The winning class will be awarded a computer for their room and will work with a PTA committee to carry out the plan. Your fifth-grade class decided that they really want that computer, and they are determined to submit a superior plan. As you study this chapter, decide how they can learn about or review measurement ideas and skills as they design the plan.

INTRODUCTION

It may seem that children would have no difficulties learning about measurement. However, the results of the fourth National Assessment of Educational Progress (NAEP) show that children do have difficulties. When given items showing pictures of rulers next to segments to be measured, about 75% of the seventh graders could read the ruler to the nearest one-fourth inch, but when the ruler was not aligned with the end of a line segment, only about 50% of the seventh-grade students and fewer third graders gave a correct measurement of the segment. When given a diagram of a rectangle with square units shown, only 46% of the seventh graders and 5% of third graders could give the area of the rectangle. Students performed similarly on other thought-provoking or nonroutine problems (Kouba, Brown, Carpenter, Lindquist, Silver, and Swafford, 1988). These responses indicate that children had not developed an understanding of measurement. Skill in the use of measuring instruments and knowledge of formulas are necessary, but without an understanding of measurement concepts, learners cannot solve measurement problems in mathematics, science, and social science. They will be handicapped in pursuing advanced studies in these areas, and many careers will be closed to them.

This chapter begins with two sections: Understanding Measurement and Instructional Sequence for Measurement. The third section, Activities for Learning Measurement Concepts and Skills, has subsections that deal with teaching various measurement topics. Assessment of Learning and a Summary end the chapter.

UNDERSTANDING MEASUREMENT

If children are taught only the skills of measurement, they do not develop the conceptual basis necessary to solve measurement problems (NCTM, 1989). Therefore, new directions in elementary school instruction emphasize developing understanding before learning skills. This section discusses areas of conceptual knowledge and readiness for learning measurement concepts and skills.

Areas of Conceptual Knowledge

Six areas of conceptual knowledge deal with measurement and can be considered general learning objectives for understanding measurement concepts:

1. **Knowledge of attributes.** Characteristics of objects or phenomena to be measured are usually referred to as *attributes*. Length, area, volume, weight (mass), and time are examples of attributes. Children construct concepts of attributes and learn the words they need to express their understanding.
2. **Knowledge of the measuring process.** To measure, a unit with the same attribute (e.g., length) as the thing to be measured is chosen. The attribute of the measurable object is compared to the attribute of the unit. This entails "covering" or "fitting" the unit to the object and counting the resulting number of units. Related to knowledge of the measuring process is the idea that the smaller the unit, the more units are needed to measure the attribute of an object.
3. **Knowledge of the approximate nature of measurement.** Because it is possible to choose smaller and smaller units, a measurement is never exact. Measurements are always approximate. There is always some error.

4. **Knowledge of estimation.** Estimation involves giving a measurement without using the measurement process. It relies on an immediate awareness of the extent of an attribute of an object. In addition to being a skill useful in real life, estimation helps learners focus on attributes and develops ideas of units. The ability to estimate is related to a "measurement sense," an intuitive notion of units of comparison. These units are sometimes referred to as *reference measurements* and would include measurements such as the distance from home to school, a 25-centimeter length, or the area of a 3″ × 5″ index card.
5. **Knowledge that some units can be added or subtracted.** To add or subtract measurement units, it must be possible to combine like attributes of different objects or parts of one object. For example, two distances or the areas of five rooms of a house can be combined and the units added or subtracted. Length, area, volume, and weight are examples of measures that can be combined. Temperatures do not combine. For example, mixing cold water and boiling water is more complex than simply determining the difference of the temperatures.
6. **Knowledge that instruments and formulas simplify the process of measuring.** Counting the units that have been arranged to cover an object is a tedious process. Students learn that rulers, scales, and formulas can make counting units unnecessary and thus simplify the measuring task.

Reader Activity 12.1

Study learners' textbooks or teachers' manuals, one for primary grades and one for upper grades, to determine how the six outcome objectives for measurement listed are presented in the books.

Readiness for Learning Measurement Concepts and Skills

A fundamental principle of learning is that children must be ready, that is, able to learn. They must have a level of intellectual maturity and appropriate background experiences to enable them to incorporate new material into their schemata. Research, however, has not established what readiness for learning measurement entails (Wilson and Osborne, 1992). For example, Piagetian theory would lead to the conclusion that children must be able to conserve length to study length measurement (Figure 12.1). However, Hiebert (1984) concluded from his research that length measurement can be learned by children who cannot conserve length.

Because research is inconclusive, instructional guidelines would suggest that you be aware of children's misconceptions, prior learning, and ability to profit from instructional activities. Use interactive teaching, questioning, listening, and observing to determine what meanings children have acquired. Then, provide experiences that challenge children so that they progress in learning about measurement.

INSTRUCTIONAL SEQUENCE FOR MEASUREMENT

An instruction sequence for any measurement system enables children to attain three broad objectives: (1) learning about measurable attributes; (2) forming concepts of nonstandard and standard units and developing skill in the use of instruments; and (3) understanding and using formulas (see Standard 10 in Curriculum Standards for Grades K–4 and Standard 13 for Grades 5–8, Appendix A). The objectives are related and enable children to construct the conceptual knowledge outlined previously and to develop the skill needed to measure. This section gives an overview of these three objectives.

Learning about Measurable Attributes

To learn about measurable attributes, children first engage in activities that require making qualitative or nonnumerical comparisons (Liedtke, 1990; Wilson and Osborne, 1992). To begin, they make judgments based on observations, perceiving dif-

FIGURE 12.1 Assessment of Conservation of Length

1. Show the child two strips of paper the same length. Place the strips side by side.

Discuss that the strips are the same length.

2. Rearrange the strips.

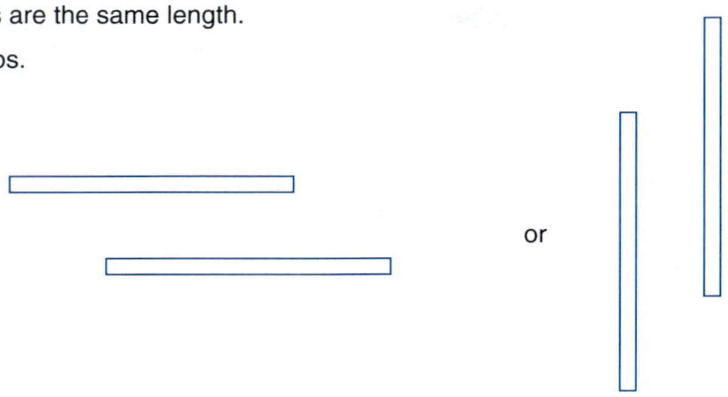

3. Ask: Now are the strips the same length or is one longer or shorter? Why do you think so?

4. If the child responds that the strips are the same length and gives a sensible reason for his or her response, he or she is said to conserve length.

5. To assess further, use two longer strips. Cut one into several short strips to compare to the other long strip and follow the same procedure.

ferences in the length or other attributes of objects. Soon, they focus on attributes by sorting objects with like attributes. Children solve the problem, for example, of placing objects together that are *the same length*. Subsequently they make a two-way sort—*as long as* and *longer than*—and later a three-way sort—*as long as, longer than*, and *shorter than*. Later, children order objects by length.

The next comparison problem is to determine which of two objects that cannot be compared directly is higher or longer. The problem can be: Which is higher, the window ledge or the cabinet? To solve the problem, a third object must be used. Often children use their bodies. For example, a child could determine that the window ledge is the height of his or her shoulder and the cabinet comes only to his or her waist. Instead of their bodies, they may use another object. For example, to compare the height of the window ledge to the height of the cabinet, children could use string. String should be given to small groups with the direction to use it if it helps. Children could decide to cut the string to show the length of one object and then compare the string length to the length of the other object.

Children can also find an object that is about as long or covers almost as much surface as a given object. This type of comparison activity gives children the opportunity to make estimates in the course of problem solving. For example, to find a book with about the same surface as a window pane requires making judgments about which book to select. Activities that involve making qualitative comparisons are planned for the beginning study of length, weight, capacity, volume, temperature, and, in the upper grades, angles.

Vocabulary is introduced and used in natural settings as children discuss their work with you or among themselves. For example, you can ask, "How did you measure to find pencils that are longer than the red pencil?" Children's responses will require the use of the words, "measure" and "longer." As they work together, children will also need to use measurement words to communicate.

Learning about Units

After a unit is selected to measure an attribute of an object and used to cover the object, units are counted to determine how many comprise the measurement. *Nonstandard units* are used in beginning measurement activities. Straws, toothpicks, or paper clips can serve as nonstandard units for length (Figure 12.2); index cards or triangular or rectangular regions for area; and marbles, bars of soap, or nails for weight. Nonstandard units for length or area can be body parts such as fingers, hands, or arms. In the middle grades, students use wedges to measure angles.

Nonstandard units help focus attention on the process of assigning a number of units to obtain a measurement. Using nonstandard units, children can think about the numerical aspects of a measurement and not be concerned with learning standard units. Nonstandard units also help children be attentive to the attribute being measured and the process of measuring and contribute to the development of an intuitive understanding of measurement. In the early primary grades more time is devoted to work with nonstandard units before introducing standard units than will be given to the use of nonstandard units in the middle grades.

A series of nonstandard units or only one unit used repeatedly will measure an object. Children begin by using as many nonstandard units as necessary to find a measurement. Next, they solve the problem of using only one unit to find a measurement.

Making measuring instruments is the final step in the study of nonstandard units. Liedtke (1990) suggests that children make hand or finger rulers (Figure 12.3). Rulers can also be constructed to measure length by cutting congruent strips from paper of two different colors and taping them end to end. Rulers with nonstandard units help children learn to measure correctly (Figure 12.4). Van de Walle (1990) would have children construct rulers with units that do not begin at the end of the ruler to help children learn that, in measuring length, it is necessary to begin by determining the front-end point of the first unit.

When children demonstrate an understanding of the process of measuring using nonstandard units, they are guided to realize that different nonstandard units give different measurements and that, therefore, *standard units* are needed. Learning about standard units involves relating knowledge of the process of measuring developed from work with nonstandard units to measurement with standard units. After children are introduced to standard units, they develop familiarity with them by using them in many settings. During elementary school they study both the metric and customary systems.

Working with nonstandard and standard units enables children to construct measurement concepts and to develop skill. They learn that the use of units involves *approximation*. Children become aware that a measurement is only about 5 hands or about 7 centimeters, and they are encouraged to report their measurements using words such as "almost," "a little longer (or shorter) than," or "about."

Measuring with nonstandard and later standard units helps children learn to *estimate* measurements. Estimation is important because it serves as a check on the reasonableness of a measurement. It also helps children develop a measurement sense. Those with good measurement sense can estimate in real-world situations. For example, they can decide that a room is about 10 feet long or that the distance to a friend's house is about 2 miles. They have internalized certain reference measurements that serve as the bases for comparisons.

As children work with nonstandard and standard units, they also become aware of the *relation* between the size of the unit and the number of units needed

FIGURE 12.2 The Pencil Is Three Toothpicks Long

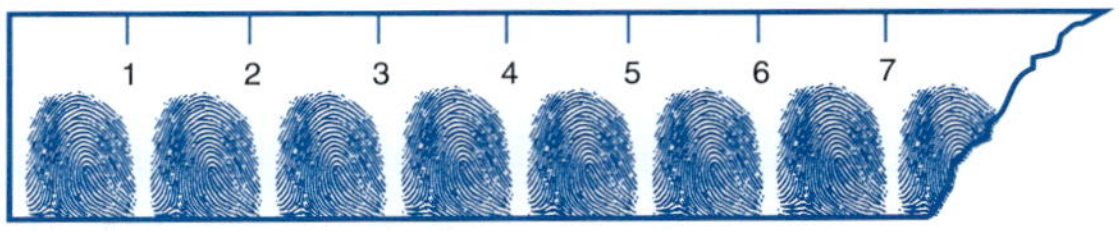

FIGURE 12.3 A Ruler Made from Index Finger Prints

to measure the attribute. They learn that when measuring an attribute of an object, more small units are needed to complete the measure than large units.

Children become *skillful* in using instruments by using rulers they make and commonly used instruments with standard units, such as rulers and scales. Many experiences enable them to become proficient in measuring.

As noted, nonstandard units are stressed in the primary grades as children measure and compare lengths, areas, and weights, but they also learn about standard units for length, weight, and capacity. In addition, children in the primary years learn to tell time, read thermometers, and use money. In the middle and upper grades standard units for area and volume are introduced. Standard units for area are studied in grades 4, 5, and 6; standard units for volume are studied in grades 5 and 6 (Reys, Suydam, and Lindquist, 1992).

Understanding and Using Formulas

In the upper grades, after children have used standard units in many activities to measure perimeter or area by covering and counting, they begin to realize that a more efficient procedure is needed. Often, they invent shortcuts. From their invented shortcuts and a study of examples, they induce the rules or formulas by generalizing from their experiences (Holmes, 1985; Wilson and Osborne, 1992).

Knowing when to use formulas is another learning distinct from knowing the formula. Many activities are used to enable children to focus on cues that trigger retrieval of an appropriate formula. Discussion is an important part of the activities that help children learn to choose a formula that leads to a correct problem solution.

ACTIVITIES FOR LEARNING MEASUREMENT CONCEPTS AND SKILLS

This section describes activities for learning measurement. Subsections are Length, Area, Capacity and Volume, Weight (Mass), Time, Temperature, Money, Angles, Formulas, and Relating Measurements. A final subsection deals with the Metric and Customary Systems. The activities use interactive approaches to teaching and learning. Learners solve measurement problems, often working together in groups, discuss their work to attain new insights and understanding, and complete assignments to develop skill.

The subsections Length, Area, Volume, Weight, and Angles include activities related to the sequence of instruction discussed. Children learn about a measurable attribute by comparing, using nonstandard units, and using standard units. The subsections Time, Temperature, and Money do not include activities for using nonstandard units as such units cannot readily be constructed by children. More ac-

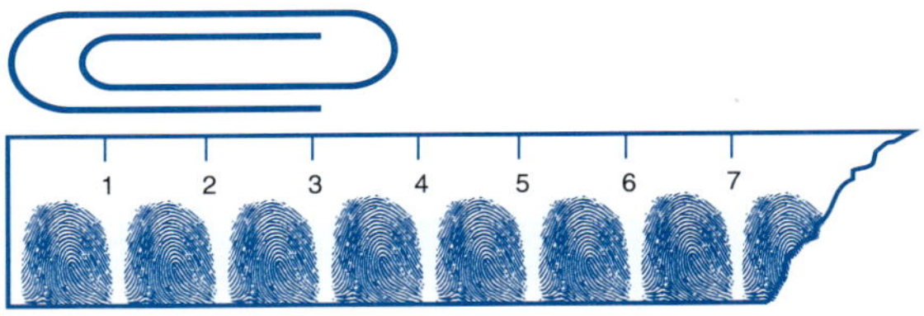

FIGURE 12.4 Measuring a Paper Clip Correctly

tivities are given for the study of length than for other measures, because these activities can be adapted to studying other types of measures.

To learn about measurement, children must measure. To engage all learners in measuring experiences, you can organize learning around learning centers or divide the class into groups of two or three children with similar objects available to all groups. Learning centers provide opportunities for different experiences at different centers. If there are not enough centers to engage all children, some can work on other projects at their desks while waiting their turn at the centers. If the groups are measuring and only one object, such as the teacher's desk, is a part of a measurement assignment, there must be a plan so that all groups can work with the object at different times. Each group could be given a ticket with a number on it. The groups would measure the object in the order of the numbers on their tickets. A member of the group would write the number on the chalkboard when they begin and cross it out when they finish, thus signaling that the next group can begin. While children work at centers or in groups, you circulate, observing children's progress and helping them clarify ideas and correct misconceptions.

The measuring activities can be motivated by having children choose objects to measure, whenever it is possible to give them choices. You can also introduce many activities by arousing interest about the measurements of objects in their environment by saying, "Let's see what we can find out" or "What do you think we will find out about . . . ?"

Length

Learning about Length by Comparing

ACTIVITY 12.1
Looking around the School.

Give children several days to find on the school campus the largest (smallest) window; widest door; tallest (shortest) tree, bush, or plant; and longest (shortest) walkway. Objects in the classroom can also be compared. Examples are: the height of the door and your height; the length of the bulletin board and the length of the chalkboard; the length of the library table and the length of your desk. Ask children for other suggestions of objects to compare. Have children share their discoveries after they have had time to think about their responses.

ACTIVITY 12.2
Comparing Body Parts.

Have children work in pairs to compare their heights, handspans, thumb lengths, and right foot lengths. (Select children for pairs so that the findings will not be embarrassing to either child.) Have them write a report using pictures to give their findings.

ACTIVITY 12.3
Measurement Sort.

Prepare boxes that contain some of several objects, such as pencils, crayons, combs, paper clips, nuts, bolts, and nails. Have children work in pairs to sort the objects into three piles. Children take turns choosing an object in a box to be the reference. Together they find objects the same, shorter, or longer than the chosen reference object.

The objects in the boxes can also be used to order objects. The activity directions are: Each child picks five objects and gives them to his or her partner to order by size. The children then discuss their work. If there is time, they repeat the activity.

ACTIVITY 12.4
How Do These Compare?

Have children form groups of two or three. Groups will estimate and then decide which of two objects is longer. Examples of objects that groups will need to take turns comparing (or groups can choose to compare and report their finding to the class) are: the height of the chalkboard from the floor and the width of your desk; the width of a window and the width of the door; and the length of the computer keyboard and the length of your arm to your elbow. Examples of objects that groups do not need to take turns to compare are: the height of their desk chair back and the width of their desk top; and the width of their chair back and the height of their desk top. Do not suggest how to solve these problems, but supply string, ribbon, long dowel rods, or long strips of paper. Say, "You may use one or more of these to solve the problems." After groups finish, discuss how they solved the problems and their conclusions.

ACTIVITY 12.5
Which Curvy Line Is Longer?

Draw two curvy lines on a piece of paper. Duplicate the drawings and distribute them to pairs of children. Have them decide which is longer. Give children the opportunity to solve the problem as in Activity 12.4 by supplying materials, but do not tell them how to use the materials.

ACTIVITY 12.6
Which Is Longer?

Children work in pairs to answer questions such as, "Which is longer—the distance around your ankle or around your wrist? The distance around your head or around your waist? The distance around your elbow or around your ankle? The distance from your desk to the pencil sharpener or to the teacher's desk?" Have them estimate before finding the answers to the questions. Supply materials as in Activity 12.4, but let children decide how to complete the task.

Using Nonstandard Units. The use of nonstandard units introduces children to measurement. By covering or fitting the object to be measured with small nonstandard units that have the same attribute as the attribute to be measured and counting the number of units used, learners develop an intuitive idea of the process of measuring. Children also discover that the units usually do not fit exactly, and the approximate nature of measurement is thus introduced. Making rulers with nonstandard units extends their knowledge.

ACTIVITY 12.7
Measuring with Blocks.

Distribute blocks or Cuisenaire rods to groups of children. Give different groups different-size materials. Ask them to solve the problem of finding the length of their desks using the materials. Tell them they will often use the word "about" when they report a measurement. (Children in grade 1 can work on this problem, and one or more groups will decide to line up the blocks or rods.)

When they have solved the problem, discuss the strategies they used and their results. Include the question, "Why do we have different answers?" to help children realize that different units give different results.

ACTIVITY 12.8
Measuring with Nonstandard Units.

Straws, toothpicks, paper clips, and the like are useful for studying measurement because all students using the same unit will arrive at the same number of units, but if they use different units, their measurements will differ.

Distribute straws to groups. Ask the groups to solve the problem of finding the length of their desks using straws. After they have had time to solve the problem by lining up the straws and counting, have groups report on how they measured and their results. Ask questions to help children realize that when all use same-sized straws, they get the same answer.

Have children solve the problem of measuring the length of different objects in their desks with toothpicks (pencils, etc.). Help them realize that when everyone uses toothpicks and measures the same objects, the measurements are the same.

Next, ask what objects in the classroom could be measured with straws and with toothpicks. Books, plants, table tops, windows, table legs, wastepaper baskets, lunch boxes, and other common classroom objects will be mentioned. Have children choose five of these to measure with both straws and toothpicks.

When children finish their work, discuss the results. Ask questions that help children focus on relations. For example, ask, "What did you notice about the number of straws and the number of toothpicks needed to measure your reading book? Why do you think the numbers are different?" "Predict the number of straws and toothpicks needed to measure my desk. Why did you predict more toothpicks than straws?" "Jenny and Patrick can each measure with both straws and toothpicks so that we can decide how close our estimates are."

ACTIVITY 12.9
Using Only One Nonstandard Unit.

Give groups one straw, saying, "How can we measure our desks with one straw?" Do not model the procedure. Let children work on the solution to this problem. Discuss their solutions. (A first-grade teacher I know used this approach, and the children were able to solve the problem.)

Repeat using one block and one toothpick. Have children measure other objects with only one nonstandard unit. After they have measured with different nonstandard units, ask questions so that they relate the number of units to the size of the unit used to measure the length of an object.

ACTIVITY 12.10
Measuring with Body Parts.

Say, "How can you use one hand to find the length of your desk?" Before they begin the task, groups of children discuss how to solve the problem and share their ideas in a class discussion. Then, they measure their desks using hands. Later, ask them to make suggestions for using other body parts to measure. Their ideas could include thumbs to measure books or feet to measure the length of the room. Follow through by asking them to use their ideas to measure objects.

Children can trace around one of their hands (open or closed), cut out the drawing, and use this handprint to find the length of other objects. They make an "X" at each end of the dimension of the handprint used to measure. A footprint rather than a hand pattern can also be used. Have each child take off a shoe and trace around his or her foot to make a footprint pattern. Ask, "What can we measure with a footprint pattern?" Groups use the patterns to measure objects mentioned by members of the class. Different groups should measure the same three or four objects with the footprint of each child in the group and report their findings. Say, "You all measured the same table (or other object). Why are your measurements different?" Discuss the relation of the footprint pattern length to the number of units in the measurement.

ACTIVITY 12.11
Making Measurement Instruments.

Suggest that measuring can be done more easily with a measuring bar than with hands, straws, or other objects (Figure 12.5). On the overhead, show a measuring bar. (The units can be the length of toothpicks, and the instrument called a toothpick-length measuring bar.) Ask children to examine the measuring bar, decide how it was made, and comment on its advantages. After they have explained that there are paper strips of two colors on the bar and noted how and why the bar is used, tell them that they can each make a measuring bar. Use two colors for the paper strips you give to each child. Each also gets a piece of cardboard a little longer than the strips placed end to end. The task is to begin close to one end of the cardboard bar, place the strips on the bar, alternating colors of strips, and then paste the strips on the bar. (Check their work before they paste the strips. Children could be engaged in another activity while you help a few paste strips.) Next, discuss how to write the numerals at the end of the strips. Before they write numerals on the bars, make certain that they know how and why to begin with 0.

The bars should be used in a number of measuring activities. Children can measure the "junk" collected for counters and other small objects of their own choosing. As they use the bars, the ideas of approximation and estimation are enhanced, and the relation between the size of a unit and the number of units in a measurement becomes more meaningful.

Activity for the Classroom 12.1. Teach one or more lessons during which each child makes a measuring bar and measures several objects with it. What meanings should children construct from this experience? Before teaching the lesson, write out questions to ask children while they are using their measuring bars so that they develop these meanings.

Using Standard Units. After children have worked with nonstandard units and have an intuitive understanding of the process of measuring, they are introduced to standard units. A discussion that emphasizes the need for units that everyone agrees on begins the study of standard units. Children are helped to reflect on the problems that arose when they used body parts or different units to measure the same objects. They discuss that if everyone used the same straw or toothpick measuring bar, the measurements would be the same. The question is then asked, "What *do* people use to measure?" Children report what they know (some may have heard of inches), but if no child answers the question, you tell them there are two kinds of units, metric and customary, and they will learn about both, beginning with metric units.

FIGURE 12.5 A Measuring Bar

ACTIVITY 12.12
Introduction to Decimeters and Centimeters.

Give each child a strip of paper 1 decimeter in length. Tell them that the strip can be used to measure a decimeter, and write the word *decimeter* on the chalkboard. To develop an intuitive understanding of the unit, students find objects in the class or line up objects to show a decimeter. For example, they can line up paper clips, play money, or checkers. Next, groups can choose objects longer than a decimeter to measure, compare their measurements, and report their measurements to the class. Usually the measurements will be reported as "about" a number of decimeters.

To introduce centimeters, have children find how many Cuisenaire unit rods line up to make a decimeter. When children make the interesting discovery that 10 unit rods have the same length as a decimeter, give them the name of the new unit.

ACTIVITY 12.13
Making a Metric Ruler.

Ask what could be done to make a metric measuring bar or ruler and why such an instrument would be useful. They may recall how they made measuring bars for nonstandard units, and they may suggest the same procedure for a metric ruler. If they do not remember the plan, you remind them of their previous work. After they decide how to make the metric rulers, give each child three paper decimeters of two different colors. They alternate the decimeters on the ruler before they paste them on the cardboard. When finished, they can use their decimeter rulers to measure and report the length of many classroom objects.

ACTIVITY 12.14
Using a Metric Ruler and Tape.

Give children commercially produced metric rulers. Ask them to examine the instrument and tell how it is like and different from the rulers they made. Ask them to draw lines whose measures will be whole numbers of centimeters. (E.g., the lines can be how far you saw a fly walk in 3, 5, or 8 seconds.) Children can study each other's lines and compare what they did. Also ask them to draw lines whose lengths are given in centimeters (e.g., lengths of footprints in the snow) and to draw lines of given lengths that begin at 3 (4, etc.) centimeters. Discuss how they know what to do. Partners can ask each other to draw lines of specified lengths to vary the activity.

To provide experiences with measuring circumference, give children cloth or metal tapes, and ask them to find distances around circular objects, such as the wastepaper basket, plates, or a pot holding a plant. Introduce the word *circumference* at an appropriate time. After a few experiences measuring circumference, they can estimate the distance around other circular objects and measure to compare their estimates with the measurements.

When children become familiar with unit names and use them in their discussions and reports, introduce the abbreviations, cm for centimeter, dm for decimeter, and later m for meter and km for kilometer.

ACTIVITY 12.15
What's My Measurement?

Each pair or small group of children is given an activity sheet with a list of classroom objects ranging from a few centimeters to 25 centimeters in length. Erasers, pencils, books, writing paper, desk tops, window panes, and distances are listed. They are to choose 10 of these objects or distances (or others of their own choice), estimate their lengths, and then measure them to decide how close their estimates were to the actual measurements. If children understand measuring to one-half unit, directions for the activity can state that the measurement should be to the nearest one-half centimeter. A discussion of their work completes the activity.

ACTIVITY 12.16
Object Hunt.

Groups of children work together to find classroom objects whose measurements you have written on an "Object Hunt List." Several different lists can be used so not all groups are trying to measure the same objects.

Include distances around some objects to give pupils intuitive experiences with perimeter. For example, children can measure the distance around the surface of their desks, a book, or a window pane. Introduce the word *perimeter* when children are discussing these measurements.

ACTIVITY 12.17
Estimate Myself.

Each pupil receives a record sheet such as in Table 12.1 and fills in the estimate column. Two children work together with a string and a ruler, each measuring the body part of the other child and filling in the measurement column. Together they decide how close the estimates were to the actual measurements.

ACTIVITY 12.18
Centimeter Book.

Children choose about 10 to 15 objects to measure with their metric rulers for inclusion in their books. Have them include the perimeter measurements of several objects. They can use objects found at school or at home. For the pages of their books, they draw a picture of the object, label the picture with the object's name, write an estimate of the object's measurement, and give the measurement they found using a metric ruler. Children can give measurements to the nearest centimeter or one-half centimeter.

ACTIVITY 12.19
Introducing Meters.

Introduce the meter by having children examine meter sticks. They should notice that a meter is 10 decimeters and 100 centimeters. They can "measure" their meter sticks using their decimeter rulers to help them focus on metric relations.

TABLE 12.1 Activity Sheet for Length

Record of Estimates of Myself

Length	Estimate	Measurement	Difference
Ear			
Wrist			
Ankle			
Handspan			
Foot			
Arm			

Groups then choose what to measure using meter sticks. The lengths and perimeters of chalkboards, bulletin boards, and the classroom floor should be suggested, if they are not mentioned by students.

ACTIVITY 12.20
Measuring Jumps.

Pairs of children can work together on the playground for this activity. In turn, they take a standing and a running jump. The partner measures the jump and records the measurement. When the children return to the classroom, they discuss the measurements and the differences and similarities they observed.

ACTIVITY 12.21
Introducing Kilometers or Miles.

Discuss the need for larger units when measuring long distances. Children probably know about miles. Introduce the kilometer, 1000 meters, as another measure of long distances. Have children make records of distances they have traveled using kilometers or miles. If possible, include school bus rides. Have them give the place the trip began and ended. Make a chart of the reports of their measurements. Emphasize distances commonly traveled in the chart. Encourage children to use the chart to develop reference measurements.

Area

Learning about Area by Comparing

ACTIVITY 12.22
Looking at Our Room.

Ask pairs of children to decide what surfaces in the room are larger and smaller than their desk tops. Have them make lists by drawing sketches. Groups report their findings and their decision processes in a class discussion.

ACTIVITY 12.23
Paper-Eater Ant.

Give pairs of children paper strips that differ in length and width. Say, "Arrange these paper strips for the paper-eater ant to gobble up so that she begins with the smallest and eats the strips in order of size." Have children explain how they decided the order of the strips.

ACTIVITY 12.24
Triangle Rearrangement.

Give children an isosceles triangle. Ask them to fold it in half and cut along the fold to make 2 right triangles. Each child rearranges the two triangles to make new figures (the sides of the triangles must touch) (Figure 12.6A). As they work and in a class discussion following the activity, ask them to compare the surfaces (areas) of the figures. If they can conserve area, they will recognize that the areas of all their figures are the same.

One-half of the class can cut another isosceles triangle congruent to the first and give one-half to another child so that all children have 3 triangles to rearrange (Figure 12.6B).

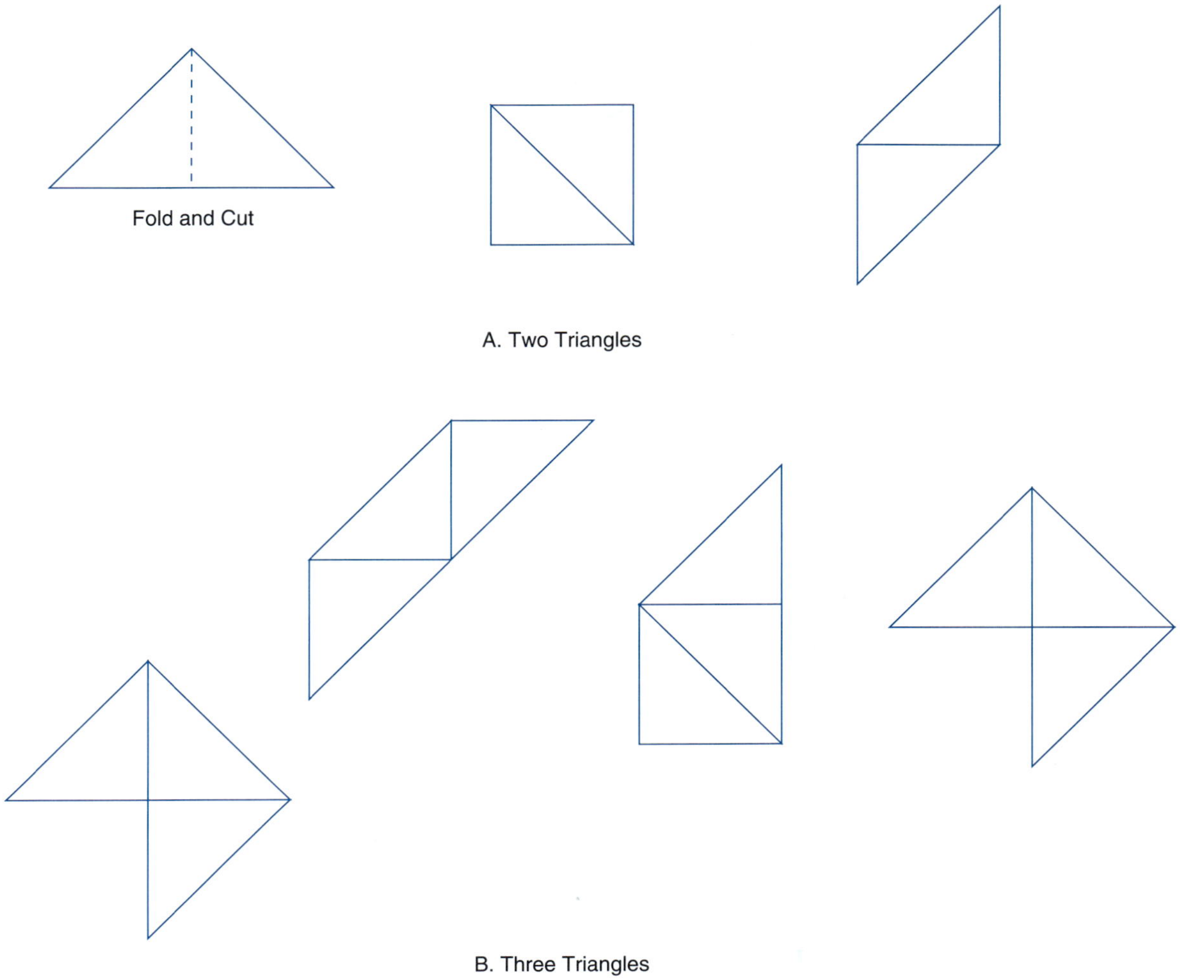

FIGURE 12.6 Rearrangement of Isosceles Triangles. A, Two Triangles. B, Three Triangles

ACTIVITY 12.25
Ordering Octagonal Regions.

Give each child an activity sheet with different octagonal shapes (Figure 12.7). Ask them to cut out the shapes and to arrange them in order of the size of their surfaces. After they finish their work, ask them to tell how they decided the order of the shapes. The word *area* can be introduced during this activity or Activity 12.26.

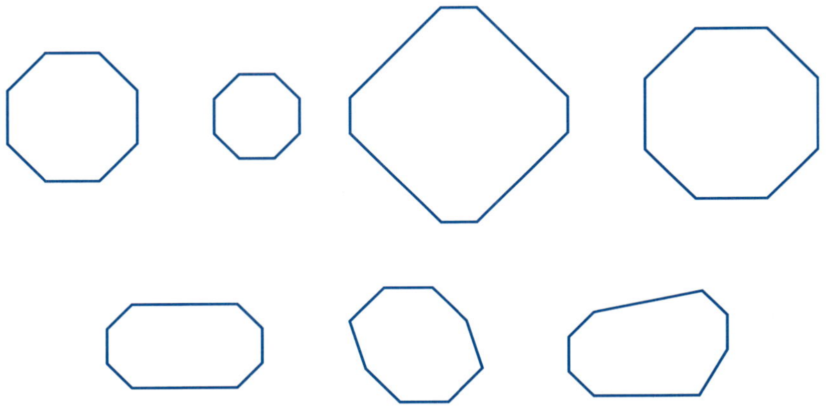

FIGURE 12.7 Activity Sheet for Ordering Octagonal Regions

ACTIVITY 12.26
Which Has More Area?

Pose problems such as: Which has more area, a window pane or the top (side) of the aquarium? The window or the table top? The chair back or the chair seat. Give each group of two or three children sheets of paper to use to solve the problem, but do not demonstrate how to measure using the paper. Let them solve the problem in their groups. Later, discuss how they solved the problems by covering the surface with sheets of paper.

Using Nonstandard Units. Measuring the area of a region with nonstandard units or standard units can involve covering the region with one or more units and counting the units. However, using only one unit is too difficult for most children, but they can work with two units, alternating the units and counting them as they measure.

ACTIVITY 12.27
Covering.

Ask children to find the area of various classroom objects they would like to measure. (If different groups measure the area of different objects, reporting to the class gives purpose to the discussion.) Have children choose from among sheets of paper, index cards, or business cards to carry out the assignment. As they report their measurements, ask questions that help them focus on the relation of the size of the unit to the number of units in the measurement.

ACTIVITY 12.28
Using Different Regions to Measure Area.

Have children use nonstandard units such as handprints, footprints, triangles, rectangles, pentagons, and hexagons, as well as squares to measure classroom objects. Stress estimating before measuring. Different groups can choose different nonstandard units, but at some time all children should have the opportunity to work with square units. After several experiences with measuring surfaces with nonstandard units, they decide what shape unit is best for measuring area. They should conclude that a square unit is best and be able to give reasons for this conclusion.

ACTIVITY 12.29
Room Measurement.

Have children use sheets of newspaper to measure one or more rooms in their house. Before making this assignment, have them measure a section of the classroom so that they understand the process. Have them write up their findings and how they carried out the task. They can read their reports to a small group or the class.

ACTIVITY 12.30
How Many Figures?

Ask children to use square dot grid paper to make as many figures as possible with four squares, edges touching (Figure 12.8). Have them share their figures. As the class discusses the figures, ask about the areas of the figures. The students should realize that all the figures have the same area, but are different shapes.

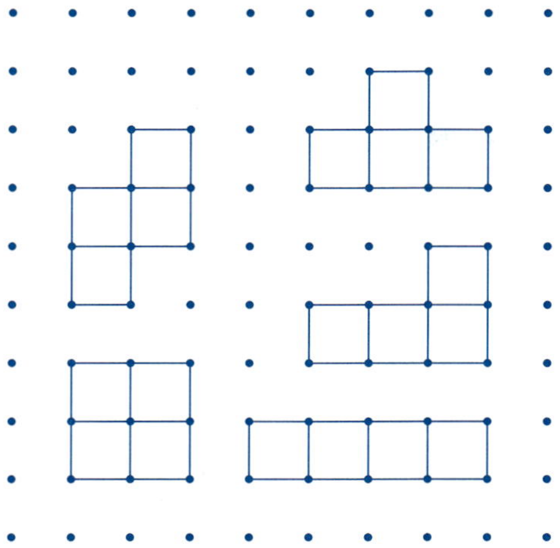

FIGURE 12.8 Figures from Four Squares Shown on Dot Paper

ACTIVITY 12.31
Areas of Irregular Figures.

Give children pictures of figures with irregular shapes whose area can be found by determining the number of squares that make up the figure (Figure 12.9). Have children find the areas. During the class discussion, ask children how they thought to find the areas. Help them realize that the area of parts of figures can be combined.

Reader Activity 12.2

Use a nonstandard unit to find the area of a region of your own choosing. Did using a nonstandard unit for measuring area help you understand how children learn area measurement? Why or why not?

Using Standard Units

ACTIVITY 12.32
Using Square Centimeters (Decimeters) to Cover.

After children have experienced using square units to measure area, show square centimeters and square decimeters, and give their names. Give each child a transparent square grid measuring 10 by 10 centimeters. Ask why it is useful for measuring area. Have children in pairs select objects to measure, using two grids if necessary. Stress estimating before measuring. Oral reports can summarize the activity.

ACTIVITY 12.33
Objects and Figures with Given Areas.

Pose the problem of finding classroom objects with a given area. While some groups are searching, other groups can be using square grid paper to solve the problem of making figures with a given number of sides and a given area (e.g., 1. a figure with 6 sides and an area of 5 squares; 2. a figure with 12 sides and an area of 8 squares—solutions are in Figure 12.10).

Activity for the Classroom 12.2. Write three problems for making figures such as described in Activity 12.33. Use these problems with your class. Then, ask groups

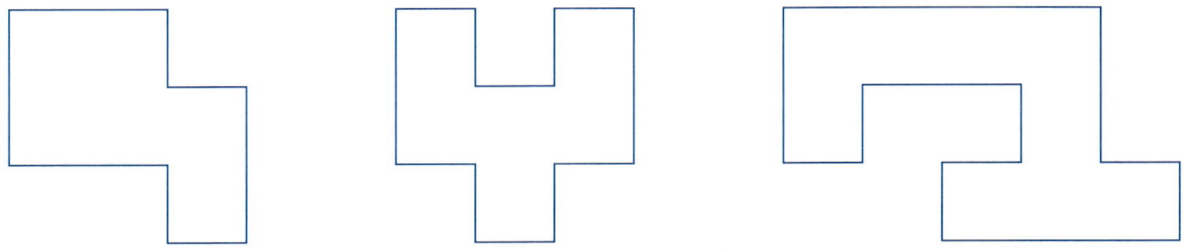

FIGURE 12.9 Areas of Irregular Figures

FIGURE 12.10 Figures with Given Properties

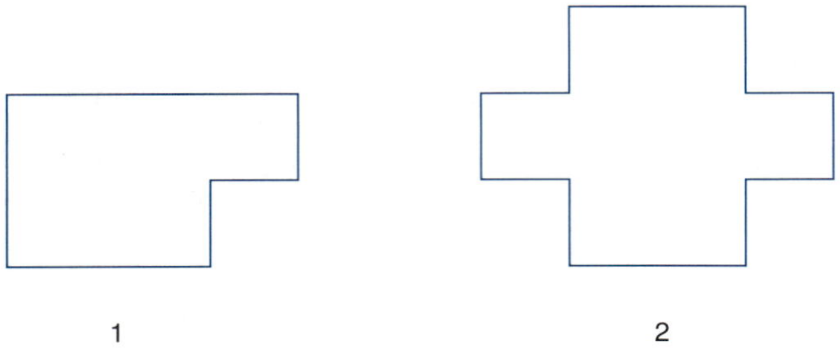

of learners each to write three such problems for other groups to solve. Have them tell what they learned from writing and solving these problems.

Capacity and Volume

Both capacity and volume tell how much a vessel contains. Capacity is expressed in units such as gallons or liters. Volume is given in cubic units related to length units, such as cubic centimeters or cubic inches.

Learning about Capacity and Volume by Comparing

ACTIVITY 12.34
Which Holds the Most?

Use different-size boxes or jars. Pairs of children should have two or more such objects for this activity. Have available many small objects, such as plastic shipping particles, marbles, blocks, pinto beans, or rice. Water can also be used by a group working at a sink (You will probably want to avoid using sand, as it is very difficult to remove from the floor.) Children should solve the problem of finding which of their objects holds the most of one kind of "filler" and report their solutions to the class.

ACTIVITY 12.35
Ordering Jars by Capacity.

Use the jars or boxes and the "filling materials" in Activity 12.34. Ask groups of children to solve the problem of ordering four jars or boxes by "what they hold filled to the top." After groups finish the task, have them report how they solved the problem.

Using Nonstandard Units

ACTIVITY 12.36
Using a Jar Measure.

Give groups several jelly or candy jars, each labeled with a numeral, and a baby food jar. Pose the problem: How many baby food jars of rice do you estimate each of these jars will hold? How close will your group's estimates be to the actual measurements? Give each group a recording sheet to help solve the problem (Table 12.2). Groups will list the numerals on the jars and write their estimate for each jar. They complete the activity by finding the capacity of each jar using the baby food jar and filling in the recording sheet. They then determine how close their measurements were to their estimates.

TABLE 12.2 Activity Sheet for Capacity

Record of Use of Baby Food Jar Measurement			
Jar	Estimate	Measurement	Difference
1			
2			
3			
4			
5			

ACTIVITY 12.37
Using Blocks for Volume Measurement.

Repeat activity 12.36 using boxes and blocks. (Sugar cubes can also be used for units.) Observe if children count the number of blocks in a layer, and repeatedly add the number of blocks in a layer as a new layer is constructed or if they continue counting the blocks as they fill the box.

ACTIVITY 12.38
Making and Using a Scale on a Paper Cup.

Children can make a paper cup scale to determine the capacity of objects. Groups use a transparent plastic cup, stick a tape to one side, and mark the tape with a felt pen to show each 10 thimbles or 10 soap-bottle caps full of rice. They can use their "measuring cup" to find the capacity of various objects that they or you bring to class. Encourage estimating before measuring and determining the difference between the estimate and the measurement.

Using Standard Units

ACTIVITY 12.39
Using Cup, Pint, Quart, and Gallon Measures.

Show children standard measuring cups, pints, and quarts. Ask them if they have seen or used these. As they report what they know, they introduce the labels for the units to the class. If children do not know the units, you give the names. Have children use each of these to measure the capacity of a variety of objects, and discuss their observations. Stress estimating before measuring when children have an awareness of the units. Help them generalize that the smaller the unit, the more are needed to fill an object.

Children can find out how many cups of water they should drink a day and measure this amount into a jug. They can research how much water different animals drink in a day (perhaps write to a zoo) and show this amount in a jar or jug. They can estimate how many quarts are needed to fill a sink and measure the amount. A homework activity can be to determine how many gallons of water are needed to take a bath.

Because children usually have had experiences with cups, pints, and quarts, they should probably be used by learners before liters. When liters are introduced, children should have many measuring experiences with liters to enable them to become familiar with this unit.

ACTIVITY 12.40
Using Cubes.

Introduce cubic units by showing a cubic centimeter and a cubic decimeter and giving their names. Cuisenaire materials are useful for this purpose. To become familiar with these units, have groups estimate the volume of several boxes, measure them with cubes, and determine the closeness of their estimates. Each student can write a summary of the activity.

Suggest that each cubic centimeter represents a room. Have students solve the problem of building as many houses as possible with a given number of rooms. Have them share their solutions to this problem.

Have students estimate how many small objects, such as checkers, dimes, or chips, placed in a stack would equal about two cubic centimeters, and have them place the objects in a stack to evaluate their estimates.

ACTIVITY 12.41
Making a Cubic Meter.

A class project is for students to assume different responsibilities in connection with making a frame for a cubic meter using meter sticks and covering the frame with wrapping paper. Some classes or groups could decide how to determine the volume of the classroom or of a space such as the library corner by using their cubic meter. Joslyn (1990) describes the construction of such a model in connection with the study of large numbers (see Activity 4.38).

Weight (Mass)

Weight is the measure of the pull of gravity; mass, the amount of material an object contains, and thus the force needed to accelerate it. In this section, the word *weight* is used, although either concept may be the basis of an activity.

Learning about Weight by Comparing

ACTIVITY 12.42
Which Weighs More?

Holding an object in each hand with their arms extended, children decide which of the two objects weighs more. Objects to use include books, tools such as screw drivers or pliers, and hand mirrors. Ask children how they knew which was heavier or lighter.

ACTIVITY 12.43
Hidden Weights.

Place different numbers of nails (or metal washers) in discarded 35-mm film cans. Label the cans with numerals. Have groups in turn order the cans. To make a record of their ordering, a child, designated as the group secretary, writes down the numerals when the group completes the work. When all groups have had a chance to order the cans, have them compare their ordering and tell how they made their ordering decisions. Open the cans so that they can check their ordering.

Using Nonstandard Units

ACTIVITY 12.44
Experimenting with Scales.

Groups in turn should experiment with balance scales (those purchased from supply houses are more durable and easier to use than home-made versions, although scales can be made with clothes hangers). Children select small classroom objects or objects brought from home (e.g., toys) and determine their weight in metal washers, nails, marbles, or the like. Encourage estimation after children have had some experience with nonstandard units.

Using Standard Units

ACTIVITY 12.45
Using Scales.

Obtain weights for metric or customary units, or use plastic sacks of dried beans, flour, sugar, or rice that weigh amounts such as 1 ounce, 8 ounces, 1 pound, 1 gram, 10 grams, or 1 kilogram. Balance scales or spring scales are used by children to weigh small objects.

Pupils can weigh objects to obtain measurements of interest to them; for example, they can weigh fruit to see how much is eaten. They can find classroom objects that weigh a given amount. This activity can be called "Secret Weights." After some familiarity with units of weight, children should estimate weights of objects and weigh the objects to evaluate their estimates.

Pupils can also make up packages of small objects—marbles, popcorn, lima beans, rice, and so on—to weigh a given amount. A display of these packages with labels can be made. Class discussions in connection with weighing objects should focus on the relation of the sizes of packages of different objects to their weights (e.g., a pound of popcorn vs. a pound of flour) and the reasons for these relations.

Time

Learning about time involves learning both calendar and clock time. Children are helped to understand calendar time beginning in kindergarten as they mark a calendar each day and note the passage of days, weeks, and months. Ask questions about the calendar to help children learn the number of days in a week and, possibly, the number of days in different months. For example, say, "We know the names of the days of a week. How could we find out how many days pass before we have another Monday and start another week?"

Birthdays are useful for studying calendar time. All children's birthdays for a month are shown on the calendar. Children can be asked the month and day of the week for one another's birthdays. The names of the days between birthdays can also be noted.

Telling clock time is complex and often difficult for children. It requires dealing with hours and minutes, that is, relating the two hands in different ways to the marks on a clock. Teaching children to tell time involves a sequence of eight instructional steps that help children: (1) develop an awareness of time by comparing; (2) understand the duration of an hour; (3) learn to tell hour time; (4) understand the duration of a minute; (5) learn to tell minute time after the hour; (6) relate clock reading to digital notation; (7) learn to tell minute time before an hour; and (8) learn to add or subtract times. Activities deal with these goals in order. The sequence can begin in grade 1, but the emphasis on telling time is in grade 3.

ACTIVITY 12.46
What Is a Long (Short) Time?

Discuss what takes a long time to finish and what takes a short time. Include questions such as: "Does it take longer to write your name than to say your name?" "Is school shorter in the morning or in the afternoon? How do you know?" Have children draw pictures of what takes a long time and what takes a short time to complete.

Using Standard Units

ACTIVITY 12.47
What Do Clocks Do?

Ask children what clocks do and why we use clocks. Help children realize the importance of knowing the time of day and the need to tell time. Have children watch the clock over a period of time and notice the moving hands. Give the names minute and hour hands to the long and short hands, respectively.

ACTIVITY 12.48
What Happens in an Hour?

Children are asked to tell what they know about an hour. A subsequent question that involves the study of the clock is: "How do we know when an hour has passed?" A demonstration clock is available for any child who volunteers to show how the clock looks before and after an hour has passed. If no child volunteers, you point out the hour and minute hands and how the clock tells an hour has passed. That the hour (short) hand moves one large space in one hour is emphasized. Have children look at the clock from time to time as the hour hand moves from one numeral to another.

Later, ask, "What can you do in an hour?" Children watch the clock to determine how much they do in an hour and what takes less or more time than an hour. (The clockwatch must begin on the hour.) Have children draw pictures of "Hour Activities" and "Less (More) than 1 Hour Activities."

ACTIVITY 12.49
Making and Using Play Clocks.

All children make play clocks from pie plates. A marked face is given to each child to paste on the pie plate because they usually cannot judge where to position the numerals so they are equidistant around the disk (Figure 12.11A). Children finish the clock by writing the numerals and attaching the hands with paper fasteners (Figure 12.11B).

After the clocks are completed, the children discuss how to show hour times (long hand on 12, small hand on the hour). They show different hour times on their

A. B. C.

FIGURE 12.11 Making Play Clocks

play clocks. Pairs of children can take turns asking each other to show different hour times.

When children can show different hour times, have them review how the hour hand moves to show an hour has passed. Talk about what it means when the hour hand is between two numerals. Children should be aware that when the hand moves from 2 to 3, the time is between 2 o'clock and 3 o'clock; for example, the time can be a little past 2 o'clock or almost 3 o'clock.

ACTIVITY 12.50
What Happens in a Minute?

Have the class watch the minute hand on the class clock. Then have children tell what they can do in school in 1 minute, more than 1 minute, or less than 1 minute. They verify their ideas by watching the clock. A class book can be made with pictures of events of less than 1 minute duration, about 1 minute, and more than 1 minute. Examples can include: time to write my name, time to walk to the pencil sharpener, time to sharpen a pencil, and time to open a book and find a given page.

ACTIVITY 12.51
Counting Clock Minutes.

Children observe that the class clock and their play clocks have many small minute spaces. They count the number of minutes on the face of their clocks by both ones and fives. Then they write numerals for the multiples of five on their play clocks (Figure 12.11C).

Show how the minute hand moves around the clock while the hour hand moves one large space. Ask who can tell hour and minute time and have them explain how they tell time. If no child volunteers to explain how he or she tells both hour and minute time and probably even if a child does explain how to tell time, you will need to use the demonstration clock to show that when the minute hand has gone past 12, we know how many minutes past an hour have gone by. Ask the children to look at the class clock to see the hour and the minute hand. Next, give an hour time for the children to show on their clocks, and then give a time 5 minutes past that hour for the children to show. Children report how they solved the problem of showing the hour and minute time and discuss how the clock hands show both hour and minute time. They next show 5, 10, 15, . . . , 60 minutes past a given hour. If they can do so, have them show times that are not multiples of 5 past a given hour and use their play clocks to show such times.

The terminology "quarter-" and "half-past" an hour are introduced in the middle grades when children understand that fractional parts can be shown on the circular regions making up the clock.

ACTIVITY 12.52
Digital Time and Clock Time.

A digital clock is needed for this activity which helps children learn to read and write the notation for time. Have children tell the time on the class clock, for example, 10:15. Show the digital clock for the same time. Ask children to think how the two clocks are the same and different. Tell children that clock time is written as digital time. Change the digital clock, saying this is a pretend time. Have children read the time on the digital clock and set their play clock to that time. Do this several times. Discuss how they knew what to do, asking often what the two dots (colon) tell us—the minutes after the hour.

Next, ask them to write a time and when they have finished, ask someone to show the time on the digital clock so that the children can compare what they wrote with the digital time. Do this several times, often discussing how they knew what to do.

A game, *Clock Bingo*, can be played by the class to give practice experiences. The cards show times in the cells (e.g., 4:45). "IT" (you or a child) reads a time, and children use markers on their cards. The rules that determine a winner are the same as for any *Bingo* game.

ACTIVITY 12.53
Important Times in My Life.

Ask each child to think of five or more important times in his or her daily life (awaken, eat breakfast, come to school, etc.) and to write the event and the time. Have them make a booklet of these times, each page showing a picture of the event and the time displayed on a digital and regular clock. (Ditto clocks for these pages as children cannot correctly make spaces equidistant when drawing a clock.)

ACTIVITY 12.54
Before the Hour.

Have children look at the class clock when the hour hand is between two numerals and the minute hand shows 50 minutes past the hour. Say, "What hour will it be next? How do you know? Is there a way to decide how many minutes it is before that hour? Solve this problem with your desk partner." After a few minutes, ask for solutions and how children thought to decide on the solutions. If no group has the answer, give a hint, "How can we count the minutes up to the hour?" Children may report that they count minutes before the hour starting at 12 and count counterclockwise, or they count minutes from the minute hand up to 12. Emphasize that either way makes sense. The activity concludes with children showing times before the hour using their play clocks. The times are given by you or children in the class.

ACTIVITY 12.55
How Much Time?

Children in the middle grades can use their play clocks to show solutions to problems that require adding or subtracting times. To begin, children count the minutes as they move the hands. Later, they can mentally compute a change in time.

Ask children how long it takes to eat a meal, write spelling words, and other activities of interest to children. Write their responses on the chalkboard. Have them verify their responses during the next day at home or at school. After they give their reports, have them set their clocks for the time of one of the activities. Ask how they would show the time the activity ended. They should decide that they can count the time that passed until they would have finished the activity, moving the hands as they count until the number of minutes reported has passed. The time displayed at the end of the count shows the ending time. Have one child use the demonstration clock to model the procedure, and all use their clocks to carry out the task. Later, have them show the time an activity is completed and decide how to change the clock to show the time the activity started.

Often call attention to the class clock when a school activity begins and ends. If the demonstration clock is set for the beginning time, the class can decide how long the activity took by noting the finishing time on the class clock. They may need to use their individual play clocks to solve this problem.

Temperature

Children need to learn to read both Celsius and Fahrenheit scales. Because most media reports are in Fahrenheit, children should probably be introduced to Fahrenheit scales first. Figure 12.12A shows how Celsius and Fahrenheit scales compare. Children can read thermometers that give both scales to make a chart of comparison temperatures useful to them (Figure 12.12B).

Learning about Temperature by Comparing

ACTIVITY 12.56
Hot and Cold.

Have children discuss what they know about hot and cold things. Before the discussion ends, make sure that hot and cold days are mentioned. If necessary, ask questions such as, "Is this a cold day? How do you know?" Children can make a chart

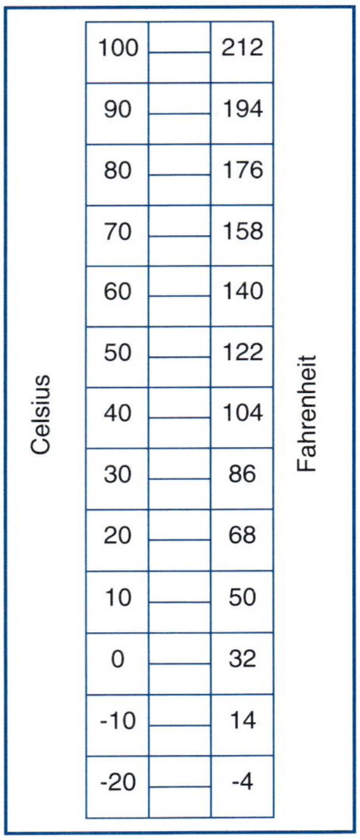

A.

	Celsius Degrees	Fahrenheit Degrees
Cold Day	0	32
Cool Day	20	68
Warm Day	30	86
Very Hot Day	40	104

B.

FIGURE 12.12 Celsius and Fahrenheit Scales. A, Two Scales on a Thermometer. B, Temperatures We Could Experience with pictures showing hot and cold objects and clothes and activities appropriate for hot and cold days.

Using Standard Units

ACTIVITY 12.57
Reading and Recording Temperatures.

Some children will have noticed that people read thermometers to determine temperatures. Ask students what they know about measuring heat and cold. Have a demonstration thermometer or an overhead of a thermometer to use during this discussion. Use the Fahrenheit scale on the thermometer. You can easily make a "play" (demonstration) thermometer with a scale of red ribbon fastened to white ribbon that moves around the thermometer frame (Figure 12.13).

To help children learn to read the thermometer, distribute a picture of a thermometer showing a temperature (e.g., 60°). Tell the class that the thermometer measures heat and cold in degrees, so we give the temperature as a number of degrees. Ask children to give the number of degrees shown on the thermometer. (They solve the problem by deciding that they count by twos when reading the scale.) Have children read different temperatures on the demonstration thermometer and explain how they knew what to do. Next, ask children to locate other temperatures on their picture thermometer, marking each one with a different color crayon you name. Have them explain how they knew what to do.

Have two different children work together to read the temperature on a class thermometer at the same time each morning and each afternoon, report the temperature to the class, explain what it signifies to them (hot, cold, balmy, chilly, etc.),

FIGURE 12.13 Demonstration Thermometer with Fahrenheit Scale

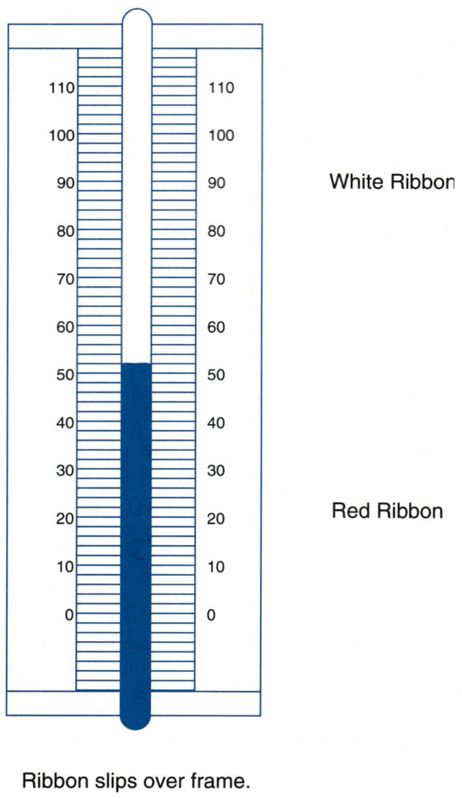

show it on your demonstration thermometer with the red ribbon, and record it on a chart. Later, children can compare the recorded temperatures on the chart.

ACTIVITY 12.58
What's the Right Temperature?

Children can make posters that show a picture of an activity and a temperature that would relate to that activity. For example, pictures could show water boiling, a child swimming, or a child skiing. The posters should be discussed and displayed.

ACTIVITY 12.59
Temperatures Everywhere.

This activity can be used in connection with the study of the United States or another country. Have children decide on criteria for choosing cities to use to compare temperatures in different places (e.g., cities at sea level and north of the equator). They choose five or six cities based on their criteria. They use the weather chart in the daily newspaper and record the temperatures in the cities selected. The temperatures in different cities are then compared, and the class discusses how the temperatures would affect daily life. Social studies concepts such as land use could be discussed in connection with this activity.

Money

Initially, children study money by using coins and paper money in purchasing and making change. For their work with money, each child needs play money to handle. Pictures of money do not reflect real-life experiences with money. Later work involves computing to solve problems involving money.

Learning about money in the primary grades involves attaining these objectives: (1) classifying coins; (2) giving the value of coins and paper money; (3) knowing the value of coins in terms of each other; (4) ordering coins and paper money in terms of increasing value; (5) counting the value of coins of like value (this involves counting by ones, fives, tens, and twenty-fives); (6) relating the value of a set of coins to paper money; (7) counting the value of a set of coins of unlike value; (8) using money in simulated purchasing activities; and (9) reading and writing money amounts.

Many children come to school knowing the names and values of coins. Assess this knowledge, and plan activities if children do not know about different coins and paper money. These activities can be play experiences or games that involve working or shopping. For example, you can say, "Each has a set of coins. If you worked in a bank, you would need to put like coins in paper rolls (if possible, show a roll of pennies). Put the coins on your desk in piles so that you could roll them in papers like bank workers." When they finish, ask them to name the coins in piles, or name the coins if they cannot.

ACTIVITY 12.60
Chorus Counting.

To help children learn to count coins, chorus count by fives or tens from a multiple of 5 or 10. For example, begin at 15, and count by fives to 55; begin at 35 and count by tens to 75. They can also count back from a multiple of 5 down to 5 (e.g., 65 to 5). Chorus counting can be a pre- or post-lesson activity or an activity to fill a few minutes before dismissal.

ACTIVITY 12.61
Coin Count Game.

Four or five children play together. A stack of cards in the center of the playing area gives an amount less than $1 and a multiple of 5 (e.g., $.35). Each child in a group gets a nickel or dime play coin. "IT" picks a card and begins counting money by giving the amount of his or her coin. The child to the left "counts on" by the amount of his or her coin. The child who reaches the amount on the card when it is his or her turn to "count on" keeps the card. (If a player must count 5 beyond the amount, he or she also keeps the card.) The child to the left of "IT" picks the next card from the pile and begins the procedure another time. At the end of the game, the child with the most cards wins.

ACTIVITY 12.62
I'm Richer (I'm Poorer) Game.

Cards showing amount of money (e.g., 3 nickels and 2 pennies) are used by two children. The game is played like *War*. In *I'm Richer*, the children picking the card showing the larger amount gets both cards; in *I'm Poorer*, the child picking the card displaying the smaller amount gets both cards.

ACTIVITY 12.63
Coins to Make Amounts.

Ask children to use play coins or paper money to make amounts of money in as many ways as possible (e.g., 87 cents or 1 dollar). You name the kind and number of coins they have to solve this problem to ensure a limited number of solutions. They should make records of their work and share their solutions in a class discussion. This is a good problem for students to work on when other work is finished or for homework, because they will need time to find the different solutions.

Angles

Children are introduced to angles when studying geometric figures (Chapter Eleven). They know that a turn makes an angle and have learned the names of right and straight angles. In grades 5 and 6, they learn to measure angles. The sequence follows that of other instruction in measurement: comparing, using nonstandard units, making protractors for nonstandard units, and last, learning about and using standard units.

Learning about Angles by Comparing

ACTIVITY 12.64
Comparing Angles.

Have children solve the problem of finding the largest or smallest angle in pairs of angles such as shown in Figure 12.14. The size of these angles should be evident from inspection. Have them discuss their choices among themselves and then share their ideas with the class. Have them report how they made their choices.

Next, give children angles with rays drawn so that the sizes of the angles may not be evident from inspection (Figure 12.15). Have children in groups decide how to compare these and report how they solved the problem. If children have difficulty solving the problem, say, "What could you do to compare them?" If more hints are

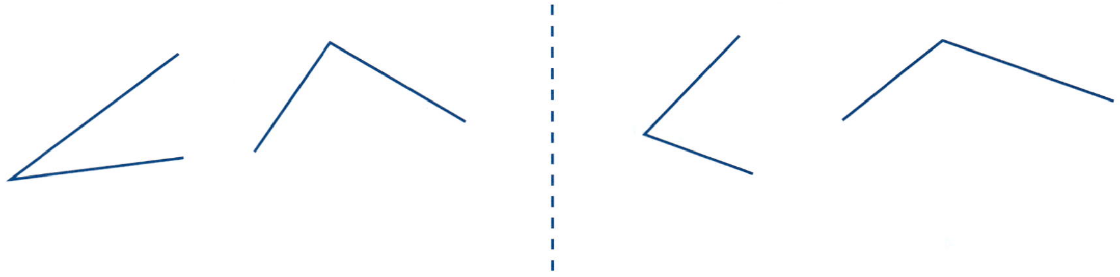

FIGURE 12.14 Which Angle in Each Pair Is Greater?

needed, say, "What about tracing? How would that help?" Have them use very lightweight paper. Let them report how they traced one angle and superimposed the tracing on the other angle to find the larger or smaller angle.

Using Nonstandard Units

ACTIVITY 12.65 *Wedges.*

Give groups of children several wedges. Explain that wedges can be used to measure the "spread" of the rays that form an angle. (Figure 12.16). Also distribute to each student an activity sheet showing three or four pictures of angles. Say, "How can we use one of these wedges to measure the angles on your study sheet?" Let them solve this problem and report their solutions. Include angles that are not a whole number of wedges (e.g., about $2\frac{1}{2}$ wedges).

Wilson and Adams (1992) suggest giving each child a circular region marked in sixths (Figure 12.17). The children cut the region in half and use one-half to make their own wedges. Children fold the one-half circular region along the marks provided, giving three wedges. Each of the three wedges is folded in half and cut to make six wedges for each learner. Later, children use the other half to make a protractor (Activity 12.67).

Activity for the Classroom 12.3. Prepare a study sheet that includes various kinds and sizes of triangles (Figure 12.18). Include equilateral triangles that are similar to

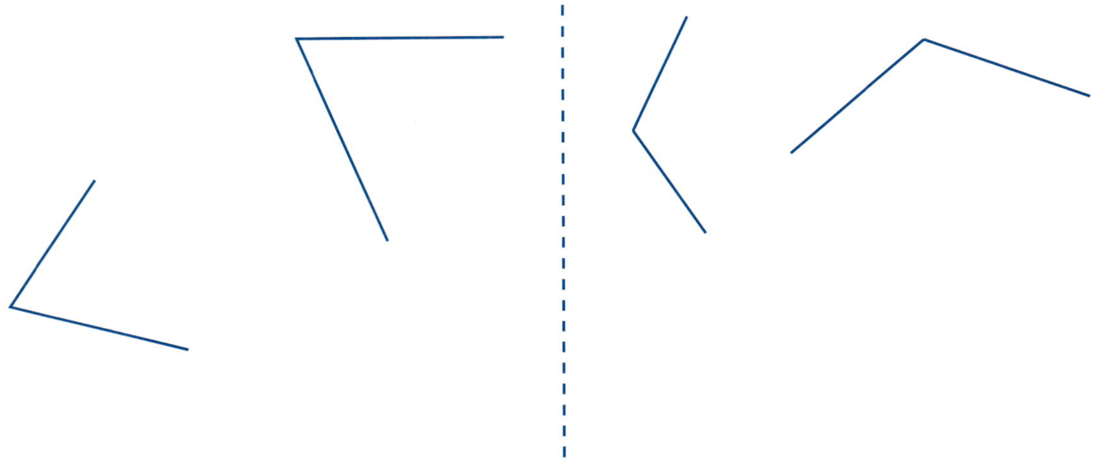

FIGURE 12.15 Which Angle in Each Pair Is Greater?

FIGURE 12.16 Wedges

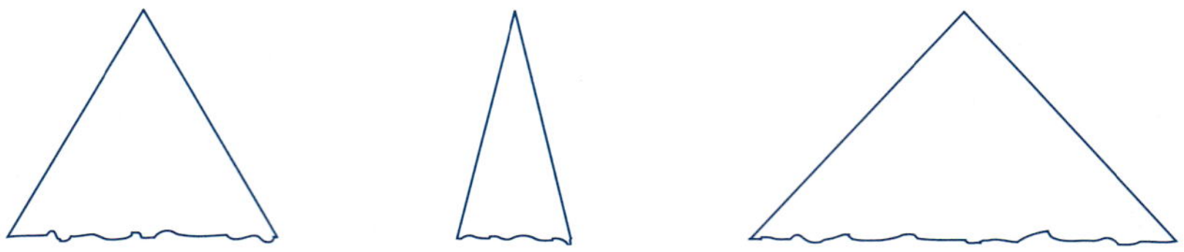

help children realize that the sizes of angles in equilateral triangles do not depend on the length of the sides or the areas of the triangles. The directions on the sheet are: "Use your wedges to study and compare these triangles and their angles." Children should share their work and conclusions with the class.

ACTIVITY 12.66
Ordering Angles.

Give children a set of angles, and have them decide how to order these by size, using wedges.

ACTIVITY 12.67
Making and Using Protractors with Nonstandard (Wedge) Units.

Have children discuss the problems connected with using loose wedges. If they do not suggest making a scale with several wedges, do so yourself. Have children fold the half-circle left from making wedges (Activity 12.65) along the marks provided and then again to give a protractor with six wedges. Have the children label the divisions as shown in Figure 12.19.

Have children use their wedge protractors to measure angles. Discuss how to use the wedge protractor correctly: The vertex of the angle must coincide with the center of the protractor, and the 0 point of the scale must be placed on a point on one ray of the angle; the point on the scale where the other ray lies gives the number of wedges of the angle. Model how to use the wedge protractor for those who need help.

Children should measure, compare, and draw angles using their wedge protractors. The angles they use should not always be whole numbers of wedges. Discuss with students how to measure wedges to the nearest half-wedge.

FIGURE 12.17 Pattern for Wedges and Wedge Protractor

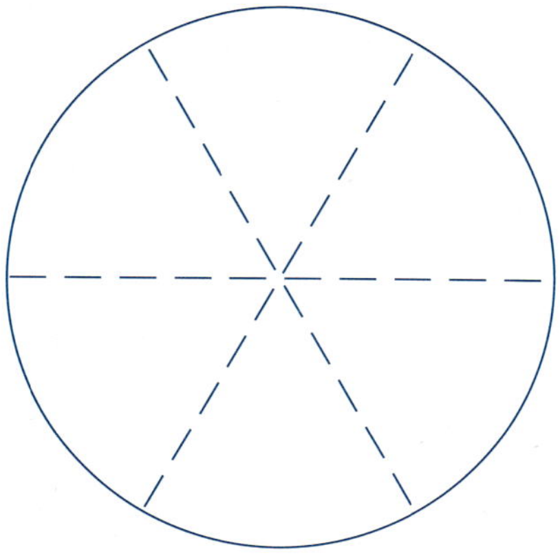

FIGURE 12.18 Activity Sheet: Compare Angles of Triangles by Using Wedges

Using Standard Units

ACTIVITY 12.68
Standard Units and Protractors.

When children recognize the inadequacy of their wedge protractors and the need for standard units, they are introduced to degrees and commercially produced protractors. Show a circle and a half-circle protractor on the overhead. Children study both kinds to learn that 360° measure a circle and that half-circle protractors can be used to measure any angle spread. If commercially produced protractors are not available for each child, give each child a paper protractor to paste on cardboard and cut out (Figure 12.20—See Appendix G for pattern). Model its use, and have children measure and draw angles using their protractors. Help children recall the proper use of the wedge protractor so that they will use the standard protractor correctly.

After learners have discovered that the angles of a triangle when joined make a straight angle (Activity 11.43), they can draw triangles with a given number of degrees for each angle by making the sum of the angles 180°. A variation is for children to make up questions for other group members to answer. An example is: "Can a triangle have angles that are 45°, 35°, and 55°? If so, draw the triangle. If not, change one of the angle degrees to make a new triangle you can draw."

FIGURE 12.19 Wedge Protractor

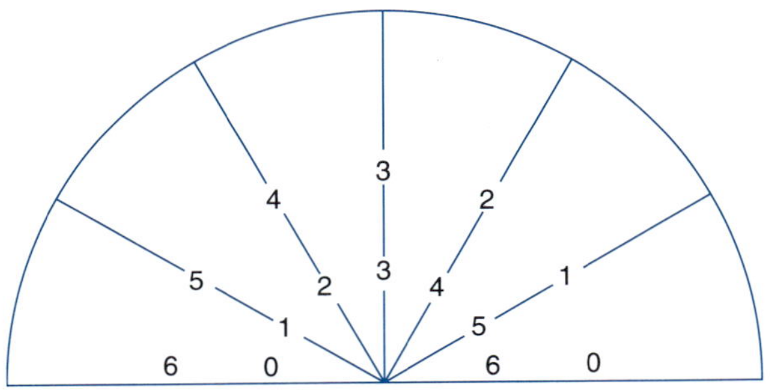

FIGURE 12.20 Paper Protractor

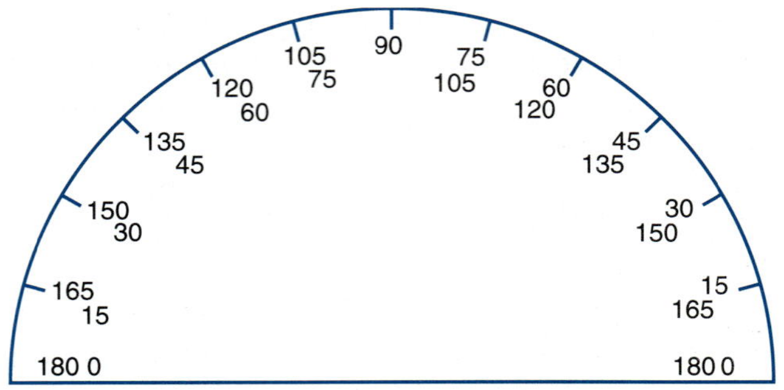

Formulas

Students study formulas in grade 6 after many experiences with measuring that involve counting units. To understand formulas, they must also have constructed the concepts of length, perimeter, area, and volume, and they must know how to use both nonstandard and standard units to measure these attributes of objects.

Sequence for Introducing Formulas

1. Assess knowledge of attributes by asking students to describe and give examples of the perimeter, area, and volume of objects and to give estimates and measurements of the attributes of some objects.
2. Give problems that require students to look for shortcuts to the counting process.
3. Lead discussions that provide opportunities for children to present their shortcuts, which can be called rules.
4. Help students write formulas to summarize the shortcuts.
5. Give assignments that enable students to use the formulas in a variety of settings. Help them learn the cues that tell which formula to use.

Reader Activity 12.3

Find three story problems in students' texts involving formulas for measurement, solve the problems, and decide the cues that enabled you to decide the formula to use to solve each problem. Write down two or three questions that you would use to help children focus on the cues in each of these problems.

Steps 2 through 5 of this sequence for developing various formulas are discussed in the following subsections: Formula for the Perimeter of a Rectangle, Formula for the Area of a Rectangular Region, Formulas for the Area of a Parallelogram and for the Area of a Triangle, Formula for the Volume of a Rectangular Solid, and Formulas for the Circumference of a Circle and for the Area of a Circular Region.

Formula for the Perimeter of a Rectangle. After students have solved perimeter problems involving rectangles by estimating and counting units, groups are given the assignment of determining shortcuts for finding the perimeter. Each group works with a different rectangle (Figure 12.21). If they need a hint during their deliberations, say, "How will multiplication make a shortcut possible?"

The discussion following their work enables them to describe in words how they solved the problems. They explain their ideas in statements, such as: "Look at the numbers that are the same, like 4 and 5 in our problem. Multiply each one of

FIGURE 12.21 Rectangles to Construct the Formula for the Perimeter of a Rectangle

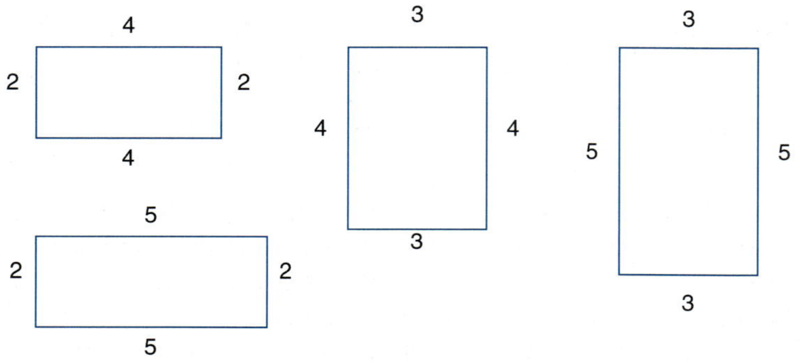

those numbers by 2, and add the products. Two times 4 equals 8 and 2 times 5 equals 10. The perimeter is 18." Another group might say, "Add the numbers on 2 adjoining sides, like 3 and 5 in our problem, and multiply the sum by 2 to get the perimeter: 3 + 5 = 8; 8 × 2 = 16."

Students develop the formula $P = 2(l \times w)$ during a discussion after the activity and sharing. The communication between teacher and students would be similar to the following:

> MR. CARILLO: We all like shortcuts! We can work out a rule for our shortcut. Let us write down what you have said to begin. You said, "Add the length and width numbers, and then multiply the sum by 2." I'll write
>
> $$3 + 5 = 8$$
> $$2 \times 8 = 16$$
>
> Think how we can rewrite these two math sentences to make them one sentence. Who will write the sentence on the board? (If no one responds, say, "Think about using parentheses.")
>
> JACKIE: I'd say use the parentheses around the 3 + 5, and write 2 in front of parentheses, like this:
>
> $$2\,(3 + 5) = 16$$
>
> MR. CARILLO: That will do it! Each of you please write one math sentence for your group's problem, or if you were in Jackie's group, make up a perimeter problem, and write the math sentence.
>
> MR. CARILLO: Let's share our work. (Pupils write their sentences on the chalkboard and explain them.)
>
> MR. CARILLO: We can give a rule useful for any problem. This kind of rule is called a formula. We do this by using the letters P for perimeter, l for length, and w for width instead of the numbers in a particular problem. Exchange these letters for the numbers in your math sentence to write the formula for the perimeter of a rectangle. Work together in your groups to do this. When you have written your formulas, we will share our thinking and formulas.

After they share their ideas and decide on the formula, they discuss how to use the formula to solve problems. After the procedure is clarified, students solve perimeter problems using the formula. They find the perimeters of rectangular regions given on activity sheets (the length and width is given on only two sides of the rectangle) and solve story perimeter problems that reflect real life. Later, students can make rectangular regions with length and width labels on only two sides or write story problems involving perimeter, exchange these with partners, and discuss their solutions among themselves. Students should be asked to find the perimeter of some irregular figures (Figure 12.22) so that they do not think that all perimeter problems can be solved by using the formula.

ACTIVITY 12.69
Developing the Perimeter of a Square.

Ask groups of students to write a formula for the perimeter of a square, $P = 4s$ (s = side), using their formula for the perimeter of a rectangle. Give students figures as in Figure 12.23. When they have decided on a formula, they share their work and their thinking.

Formula for the Area of a Rectangular Region. The formula for the area of a rectangular region is $A = l \times w$ (A = area, l = length, and w = width). This formula is derived from the rule for finding the area of a rectangular region: Multiply the number of square units in a row by the number of rows in the region. It is based on the fact that the number of length units of a rectangle is the same as the number of

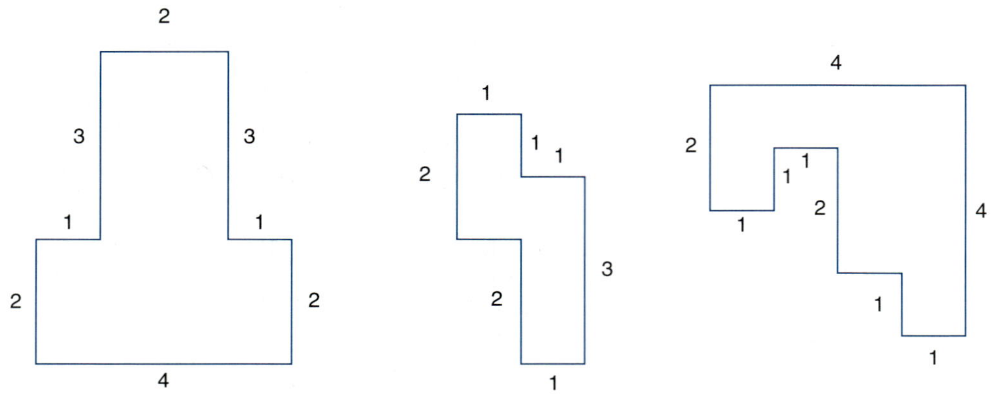

FIGURE 12.22 Finding the Perimeters of Irregular Figures

square units in a row of the rectangular region and the number of width units is the same as the number of rows in the rectangular region.

When students can estimate areas and can count square units to find the area of a rectangular region (Activities 12.28, 32–33), they develop the rule and the formula for the area of a rectangular region by generalizing from their experience.

ACTIVITY 12.70
Finding a Shortcut or Rule for Determining Area.

Ask if any student does not need to count all the square units in a rectangular region but has discovered a shortcut. If so, use his or her ideas as the basis for the discussion that involves the use of the diagrams in Figure 12.24. If not, give groups of students the diagrams. Ask them to find a shortcut for the area of each rectangular region by studying what the diagrams show. After they have had sufficient time to solve the problem, have them report their thinking and solutions and write the rule: The area of a rectangle is the number of square units in a row multiplied by the number of rows. In the next few days, pupils use the rule to find the area of rectangular regions.

If no group presents the shortcut, give guidance by asking questions similar to: "How could you use multiplication in a shortcut?" or "Look at one row. How many square units are in the row? How would you find the square units in all the rows?"

ACTIVITY 12.71
Writing a Formula for the Area of a Rectangular Region.

To reformulate the rule in Activity 12.70 as a formula, students must understand that the number of length units of the rectangle is the same as the number of square units in a row and that the number of width units is the same as the number of rows. Pupils should have an activity sheet with pairs of diagrams. (One pair is given Figure 12.25.) Mention that the class rule for finding an area can be used to write a formula. To guide learners to devise the formula from the rule, ask questions such as: "What do you notice about the number of square units in a row in Figure A and the number of length

FIGURE 12.23 Square to Develop the Formula for the Perimeter of a Square

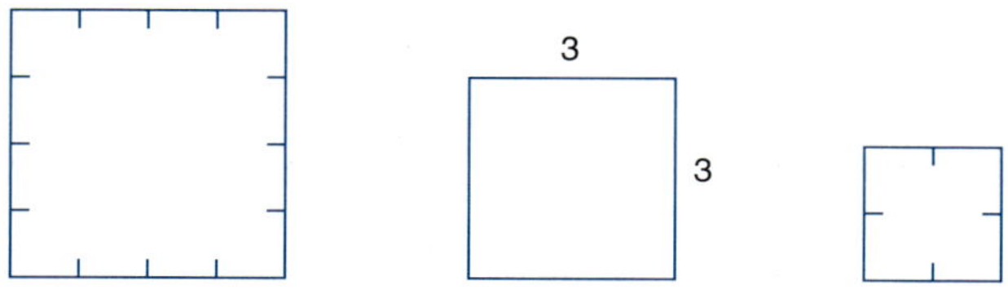

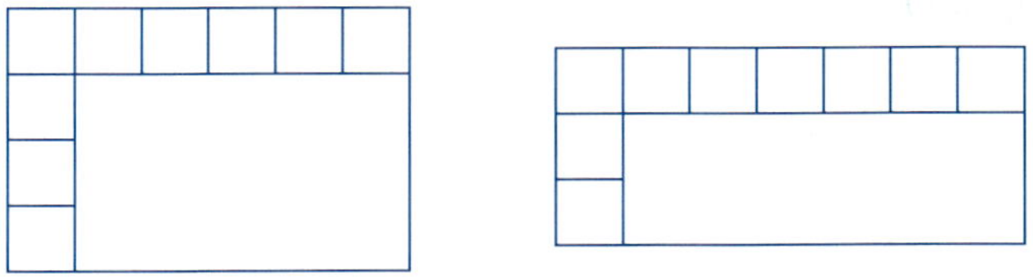

FIGURE 12.24 Rectangles to Develop the Rule for the Area of a Rectangular Region

units of Figure B?" "What is true of the number of rows in the Figure A and number of width units of Figure B?" Similar questions are asked for each figure used in the activity. When they understand how the numbers in each pair of figures are related, they can be asked to rewrite their rule using *A* for area, *l* for length, and *w* for width.

ACTIVITY 12.72
Developing the Formula for the Area of a Square.

Ask students to find the formula for the area of a square using diagrams such as in Figure 12.26. They should realize that the number of units of only one side is needed to give the formula for the area of a square, $A = s \times s$.

Formulas for the Area of a Parallelogram and for the Area of a Triangle. Students develop the formulas for the area of a parallelogram ($A = b \times h$) and for a triangle ($A = \frac{1}{2} b \times h$) as they solve problems. Before problems are assigned, however, students learn that the word *base* is the term used for any side or flat surface of a figure and that the word *height* means the perpendicular distance to the base from the vertex opposite the base. Students decide that in rectangles and squares the height can be the width and the base can be the length. They revise the formula for the area of a rectangle: $A = b \times h$.

ACTIVITY 12.73
Developing the Formula for the Area of a Parallelogram Region.

Assign groups of students the problem: Find the area of the parallelogram regions on your activity sheet (Figure 12.27A). Use any materials you want. You may even want to use scissors. After you have decided how to find the areas of these parallelograms, think about the formula. They should solve the problem by cutting and rearranging the parts of a parallelogram as shown in Figure 12.27B. When students have had time to solve the problem, discuss their ideas.

If no group has solved the problem, suggest cutting along the line labeled height, ask how this piece could be attached to make a rectangle, and how the letters *b* and *h* can be used in the area formula for a rectangle to give the new formula. Review the meaning of the height of a figure.

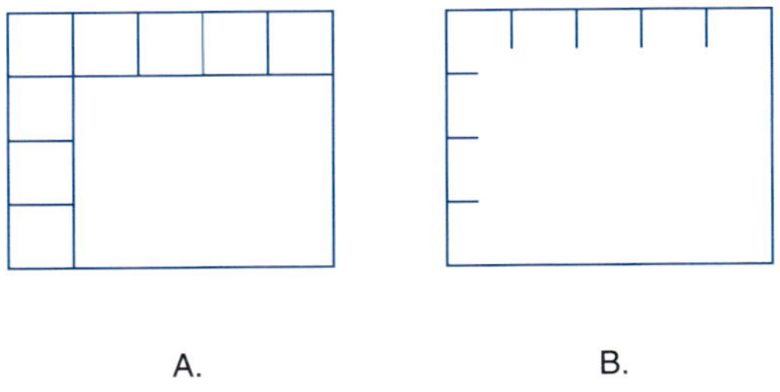

FIGURE 12.25 Diagrams to Develop the Formula for the Area of a Rectangular Region

FIGURE 12.26 Diagrams to Develop the Formula for the Area of a Square Region

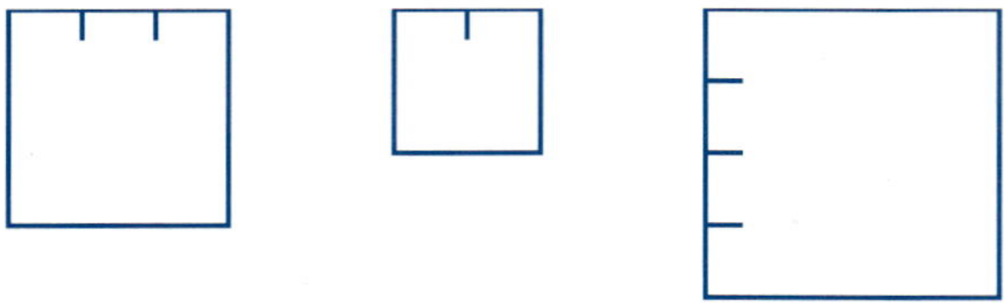

ACTIVITY 12.74
Developing the Formula for the Area of a Triangular Region.

Follow the same procedure as in Activity 12.73. Give groups several triangles so that they can experiment (Figure 12.28A).

It is expected that some groups will see how two congruent triangles form a rectangle or parallelogram, which means that the area of the triangular region is $\frac{1}{2}$ of the newly formed rectangular or parallelogram region and that the formula for the area of a triangular region can be written: $A = \frac{1}{2}\, b \times h$ (Figure 12.28B).

If students are unable to derive the formula, say, "How can you use what you know about the area of a rectangular region or a parallelogram region to find the area formula for a triangle?"

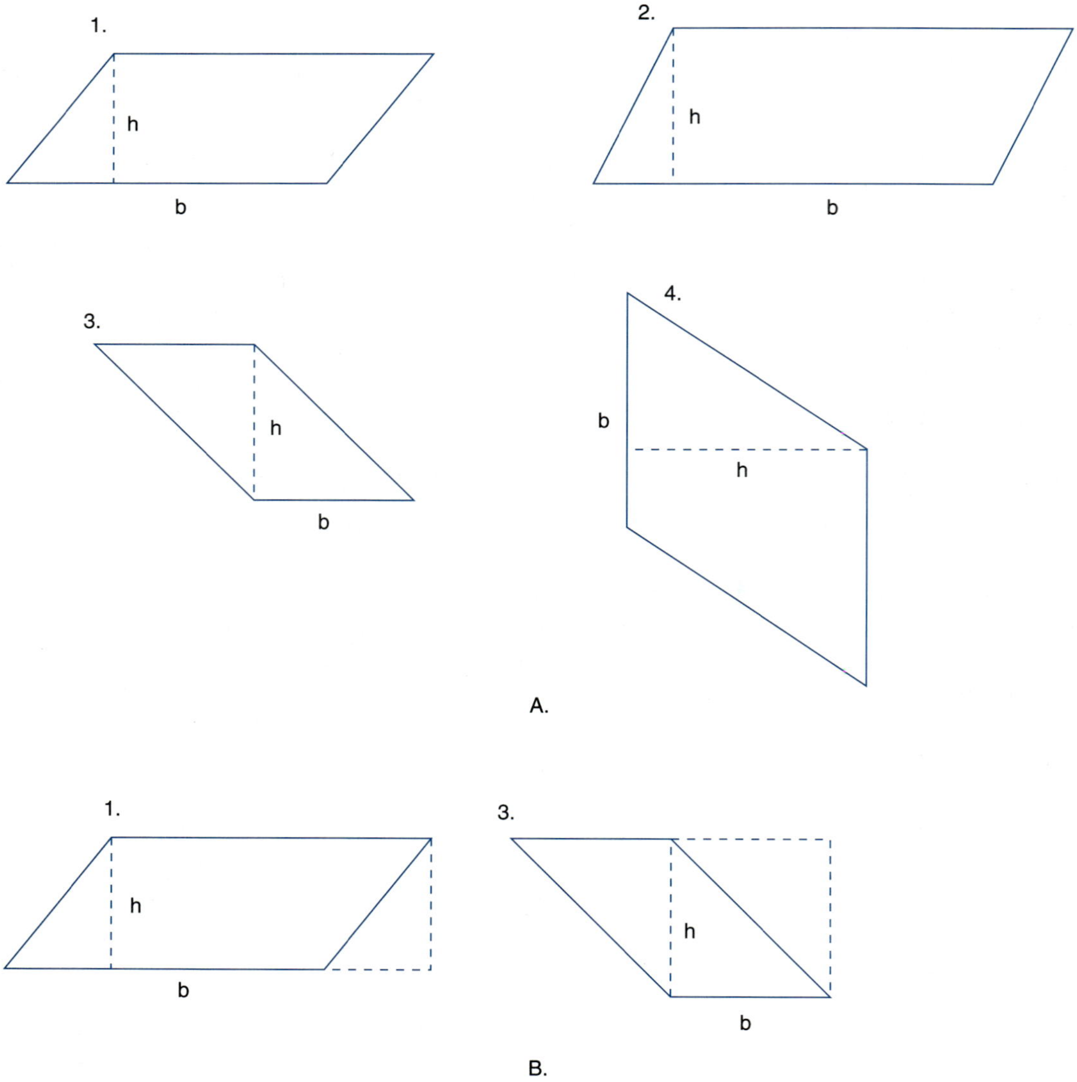

FIGURE 12.27 Diagrams to Develop the Formula for the Area of a Parallelogram Region

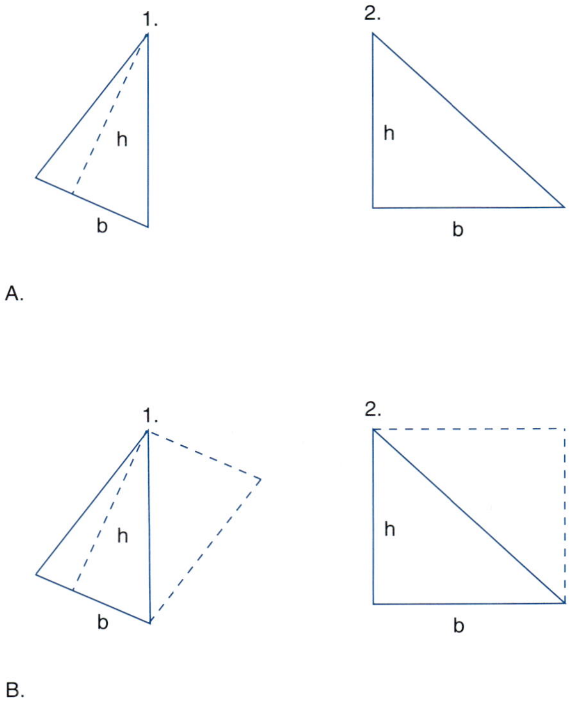

FIGURE 12.28 Diagrams to Develop the Formula for the Area of a Triangular Region

ACTIVITY 12.75
Areas of Unusual Figures.

When students can use the formula to find the area of rectangular regions, ask them to find the area of unusual figures (Figure 12.29). Remind them to estimate the areas before computing. After they complete their work, discuss how they broke the figure into parts, found the area of each part, and added the numbers.

When they understand the breaking-into-parts strategy, students can create unusual figures and after determining the area of each figure, ask other students to find the areas of their figures.

Reader Activity 12.4

Draw three unusual figures, and determine how the area of each figure could be determined if area formulas are known. The figures should be usable for sixth-grade learners. Explain the ease or difficulty of making these figures.

Formula for the Volume of a Rectangular Solid. The formula for volume is $V = l \times w \times h$ (V = volume, l = length, w = width, and h = height). After students can find the volume of an object by arranging layers of cubic centimeters in a box and counting the number of cubes in all the layers (Figure 12.30), they study the formula for volume. An interactive lesson to help learners understand the meaning of the formula begins with a problem. Give a group of students only enough cubic

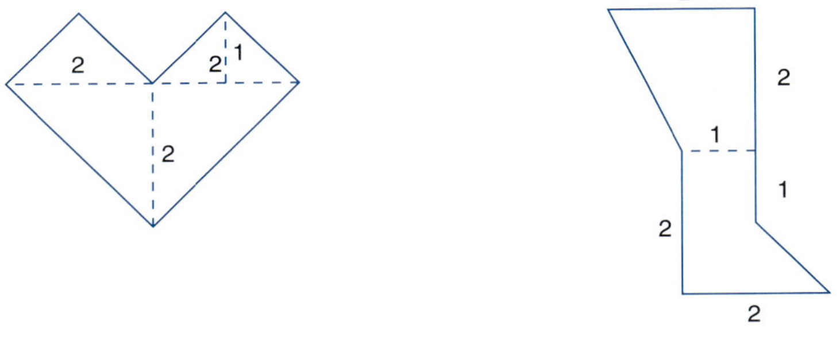

FIGURE 12.29 Find the Area of Odd-Shaped Figures

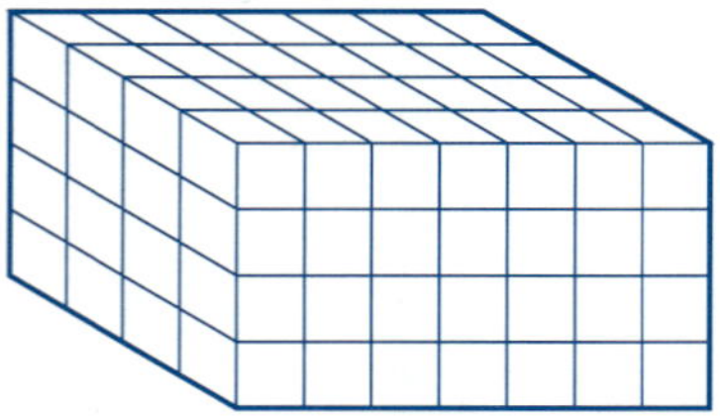

FIGURE 12.30 Cubes in a Rectangular Box to Use in Counting Units to Determine Volume

centimeters to fill one layer of a box. Ask them to estimate the volume and then find the volume using the cubic centimeters you have provided. If a group needs guidance, say, for example, "After you find the number of cubic centimeters in a layer, how can you find the number of layers of cubes in the box? When you know the number of layers, how can you find the total number of cubic centimeters?"

After working with this problem, students share their solutions. Some students will point out that they can count the number of cubic centimeters in a layer, then line up the cubes against one side of the box to determine the number of layers in the box, and finally multiply the number of cubic centimeters in a layer by the number of layers. (If someone suggests repeatedly adding the number of cubes in a layer until all layers have been accounted for, help him or her think of multiplication as repeated addition.)

A class discussion then involves finding a formula for the volume of a rectangular solid. Some students may immediately give the formula because of their earlier work with the formula for the area of a rectangular region. If they cannot do so, ask questions such as: "What do you know about the number of the length units and the number of cubic centimeters in a row?" "What do you know about the number of width units and the number of rows?" After learners determine that these corresponding numbers are the same, tell them that the number of layers is called the height of the box. Ask them what letter would be good to designate the number of height units (h). Then ask, "How can we put these ideas together to give the formula for volume?" They decide in response to your questions and comments that the formula is $V = l \times w \times h$.

After students have developed the formula, have them explain how to use it to find the volume of boxes previously found by counting blocks. Activities then involve finding the volume of various boxes and of a desk drawer and considering how to find the volume of their room. Students also find the volume of other three-dimensional rectangular objects of their own choice. They consider the reasonableness of their solutions and review the meaning of the formula in terms of the problems solved.

Formulas for the Circumference of a Circle and for the Area of a Circular Region. Estimation of the circumference of a circle and of the area of a circular region is the first step in working with the formulas for these measures. Use diagrams such as the one in Figure 12.31. Because the circle is inscribed in a square bounding a region of 4 large and 36 small squares, it is possible for students to estimate the circumference of the circle and the area of the circular region. Their estimations will enable them to give meaning to the formula. They will note that the circumference is not 4 times but probably about 3 times the diameter and that the area is not 4 times the radius times the radius, but probably about 3.

Save students' estimates. After they develop the formulas for the circumference of a circle and for the area of a circular region, students should compare their estimates with the computed measurements.

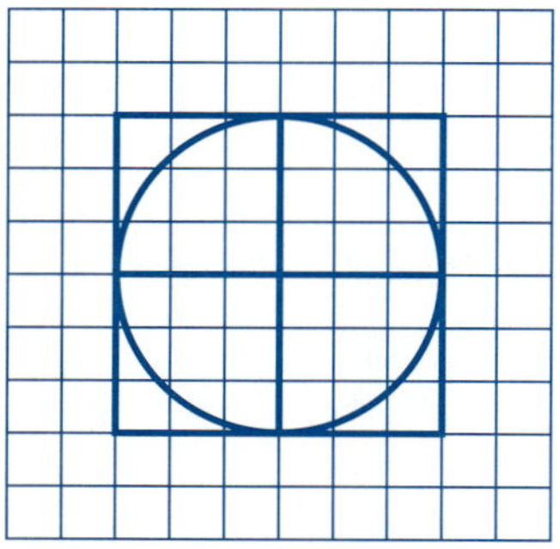

FIGURE 12.31 Circle Inscribed in a Square

ACTIVITY 12.76
Developing the Formula for the Circumference of a Circle.

After students have estimated the circumference of several circles, say, "What number do we predict is the ratio of the circumference to the diameter? (About 3.) Let's experiment to find the ratio of the circumference to the diameter and use it to give a rule for the circumference of a circle."

Give groups of children five plates or pots, labeled A through E, and a measuring tape. Ask them to find the circumference of each plate or the measure at the top of each pot and to fill in a table such as Table 12.3 (diameters are given). Suggest that they can write a rule for the circumference after they have completed the

TABLE 12.3 Completed Table to Compare Diameter of a Circle to Its Circumference

Plate	Circumference (cm)	Diameter (cm)	C/D
A	22	7	3.14
B	28.25	9	3.14
C	18.75	6	3.13
D	12.5	4	3.13
E	11	3.5	3.14

table. Questions to ask if they need more guidance are, "How does the circumference compare to the diameter? What number times the diameter gives the circumference of a circle? How can we use the ratio to find the circumference for any circle?" They discuss their solutions and arrive at the idea that the diameter times 3.14 will give a good approximation of the circumference of any circle. Question them so that they understand that the diameter is 2 times the radius and the latter number can be used in their rule. They use their rule to write *their* formula $C = 3.14 \times d$ or $C = 3.14 \times 2r$. Have them react to their earlier predictions regarding the ratio of the circumference to the diameter.

The formula for the circumference of a circle is $C = \pi \times d$ or $C = \pi \times 2r$. The ratio students develop from the activity will not give them the constant π to use in their formula, but a good approximation. They are told that π (pi) represents the exact ratio of the circumference to the diameter, which is close to 3.14, and that π is used in the formula. (Some student may wish to research other approximations of π.) They use the formula, with 3.14 for π, to solve problems, and they can write problems that involve use of the formula for others to solve.

Reader Activity 12.5

Measure the diameter and circumference each of five round objects, and complete a table such as Table 12.3. Why would this be a valuable activity for learners?

ACTIVITY 12.77
Developing the Formula for the Area of a Circular Region.

After students have estimated the areas of circular regions (the diagram in Figure 12.31 is an example), they develop the formula for the area of a circular region by engaging in the following activity: Cut a circular region in half, fold each piece in half twice, cut the eight pieces, rearrange the parts, and consider that the rearranged parts resemble a parallelogram (Figure 12.32). The directions can be given in writing for this activity or you can give them orally to the class. The key to developing the formula is in noticing that the rearranged parts look like a parallelogram whose height is the radius of the circle, recognizing that the base of the "parallelogram" is $\frac{1}{2}$ the circle's circumference, and substituting in the formula for the area of a parallelogram region. Most students need to be helped to make these observations as well as to develop the formula because the algebra needed to accomplish the task has not yet been learned by upper elementary grade children:

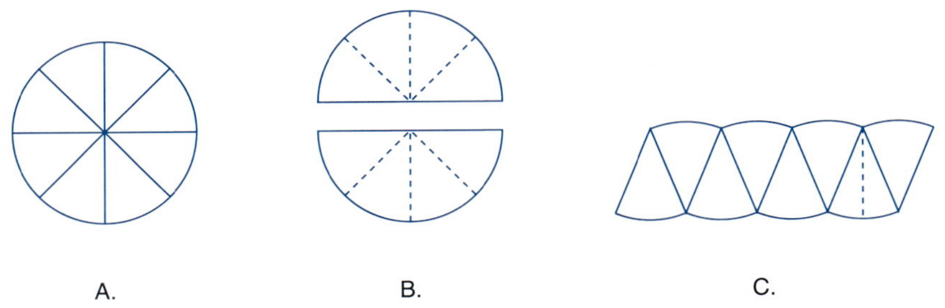

FIGURE 12.32 Developing the Formula for the Area of a Circular Region

Parallelogram region: $A = b \times h$

Circular region: $b = \frac{1}{2} \times C$ (circumference)

$= (\frac{1}{2} \times \pi 2r) = \pi r$

$h = r$

$A = \pi r \times r$

They compare their earlier predictions of the areas of circular regions to the computed areas and discuss the reasonableness of the formula they developed.

After formulas for perimeter, area, and volume have been learned, children will need to learn the cues in a problem that help them decide which formula to use. Discussions involving an exchange of ideas can help students learn how to analyze a problem to determine which formula should be used. The discussions should emphasize visualizing the problem so that the appropriate formula can be chosen.

Relating Measurements

Students can make interesting discoveries about the relation of attributes in figures as they engage in activities. The three activities described here help students learn that if the shape of a figure is changed, one measurement can change while the other remains the same.

ACTIVITY 12.78
Area and Perimeter.

Children use square centimeter paper for this activity. The directions on an assignment sheet are: Use an area of 2 square centimeters. Draw as many rectangles as you can with this area, and determine the perimeter for each rectangle. Label each new rectangle for a given area with a letter, and record the results in the table on your study sheet; separate different perimeters with commas (Table 12.4). When you finish, repeat the activity three times, using in turn 4, 8, and 12 square centimeters. Study your record to make an interesting discovery. (The area of a rectangle can remain the same and the perimeter of the rectangle change.) Who would be interested in knowing this? (Perhaps house or building planners.)

ACTIVITY 12.79
Perimeter and Area.

This activity is similar to 12.78, except that children use perimeters of 6, 8, 12, and 16 centimeters. The assignment is: Using square centimeter paper, draw as many rectangles as possible each with a perimeter of 6 centimeters, determine the area of each rectangle, and make a record using the table on your assignment sheet. Separate the areas with commas (Table 12.5). Repeat the activity three times, using perimeters of 8, 12, and 16 centimeters. Study your record to make an interesting

TABLE 12.4 Activity Sheet for Relating Areas of Rectangular Regions and Perimeters of the Rectangles

Rectangular Regions (cm^2)	Perimeters of Rectangles
2	
4	
8	
12	

TABLE 12.5 Activity Sheet for Relating Perimeters of Rectangles and Areas of the Rectangular Regions

Perimeters of Rectangles (cm)	Areas of Rectangular Regions
6	
8	
12	
16	

discovery. (The perimeter of a rectangle can remain the same and the area of the rectangle change.) Who would be interested in knowing this? (Perhaps house or building planners.)

Variation: Repeat Activities 12.78 and 12.79, but use irregular figures instead of rectangles.

Metric and Customary Systems

Metric System. Children learn some metric relations as they work with instruments. In grade 6 children examine what they know and develop new understandings about the metric system. They learn the meaning of prefixes, develop images or mental pictures of units, and learn to make conversions in order to solve problems. They learn the meaning of prefixes in the metric system by studying a chart for units of length (Table 12.6).

Images of units that students have developed in earlier grades are reexamined and extended. Children are asked to create a mind picture or mental image of a centimeter, a decimeter, and a meter and to discuss what they "see." Square and cubic metric units are explored in the same way after students have studied some metric relations. Activities 12.80–12.82 can be used to develop the meaning of units and their relation to other units. After students have explored metric units for length, area, and volume, they can make charts to summarize their learning.

ACTIVITY 12.80
What Are Square Units?

Have a group draw a square meter on a piece of newsprint or cloth, marking each square decimeter. The children who are not engaged in this activity each draw a square decimeter, marking each square centimeter. The square decimeters can be placed on the square meter for students to examine. After the models are completed, children answer questions such as, "Why is a square decimeter 100 square centimeters?" "Why is a square meter 100 square decimeters or 10,000 square centimeters?" "Why is a square centimeter 100 square millimeters?"

TABLE 12.6 Metric System

Prefixes	Units of Length	Abbreviation
Milli = .001	Millimeter =.001 meter	mm
Centi = .01	Centimeter = .01 meter	cm
Deci = .1	Decimeter =.1 meter	dm
	1 meter	m
Deka = 10	Dekameter =10 meters	dkm
Hecto = 100	Hectometer =100 meters	hm
Kilo = 1000	Kilometer =1000 meters	km

ACTIVITY 12.81
What Is a Cubic Unit?

The cubic meter constructed by students (Activity 12.41) can be examined to decide the relations among cubic centimeters, cubic decimeters, and cubic millimeters that comprise the cubic meter. Students should have many opportunities to communicate their understanding of the base ten relations that are the basis for cubic units.

ACTIVITY 12.82
Volume, Capacity, and Weight Relations.

A class project helps students learn that a liter of water will fill a box whose volume is 1 cubic decimeter or 1000 cubic centimeters, and that the water weights 1 kilogram. Use heavy cardboard and tape to make a box that holds 1000 cubic centimeters, and line the box with a plastic bag. Discuss the size of the box with the class. Fill the box with water, and have a student measure the amount the box holds (1 liter). Pour this amount into a plastic bag and determine that the weight is 1 kilogram. (These results will occur only if the experiment is carried out at sea level with water at 4° Celsius. Allowances must be made if elevations and temperature differ from these.) Have each student write up the experiment and his or her reaction to it.

Because of their frequent use of instruments and formulas, pupils should have an intuitive understanding of some conversions. For example, they should know that 2 meters are 200 centimeters. Knowledge of base ten makes conversions in the metric system quite easy, and some, although probably not all, students can construct conversion rules (Activity 12.83).

ACTIVITY 12.83
Learning Conversions.

Ask students to use metric rulers to complete an activity sheet that requires making conversions and to find patterns that would make rules for converting from one unit to another. Examples for the activity sheet are:

- 3 centimeters = _______ millimeters
- 60 millimeters = _______ centimeters
- 5 decimeters = _______ centimeters
- 20 centimeters = _______ decimeters

Some students will generalize from the examples completed on the activity sheet and understand the rules: to convert smaller metric units to larger metric units, divide by 10, 100, or 1000; and to convert larger metric units to smaller metric units, multiply by 10, 100, or 1000. These generalizations requires a high level of thinking, and some students will not be able to grasp them until they study mathematics in the middle school. However, these students can usually convert specific metric units from one to the other (e.g., centimeters to decimeters or meters to centimeters) because they know the base ten relations developed from many measuring experiences.

Problem solving should entail real-life problems or be coordinated with other curricular areas such as science and social studies. Fay and Tsairides (1989) give a description of a unit, Metric Mall, that integrated mathematics with "retailing" experiences for students in grades 3, 4, and 5. Creative problems were designed for use in learning centers. Students used knowledge of metric units and measuring instruments to solve the problems. Fay and Tsairides report that students were motivated by the unit and often asked when they could return to the centers.

Customary System. The customary system is used in no industrialized country except the United States. In 1974 the United States House of Representatives defeated a bill that would have required conversion to the metric system in the United States. Therefore, American children must learn both systems. In general, textbooks contain materials devoted to both systems, and children learn to use both systems concurrently.

Units in the customary system commonly used in the United States are given in Table 12.7. The relations between units for an attribute are for the most part arbitrary, and therefore children must memorize the equivalences. Conversions within the system are awkward; for example, 3 feet 13 inches equals 4 feet 1 inch. Experience usually teaches conversions, and drill to learn conversions is not recommended.

Children do not learn to convert from one system to the other. However, many children relate the two systems as they use instruments in and out of school. Common comparisons are:

- 1 meter is about 39 inches
- 1 kilometer is about .6 mile
- 1 mile is a little more than 1.5 kilometers
- 1 quart is about 1 liter
- 1 cup is about 250 milliliters

ASSESSING MEASUREMENT LEARNING

As with all assessment of mathematical learning, assessment of measurement learning involves observation, interviews, examination of children's work product, and quizzes and tests, the latter mainly in the middle and upper grades. You assess children's ability to make qualitative comparisons, their ability to use nonstandards units and standard units, their skill in using measuring instruments, and their understanding and use of formulas. You also assess their attitudes.

Qualitative Comparisons

Observations enable you to determine if children can decide which one of two objects is greater (lesser) or the same in length, area, size, capacity, or weight as the other object. To make their judgments, children use direct comparison, or if the objects cannot be compared directly, they show that they can use a third object to make the comparison. Observations are made as children complete activities described in this chapter that deal with qualitative or nonnumerical comparison. To gather information regarding the meanings a child has of the process, ask questions such

TABLE 12.7 Customary System

Measures		Corresponding Unit
12 inches	=	1 foot
3 feet	=	1 yard
2 pints	=	1 quart
4 quarts	=	1 gallon
16 ounces	=	1 pound
24 hours	=	1 day
7 days	=	1 week
144 square inches	=	1 square foot
9 square feet	=	1 square yard

as, "How did you decide what to do?" The explanations children give help you decide if they understand the comparison idea involved in measurement well enough to work with nonstandard units.

Nonstandard Units

Similarly, when assessing children's work with nonstandard units, watch children use nonstandard units and listen to their explanations of the process involved to gain insight regarding students' understanding. Also assess children's work products that result from the use of nonstandard units.

Notice particularly when children are able to measure using only one nonstandard unit repeatedly to measure an attribute of an object. Also study children's understanding by asking a question that requires students to choose a nonstandard unit because children's responses tell whether or not they recognize that the attribute of an object is measured by a unit having the same attribute as that being measured. An example of such a question is: "What can you use to measure the distance from our room to the playground?"

Listen for children's use of words such as "about," "almost," and "a little more" to assess their awareness that measurements are approximate. Ask learners to estimate and to decide whether their estimates are reasonable.

Standard Units and Formulas

Observations, interviews, work products, and quizzes and tests are used to assess children's ability to use instruments such as rulers, meter sticks, and clocks and solve problems using formulas. Pupils' responses to an item such as in Figure 12.33A indicate whether they can use instruments, whereas responses to an item such as in Figure 12.33B tell how well they understand the use of instruments.

Of special importance in assessing children's understanding and ability is determining their ability to estimate. Children are frequently asked to tell about how long, big, or heavy an object seems to be. They should know distances and areas frequently encountered in their lives, such as how far they live from school.

FIGURE 12.33 Quiz Items

Give the length of the line. ____ cm

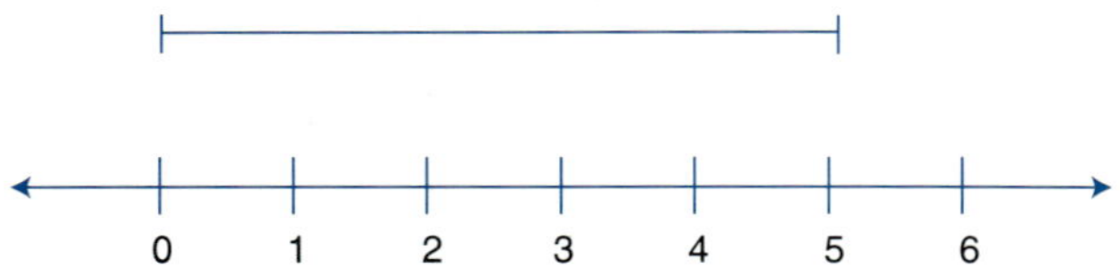

A

Give the length of the line. ____ cm

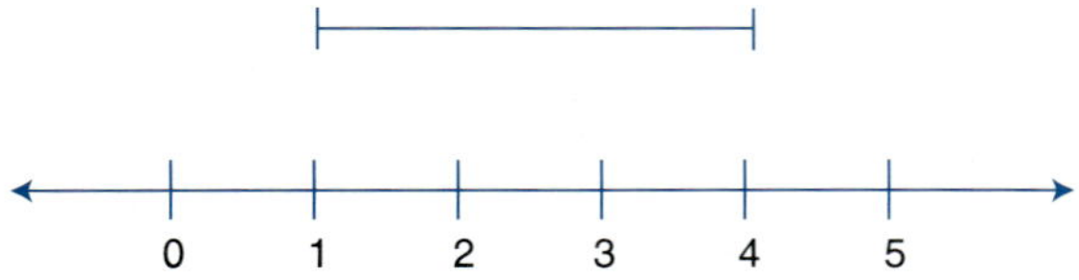

B

Students' solutions to story and number problems on tests and quizzes give information about their knowledge of formulas. However, assessment should also include questions that provide information about children's understanding of the cues to use to determine which formula to use. Examples of such questions are: In these problems, write up how you decided what formula to use and give the formula. Do not solve the problem:

1. Mary wanted to make a hooked rug for beside her bed. The space is 3 feet by 5 feet. How big will she make her rug?
2. Mr. and Mrs. O'Brien decided to build a fence to keep their dog in the yard. The space for the dog was to be 4 m by 5 m. How much fence did they build?

Records are kept to give a picture of children's progress. Records give the date, type of assessment, results, and usually your interpretations of your observations, interviews, the child's work products, and his or her responses to assessment questions.

Attitudes

Children's attitudes toward measurement learning are assessed mainly by observation. Note children's enthusiasm when engaging in measurement activities and any references to measurement they make when discussing other school subjects or out of school life. A few interview questions or write-up assignments can ask children to tell about their interest in learning about measurement. If children do not express positive attitudes, they can be asked why the study of measurement is not interesting to them. Their comments will enable you to revise your curriculum to make the study of measurement more meaningful and thus interesting to learners.

SUMMARY

This chapter described how instruction enables children to construct the conceptual knowledge necessary to solve measurement problems and acquire skill based on understanding. Six areas of conceptual understanding were outlined: (1) knowledge of attributes; (2) knowledge of the measurement process; (3) knowledge of the approximate nature of measurement; (4) knowledge of estimation; (5) knowledge that some units can be added or subtracted; and (6) knowledge that instruments and formulas simplify the process of measuring.

A sequence for learning measurement was described that provided for instruction dealing with qualitative comparisons of attributes, the study of nonstandard units, the use of standard units, making and using instruments, and generating and using formulas. The activities incorporated learning experiences and problems for studying length, area, capacity and volume, weight (mass), temperature, time, and angle measurement. Activities for helping learners develop formulas and relating measurements were also given. The use of both the metric and customary systems was described. Assessment of learning dealt with the key measurement concepts and skills taught in elementary schools and attitudes toward learning measurement.

REFERENCES

Fay, Nancy, and Catherine Tsairides. (September 1989). "Metric Mall." *Arithmetic Teacher* 37: 9–11.

Hiebert, James. (March 1984). "Why Do Some Children Have Trouble Learning Measurement Concepts?" *Arithmetic Teacher* 31: 19–24.

Holmes, Emma E. (1985). *Children Learning Mathematics: A Cognitive Approach to Teaching*. Englewood Cliffs, NJ: Prentice-Hall.

Joslyn, Ruth. (November 1990). "Using Concrete Models to Teach Large-Number Concepts." *Arithmetic Teacher* 38: 6–9.

Kouba, Vicky L., Catherine A. Brown, Thomas P. Carpenter, Mary M. Lindquist, Edward A. Silver, and Jane O. Swafford. (May 1988). "Results of the Fourth NAEP Assessment of Mathematics: Measure, Geometry, Data Interpretation, Attitudes, and Other Topics." *Arithmetic Teacher* 35: 10–16.

Liedtke, Werner W. (1990). "Measurement." In *Mathematics for the Young Child*, edited by Joseph N. Payne, pp. 229–249. Reston, VA: National Council of Teachers of Mathematics.

National Council of Teachers of Mathematics. (1989). *Curriculum and Evaluation Standards for School Mathematics.* Reston, VA: Author.

Reys, Robert E., Marilyn Suydam, and Mary M. Lindquist. (1992). *Helping Children Learn Mathematics,* 3rd ed. Englewood Cliffs, NJ: Prentice-Hall.

Van de Walle, John A. (1990). *Elementary School Mathematics: Teaching Developmentally.* New York: Longman.

Wilson, Patricia S., and Verna M. Adams. (January 1992). "A Dynamic way to Teach Angle and Angle Measure." *Arithmetic Teacher* 39: 6–13.

Wilson, Patricia S., and Alan Osborne. (1992). "Foundational Ideas in Teaching about Measure." In *Teaching Mathematics in Grades K–8: Research Based Methods,* 2nd ed., edited by Thomas R. Post, pp. 89–121. Boston: Allyn & Bacon.

SOFTWARE RESOURCES

Explorer Metros
Company: Sunburst
Computer: Apple
Grade level: 4–8

Games give experience with estimation of metric capacity, mass, length, and temperature.

Clock Works
Company: MECC
Computer Apple
Grade level: 1–4

Practice in telling time and setting clocks on dial and digital clocks.

Money Works
Company: MECC
Computer: Apple
Grade level: 1–4

Practice in counting money and making change. Students can design money for special occasions.

IBM Elementary Mathematics Series: Math Concepts
Company: IBM/EduQuest
Computer: IBM
Grade level: 4–8
Level II, Unit 5, Lesson 24

Deals with perimeter and area. Students count unit squares before developing formula for area.

Level III, Unit 6, Lesson 23

Use of formulas for perimeter, rectangle, parallelogram, and triangle.

Level III, Unit 6, Lesson 24

Deals with terms for a circle and for circumference formula.

CHAPTER 13

Studying Ratio, Proportion, and Percent

▪ INTRODUCTORY PROBLEM ▪

Your class is studying the body in their science unit. They are learning the kind and amount of food children and adults should eat for good health, and they are studying the makeup of the body—blood, water, bones, and so on. As you study this chapter, list the possibilities for studying ratios, proportions, and percents that can be found in this science unit.

INTRODUCTION

Proportional reasoning involves the study of ratio and proportion. It is often difficult for learners (Behr, Lesh, Post, and Silver, 1983). Their difficulties are related to the fact that proportional reasoning is based on grasping the concepts of covariation and multiple comparisons and relies on the capacity to store and manipulate several aspects of a problem (Post, Behr, and Lesh, 1988).

To understand the complexity of proportional reasoning, reflect on your thinking as you solve these problems:

1. James ate more toast for breakfast today than yesterday, but he took the same amount of time as yesterday. Did he eat more or less slowly yesterday?
2. Last week oranges cost 12 for \$3.35. This week they were 8 for \$1.99. Which was the cheaper price?

Proportional reasoning is believed to develop during adolescence, but many adults cannot deal with proportions (Hoffer and Hoffer, 1992). This is unfortunate because the ability to work with proportions is necessary for understanding aspects of subjects such as algebra, geometry, economics, accounting, finance, biology, chemistry, and physics; thus, dealing with proportions is required for careers in social science, business, science, medicine, and technology. Furthermore, proportions occur in daily life in shopping, personal finances, cooking, and home-improvement projects. Being unable to solve problems involving proportions thus precludes individuals from pursuing many careers and from relating to the demands of daily life in a fulfilling manner.

Because proportional reasoning can involve relating ratios, formal thought is considered necessary for using symbols for proportions. Rule-based approaches for solving proportion problems would therefore be delayed until the seventh or eighth grade, or for some learners, sixth grade. However, children in the elementary school can construct intuitive ideas of ratios and proportions by working with concrete materials and graphic representations of these concepts (NCTM, 1989). This chapter emphasizes teaching to enable children to develop a foundation for the study of proportion in adolescence or the years just preceding this period of life (see Standards 5, 7, and 9, in Curriculum Standards for Grades 5–8, Appendix A). A few activities to use with learners ready for paper-and-pencil work are also included. The sections are: Fractions and Ratios, Learning Ratio Concepts, Learning Percent, and Assessing Ratio, Proportion, and Percent Learning. A summary section ends the chapter.

FRACTIONS AND RATIOS

Fractions are numbers that deal with comparisons of a part to a whole or to a set that has been partitioned into equal parts. A ratio is a relative comparison between two numbers or measurements. Examples of ratios are 2 to 6—for example, to make orange juice, 2 parts of orange concentrate to 6 parts of water; or 2 to 3—for example, 2 hits for 3 times at bat. Fractions and ratios differ in many respects.

- A fraction expresses a part–whole relation; a ratio states a part–whole or a part–part relation. Thus, a fraction is a ratio, but not all ratios are fractions.
- Fractions and ratios are read differently. For example, $\frac{3}{4}$ as a fraction is read "three-fourths." The ratio $\frac{3}{4}$ is read 3 to 4.

- Fractions are symbolized in one way, ratios, several; for example, the fraction four-fifths is given by $\frac{4}{5}$. Ratios are written one of four ways: 4:5, $\frac{4}{5}$, (4,5), and $4 \to 5$. Each is read 4 to 5, 4 for 5, or 4 per 5.
- The second number in a fraction cannot be zero, but the second number in a ratio can be zero. For example, if the only two third-grade teachers in a school are females, the ratio of third-grade female teachers to male teachers is 2 to 0.
- The rules for combining ratios do not apply to fractions. For example, if Jack bought 2 peppermint candies for $.07 (2:7) and 2 chocolate candies for $.09 (2:9), the ratios are combined to give 4:16 or 4 candies for $.16. The fractions $\frac{2}{7}$ and $\frac{2}{9}$ cannot be combined by adding both the first and the second numbers of the pairs.

LEARNING RATIO CONCEPTS

Concrete thought is characteristic of most children in the elementary school, and many continue at this level. Harrison, Brindley, and Bye (1989) report that in their research 50% of a sample of junior high school children operated at the concrete level when dealing with ratio and proportion. To enable learners to develop the foundation for a study of ratio, instruction for elementary school children and even many middle-school students should provide opportunities for them to use objects and diagrams to develop the ratio concept.

Karplus, Pulos, and Stage (1983) suggests beginning instruction with experiences that help children understand the concept of variables and their relationship. They also recommend that the exploration, concept development, and concept application instructional sequence be used. Quintero (1987) also recommends helping children learn the vocabulary of ratio.

The simplest ratio is a unit ratio. One number in a unit ratio is 1; the other, a whole number (e.g., 3 to 1). An integer ratio can be a unit ratio or equivalent to a unit ratio ($\frac{3}{12} = \frac{1}{4}$) and cannot include fractions. A noninteger ratio is not equivalent to a integer ratio (e.g., $\frac{2}{3}$); when renamed with one number equal to 1, it includes a fraction (e.g., $\frac{2}{3}$ to 1). Children should begin their study of ratios with unit ratios. Noninteger ratios are introduced after children can represent unit and integer ratios.

The following activities are designed to help children develop an intuitive understanding of ratios. They are appropriate for the late primary grades but can also be used in the upper elementary school. They are assigned as part of instruction characterized by interactive teaching. Scaling, proportions, learning to solve proportions, and comparing ratios are discussed after activities to introduce ratios.

Activities for the Introduction of Ratios

ACTIVITY 13.1
Changing Shadows.

To develop an intuitive idea of variables, children can explore their shadows. Later they experiment to determine what variables change the length of the shadow of a pencil on their desks (Karplus et al., 1983).

On a sunny day go outside at different times, and ask children to find out how they can change the length of their shadows. Repeat the activity on a cloudy and partly cloudy day. After students observe the variables that influence the length of shadows, such as their heights, the time of day, the weather, and the angle of the sun, have them write up their observations. Discuss their write-ups. During the discussion, help children focus on the concept of variable, the thing that relates to changes in their shadows, by asking questions such as, "What makes your shadow get longer (shorter)?" "What is related to (goes with) a long (short) shadow?" When children express the idea that a shadow's length is influenced by one or more factors, introduce the term *variable.*

Follow up the exploration of their own shadows by asking students to experiment with pencils and shadows. They work alone or together with one or more pencils to determine the variables, and they discuss their investigations with one or two learners before a class discussion of their observations. Help children observe that when all the variables have the same value (e.g., pencil length, angle to the desk, and the time of day), the shadows have the same length.

Activities to teach the notion of variable include observing the variables that influence (1) the speed of the school bus that takes them home; and (2) the number of cars passing the school.

ACTIVITY 13.2
Developing Intuitive Understanding.

To develop an intuitive understanding of ratios, children can investigate unit ratios when studying content such as transportation in a social science unit, food or their bodies in a science unit, and money in a mathematics unit. They can use counters or draw diagrams to solve problems. Model how to use an arrow in the representations of their solutions. Paper arrows should be distributed for use with manipulatives (Figure 13.1). Problems to use include:

1. How many wheels go with one car?
2. How many wheels go with a truck and trailer?
3. How many fingers for one hand?
4. About how many cents per one apple (orange, carton of milk, etc.)?
5. How many quarters go with one dollar?
6. How many nickels for one dime?
7. How many children for one teacher?
8. How many crayons for one box?
9. How many walls for one classroom?

After children work in small groups or alone to solve the problems, have them share their work.

Integer ratios and noninteger ratios are also introduced with problems students can solve with counters or drawings. Examples of problems are:

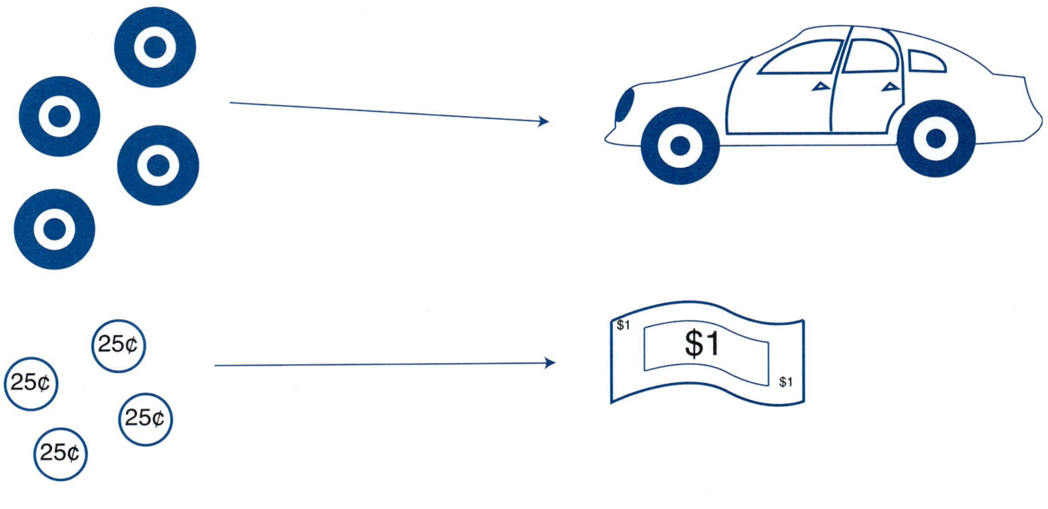

FIGURE 13.1 Showing Relations

1. How many arms for 3 people?
2. How many recesses for 5 days?
3. How many pillows on 2 beds?
4. How many legs on 3 cats?
5. How many hours of sleep for a 5-day school week?
6. How many legs on two 3-legged stools?
7. How many nickels for 3 quarters?
8. How many ears on 4 monkeys?
9. How many people to the number of rooms in your house?

As with unit ratios, students explain to each other how they solved the problems.

When children can solve problems involving ratios by using materials and can explain the meaning of their work, ask them to think about what is alike in all the problems. They can share their ideas in small groups and then in a class discussion. The ideas expressed in the whole class should include the notion that in the problems two numbers are related, although children will probably use words such as *belong to* or *go with*. When they indicate a grasp of the concept, tell them that they are working with ratios.

Show learners the three most common notations for ratios: 3:6, $\frac{3}{6}$, 3 → 6. Have them use all of them to express several ratios of their own choice.

A follow-up to the introduction of ratios is for learners to find examples of things that go together at school or outside of school. They can draw diagrams of their discoveries, share them with others, and post them on the bulletin board. Sharing can be planned so that a child shows his or her diagram, and the other children decide what the drawing tells.

ACTIVITY 13.3
Vocabulary for Ratios.

When children can show that they can represent ratios with counters or diagrams, have an awareness of the meaning of ratios, and can use a notation for ratios, have them review the words used in the ratios that have been studied in one or more lessons. List these. Have the children restate several ratios discussed previously using the words *per, for,* and *to.* Discuss how the words all mean the same thing.

Scaling

Scaling involves constructing a list of items that are related in a certain way. In *scaling up* the numbers in the related items get larger; in *scaling down,* the numbers get smaller. For example, students are scaling up when they complete the following ratios:

- 1 nickel → 5 pennies
- 2 nickels → 10 pennies
- 3 nickels → pennies
- 4 nickels → pennies

Scaling down is involved in

- 8 dimes → 16 nickels
- 4 dimes → 8 nickels
- 2 dimes → 4 nickels
- 1 dime → nickels

Scaling-up activities are completed by using repeated addition or multiplication; scaling-down activities by using repeated subtraction or division. After completing several scaling tasks, students should be asked to explain the processes they used. The discussion should bring out that multiplication or division is the most efficient approach to scaling. Children should also be questioned so that they express the idea that they must decide how the numbers in the list are related before they can complete the list.

ACTIVITY 13.4
Background for Scaling.

Before beginning scaling activities, children need opportunities to double and halve quantities by using materials and diagrams. Give problems such as the following. Ask learners to use counters or diagrams to solve the problems (Figure 13.2). Supply arrows for use with counters.

1. If 3 pieces of gum cost $.25, what is the cost of 6, 12, and 24 pieces?
2. If 8 cookies cost $.64, what is the cost of 4, 2, and 1?
3. How many days are in 1, 2, and 4 weeks?

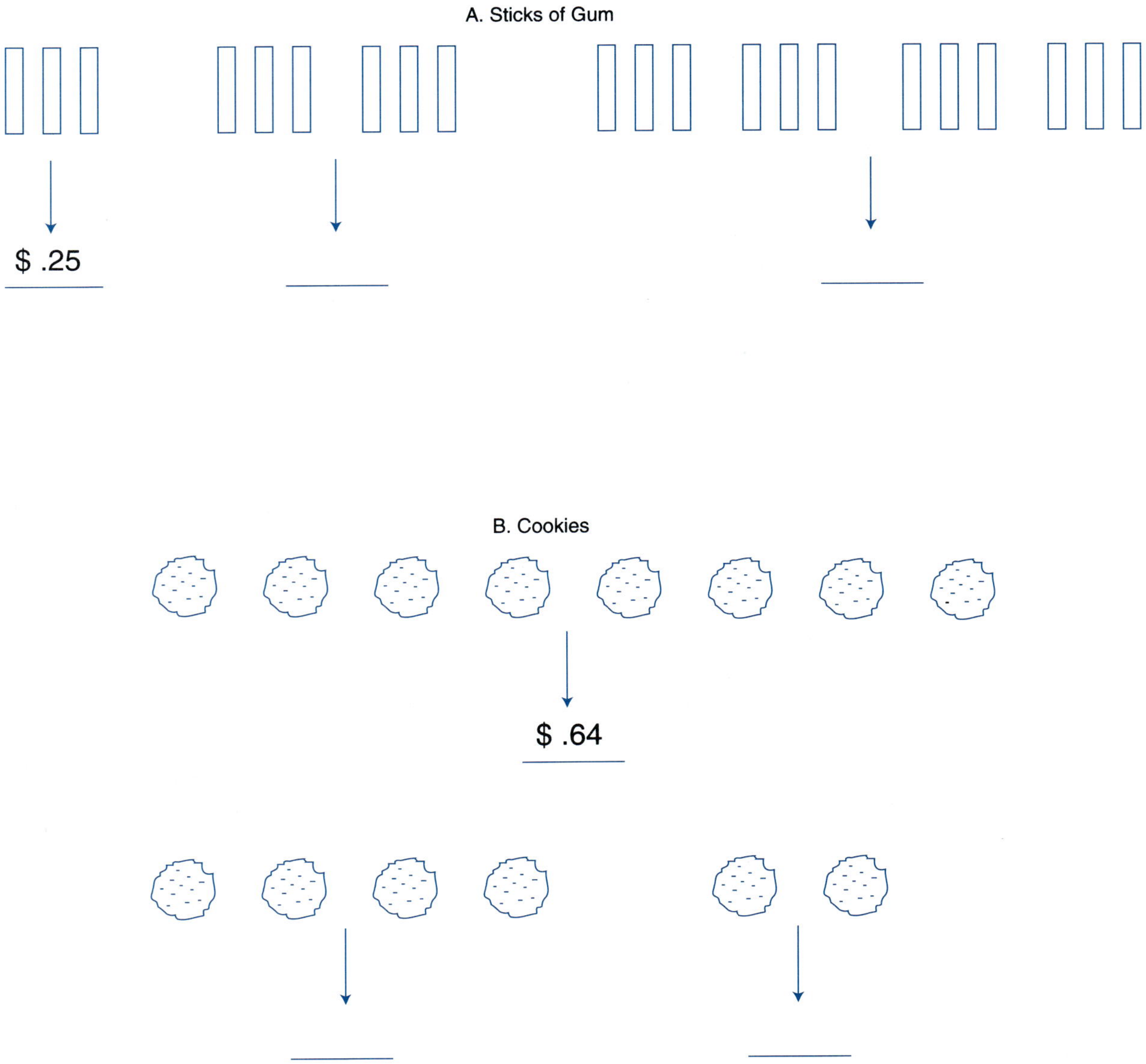

FIGURE 13.2 Scaling

After children complete their work, discuss how they found the answers. During the discussion, ask questions to help children realize that they were doubling (halving), which is the same as multiplication (or division) by 2. For example, ask, "What operation did you use when you doubled (halved) the number?" "Is doubling (halving) like multiplying (dividing)? Why?"

ACTIVITY 13.5
Studying Scaling.

Scaling tasks help develop a foundation for learning ratio and proportion concepts. An example of a scaling task using money is:

- 1 dime → 10 pennies
- 2 dimes → 20 pennies
- 3 dimes → pennies
- 4 dimes → pennies
- 5 dimes → pennies

Scaling activities for children can deal with:

- *Capacity:* 1 cup → 8 ounces; 1 pint → 2 cups; 1 quart → 2 pints; 1 gallon → 4 quarts
- *Time:* 1 minute → 60 seconds; 1 hour → 60 minutes; 1 day → 24 hours; 1 week → 7 days; 1 month → 4 weeks; 1 year → 12 months; 1 decade → 10 years; 1 century → 100 years
- *Money:* 1 nickel → 5 pennies; 1 dime → 10 pennies; 1 dime → 2 nickels
- *Other:* 1 table → 4 legs; 1 stool → 3 legs; 1 chicken → 2 legs; 1 goat → 4 legs; 1 mouse → 2 ears

After children understand scaling, have them choose items to use in constructing a scaling task. They can have fun thinking of examples to use in exercises. They may complete the list or exchange their exercise with another person.

Scaling does not need to involve unit ratios, as shown in the following examples:

- 2 tablespoons sugar → 5 tablespoons lemon juice
- 4 tablespoons sugar → 10 tablespoons lemon juice
- 6 tablespoons sugar → tablespoons lemon juice
- 8 tablespoons sugar → tablespoons lemon juice

ACTIVITY 13.6
Scaling with Graphing.

After children complete a scaling task, they can make a graph of the numbers in their list (Figure 13.3). To ensure that they understand how to proceed even if they have been introduced to graphing, complete a graph as a group. Then ask children to choose a scaling task they have completed for their graphing. After all have finished, have them share graphs and read several ratios from their graphs.

Later, ask them to compare the shape of their graphs. Distribute scaling work they completed earlier. Ask them to predict the shape of the graph drawn by using the numbers in their earlier scaling assignment. After they draw these graphs, discuss the goodness of their predictions.

Activity for the Classroom 13.1. Write three scaling tasks with five items in each task. Assign them to learners. Ask them to tell how they thought to carry out the tasks. If you teach advanced students, ask them to make a graph for each task. Have them compare their graphs and share their conclusions about the shapes of the graphs.

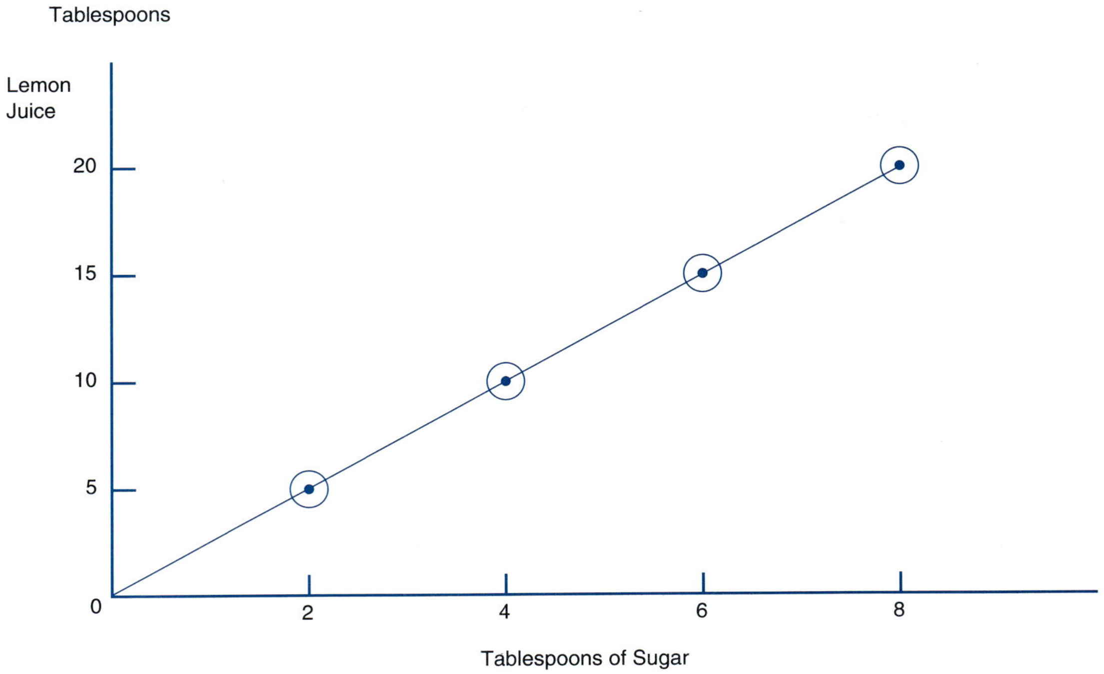

FIGURE 13.3 A Graph for Numbers in a Scaling Task

Proportion

A proportion expresses an equality between two ratios (written as $\frac{3}{4} = \frac{6}{8}$ or in the form, 3:4 = 6:8). In the form a:b = c:d, the first and fourth numbers, a and d, are called the extremes and the second and third numbers, b and c, the means. Solving a proportion involves finding the missing number when three numbers are given. For example, finding $N = 12$ in $\frac{3}{4} = \frac{9}{N}$ entails solving the proportion. There are three approaches for solving proportions: unit-rate method, factor-of-change approach, and the cross-products approach. Mental calculation, paper-and-pencil computation, or solution with a calculator can be used with any of the approaches.

Examples of the approaches are:

Jim made 2 baskets out of 4 throws. If he continued at this rate, how many baskets would he make in 12 throws?

Unit-Rate Method:

$\frac{2}{4} = \frac{H}{12}$

$\frac{1}{2} = \frac{H}{12}$

$\frac{1}{2} = \frac{6}{12}$

$H = 6$

This approach involves finding a unit ratio, and then solving for the missing value by using the notion of equivalent ratios (divide the second numbers to determine the multiplier of 1, which is 6).

The unit-rate method is particularly useful in problems such as: Anna noticed that socks were on sale for $2.98 for 2 pairs. She wanted 5 pairs. How much would she pay for that many? The solution involves finding the cost of one pair—$1.49—and determining 5 × $1.49 = $7.45.

Factor-of-Change Method:

$\frac{2}{4} = \frac{H}{12}$

3 × 4 equals 12, so the answer is 3 × 2, or 6.

This method is most useful when one of the corresponding numbers in one ratio is a whole-number multiple of the other. It would not be too useful in an example such as: $\frac{3}{4} = \frac{10}{x}$, although a student could think $10 \div 3 = 3\frac{1}{3}$; $3\frac{1}{3} \times 4 = 13\frac{1}{3}$

Cross-Products Method:

$\frac{2}{4} = \frac{H}{12}$	$2:4 = H:12$
$2 \times 12 = 4 \times H$	$2 \times 12 = 4 \times H$
$\frac{24}{48} = 4 \times H$	$24 = 4 \times H$
$6 = H$	$6 = H$

In the right-hand solution, the product of the extremes (end numbers) equals the product of the means (inside numbers). This cross-products procedure is often taught to learners as an algorithm, but they develop little understanding of the process.

The cross-products method can be rationalized in the preceding problem by (1) noting that the solution can be found by renaming both ratios so that the second number in each ratio is 48:

$$\frac{2}{4} = \frac{H}{12}$$
$$\frac{(2\times 12)}{(4\times 12)} = \frac{(H\times 4)}{(12\times 4)}$$
$$\frac{(2\times 12)}{48} = \frac{(4\times H)}{48}$$
$$\frac{24}{48} = \frac{4H}{48}$$
$$24 = 4H$$
$$6 = H$$

and (2) thinking that a shortcut for this computational solution, is the cross-products method.

The cross-products approach should probably not be introduced in the elementary school because it is often approached in a mechanical way. Elementary school children would find it difficult to understand the reasoning that makes the approach sensible.

When writing a proportion to solve a problem, the equality can involve ratios within or between a situation (Karplus et al., 1983). Within ratios differ in labels; between ratios have the same labels. For example, in the problem "If 3 apples cost 42 cents, what do 5 apples cost?" using within ratios, the proportion is: $\frac{3}{42} = \frac{5}{\text{Cost}}$. The between ratios give the proportion $\frac{3}{5} = \frac{42}{\text{Cost}}$. Students can use within or between ratios when writing math sentences for problems. Both will give the same answer. The concept to be learned is that the same relation is expressed in either form. For example, apples to cost *relates to* apples to cost (within ratios) or cost to cost *relates to* apples to apples (between ratios).

Reader Activity 13.1

Write three ratio problems. Solve them using both within and between ratios. Decide if you prefer using within or between ratios or if you have no preference. Give reasons for your answers. If possible, discuss your ideas with others.

Learning to Solve Proportions

As elementary school children learn about solving proportions, they have a series of experiences that enables them to deal with proportions on a concrete level before using symbolic representations to solve proportions. They:

1. Explore proportions using manipulatives and solve story problems involving proportions using diagrams or scaling.
2. Use mental computation and estimation to solve proportion problems involving mainly halving or doubling.
3. Make records of their problem solving.
4. Explore solution strategies to use with symbolic representations.
5. Use the unit-rate or factor-of-change method to solve proportion problems.

Gifted learners can be introduced to the cross-products approach for solving proportions, but most students will learn this method in the middle school.

ACTIVITY 13.7
Studying Special Polygons.

Similar triangles, rectangles, and squares have sides with lengths in the same ratio. The study of these special polygons enables students to explore proportional ideas in a geometric setting.

Give each student an activity sheet of similar polygons, three or more each of triangles, rectangles, and squares (Figure 13.4). Ask groups of students to find out how the triangles are related. Say, "You can cut out the triangles and rearrange them, measure the triangles, or solve the problem in another way. When you have decided how the triangles are related, solve the same problem with the rectangles and with the squares." Have them discuss their solutions and how they solved the problems. Tell students that when the lengths of their sides have the same ratio, we say that the triangles, rectangles, and squares are similar.

ACTIVITY 13.8
All Squares Are Similar.

Ask students whether all triangles are similar. Repeat the question for rectangles and for squares. Discuss learners' ideas, and suggest that they test their hypotheses. To aid in their work, give them materials such as those used in Activity 13.7, but include

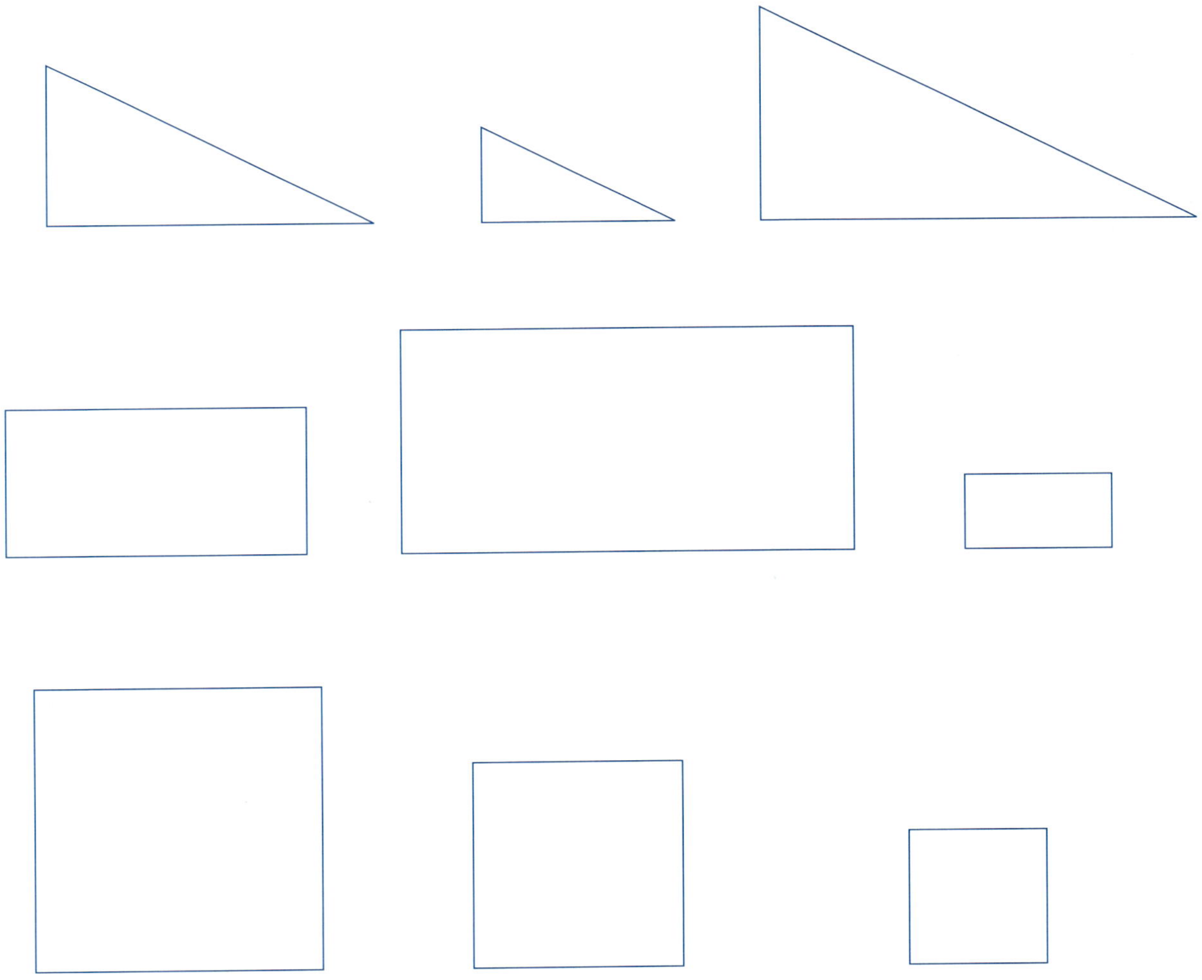

FIGURE 13.4 Similar Polygons

rectangles and triangles that are not similar. They should conclude from their investigation that all squares are similar, but that not all rectangles or triangles are similar.

ACTIVITY 13.9
Introduction to Solving Proportions.

Ask children in groups to solve story problems such as the following that involve proportions. The ratios should be unit or integer ratios. Before beginning, ask them what different strategies they know for solving problems—materials, tables, diagrams, or mental computation. Have them use any method they understand. Ask them to make records of their work (Figure 13.5).

1. Mother bought 4 pillow cases for $16.00. What did she pay for each one?
2. Sam's brother runs once around the track in 7 minutes; how many minutes does it take to run around 3 times?
3. Oranges are on sale for 3 pounds for $.99. What does 1 pound cost?
4. The school nurse reported that 1 child in 6 in the two kindergartens was absent because of the measles. If there are 48 children in kindergarten, how many were absent because of this illness?

After groups complete their work, they discuss the strategies used for finding solutions. Children should use the overhead to demonstrate their use of materials and diagrams. Ask those who used mental computation to tell about their thinking.

In following lessons, proportions are used that do not always involve integer ratios. Examples of problems with noninteger ratios are:

1. Herman delivers 6 newspapers in 15 minutes. At that rate how many minutes will it take to deliver 30 papers?
2. Charles bought 3 apples for $.40. What would 6 cost at that rate?

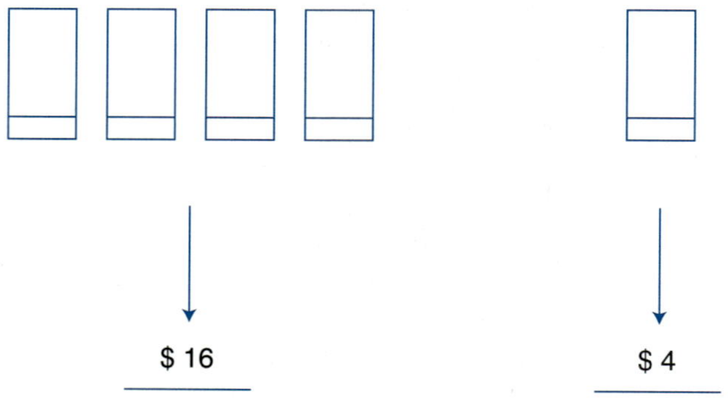

Pounds of Oranges	3	2	1
Cost	$.99	$.66	$.33

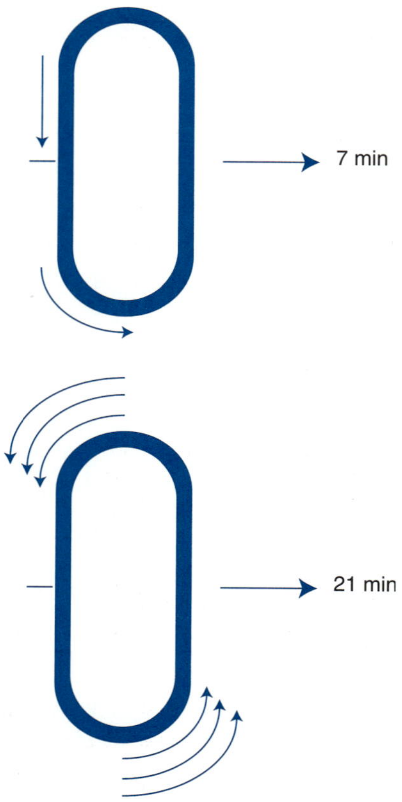

FIGURE 13.5 Records of Solving Proportion Problems

3. Nancy was collecting rocks. She hoped to collect at least 20 unusual rocks when her family was visiting the desert. If she collected 4 special rocks every 25 minutes, how long would it take her to collect 20 rocks at that rate?
4. Sophia noticed that she missed 2 spelling words on a test of 25 words. She wondered how many she would miss on the review test of 100 words if she missed at that rate. When she figured this out, she decided she should study a little more for the review test. Do you agree with her decision? Why?

When children understand how to solve proportions and show that they have constructed the idea of relative comparisons, ask them to *estimate solutions* before solving the proportions. Class discussion of estimation strategies will give some students opportunities to model their thinking for others to observe. Students should be able to estimate and judge the reasonableness of solutions before they are introduced to writing proportions for problems.

After several lessons in which children solve problems involving proportions using materials, tables, diagrams, or mental computation and demonstrate that they can estimate solutions, they study writing proportions. Distribute the papers they completed recently showing their solutions with tables or diagrams. Ask them to write math sentences for these problems. Remind them that they know how to write ratios and math sentences that show equalities. After time to solve the problem of writing proportions, have them share their ideas. If they do not work out the standard format, $\frac{a}{b} = \frac{c}{d}$, introduce it using numbers from one problem by saying, "This is the way many people write math sentences for problems of this type, and it will be useful for you to know about it."

Continue the lesson in the same or another period to help them understand the unit-rate and factor-of-change methods for solving proportions. (These methods will have been used intuitively as strategies by students when they solved proportions using materials, tables, diagrams, or mental computation.) They learn that: (1) Using the unit-rate method, you rename the known ratio so that one number in the ratio is 1, and you solve for the missing number by finding equivalent ratios. For example, to solve $\frac{2}{6} = \frac{4}{x}$, think $\frac{2}{6} = \frac{1}{3} = \frac{4}{12}$, so x is 12. (2) Using the factor-of-change method, you determine how many times greater one number in one ratio is than its corresponding number in the other ratio and use that factor to find the unknown. For example: to solve $\frac{4}{5} = \frac{12}{x}$, think $4 \times 3 = 12$, so $x = 3 \times 5 = 15$. Help them relate the methods to their knowledge of equivalent fractions.

A chart summarizing the discussion can be made and posted. The chart should mention that the solution should be estimated as a check on computation.

Ask groups to write math sentences to solve several story problems involving proportions and to find solutions. Have them share their math sentences and strategies for solution and explain the reasonableness of their solutions.

ACTIVITY 13.10
Writing Proportions.

Children learn that proportions can be written to reflect within-ratios or between-ratios by reflecting on their work and that of others in their class. Using problems such as in Activity 13.9, ask groups of learners to solve the problems by writing proportions whenever possible in more than one way. If they cannot do this for a problem (e.g., Charles bought 3 apples for $.40. What would 6 cost at that rate?), ask probing questions, such as, "You have written your proportions as apples to cost. What about known apples to apples and cost to unknown cost? How would you write that math sentence? Would that give you the same solution? Let's try it." Guide pupils to notice that the labels attached to the numbers in the proportions are dissimilar in one case and similar in the other. Ask them to write proportions both ways for other problems.

When they finish their work, students share their proportions, solution strategies, and solutions. It should become evident that both approaches give the same answer. The evidence from working with proportions rather than a proof is appropriate for young learners.

Continue the activity on another day by asking one half of the class to use dissimilar labels when setting up proportions (within ratios) and the other half of the class to use similar labels (between ratios). Compare solutions and strategies, helping learners realize that one approach may lend itself to an easier solution than the other in a particular problem but that the answers are always the same.

ACTIVITY 13.11
Using Calculators to Solve Proportions.

Most proportions do not involve whole-number division and multiplication as in the problem examples given so far in this section but, rather, proportions such as $\frac{3}{4} = \frac{5}{x}$ that entail work with fractions. They should usually be solved using the calculator. Deciding which operations to use when working with the calculator contributes more to students' understanding of mathematics than computing the answer with paper and pencil.

Give students story or number problems that involve proportions to solve using their calculators. After they complete their work, discuss the thinking involved in solving the problem before they used their calculator, in estimating the solutions, and in deciding if the answers made sense. Four such story problems are:

1. Every 3 minutes 8 drops of water drip from my faucet. If the plumber takes 95 minutes to arrive to fix the leak, how many drops of water have been wasted?
2. Plastic spoons cost 3 for $.10. We need 250 for the school ice cream social. How much will they cost?
3. Franklin School is going to sell stickers that show the school logo. They will cost 2 for 7 cents. How many can I buy for $.50?
4. If my pet parrot eats 145 milliliters of nuts in 3 days, how many milliliters will she eat in a week?

ACTIVITY 13.12
Making up Silly Proportion Problems.

Ask children in groups or in pairs to write 2 or 3 silly problems that involve proportions and to solve their problems. Groups or individuals then exchange problems to solve. Examples that would involve the use of calculators are:

1. If there are 455 beans per 7 chili servings, how many beans are there for 19 servings?
2. If there are 176 leaves per 4 rose bushes, how many leaves are there per 18 rose bushes?
3. If 40 clowns go with 90 hula hoops, how many hula hoops go with 8 clowns?
4. There are 55 buckets for 165 mops at the Sure-Thing Cleaning maintenance center. For a large commercial building cleanup, 21 mops are needed. If the relation of buckets and mops is the same in their cleaning operation as in storage, how many buckets would go with those mops?

As children report on the solutions to these problems, have them explain why the answers makes sense. As mentioned previously, developing this habit is an important aspect of learning.

ACTIVITY 13.13
Change the Ratio.

Have students study the ratio of parts of their bodies, for example, hand to forearm or foot to hand, or they can investigate the ratios of the parts of bodies of animals.

Next, they make drawings of imaginary animals or people with parts of their bodies in ratios different from those they discovered. Kilman (1993) suggests relating the study of stories involving giants, such as *Gulliver's Travels,* to the study of scaling and ratio.

Activity for the Classroom 13.2. Write three proportion problems. Ask four upper-grade children to solve these problems any way they wish and think out loud as they solve them. Write up your reactions to their thinking about the proportion problems and their solutions.

Comparing Ratios

Learners can compare ratios by using scaling or solving proportions. In the first lessons, groups solve easy comparison problems such as the following. The class can be reminded of scaling strategies and solving proportions before they begin their work.

1. Stephen bought 3 red apples for $.99 and 2 green apples for $.60. Did one green or red apple cost more?
2. Two cans of tomatoes at one supermarket cost $.98. At the other store, the same brand sells for 3 cans for $1.35. Which store has the better buy on canned tomatoes?
3. The zoo keeper in the Harbor Zoo gives the 4 monkeys 16 bananas each day. The zoo keeper in the Central Zoo gives the 2 monkeys 10 bananas each day. Which monkeys get the most bananas?
4. Erika plays ball 2 afternoons out of 4. Connie plays ball 4 afternoons out of 7. Who plays ball more often?

After groups complete their work, they share solutions and strategies.

Students who use alternate strategies are always given time to explain their thinking. The question, "Why does your answer make sense?" is asked frequently to give pupils opportunities to estimate and to use inexact quantities in their comparisons. For example, in Problem 4, a student might say, "Two out of 4 is 1 out of 2; 1 out of 2 would be 4 out of 8, but Connie plays 4 out of 7 afternoons, which is playing more than 4 out of 8 afternoons, so she plays more often than Erika."

When ratios in comparison problems are not equivalent, children can be asked to tell how to make the ratios equivalent. For example, in the monkey problem, so that the monkeys at both zoos would get the same number of bananas, the zoo keeper at Harbor Zoo would need to give his monkeys 4 more bananas each day or the zoo keeper at Central Zoo would need to give his monkeys 2 less bananas each day. (Why?) Pupils can also be asked to write problems comparing ratios.

After working with problems that can be solved with unit ratios and do not involve fractions in the comparison, more complex comparison problems can be introduced to learners that have the ability and confidence to be challenged by such problems. Calculators should be used to solve these problems. After solving the problems, students should share their solutions and discuss the reasonableness of their solutions and their solution strategies. The problems would be similar to:

1. At the Harden School picnic, there were 3 adults for every 20 students. At the Beacon School picnic, there were 4 adults for every 25 students. Two hundred students attended each picnic. Which school picnic had fewer adults in attendance?
2. Sally made lemon concentrate for her tables at the school picnic by using 2 tablespoons of sugar for 5 tablespoons of lemon juice. Frank used 4 tablespoons of sugar for 9 tablespoons of lemon juice. Which concentrate was sweeter? How could they make their lemonade have the same sweet taste?
3. At the picnic, Grace used lemon concentrate and water in the ratio of 2 parts concentrate to 7 parts water to make lemonade for her table. George made the

lemonade for his table in the ratio of 3 parts of concentrate to 12 parts of water. Which lemonade was more "lemony?"

4. Bill paid $12.56 for 4 sandwiches for the people at his table at the school picnic. Deborah paid $15.30 for 5 sandwiches for the people at her table. Whose sandwiches were more expensive?

LEARNING PERCENT

Percent is a ratio concept involving the comparison of a number to 100. For example, *20 percent* means 20 per 100 or 20 for 100. The percent symbol is %. For computational purposes, a percent is expressed as a decimal (.20) or a fraction (20/100). Problems involving percents are often written in equation form, and the numbers given special names.

- 20% of 60 = .20 × 60 = 12
- 20% (.20; $\frac{20}{100}$) is the *rate*
- 60 is the *base*
- 12 is the *percentage*

Percents abound in real life. For example, merchandise for sale, taxes to be paid, and reports of surveys are given in percents. However, percent is not well understood by learners and students performed rather poorly on percent items included in the fourth National Assessment of Educational Progress (NAEP). For example, only 30 % of seventh-grade students could give .9 as a percent and only 32% correctly answered the question, "What is 4% of 75?" (Kouba, Brown, Carpenter, Lindquist, Silver, and Swafford, 1988).

There are three types of percent problems. Examples with the two commonly used solution formats, proportion and equation, follow.

Find percent of a number (percentage). The price of Jose's dad's new car was listed as $15,000, but he got a discount of 10%. What was the discount in dollars?

Proportion	Equation
$\frac{10}{100} = \frac{N}{\$15{,}000}$	$.10 \times \$15{,}000 = N$

Find the percent (rate). Jose's dad got $1,500 off the $15,000 price of his new car. What percent did he get off?

Proportion	Equation
$\frac{\$1{,}500}{\$15{,}000} = \frac{N}{100}$	$N \times \$15{,}000 = \$1{,}500$

Find the original number (base). Jose's dad got 10% off the listed price of his new car. That amounted to $1,500. What was the original price?

Proportion	Equation
$\frac{10}{100} = \frac{\$1{,}500}{N}$	$.10\,N = \$1{,}500$

Percent is usually studied in grade 5 or 6. Elementary school children learn to solve only problems involving finding the percent of a number.

Introduction to Percent

The introduction to percents discussed here suggests using children's knowledge of problem solving with proportions or decimals, rather than beginning with percent as an idea that is learned and then applied to problem solving. In this way, children can reexamine their understanding of problem solving with known concepts and gain insight into a new idea that is really only new terminology and notation. Instruction stressing prior knowledge of ratio and proportion is discussed first; instruction based on knowledge of decimals, the equation approach, second.

Proportion Approach. Proportion problems in which one ratio has 100 as the second number begins students' study of percents when the proportion approach is used. Several lessons should include such problems. The vocabulary of percent is not introduced at this time. Examples of problems are:

1. A newspaper report says that in our town the unemployment rate is 10 out of 100 workers. If 30,000 people are employed in our town, how many are out of work?
2. Ira paid $5.00 for school supplies. The sales tax on his purchase was 5 cents for every dollar? How much sales tax did he pay?
3. Hanna had a coupon for corn flakes that said 25 cents off for every dollar of cost. The corn flakes cost $2.00? How much less did she pay for the corn flakes?

Students solve these problems in groups or pairs so that they can discuss their strategies with others. After most have completed their work, they share solutions and strategies. It is expected that children will use the unit-rate or the factor-of-change method.

After students successfully solve these problems in one or more lessons, they are told that there is a special name and symbol to designate ratios with 100 as the second number: "percent" and "%." Some of the problems are reintroduced with the new words or symbols, and students compare the earlier wording and the percent language. They also discuss how their previous solutions apply to the reworded problems. They practice rewriting ratios in the form $\frac{N}{100}$ as percents and show the meaning of percents using hundred squares (Figure 13.6). The task directions are to think the answers to items such as the following and to show the meaning of their responses using hundred squares:

- $\frac{22}{100} = \ \%$
- $\frac{3}{100} = \ \%$
- $\frac{N}{100} = 6\%$
- $\frac{N}{100} = 72\%$

When students demonstrate that they understand the meaning of percent and can write ratios as percents, they write math sentences for several story problems in which the percent of a number is to be found. They work in pairs or groups for this task. When finished, they share their math sentences and explain their meaning. Finally, they write math sentences and solve the percent problems.

Equation Approach. Some would introduce learners to the equation approach first. If your school's curriculum calls for such a sequence, you can use the same steps as outlined for first teaching percent as a ratio with 100 as the second number:

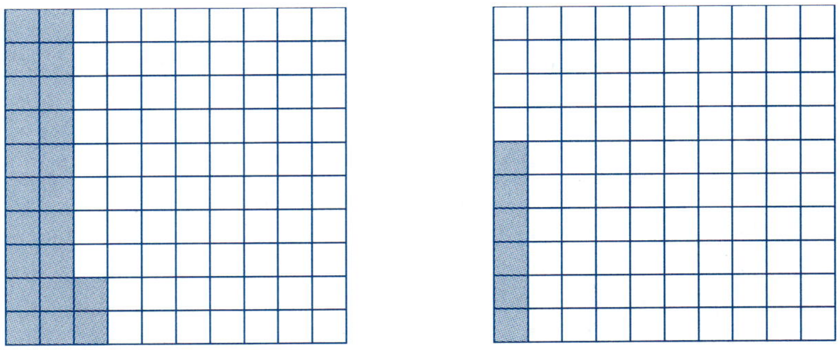

$\frac{22}{100} = 22\%$ $\frac{6}{100} = 6\%$

FIGURE 13.6 One Hundred Squares Representing Percent

1. Give story problems from real life involving hundredths of a number for students to solve in groups. The problems should make sense when rewritten with percents. A problem example is: In a recent survey, .65 of 70 students polled said they would vote for Suzanne Jones for Central School Council. How many claimed they would vote for Suzanne?
2. After students solve such problems successfully, explain that percents are hundredths. Distribute the problems rewritten so that the hundredths numbers are replaced by numbers with the percent symbol. Tell students that both versions mean the same. Have them read both versions and compare them.
3. Have students complete exercises that ask them to write hundredths as percents and percents as hundredths and to show the meaning of what they have done using hundred squares.
4. Have students write math sentences for story problems for percent of a number and explain the meaning of the math sentences. The sentences are rewritten using decimals.
5. Have students solve story problems that involve percent of a number.

Students should be involved in learning activities for extension of percent concepts during the time when the preceding sequence is being followed. Examples of such activities follow.

ACTIVITY 13.14
Percent Games.

Prepare cards for a matching game. The cards show percent, diagrams of hundredths shaded on hundred squares, or symbols naming hundredths (Figure 13.7). The game is played like *Fish* or *Rummy*. *War* (see Box 3.1) can also be played with these cards.

ACTIVITY 13.15
Newspapers and Percents.

Have children prepare a bulletin board that gives examples of percents in newspaper or magazine articles. Beside each clipping, the meaning of the percent reported can be explained in a sentence or two.

ACTIVITY 13.16
Using Decimal Wheels.

To help students relate percents to decimals, ask them to show percents on the decimal wheels introduced when they studied decimals (Figure 13.8). If they work in pairs, one student can name a percent and the other can show it on the wheel. Discuss their reactions to the activity.

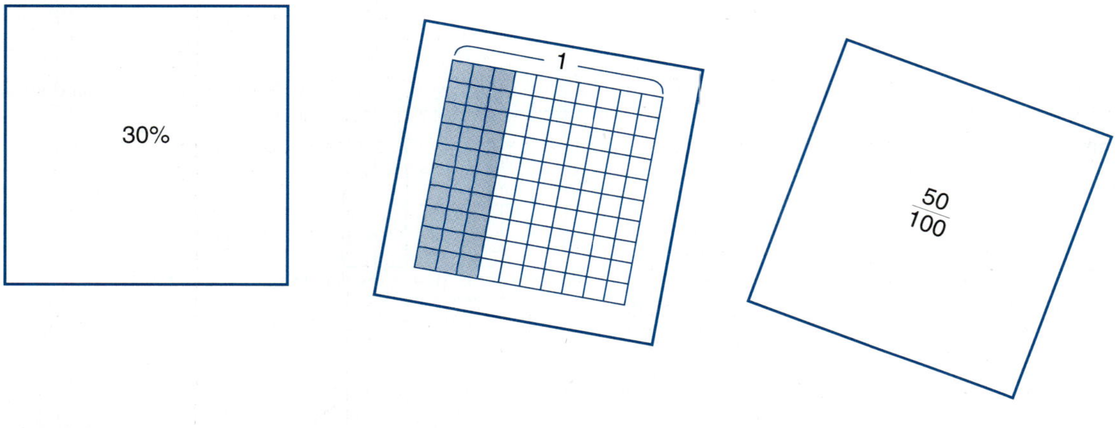

FIGURE 13.7 Cards for Percent Games

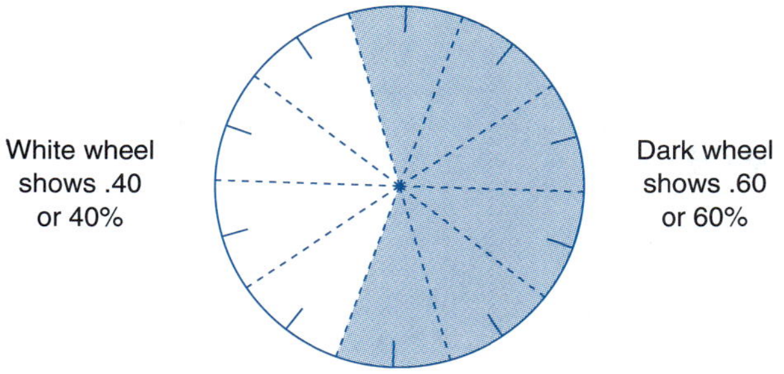

FIGURE 13.8 Decimal Wheels Showing Percents

ACTIVITY 13.17
Common Fractions, Decimal Equivalents, and Percents.

Begin by asking groups to choose and list three fractions equivalent to decimal fractions (e.g., $\frac{1}{2} = .5$). When they finish the task, ask them to use their lists to give fractions equivalent to percents. When learners realize that $\frac{1}{2} = .5 = .50 = 50\%$ and that $\frac{1}{4} = .25 = 25\%$, ask them how they would determine the percents equivalent to other common fractions. Approaches include finding equivalent fractions and renaming ($\frac{1}{5} = \frac{20}{100} = 20\%$), using decimal wheels, and using calculators to divide. Let them choose some common fractions and any approach they choose to find percents equivalent to these common fractions.

Those who use calculators will be introduced to terminating and repeating decimals. Have them discuss their findings and suggest that all learners use calculators to confirm the findings reported. Ask questions so that all learners understand these decimals. Tell students that these decimals are called *terminating decimals* and *repeating decimals*. For follow-up, have students work in groups to make charts of common fractions and percent equivalents (Table 13.1). Display the charts for student reference.

Reader Activity 13.2

Use your decimal wheels to determine decimals and percents equivalent to common fractions. Evaluate this approach for learners.

ACTIVITY 13.18
More Than One Hundred Percent.

Give students percents that are more than 100%, and ask them to show the meaning of these percents using grid paper (Figure 13.9). Working in groups, different learners can complete different examples. As they complete their examples, they should discuss how they thought to complete the assignment.

ASSESSING RATIO, PROPORTION, AND PERCENT LEARNING

Assessing the learning of ratio, proportion, and percent takes place as you observe, interview, and test children and study their work products. It involves mainly noting how students approach proportion problems. The most important question to be answered is, "Can students use proportional reasoning?" You also notice stu-

TABLE 3.1 Percent Equivalents for Common Fractions

$\frac{1}{2} = .50 = 50\%$	$\frac{1}{6} = .166\ldots = 16\frac{2}{3}\%$
$\frac{1}{3} = .333\ldots = 33\frac{1}{3}\%$	$\frac{1}{7} = .142857142857\ldots = 14\frac{2}{7}\%$
$\frac{2}{3} = .666\ldots = 66\frac{2}{3}\%$	$\frac{1}{7} = .125 = 12.5\%$
$\frac{1}{4} = .25 = 25\%$	$\frac{1}{9} = .111\ldots = 11\frac{1}{9}\%$
$\frac{1}{5} = .20 = 20\%$	$\frac{4}{10} = .10 = 10\%$

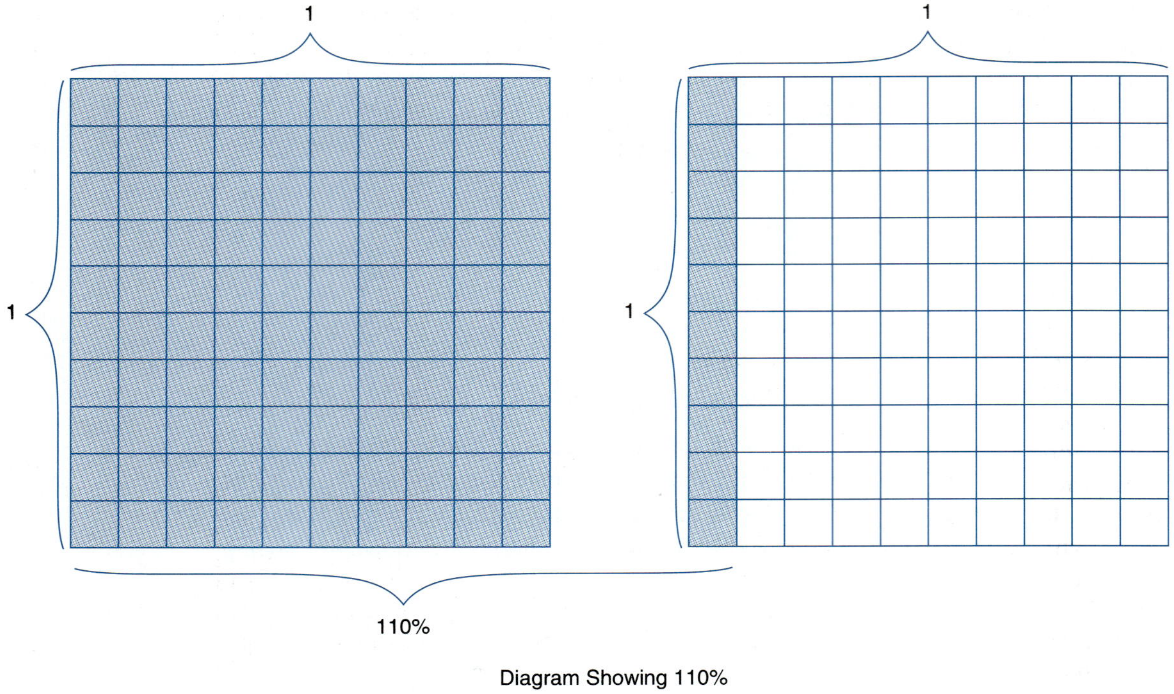

FIGURE 13.9 Grid Paper Representation of Percent Greater Than 100%

dents' interest in studying ratio, proportion, and percent ideas, and you observe if they relate their knowledge of these concepts to events or reports of events in and out of school.

Noting How Students Approach Problems

Ask children to find ratios in everyday life and to draw diagrams to illustrate these ratios. Have them find examples of percent in newspapers or TV ads or in social studies material; ask them to explain the meaning of their findings.

Have children explain how they solved a problem, or have them write out their thinking to find a solution and decide if they used proportional reasoning. Students often solve proportion problems by using difference comparisons and subtraction rather than using proportional reasoning, which involves dividing and multiplying. For example, they solve the comparison problem given earlier (Bill paid $12.56 for 4 sandwiches for the people at his table at the school picnic. Deborah paid $15.30 for 5 sandwiches for the people at her table. Whose sandwiches were more expensive?) by computing $15.30 – 12.56 = $2.74 and 5 – 4 = 1, and they say that Deborah paid more for her sandwiches. A correct solution is: If Bill paid at Deborah's rate, $15.30 for 5, which equals $3.06 for 1, he would pay $12.24 for 4 sandwiches, which is less than he paid, so his sandwiches were more expensive.

Other assessment suggestions are:

1. Give children numbers, and ask them to write proportion or percent problems using the numbers and to solve one or more of the problems they have written. Note the extent to which their thinking involves proportional reasoning.
2. Ask children to estimate solutions to proportion or percent problems or to explain orally or in writing why their solutions are reasonable.
3. Have them make comparisons between ratios as is to be done in several of the problems that were presented. When ratios are not equivalent, ask children how to make them equivalent and to note the thinking involved.

Children who do not understand proportional reasoning should have experiences with manipulatives and diagrams and opportunities to reflect on their experiences. They also need to discuss their ideas with other students who can challenge their illogical thinking and thus encourage them to examine their ideas more critically.

SUMMARY

This chapter gave ideas for introducing students to ratios, proportions, and percent. The final section discussed assessing proportional reasoning. The discussion emphasized that instruction should begin with experiences familiar to learners and include work with materials, scaling, tables, and diagrams. Interactive teaching here, as well as in other chapters, stresses that problems are the vehicle for introducing concepts. The problems assigned should be those that children can solve using prior learning. After children solve problems, they discuss their solutions and their thinking. During some discussions, the concepts embedded in the problems are highlighted and new vocabulary is introduced.

Because dealing with ratios, proportions, and percent involves proportional reasoning, these topics are difficult for many elementary school children. Only when learners demonstrate understanding at a concrete level should symbols and notation be introduced.

REFERENCES

Behr, Merlyn J., Richard Lesh, Thomas R. Post, and Edward A. Silver. (1983). "Rational Number Concepts." In *Acquisition of Mathematics Concepts and Processes,* edited by Richard Lesh and Marsha Landau, pp. 91–126. New York: Academic Press.

Harrison, Bruce, Selwyn Brindley, and Marshall P. Bye. (May 1989). "Allowing for Students' Cognitive Levels in the Teaching of Fractions and Ratios." *Journal for Research in Mathematics Education* 20: 288–300.

Hoffer, Alan R., and Shirley Ann K. Hoffer. (1992). "Ratios and Proportional Thinking." In *Teaching Mathematics in Grades K–8: Research Based Methods,* 2nd ed., edited by Thomas R. Post, pp. 303–330. Boston: Allyn & Bacon.

Karplus, Robert, Steven Pulos, and Elizabeth K. Stage. (1983). "Proportional Reasoning of Early Adolescents." In *Acquisition of Mathematics Concepts and Processes,* edited by Richard Lesh and Marsha Landau, pp. 45–90. New York: Academic Press.

Kilman, Marlene. (February 1993). "Integrating Mathematics and Literature in the Elementary Classroom." *Arithmetic Teacher* 40: 318–321.

Kouba, Vicky L., Catherine A. Brown, Thomas P. Carpenter, Mary M. Lindquist, Edward A. Silver, and Jane O. Swafford. (April 1988). "Results of the Fourth NAEP Assessment of Mathematics: Number, Operations, and Word Problems." *Arithmetic Teacher* 35: 14–19.

National Council of Teachers of Mathematics. (1989). *Curriculum and Evaluation Standards for School Mathematics.* Reston, VA: Author.

Post, Thomas R., Merlyn J. Behr, and Richard Lesh. (1988). "Proportionality and the Development of Prealgebra Understandings." In *The Ideas of Algebra, K–12,* edited by Arthur F. Coxford and Albert P. Shulte, pp. 78–90. Reston, VA: National Council of Teacher of Mathematics.

Quintero, Ana Helvia. (May 1987). "Helping Children Understand Ratios." *Arithmetic Teacher* 34: 17–21.

SOFTWARE RESOURCES

Conquering Percents
Company: MECC
Computer: Apple
Grade level: 5–8

Explore percents, and solve percent problems by estimating and painting percents of a figure. Includes game using percents, fractions, and ratios.

Gears
Company: Sunburst
Computer: Apple, IBM, Tandy
Grade level: 6 and up

Working with gears and building a gear factory give experiences with ratios and decimals.

IBM Elementary Mathematics Series: Math Concepts
Level III, Unit 6, Lesson 25
Company: IBM/EduQuest
Computer: IBM
Grade level: 6–9

Work with equivalent fractions and percents. Use number lines for estimation of percent. Teaches changing decimals to percents and comparing fractions, decimals, and percents.

CHAPTER 14

Studying Statistics and Probability

▪ INTRODUCTORY PROBLEM ▪

Your class is divided into committees to study environmental issues. Two committees are studying air quality, two, water quality, and two, the land and its use. The committees have decided that they will not duplicate each other's research. The two air quality committees will share research on precipitation and pollution; the two water quality committees will share research on pollutants, their sources and kinds, as well as information regarding the condition of state lakes, rivers, and streams. The two committees studying the land will share research on the wildlife of fields, woods, and wetlands, endangered species, and information that is available on changes in the world population of birds, animals, insects, fish, and plants. As you study this chapter, decide how you would help the committees use statistics and probability in their reports.

INTRODUCTION

The National Council of Teachers of Mathematics (1989) recommends that statistics and probability be included in the curriculum at all grades (see Standard 11 in Curriculum Standards for Grades K–4, and Standards 10 and 11 for Grades 5–8, Appendix A). Children should study these topics to relate to the world in which they live, understand content subjects, develop mathematical knowledge and thinking processes, and form positive attitudes toward mathematics.

To understand their world, students must deal with information that often includes references to statistics and probability concepts. For example, knowledge of statistics and probability is needed to understand reports such as:

- Probability of heavy snow by weekend is 40%.
- Principal reports that students at Tyler School all score above the 75th percentile in mathematics.
- Students in the state are reported to spend an average of 5 hours 10 minutes in elementary school each day.
- Agency survey says that 50% of population not prepared for major disaster.
- Population growth in Third World countries is estimated to be 4% yearly.

Science and social studies are more meaningful when integrated with mathematics. For example, the study of plant growth and animal populations, community characteristics, and environmental problems are clarified by statistical and probability concepts.

The concepts and skills developed while studying statistics and probability contribute to mathematical knowledge and enable learners to make further progress in their study of mathematics. The study of statistics and probability involves mathematical problem solving and reasoning, as well as work with counting, whole and fractional numbers, and ratios.

Certain psychological outcomes also result from the study of statistics and probability. These content areas can be interesting and exciting for children (Leutzinger, 1990). Collecting and presenting data is enjoyable, and playing games with an element of chance is fun. From an initial positive experience with statistics and probability, motivation to learn more mathematics and a favorable attitude toward it can develop.

The role of statistics and probability in the elementary school curriculum is discussed in the two main sections of this chapter, Studying Statistics and Studying Probability. Each section gives an overview of what is to be learned and describes interactive teaching approaches and activities to enable children to develop a knowledge of statistics and probability appropriate for their developmental level. The third section, Assessing Learning of Statistics and Probability, and the fourth, Summary, conclude the chapter.

STUDYING STATISTICS

Statistics involves collecting, organizing, representing, analyzing, and interpreting numerical information, called data. Learning statistics occurs over time. Each year children learn more about dealing with data (Russell and Friel, 1989).

Students begin their study of statistics by engaging in a variety of activities that involve real-life data. It is by collecting and handling data meaningful to them that children learn statistical concepts (Shaw, 1984). Work with data relevant to their lives enables learners to analyze and interpret data collected by others and presented in the media and textbooks.

Teachers use an interactive teaching approach to help children become familiar with statistical concepts. Five steps, adapted to the developmental level of learners, make up the teaching sequence:

1. Help children understand or formulate problems that are solved by gathering information.
2. Help children plan and carry out the collection of data.
3. Guide children in organizing and representing their data.
4. Question children to enable them to analyze and interpret their data. Listen to them, and use their responses in the discussion.
5. Provide opportunities for children to extend their experiences.

How to use these steps is illustrated in the sections, Beginning Work with Data Collection and Representation, Later Work with Data Collection and Representation, Analyzing and Interpreting Data, and Extending Understanding of Graphs.

Beginning Work with Data Collection and Representation

Graphs communicate numerical information through diagrammatic representation. They combine numerical, visual, and verbal information in ways that enable readers to grasp relationships among data. Choate and Okey (1981) claim that graphing in the primary grades can enrich every unit of study. For example, graphs can be made of temperatures (inside/outside), leaf perimeters, sinking or floating objects, and frequency counts of words or letters in reading material. Beginning work with data collection and representation involves making real-people graphs, chart graphs, and bar graphs.

It is important for learners to be involved in decisions about what to graph rather than being told what information they will gather and work with. Making choices fosters independence and responsibility and leads to intrinsic motivation to learn (deCharms, 1984). However, young children need some direction in working with graphs.

Initially, ask a question whose answer can be given by you and the class working cooperatively. For example, you can say, "We will be a school family for many weeks. We need to know about each other so that we can enjoy being with one another. What will help us know about each other?" You and the children (they may need some prompting) tell what you and they would like to know. *Real-people graphs* are introduced as a way to help answer the questions.

Generally real-people graphs include only two categories so that young children will be able to make comparisons. Characteristics to examine using real-people graphs include:

- Boys and girls in the class
- Children who live in houses and children who live in apartments
- Children who ride the bus to school and children who walk
- Children who have pets and children who have no pets
- Children who have brothers (sisters) at the school they are attending, and those who do not have brothers (sisters) at the school they are attending

To make real-people graphs, children sort themselves by moving to a part of the room designated for those with a certain characteristic. Then each group sharing a like attribute makes a line. After children are arranged in lines, they count the children in each line and determine which is the greater (and lesser) group. At first, qualitative comparisons are made. For example, there are more boys than girls in our class. After children study numbers greater than ten, quantitative comparisons are made.

Ask children in what way they are alike and to look carefully at those in their line so that they will know who are like them. Next, ask them to look at those in the other line so that they will find out about them. Continue to ask questions until children understand that each group has individuals alike in a certain way. Some children can be asked to name two or three children near to them who are both like and unlike them in the characteristic being examined.

Children next participate in making *chart graphs.* Such graphs are made by fastening pictures or objects in rows or columns to large sheets of paper or a small bulletin board. The paper can have grids or be plain (Figure 14.1). Cuphooks for holding objects can be attached to the bulletin board. Objects used include paper clips, clothes pins, curtain rod rings, stickers, or tags on which pupils can write their names. Sticky notes are very useful for chart graphs. Each child can write or draw on his or her own sticky note. Chart graphs do not have numbers or scales. Children count the objects on the chart graph to analyze the data.

Chart graphs can be introduced by suggesting that a permanent record be made of the people graph so that others will know about the class. Children are

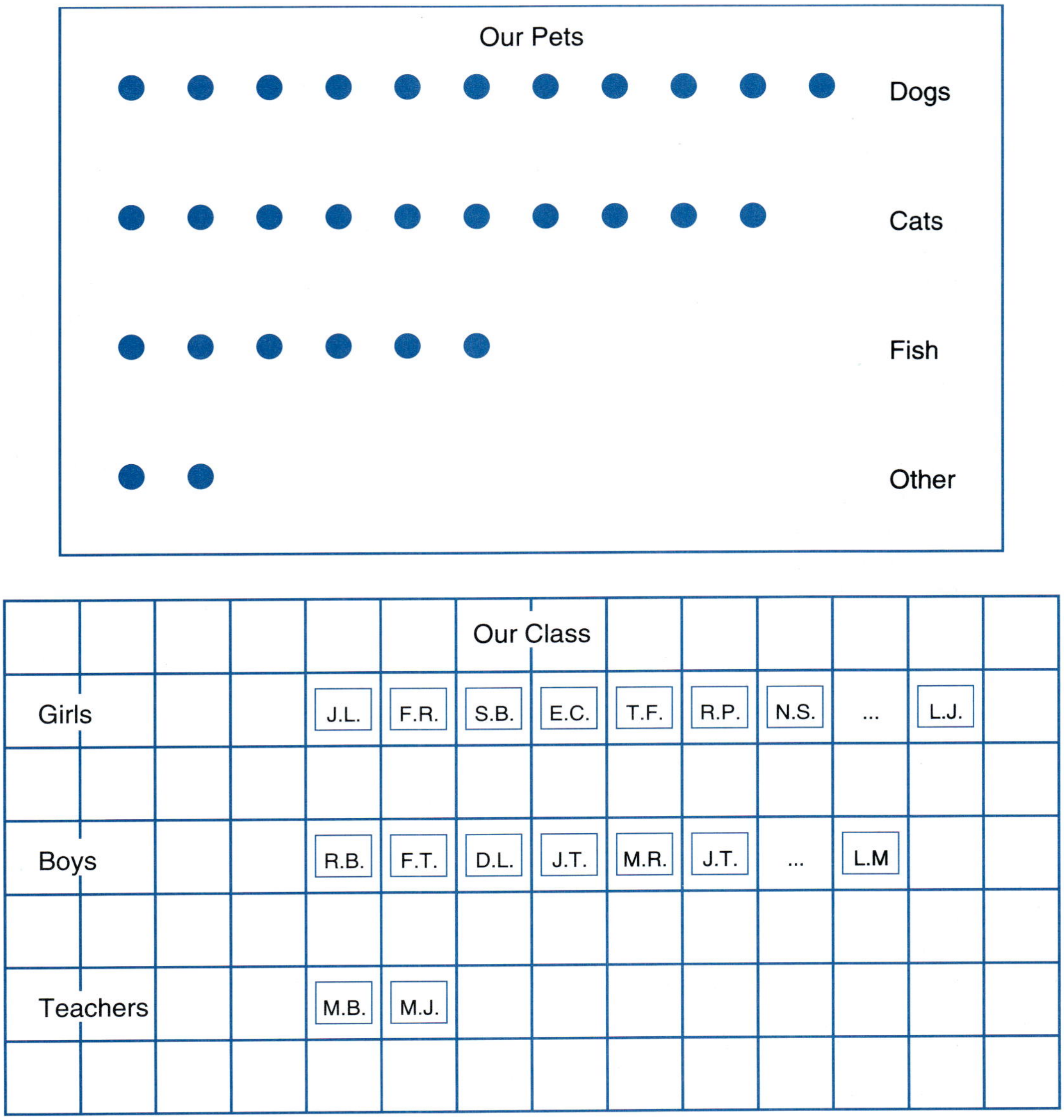

FIGURE 14.1 Chart Graphs

given objects to use on the chart graph to represent them. Children discuss the difference between the people graph and the chart graph, noting that an object stands for a child.

Chart graphs can also be introduced by asking children what they could tell their parents about the class. Their suggestions are the basis for chart graphs. Chart graphs can be displayed for "Open House" or duplicated and sent home in a newsletter to inform the parents about the class.

Chart graphs provide opportunities for counting and comparing. They are useful for teaching number in a setting meaningful to learners. They can be made for data such as:

- Sex of children
- Hair color
- Birthdays by months
- Eye colors
- Alphabet letters that begin children's names
- Number of members in children's families

ACTIVITY 14.1
Making Chart Graphs.

Fill discarded plastic margarine tubs or plastic or paper bags with any free or inexpensive material such as blocks, bolts, nuts, jar lids, keys, rocks, shells, pasta, beans, play coins, small plastic toys, and the like to prepare Make-a-Graph tubs or bags. For the youngest children, have only two categories of a single attribute, such as shape or color. Later, include objects that can be sorted by more attribute categories, for example, green, orange, and white pasta. Put 12 or less objects in a bag. Make reusable grids of plastic or oilcloth. The size of the grid is determined by the space available for children to use and the materials supplied for graphing. The cells of the grids should be large enough for any material in a Make-a-Graph tub or bag.

Children individually use the materials in a tub or bag, placing them on the grid, one object to a square, after deciding how they will be sorted and "graphed." Each child should have an opportunity to tell about his or her graph, communicating two or three observations to you, an aide, or another child, saying for example, "There are more black beans than white beans. There are more black beans than red beans."

Bar graphs are introduced next (Figure 14.2). Bar graphs for use in beginning instruction are made on grids and have labels giving data characteristics on one axis and a number line on the other axis. An object is designated by making a mark or by coloring in a square. You can introduce bar graphs by showing a chart graph made by the class and a bar graph you make for the same data. Ask the children to study the two graphs to determine how they are alike and different and to read the bar graph.

During the discussion, model the procedure for making a bar graph, stressing how to choose and write labels and how to make and use a number line. The class discusses the procedure, and the steps are listed on a chart:

How to Make a Bar Graph

1. Determine what data I have.
2. Name my graph.
3. Decide on the groups.
4. Sort by groups.
5. Count each group.

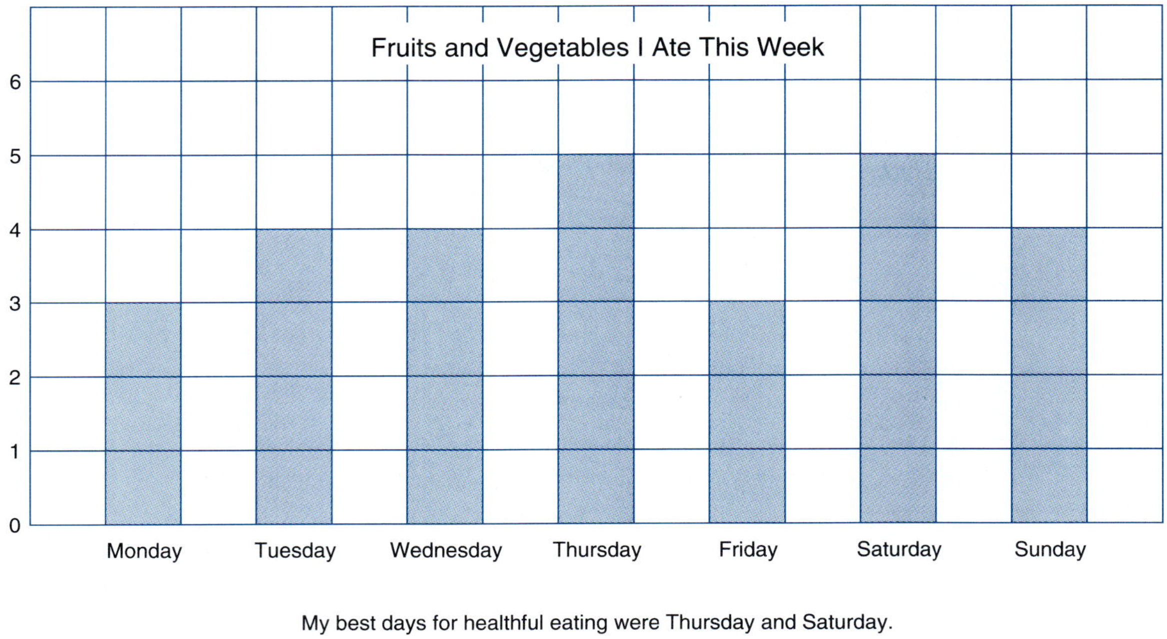

FIGURE 14.2 Bar Graph

6. Make a table or list of the number in each group.
7. Choose a grid large enough for the graph.
8. Use labels on the bottom of the grid.
9. Use the left side of the grid as a number line and write numbers. (Labels and numbers can be reversed.)
10. Make bars by filling in squares on the grid to show the groups and the number in each group that are given on the table or list I have made. Make the bars the same width.
11. Check my work.
12. Write a sentence to tell about the graph.

Following these steps, children (individually or in pairs) make bar graphs with your guidance. (The materials for the Make-a-Graph activity can be used in the first five steps.) They share their graphs with the class by explaining the data shown on the graphs. An alternative is for children to ask class members to read the graphs.

ACTIVITY 14.2
Making Bar Graphs.

When children have had experience with making graphs, they are able to work more independently. A possible procedure is: You introduce a topic, suggesting some data to be collected and the reason for its collection, and ask pupils to think of information they would find interesting to collect and study (Sullivan and O'Neil, 1980). For example, again at the beginning of a school year (or at a later time), say, "We are a special group. We have different likes and favorite things. I will give some preferences I would like to know about, and you can give some you would like to know. I think it would be interesting to know your favorite colors so that we can use those colors in our work. If I know your favorite pets, I will try to find stories about those animals. What other favorites would it be interesting to know about?" To get children started, you may need to state many options, from which they can choose a favorite of interest to them. Favorites include, among many:

TV show	Zoo animal
Ice cream flavor	Farm animal
Dessert	Story character
Fruit	Number
Vegetable	Song
Meat	Game
Candy	School subject

After class members have listed categories of favorites, one of two plans can be followed for collecting and representing the data. The first is for younger children, the second for older, more independent learners.

1. The class decides by voting what information to collect first (e.g., ice cream flavors preferred by class members). The data are collected by a show of hands, and you tabulate the responses on the chalkboard. The class reviews how to make graphs, and groups or pairs each make a bar graph of the data listed on the chalkboard. When finished, they share their work.
2. Groups are formed. Each group decides on a "favorite" to graph and reports its choice to you. You write a questionnaire that asks for information about these favorites. Each child fills out the questionnaire by writing his or her favorite for the categories requested. The questions together with responses on the questionnaire are cut apart. Each group is given: (1) responses to the question it is investigating; (2) a table format to use to organize the data; and (3) a grid for use to represent the data. After groups complete their graphs, they share them with the class. The graphs of favorites are displayed on a bulletin board and discussed.

Often, children in the late primary or middle grades can collect information independently or in groups for use in graphs. Examples are:

- The number of cars, trucks, or motorcycles I counted coming to school
- Temperature each hour of the school day

Activity for the Classroom 14.1. Give groups the same or different graphs to interpret. Have them report their conclusions. Decide if they have developed abilities to read and interpret graphs appropriate for their grade level or if they need further instruction.

Later Work with Data Collection and Representation

Reader Activity 14.1

Locate graphs in students' textbooks in subjects other than mathematics. Assess the use of these graphs by learners. Use your findings from *Activity in the Classroom 14.1* to make your assessment.

Children who can make bar graphs independently learn other graphing formats. Then they collect data independently, organize it in tables, and choose the type of graph useful for representing their data. They use school, community, science, historical, current event, and consumer information in their study. This section discusses New Types of Graphs, Introducing New Types of Graphs, Making a Graphing Assignment, and What to Graph.

New Types of Graphs. Older children study histograms, line graphs, stem-and-leaf plots, box-and-whisker plots, pictographs, and pie graphs. Stem-and-leaf plots and box-and-whisker plots are new forms of representation that have interesting potential use in elementary schools (Maher, 1981).

Histograms (also called bar graphs) give quantitative information on the vertical and horizontal axes (Figure 14.3). Variations of histograms are often found in

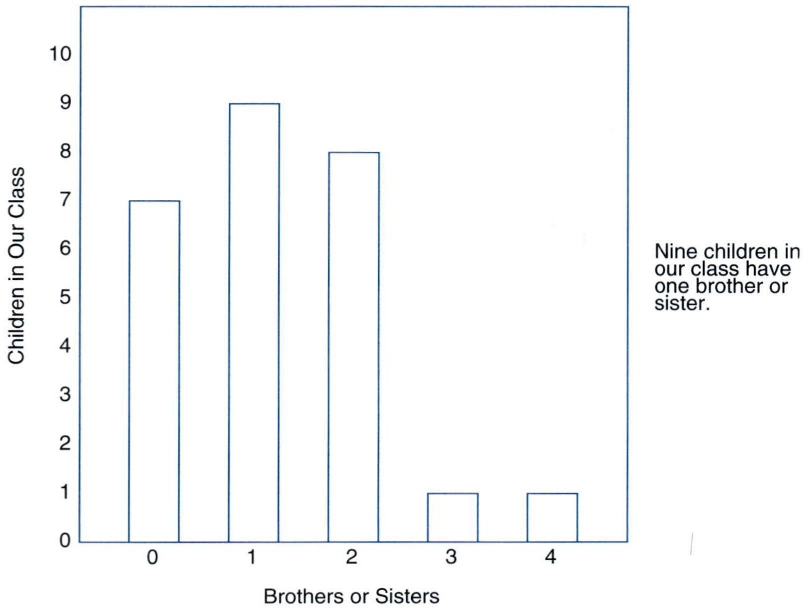

FIGURE 14.3 Histogram

printed material and include those in which: increments on the scales are greater than 1; a scale does not begin with 0; and a grid background is not used.

Line graphs are essentially bar graphs with the bars erased and the center points of the bars connected. Line graphs should be used to show continuous data, that is, data for which values on the graph could exist for any point between the points designated. Line graphs effectively show trends, such as temperature or population change, but different scales can give different impressions (Figure 14.4A and B).

Stem-and-leaf-plots can be constructed quickly. When the data are listed, the stem is made by noting the range of the tens numbers in the data and writing the tens digits of each number in sequence in a column of squares. The leaves are the ones digits of each number. The leaves are written in squares in the row beside their respective tens number in the stem of the graph. The stem numbers can be greater than tens and the leaf numbers greater than ones (e.g., the stem numbers can be rounded to hundreds and the leaves to tens). Figure 14.5 gives a stem-and-leaf plot for the number of pounds of paper collected by the students in

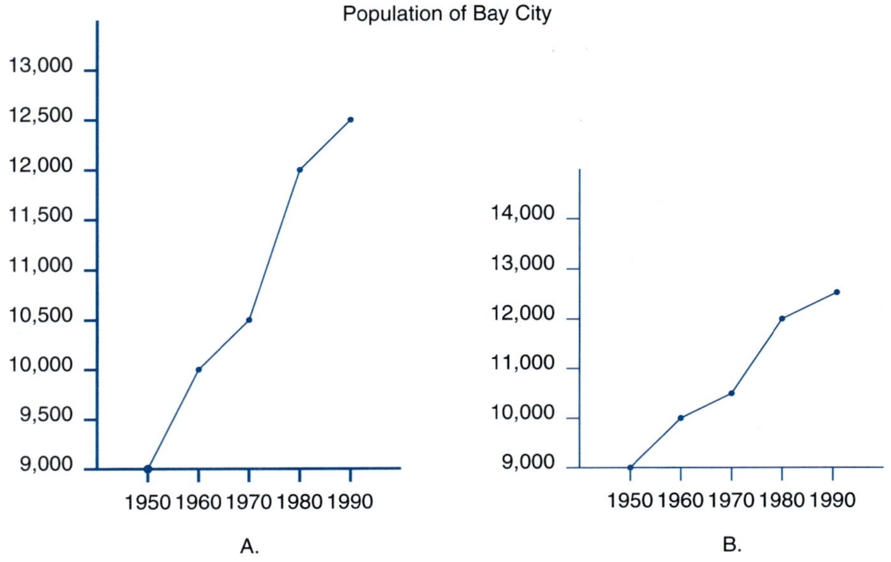

FIGURE 14.4 Line Graphs

FIGURE 14.5 Pounds of Newspapers Collected per Student in Ms. Girard's Class, Unordered Data, Stem-and-Leaf Plot

9	1			
8	3	3	8	0
7	2	0	6	
6	5	7	1	
5	2	8	5	
4	6	9	2	
3	5			
2	7	3		
1	4	7		
0	9			

Unordered Data
Stem-and-Leaf Plot

Ms. Girard's class. A list of the students in alphabetical order with the pounds of paper each collected is:

S. A., 83; E. B., 9; H. C., 46; F. D., 35; R. D., 83; R. E., 27; G. G., 72; L. H., 52; E. J., 88; C. K., 70; I. L., 14; J. M., 91; M. M., 65; K. N., 58; L. N., 67; N. P., 55; S. R., 76; T. R., 49; D. S., 80; J. V., 61; N. V., 17; E. W., 23; L. Z., 42.

Grouping or ordering of the data is not necessary, which makes the graph easy to prepare. The leaves can be ordered on a redo of the graph to order the data (Figure 14.6).

The stem-and-leaf plot can be used to compare data. The number of pounds collected by the students in Mr. Lewis's class and used in comparing Mr. Lewis's and Ms. Girard's classes are (Figure 14.7):

L. B., 95; M. B., 12; C. C., 19; D. C., 8; D. D., 41; K. D., 62; G. E., 88; S. E., 69; B. H., 59; L. H., 76; N. J., 75; S. L., 56; T. L., 70; R. M., 38; E. N., 28; C. O., 49; A. P., 27; D. P., 6; H. R., 66; V. R., 32; A. S., 83; W. V., 40.

The advantages of a stem-and-leaf plot are simplicity of construction and the visual picture of the clustering of the data shown by the plot.

Box-and-whisker plots (sometimes called box plots) reveal at a glance information about the center, distribution, and range of data. Figure 14.8 shows a box-and-whisker plot for the same data as shown by the stem-and-leaf plot in Figure 14.7. The box represents the center half of the data, one-fourth to the left and one-fourth to the right of the median, which is shown by a vertical line in the box. The mean can be shown by short lines outside the box. The lower quarter is shown by a whisker (line) to the left of the box and the upper quarter by a line to the right. Thus, the end points of the lines indicate the range.

FIGURE 14.6 Pounds of Newspapers Collected per Student in Ms. Girard's Class, Ordered Data, Stem-and-Leaf Plot

9	1			
8	0	3	3	8
7	0	2	6	
6	1	5	7	
5	2	5	8	
4	2	6	9	
3	5			
2	3	7		
1	4	7		
0	9			

Ordered Data
Stem-and-Leaf Plot

In *pictographs,* pictures represent values (Figure 14.9). Each picture can represent a large number. The values are estimated by rounding for ease of representation. The pictures chosen should lend themselves to division by halves, possibly fourths. A key gives the value of each picture.

Pie or circle graphs (Figure 14.10) show at a glance the relative value of categories of the data because the sections or wedges of the graph give fractions or percents of the circular regions (frequency may also be shown). To construct their own pie graphs, students must understand fractions, possibly percents, and angular measurement.

Introducing New Types of Graphs. If a *histogram* is an appropriate graph for representing data students have collected, they will probably be able to construct the histogram with little direction because of the similarity between the simple bar graphs they constructed in the primary grades and histograms. Both use "bars," but simple bar graphs have a number line on one axis, whereas histograms have numerical scales on two axes. If students need direction to construct the histogram, you can say, "How will your graph be like and different from a bar graph? What is needed on each dimension? Why? How will you make your scales?"

To introduce *line graphs,* suggest that students connect the midpoints of each bar to get a different picture of the data. After students carry out this suggestion on histograms they have produced, they discuss the kind of information given by the line graph and why the line graph is or is not superior to the histogram. Ask questions to bring out the fact that line graphs are used to represent continuous data. Discrete data should be represented by histograms so that the graph reader does not interpret discrete data as continuous.

FIGURE 14.7 Pounds of Newspapers Collected per Student in Two Third-Grade Classes, Stem-and-Leaf Plot

			5	9	1			
		8	3	8	0	3	3	8
	6	5	0	7	0	2	6	
	9	6	2	6	1	5	7	
		9	6	5	2	5	8	
	9	1	0	4	2	6	9	
		8	2	3	5			
		8	7	2	3	7		
		9	2	1	4	7		
		8	6	0	9			

Mr. Lewis Ms. Girard

The procedure for introducing either a *stem-and-leaf plot* or a *box-and-whisker plot* is: After children graph data using a histogram or line graph, point out that the same data may look different on a different kind of graph. Show the same data you have collected on a histogram and the new graph (stem-and-leaf or box-and-whisker plot). Ask students to study the two graphs. Question them so that they note the distinguishing characteristics of the new graph and understand how to read it. Point out features they have difficulty observing. Next, ask questions that students can answer by examining data on the new type graph or on the histogram. Have children tell which graph they read to give a response and why they used that graph. Help them focus on the possible different meanings that can be gained from a histogram and the new type graph, and encourage them to point out the benefits of the new type. Next, help learners construct a stem-and-leaf or box-and-whisker plot to show data they have collected or found in a book or magazine (Activity 14.3 or 14.4).

FIGURE 14.8 Pounds of Newspapers Collected by Two Third-Grade Classes, Box-and-Whisker Plot

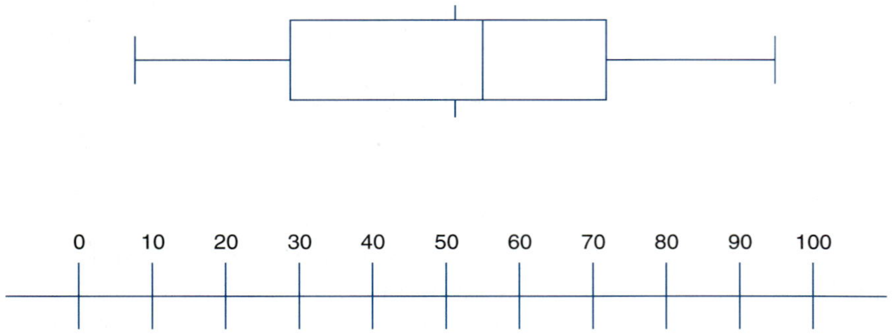

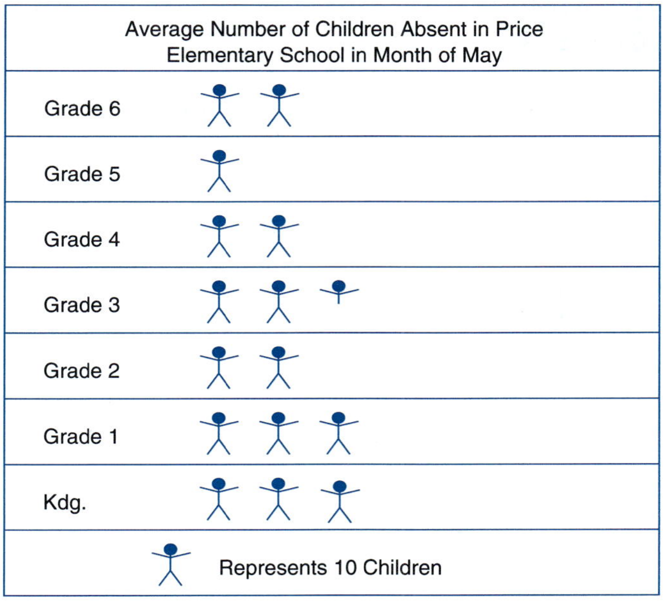

FIGURE 14.9 Pictograph

ACTIVITY 14.3
Making Stem-and-Leaf Plots.

As they study a stem-and-leaf plot, help children make a chart of the steps to make such a graph. They begin with tens and ones numbers. Later, when dealing with larger numbers (such as populations of countries), the students extend the possibilities for stem-and-leaf plots. The chart has these entries:

1. Use a piece of square grid paper.
2. Use a ruler to make a column for the stem.
3. List the tens in order in the stem.
4. Group the data by tens.
5. Write the ones in the leaves.
6. If useful, reorder the data.
7. Interpret the data; share it in writing or orally.

Children then choose data to graph using a stem-and-leaf plot.

The construction of box-and-whisker plots is more difficult, but upper-grade students can find it a challenging experience. (The measures of central tendency displayed by box-and-whisker plots are discussed later in this chapter.)

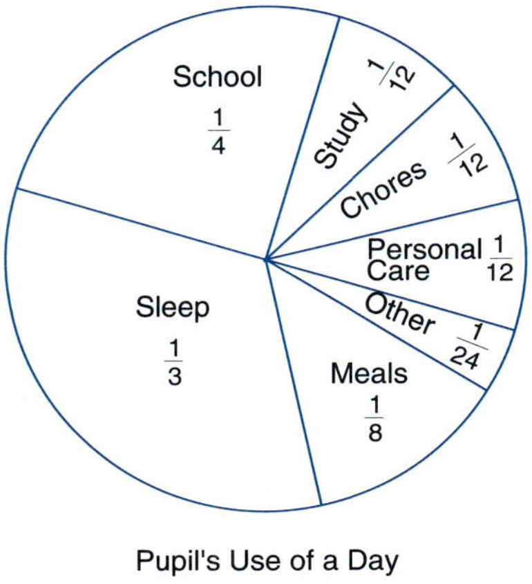

FIGURE 14.10 Circle Graph

ACTIVITY 14.4
Making Box-and-Whisker Plots.

Your introduction to box-and-whisker plots should have helped students learn that this type of graph gives information about range, the median (midpoint), and the quartiles (midpoints of the upper and lower halves of the distribution). Ask students to think about how to construct a box-and-whisker plot. As they share their ideas and you make suggestions, a list of steps should emerge that is similar to:

- Study the data to determine the range.
- Use the list of values arranged in order of size.
- Determine the median of the distribution by marking off values from the top and bottom of the distribution at the same time until the midpoint of the distribution is reached.
- Determine the upper and lower quartiles. Omit the median from the values to be considered; mark off the values in the lower and in the upper half in the same way as with the whole distribution. The midpoints of lower and upper halves designate the lower and upper quartiles, respectively.
- Make a number line that includes the extreme values.
- Above or below the number line, make a box with sides at the median values of the upper and lower halves. Make a line in the box to indicate the median.
- Draw whiskers from the box to the lower and upper extremes.
- Draw lines outside the box to show the mean.

Have students make box-and-whisker plots using data that they have collected or you supply. When the students have finished their work, display the box-and-whisker plots. Have them interpret their graphs. Encourage them to observe whether the values between quartiles are bunched (the word *clumped* can also be used) or whether the quartiles have the same differences. Discuss possible reasons for their observations.

Reader Activity 14.2

Collect data from 10 classmates or friends, and make a stem-and-leaf plot and a box-and-whisker plot to enable you to interpret the data. Compare the graphs and the meanings they convey. If possible, carry out this activity in a group.

Many students in the upper grades can figure out the meaning and usefulness of *pictographs and pie graphs* if they are asked to study such graphs and explain what they can learn from them. If they are unable to do so, the procedure for introducing stem-and-leaf and box-and-whisker plots is used. Very few children will be able to construct pie graphs in the elementary school. (Why?) They are introduced so that children can read the graphs shown in textbooks or other materials.

Making a Graphing Assignment. Bankard and Fennell (1991) describe activities for all grade levels that involve collecting and graphing data to help students become acquainted with one another. Dickinson (1986) points out that students in the upper elementary school enjoy projects that involve investigating the world of information by devising a problem, collecting information, organizing and representing the information, and interpreting their findings. The projects begin with an assignment to choose a research topic from one of three categories: personal preferences, interest areas, or original ideas. *Personal preferences* involve making a survey such as would be done by a marketing or advertising firm. Topics researched could involve consumer preferences and include: pizza toppings, video games, TV shows, or fashion designers. *Interest area* projects involve working with data that have already been collected and usually relate to health, science, and social studies. Topics to research could include animal populations in any country in the world, records of local Christmas bird counts, World Series or Super Bowl winners, speed of land animals, or length of longest rivers in any country in the world. *Original research* ideas involve topics that require the researcher to gather data. Dickinson reports that one of his students collected information on milk wasted in the school cafeteria during one week.

Assignments such as described by Dickinson should begin with a discussion of how to conduct a survey (for suggestions, see Newman and Turkel, 1985) or of how to locate data collected by others. The usefulness of different kinds of graphs for displaying data is reviewed. If students have not studied tables and graphs, a "detour" involving an introduction to organizing and graphing data will need to be taken. The assignment should be clearly written and distributed to students so that they will understand the expectations. The assignment should include the importance of using multiple forms of representation to view the data from different perspectives (Russell and Friel, 1989).

What to Graph. Many kinds of data can be graphed by children. Some have been listed previously in this chapter. Others are given here. Klitz (1981) gives suggestions for projects in statistics and probability, some of which are appropriate for elementary school learners. You and your students will think of many others. Information can be collected by students or obtained from libraries or encyclopedias. Students need to have many options for choosing data so that they will be excited about carrying out a project.

- *School data.* PTA attendance, number eating in cafeteria by grade, absences or tardiness by grades or sexes, number of tests given weekly by grade, hours of TV watching by grade or day, and living grandparents by grade.
- *Class data.* Handspan, foot length, eye color, arm length, height, weight, type of fingerprint, hours of TV watching by day or sex, country of ancestors, and states of residence of class members during their lifetime. Care *must* be taken in collecting class data not to embarrass any child because he or she is (or thinks he or she is) singled out as different. For example, an overweight child could find the experience of being graphed at the end of the range a very painful experience. There is so much information to work with in the elementary school that you can be sensitive to the feelings of children and avoid the selection of certain information for use by the class if it would be embarrassing to any child.
- *Consumer data.* Number of candies of different colors (e.g., M&Ms) or number of raisins in a small package, weights of candy bars, prices of items (e.g., tapes) at different stores, and prices of pets.
- *Current events and social studies.* Crime in our city, pollution levels in our area, political parties in or out of power, and population by states.
- *Sports.* National baseball (football or basketball) league or little league statistics, states of bowling or tennis stars, and track or pole vault records.

Analyzing and Interpreting Data

Analyzing and interpreting data involve deciding if the graph answers the question that prompted the collection of data, deciding what else the graph tells about the information displayed, what can be inferred, and what measures of central tendency and variability will summarize the data.

What Questions Does the Graph Answer? Those who read graphs learn to ask questions that can be answered by studying graphs. If children are to learn to analyze graphs, they must not only use a graph to answer an original question but also construct questions after the graph is made and use the graph to answer these questions. Children learn this step if you ask them to examine their graphs and decide what new questions can be answered by studying the graphs.

Graphs can answer *descriptive and comparative questions* that are usually not children's original questions. Answers to descriptive questions tell how many. For example, if children have collected data on their favorite pets, displayed the data in a bar graph, and used the graph to tell the number of different kinds of pets owned by class members, they can now ask and answer the descriptive questions: "What is the most favorite pet? What is the least favorite pet?" Answers to comparative questions tell what category or characteristic is more or less than another category and often give the comparison. For example, the favorite pets graph can answer the questions," Do more children like dogs or cats? How many more like dogs?"

If children do not ask either descriptive or comparative questions in response to your request to examine the graph and ask a new question, you can get them started by saying, "I have a question about these data. The answer is dogs (more dogs)? What could my question be? . . . Let's think of other questions."

Graphs can also answer *relational questions* or enable the reader to *discern patterns.* Answers to relational questions enable us to see relations or connections among categories or characteristics. For example, if the length of the handspan of members of the class is tabulated and graphed, a relation between handspan and sex may be observed. Data also often reveal patterns if the reader asks, "What is going on here?" For example, if children graph absences each day of the week for several weeks, a pattern of more absences on Mondays may be evident.

Inferring from Graphs. Students also learn to make inferences from graphs. Reasons for certain observations can often be hypothesized. For example, if more children have goldfish than dogs or cats for pets, children can decide that the reason could be that the owners live in apartments that have rules against owning dogs and cats. Of course, another reason could be that last week there was a coupon in the paper for two free gold fish with the purchase of a fish bowl at the grand opening of a pet store in the mall and that many bought the fish bowl and redeemed the coupon. Children should be helped to examine all possible interpretations of data they collect and display.

Measures of Central Tendency and Variability. Children in the elementary school often study the mode, median, and mean—measures of central tendency—and the range and difference between quartiles—measures of variability.

Measures of Central Tendency. Initial work does not introduce the labels for these statistics but helps children develop the concepts.

The *mode* is the value that occurs most frequently in a set of data and usually is of interest to children. Learners can easily determine from any graph which category or characteristic has the greatest frequency. They should be encouraged to ask the question, "Which is most?" In the upper grades, they learn that the name of this statistic is "mode." Older students may notice that some distributions are bimodal (have two modes), and they discuss the reasons for this occurrence.

The *median* is the middle value in a distribution. To interest children in finding the middle, you can ask, for example, about values of foot lengths students have graphed, "Who has the foot length that is in the middle of our graph? How can we find out?" Elementary school children will decide that to find the middle value, they can mark off the same number of values from the top and the bottom of a list of values arranged in order. (Perhaps they will need the hint, "If we start by checking off at the same time the top and bottom numbers in our list of ordered values, how will we reach the middle?")

If there is an odd number of values, the median has an equal number of values below and above. If there is an even number of values in the distribution, the median is the midpoint between the two.

The formula for finding the median is

Median = $\frac{(N+1)}{2}$th score in order of size (N = the number of values in the distribution).

For example, if the distribution is 3, 6, 8, 9, 10 (an odd number), the formula gives the third value—8—as the median. If 3 is not in the distribution, there is an even number of values in the distribution. The formula then gives 2.5, and the median is the midpoint between the second and third number, or 8.5. Some upper-grade learners may study the formula to decide why it makes sense, but most elementary school children use the manipulative method of discarding values simultaneously at both ends of the ordered distribution to find the median.

The *mean* is the arithmetic average of the values. It is found by adding the values in the distribution and by dividing by the number of values. Children first learn about the mean by participating in activities such as described in Activities 14.5 and 14.6.

ACTIVITY 14.5
What Is a Fair Distribution?

Give each in a group of three or four a bag of cardboard cookies each containing a different number of cookies (Goldman, 1990). (Each may be given a handful of crayons. Handfuls must contain different numbers of crayons.) Ask the groups to make the distribution even or fair for each child in the group. Discuss their thinking and results when they finish the assignment.

Repeat the activity with different numbers, and have students reflect on the differences arising because the numbers were different.

ACTIVITY 14.6
If All Prices Were the Same.

For this activity students first make bar graphs. Bars composed of small sticky notes indicate the prices of different brands of cereals, candy bars, or snacks. Students use a bar for each brand. (Help learners use about the same amount for each kind of food on their graphs, e.g., a pound of each kind of cereal.) Each group chooses a different product and makes its own graph. For extension, ask them to decide what the price would be if it were adjusted so all brands had the same price, but no money was lost or gained in the price adjustment, and the total cost of the food remained the same. Remind them that they can move their sticky notes and make new bars if needed to answer the question. When they finish the assignment, have them report their results and the strategies they used to answer the question. Tell them that the number they found is called the *average*. They can explain why they think this is a good label.

To enable learners to construct the rule for finding the average, display the numbers they reported for activities such as 14.5 and 14.6. Ask the students to play around with the numbers to determine how to obtain the same solutions using only numbers. Say that this will be their rule for finding the average.

If no group discovers the rule, give math sentences related to their work, such as $7 + 5 + 4 + 8 = 24$ and $24 \div 4 = 6$. Ask them to study the equations for a hint about the rule. Students can relate the rule to their "even-up experiences" to determine the sense of the rule. To connect the experience with the rule, they may need to connect a math sentence to the experience. For example,

$$7 + 5 + 4 + 8 = (7 - 1) + (5 + 1) + (4 + 2) + (8 - 2) = 24$$

shows the even-up idea with numbers.

ACTIVITY 14.7
Averaging Game.

Prepare cards each with a number 10 to 34 for four players. Players choose an "IT." "IT" shuffles and deals the cards. When "IT" gives the signal, each player places a card in the center of the playing area. "IT" estimates the average in 20 seconds (designate a time keeper to watch the clock and "call time") and computes the average on a calculator. If the average estimated is within 3 (4 for some groups) of the computed average, "IT" gets a point or a counter. The person to the right of "IT" becomes the next "IT", and the estimating and calculating procedure is repeated. When one person has 5 points, he or she is the winner of that round, and another round is played.

Measures of Variability: Range and Quartiles. The *range* is usually introduced naturally as children examine their data to determine the lowest and highest values. In any distribution, these extremes and their differences are of interest and will probably be noted by learners as they study their tables and graphs. If not, ask students to find the difference between these two numbers and decide why the difference is important. Tell them the difference of the extremes is called the *range.*

Quartiles divide the values of a distribution ordered by size into fourths. The quartiles are labeled first (bottom), second (median), and third. As discussed, after the values in a distribution are arranged in order of size, quartiles are determined by finding the median of the distribution and the median of the lower and upper halves. The differences between the quartiles can give interesting information about the distribution.

Extending Understanding of Graphs

After children have made a graph, they should be encouraged to ask questions that extend their understanding of the data collected and displayed. Extensions include:

- Deciding if the data answer our question(s) (e.g., "Do the data tell something about our class?")
- Asking if we have enough data to answer our question (e.g., "Do we need more packages of M&Ms?")
- Posing questions the graph could answer other than those whose answers were sought by collecting the data displayed
- Asking if data from other classes (schools, cities, etc.) would show the same relations or patterns
- Asking why the data do not fit with what we already know
- Asking how to explain certain aspects of the data (e.g., differences in mean, median, and mode)
- Deciding where to find more information about this topic

After collecting data and constructing their own graphs, learners apply their knowledge of data collection and representation to the study of graphs in textbooks and other materials. Graphs found in textbooks that students are using should be examined and explained. Students should be encouraged not only to read the graph for obvious information but also to interpret the data. They may decide to use the data to construct a different graph to see if it tells a different story.

Extension includes developing an intuitive understanding of sampling. Have children consider the population sample and the size of the collection by asking questions such as:

- Do our data tell us that all third graders have more dogs than cats? Why or why not?
- We have counted the number of words that begin with vowels on five pages. What do our findings tells us about the words that begin with vowels in the entire book?
- About how many lizards would we need to measure before we could get a good idea of the average size of lizards?
- We have charted the temperature for a week. What does that tell us about other weeks this month? This year?

ACTIVITY 14.8
Finding Graphs.

Assign students in the upper grades to bring in a graph found in a newspaper or magazine and to write a short report telling what the graph tells. Have them explain their graphs and share their reports in small groups. Display the graphs, and ask students to tell about graphs that give information of interest to the whole class.

ACTIVITY 14.9
Should We Know This?

Have students bring in graphs from newspapers or magazines for use by other students. In pairs they exchange graphs. After each student in a pair has had time to study his or her graph, they share their ideas with each other. They decide whether the information is useful to them and why or why not. Pairs who have studied graphs giving information important to their age group report their ideas to the class. They may also report why the information in a graph is not useful to them.

ACTIVITY 14.10
Comparing Measures of Central Tendency.

This activity is appropriate for students who understand the mean, median, and mode. Have students find prices of houses in a metropolitan newspaper real estate or classified ad section (prices or cars, etc., could be used). Choose advertisements for them to use so that there are prices at all levels, including at least one very expensive home. Have students use about 20 house prices. The first assignment is to find the mode, median, and mean of the distribution. Different groups could find different statistics and compare their work. A graph and a table of ranked prices will enable students to find the mode and median of the distribution. Calculators are used to determine the mean. The second assignment is to remove the most expensive house and to recalculate the mode, median, and mean. The results of both assignments are posted. Groups, and then the class, discuss how these statistics differ in each assignment and the reasons for the differences. They should be able to determine that a very high value influences the mean to a much greater extent than it affects the median and the mode.

STUDYING PROBABILITY

As one observes events, records observations, and works with data, it is natural to ask, "What is the probability of this event occurring? How can I predict its occurrence?" Thus the topics of statistics and probability—the study of chance—are naturally related. In the elementary school the study of probability mainly involves gaining an intuitive understanding of some probability ideas by engaging in related activities. This section discusses the nature of probability and gives activities for elementary school children that enable them to construct an awareness of rudimentary probability ideas.

Introducing Probability

Probability is the likelihood that an event will occur. The probability of an event can be from 0 to 1. It is stated as a ratio:

$$\frac{\text{Number of ways a particular event can occur}}{\text{Total number of possible events}}$$

For example, if a checker with a star (S) on one side and a crown (C) on the other is flipped, the probability of getting a circle is $\frac{1}{2}$ or 1 out of 2 possible events. If the checker is flipped 10 times, one can reason that the probability of getting a star is 5 out of the 10 flips. This is the theoretical probability. However, actual flipping of the checker 10 times may not give a star 5 times. There is a chance that 6 or another number of stars will occur, even a remote possibility that 10 stars would turn up. The experimental results do not always agree with the theoretical results, but if a very great number of experiments were conducted, the experimental and the theoretical results should agree if the event occurs randomly.

Children experiment with many different materials to get an intuitive understanding of the concept of probability. They learn that events are not related to their wishes but that chance is a factor in events. As they discuss their experiments, they talk about what they thought would happen (predictions) and the experimental results. They become intuitively aware that the theoretical probability of an event occurring is related to all possible outcomes (sample space). They begin to realize that their experiments may not, in the short run, mirror the theoretical probability of an event. They learn the difference between fair and unfair situations and thus develop an intuitive awareness of randomness or equal chance. Later, they begin to develop an awareness of the shape of a distribution of random events—the normal curve. In the upper grades, by working with models, they develop an experiential background for mathematical rules used to determine the probability of a random event.

Activities with Probability

ACTIVITY 14.11
Will It Happen?

With very young children talk about events that could happen, maybe happen, and not happen. Ask them to react to examples and explain why they would say "yes," "no," or "maybe." Some examples are:

1. The night will go away tomorrow morning.
2. There will be school next Monday.
3. It will rain tomorrow.
4. You will have a winter or Christmas holiday (spring or summer vacation).
5. An elephant will come to visit our room in one hour.
6. Our pet white rat is alive.
7. The sun is shining now.
8. Dogs talk my language.

Give children statements similar to those above, and have them shake their heads for "yes" and "no" and not move their heads for "maybe" in response to these statements. The words *possible* and *impossible* may be used. As soon as possible, children should think of examples.

With older children introduce the notions of certain, likely, unlikely, and impossible, and ask students to give any words or phrases they know that can be used to describe these concepts. Have student give examples and draw pictures of events that fall in these categories. Later, learners can review these ideas by sorting statements class members have written into the categories "certain," "likely," unlikely," and "impossible."

ACTIVITY 14.12
What Could Happen?

Give each pair of children two blocks (marbles can be used) that do not have the same color (e.g., one blue and one yellow). Ask them to put the blocks in a paper sack. Have one child in a pair decide what could happen when the partner takes a block out of the sack. The child who did not decide what would happen, shakes the sack, and without looking takes a block out of the sack. The children note the color of the block and compare the prediction with what actually happened. The block is returned to the sack, and they repeat the procedure, but trade tasks. In a whole-class discussion, review what they thought would happen, why they thought that, and what did happen. In the course of the discussion, ask, "Why did some say a blue block would be drawn and others say a yellow block would be drawn?" Over time your questions should enable them to develop the understanding that the possible outcomes are a blue or a yellow block. "Could anything else happen?" is a good question to ask to get children to think about all possible outcomes.

It is important to notice the reasons they give for their "predictions." Do they give egocentric reasons (e.g., I like blue), or do they show a high level of thinking by claiming that either a blue or a yellow block will be drawn out of the bag, that is, half of the time a blue will be drawn, and half the time, a yellow. If they give the latter response, it appears that they can reason about all possible outcomes.

Later, each child in a pair should make a prediction for 10 draws of the blocks, follow the procedure, always remembering to return the block to the bag after it is drawn, and then compare the predictions of each child with the experimental results. Soon children work with a variety of objects, such as coins or checkers. Coins show heads or tails. Checkers usually have a star on one side, a crown on the other.

The next step is to put several blocks of one color and the same number of blocks of another color in the sack and repeat the activity. Children may not realize that the same results will be determined by an equal number of each color of blocks, no matter what the number.

ACTIVITY 14.13
Adaptation of What Could Happen?

Have older children place more objects with varying numbers of each color in the sack and repeat Activity 14.12. The withdrawn object must be replaced each time. The discussion that compares their ideas about what could happen with the results of the actual experiment is important. The ratio of colors in the sack is noted and thus the theoretical probability established. (E.g., if there are 3 blue blocks and 1 green block in the sack, the probability of drawing a blue is $\frac{3}{4}$; a great number of experiments, say 500, will give approximately 3 blue for every 1 green drawn.)

If children have studied ratios, on the chalkboard or overhead, write the ratio that gives the probability discussed (e.g., $\frac{3}{4}$). When the notation is first introduced, you should do so informally, with no more explanation than this is the way we write the results of our prediction (e.g., the prediction is 3 blue out of 4 blocks).

Question learners so that they gradually develop an awareness that the events are independent. They need to develop the idea that one drawing does not affect the next drawing. For example, if the mixture is half red and half blue and a red block is drawn and put back, it does not follow that a blue block will be drawn next. The fact that a red block was drawn first does not influence the color of the next block to be drawn.

ACTIVITY 14.14
What Is Happening in These Games?

Make three or four spinners for each group so that all students in the class can play three or four spinner games with the same partner, each time using a different spinner. (If the game is adapted to more than two players, there will be more than two colors to a spinner, but each color will have the same number of sections.) Only some of the spinners lead to a fair game, that is, each player has an equal chance of winning (Figure 14.11). To begin, each pair is given different spinners to use in different games. (The students can play at different times, and thus the spinners can be passed from group to group.) Each student chooses a different colored section of the spinner. The order of choice can be determined by the length of the players' names, and the player with the shortest first name, for example, can choose first. The game

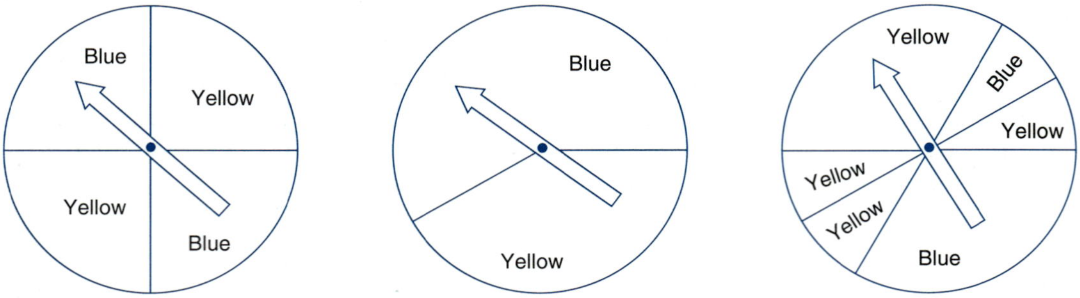

FIGURE 14.11 Various Types of Spinners

is played by moving on a board game (Figure 3.14) or collecting a token when the spinner lands on a player's color. The winner is the player who completes the path first or collects 10 tokens. Players can change colors after each game. They keep track of their colors and of who is the winner.

After all the members of the class have played games with different spinners, a whole-class discussion is held. During the discussion ask questions such as, "What did you notice about winning and losing?" "Could you tell who would win before the game began? Why?" "What did you learn from this game?" Use prompting questions as needed to help students become aware that the players did not always have an equal chance of winning and thus that some games were not fair. Stress that fairness depends on each having an equal chance.

Many games that deal with this idea are given by Bright, Harvey, and Wheeler (1981). The variety of games students can play would add zest to this learning.

Sue's Record

Red Kidney	6
Pinto	7
White	5
Black	9
Total	27

FIGURE 14.12 Record of Beans in Scoop

ACTIVITY 14.15
Lots of Beans (Bruni and Silverman, 1986).

Use a pound or a half-pound of each of four kinds of dried beans (e.g., black, lima, pinto, and red) or three kinds of dried beans and popcorn—not popped). Mix them together in a large sack. Have each student take a small scoop or cup and predict how many of each kind is in his or her "sample." Each child counts the number of each kind of food in his or her scoop and makes a record as in Figure 14.12. They should reason why more or less of a kind of bean or corn is in the scoop. (Because size varies, the beans do not have an equal chance of occurring.)

To help older students develop an intuitive awareness of random events, ask groups to combine their records and make graphs (Figure 14.13). They can determine the mean, mode, median, and range of each distribution if they have been introduced to these measures.

ACTIVITY 14.16
What's in the Bag?

Repeat *What Could Happen?* (Activity 14.12), with the variation that one child in each pair puts objects (blocks, chips, or marbles—8 or less) of two colors in a bag without the other child looking. The child who did not see the objects hidden in the bag (1) makes 20 draws (returning the object each time); (2) tells the other child what color to record on the record sheet (Figure 14.14); (3) predicts on the basis of the experimental record what number of each color of objects was put in the bag; (4) looks in the bag; and (5) compares his or her prediction with the actual number in the bag. The roles are exchanged, and the procedure is repeated. In a whole-class discussion, students report on the ideas they gained by carrying out the activity.

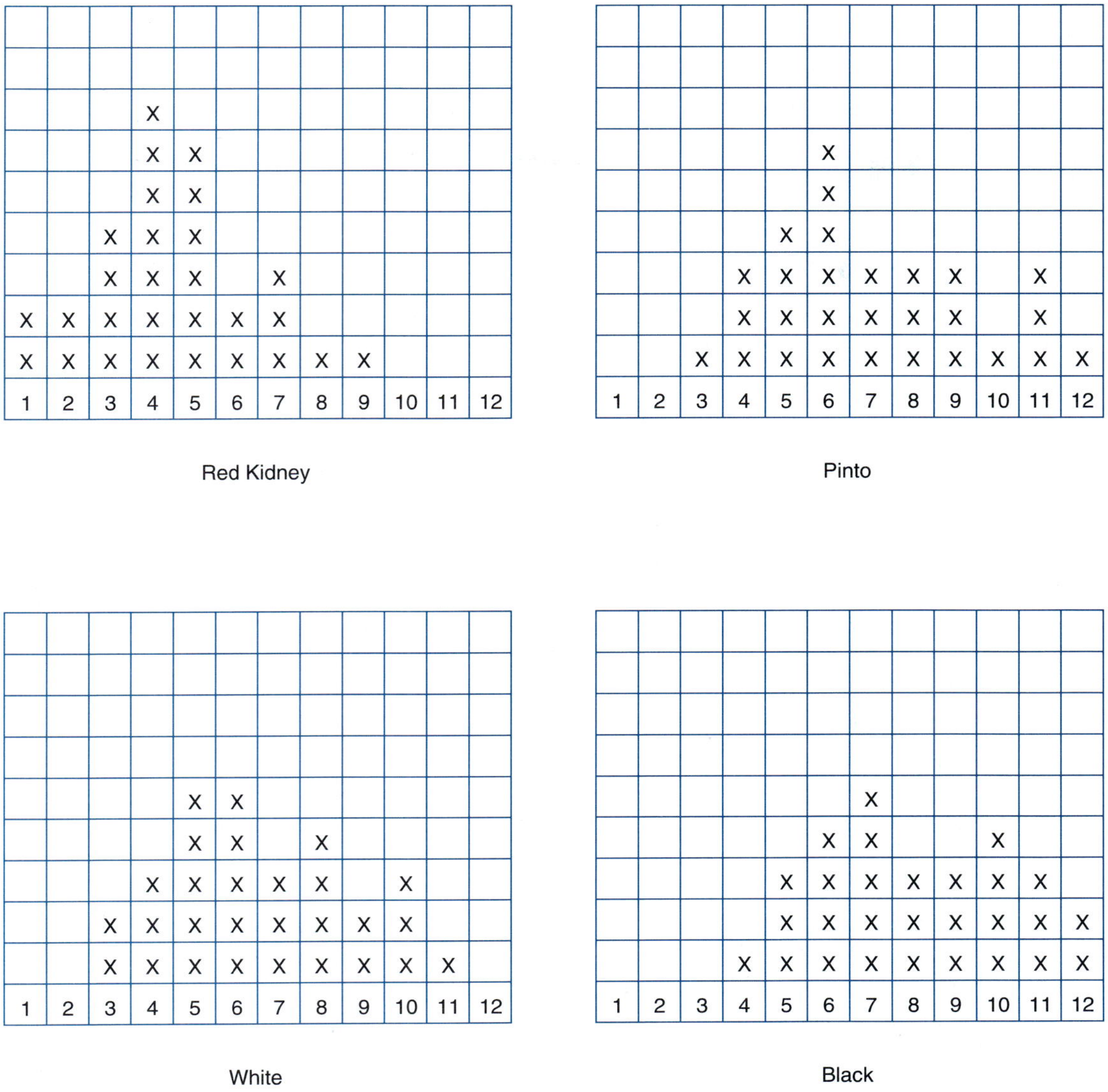

FIGURE 14.13 Class Record of Beans in Scoop by Type of Beans (x = 1 Student)

ACTIVITY 14.17
Making 10-Square Strip Records (Bruni and Silverman, 1986).

Children can repeat the last task in the *What Could Happen?* Activity (14.12) with 5 blocks of one color and 5 of another color, and make records of their draws of blocks of one color on strips of 10 squares cut from grid paper. When each child in a pair has made at least one strip, display the strips as in Figure 14.15. Discuss the display, asking questions such as, "What do the strips show?" (Five blues out of 10 draws happened most often.) "Why do you think that happened? What prediction will you make? How does our prediction compare with the actual results?"

ACTIVITY 14.18
Drawing Two Objects in Order.

Use 40 cards, half of the cards marked on one side with a red star (R), half with a black star (B). Have pairs of children shuffle the cards, take turns drawing one card,

FIGURE 14.14 What's in the Bag?

Draw	Color	Draw	Color	Draw	Color
1		8		15	
2		9		16	
3		10		17	
4		11		18	
5		12		19	
6		13		20	
7		14			

returning it to the pack, shuffling the cards, drawing another card, and recording the results of the two cards drawn. This procedure is carried out 20 times, 10 for each child. (They can take turns during the day carrying out the activity so that only 40 cards need to be made.) Before any group begins, students should list what they think the possible outcomes are and make predictions. They carry out the experiment, and, using a calculator, a committee combines the results of all the groups. Help the class estimate the probabilities in lowest terms (e.g., $\frac{69}{300}$ is about $\frac{75}{300}$, which is $\frac{1}{4}$—calculators could help). The class then compares their predictions and the experimental results. Repeat the activity using a red and a black checker in a bag.

After carrying out these activities, children can be helped to list the possible outcomes: BB, RR, BR, RB. Then, ask, "What are the chances of drawing two blacks in a row?" Help them reason that it is 1 out of 4. Have them compare the theoretical probability with the experimental results.

The activity may be extended by thinking of the possibility of tossing three checkers of the same color or one three times and determining the possibilities of a star (S) or a crown (C) being face up. There are eight possibilities: SSS, CCC, SSC, SCS, CSS, CCS, CSC, SCC. The probability of any one of the sequences is $\frac{1}{8}$, or 1 out of 8.

ACTIVITY 14.19
Tree Diagrams (for Older Learners).

Tree diagrams make probabilities of ordered events very clear to many individuals. Introduce tree diagrams as a follow-up to the checker experiment in Activity 14.17. After students have participated in the activity, say, "We can figure out the possible outcomes by making a tree diagram. We begin with two branches (show branches). We will label one branch B for black checker; the other R for the red checker (Figure 14.16A). Let's look at the possibilities for the next event. What are the possibil-

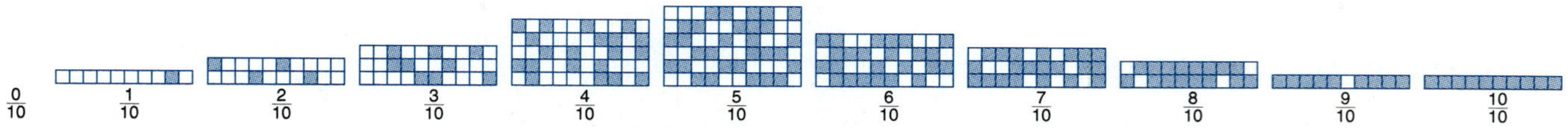

FIGURE 14.15 Number of Blue Blocks in Ten Trials (▪ = blue block; blank = yellow block)

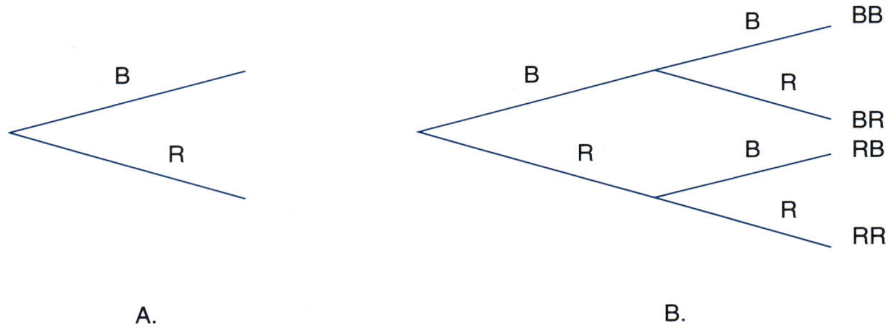

FIGURE 14.16 Tree Diagram for Number of Outcomes for Ordered Events

ities for the second toss?" After they agree that it is either a red or black checker, say, "We use two more branches on each of the first branches (Figure 14.16B). Would that make sense? Why?" After the students decide that the two new branches stand for the outcomes of the second toss, they study the tree diagram to decide the possibilities. They should be helped to read the four possibilities by examining the branches.

ACTIVITY 14.20
Die Toss.

Have each pair of students predict the probability of getting a 4 when a die is tossed or flipped. They should write their predictions and the reasons for their conclusion in a short report. Next, have each pair of students toss the die 20 times (10 times for each student) and keep a record of the result of each toss. When all have completed the experiment, make a record on a chart of the results of all the students' work. By combining the results of all the class, you will have about 300 tosses for the students to use to compare the theoretical and the experimental probabilities. Ask them to react to the record, compare their predictions and the results, and give reasons for similarities and differences.

ACTIVITY 14.21
Toss the Die Twice.

Repeat Activity 14.19 but change the directions so that they predict the probability of tossing a 4 followed by a 3. After they write their reports and carry out the experiment, have them compare their predictions and the experimental results.

Reader Activity 14.3

Make a tree diagram for the theoretical probability, if you used a die, of tossing a 2 followed by a 4.

ACTIVITY 14.22
Diagram for Die Tossing.

Have students work cooperatively or as a class to make a tree diagram for the probability of tossing a 4 followed by a 3 (Figure 14.17). Help them discover that the diagrams gives 36 possibilities, so the probability of a 4 followed by a 3 is $\frac{1}{36}$.

A few students may be able to reason that the probability of one number tossed followed by another number tossed is the probability of the second toss ($\frac{1}{6}$) *of* the probability of the first toss ($\frac{1}{6}$). For example, if a 4 is tossed first (probability $\frac{1}{6}$), the probability of the second toss being a 3 (probability $\frac{1}{6}$) is $\frac{1}{6}$ of $\frac{1}{6}$, or $\frac{1}{36}$. If students can grasp the concept, give time to a discussion of the probability of tossing other numbers on a die in order. They can use a tree diagram to explain their thinking.

ACTIVITY 14.23
Car Colors (Fennell, 1990).

Have students list four exterior car colors and four interior colors. In groups of two have them decide what is the chance of walking onto a car lot that has cars with all

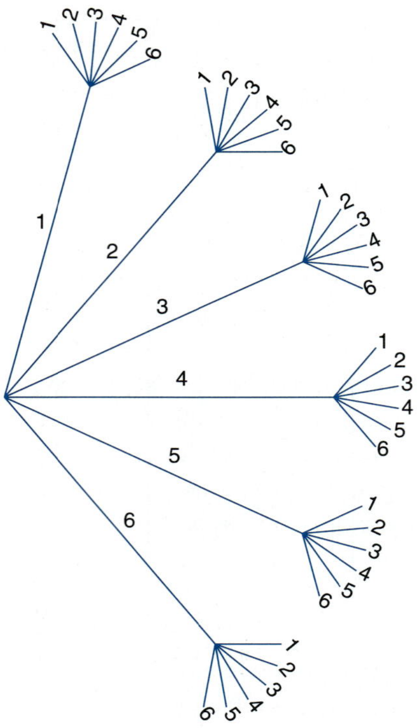

FIGURE 14.17 Tree Diagram for Probability of Tossing a 4 followed by a 3

possible color combinations, selecting a car at random, and choosing a car that has their favorite interior and exterior colors. Have them draw a tree diagram (Figure 14.18) to show the probability ($\frac{1}{16}$).

Variation: Use four colors of shirts and four colors of jeans instead of exterior and interior car colors. Children can write all the different combinations on index

FIGURE 14.18 Tree Diagram for Probability of Car Color Combinations

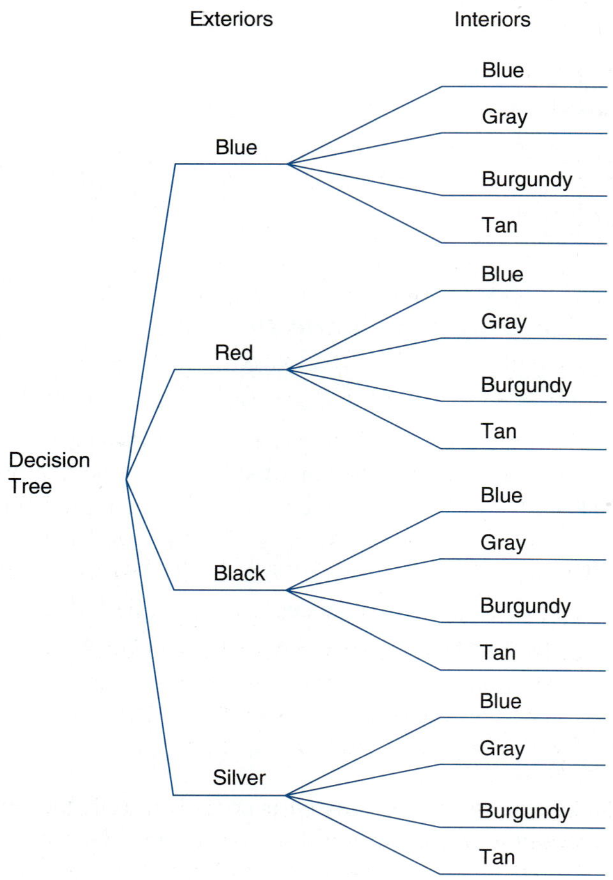

cards. The question becomes: "What is the probability of choosing at random my favorite combination from the cards in a bowl?" Have them set up an experiment to determine the experimental probability and draw a diagram to show the theoretical probability. They should compare the experimental and theoretical probabilities.

Activity for the Classroom 14.2. Ask older students in groups to list three different meats and three different vegetables that they might find at a cafeteria where all the serving dishes are covered. Have the groups draw a diagram to show the probability of choosing at random a certain combination of their own choosing of one meat and one vegetable from the three meats and three vegetables. Have them share their work.

ASSESSING LEARNING OF STATISTICS AND PROBABILITY

Assessing work with data is often informal. Observe children's work in small groups, their contributions to class discussions, and some work products. In the primary grades, look for the following evidence:

1. A child volunteers characteristics to be graphed.
2. A child can interpret a graph made on a grid (Activity 14.1) by explaining what the graph shows and by making comparisons based on the graph.
3. A child can make a bar graph independently if given data, a table format, and a grid format.
4. A child is interested in making and interpreting a graph.

Older children can be assessed using the same indicators. Formal assessment of a student's statistics project is also important:

1. Did the student devise the project independently?
2. Is he or she conscientious about collecting information to use to answer the project question?
3. How much help does he or she need to organize the data in a table?
4. Does the student use more than one appropriate representation for the data?
5. Does the student's analysis show ability to deal with comparisons, the range, a possible trend, and one or more measures of central tendency?
6. Can the student infer from the data?
7. Does the learner ask questions that shows a willingness to extend his or her understanding of the data collected and displayed?
8. Did the student undertake the project with enthusiasm?

Older children should also be assessed on their ability to read graphs in texts or children's newspapers. Questions 5, 6, and 7 are used to assess students' ability to read graphs.

Student's understanding of probability is evaluated by gathering evidence through observations and examination of work products:

1. Does the young child understand the concepts of *possible* and *impossible?* Do older children also understand the meaning of *likely* and *unlikely?*
2. Do students find probability activities interesting?
3. Do they make reasonable predictions of what is most or least likely?
4. By playing "fair' and "unfair" games, do they show an awareness of the concept of equal chance.
5. Can older children state the probability of an event? Are they curious to find all possible outcomes and the probability of a given event?
6. Can they draw diagrams to indicate the probability of an event.

SUMMARY

The study of statistics and of probability enables children to live in the modern world because these topics play an important role in our lives. New directions in teaching and learning mathematics give students problem-solving experiences that involve collecting, organizing, representing, analyzing, and interpreting data. Initial work involves making, analyzing, and drawing simple conclusions from people graphs, chart graphs, and bar graphs.

Older learners study other types of graphs: histograms, line graphs, stem-and-leaf plots, box-and-whisker plots, pictographs, and pie graphs. Students analyze and infer from the data given in graphs they and others make. They carry out projects that involve all the steps connected with working with data. They also learn about measures of central tendency—mean, median, and mode—and measures of variability—range and difference between quartiles.

The study of probability in the elementary school first involves becoming aware that chance does not depend on wishes. Later, students develop an intuitive understanding of equal chance, all possible outcomes, independence of events, the probability of an event, theoretical and experimental results, and ordered events. Advanced learners may study tree diagrams to understand probability. Children do not study definitions or rules. Rather, they engage in many activities, examples of which were described in this chapter. Being engaged in activities and communicating with their peers and teachers enable students to construct concepts by abstracting from experience and reasoning informally about what they have done.

Observing of students as they work with data and examining work products and projects are useful approaches to assessment. Examples of questions to answer in the assessment process were given in the section dealing with assessment of statistics and probability learnings.

REFERENCES

Bankard, Dianne, and Francis (Skip) Fennell. (September 1991). "Ideas." *Arithmetic Teacher* 39: 24–33.

Bright, George W., John G. Harvey, and Margariete Montague Wheeler. (1981). "Fair Games, Unfair Games." In *Teaching Statistics and Probability,* edited by Albert P. Shulte and James R. Smart, pp. 49–59. Reston, VA: National Council of Teacher of Mathematics.

Bruni, James V., and Helene J. Silverman. (February 1986). "Developing Concepts in Probability and Statistics—and Much More." *Arithmetic Teacher* 33: 34–37.

Choate, Laura Duncan, and JoAnn King Okey. (1981). "Graphically Speaking: Primary-Level Graphing Experiences." In *Teaching Statistics and Probability,* edited by Albert P. Shulte and James R. Smart, pp. 33–40. Reston, VA: National Council of Teacher of Mathematics.

deCharms, Richard. (1984). "Motivational Enhancement in Educational Settings." In *Research on Motivation in Education Vol. 1: Student Motivation,* edited by Russell E. Ames and Carole Ames, pp. 275–310. New York: Academic Press.

Dickinson, J. Craig. (December 1986). "Gather, Organize, Display: Mathematics for the Information Society." *Arithmetic Teacher* 34: 12–15.

Fennell, Francis (Skip). (December 1990). "Probability." *Arithmetic Teacher* 38: 18–22.

Goldman, Phyllis H. (March 1990). "Teaching Arithmetic Averaging: An Activity Approach." *Arithmetic Teacher* 37: 38–43.

Klitz, Ralph H., Jr. (1981)."Projects." In *Teaching Statistics and Probability,* edited by Albert P. Shulte and James R. Smart, pp. 239–246. Reston, VA: National Council of Teacher of Mathematics.

Leutzinger, Larry P. (1990). "Graphical Representation and Probability." In *Mathematics for the Young Child,* edited by Joseph N. Payne, pp. 251–163. Reston, VA: National Council of Teachers of Mathematics.

Maher, Carolyn Alexander. (1981). "Simple Graphical Techniques for Examining Data Generated by Classroom Activities." In *Teaching Statistics and Probability,* edited by Albert P. Shulte and James R. Smart, pp. 109–117. Reston, VA: National Council of Teachers of Mathematics.

National Council of Teachers of Mathematics. (1989). *Curriculum and Evaluation Standards for School Mathematics.* Reston VA: Author.

Newman Claire M., and Susan B. Turkel. (May 1985). "The Class Survey: A Problem-solving Activity." *Arithmetic Teacher* 32: 10–12.

Russell, Susan Jo, and Susan N. Friel. (1989). "Collecting and Analyzing Real Data in the Elementary School Classroom." In *New Directions for Elementary School Mathematics,* edited by Paul R. Trafton and Albert P. Schulte, pp. 134–148. Reston, VA: National Council of Teachers of Mathematics.

Shaw, Jean M. (May 1984). "Dealing with Data." *Arithmetic Teacher* 31: 9–15.

Sullivan, Delia, and Mary Ann O'Neil. (September 1980). "This is Us! Great Graphs for Kids." *Arithmetic Teacher* 28: pp. 14–18.

SOFTWARE RESOURCES

Exploring Tables and Graphs
Company: Silver Burdett-Ginn
Computer: Apple
Grade level: 2–6

Gives examples of line, bar, picture, and circle graphs. Learners make their own graphs.

Bumble Games
Company: The Learning Company
Computer: Apple
Grade level: 1–4
Six games involve using number lines, number pairs, and plotting on a graph. Feedback.

Probability
Company: MECC
Computer: Apple
Grade level: 6–9
Coin tossing simulations and games involving study of expected events in rolling dice.

Taking Chances
Company: Sunburst
Computer: Apple
Grade level: 3–8
Exploration of probability. Prediction of numbers of colored marbles that will fall out of a machine. Some marbles are replaced; others are not. Can develop an intuitive understanding of probability.

CHAPTER 15

Mathematics for Children with Special Needs

▪ INTRODUCTORY PROBLEM ▪

Your school is sponsoring a Diversity Festival two evenings in March. Each class is to use charts, exhibits, or videotapes to present information in its room, and it will participate in a program to be held in the cafeteria. Your class has decided it will use the theme Holidays of the Peoples in Our Community. List four or more holidays familiar to the children of majority and minority groups in your class. As you study this chapter, decide how you can include mathematics for children with special needs in this project for the Diversity Festival.

INTRODUCTION

To realize their full potential, some children require instruction different from that provided for other children at their grade level. These children have special needs. They include minority children, girls, learning disabled children, slow learners, and mathematically gifted children. To instruct these students, teachers may need to modify their instruction. Four main sections of the chapter discuss how teachers can instruct children with special needs so that they become interested in learning mathematics and reach the goals of the program in which they are enrolled: Mathematics for Minority Children, Gender and Mathematics Learning, Mathematics for Exceptional Children, and Assessing Mathematics Learning of Children with Special Needs. A Summary section ends the chapter.

MATHEMATICS FOR MINORITY CHILDREN

Minority children are those whose culture is different from the mainstream culture of the United States. They speak a language other than English, or they use an English dialect. Children who speak other languages include Hispanic and American Indian children and in smaller numbers those who speak Chinese, Vietnamese, Lao, Thai, French, Arabic, and other languages. Children who speak a dialect are those who speak black English and dialects found in various regions of the United States. By the year 2000 about 40% of American school children will belong to minority cultures (Secada, 1990).

The mathematics achievements of many of these children is below that of white children proficient in standard English. The 1986 National Assessment of Educational Progress (NAEP) tested 9-year-old students at four levels: (1) simple arithmetic facts; (2) beginning operations and problem solving; (3) beginning skills and understanding; and (4) moderately complex procedures. At ages 13 and 17, students were tested at these levels and at another level, multi-step problem-solving and algebra. Results are reported for whites, blacks, and Hispanics. The results of the NAEP for 1986 showed Hispanics and blacks were below whites at the four levels of assessment at age 9, though the difference for simple arithmetic facts was minimal. (In the simple arithmetic facts category, whites scored at or above 98.9%, Hispanics 96.4%, and blacks, 93%.) At ages 13 and 17, blacks and Hispanics showed almost no difference from whites in the simple arithmetic facts category. For all other levels at ages 13 and 17, minorities scored noticeably lower than whites. At all ages, however, statistically significant increases in 1986 mean scores over the 1977 and 1982 scores on the NAEP were reported for blacks. Hispanics' scores improved at the older ages, but the increases were not statistically significant. (Dossey, Mullis, Lindquist, and Chambers, 1988). Asian-Americans have scored higher than whites on the Scholastic Aptitude Test (SAT) and the quantitative section of the Graduate Record Examination (GRE) (Tsang, 1984).

The poor achievement of blacks and Hispanics has been related to language, to attitude, to cognitive style, and to experiential background. These factors are discussed in this section, and guidelines are given for helping minority children attain higher levels of mathematics learning than they have in the past.

Language and Mathematics Learning

Many believe that mathematics is a universal language involving mainly the use of symbols and that children whose language is not standard English can begin to learn mathematics with little proficiency in standard English. This may be true for speakers of black English because it appears that they can understand standard English and read it with comprehension using black English (Leu and Kinzer, 1991). However, Orr (1987) has documented for high school students that speaking black English makes it difficult to understand certain mathematical language. For example, the constructions "one-fourth less than" and "one-fourth larger than" are often interpreted as subtraction or as addition. Even though she does not discuss problems that speakers of black English may have learning mathematics in the elementary school, her reports of high school learners indicate that teachers of elementary school mathematics should give close attention to these students' interpretations of standard English mathematical expressions to detect misinterpretations. Teachers must then work with students who show misunderstanding, so that misinterpretations do not persist in learners' thinking.

The situation is different for those children who are proficient in a first language (L1) and are learning English as a second language (L2). These children must attain a sufficient level of proficiency in English to profit from mathematics instruction (Spanos, Rhodes, Dale, and Crandall, 1988). They must be able to receive information, follow directions, and communicate ideas. This is a *functional* use of language. They must also have *notional* language abilities. This is knowledge of language specific to mathematics and involves language to communicate mathematics ideas such as the meaning of fractions (Cuevas, 1984).

Language is also said to be conversational or cognitive/academic (Cummins, 1981; 1989). *Conversational;* or surface, language is contextual. It involves gaining meaning from gestures, body language, intonation, and situational clues as well as words. *Cognitive/academic language* is decontextual and cognitively demanding. Decontextualized language conveys information through words, and there is a logic to the communication which must be understood by the participants. Success in school is related to cognitive/academic language proficiency. Both bilingual and monolingual children come to school with different degrees of cognitive/academic language. If instruction assumes that children have a cognitive/academic language proficiency and they do not, a mismatch occurs, and learning is adversely affected.

Cummins states that if children learn concepts in their first language, instruction in English can emphasize learning new labels for the concepts. The concepts transfer to English, and the concepts developed in the first language facilitate learning subject matter in the second language.

Some cultures do not have words for certain ideas, and thus the concepts cannot be communicated with words. Bradley (1984) notes that the Navajo language does not have words for *multiply, divide,* and *if.*

A concept can be expressed in a foreign language so that it does not appear to be the same idea when the words are translated into English. For example, the English, *4 goes into 9* is given in Spanish as *9 into 4* meaning 9 into 4 parts (Castellanos, 1980).

Attitudes and Mathematics Learning

It is believed that attitudes of minorities toward mathematics and toward the learning of mathematics have been related to their low achievement (Stiff and Harvey, 1988). However, studies show that minority students like mathematics, are interested in it, have little mathematics anxiety, and plan to pursue the study of mathematics. Nevertheless, they do not perceive the usefulness of mathematics in their future work or in further schooling (Matthews, 1984). The percentage of students taking algebra II and precalculus or calculus courses is lower for blacks and Hispanics than whites (Dossey et al., 1988).

Attitudes and behaviors of significant others—parents, teachers, and counselors—influence students' attitudes toward mathematics (Matthews, 1984). Many parents of minority students want their children to do well in mathematics, but they often do not know how to encourage their children to study mathematics, nor do they know how to help with planning for careers that involve knowledge of mathematics. Teachers interested in mathematics can serve as role models, and counselors can provide career counseling that emphasizes the need for continuing the study of mathematics in the middle school, high school, and college.

Cognitive Style

Cognitive style refers to the manner in which one perceives and organizes information. Field dependence and field independence are two aspects of cognitive style that have been examined in relation to the learning of minorities. *Field-dependent* individuals perceive the world in wholes and tend to relate more comfortably to people than objects. *Field-independent* people are analytical and task-oriented. They tend to impose their own structure on a situation rather than seek structure from the environment. They like to solve problems without guidance (Kaplan, 1990).

Whether minorities are more field dependent than nonminorities and whether teachers should make provision for these differences has been discussed by different educators. Ramirez and Castaneda (1974) claim that Hispanics are generally field dependent. On the other hand, De Avila (1988) reports that when language proficiency differences are controlled, cognitive style does not differentiate language minority students from other students. Lovett (1980) suggests taking cognitive style into consideration in teaching bilingual children but advises teachers to plan programs that enable children to use both cognitive styles in learning mathematics. Stiff (1990) notes that blacks approach problems holistically. He claims they defer, but do not neglect, analytical approaches and they prefer working with others. Adapting instruction to accommodate the field-dependent cognitive style of blacks is advocated by Stiff and Harvey (1988).

Experiential Background

All young children have real-life experiences that introduce them to mathematical concepts (Charbonneau and John-Steiner, 1988). These include playing games involving counting and scoring, enjoying toys such as balls that develop intuitive ideas of shapes, and participating in family activities that introduce children to time and space. Children from rural and urban environments have different experiences, but they enter school with knowledge that is useful in subsequent mathematics learning. Charbonneau and John-Steiner also claim that all children have difficulty relating their informal learning to school learning but that making the needed connections is particularly difficult for minority children.

Minority children can bring cultural learnings to school that interact with school learning in negative ways. For example, Bradley (1984) notes that the American Indian culture teaches children to listen, to be silent, and they are uncomfortable with "discovery learning" that stresses verbal responses. She also points out that traditional Indian culture stresses memorization to pass on the culture to the next generation but that in mathematics those who rely on memorization are not creative problem solvers.

Cultural experiences can teach children not to deal with situations that do not conform to reality. For example, Leap (1988) relates the story of a Ute Indian boy who, when asked to solve a problem involving finding the cost of gasoline for a trip his brother would take in his pickup, replied that his brother did not have a pickup.

Guidelines for Teaching Mathematics to Minority Children

To help children of minority cultures succeed in learning mathematics, teachers usually must modify some aspects of their instruction. Six guidelines for teaching mathematics to minority children are discussed in this section. The guidelines are based on the factors, outlined in the previous sections, that are related to the learning of minority children and on the concepts of interactive teaching and learning.

1. Begin mathematics instruction in the child's native language.
2. Teach mathematics to develop mathematical thinking and problem-solving abilities.
3. Develop a classroom climate conducive to each child's learning mathematics.
4. Be alert to individual and possible cultural differences that could influence the learning of mathematics.
5. Use culturally relevant materials.
6. Enlist the cooperation of parents and caretakers.

Activity for the Classroom 15.1. Determine the percents of different minority populations in your classroom and your school. Ask school officials if the populations in the school have changed in the past five years and how the school has responded to changes.

Begin Mathematics Instruction in the Child's First Language. Most educators advocate teaching mathematics in a children's second language only after they have developed some fluency in their first language (Cuevas, 1984; Cummins, 1981, 1989; Lass, 1988). It is believed that if children begin instruction in L1, when they have acquired sufficient English to understand and communicate, they can learn English labels for concepts constructed in L1 and profit from instruction in L2.

Instruction to advance understanding of mathematics concepts in L1 and later L2 should employ the interactive approach. Working individually or cooperatively, children use materials to solve problems and complete activities, and they share their work and thinking processes in group discussions. To detect sources of confusion that arise mainly because of language or cultural background, teachers listen carefully to children's "talk" when they are working together and in a whole-class setting. They can ask children proficient in L1 and L2 to help children who are just beginning to use L2 in mathematics and may have formed misconceptions. Children can also be paired for problem solving, so that one who is strong in L1 and L2 can be paired with a child who is not yet fully proficient in L2.

Instruction should also teach vocabulary directly. Children need to learn the English labels for the concepts they have constructed when studying mathematics in L1. Lessons would employ objects and pictures, with words given by the teacher orally and in writing and repeated by the children. Children should have many opportunities to use the English words in games and activities. The games and activities can involve matching oral or written words in L1 and L2. However, children should not begin to believe that mathematics is the study of vocabulary because vocabulary has been overemphasized.

Garbe's (1985) research involving Navaho Indians led him to conclude that students can have trouble with sound-alike words such as "sum" and "some." He advises teachers to be alert for possible pupil difficulties with sound-alike words.

Teach Mathematics to Develop Mathematical Thinking and Problem-Solving Abilities. To enable elementary school bilingual children to develop cognitive/academic proficiency in mathematics, teaching should provide opportunities to develop mathematical thinking and to solve problems. To achieve this goal, teachers should base their instruction on the four principles used by Spanos et al. (1988) to develop written materials for bilingual students of beginning algebra. The principles can serve as guides to develop mathematics thinking in younger as well as older learners. They reflect the recommendations of the *Curriculum and Evaluation Standards for School Mathematics* (NCTM, 1989) and are in line with current thinking in the field of mathematics education.

1. Have children talk through problems together to become comfortable with listening to and speaking English mathematical language. Many opportunities should be given to discuss solution strategies used to arrive at solutions to the problems.
2. Have children formulate story problems using information from their lives or provided by the teacher.
3. Ask children to write essay-type answers to questions on quizzes and tests to enable them to use mathematical language.
4. Have students keep journals to describe their thinking about mathematical problems or topics.

Instruction incorporating these principles makes it possible for learners to develop both the language and thinking structures of mathematics because they use mathematical language in solving problems and learning mathematics.

Stiff (1990) recommends that instruction for black students be developed along similar lines. He claims that group work related to investigations and projects would benefit black students and improve their performance in mathematics. He points out that the *Standards* with their emphasis on connections and communication are particularly suited to the needs of black learners.

Develop a Classroom Climate Supportive of Each Child's Learning Mathematics. A classroom climate that encourages mathematics learning is characterized by a supportive environment in which trust and respect for others are demonstrated throughout the day and in which children are given time and encouragement to explore mathematical ideas and share their investigations. Campbell and Langrall (1993) report on a project that is built around such objectives. The project, Increasing the Mathematical Power of All Children and Teachers (IMPACT), was implemented for children in three Washington, DC, schools with populations that are racially and ethnically diverse and speak different languages. The project focused on children in kindergarten through grade 3. It stressed:

- Doing investigative activities
- Building on learner's prior knowledge
- Asking open and justification questions to enable learners to communicate meanings
- Encouraging learners to trust their thinking and to risk exposing their thoughts
- Being sensitive to each child's feelings
- Withholding judgment; letting children exchange ideas to clarify thinking
- Integrating mathematics with all subjects
- Raising the expectations of teachers for children's mathematical learning

A commitment to implementing these goals would provide a classroom climate in which children from all cultures would be free to employ mathematical thinking, construct mathematical concepts, and develop skills.

Be Alert to Individual and Possible Cultural Differences That Could Influence the Learning of Mathematics. Children process and organize material in different ways. Although cognitive styles may not be identified with cultural groups, there may be a tendency for children from a particular culture to share characteristics such as a desire to work together, a need for structure and direction, and a propensity to relate to people more than tasks. Because children from all cultures show differences in cognitive style, look at all children as individuals to determine how to accommodate these differences.

Use Culturally Relevant Materials. Culturally relevant materials enable children to identify with their own culture and give children of all cultures opportunities to broaden their understanding of other cultures. Taylor, Stevens, Peregoy, and Bath (1991) suggest using tessellations and Pascal's triangle to explore designs meaningful to American Indian children. Navaho Indian designs can be created with LOGO (Bradley, 1993). Zaslavsky (1991) describes two intriguing projects for upper elementary school children based on African culture: (1) an investigation of the relation of area and perimeter in round houses; and (2) a study of networks. She illustrates how mathematics can help children recognize the contributions of all peoples to mathematics and can help children of different cultures take pride in the accomplishments of their people. The NCTM publication, *Multicultural Mathematics Materials* (Krause, 1983), gives interesting activities and games from Africa, Asia, Oceania, Europe, Middle East, South America, and different Indian tribes of North America. The booklet includes diagrams that enable teachers easily to incorporate the suggestions in their mathematics classes.

Enlist the Cooperation of Parents and Caretakers. Parents and caretakers can be powerful allies in helping children learn mathematics. They can be given information in their language that helps them understand the usefulness of mathematics for their children as they enter the work world. They can be urged to help their children develop positive attitudes toward the study of mathematics by discussing with their children the importance of studying mathematics and continuing to enroll in mathematics courses through high school and college.

Minority parents and caretakers can help in the classroom by serving as bilingual aides. Moyers (1993) describes a program organized by a third-grade classroom teacher in which mentor parents helped non-English-speaking children adjust to their new life in an American classroom and particularly helped them with language skills and subject matter learning. Such mentors would be particularly useful for children for whom no L1 instruction is available because no teacher proficient in a language can be found (e.g., Hmong).

Workshops for minority parents and caretakers can encourage them to learn to include mathematics in the everyday lives of their children. *Family Math* (Stenmark, Thompson, and Cossey, 1986) gives ideas to use with children at home and can be the basis of workshop activities. Teachers can also encourage workshop participants to think of instances in their lives in which number, shapes, time, and space make situations comprehensive, and teachers can encourage parents and caretakers to decide how to share these situations with their children.

GENDER AND MATHEMATICS LEARNING

Less women enroll in advanced courses in mathematics and pursue careers in mathematics and science than men (Leder, 1990). This situation is unfortunate because it is a loss to the nation and can create economic problems for women. Boys and girls in the elementary school achieve at the same level in mathematics, but by age 17 boys outperform girls (Dossey et al., 1988). Thus, it appears that events in elementary school mathematics classes could be related to the greater mathematical achievement of males in high school and in later life.

Many researchers have studied interaction patterns between teacher and students to find reasons for older boys' greater achievement in mathematics. Summaries of such research related to learning mathematics in the elementary school are found in Brophy (1985), Fennema and Peterson (1985), (1987), and Koehler (1990). Major findings are:

1. Boys receive more mathematical instructional time than girls.
2. Teachers ask boys more high-level (thought-provoking) questions in mathematics than they ask girls.
3. Boys are praised more for intellectual abilities; girls for nonacademic qualities such as neatness.
4. Boys respond more because they are asked more questions and volunteer more than girls.

Others claim there are genetic differences related to the difference in mathematics performance of males and females after elementary school. Difference in spatial skill has often been cited as a factor contributing to males' higher achievement. The research of Fennema and Tartre (1985) and Tartre (1990) examined two aspects of spatial skill: spatial visualization, the ability to mentally manipulate all or part of objects, and spatial orientation, the ability to recognize change in the orientation of an object or comprehend two different representations. They demonstrated that middle-grade and high school males with either high or low spatial skills (both spatial visualization and orientation) performed equally well on mathematics problems or low spatial males outperformed high spatial males. The pattern was different for females. Low spatial females had difficulty with the mathematics problems, whereas the high spatial females scored as high as or higher than the male subjects. Tartre concludes that females who lack spatial skills may have caused the mean of all females to be lower than that of males and confused the issue of gender differences in spatial skills and mathematics achievement.

The differences in mathematical performance of males and females has often been attributed to attitudinal factors. Women as a group have been shown to:

1. Have less confidence in their ability to learn mathematics.
2. Believe that mathematics is less useful to them than boys do.
3. Stereotype mathematics as a male activity.
4. Be less autonomous learners; they do not show independence in mathematical problem solving.
5. Believe that their success is not due to their ability but to other factors such as luck. Males, on the other hand, generally attribute success to ability and thus would exhibit greater control over their lives (Fennema, 1982; Meyer and Fennema, 1992).

Meyer and Fennema hypothesize that such attitudes interfere with girls' interest in studying mathematics and persisting in that study. It is important to remember, however, that individual females may not exhibit these attitudes and that many women study advanced mathematics and are very successful.

Elementary school teachers can help girls develop attitudes that contribute to their confidence in studying mathematics, their belief in their own ability, and the knowledge that more careers are open to them if they pursue the study of advanced mathematics. Three guidelines for teachers are discussed in the remainder of this section.

Guidelines to Ensure Equity for Girls in Mathematics Instruction

Monitor Your Behavior. Teachers often believe they do not interact differently with boys and girls in mathematics classes. One of my students reported that a friend in her building denied she interacted differently with students. The friend challenged my student to observe in her class to verify her claim that she showed no difference in interacting with boys and girls. The friend was amazed that the observation record showed she did call on boys more frequently than girls and did give boys more opportunities to solve challenging problems.

It takes effort to monitor one's behavior. It appears easier to monitor students' behavior than one's own behavior. It can be done, however, if one has an interest in doing so (Fennema and Peterson, 1985). If you believe that girls should develop attitudes and skills required for the advanced study of mathematics, you will monitor your behavior. If your self-observation reveals inequities in your instruction, you will change your interactions with girls. You will start giving girls more opportunities to respond and will avoid letting boys speak out and volunteer more than girls during class discussions. Keeping a record of your self-observations can help in the process of monitoring and changing your behaviors.

Activity for the Classroom 15.2. Ask a friend or the teacher with whom you work to observe and make a record of your interactions with boys and girls. Study the record to determine how you rate on dealing with both sexes equitably.

Encourage Girls to Be Independent Problem Solvers. Girls must be given many opportunities to engage in high-level thinking to learn to solve challenging problems. Learning high-level thinking occurs over a long time by engaging in many problem-solving experiences, persisting, and succeeding (Fennema and Peterson, 1985).

To help girls become confident, autonomous problem solvers, give hints about problem-solving strategies rather than about answers, encourage girls to persist in problem solving, and frequently ask them "why" and "how" questions. Give feedback that stresses girls' intellectual ability. Help them take credit for their successes (Fennema and Peterson, 1987).

Interactive teaching can provide a format for helping girls become problem solvers. In the problem-solving phase, vary the format so that sometimes individuals solve problems and sometimes problems are solved by groups. Discuss why all should participate when groups solve problems. Students can be taught to include everyone in cooperative groups by learning the skill of asking for contributions and giving positive feedback to others. Role playing is a technique to teach these skills. To help students learn to give and accept contributions, you can also occasionally have one group member serve as an observer and report how the group worked as a team. Follow-up discussions can emphasize how to make further progress in including everyone in group problem solving.

Use Class Activities to Promote Awareness of the Usefulness of Mathematics for Women. All students, but particularly girls, should study the usefulness of mathematics in careers. Although many children recognize that consumers use mathematics, few are aware of the need for mathematics in many lines of work. Individuals in different careers can be asked to speak to students and point out how they use mathematics. For example, medical workers—doctors, nurses, and lab technicians—accountants, biologists, ecology scientists, engineers, and building contractors can tell a class the need for mathematics in their work. At least as many women as men should be scheduled to speak to your class. Discussions following such presentations can help focus on the need to study mathematics in future years to be prepared for life's work.

Reader Activity 15.1

Write a short report on a female mathematician. How did you decide whom to choose?

Students can report on the lives of famous women and men mathematicians. Three sources of information are:

Osen, Lynn M. (1974). *Women and Mathematics.* Cambridge, MA: MIT Press.
Perl, Teri Hoch. (1978). *Math Equals.* Menlo Park, CA: Addison-Wesley.
Voolich, Erica Dakin. (September 1993). "Using Biographies to 'Humanize' the Mathematics Class." *Arithmetic Teacher* 41: 16–19.

The reports on women mathematicians students write and present to the class can help both boys and girls become aware of the contributions of women to mathematics, give girls role models, and help build pride in the accomplishments of women.

MATHEMATICS FOR EXCEPTIONAL CHILDREN

Exceptional children are handicapped children and gifted learners. Their instructional needs are different from those of most children. Two federal laws have dealt with the education of exceptional children (MacMillan, Keogh, and Jones, 1986; Spicker and McLeskey, 1981). Public Law 94–142 gave certain rights and protections to handicapped children. It provided for due process in classification and assignment in a school, protection against assessment procedures that are discriminatory, assurance of placement in an educational environment that is the least restrictive, and the preparation of individualized education programs (IEPs). Handicapped children covered under the law include several subcategories of physically handicapped, mentally handicapped, and learning handicapped. The Gifted and Talented Children's Act, passed in 1978, authorized the expenditure of funds until 1983 to assist public and private agencies and organizations to provide programs for the educational needs of the gifted and talented. Although this law is no longer in effect, from time to time Congress appropriates funds for the education of the gifted and talented. Your district should keep you informed regarding federal and state funds that become available for special programs for educating the gifted.

This main section discusses mathematics for children with learning disabilities, for slow learners, and for mathematically gifted children. One or more children from these groups are found in most classrooms. The parts of the section are: Characteristics of Learning Disabled Children and of Slow Learners, Mathematics Instruction for Learning Disabled Children, Mathematics Instruction for Slow Learners, Identifying Mathematically Gifted Learners, and Mathematics Instruction for Gifted Learners.

Characteristics of Learning Disabled Children and of Slow Learners

Children with *learning disabilities* include those with perceptual and cognitive processing deficits. Many different disabilities have been identified. Learners with disabilities can have difficulties attending and are distracted by the stimuli bombarding them. They can make figure-ground reversals, have visual or auditory perceptual difficulties, show inability to discriminate or sequence, or have memory dysfunctions. Learning disabled children are found at all levels of intelligence, from low to high (Glennon and Cruickshank, 1981).

Slow learners learn more like normal learners, but at a slower rate. They will learn to compute at the level expected for their mental age, but have difficulties with mathematical reasoning. They have difficulty attending to tasks, determining key elements in problems, and organizing incoming stimuli. Short-term memory is poor, but if they "overlearn" material, they will retain it quite well . Because they have often experienced failure, they may expect failure and will not exert the effort necessary to complete a task successfully (Callahan and MacMillan, 1981).

It is often difficult to determine a child's problem in learning mathematics. If a child in your class has difficulty learning mathematics, first determine if the child lacks the background learning to profit from your instruction (Glennon and Cruickshank, 1981). If children have not had appropriate instruction in previous grades, they have no prior learning to connect with new information and are unable to construct the meanings necessary for advancing in the study of mathematics. In general, if a child is performing at an immature level (such as counting an easy addition fact at age 11), it may be that he or she was never helped to develop strategies or learn the facts for immediate recall. Or, if the student is unable to solve a problem by drawing a diagram, he or she may have never learned the draw-a-diagram strategy for solving problems or was discouraged from drawing diagrams to solve problems. Discussion with the child can often clarify what he or she was taught in previous grades, and a few short individual lessons or the use of special study materials can help the child use age-appropriate procedures. If the child continues to have problems learning mathematics, he or she should be referred to the school or district psychologist. His or her specific learning problem can then be determined and a plan developed to enable him or her to learn mathematics in your classroom.

Mathematics Instruction for Learning Disabled Children

Children with handicaps are frequently *mainstreamed* into regular classes to comply with Public Law 94-142. Mainstreaming provides a least restrictive environment for every child and gives attention to the educational needs of children rather than diagnostic labels. Mainstreaming should provide for instruction in a regular classroom as well as provide support services such as itinerant teachers, consulting teachers, and resource room teachers (Caster, 1975). Your curriculum and pedagogy will reflect the IEP that must be prepared for each child mainstreamed into your class. Guidelines for instruction for those mainstreamed are given later in this section. They are general in nature and do not take the place of an IEP.

Problem solving is important for all children, and the learning disabled are no exception. Being able to solve problems is the most important instructional objective for these children. Living in the real world will require them to solve problems (Bley and Thornton, 1989; NCTM, 1989). To develop the meanings necessary to analyze and solve problems, learning disabled children use concrete aids and graphic materials as do all children. However, they usually need more structured instruction and study materials than others. They may need specific suggestions for the use of concrete and graphic materials. To help such children develop their problem-solving skills, Bley and Thornton suggest assigning them story problems together with several choices related to a strategy for solving the problems, to operations to use to solve the problems, or to solutions. They say that similar choice-type materials can also be used to help the learning disabled determine if the answer is reasonable by giving choices for estimations or logical reasons. If children have opportunities to explain their choices to others or to you, they will gain understanding so that later they can solve problems without the guidance provided by choices at each step in problem solving. Bley and Thornton point out that learning disabled children need to discuss their work and to explain their thinking to others to internalize meanings. Thus, they can profit from interactive teaching if this approach is adapted to their specific needs. For example, a learning disabled child could explain why he or she chose a certain operation to use to solve a problem assigned to all members of the class.

Many learning disabled children have difficulty learning basic facts and remembering steps in computational procedures, even though they can reason about mathematical relations. They should use tables of facts and calculators for coping with their specific memory problem.

Activity for the Classroom 15.3. Write three study sheets, each with four different story problems and four choices for each problem. One study sheet should deal with strategies for solution, one with operations, and one with answers to the problems. If possible, use these study sheets with learning disabled children; if you do not teach learning disabled children, use them with the children you teach. Ask the children to tell why they selected certain choices.

Guidelines for Instruction. Bley and Thornton and Glennon and Cruickshank (1981) give many suggestions for helping the learning disabled. Their ideas are incorporated in the following guidelines:

1. *Help the child format a study sheet.* Have him or her use a marker or plain side of a ruler to keep his or her place in a written story problem or provide a template for blocking out all but the number problem presently being considered.
2. *Make directions short and specific.*
3. *Help him or her find a quiet place to work.* When he or she is working in a group, make certain the group is in a part of the room where there is the least distraction (e.g., not facing bulletin boards as these often distract those who have difficulties blocking out distracting stimuli).
4. *Allow the child to take quizzes or tests orally.*
5. *Give the child the time he or she needs to complete an assignment.*
6. *Help him or her keep the work space uncluttered so that distractions are minimized.*
7. *Include a learning disabled child in small group work (e.g., games) to enable him or her to know he or she belongs.* It will probably be necessary to have someone in the group be a "study-buddy." A study-buddy can help a learning disabled child by asking a member of the group to repeat what he or she said if the study-buddy thinks the learning disabled child did not follow the speaker; quietly explaining the work of the group, when needed, particularly at the beginning or end of the problem-solving session; asking the learning disabled child for contributions; and thanking him or her for the ideas expressed. A learning disabled child and a study-buddy can also solve problems together. Study-buddies should probably be volunteers. You must discuss with them how to carry out the helping role and give them positive informational feedback so that they can develop pride in their contributions to the learning of another child.
8. *Inform the parent(s) or caretaker(s) of the procedures used with their child and the reasons why the procedures were selected.* Encourage them to continue with the approaches at home; for example, keeping the environment as free of distractions as possible.

Mathematics Instruction for Slow Learners

Callahan and MacMillan (1981) suggest a program for slow learners that minimizes feelings of inadequacy and anxiety over failure and maximizes opportunities to acquire the mathematics knowledge and problem-solving strategies necessary for living. They state that problem solving should be the center of the curriculum and suggest teaching a strategy for one-step problems that focuses on the relations between part and whole. Children learn whether the problem question involves (1) combining parts (addition); (2) separating a whole into parts or comparing a part to the whole (subtraction); (3) finding the whole when a number of parts of the same size is referred to in the problem (multiplication); or (4) finding the size of equal parts or the number of equal parts when the whole is given in the problem (division). After children examine many problems in terms of the part-whole connections and can identify relations, they learn to associate operations with the part–whole relations in problems.

Guidelines for Instruction. Twelve guidelines for teaching slow learners that incorporate the ideas of Callahan and MacMillan follow:

1. *Emphasize counting and using counting strategies.* Counting helps develop a sense of number, number relations, and can be applied to solving real-life problems. Teach counting by ones and tens (forward and backward). Help children learn strategies for finding answers for basic facts and for sums greater than 10, such as counting on first with tens and then ones. These strategies can be developed by using base ten materials (e.g., $45 + 23 = N$; use number bars to count 45, 55, 65, 66, 67, 68).
2. *Teach the use of the calculator for computation.* If possible, purchase calculators that compute with fractions as well as whole numbers and decimals.

3. *Give hints during problem-solving lessons.* To help slow learners become independent workers, refrain from giving answers.
4. *Use the same type of concrete materials in different lessons.* Slow learners cannot profit from the use of a great variety of materials because they cannot transfer learning with one kind of materials to learning with other materials. A few types of materials that can be used with different content should be chosen for use by slow learners.
5. *Be consistent in the use of mathematical vocabulary.* Different terms for a concept, for example, using both "take away" and "less" in talking about subtraction tends to confuse slow learners and interferes with learning. If possible, terms should be selected by teachers of different grades and the terms used consistently by the teachers at all grades. The terms should be mathematically correct and used in the middle grades as well as in high school.
6. *Emphasize patterning with slow learners.* Perceptual patterns that involve the use of concrete materials are particularly important to slow learners' understanding of numbers. For example, if students are showing four rows of trees with two in a row, you can ask, "What would happen if we had three rows of trees with two in a row?" After children find the answer to this question, continue with the "What would happen if . . ." question with two rows, then one row with two trees in a row. Learners should use concrete materials to answer all the questions. By examining the pattern that appears in the concrete materials (Figure 15.1), slow learners can often recognize a pattern in numbers as well as in the perceptual field.

   Patterns in numbers can be an extension of patterns with objects and geometric figures. Ideas for beginning patterning activities are given in Chapter Three.
7. *Give experiences for extending ideas.* For example, after a story problem is solved, ask children to solve problems with the same part–whole relation but different settings.
8. *After meaning is constructed, slow learners need repetitive practice to attain mastery.* Vary the practice format and make it interesting. Games make practice enjoyable.
9. *Teach real-life mathematics that involves geometry and measurement.* Ask slow learners to identify shapes in their environment. Have them work with coins, clocks, rulers, scales, and volume measures such as pints, quarts, and gallons.

Reader Activity 15.2

Compose three problems that involve different settings but are based on the same numerical relation. How could you use these problems in most classrooms?

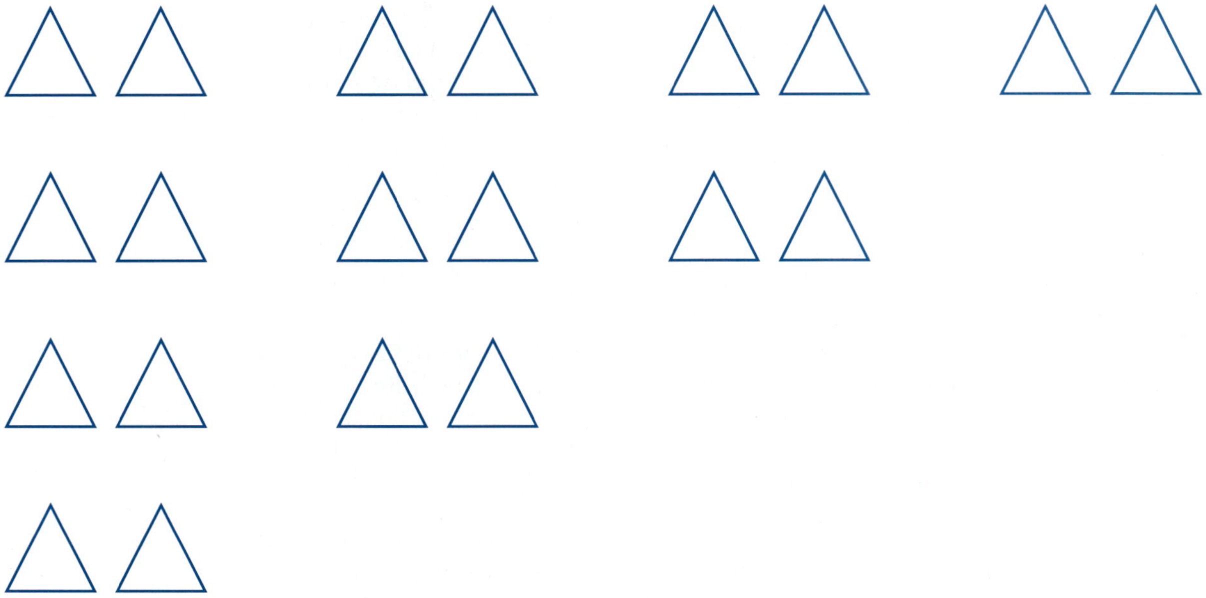

FIGURE 15.1 Rows of Trees with Two in a Row (Use Pattern Blocks for Trees)

10. *Include slow learners in group work.* Slow learners, as all learners, need to feel that they belong to a class and are important to the group's functioning. A study-buddy can work with a slow learner to solve problems. Help study-buddies learn to listen to slow learners' explanations.

    Group games that involve a great deal of chance, as many card games do, can be played by a heterogeneous group that includes slow learners. If necessary, pairs can play together in a group game. A slow learner can play with a study-buddy, receiving help and support when needed.
11. *Keep the parent(s) or caretaker(s) informed of your program and of their child's progress.* Give them suggestions for using real-life experiences with numbers and measurement to help their child understand mathematics.
12. *Provide success experiences for slow learners.* Let them know they have made progress. Tell them specifically what mathematics they have learned.

Identifying Mathematically Gifted Learners

No less than other exceptional children, gifted learners need special opportunities and programs to nurture their latent abilities. Gifted individuals can make important contributions to society and experience a sense of fulfillment only if their potential is realized. Without programs designed to meet the special needs of gifted learners and teachers sensitive to their needs, gifted children can be frustrated and feel misunderstood. Society loses because the talent of these gifted individuals has not been harnessed for the greater good. Gifted individuals can lose because they do not feel a sense of accomplishment.

Identifying mathematically gifted learners involves becoming aware of general characteristics of gifted children and the specific characteristics of mathematically gifted learners. Ridge and Renzulli (1981) state there are three components of giftedness; above-average ability, creativity, and task commitment, and that no single component defines giftedness. It is the interaction of these components that makes it possible for gifted individuals to perform in some valuable area of human endeavor at levels not attained by most individuals.

Identifying gifted learners is the shared responsibility of district personnel and classroom teachers. Many different sources of information should be used, including test scores, anecdotal records, samples of creative work, checklists, rating scales, and parental assessments. If your district does not have a plan for identifying the mathematically gifted, you will need to make careful observations and records to determine the student or students in your class who should have special instruction in mathematics. Your observations will note particularly behaviors discussed by House (1987) and Ridge and Renzulli (1981) and summarized in the following list:

- Shows superior memory and reasoning ability in area of mathematics.
- Masters skills and develops concepts earlier and more quickly than other children their age.
- May solve problems in unusual ways.
- Likes to look for patterns; enjoys mathematical puzzles.
- Shows interest in numbers, clocks, calendars, and measurement.
- Will spend long periods of time on mathematical problems without tiring.
- Often chooses activities dealing with mathematics during free time.

Mathematics Instruction for Gifted Learners

Educational opportunities for the gifted include magnet schools with a focus on science and mathematics; special regional or state schools for the gifted; learning centers in a school, district, or region where students go for special instruction and teachers find resources for use in their classes; and special classes in a pullout program in a school or district. However, these plans are not common for elementary school children. Because most teachers are responsible for the mathematical instruction of the gifted children in their classes, the following suggestions will be most helpful for teachers who have a few students they identify as mathematically gifted.

Acceleration and Enrichment. Authorities suggest that good programs have elements of both acceleration and enrichment. *Acceleration* makes it possible for children to study topics normally introduced at higher grade levels. Acceleration does not mean that mathematically gifted children only use the textbook for the next grade; when they study advanced topics, they should construct deeper meanings than are developed by children in a regular classroom. They construct these meanings by looking at the logic of procedures and by applying concepts to a wide range of situations. *Enrichment* enables children to study topics at their grade level in a broader or more comprehensive way than other children, to explore topics that are not a part of the regular school curriculum, or to carry out investigations related to topics studied at a higher grade. Enrichment will predominate in a program for the mathematically gifted carried out by a classroom teacher.

Class Organization. Depending on the topic under consideration, gifted students will be included in whole-class mathematics instruction, study independently, or work with others in small groups. They can be a part of the class for the introduction to a topic such as probability but be assigned follow-up work that gives them the opportunity to explore a topic in greater depth than is done by others in the class. They also need time independently to explore and investigate topics of interest. Working with others is a valuable experience for all learners because of the opportunities it provides for communicating mathematical ideas, and the mathematically gifted should have opportunities to participate with others in problem solving and carrying out projects.

Guidelines for Instruction. Six guidelines summarize the ideas of House and Ridge and Renzulli regarding instruction for the mathematically gifted. These guidelines should be the basis for the program you plan for gifted learners you teach:

1. *The gifted need guidance as do all children.* They are not always self-starters. You must provide direction and high-quality instruction. Interactive teaching is appropriate for these learners with its emphasis on problem solving and questioning. Mathematically gifted learners need you to interact with them as they work on problems and activities and when they are planning, carrying out, and evaluating a project. To extend their thinking and challenge them to defend their ideas, you ask the "Why," "How," and "Is it always true?" questions.
2. *The enrichment program for the mathematically gifted should not be a random collection of fun puzzles, computer activities, or problems.* It must be organized and sequential.
3. *The gifted need to work with concrete materials to develop concepts as well as to learn to appreciate the value of modeling.* Work with materials and diagrams helps them realize that not all mathematics is abstract.
4. *The gifted must master the concepts and skills expected of all students at a grade level.* Enrichment should not be the total program. Although they often dislike repetitive work, gifted children need periodic reviews of fundamental learnings. Often, review can be a part of a challenging activity.
5. *Problems solving should be the center of the curriculum for the gifted as it is for all children.*
6. *Applications and integration with other subjects should be stressed.*
7. *Mathematically gifted should have opportunities to read and write mathematics.* They should be expected to use good English and write well.

8. *Communicate with the parent(s) or caretaker(s) about your program for their mathematically gifted learner.* You are responsible for telling parent(s) or caretaker(s) how your program will enable their mathematically gifted child to develop to their full potential.

Activities in the Enrichment Program. The program should incorporate the three types of activities suggested by the Enrichment Triad Model. This model developed by Renzulli (1977) describes Types I, II, and III enrichment.

Type I activities are exploratory. Learners choose from different Type I activities to develop new interests. Learning centers can be set up with a variety of materials to give learners opportunities to explore. They can include:

- Manipulative materials such as pattern blocks, geoboards, tiles, geometric solids, Cuisenaire rods, base ten blocks, linking blocks or shapes, and tangrams
- Task cards or activity books that give suggestions for investigations involving, for example, probability or data collection
- Task cards or activity books that give puzzles and problems
- Calculators
- Computers
- Books on the history of mathematics

Appendix E gives suppliers of the type of commercial materials listed in the first four categories. You can request a catalog of the merchandise offered by these companies to study what would be useful to you in setting up an interest center for gifted learners.

Renzulli labeled *Type II enrichment activities* "group training activities." They are structured tasks designed so that learners develop high-level thinking processes, including analyzing, synthesizing, comparing, classifying, elaborating, hypothesizing, interpreting, and inferring. They should relate to the interests students express after engaging in Type I activities. Examples of Type II activities are:

- Investigating with pattern blocks to develop an awareness of proportional figures and develop concepts of similarity and ratio.
- Extending an investigation; for example after working with pentominoes, consider all possible arrangements of different polyominoes. Later, extend the investigation to arrangements of different numbers of cubes.
- Using and comparing different types of graphs for organizing and presenting data (e.g., stem-and-leaf plots, bar-and-whisker plots, pictographs, histograms, and circle graphs). Learn statistical techniques.
- Conducting experiments that give insight into basic probability ideas.
- Examining strategies for winning games or solving puzzles.
- Learning a computer language, for example, Logo.
- Studying notational systems or computational procedures used by people in times past.
- Studying the development and use of perspective in works of art.

Reader Activity 15.3

Write an activity based on one of the ideas given for Type II enrichment. Was writing the activity interesting and challenging? Why or why not?

Type III enrichment activities involve investigating and posing real problems and presenting the findings to others. Often, these problems relate to life outside of school.

- Invent new algorithms, and explain them to others.
- Write a computer program for students in your own or another grade.
- Investigate real-world problems; for example, determine which menu in the cafeteria is most liked or disliked and reasons for the choice. Present the findings to interested school personnel or students.
- Write logic or other nonroutine problems for the school paper. (See Chapter Two for examples of nonroutine problems.)

ASSESSING MATHEMATICS LEARNING OF CHILDREN WITH SPECIAL NEEDS

The assessment of the mathematics learning of children with special needs should relate to the guidelines for instruction discussed in each section of the chapter. The guidelines can be considered objectives against which mathematics instruction is assessed. Assessment also looks at the attainments of learners and their attitudes toward mathematics.

Work products, written materials, observations, interviews, and quizzes and tests are used to assess minority children's academic learning and their attitudes toward mathematics. These may be in the child's native language or in English depending on the child's language abilities. Culturally relevant materials and questions should be considered for inclusion in assessment. Children should have opportunities to tell how they think to solve problems and how they feel about learning mathematics.

Assessment of mathematics instruction for girls involves deciding if instruction is equitable. Teachers can work together to observe their behaviors before and after efforts are made to provide equity for boys and girls. Teachers can also work together to assess what they did to help girls become independent problem solvers and develop positive attitudes toward mathematics.

The assessment of the academic achievement of girls is like that for boys and includes compiling and recording information from observations and interviews, critically examining work products and journal entries, and evaluating responses on quizzes and tests. To assess change of attitude, observations and interview questions can be used.

The achievement of the learning disabled and slow learners should be in terms of the progress they have demonstrated. Observations, work products, test results, and their oral or written reports of how they solved problems are used to give evidence of progress. Children should also be interviewed to determine their progress and feelings about learning mathematics. Assessment for these children relates directly to the IEPs that guide their instruction.

Assessment of learning for mathematically gifted learners should include more than achievement tests for they generally perform well on such tests. Work products, journals, notebooks of problem solving, records of activities selected from learning centers, and the reports given to others can be used to assess learning. Interviews in which gifted learners are asked to explain their thinking are useful in determining progress. Examples of creativity and reasoning should be observed in work products and responses during interviews. Interviews and questionnaires can be used to question learners about attitudes. Motivation and persistence demonstrated as gifted learners carry out assignments and projects should be noted and records made of the behaviors observed.

SUMMARY

Mathematics instruction for minority children, the learning disabled, slow learners, females, and mathematically gifted children was discussed. Characteristics of learners in each category were presented and instructional guidelines given to meet their different learning needs. Problem solving and instruction to promote mathematical thinking were emphasized for children with special needs and interactive approaches to teaching and learning mathematics were stressed. The importance of communication with parents and caretakers was discussed. Of course, all programs should include communication with parents and caretakers, but informing them of programs and children's progress is of particular importance when students have special needs. The importance of attitudes toward learning mathematics was noted, and suggestions for developing positive attitudes were given. The final section of the chapter dealt with the assessment of learning of children with special needs.

REFERENCES

Bley, Nancy S., and Carol A. Thornton. (1989). *Teaching Mathematics to the Learning Disabled,* 2nd ed. Austin, TX: Pro-Ed.

Bradley, Claudette. (March 1984). "Issues in Mathematics Education for Native Americans and Directions for Research." *Journal of Research for Mathematics Education* 15: 96–106.

Bradley, Claudette. (May 1993). "Making a Navaho Blanket Design with Logo." *Arithmetic Teacher* 40: 520–523.

Brophy, Jere. (1985). "Interactions of Male and Female Teachers with Male and Female Students." In *Gender Influences in Classroom Interaction,* edited by Louise Cherry Wilkinson and Cora B. Marrett, pp. 115–142. New York: Academic Press.

Callahan, Leroy G., and Donald L. MacMillan. (1981). "Teaching Mathematics to Slow-Learning and Mentally Retarded Children." In *The Mathematics Education of Exceptional Children and Youth,* edited by Vincent J. Glennon, pp. 146–190. Reston, VA: National Council of Teachers of Mathematics.

Campbell, Patricia F., and Cynthia Langrall. (October 1993). "Making Equity a Reality in Classrooms." *Arithmetic Teacher* 41: 110–112.

Castellanos, Gloria G. (November 1980). "Mathematics and the Spanish-Speaking Student." *Arithmetic Teacher* 28: 16.

Caster, Jerry. (November 1975). "Share Our Specialty: What Is 'Mainstreaming'?" *Exceptional Children* 42: 174.

Charbonneau, Manon P., and Vera John-Steiner. (1988). "Patterns of Experience and the Language of Mathematics." In *Linguistic and Cultural Influences on Learning Mathematics,* edited by Rodney R. Cocking and Jose P. Mestre, pp. 91–100. Hillsdale, NJ: Erlbaum.

Cuevas, Gilberto J. (March 1984). "Mathematics Learning in English as a Second Language." *Journal for Research in Mathematics Education* 15: 134–144.

Cummins, James. (1981). "The Role of Primary Language Development in Promoting Educational Success for Language Minority Students" In *Schooling and Language Minority Students: A Theoretical Framework,* edited by David P. Dolson, pp. 3–49. Los Angeles, CA: Evaluation, Dissemination and Assessment Center, California State University.

Cummins, James. (1989). *Empowering Minority Students.* Sacramento, CA: California Association for Bilingual Education.

De Avila, Edward A. (1988). "Bilingualism, Cognitive Function, and Language Minority Group Membership." In *Linguistic and Cultural Influences on Learning Mathematics,* edited by Rodney R. Cocking and Jose P. Mestre, pp. 101–121. Hillsdale, NJ: Erlbaum.

Dossey, John A., Ina V. S. Mullis, Mary A. Lindquist, and Donald L. Chambers. (1988). *The Mathematics Report Card: Are We Measuring Up? Trends and Achievements Based on the 1986 National Assessment.* Princeton, NJ: Educational Testing Service.

Fennema, Elizabeth. (1982). "Girls and Mathematics: The Crucial Middle Years." In *Mathematics for the Middle Grades (5–9),* edited by Linda Silvey and James R. Smart, pp. 9–19. Reston, VA: National Council of Teachers of Mathematics.

Fennema, Elizabeth, and Penelope Peterson. (1985). "Autonomous Learning Behavior: A Possible Explanation of Gender-Related Differences in Learning Mathematics." In *Gender Influences in Classroom Interaction,* edited by Louise Cherry Wilkinson and Cora B. Marrett, pp. 17–35. New York: Academic Press.

Fennema, Elizabeth, and Penelope Peterson. (1987). "Effective Teaching for Boys and Girls: The Same or Different?" In *Talks to Teachers,* edited by David C. Berliner and Barak V. Rosenshine, pp. 111–125. New York: Random House.

Fennema, Elizabeth, and Lindsay A. Tartre. (May 1985). "The Use of Spatial Visualization in Mathematics by Girls and Boys. *Journal for Research in Mathematics Education* 16: 184–206.

Garbe, Douglas G. (October 1985). "Mathematics Vocabulary and the Culturally Different Student." *Arithmetic Teacher* 33: 39–43.

Glennon, Vincent J., and William M. Cruickshank. (1981). "Teaching Mathematics to Children and Youth with Perceptual and Cognitive Processing Deficits." In *The Mathematical Education of Exceptional Children and Youth,* edited by Vincent J. Glennon, pp. 50–94. Reston, VA: National Council of Teachers of Mathematics.

House, Peggy A. (Ed.). (1987). *Providing Opportunities for the Mathematically Gifted, K–12.* Reston, VA: National Council of Teachers of Mathematics.

Kaplan, Paul S. (1990). *Educational Psychology for Tomorrow's Teacher.* New York: West Publishing.

Koehler, Mary Schatz. (1990). "Classrooms, Teachers, and Gender Differences in Mathematics." In *Mathematics and Gender,* edited by Elizabeth Fennema and Gilah C. Leder, pp. 128–148. New York: Teachers College Press.

Krause, Marina C. (1983). *Multicultural Mathematics Materials.* Reston, VA: National Council of Teachers of Mathematics.

Lass, Mary Jo. (October 1988). "Suggestions from Research for Improving Mathematics Instruction for Bilinguals." *School Science and Mathematics* 88: 480–487.

Leap, William L. (1988). "Assumptions and Strategies Guiding Mathematics Problem Solving by Ute Indian Students." In *Linguistic and Cultural Influences on Learning Mathematics,* edited by Rodney R. Cocking and Jose P. Mestre, pp. 161–186. Hillsdale, NJ: Erlbaum.

Leder, Gilah C. (1990). "Gender Differences in Mathematics: An Overview." In *Mathematics and Gender,* edited by Elizabeth Fennema and Gilah C. Leder, pp. 10–26. New York: Teachers College Press.

Leu, Donald J., Jr, and Charles K. Kinzer. (1991). *Effective Reading Instruction, K–8,* 2nd ed. New York: Merrill.

Lovett, C. James. (April 1980). "Bilingual Education: What Role for Mathematics Teaching." Arithmetic Teacher 27: 14–17.

MacMillan, Donald L., Barbara K. Keogh, and Reginald L. Jones. (1986). "Special Educational Research on Mildly Handicapped Learners." In *Handbook of Research on Teaching,* 3rd ed., edited by Merlin C. Wittrock, pp. 686–724. New York: MacMillan.

Matthews, Westina. (March 1984). "Influences on the Learning and Participation of Minorities in Mathematics."*Journal for Research in Mathematics Education* 115: 84–95.

Meyer, Margaret R., and Elizabeth Fennema. (1992). "Girls, Boys, and Mathematics." In *Teaching Mathematics in Grades K–8: Research Based Methods,* 2nd ed., edited by Thomas R. Post, pp. 443–464. New York: Allyn & Bacon.

Moyers, Suzanne. (January 1993). "Bridging the Culture Gap." *Instructor* 102: 31–33.

National Council of Teachers of Mathematics (1989). *Curriculum and Evaluation Standards for School Mathematics.* Reston, VA: Author.

Orr, Eleanor Wilson. (1987). *Twice As Less: Black English and the Performance of Black Students in Mathematics and Science.* New York: Norton.

Osen, Lynn M. (1974). *Women and Mathematics.* Cambridge, MA: MIT Press.

Perl, Teri Hoch (1978). *Math Equals.* Menlo Park, CA: Addison-Wesley.

Ramirez, Manuel, and Alfredo Castaneda. (1974). *Cultural Democracy, Bicognitive Development, and Education.* New York: Academic Press.

Renzulli, Joseph S. (1977). *The Enrichment Triad Model: A Guide for Developing Defensible Programs for the Gifted and Talented.* Wethersfield, CT: Creative Learning Press.

Ridge, H. Laurence, and Joseph S. Renzulli. (1981). "Teaching Mathematics to the Talented and Gifted." In *The Mathematical Education of Exceptional Children and Youth,* edited by Vincent J. Glennon, pp. 191–196. Reston, VA: National Council of Teachers of Mathematics.

Secada, Walter G. (1990). "The Challenges of a Changing World for Mathematics Education." In *Teaching and Learning Mathematics in the 1990s,* edited by Thomas J. Cooney and Christian R. Hirsch, pp. 135–143. Reston, VA: National Council of Teachers of Mathematics.

Spanos, George, Nancy C. Rhodes, Theresa Corasaniti Dale, and JoAnn Crandall. (1988). "Linguistic Features of Mathematical Problem Solving." In *Linguistic and Cultural Influences on Learning Mathematics,* edited by Rodney R. Cocking and Jose P. Mestre, pp. 221–240. Hillsdale, NJ: Erlbaum.

Spicker, Howard H., and James McLeskey. (1981). "Exceptional Children in Changing Times." In *The Mathematical Education of Exceptional Children and Youth,* edited by Vincent J. Glennon, pp. 1–22. Reston, VA: National Council of Teachers of Mathematics.

Stenmark, Jean Kerr, Virginia Thompson, and Ruth Cossey. (1986). *Family Math.* Berkeley, CA: University of California Regents.

Stiff, Lee V. (1990). "African-American Students and the Promise of the *Curriculum and Evaluation Standards.*" In *Teaching and Learning Mathematics in the 1990s,* 1990 Yearbook of the National Council of Teachers of Mathematics, edited by Thomas J. Cooney and Christian R. Hirsch, pp. 152–158. Reston, VA: National Council of Teachers of Mathematics.

Stiff, Lee V., and William B. Harvey. (December 1988). "On the Education of Black Children in Mathematics." *Journal of Black Studies* 19: 190–203.

Tartre, Lindsay A. (1990). "Spatial Skills, Gender, and Mathematics." In *Mathematics and Gender,* edited by Elizabeth Fennema and Gilah C. Leder, pp. 27–59. New York: Teachers College Press.

Taylor, Lyn, Ellen Stevens, John J. Peregoy, and Barbara Bath. (February 1991). "American Indians, Mathematical Attitudes and the *Standards.*" *Arithmetic Teacher* 38: 14–21.

Tsang, Sau-Lim. (March 1984). "The Mathematics Education of Asian Americans." *Journal for Research in Mathematics Education* 115: 114–122.

Voolich, Erica Dakin. (September 1993). "Using Biographies to 'Humanize' the Mathematics Class." *Arithmetic Teacher* 41: 16–19.

Zaslavsky, Claudia. (February 1991). "Multicultural Mathematics Education for the Middle Grades." *Arithmetic Teacher* 38: 8–13.

In Conclusion

All the chapters in this book have discussed an interactive approach to teaching and learning. As you know, interactive teaching enables children to construct knowledge and develop positive attitudes by:

- Solving problems
- Answering questions
- Investigating and relating mathematical ideas
- Formulating problems
- Reasoning
- Connecting mathematics with their lives and other school subjects
- Understanding procedures and acquiring needed skills
- Communicating meanings

You also know that your role is to:

- Provide learners with experiences so that they construct knowledge and develop positive attitudes
- Question them so that they think critically about their work
- Assess their progress
- Decide what further activities would advance their learning

Your questioning is crucial in interactive teaching and learning. Your questions help learners make connections among ideas and construct new ideas. In order to ask learners thought-provoking questions, *you yourself think critically.* You analyze learners' responses to determine the mathematical meanings they have developed. Your interpretations of what they say and do enable you to stimulate learners to higher levels of mathematical thought and understanding.

Interactive approaches are not as easy to practice as explanatory methods, but they are more fulfilling. You will always need to seek out new problems and activities for learners, monitor your questioning, examine your assessment techniques, and think critically about your mathematics teaching so that you can meet the criteria for interactive teaching. As you grow professionally in the process of fine-tuning this approach to teaching, you will find greater and greater satisfaction in your work. You will know that you have contributed to learners' attaining mathematical knowledge for the present and for the future. You will realize that they are making sense of mathematics, are developing useful procedures, and are motivated to learn more mathematics. You will feel gratified that your teaching helped them build a good foundation for using mathematics and learning more mathematics as they advance in school.

APPENDIX A

A

National Council of Teachers of Mathematics Curriculum Standards, Evaluation Standards (1–10), and Assessment Standards

CURRICULUM STANDARDS FOR GRADES K–4*

Standard 1: Mathematics as Problem Solving

In K–4, the study of mathematics should emphasize problem solving so that students can:

- use problem-solving approaches to investigate and understand mathematical content;
- formulate problems from everyday and mathematical situations;
- develop and apply strategies to solve a wide variety of problems;
- verify and interpret results with respect to the original problem;
- acquire confidence in using mathematics meaningfully. (p. 23.)

Standard 2: Mathematics as Communication

In grades K–4, the study of mathematics should include numerous opportunities for communication so that students can:

- relate physical materials, pictures, and diagrams to mathematical ideas;
- reflect on and clarify their thinking about mathematical ideas and situations;
- relate their everyday language to mathematical language and symbols;
- realize that representing, discussing, reading, writing, and listening to mathematics are a vital part of learning and using mathematics. (p. 26.)

Standard 3: Mathematics as Reasoning

In grades K–4, the study of mathematics should emphasize reasoning so that students can:

- draw logical conclusions about mathematics;
- use models, known facts, properties, and relationships to explain their thinking;
- justify their answers and solution processes;
- use patterns and relationships to analyze mathematical situations;
- believe that mathematics makes sense. (p. 29.)

Standard 4: Mathematical Connections

In grades K–4, the study of mathematics should include opportunities to make connections so that students can:

- link conceptual and procedural knowledge;
- relate various representations of concepts or procedures to one another;
- recognize relationships among different topics in mathematics;
- use mathematics in other curriculum areas;
- use mathematics in their daily lives. (p. 32.)

Standard 5: Estimation

In grades K–4, the curriculum should include estimation so students can:

- explore estimation strategies;
- recognize when an estimate is appropriate;

* National Council of Teachers of Mathematics. *Curriculum and Evaluation Standards for School Mathematics.* Reston: VA: Author, 1989. Reprinted by permission.

- determine the reasonableness of results;
- apply estimation in working with quantities, measurement, computation, and problem solving. (p. 36.)

Standard 6: Number Sense and Numeration

In grades K–4, the mathematics curriculum should include whole number concepts and skills so that students can:

- construct number meanings through real-world experiences and the use of physical materials;
- understand our numeration system by relating counting, grouping, and place-value concepts;
- develop number sense;
- interpret the multiple uses of numbers encountered in the real world. (p. 38.)

Standard 7: Concepts of Whole Number Operations

In grades K–4, the mathematics curriculum should include concepts of addition, subtraction, multiplication, and division of whole numbers so that students can:

- develop meaning for the operations by modeling and discussing a rich variety of problem situations;
- relate the mathematical language and symbolism of operations to problem situations and informal language;
- recognize that a wide variety of problem structures can be represented by a single operation;
- develop operation sense. (p. 41.)

Standard 8: Whole Number Computation

In grades K–4, the mathematics curriculum should develop whole number computation so that students can:

- model, explain, and develop reasonable proficiency with basic facts and algorithms;
- use a variety of mental computation and estimation techniques;
- use calculators in appropriate computational situations;
- select and use computation techniques appropriate to specific problems and determine whether the results are reasonable. (p. 44.)

Standard 9: Geometry and Spatial Sense

In grades K–4, the mathematics curriculum should include two- and three-dimensional geometry so that students can:

- describe model, draw, and classify shapes;
- investigate and predict the results of combining, subdividing, and changing shapes;
- develop spatial sense;
- relate geometric ideas to number and measurement ideas;
- recognize and appreciate geometry in their world. (p. 48.)

Standard 10: Measurement

In grades K–4, the mathematics curriculum should include measurement so that students can:

- understand the attributes of length, capacity, weight, area, volume, time, temperature, and angle;
- develop the process of measuring and concepts related to units of measurement;
- make and use estimates of measurement;
- make and use measurements in problem and everyday situations (p. 51.)

Standard 11: Statistics and Probability

In grades K–4, the mathematics curriculum should include experiences with data analysis and probability so that students can:

- collect, organize, and describe data;
- construct, read, and interpret displays of data;
- formulate and solve problems that involve collecting and analyzing data;
- explore concepts of chance. (p. 54.)

Standard 12: Fractions and Decimals

In grades K–4, the mathematics curriculum should include fractions and decimals so that students can:

- develop concepts of fractions, mixed numbers, and decimals;
- develop number sense for fractions and decimals;
- use models to relate fractions to decimals and to find equivalent fractions;
- use models to explore operations on fractions and decimals;
- apply fractions and decimals to problem situations. (p. 57.)

Standard 13: Patterns and Relationships

In grades K–4, the mathematics curriculum should include the study of patterns and relationships so that students can:

- recognize, describe, extend, and create a wide variety of patterns;
- represent and describe mathematical relationships;
- explore the use of variables and open sentences to express relationships. (p. 60.)

CURRICULUM STANDARDS FOR GRADES 5–8*

Standard 1: Mathematics as Problem Solving

In grades 5–8, the mathematics curriculum should include numerous and varied experiences with problem solving as a method of inquiry and application so that students can:

- use problem-solving approaches to investigate and understand mathematical content;
- formulate problems from situations within and outside mathematics;

* National Council of Teachers of Mathematics. *Curriculum and Evaluation Standards for School Mathematics*. Reston: VA: Author, 1989. Reprinted by permission.

- develop and apply a variety of strategies to solve problems, with emphasis on multistep and nonroutine problems;
- verify and interpret results with respect to the original problem situation;
- generalize solutions and strategies to new problem situations;
- acquire confidence in using mathematics meaningfully. (p. 75.)

Standard 2: Mathematics as Communication

In grades 5–8, the study of mathematics should include opportunities to communicate so that students can:

- model situations using oral, written, concrete, pictorial, graphical, and algebraic methods;
- reflect on and clarify their own thinking about mathematical ideas and situations;
- develop common understandings of mathematical ideas, including the role of definitions;
- use the skills of reading, listening, and viewing to interpret and evaluate mathematical ideas;
- discuss mathematical ideas and make conjectures and convincing arguments;
- appreciate the value of mathematical notation and its role in the development of mathematical ideas. (p. 78.)

Standard 3: Mathematics as Reasoning

In grades 5–8, reasoning shall permeate the mathematics curriculum so that students can:

- recognize and apply deductive and inductive reasoning;
- understand and apply reasoning processes, with special attention to spatial reasoning and reasoning with proportions and graphs;
- make and evaluate mathematical conjectures and arguments;
- validate their own thinking;
- appreciate the pervasive use and power of reasoning as a part of mathematics. (p. 81.)

Standard 4: Mathematical Connections

In grades 5–8, the mathematics curriculum should include the investigation of mathematical connections so that students can:

- see mathematics as an integrated whole;
- explore problems and describe results using graphical, numerical, physical, algebraic, and verbal mathematical models or representations;
- use a mathematical idea to further their understanding of other mathematical ideas;
- apply mathematical thinking and modeling to solve problems that arise in other disciplines, such as art, music, psychology, science, and business;
- value the role of mathematics in our culture and society. (p. 84.)

Standard 5: Number and Number Relationships

In grades 5–8, the mathematics curriculum should include the continued development of number and number relationships so that students can:

- understand, represent, and use numbers in a variety of equivalent forms (integer, fraction, decimal, percent, exponential, and scientific notation) in real-world and mathematical problem situations;

- develop number sense for whole numbers, fractions, decimals, integers, and rational numbers;
- understand and apply ratios, proportions, and percents in a wide variety of situations;
- investigate relationships among fractions, decimals, and percents;
- represent numerical relationships in one- and two-dimensional graphs. (p. 87.)

Standard 6: Number Systems and Number Theory

In grades 5–8, the mathematics curriculum should include the study of number systems and number theory so that students can:

- understand and appreciate the need for numbers beyond the whole numbers;
- develop and use order relations for whole numbers, fractions, decimals, integers, and rational numbers;
- extend their understanding of whole number operations to fractions decimals, integers, and rational numbers;
- understand how the basic arithmetic operations are related to one another;
- develop and apply number theory concepts (e.g., primes, factors, and multiples) in real-world and mathematical problem situations. (p. 91.)

Standard 7: Computation and Estimation

In grades 5–8, the mathematics curriculum should develop the concepts underlying computation and estimation in various contexts so that students can:

- compute with whole numbers, fractions, decimals, integers, and rational numbers;
- develop, analyze, and explain procedures for computation and techniques for estimation;
- develop, analyze, and explain methods for solving proportions;
- select and use an appropriate method for computing from among mental arithmetic, paper-and-pencil, calculator, and computer methods;
- use computation, estimation, and proportions to solve problems;
- use estimation to check the reasonableness of results. (p. 94.)

Standard 8: Patterns and Functions

In grades 5–8, the mathematics curriculum should include explorations of patterns and functions so that students can:

- describe, extend, analyze, and create a wide variety of patterns;
- describe and represent relationships with tables, graphs, and rules;
- analyze functional relationships to explain how a change in one quantity results in a change in another;
- use patterns and functions to represent and solve problems. (p. 98.)

Standard 9: Algebra

In grades 5–8, the mathematics curriculum should include the explorations of algebraic concepts and processes so that students can:

- understand the concepts of variable, expression, and equation;
- represent situations and number patterns with tables, graphs, verbal rules, and equations and explore the interrelationships of these representations;

- analyze tables and graphs to identify properties and relationships;
- develop confidence in solving linear equations using concrete, informal, and formal methods;
- investigate inequalities and nonlinear equations informally;
- apply algebraic methods to solve a variety of real-world and mathematical problems. (p. 102.)

Standard 10: Statistics

In grades 5–8, the mathematics curriculum should include exploration of statistics in real-world situations so that students can:

- systematically collect, organize, and describe data;
- construct, read, and interpret tables, charts, and graphs;
- make inferences and convincing arguments that are based on data analysis;
- evaluate arguments that are based on data analysis;
- develop an appreciation for statistical methods as powerful means for decision making. (p. 105.)

Standard 11: Probability

In grades 5–8, the mathematics curriculum should include explorations of probability in real-world situations so that students can:

- model situations by devising and carrying out experiments or simulations to determine probabilities;
- model situations by constructing a sample space to determine probabilities;
- appreciate the power of using a probability model by comparing experimental results with mathematical expectations;
- make predictions that are based on experimental or theoretical probabilities;
- develop an appreciation for the pervasive use of probability in the real world. (p. 109.)

Standard 12: Geometry

In grades 5–8, the mathematics curriculum should include the study of the geometry of one, two, and three dimensions in a variety of situations so that students can:

- identify, describe, compare, and classify geometric figures;
- visualize and represent geometric figures with special attention to developing spatial sense;
- explore transformations of geometric figures;
- represent and solve problems using geometric models;
- understand and apply geometric properties and relationships;
- develop an appreciation of geometry as a means of describing the physical world. (p. 112.)

Standard 13: Measurement

In grades 5–8, the mathematics curriculum should include extensive concrete experiences using measurement so that students can:

- extend their understanding of the process of measurement;
- estimate, make, and use measurements to describe and compare phenomena;

- select appropriate units and tools to measure to the degree of accuracy required in a particular situation;
- understand the structure and use of systems of measurement;
- extend their understanding of the concepts of perimeter, area, volume, angle measure, capacity, and weight and mass;
- develop the concepts of rates and other derived and indirect measurements;
- develop formulas and procedures for determining measures to solve problems. (p. 116.)

EVALUATION STANDARDS THAT PERTAIN TO LEARNING*

Standard 1: Alignment

Methods and tasks for assessing students' learning should be aligned with the curriculum's:

- goals, objectives, and mathematical content;
- relative emphases given to various topics and processes and their relationships;
- instructional approaches and activities, including the use of calculators, computers, and manipulatives. (p. 193.)

Standard 2: Multiple Sources of Information

Decisions concerning students' learning should be made on the basis of a convergence of information obtained from a variety of sources. These sources should encompass tasks that:

- demand different kinds of mathematical thinking;
- present the same mathematical concept or procedure in different contexts, formats, and problem situations. (p. 196.)

Standard 3: Appropriate Assessment Methods and Uses

Assessment methods and instruments should be selected on the basis of:

- the type of information sought;
- the use to which the information will be put;
- the developmental level and maturity of the student.

The use of assessment data for purposes other than those intended is inappropriate. (p. 199.)

Standard 4: Mathematical Power

The assessment of students' mathematical knowledge should yield information about their:

- ability to apply their knowledge to solve problems within mathematics and in other disciplines;
- ability to use mathematical language to communicate ideas;
- ability to reason and analyze;
- knowledge and understanding of concepts and procedures;

* National Council of Teachers of Mathematics. *Curriculum and Evaluation Standards for School Mathematics.* Reston: VA: Author, 1989. Reprinted by permission.

- disposition toward mathematics;
- understanding of the nature of mathematics;
- integration of these aspects of mathematical knowledge. (p. 205.)

Standard 5: Problem Solving

The assessment of students' ability to use mathematics in solving problems should provide evidence that they can:

- formulate problems;
- apply a variety of strategies to solve problems;
- solve problems;
- verify and interpret results;
- generalize solutions. (p. 209.)

Standard 6: Communication

The assessment of students' ability to communicate mathematics should provide evidence that they can:

- express mathematical ideas by speaking, writing, demonstrating, and depicting them visually;
- understand, interpret, and evaluate mathematical ideas that are presented in written, oral, or visual forms;
- use mathematical vocabulary, notation, and structure to represent ideas, describe relationships, and model situations. (p. 214.)

Standard 7: Reasoning

The assessment of students' ability to reason mathematically should provide evidence that they can:

- use inductive reasoning to recognize patterns and form conjectures;
- use reasoning to develop plausible arguments for mathematical statements;
- use proportional and spatial reasoning to solve problems;
- use deductive reasoning to verify conclusions, judge the validity of arguments, and construct valid arguments;
- analyze situations to determine common properties and structures;
- appreciate the axiomatic nature of mathematics. (p. 219.)

Standard 8: Mathematical Concepts

The assessment of students' knowledge and understanding of mathematical concepts should provide evidence that they can:

- label, verbalize, and define concepts;
- identify and generate examples and nonexamples;
- use models, diagrams, and symbols to represent concepts;
- translate from one mode of representation to another;
- recognize the various meanings and interpretations of concepts;
- identify properties of a given concept and recognize conditions that determine a particular concept;
- compare and contrast concepts.

In addition, assessment should provide evidence of the extent to which students have integrated their knowledge of various concepts. (p. 223.)

Standard 9: Mathematical Procedures

The assessment of students' knowledge of procedures should provide evidence that they can:

- recognize when a procedure is appropriate;
- give reasons for the steps in a procedure;
- reliably and efficiently execute procedures;
- verify the results of procedures empirically (e.g., using models) or analytically;
- recognize correct and incorrect procedures;
- generate new procedures and extend or modify familiar ones;
- appreciate the nature and role of procedures in mathematics. (p. 228.)

Standard 10: Mathematical Disposition

The assessment of students' mathematical disposition should seek information about their:

- confidence in using mathematics to solve problems, to communicate ideas, and to reason;
- flexibility in exploring mathematical ideas and trying alternative methods in solving problems;
- willingness to persevere in mathematical tasks;
- interest, curiosity, and inventiveness in doing mathematics;
- inclination to monitor and reflect on their own thinking and performance;
- valuing of the application of mathematics to situations arising in other disciplines and everyday experiences;
- appreciation of the role of mathematics in our culture and its value as a tool and as a language. (p. 233.)

ASSESSMENT STANDARDS*

Standard 1: Important Mathematics

Assessment should reflect the mathematics that is most important for students to learn.

Standard 2: Enhanced Learning

Assessment should enhance mathematics learning.

Standard 3: Equity

Assessment should promote equity by giving each student optimal opportunities to demonstrate mathematical power and by helping each student meet the profession's high expectations.

* National Council of Teachers of Mathematics. *Assessment Standards for School Mathematics: Working Draft.* Reston: VA: Author, October 1993, pp. 6–7. Reprinted by permission.

Standard 4: Openness

All aspects of the mathematics assessment process should be open to review and scrutiny.

Standard 5: Valid Inferences

Evidence from assessment activities should yield valid inferences about students' mathematical learning.

Standard 6: Consistency

Every aspect of an assessment process should be consistent with the purposes of assessment.

APPENDIX B

Interactive Instruction Lesson

Interactive instruction is illustrated in the following example from a fifth-grade class studying mental computation. The teacher, Mr. Hopkins, asked students to recall that they found mental computation useful when they were working on budgets for teenagers. He then showed eight math sentences on the overhead for study by cooperative groups. The directions to the groups were: Each person mentally find the sums. Then discuss your answers and methods of solution. If you can, decide on your group's preferred method. After time for group work during which Mr. Hopkins circulated to observe students, he began the class discussion.

MR. HOPKINS: Carl, please report for your group and give us your results for $39 + 41 = N$, $62 + 38 = N$, $26 + 44 = N$, and $78 + 42 = N$.

CARL: For 39 + 41, we decided the easiest way was to take the 1 from 41, add it to 39, and think 40 + 40 = 80. We agreed that you could use that method in the other examples. We made 62 + 38 = 70 + 30 = 100, 26 + 44 = 30 + 40 = 70, and 78 + 42 = 80 + 40 = 120.

MR. HOPKINS: Thank you, Carl. Did any group use another method?

JANE: In our group we decided we'd compute by subtracting and adding, like Carl's group did. But we also decided we could add the ones to get 10, then add the tens plus 10 more to get the answer.

MR. HOPKINS: Tell us how you did the first one, Jane, using your second method.

JANE: We said 9 + 1 = 10; 30 + 40 + 10 = 80.

MR. HOPKINS: OK, we have two approaches to these problems. Any others? [No responses.]

MR. HOPKINS: Let's discuss the second group of math sentences. Esther, please report for your group for $53 + 49 = N$; $75 + 26 = N$; $67 + 55 = N$; $64 + 25 = N$.

ESTHER: In the first example, we said that it was easy to take 1 from 53 to make 49 into 50. So 52 + 50 = 102. With the second example, we thought a good way to think was 75 + 26 = 75 + 25 + 1 = 101. We thought 67 + 55 = 65 + 2 + 55 = 50 + 10 + 50 + 10 + 2 = 122. For the last one we thought the fastest way was 64 + 25 = 60 + 25 + 4 = 85 + 4 = 89, but you could think 60 + 20 + 4 + 5 = 80 + 9 = 89.

ROGER: Our group did 67 + 55 = 122 by taking 5 from 67 and adding it to 55 to make 60. Then we had 60 + 62, which is 60 + 60 + 2 = 122. I don't understand what Esther's group did.

ESTHER: We thought 67 = 65 + 2. We took 5 from 65. That leaves 60. We took 5 from 55 and got 50. The two fives make 10. 60 is 50 + 10. So you add 50 + 10 + 50 + 10 + 2 = 50 + 50 + 10 + 10 + 2 = 100 + 20 + 2 + 122. I'll write that on the board. [She uses the chalkboard to show the steps.] Does that make sense, Roger?

ROGER: I get it now. Thanks, Esther.

MR. HOPKINS: How can we summarize the methods we have used for addition mental computation?

GARY: We made the big numbers easy to add by taking away enough to get tens or numbers ending in 5. Then we tacked on what we had subtracted.

MR. HOPKINS: What did you tack the ones numbers on to, Gary?

GARY: Well, let me think. . . . In the first ones we tacked it on to the other number. But our group did what Esther's group did and in some examples added the extra ones to the answer.

MR. HOPKINS: Let's write our methods on the chalkboard and see how a method goes with an example.

The class composed the statement: When you have tens and ones numbers to add, try to work with even tens or use numbers ending in 5. Make even tens or numbers ending in 5 by subtracting from one number and adding the difference to the other number. Then add to get the total. You can use another method: Add the tens and ones separately and then add those answers to get the total.

Several examples that pupils discussed as well as new examples were used to illustrate the generalization.

MR. HOPKINS: Any questions about what has been reported? [No responses.] Yesterday we did examples such as 46 + 23? How do our methods today differ from those we discussed yesterday. Look at our summaries from yesterday and today. [Gives time for students to think.]

MI LING: They are not too different. Both today and yesterday we decided that you could add the ones and tens separately and then add those answers together. Today when the ones added up to 10 or more, you could make one or both numbers even tens by subtracting and then adding to one number what you subtracted from the other number. Then you added all the numbers together. Sometimes we had even tens, and sometimes we had even tens and some ones left over to add in. Yesterday we didn't talk about using numbers ending in 5.

MR. HOPKINS: I'll write some examples on the board, so Mi Ling's answer will be clearer to us. [He writes 43 + 47 = N, 48 + 54 = N, and 43 + 44 = N on the chalkboard.] How do these differ? What does that mean for the way you mentally compute? [Gives time for students to think.] Mi Ling, please follow up on what you said by using these examples.

MI LING: You can see in the first one that 3 + 7 = 10, so you can take 3 from 43 and put it with 47 to make 40 + 50 = 90. Or you can think 40 + 40 + 10 = 90. In the second one, make 48 into 50; that leaves 52 or 50 + 2; 50 + 50 + 2 = 102. In the third one you see that 40 + 40 + 3 + 4 = 80 + 7 = 87. Or you can think 43 + 4 = 47; 47 + 40 = 87.

MR. HOPKINS: Your summary was complete, Mi Ling. It clearly states the methods we have discussed. There may be other ways. When anyone finds another approach for mentally finding a sum, please report it to the class. Tomorrow we will look into whether or not methods we discussed today are useful for other operations.

The next day Mr. Hopkins puts 10 examples on the board that involve mental computation with multiplication using numbers such as previously discussed for mental computation with addition. Examples include 31 × 29 = N and 48 × 52 = N. He also writes on the chalkboard: "Individually use your calculator to find the value of N in these open math sentences. Study the products for patterns. In your groups decide if our methods for mental calculation for addition can be used in mental calculation with multiplication or if other rules are needed. Try out your group's ideas on other examples." While the groups are working, Mr. Hopkins circulates to observe the groups' discussions. His observations enable him later to lead a class discussion summarizing what pupils have found, helping them compare mental computation for addition and multiplication, and constructing rules for finding products of special combinations of factors.

APPENDIX C

Answers for Chapter Two Selected Problems

C

6. A square 10′ × 10′
7. The two boys go to the island. One returns. Uncle Robert goes to the island. The other boy returns. The two boys go to the island.
10. 4 funny faces: red nose with green ears; red nose with red ears; blue nose with green ears; blue nose with red ears
11. 3 posts
12. Between 21 and 30; between 20 and 29
13. 3 days
14. Rectangle could have dimensions of
1 row of 30 chairs
2 rows of 15 chairs
5 rows of 6 chairs
6 rows of 5 chairs
15. 7 hours and 15 minutes
16. 14 eggs with yolks
17. 15
18. 27
19. 3 people. All 3 start together. One goes only one day, uses up 2 days of food and water coming and going back and leaves 2 days of food and water with the others. The others each have used up 1 day of supplies. Each has 3-days' supplies of his or her own and 1 from the person who went back, which they use on day 2. Person 2 gives 1 day of food and water to Person 3 and goes back with 2-days' supplies left for returning. Person 3 now has 3-days' supplies of his or her own and 1-day's supplies from Person 2, which is 4 days of food and water, the amount needed to complete the journey to obtain help.

21.

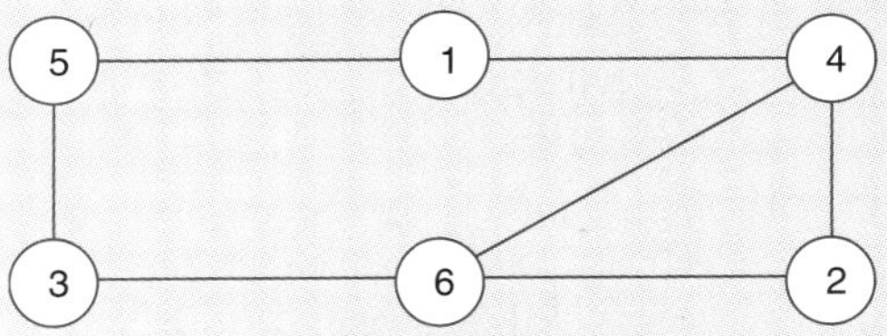

22.

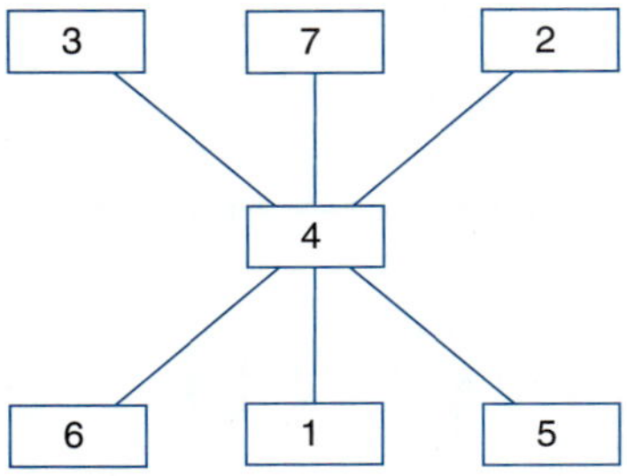

23.

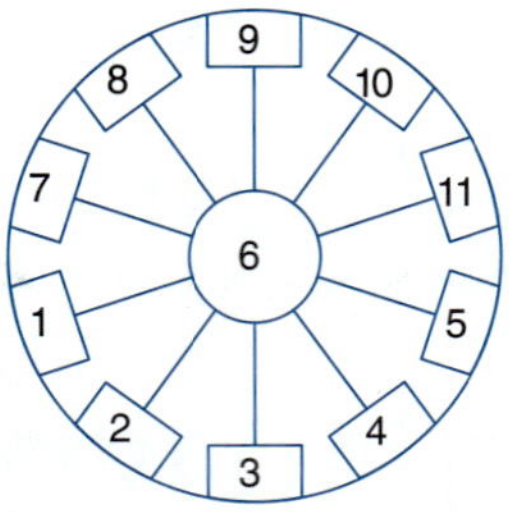

24. 26 and 27

25.

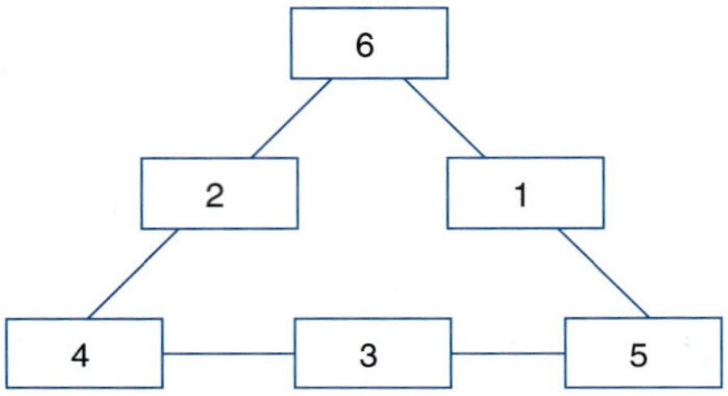

Other solutions are possible.

26. 2 of each

27.

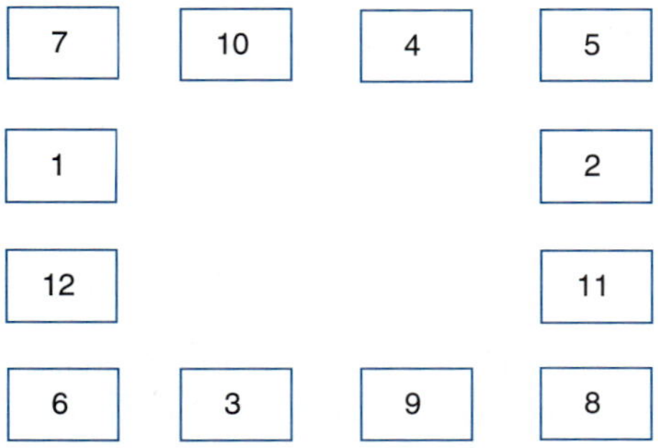

28. $2 + 3 + 6 = 11$
$6 - 2 - 4 = 0$
$6 + 4 - 6 = 4$
$2 + 3 + 4 = 9$

29. 15 and 16

30. The third number in each set is the least common multiple of the first two.

35.

QUARTERS	DIMES	NICKELS
1	1	13
2	2	6
2	1	8
3	2	1 (answer)

36.

DIMES	NICKELS	PENNIES
2	2	4
2	1	9
2	0	14
1	2	14
1	1	19

37.

CHOCOLATE (7 CENTS)	PEPPERMINT (5 CENTS)	COST	MONEY LEFT
2	1	19 cents	2 cents
1	2	17 cents	4 cents

38.

DAYS AFTER FIRST MEETING	
DAYS GAIL SWEEPS	DAYS MARIA SWEEPS
3	4
6	8
9	12
12	16

They would meet again the twelfth day.

39.

CHICKENS/LEGS	PIGS/LEGS	HEADS	TOTAL LEGS
10/20	0/0	10	20
9/18	1/4	10	22
8/16	2/8	10	24
7/14	3/12	10	26
6/12	4/16	10	28
5/10	5/20	10	30 (answer)

40.

TWO-WHEELERS VEHICLES/WHEELS	THREE-WHEELERS VEHICLES/WHEELS	TOTAL NUMBER OF WHEELS
12/24	0/0	24*
11/22	1/3	25
10/20	2/6	26
9/18	2/6	24*
8/16	3/9	25
7/14	3/9	23
6/12	4/12	24*
5/10	5/15	25
4/8	6/18	26
3/6	6/18	24*
2/4	7/21	25
1/2	7/21	23
0/0	8/24	24*

* Answer.

41. 1; 2; 3
1, 2; 1, 3; 2, 3; 2, 1; 3, 1; 3, 2
1, 2, 3; 2, 3, 1; 3, 2, 1; 1, 3, 2; 3, 1, 2; 2, 1, 3
Answer: 15

42.

QUARTERS	DIMES	NICKELS	PENNIES	TOTAL
1	1	2	5	9
1	2	0	5	8

43.

Transaction	Bought	Sold	Profit
1	3	2	1 card
2	3	2	1 card
3	0	2	$5

On 6 cards he buys and sells he makes a profit of $5; to make $25 he needs to buy and sell 30 cards or 5 × 6 cards since he makes $5 on each of 6 cards (5 × $5).

44.

Number of Hours	Dollars for Tomas	Dollars for Hernandez
1	6	8
2	12	16
3	18	24
4	24	32

The solution table shows that when Hernandez works 3 hours and Tomas works 4 hours they will have the same amount of money. Hernandez will have $24 in 3 hours, which is twice what Tomas will have in 2 hours.

45.

	Meters Run	
Minutes	Jogger 1	Jogger 2
	Start	Start
1	200	100
2	Start	200
3	200	300
4	Start	Start

4 minutes after they start, they will begin again at the same time.

46.

Days	Minutes Run
1	8
2	10
3	12
4	14
5	16
6	18
7	20
8	22
9	24
10	26

47. $N = (1 + n)\,n/2$ N = total number of dots in figure; n = number of rows. Triangle with 6 rows has 21 dots; with 24 rows, 300 dots

48. Formula is the same as in for Problem 47: 5 steps have 15 blocks; 15 steps, 120 blocks.

49. Answer: 47, 95, 191. Pattern is: Add 2 times the difference between the two last numbers.

50. Students examine squares in larger squares and make a table.

	Number of Squares of Different Sizes				
	1 × 1	2 × 2	3 × 3	4 × 4	Total
Size of square					
1 × 1	1	—	—	—	1
2 × 2	4	1	—	—	5
3 × 3	9	4	1	—	14
4 × 4	16	9	4	1	30

The pattern observed involves the sum of squares. For a square 7 × 7 there are: 1 + 4 + 9 + 16 + 25 + 36 + 49 = 140 squares.

51. 21, 34, 55, 89, 144. The pattern rule is: After the first number, add the two preceding numbers to find the next number.

53. By using 4 as a factor five times, a pattern is observed: in the ones place 4, 6, 4, 6, 4. An even number of factors has 6 in the ones place. 100 is an even number; 100 factors of 4 give a product with 6 in the ones place.

56. Dog 1 and Dog 2 go to the mainland. Dog 1 remains on the mainland. Dog 2 returns to the island and takes Cat 1 to the mainland. Cat 1 stays on the mainland with Dog 1. Dog 2 goes to the island and returns to the mainland with Cat 2. Cat 2 stays. Dog 2 goes to the island and returns with Cat 3. Cat 3 stays on the mainland. Dog 2 returns to the island and takes Dog 3 to the mainland. They stay on the mainland. Now all are on the mainland.

57. 56 times. Problem 57 differs from the handshake problem (#17) in that two people shake hands once, but two people say two hellos.

58. 36; 72

59. Tom

60. Patty is 12; Rose is 11; Masako is 10; Judy is 9.

61. Duc is the salesperson; Fred is the medical doctor; Walter is the teacher.

62. Susan owns Curley; Bryan owns Spot; Carol owns Patches; Patrick owns Beauty.

APPENDIX D

Pattern for Clown Suit

APPENDIX E

Names and Addresses of Suppliers of Mathematical Learning Materials

E

ACTIVITY AND STUDY MATERIALS

Activity Resources Company, Inc.
P.O. Box 4875
Hayward, CA 94540
(510) 782-1300

Creative Publications
Order Department
5040 West 11th Street
Oak Lawn, IL 60453
1-800-624-0822

Cuisenaire Co. of America, Inc.
P.O. Box 5026
White Plains, NY 10602-5026
1-800-237-3142

Dale Seymour Publications
P.O. Box 10888
Palo Alto, CA 94303-0879
Outside California: 1-800-872-1100
Inside California: 1-800-222-0766

Delta Education
P.O. Box 950
Hudson, NH 03051
1-800-442-5444

Didax, Inc., Educational Resources
395 Main Street
Rowley, MA 01969
1-800-458-0024

Educational Teaching Aids (ETA)
620 Lakeview Parkway
Vernon Hills, IL 60061
1-800-445-5985

Nasco Math
901 Janesville Ave.
Fort Atkinson, WI 53538-0901
1524 Princeton Ave.
Modesto, CA 95352-3837
1-800-558-9595

National Council of Teachers of Mathematics
1906 Association Drive
Reston, VA 22091-1593
1-800-235-7566

Tricon Mathematics
Box 146
Mt. Pleasant, MI 48804
1-517-772-2811

CALCULATORS

Texas Instruments Incorporated
Instructional Marketing
P.O. Box 53
Lubbock, TX 79408
1-800-842-2737

SOFTWARE

Critical Thinking Press & Software
P.O. Box 448
Pacific Grove, CA 93950
1-800-458-4849

Davidson & Associates
19840 Pioneer Avenue
Torrance, CA 90503
1-800-545-7677

IBM/EduQuest
4111 Northside Parkway
Atlanta, GA 30327
1-404-238-2000

Minnesota Educational Computing Company (MECC)
6160 Summit Drive
Minneapolis, MN 55430
1-800-685-6322

Silver Burdett-Ginn
Customer Service Center
P.O. Box 2649
Columbus, OH 43216
1-800-922-0319

Sunburst Communications
101 Castleton Street
Pleasantville, NY 10570
1-800-321-7511

The Learning Company
6493 Kaiser Drive
Fremont, CA 94555
510-792-2101

Terrapin Software, Incorporated
400 Riverside Street
Portland, ME 04103
1-800-972-8200

Tom Snyder Productions, Incorporated
80 Coolidge Hill Road
Watertown, MA 02172
1-800-342-0236

APPENDIX F

Suggested Mathematics Topics and Objectives for Kindergarten and Elementary School Grades

F

Most learners would construct concepts and develop skills at the grade level given below; in later grades, ideas would be extended and examined in new settings, and skills maintained through use and practice.

TOPICS WITH OBJECTIVES FOR KINDERGARTEN

- Develop thinking skills; classify, compare, order, conserve, pattern
- Count beyond 20
- Represent sets of objects to 10
- Begin to recognize and write numerals for sets to 10
- Statistics
  - Make and interpret people graphs
- Geometry
  - Use Level 0 thinking
- Measurement
- Understand some measurable attributes
- Make qualitative comparison of attributes
- Recognize some coins
- Problem Solving

TOPICS WITH OBJECTIVES FOR GRADE 1

- Problem solving
  - Routine problems: begin to use math sentences
  - Nonroutine problems: begin to use strategies
- Addition and subtraction facts
  - Construct meanings
  - Use strategies for recall
  - Begin to master
- Begin base and place value for numbers to 100
  - Count, group, represent, and estimate sets with numbers to 100
  - Compare numbers to 100
  - Recognize, write, and interpret numerals to 100
- Geometry
  - Use Level 0 thinking
- Measurement
  - Measure with nonstandard and some common standard units: length, area, capacity, weight, and temperature
  - Recognize value of some coins
  - Begin work with time
- Introduction to fractions
  - Develop concept of equal-sized parts
- Calculator
  - Investigate number relations
  - Use for problem solving
- Statistics
  - Make and interpret object and chart graphs
- Probability
  - Develop intuitive awareness

TOPICS WITH OBJECTIVES FOR GRADE 2

- Problem solving
  - Routine problems: begin to use math sentences
  - Nonroutine problems: use a few strategies
- Addition and subtraction facts
  - Use strategies for recall
  - Continue to master
- Base and place value
  - Count, group, represent, and estimate sets with numbers to 100
  - Compare numbers to 100
  - Recognize, write, and interpret numerals to 100
- Addition and subtraction of whole numbers
  - Begin mental computation with powers of 10
- Multiplication and division facts
  - Construct meaning
  - Use strategies for recall
- Geometry
  - Use Level 0 thinking

Measurement
- Compare and measure with nonstandard and some common standard units: length, area, capacity, weight, and temperature
- Recognize value of coins and paper money
- Tell time to the hour
- Estimate measurements

Introduction to fractions
- Represent common unit fractions
- Recognize, write, and interpret common unit fractions

Calculator
- Investigate number relations
- Use for problem solving

Statistics
- Make and interpret object, chart, and bar graphs

Probability
- Develop intuitive awareness

TOPICS WITH OBJECTIVES FOR GRADE 3

Problem solving
- Routine problems: use math sentences
- Nonroutine problems: use several strategies

Addition and subtraction facts
- Master

Multiplication and division facts
- Use strategies for recall
- Begin to master

Base and place value
- Begin numbers to 1000
  - Count, group, represent, and estimate with objects and symbols
  - Compare numbers to 1000
  - Recognize, write, and interpret numerals to 1000

Addition and subtraction of whole numbers
- Compute mentally with powers of ten
- Use estimation strategies
- Algorithms with and without regrouping
  - Construct meaning
  - Develop skill

Geometry
- Use Level 0 thinking
- Begin Level 1 thinking

Measurement
- Compare and measure with nonstandard and some common standard units: length, area, capacity, weight, and temperature
- Recognize value of coins and paper money
- Relate values of coins and paper money
- Tell time
- Estimate measurements

- Introduction to fractions
  - Represent unit fractions and common nonunit fractions
  - Recognize, write, and interpret unit fractions and nonunit fractions
  - Use reference fractions
- Calculator
  - Use for computation
  - Investigate number relations
  - Use for problem solving
- Ratio and proportion
  - Develop intuitive understanding
- Statistics
  - Collect data
  - Make and interpret bar graphs and histograms
- Probability
  - Develop intuitive awareness

TOPICS WITH OBJECTIVES FOR GRADE 4

- Problem solving
  - Routine problems: use math sentences
  - Nonroutine problems: use many strategies
- Multiplication and division facts
  - Use strategies for recall
  - Continue to master
- Base and place value
  - Numbers to 10,000
  - Represent with objects and symbols
  - Compare numbers to 10,000
  - Recognize, write, and interpret numerals to 10,000
  - Rename in different powers of 10
- Multiplication and division of whole numbers
  - Compute mentally with powers of 10
  - Use estimation strategies
  - Algorithms
    - Construct meaning
    - Develop skill
- Geometry
  - Use Level 1 thinking
- Measurement
  - Compare and measure with nonstandard (where not previously experienced) and standard units: length, area, capacity and volume, weight, and temperature
  - Estimate measurements
- Fractions
  - Represent unit fractions and nonunit fractions
  - Recognize, write, and interpret fractions
  - Compare

Addition and subtraction of fractions
- Construct meaning
- Begin study of algorithms
- Use reference fractions in computational estimation

Decimals: tenths and hundredths
- Represent, recognize, and interpret numbers
- Recognize, write, and interpret numerals
- Compare numbers

Calculator
- Use for computation
- Investigate number relations
- Use for problem solving

Ratio and proportion
- Develop intuitive understanding

Statistics
- Collect data
- Make and interpret bar graphs, line graphs, and histograms

Probability
- Develop intuitive awareness

TOPICS WITH OBJECTIVES FOR GRADE 5

Problem solving
- Routine problems: use math sentences
- Nonroutine problems: use most strategies

Multiplication and division basic facts
- Master

Base and place value
- Numbers to 100,000
  - Construct meaning
  - Represent, write, and interpret numerals
  - Compare numbers
  - Rename in different powers of 10

Addition and subtraction of fractions
- Develop skill in use of algorithms
- Use reference fractions in computational estimation

Multiplication and division of fractions
- Construct meanings of algorithms
- Begin study of algorithms
- Use reference fractions in computational estimation

Decimals: thousandths
- Construct meaning of numbers
- Read, write, and interpret numerals
- Compare numbers

Addition and subtraction of decimals
- Construct meaning
- Compute mentally with powers of ten

Use computational estimation
Use algorithms for easy examples
Geometry
Use Level 1 thinking
Begin Level 2 thinking
Measurement
Compare and measure with nonstandard (where not previously experienced) and standard units: length, area, capacity and volume, weight, temperature, and angles
Estimate measurements
Calculator
Use for computation
Investigate number relations
Use for problem solving
Ratio and proportion
Begin to construct meanings
Statistics
Data collection
Make and interpret bar graphs, histograms, line graphs, and stem-and-leaf plots
Make and interpret charts and tables
Probability
Investigate

TOPICS WITH OBJECTIVES FOR GRADE 6
Problem solving
Routine problems: use math sentences
Nonroutine problems: use all strategies
Base and place value
Numbers greater than 100,000
Construct meaning
Write and interpret numerals
Compare
Multiplication and division of fractions
Develop skill in use of algorithms
Use reference fractions in computational estimation
Decimals: ten thousandths
Construct meanings for numbers
Recognize, write, and interpret numerals
Compare numbers
Multiplication and division of decimals
Construct meaning of algorithms
Compute mentally with powers of 10
Use computational estimation
Use algorithms for easy examples
Geometry
Use Level 1 and possibly Level 2 thinking

Measurement
- Study and use formulas
- Extend knowledge of metric system

Calculator
- Use for computation
- Investigate number relations
- Use for problem solving

Ratio and proportion
- Construct meaning
- Solve problems

Percent
- Construct meaning
- Solve problems: percent of a number

Statistics
- Collect data
- Make and interpret bar graphs, histograms, line graphs, stem-and-leaf plots, and box-and-whisker plots
- Interpret pie graphs
- Make and interpret charts and tables

Probability
- Investigate

APPENDIX G

Masters for Materials to Duplicate

Lima Bean Recording Sheet

Tangram Patterns

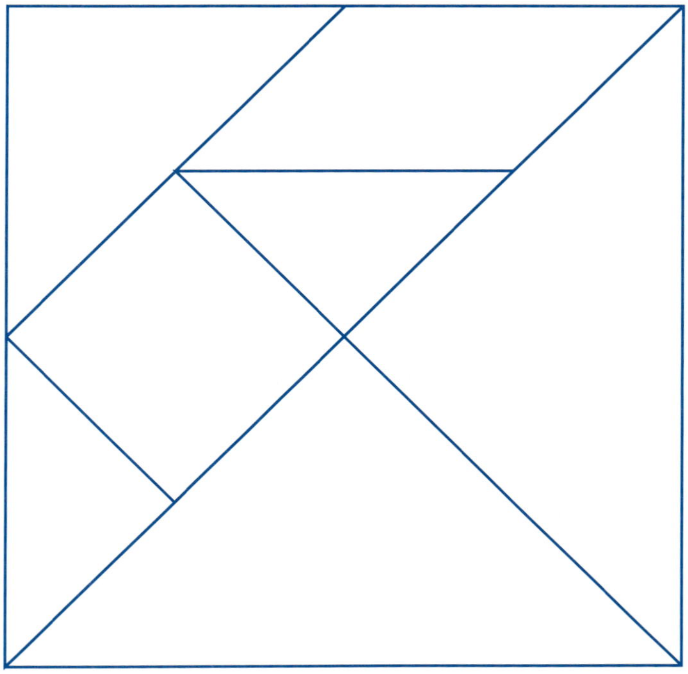

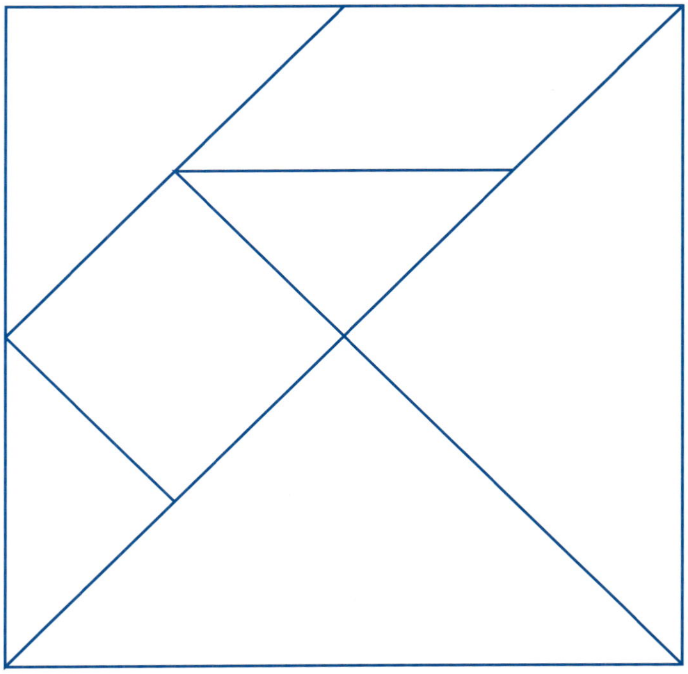

Number Bars

A, Five-Frames. B, Ten-Frames

Number Lines

Hundred Squares

1	2	3	4	5	6	7	8	9	10
11	12	13	14	15	16	17	18	19	20
21	22	23	24	25	26	27	28	29	30
31	32	33	34	35	36	37	38	39	40
41	42	43	44	45	46	47	48	49	50
51	52	53	54	55	56	57	58	59	60
61	62	63	64	65	66	67	68	69	70
71	72	73	74	75	76	77	78	79	80
81	82	83	84	85	86	87	88	89	90
91	92	93	94	95	96	97	98	99	100

Hundred Squares

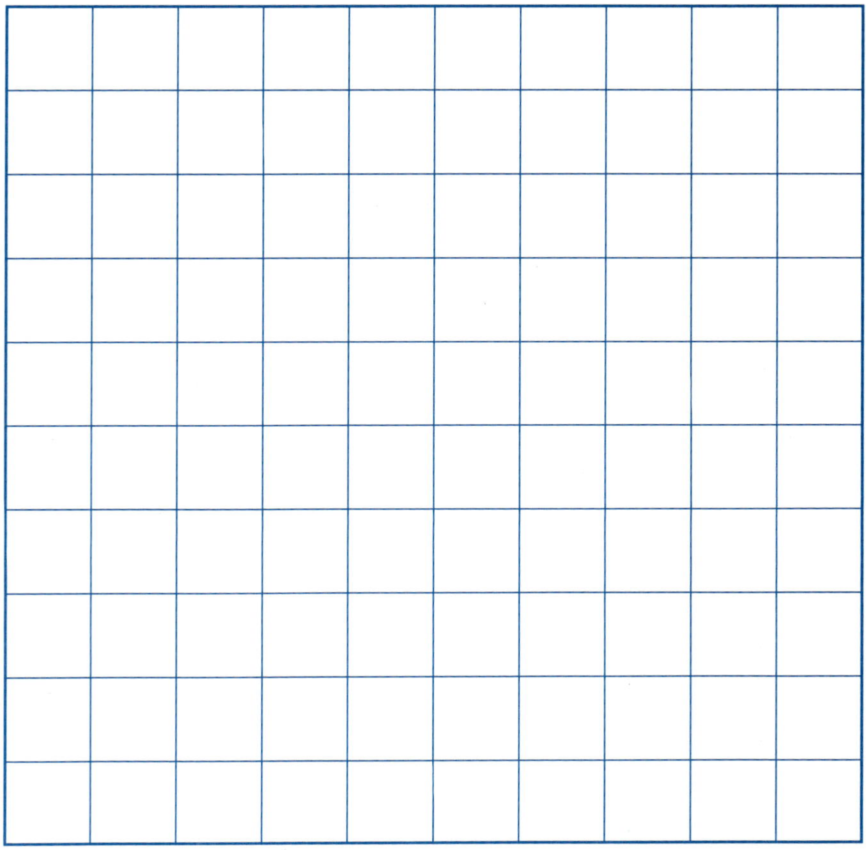

1-In Grid Paper

G

1/4-in Grid Paper

1-cm Grid Paper

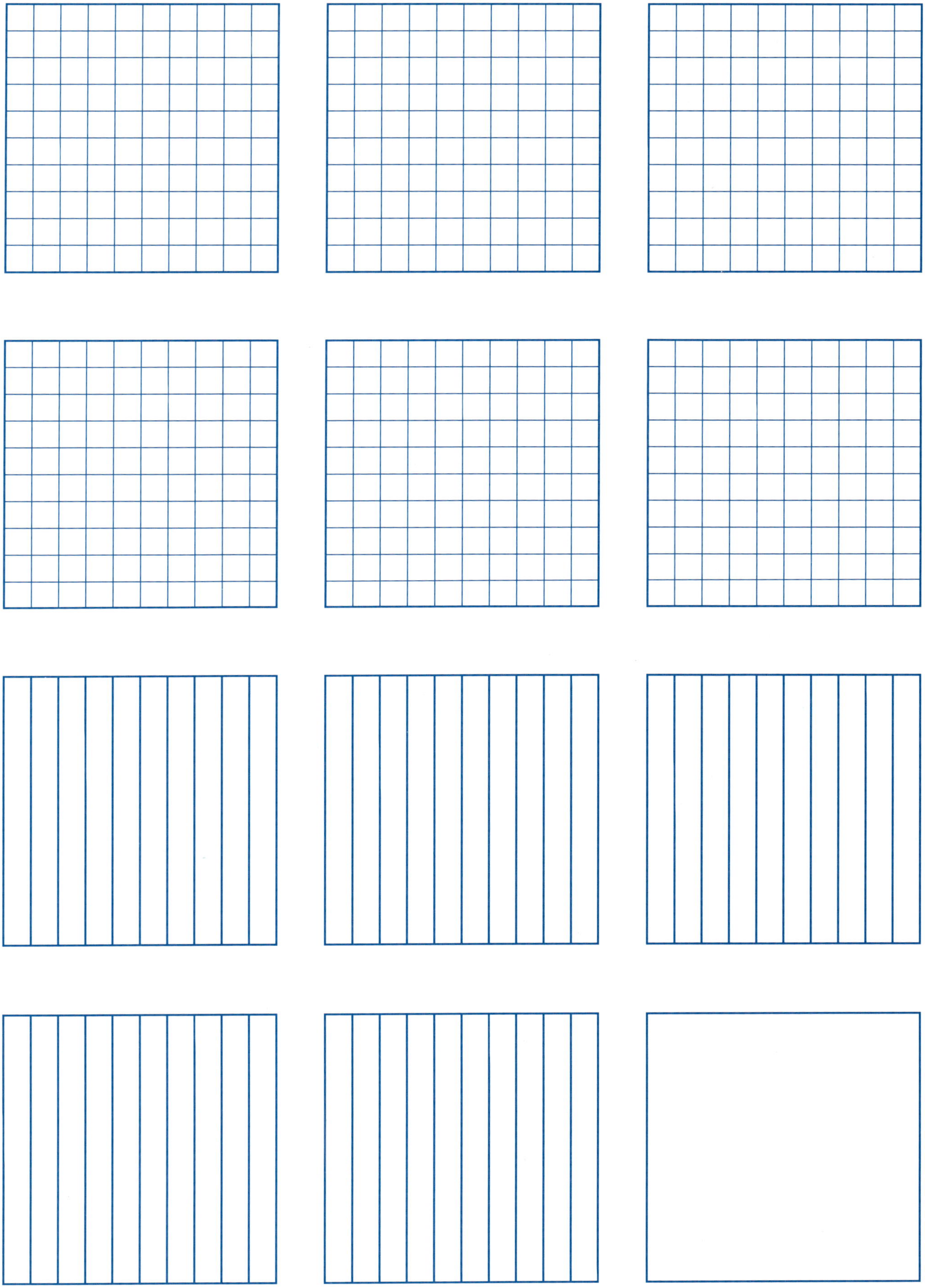

G

0.25-cm Square Grid Paper

Fraction Disks

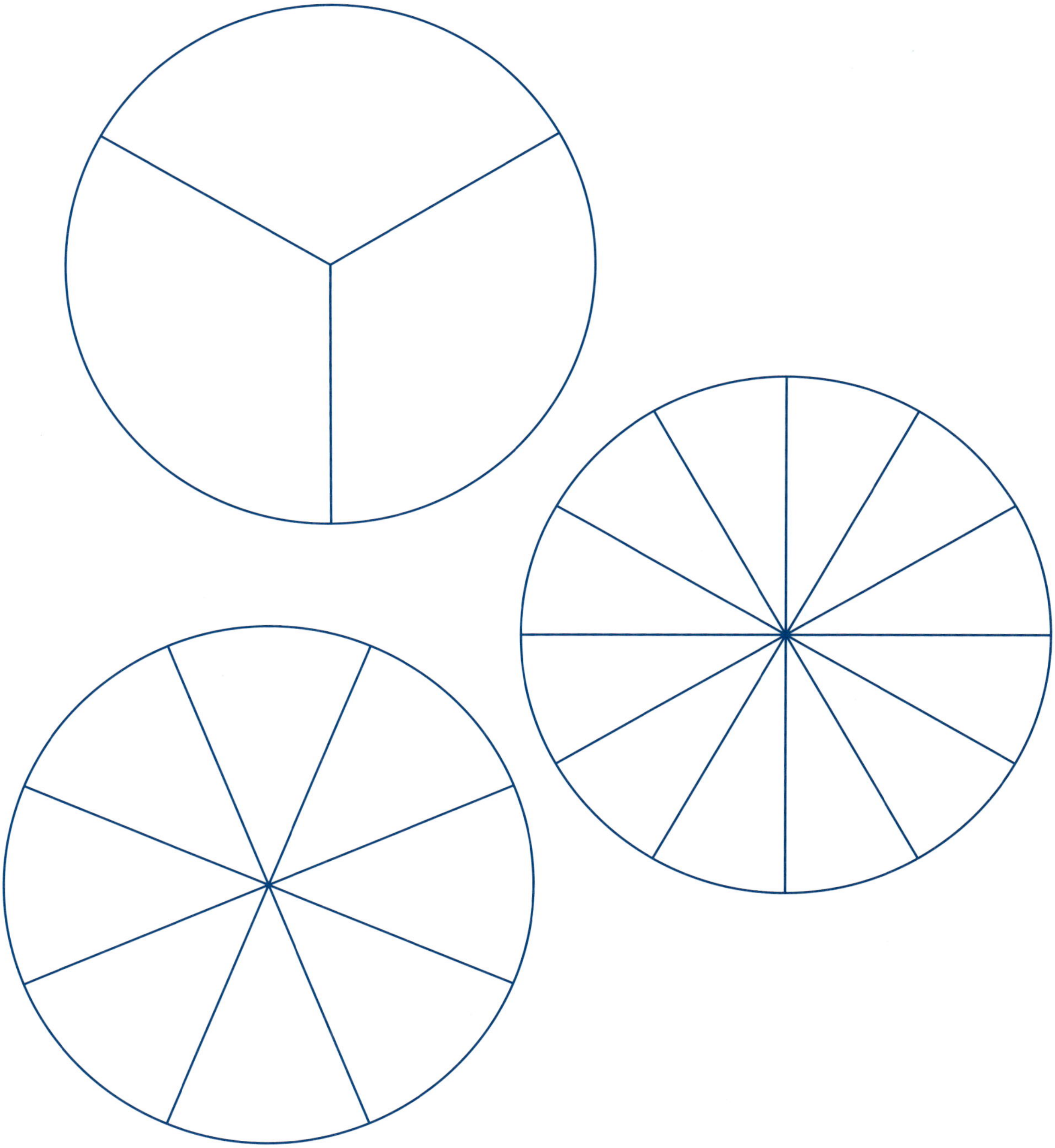

Fraction Disks

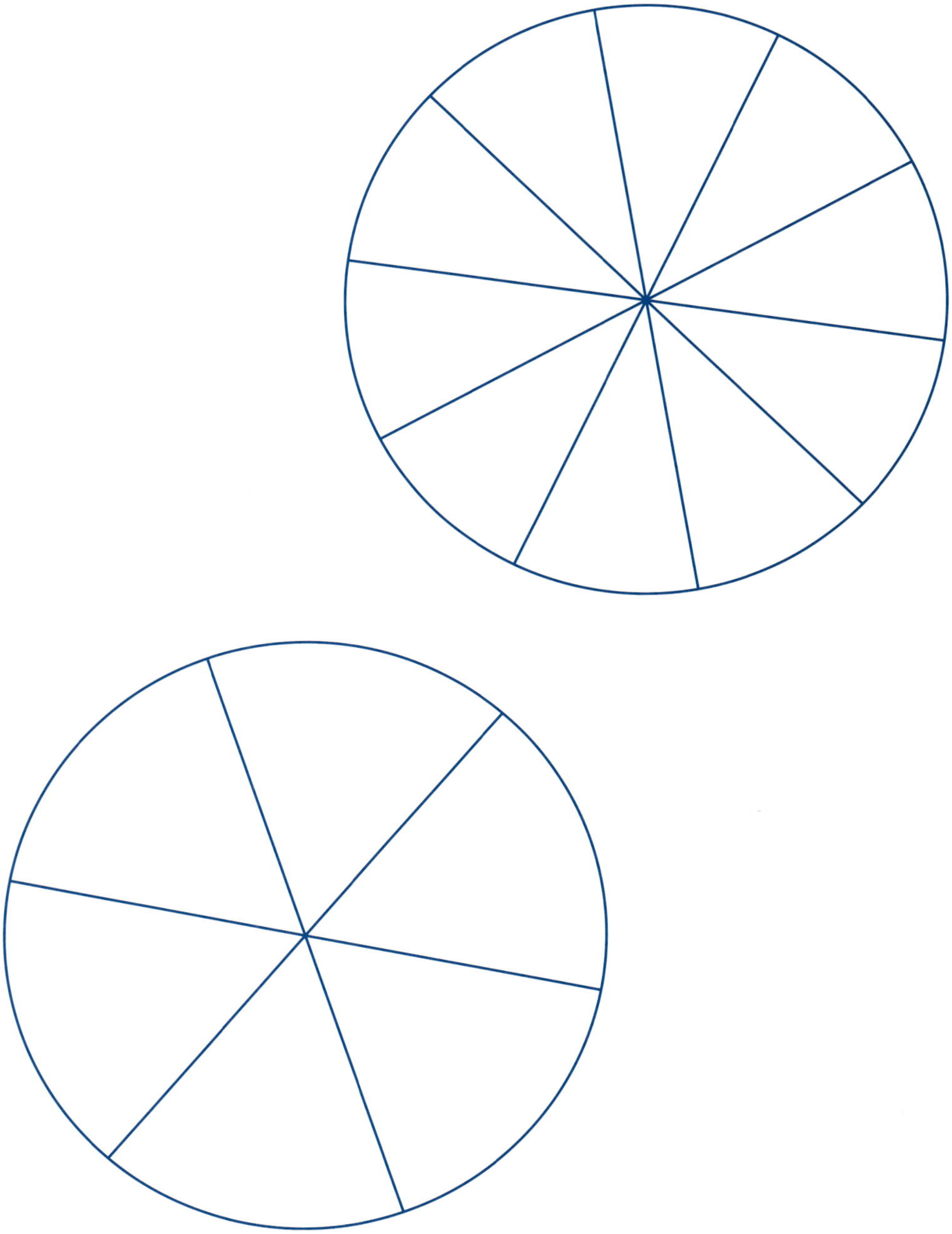

Fraction Disks

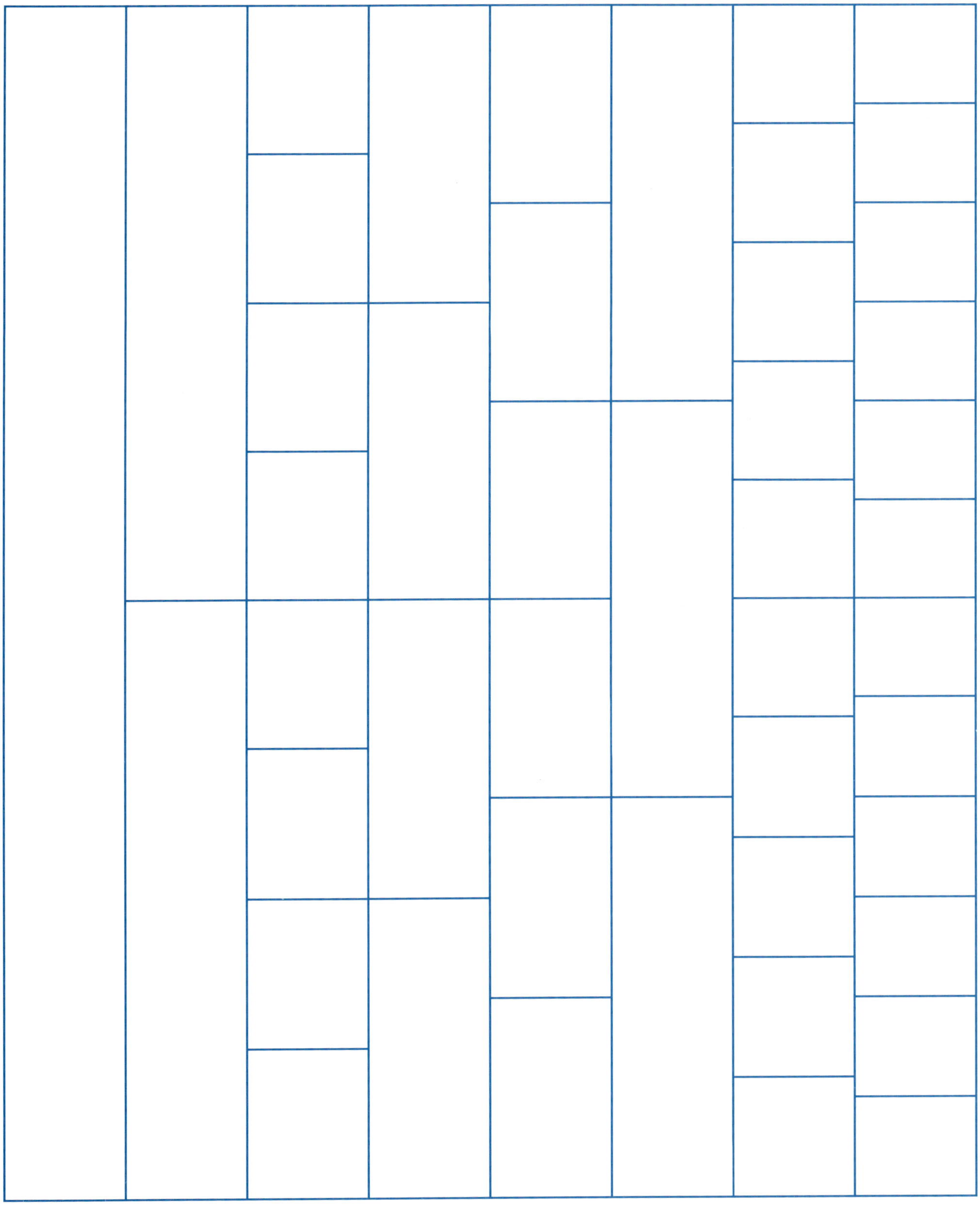

Fraction Bars

Decimal Wheels

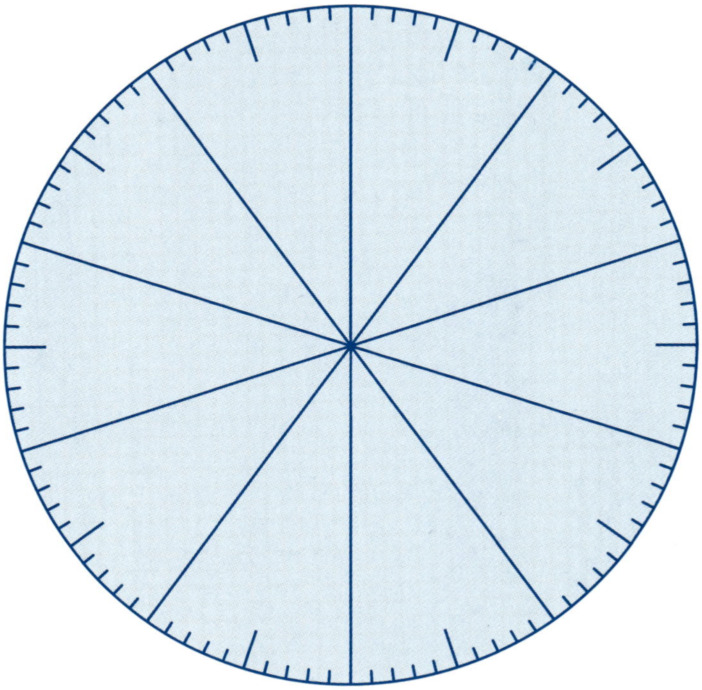

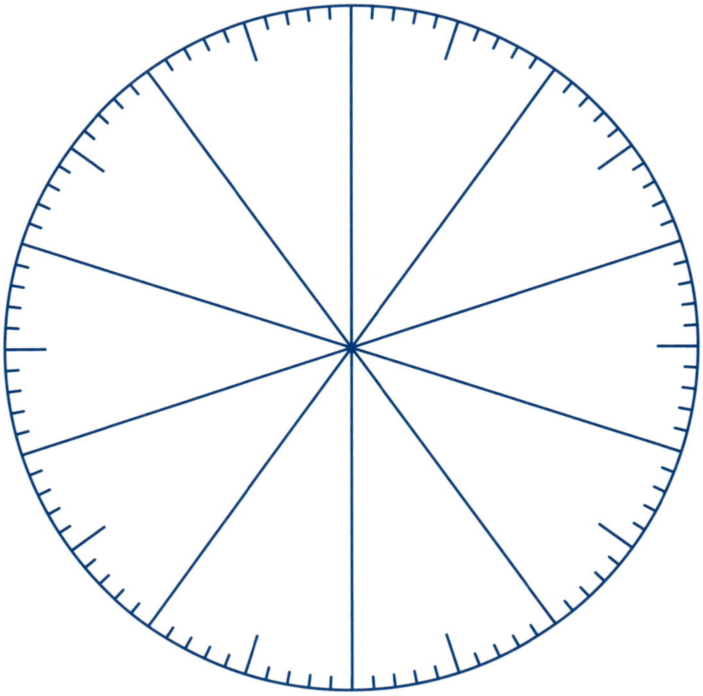

Decimal Card—One

Decimal Card—10 Tenths

Decimal Card—100 Hundredths

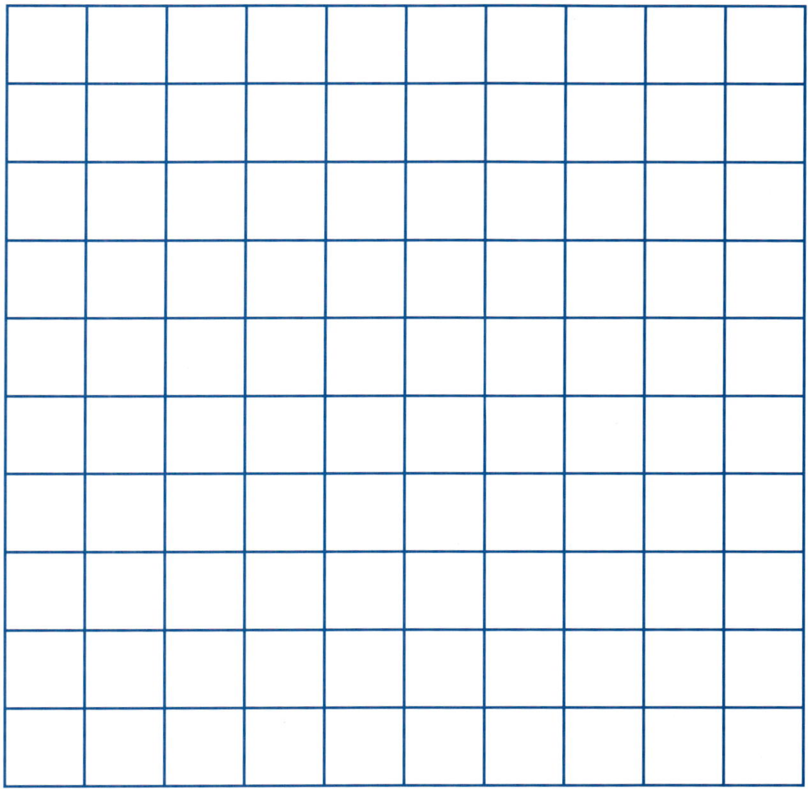

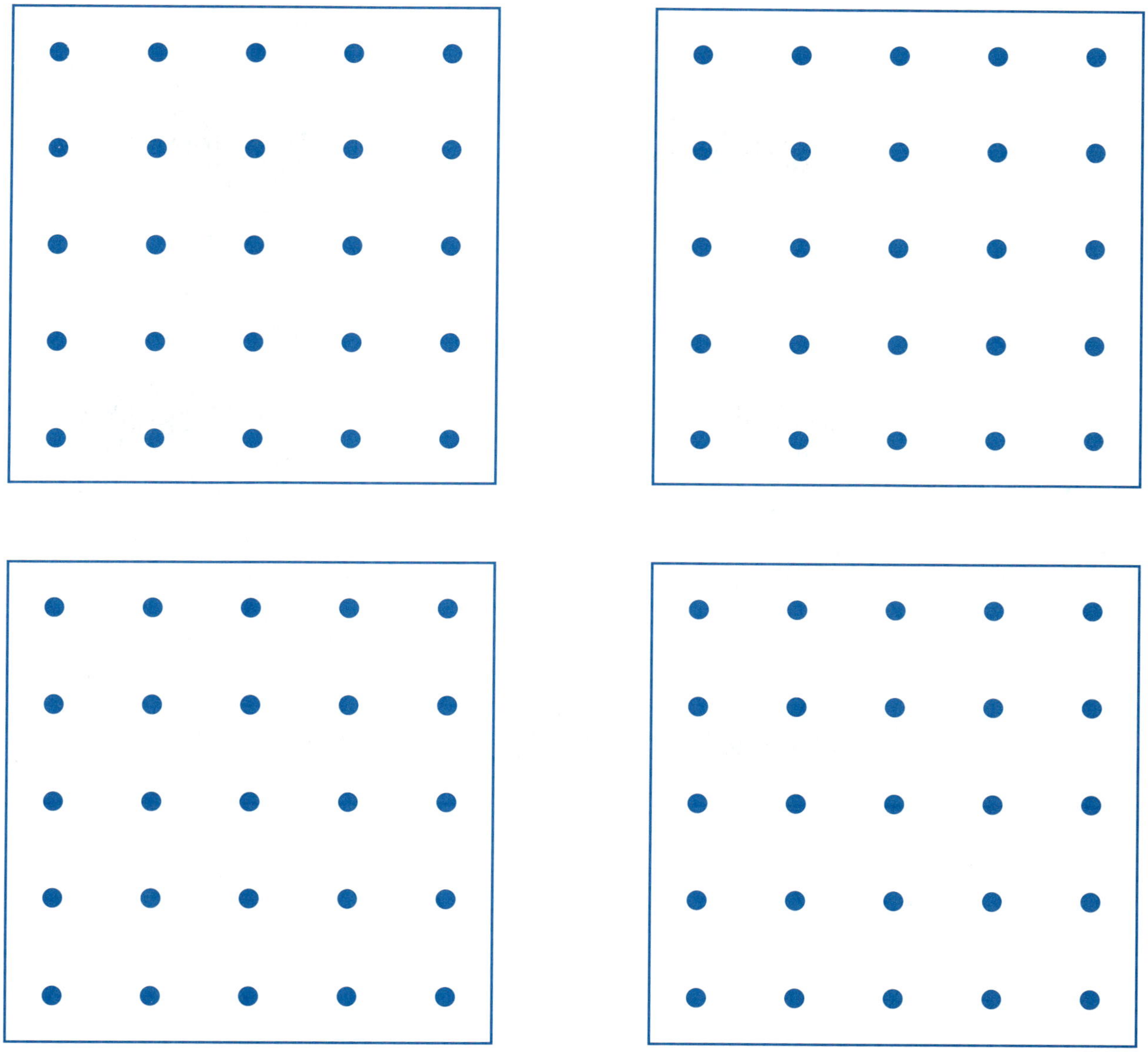

Geoboard Recording Sheet

Square/Diagonal Grid Paper

Triangle Grid Paper

Triangle Dot Grid Paper

1-cm Square Dot Grid Paper

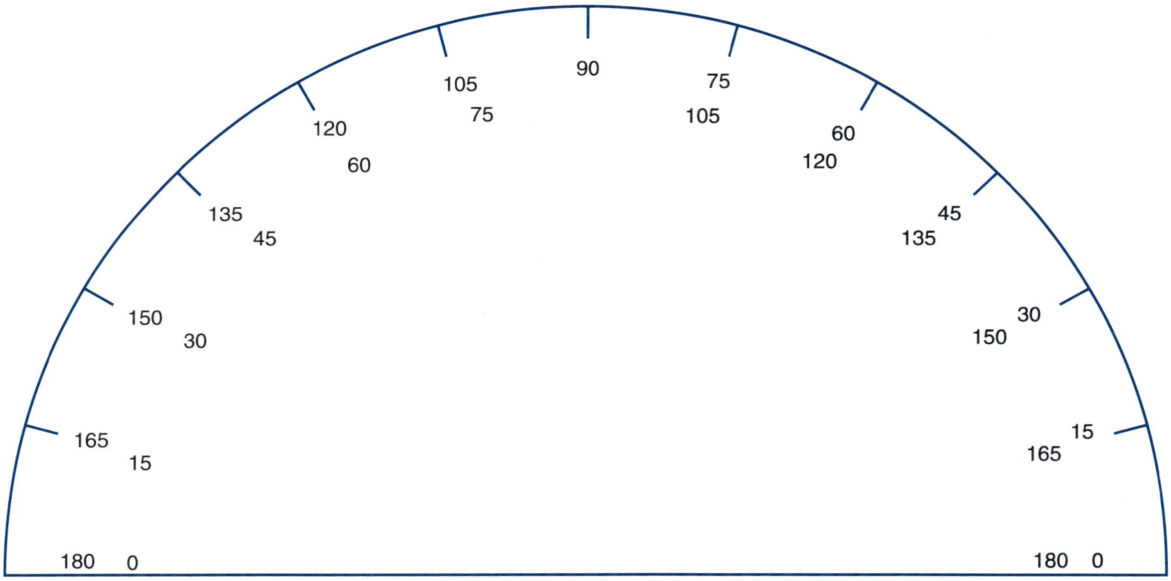

Paper Protractor

AUTHOR INDEX

SUBJECT INDEX